D0485937

Malawi

the Bradt Travel Guide

Philip Briggs

Updated by
Sean Connolly

HARRISON
MEMORIAL
LIBRARY
OCT 2 4 2013
PO BOX 800
CARMEL, CA
93921

edition
6

www.bradtguides.com

Bradt Travel Guides Ltd, UK
The Globe Pequot Press Inc, USA

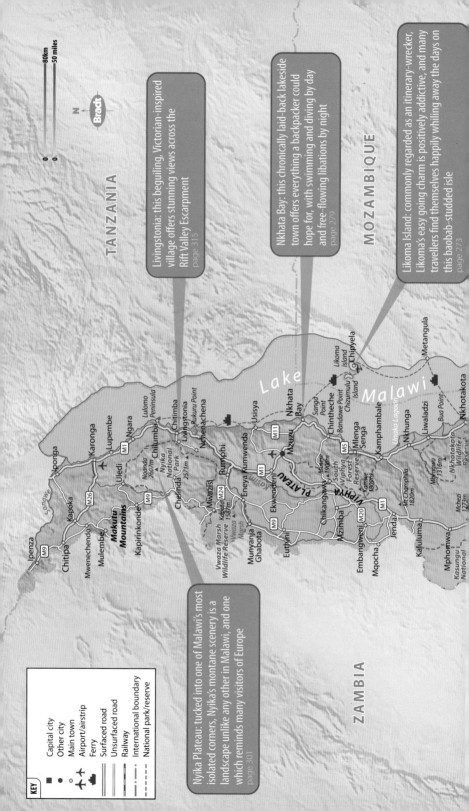

Nyika Plateau: tucked into one of Malawi's most isolated corners, Nyika's montane scenery is a landscape unlike any other in Malawi, and one which reminds many visitors of Europe
page 301

Livingstonia: this beguiling, Victorian-inspired village offers stunning views across the Rift Valley Escarpment
page 315

Nkhata Bay: this chronically laid-back lakeside town offers everything a backpacker could hope for, with swimming and diving by day and free-flowing libations by night
page 279

Likoma Island: commonly regarded as an itinerary-wrecker, Likoma's easy going charm is positively addictive, and many travellers find themselves happily whiling away the days on this baobab-studded isle
page 273

KEY

- ■ Capital city
- • Other city
- ○ Main town
- ✈ Airport/airstrip
- Ferry
- Surfaced road
- Unsurfaced road
- Railway
- International boundary
- National park/reserve

Bradt

N

0
0

80km
50 miles

TANZANIA

MOZAMBIQUE

ZAMBIA

Lake Malawi

Ipenza
Chitipa
Mwenechendo
Mulembe
Kapirinkonde
Makutu Mountains
Kaboka
Uledi
Mwenechendo
M26
M9
Songwe
Iponga
Karonga
Lupembe
Ngara
Lupembe
M1

Nyika National Park
Nganda 2607m
2571m
Chelinda
Mwazisi
Kapumbu 587m
Rumphi
M24
Eneza Kumwenda
Euthini
M9
Vwaza Marsh Wildlife Reserve
Vwaza Marsh
Munyanja
Ghabota
Lulomo Peninsula
Chitimba
Chilumba
Livingstonia
Nehenachena
Rukuru Point
Usisya
Ekwendeni
M1
Kasitu
VIPHYA PLATEAU
Mzuzu
M17
Nkhata Bay
Sanga Point
South Viphya Forest
Mapata 1906m
Kamwe 1800m
Chikangawa
Mzimba
M20
Jenda
Kajuluma
Embangweni
Mqocha
Mphomwa
Kasungu National
Mchinji 1273m
Mt Champhila 1820m
M1
Likoma Island
Chipyela
Chizumulu Island
Chintheche
Bandawe Point
Menga
Senga
Kamphambale
M5
Nkhunga
Liwaladzi
Usaka Lagoon
Mbengwa 1316m
Nkhotakota Wildlife Reserve
Bua Point
Nkhotakota
Mehezi 1273m
Metangula

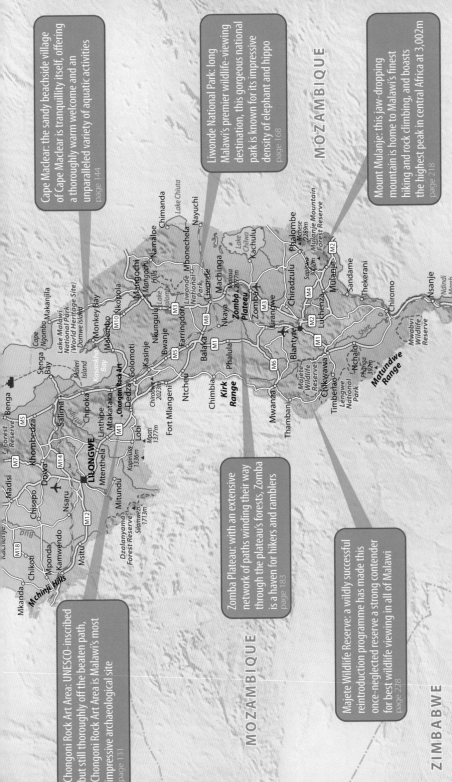

Cape Maclear: the sandy beachside village of Cape Maclear is tranquillity itself, offering a thoroughly warm welcome and an unparalleled variety of aquatic activities
page 144

Liwonde National Park: long Malawi's premier wildlife-viewing destination, this gorgeous national park is known for its impressive density of elephant and hippo
page 168

Mount Mulanje: this jaw-dropping mountain is home to Malawi's finest hiking and rock climbing, and boasts the highest peak in central Africa at 3,002m
page 218

Chongoni Rock Art Area: UNESCO-inscribed but still thoroughly off the beaten path, Chongoni Rock Art Area is Malawi's most impressive archaeological site
page 131

Zomba Plateau: with an extensive network of paths winding their way through the plateau's forests, Zomba is a haven for hikers and ramblers
page 183

Majete Wildlife Reserve: a wildly successful reintroduction programme has made this once-neglected reserve a strong contender for best wildlife viewing in all of Malawi
page 228

Malawi
Don't
miss...

Liwonde National Park
Along the atmospheric upper Shire River, this is the country's top destination for viewing big game such as hippo, buffalo and elephant
(AZ) page 168

Mount Mulanje
This spectacular massif has long been Malawi's premier hiking and rock-climbing destination, popular with residents and tourists alike for its dramatic scenery
(AZ) page 218

People and culture
A proud tradition of hospitality, friendship and courtesy permeates the entire country and warrants Malawi's epithet 'The Warm Heart of Africa'
(RPS) page 24

Nyika Plateau
The undulating Nyika Plateau affords visitors the freedom to explore a vast network of dirt roads and footpaths through an area rich in wildlife great and small
(WS) page 301

Likoma Island
With splendid beaches ringed by the mountainous Mozambican shore rising above them, Likoma has an overwhelmingly friendly atmosphere
(KM) page 273

Malawi in colour

above   Despite being one of Malawi's most neglected national treasures, the Chongoni Rock Art Area is a fascinating site containing 2,500 year-old paintings (AZ) page 131

left   A tradesman defies gravity whilst balancing traditional musical instruments on the back of his bicycle (FR) page 24

below   Masked performers re-enact a traditional funereal dance of the secret *nyau* society (WS) page 135

above Mount Mulanje towers over what is reputedly the oldest tea-growing area in Africa, centred on the small town of Thyolo midway between Mulanje and Blantyre (WS) page 225

right Dedza Pottery is one of Malawi's finest spots to pick up handcrafted ceramic tableware, figurines and other statues (DP) page 128

below The Nkwazi Boma are a *malipenga* dancing group local to Likoma Island (KM) page 276

above   Enclosed by tall, forested mountains and lush rocky islands, Cape Maclear is a beautiful spot that has long enchanted visitors (AZ) page 144

ulendo
TRAVEL GROUP

Simply no more excuses to stay at home...

e: info@ulendo.net / t: +265 1 794 555 / www.ulendo.net

AUTHOR

Philip Briggs has been exploring the highways, byways and backwaters of Africa since 1986, when he spent several months backpacking on a shoestring from Nairobi to Cape Town. In 1991, he wrote the Bradt Guide to South Africa, the first such guidebook to be published internationally after the release of Nelson Mandela. Over the rest of the 1990s, Philip wrote a series of pioneering Bradt Guides to destinations that were then – and in some cases still are – otherwise practically uncharted by the travel publishing industry. These included the

first dedicated guidebooks to Tanzania, Uganda, Ethiopia, Malawi, Mozambique, Ghana and Rwanda (co-authored with Janice Booth), all now in their fourth–seventh editions. Philip has visited more than two dozen African countries in total and written about most of them for specialist travel and wildlife magazines including *Africa Birds & Birding, Africa Geographic, BBC Wildlife, Travel Africa* and *Wanderlust*. He still spends at least four months on the road every year, usually accompanied by his wife, the travel photographer Ariadne Van Zandbergen, and spends the rest of his time battering away at a keyboard in the sleepy village of Bergville, in the uKhahlamba-Drakensberg region of South Africa.

UPDATER

Sean Connolly has been an English teacher in Somaliland, a student in Ghana, a writer in Malawi, and a backpacker across much of the African continent. When he's not discussing verb tenses, diplomatic recognition or the merits of camel meat, you may find him riding in the back of a grain truck, sampling questionable local delicacies or seeking out a country's funkiest records. Raised in Chicago and educated in New York, Sean is a full-time culture fiend (read: anthropology graduate) and stays on the move whenever possible. Check out his website at www. seandconnolly.com.

CONTRIBUTOR

Mary-Anne Bartlett, who updated the fourth edition of this guide, is a travel artist who has visited Malawi regularly since 1991, when she joined an expedition to survey the Elephant Marsh and walk the length of the Shire River from Chikwawa to Monkey Bay – following in the footsteps of her forebear Sir John Kirk and Dr David Livingstone on the original Zambezi expedition. Mary-Anne now runs a creative travel company, Art Safari, and regularly brings groups to Malawi and neighbouring countries to sketch, paint and experience the wonder and inspiration of Africa.

PUBLISHER'S FOREWORD   *Hilary Bradt*

I visited Malawi 37 years ago, in 1976. The political scene has changed (thank goodness!) but the extraordinary natural world of lake and mountain is still the same. The hiking we enjoyed on the Mulanje Plateau rivalled the best in Africa, and the lakes provided the perfect post-hiking relaxation. We also loved the warmth and friendly self-confidence of the people. It is a pleasure to know, through the descriptions of Philip Briggs and Sean Connolly, that in this respect Malawi hasn't changed. You're in for a treat.

Sixth edition published July 2013   First published 1996

Bradt Travel Guides Ltd
IDC House, The Vale, Chalfont St Peter, Bucks SL9 9RZ, England
www.bradtguides.com
Print edition published in the USA by The Globe Pequot Press Inc,
PO Box 480, Guilford, Connecticut 06437-0480

Text copyright © 2013 Philip Briggs
Maps copyright © 2013 Bradt Travel Guides Ltd
Photographs copyright © 2013 Individual photographers (see below)
Project Manager: Greg Dickinson
Cover research: Pepi Bluck, Perfect Picture

The author and publisher have made every effort to ensure the accuracy of the information in this book at the time of going to press. However, they cannot accept any responsibility for any loss, injury or inconvenience resulting from the use of information contained in this guide. All rights reserved. No part of this publication may be reproduced, stored in a retrieval system, or transmitted in any form or by any means, electronic, mechanical, photocopying, recording or otherwise without the prior consent of the publisher. Requests for permission should be addressed to Bradt Travel Guides Ltd in the UK (print and digital editions), or to The Globe Pequot Press Inc in North and South America (print edition only).

ISBN: 978 1 84162 474 7 (print)
e-ISBN: 978 1 84162 767 0 (e-pub)
e-ISBN: 978 1 84162 669 7 (mobi)

British Library Cataloguing in Publication Data
A catalogue record for this book is available from the British Library

Photographs Alamy: Imagestate Media Partners Limited – Impact Photos (I/A), John Warburton-Lee Photography (JWLP/A); Ariadne Van Zandbergen (AZ); Dedza Pottery (DP); Fisherman's Rest (FR); FLPA: David Hosking (DH/FLPA); Kaya Mawa (KM); Kayak Africa (KA); Robin Pope Safaris (RPS); Superstock (SS); Wilderness Safaris (WS)
Front cover Dhow on Lake Malawi, Cape Maclear, Malawi (AZ)
Back cover Girl balancing fish on head (RPS), Elephant in Liwonde National Park (AZ)
Title page Zebra, Nyika National Park (WS), Impala lily (SS), Member of the *nyau* secret society (WS)
Chapter openers Balancing bicycle (page 89; FR), Hippo in Liwonde (page 163; WS), Fishermen (page 243; KM), Walking safari (page 289; WS)

Illustrations Annabel Milne

Maps David McCutcheon FBCart.S; colour map relief base by Nick Rowland FRGS

Typeset from the author's disc by Wakewing, High Wycombe
Production managed by Jellyfish Print Solutions; printed in India
Digital conversion by the Firsty Group

Crafting my itinerary to update this sixth edition of Bradt's *Malawi* seemed enough of a cut-and-dried affair at the time. Eight weeks, three rental cars, a few well-planned circuits around each region, and a carefully chosen exit date to avoid excess visa renewals (cheap though they may be)! All was laid out in front of me, but as the Scottish poet Robert Burns famously wrote, 'The best laid schemes of mice and men go often awry', and from the moment I crossed the border I knew this was to be the case. 'The Warm Heart of Africa' had claimed another victim, love-struck and powerless to resist the tranquil charms of this most welcoming of countries.

Eight weeks quickly became nine, and ten, and even a few more after that. I had to skip forward several pages each time I opened my calendar. So many places made a mockery of my best laid schemes: Likoma, the uncharted island getaway of so many daydreams, Nkhata Bay's syrupy languor turning my most rigid of agendas into fanciful abstractions, and the uncrowded game reserves, thoroughly enchanting in their solitude. But even against this idyllic natural backdrop, an unfolding political drama remains on the tip of every Malawian tongue.

Recently spared the increasingly-authoritarian rule of former President Bingu wa Mutharika by his unexpected demise, the nation breathed a collective sigh of relief with the democratic transfer of power to now-President Joyce Banda. Elections take place in 2014, and any friends you meet will be happy to inform you of the latest political escapades.

Finally, while it may be a cliché that 'the people' are a country's greatest asset, in Malawi you would be hard pressed to make an argument to the contrary. Take the time to greet and shake hands, and you will be repaid with smiles, laughter, and a genuine welcome given freely and without expectations. It's the only country where I've been asked for my Facebook information more than I've been asked for money! This is why for me, and as for so many visitors, Malawi – its gentle and engaging people, stunning landscapes, and ease of travel – was an unexpected delight. Come ready to slow down, be a bit less cynical, and most importantly, leave yourself some extra time.

MALAWI UPDATES WEBSITE AND FEEDBACK REQUEST

At Bradt Travel Guides we're aware that guidebooks start to go out of date on the day they're published – and that you, our readers, are out there in the field doing research of your own. You'll find out before us when a fine new family-run hotel opens or a favourite restaurant changes hands and goes downhill. So why not write to us and tell us about your experiences? Contact us on ☎ 01753 893444 or e info@bradtguides.com. Alternatively you can add a review of the book to www.bradtguides.com or Amazon.

If you notice that information in this book has changed, or for updates to information in this guide, please go to updates.bradtguides.com/Malawi. Administered by *Malawi* author Philip Briggs, this website will supplement the printed Bradt guidebook, providing a forum whereby the latest travel news can be publicised online with immediate effect.

Acknowledgements

SEAN CONNOLLY First and foremost my thanks must go to Philip Briggs for obvious reasons. Thank you for the opportunity to take on such a fantastic project and for all your invaluable guidance along the way. It's difficult to go a day without making a new friend in Malawi, particularly if you're travelling alone as I was while researching for this update. This genuine welcome is among Malawi's most irresistible and inimitable qualities. To the multitude of people who welcomed me with open arms, pointed me in the right direction and took the time to hang around and have a laugh, my deepest thanks. *Zikomo kwambiri.*

These friends and helpers include, in no particular order: Simon Allison and Claire Waterhouse; Ariadne Van Zandbergen; Chris and Emma (Mkulumadzi); Mark and Sylvia (Casa Rossa); Danger (Mvuu Camp); Chris Badger (Wilderness Safaris); Lisa, Christine, Helen and Cheri (Latitude 13); Kate Moore (Lilongwe Wildlife Centre); Ken Smith, Fatima Bhayat and Major (Barefoot Safaris); Chris Stevens (Nyassa Lodges); John Dickinson (Bua River Lodge); Joanne, Zane and David (Tongole); John and Adila (Kande Horse); Rob Rix (Aqua Africa); Sam Singh (SS Rent A Car); Robin (Nyala Lodge); Lucila Runnacles; Floor Willemen and Jan de Groot (FloJa Malawi); Vijay Shah and Evelyn Kallweit; Thando Sibindi and Eveline Sibindi-Van Dam (Madidi Lodge); Toni Lowe and Fred (Liwonde Safari Camp); Tara and Dave (Namizimu Forest Retreat); Grant, Mareli, Kevin, Georgia and Linda (Mango Drift); Becky, Josh and Macdonald (Kaya Mawa); Lisa, Wezi and Will (Nkwichi Lodge); Nick (Wakwenda Retreat); Paul Norrish; Gilbert Mafunga and Dixon Phiri (Njaya Lodge); Kristen Burgess; Gerard Esposito (Mzoozoozoo); Remmie Lasance (Lifupa Conservation Lodge); Esau Mwamwaya, Tom and Janey (Mabuya Camp); Nizam Kasmani (Apex Rent-A-Car); Zein Dudha (Villa 33); Julie, James and Steven (Café 33); Adam Klug and Emma Rees; Lindsey Macdonald (WESM); Richard and Lauren (Makuzi Beach); Selena Gleadow-Ware; Auke Swennen (Lukwe Eco-Camp); Ryan and Dayni (Nanchengwa Lodge); Maky (Chez Maky); Lindsay McConaghy and Alan McLellan (Ulendo Safaris); Clive Bester (Kayak Africa); and Kay de Silva (Mgoza Lodge). Many thanks to all of you, and apologies if I missed anyone out!

Contents

A NOTE ON TELEPHONES

Telephone numbers seem to change with the seasons in Malawi, and have not been reliable means of communication for very long. Advance booking is rare for small guesthouses and lodges, and individuals, smaller businesses, and lodges may change their mobile-phone numbers several times over the years. This means that unfortunately there's a high possibility that some of the phone numbers we've supplied may soon be out of use – Malawi is chock-full of unused, lost, forgotten and stolen numbers. Oh, and don't forget that if you do ring you might have to try three times before you get through…

LIST OF MAPS

NOTE ABOUT MAPS

Several maps use grid lines to allow easy location of sites. Map grid references are listed in square brackets after listings in the text, with page number followed by grid number, eg: [98 C3].

Introduction

'The Land of the Lake', 'The Warm Heart of Africa', 'Africa for Beginners'... Malawi certainly attracts its share of snappy catchphrases, and these three sum up much of what makes this small African country so well liked by all who visit it.

Few countries are so dominated by a single geographical feature as the 'Land of the Lake'. Lake Malawi follows the dramatic contours of the Great Rift Valley for a distance of 585km; it is up to 100km wide in parts and it covers more than 15% of Malawi's surface area. Enclosed by sheer mountains and edged by seemingly endless palm-fringed sandy beaches, Lake Malawi is the most beautiful of Africa's great lakes and the indisputable focal point of Malawi's tourist industry.

There is much truth in the phrase 'The Warm Heart of Africa'. Not only do the climate and lush vegetation of the lakeshore conform effortlessly to every stereotypical image of tropical Africa, but the people of Malawi exude a warmth and friendliness that make most visitors feel instantly at home. Malawi may well be the most laid-back nation on earth.

And 'Africa for Beginners'? Well, certainly, Malawi would lie near the top of any list of African countries I'd recommend to a nervous novice traveller. Although crime is on the increase, Malawi remains as safe as anywhere on the continent, and it is one of a handful of African countries where English is widely spoken. The country's small size, relatively well-maintained roads and unusually nippy public transport combine to spare visitors the arduous all-day bus trips that are part and parcel of travel elsewhere on the continent. Malawi is remarkably compact, relatively cheap and hassle-free – with one qualification: the high incidence of malaria on the lakeshore.

Tourism in Malawi has developed along rather unusual lines. The country lacks the vast game reserves of East Africa and the world-class tourist facilities of southern Africa; as a result, it sees little in the way of fly-in tourism. Instead, Lake Malawi has become the ultimate venue for backpackers crossing between East and southern Africa. It also relies on being included in the itineraries of tourists visiting neighbouring countries, and has suffered in recent years as political uncertainty and chronic shortages domestically have led tourists to travel around, rather than through, Malawi, and as Zimbabwe's troubles have helped keep visitors away from the region as a whole. Thankfully, these situations are very much on the upswing and tourist numbers have rebounded in turn.

Within Malawi, tourist patterns are oddly schizophrenic. Travellers gather in their hundreds at lakeshore retreats like Cape Maclear and Nkhata Bay, yet away from the lake there are many attractive and accessible destinations which regularly go weeks on end without seeing a non-resident visitor. There is more to Malawi than a lake and, with the publication of this guide, I hope to draw attention to several exciting destinations which have previously been overlooked by visitors.

Malawi boasts a wealth of forest and mountain reserves, ranging from the relatively well-known Mulanje and Zomba plateaux to the little-visited but highly accessible mountains around Dedza, Ntchisi and Mzimba. Malawi's wildlife reserves may not compare to the very best in Africa, but several – Nyika, Vwaza, Nkhotakota, Majete and Liwonde – are easy and cheap to visit, and they have an untrammelled and unpretentious appeal, which, combined with the opportunity to watch big game on foot, should make them popular fixtures on the overland travel circuit. Add to this such currently obscure gems as Lake Chilwa and the Elephant Marsh and you realise it is one of the anomalies of African travel patterns that a country which attracts such consistently heavy traveller traffic has so much unrealised travel potential.

Perhaps the greatest of Malawi's attractions is a low-key charm that most visitors find thoroughly addictive. Many travellers fly into Africa barely aware that Malawi exists; by the time they return home a high proportion have come to regard it as their favourite African country.

Whether you're content to relax at the lake or prefer to actively explore little-visited mountains, forests and game reserves, it is difficult to think of a more agreeable place for easy, unstructured travel than Malawi.

KEY TO MAP SYMBOLS

═══════	Main road (tarred)
───────	Secondary road
═════	Track/4x4
⬜	Main road/tarred (town plans)
▪▪▪▪▪▪▪	Railway
··········	Footpath
✈ ✛	Airport/airstrip
→	One-way street
🚐	Bus station/taxis/matola
🚗	Car hire
⛴	Ferry
⛽	Filling station
🅿	Parking
ℹ	Tourist information
📧	Embassy, High Commission
🏺	Museum/art gallery
🎭	Theatre/cinema
🏛	Historic house/important building
⬆	Statue/monument
$	Bank/ATM
✉	Post office
✚	Hospital/clinic
✚	Health centre/pharmacy

⌂	Hotel/resthouse/guesthouse
⅄	Camping
✕	Restaurant
☆	Nightclub/casino
♀	Bar
☕	Café
@	Internet
✝	Church/cathedral
☾	Mosque
⬭	Cemetery
▸	Golf course
✳	Viewpoint
∭	Waterfall
♧	Woodland feature
⌓	Cave/rock shelter
▲	Summit (height in metres)
●	Other place of interest
✕═✕	Police block/gate
(⍟)	Stadium/sports facility
▦	Urban park
▨	Shopping mall
⧄	Market/square
▦	National park
▧	Forest reserve

x

Part One

GENERAL INFORMATION

Location Southern Africa, east of Zambia

Border countries Zambia, Tanzania and Mozambique

Area 118,484km²

Climate November–March, hot and wet; April–August, moderate and dry; September–October, hot and dry

Status Republic

Population 16.3 million (2012 estimate)

Life expectancy 51.5 years (men), 53.1 years (women)

Capital Lilongwe (estimated 2009 population 821,000)

Other main towns Blantyre, Mzuzu, Zomba and Karonga

Economy Predominantly agricultural. Depends on substantial inflows of economic assistance from the IMF, the World Bank and individual donor nations. Performance of the tobacco sector is key to short-term growth. Untapped oil reserves promise to fuel the energy sector.

Inflation 18.4% (2012 estimate)

Language English (official) widely spoken by most Malawians. Chichewa 57.2% (national language), Chinyanja 12.8%, Chiyao 10.1%, Chitumbuka 9.5%, Chisena 2.7%, Chilomwe 2.4%, Chitonga 1.7%, other 3.6%.

Religion Approximately 80% Christian (mostly Roman Catholic and Church of Central Africa Presbyterian (CCAP)), 13% Muslim, 4% traditional animism; remainder a selection of other faiths and sects

People About 11 groups: Chewa in Central Region; Yao along the lakeshore districts of Central and Southern regions; Lomwe mainly in the Shire Highlands; Nkonde, Lambya, Nyanja, Tonga and Tumbuka in Northern Region; Ngoni in the north and centre; Sena in Chikwawa; Nsanje in the south, as well as Asian and European

Currency Malawian kwacha (Mk)

Rate of exchange US$1=Mk400, £1=Mk620, €1=Mk525 and ZAR1=Mk45 (May 2013)

International dialling code +265

Time GMT +2

Electricity AC 240v

Flag Three equal horizontal bands of black (top), red and green with a radiant, rising, red sun centred in the black band. The flag was briefly changed from 2010–2012, with three horizontal bands of red (top), black and green with a white sun in the black band. It has since returned to the original.

Type of government Democratic republic

Head of state Joyce Banda (president)

Ruling party People's Party

Independence (from the UK) 6 July 1964

National parks Lake Malawi, Liwonde, Nyika, Kasungu and Lengwe

Wildlife reserves Vwaza, Nkhotakota, Majete and Mwabvi

Forest reserves 70, including South Viphya, Ntchisi, Namizimu, Dzalanyama, Thuma, Chongoni, Dedza, Zomba Mountain and Mulanje Mountain

Public holidays 1 January (New Year's Day); 15 January (John Chilembwe Day); 3 March (Martyrs' Day); 1 May (Labour Day); 14 May (Kamuzu Day); 14 June (Freedom Day); 6 July (Independence Day); 15 October (Mother's Day); 25–26 December (Christmas)

1

Background Information

GEOGRAPHY

LOCATION Malawi is a landlocked country in south-central Africa falling between 33° and 36°E and 9° and 18°S. It is bordered by Tanzania to the north, Zambia to the northwest and Mozambique to the east, south and southwest.

SIZE Covering an area of only 118,484km², Malawi is one of the smallest countries in sub-equatorial Africa, smaller even than England. It is 840km long from north to south, and is nowhere more than 160km wide.

CAPITAL In 1975, the centrally situated city of Lilongwe replaced Zomba as the capital of Malawi, and most government bodies and non-government organisations now have their headquarters there. Until the 21st century, Blantyre was the country's largest city and the unofficial economic capital, but Lilongwe overtook it population-wise in 2000, and it is also increasingly important as a centre of commerce.

PHYSICAL FEATURES The Malawian landscape is dominated by the Great Rift Valley, which runs through the eastern side of Africa from the Red Sea in the north to the Zambezi Valley in the south. Lake Malawi is the most southerly of the great lakes of the Rift Valley; at 585km long and up to 100km wide, it is the third-largest lake in Africa and the ninth-largest freshwater body in the world. The only outlet from Lake Malawi is the **Shire River**, which flows out of the southern tip near Mangochi and then follows the course of the Rift Valley southward, descending to an altitude of 38m above sea level near Nsanje, before it crosses into Mozambique, where it drains into southern Africa's largest river, the Zambezi.

In addition to Lake Malawi, there are three other sizeable lakes in Malawi. Lake Malombe lies in the Rift Valley south of Mangochi along the Shire River, and it can thus be seen as part of the Lake Malawi system. Lakes Chilwa and Chiuta are shallow bodies of water east of the Rift Valley near the border with Mozambique. Altogether, some 20% of Malawi's surface area is covered by water.

The Rift Valley Escarpment rises sharply to the west of the lake, in some areas reaching altitudes of above 1,500m (about 1km higher than the lakeshore). The highest and most extensive mountain range in northern Malawi is **Nyika**, protected in the national park of the same name, followed by the Viphya Plateau around Mzimba. Southern Malawi is also rather mountainous. Mulanje and Zomba are the most important mountains in the south, but there are also several smaller peaks in the Dedza and Thyolo areas. The highest peak in central Africa, **Sapitwa** (3,002m), is part of the Mulanje Massif in the southeast.

There are three distinct altitude levels in the country, the highest being the Nyika Plateau in the north, dropping down to the highlands of the Central Region and dropping again to the Shire Valley in the south.

CLIMATE

The overall climate can be characterised as tropical, with hot days and balmy nights. However, local temperature variations are influenced greatly by altitude and season. The hottest parts of the country are the Lake Malawi hinterland and the Shire Valley, which lie below 500m. Highland regions such as Mulanje, Zomba, Nyika, Dedza and Viphya are more temperate, and they can be very chilly at night during winter.

There are three seasons. The months between November and March are hot and wet, those between April and August are moderate and dry, while September and October are hot and dry. July and August can be very cold at night. Despite the large amount of surface water in Malawi, much of the country is prone to drought; the absence of any irrigation schemes means that local famines are a serious threat in years of low rainfall.

HISTORY

History has scant regard for the arbitrary political boundaries of modern Africa, and Malawi in particular throws up several problems of definition. The country took its present shape as recently as 1907, so it would be misleading to think of it as a discrete entity prior to the 20th century, and one cannot write meaningfully about its history in isolation of events that took place outside its modern boundaries.

Between 1907 and 1964, Malawi was known as **Nyasaland** and Lake Malawi was called Lake Nyasa (the name that is still in use today in Tanzania). In the history that follows, we have used the name Nyasaland where appropriate, but we have referred to Lake Malawi by its modern name throughout.

At different times we refer to Malawi as a part of southern Africa, eastern Africa and central Africa. This is simply because Malawi doesn't fit convincingly into any of these regions. Geographically, the country follows the southern end of the Rift Valley, and in prehistoric and geographical terms it feels like part of eastern Africa. In the 19th century, northern Malawi was most often influenced by events further north, and southern Malawi by events further south. During the colonial era, the term central Africa (ignoring any geographical reality) was generally applied to the grouping of Nyasaland and Northern and Southern Rhodesia. In modern Malawi, you sense a society and economy that looks south to Johannesburg rather than north to Nairobi, and we would thus tend to think of Malawi as part of southern Africa.

For the sake of clarity, when we refer to eastern Africa we generally mean Kenya, Uganda, Tanzania, Malawi and Mozambique north of the Zambezi River; when we refer to central Africa, we generally mean Zambia, Zimbabwe and Malawi; and when we refer to southern Africa we generally mean Malawi, Zambia, Mozambique and those countries south of the Zambezi River.

PREHISTORY It is widely agreed that the entire drama of human evolution was enacted in the Rift Valley and plains of eastern Africa. The details of human evolution are obscured by the patchy nature of the fossil record, but DNA evidence and recent 'missing link' discoveries suggest that the ancestors of modern humans and modern chimpanzees diverged roughly five to six million years ago. Malawi has not thrown up hominid remains of a comparable antiquity to those unearthed in Kenya, Tanzania and Ethiopia, but it seems reasonable to assume that it has supported hominid life for as long as any other part of eastern Africa. Furthermore, a 2.5-million-year-old hominid jawbone discovered near **Karonga** in 1993 has been identified as *Homo rudolfensis*, making it the oldest-known fossil relict placed in the same genus as modern humans.

Stone Age implements over one million years old have been discovered throughout eastern Africa, and it is highly probable that this earliest of human technologies arose in the region. For a quarter of a million years prior to around 8000bc, Stone Age technology was spread throughout Africa, Europe and Asia, and the design of common implements such as the stone axe was identical throughout this area. Little is known about the early Stone Age hunter-gatherers who occupied central Africa, but the only known skull of this period, found at Broken Hill in Zambia, suggests they were of completely different stock from the modern peoples of the region.

The absence of written records means that the origin and classification of the modern peoples of east and southern Africa is a subject of some academic debate. Broadly speaking, however, it is probable that the region witnessed two major human influxes in the last 3,000 years.

The first probably originated somewhere in the Congo Basin about 3,000 years ago. The descendants of these people, remembered locally as the Akafula or Batwa, were similar in lifestyle and appearance to the so-called Bushmen of southwest Africa and Pygmies of west Africa. In other words, they were slightly built hunter-gatherers, much shorter in stature than the modern occupants of the region. The **rock paintings** that are found throughout eastern and southern Africa are generally credited to people whose social customs derived from this early human influx. By the time the first Europeans settled, it is probable that the Batwa had already been exterminated in Malawi, although rumours that a few still lived on the Mulanje Massif suggest that they may have survived in small numbers into the 19th century.

The second human influx started in roughly AD100, and it apparently coincided with the spread of Iron Age technology in the region. The earliest-known **Iron Age** site in Malawi, dated to AD300, is on the South Rukuru River near Phopo Hill. There is good reason to suppose that the people who brought iron-working techniques into the region were the ancestors of the Bantu-speakers who, by AD500, probably occupied most of sub-equatorial Africa with the major exception of the arid southwest, which was still occupied by Bushmen when the Cape was settled by Europeans in 1652.

EAST AND CENTRAL AFRICA BEFORE THE 19TH CENTURY It is impossible to discuss events in Malawi prior to European colonisation without first having a general grasp of the regional history.

The eastern coast of Africa has been a hub of **international trade** for millennia. It is not known when this trade started, but the region was certainly known to the Phoenicians at around the time of Christ. By AD1000, trade between eastern Africa and the Shirazi Arabs of Persia was well established; by AD1300, more than 30 Swahili city-states had been established along the coast between Mogadishu in Somalia and Sofala in Mozambique. The most important of these cities was Kilwa, which lay on a small island 2km off the shore of what is now southern Tanzania.

The cornerstone of Kilwa's medieval trading empire was gold, and the source of this gold was the powerful Shona Kingdom of **Great Zimbabwe**. The nature of trade between Great Zimbabwe and Kilwa is obscure, but the absence of Arabic influences on Shona architecture suggests it was the Shona who organised trade as far as the coast. Great Zimbabwe alone is evidence enough that this was a well-organised and technologically impressive society. Founded in around AD1250 and abandoned 250 years later (when its inhabitants moved into the Zambezi Valley to form the Mwene Matupa Empire), the old Shona capital near Masvingo (in modern-day Zimbabwe) remains the most compelling and impressive ruin anywhere in sub-equatorial Africa.

The amiable trading relationship between the Shona, the Swahili and the Shirazi was shattered by the arrival of the Portuguese in the early **16th century**. Portugal's interest in eastern Africa was driven to some extent by the desire to check the spread of Islam, which had become the predominant religion on the coast. But this motive was rapidly subverted by simple greed: Portugal wanted to control the gold trade, not only on the coast (which it did by razing Kilwa and moving the main trading centre to Sofala near the Zambezi mouth) but also at the source of the Zambezi in the interior.

After the Portuguese captured Sofala in 1505, they decided to seek out the gold fields of Mwene Matupa, which they believed to be the fabled mines of King Solomon. In 1513, a Portuguese emissary called Antonio Fernandez was sent inland up the Zambezi Valley to locate the source of the gold. By 1540, Portugal had established official trading posts at Tete and Sena, the result of which was that the Zambezi Valley rapidly became a hotbed of **religious tensions**, with the Christian Portuguese and Islamic Swahili vying for trade with Mwene Matupa, and for converts. King Sebastian's first military incursion into the Zambezi Valley in 1569 met with dismal failure – only one-fifth of the 1,000 soldiers sent inland returned to the coast alive. A second attempt at colonisation in 1574 was only marginally more productive.

In 1596, Portugal took control of the Zambezi Valley by placing a puppet king on the Shona throne. This led to a brief flourishing of coastal trade, but also to civil war in Mwene Matupa and the eventual split of the Shona in 1665. The Portuguese were never prepared to pay fair prices to local gold traders and so production slowly dropped. Up until 1680, the Zambezi Valley produced around 16,000 ounces of gold annually. By 1800, this figure had dropped to less than 200 ounces per year. Portuguese expansion into the plateau south of the Zambezi was halted in the 1590s by the Changamire Empire, a Shona offshoot, but the Portuguese remained in control of the Zambezi Valley right up until Mozambique's independence in 1974. The net result of Portuguese interference in eastern Africa was the destruction of a trade network that had existed for centuries.

Coastal trade probably prompted the change in Malawi's social structures from loosely related clans to more centralised kingdoms. The process of **centralisation** started in the 14th century, as Malawi became an increasingly important source of ivory to coastal traders, and it gathered momentum under Portuguese influence. The most important kingdom, **Maravi** (from which the name Malawi derives), was formed in around 1480 and covered much of what is now southern Malawi, northern Mozambique and eastern Zambia. It was an agriculture- and trade-based empire, ruled by a dynastic king or Kalonga from a capital in central Malawi. The Kalonga dynasty reached its peak under Chief Masula, who ruled from about 1600 to 1650. Masula formed a strong alliance with Portugal, at one time sending 4,000 warriors to help quell a rebellion in Mwene Matupa, and by the time of Masula's death, the empire extended all the way to the coast near Mozambique Island. This vast kingdom was feared and respected by the Portuguese, but it gradually collapsed after 1650, and by 1700 it had split into several less powerful groups united under a breakaway Kalonga known as Undi. Many of Malawi's modern ethnic groups, most notably the Chewa, share a common Maravi heritage.

Centralisation was less of a feature in northern Malawi, where the Tumbuka people lived in loosely related clans, united by language and culture rather than politics. In around 1775, a group called the Balowoka established a major trading post in Tumbuka territory, but they had no imperial ambitions and were regarded by the Tumbuka as fair and honest in their dealings. The Balowoka were probably Swahili people from the Kilwa area, whose main interest was to maintain the **ivory trade** between northern Malawi and the coast.

Although Portugal had no sustained physical presence in what is now Malawi, a Portuguese trader called **Gaspar Boccaro** was probably the first European to enter the country. In 1616, Boccaro marched the 1,000km stretch between Tete and Kilwa in seven weeks, a remarkable, if now largely forgotten, feat of exploration. Boccaro crossed the Shire River near Chiromo and he also passed close to Lake Chilwa. His journals mention 'a lake which looks like the sea, from which issues the river Nhanha, which flows into the Zambezi below Sena and there it is called the Chiry', a clear reference to **Lake Malawi** and the Shire River. It is uncertain whether Boccaro ever saw the lake, and, rather oddly, the Portuguese showed no apparent interest in his report, though after his journey Lake Malawi appeared on several of their maps.

THE SLAVE TRADE The 19th century was a period of rapid and destructive change in Malawi, as the previous relative stability of the region was shattered by brutal incursions from all sides.

In 1824, Sultan Said of Muscat captured Mombasa and effectively ended Portugal's dominance of the eastern African coast north of Mozambique. By 1840, when the sultan moved his capital from Muscat to Zanzibar, coastal trade and commerce was dominated by newly arrived Omani Arabs, who established trade routes deep into the interior, most significantly from Bagamoyo to Lake Tanganyika and from Kilwa to Lake Malawi.

Slavery had always played a role in eastern Africa's coastal trade, both under the Shirazi-Swahili and later under the Portuguese, but prior to the 19th century it was subservient to the trade in gold and ivory. Under Omani rule, which coincided not only with the abolition of slavery in Europe and America but also with the decline of gold output from Zimbabwe, the slave trade took on fresh and quite horrific dimensions. By 1839, over **40,000 slaves** were sold annually at Zanzibar's slave market, and perhaps five times as many Africans died every year in slave raids and on the long march from the Rift Valley lakes to the coast.

Several coastal slave traders established themselves in what is now Malawi. The most important was **Jumbe**, who moved to Nkhotakota in around 1845, founding a dynasty which ruled over the local Tonga for three generations. Under the Jumbe dynasty, Nkhotakota became the main slave terminus out of Malawi, shipping thousands of slaves annually across the lake to Kilwa.

The Omani slavers were methodical and ruthless. Their night raids, known as *chifwamba*, were initiated by letting off a volley of gunshots around the targeted village. The slavers would then wait outside hut entrances to club or spear to death the village's men, who would rush from their huts to see what was happening. The fittest and healthiest women and children were selected as captives and tethered together using iron neck bracelets; the rest were killed on the spot. The captives would be herded to the nearest slave stockade until they numbered around 1,000, when they were shipped across the lake. After crossing Lake Malawi, the captives were forced to march for three or four months to Kilwa, generally carrying heavy loads of ivory and other goods. If any of the captives became ill or expressed tiredness along the way, they were instantly beheaded so that their neck bracelet could be re-used. At Kilwa, males were castrated, because eunuchs fetched higher prices. Eventually, the captives would be shipped to **Zanzibar** in conditions so crowded and dirty that a cargo of 300 people might be reduced to fewer than 20 on arrival.

The devastation that was caused to eastern African societies by the Omani slave trade cannot be underestimated. For Malawi, it was exacerbated by the arrival of the Yao, an itinerant group who originally came from the Ruvumu River Valley east of the lake. In the 1840s, the Yao were converted to **Islam** by Zanzibari Arabs, who also gave them weapons and agreed to buy any slaves they could capture. From 1850 onwards, many Yao settled in southern Malawi operating as a kind of fifth column, repaying the hospitality shown to them by the local Maganja and Chewa by capturing and killing them in their hundreds, and in a manner only slightly less ruthless than that of their mentors. The Yao also sold their captives to the Portuguese, whose trade in slaves grew greatly after about 1850.

THE MFECANE Nineteenth-century Malawi was further rocked by the aftermath of events in what is now the Zululand region of the KwaZulu-Natal province of South Africa. Prior to the turn of the 19th century, Zululand was populated by around 20 small, decentralised **Nguni-speaking clans**. Between 1800 and 1830, the nature of this society was transformed by the cataclysmic series of events which became known as the Mfecane – 'The Crushing'. The roots of the Mfecane remain a subject of debate, but modern theorists believe they had more to do with the influence of the Portuguese slave and gold trade in what is now Mozambique than with the more distant European settlement in the Cape. For whatever reason, there is no doubt that the first few years of the 19th century saw Nguni society become highly **militarised**, the result of which was the formation of three centralised kingdoms: Ngwane, Mdwandwe and Mthethwe.

In 1816, the Mthethwe Kingdom fell under the rule of Shaka, a member of the previously insignificant Zulu clan. Shaka revolutionised Nguni warfare by replacing the traditional throwing spear with a shorter stabbing spear, and instructing his troops to surround their foes in a U-formation and stab them to death. The result was an extended massacre which reverberated across the country and depopulated vast tracts of the southern African interior. As many as **two million** people died in the Mfecane, and those who were not killed by Shaka's marauding army either joined its ranks or fled, taking with them the Zulus' frenzied militarism and deadly tactics.

In 1818, the Mdwandwe Kingdom collapsed beneath Shaka's military onslaught. Under the leadership of Zwangendaba, a Jere chief, various Mdwandwe clans fled north into Mozambique, where they attacked and co-opted the local Tonga people to form a mighty migrating army known as the Jere-Ngoni. Northwards they marched, into the Zambezi Valley, where they ran riot over the Portuguese settlements at Tete and Sena, and destroyed the powerful Changamire Empire. The Ngoni raided every village they passed through, killing everybody but young men (who were drafted into their army) and women of marriageable age. Their methods of killing were without mercy: men were bludgeoned to death and unwanted women had their breasts cut off and were left to die of blood loss.

The Jere-Ngoni crossed the Zambezi in November 1825, settling for many years in the area west of Lake Malawi, where they terrorised the Tumbuka of the highlands and the Tonga of the lakeshore. This period is still remembered by the people of northern Malawi as 'The Time of Killing'. In 1845, Zwangendaba died on the southern tip of Lake Tanganyika. After his death, the Ngoni split into several factions, two of which returned to what is now Malawi. The most significant of these, the Mombera-Ngoni, subjugated the Tumbuka, Tonga and Nkonde people of northern Malawi, killing their chiefs and massacring huge numbers of people at the first sign of rebellion.

LIVINGSTONE AND THE ZAMBEZI EXPEDITION By the middle of the 19th century, the combined efforts of the Ngoni, the Yao, and the Omani and Portuguese slave traders had turned Malawi into something of a bloodbath. And so it might have remained but for the arrival in 1859 of David Livingstone, a Scottish **missionary** turned explorer who, perhaps more than any one man until Banda (see page 16), was to shape the future course of events in Malawi.

David Livingstone was born at Blantyre, Scotland, in 1813. He trained as a medical doctor at Glasgow University and then as a missionary at the London Missionary School. In 1840, he joined Robert Moffat's mission station at Kuruman in South Africa, where he married Moffat's daughter Mary. While at Kuruman, Livingstone came to perceive his role in Africa as something grander than merely making a few more converts: his ambition was to open up the African interior so that other missionaries might follow in his wake.

Between 1853 and 1856, Livingstone became the first European to cross Africa from west to east, starting at Luanda in Angola and then following the course of the Zambezi to its mouth in Mozambique. Livingstone was a first-hand witness to the suffering caused by the brutal slave trade; he became convinced that the only way to curb slavery was to open Africa to **Christianity, colonisation** and **commerce**. Livingstone's faith in the so-called 'three Cs' was not untypical of Victorian attitudes to Africa, but, more unusually, Livingstone was fuelled neither by greed nor by arrogance, but by plain altruism.

In 1858, Livingstone convinced the British government to finance an expedition to search for a navigable river highway upon which European influences might be brought to the African interior. This was the second 'Zambezi Expedition'; it lasted for six years, with the diverse crew of botanist and physician Dr John Kirk, navy officer Captain Norman Bedingfield, geologist Richard Thornton, Livingstone's younger brother Charles as evangeliser, the artist Thomas Baines and the engineer George Rae.

Livingstone's firm belief that the **Zambezi** would prove to be this highway was crushed by the end of 1858, when the Kebrabasa Rapids west of Tete proved to be impassable by steamer. In 1859, Livingstone turned his attention to the Shire, a tributary of the Zambezi and, though he did not know it at the time, the sole outlet from Lake Malawi. Livingstone's steamer made several trips up the river, but his projected highway to the interior was again blocked, this time by the Kapichira Rapids. Nevertheless, Livingstone, together with his companion John Kirk, explored much of southern Malawi on foot in 1859, including mounts Mulanje and Zomba, as well as Lake Chilwa and the southern part of Lake Malawi.

In 1861, Livingstone was sent a new boat by the British government. It arrived at the Mozambican coast carrying a party of clergymen, who had been sent by the Universities' Mission to Central Africa (UMCA) at Livingstone's request to establish the first mission in central Africa. Livingstone deposited the party, led by Bishop Mackenzie, at Magomero near Chiradzulu Mountain (between the modern towns of Blantyre and Zomba).

On 2 September 1861, Livingstone sailed up Lake Malawi in a local boat, a trip that John Kirk was to describe as 'the hardest, most trying and most disagreeable of all our journeys'. Livingstone stopped at Jumbe's slaving emporium at Nkhotakota, which he called 'an abode of bloodshed and lawlessness'. Further north, the lakeshore was 'strewed with human skeletons and putrid bodies', victims of the marauding Ngoni. By the time he reached Nkhata Bay, the depressed and exhausted doctor feared for his life, and he decided to turn back south, thus underestimating the length of the lake by 100km.

From here on, the Zambezi Expedition went from disaster to disaster. Disease claimed the lives of several of the Magomero missionaries, including Bishop Mackenzie himself in late 1861, and the UMCA eventually **withdrew the mission** to Zanzibar. Days after Bishop Mackenzie's death, Mary Livingstone, who had only shortly before joined her husband in central Africa, died of malaria. In 1863, the last time Livingstone sailed up the Shire, the river was described by a member of the expedition as 'literally a river of death'. The boat's paddles had to be cleared of bloated corpses every morning. Livingstone realised that in attempting to open the Shire to the three Cs, he had unwittingly opened the way for **Portuguese slave raids**. The British government withdrew their support for the expedition in 1864, and Livingstone returned to Britain.

Livingstone is now best remembered as the recipient of Henry Stanley's immortal greeting, 'Doctor Livingstone I presume', and as one of the many explorers of his era obsessed with the search for the source of the Nile. Neither memory does him justice: Livingstone had been exploring Africa for more than two decades before he turned his thoughts to the Nile (on his last African trip between 1867 and 1874), and the posthumous reward for his earlier efforts was indeed the abolition of slavery through the influence of the three Cs. Somewhat ironically, it was only after Livingstone's death near Lake Bangweula in 1874 and his emotional funeral at Westminster Abbey that Britain finally made serious efforts to end the slave trade around Lake Malawi.

CHRISTIANITY, COMMERCE AND COLONIALISM Livingstone's Zambezi Expedition was, on the face of it, an unmitigated disaster. In time, however, it was to prove the catalyst that put an end to the slave trade. Livingstone's published descriptions of the atrocities he had witnessed in Malawi heightened public awareness in Britain. In the year that Livingstone died, John Kirk, a leading member of the Zambezi Expedition and now Consul General of Zanzibar, succeeded in convincing the Sultan of Zanzibar to close Zanzibar's slave market and ban the highly lucrative slave trade.

The UMCA returned to Malawi in 1875, establishing a chain of missions, the most important of which was on Likoma Island. In 1874, the Free Church of Scotland established the Livingstonia Mission at Cape Maclear under the leadership of Dr Robert Laws, but due to the high incidence of malaria at Cape Maclear the mission moved to Bandawe in 1881, where Dr Laws made the significant breakthrough of persuading the Ngoni to cease their endless harassment of the more peaceable Tonga. The **Livingstonia Mission** moved to its current position on the Rift Valley Escarpment above the lake in 1894. The other important mission established in 1875 was the Blantyre Mission in the Shire Highlands, eventually to become the site of Malawi's largest city.

As a rule, the arrival of missionaries in Africa was at best a mixed blessing. Many were unbelievably arrogant in their handling of Africans. Often they collaborated with would-be colonisers against the interests of their purported congregation, and the use of violence to create converts was commonplace. The Scottish Missions in Malawi were a happy exception. Inspired by Livingstone's humanitarian values and his respectful attitude towards Africans, they made great efforts to end local wars and to curb slavery, often risking their lives in the process.

The **Scottish missionaries** offered education to thousands of Africans. Malawi's northern province had at one time the highest educational standards anywhere in central Africa, and Likoma Island boasted the only **100% literacy rate** on the continent. The missionaries introduced new crops and farming methods as well as passing on practical skills such as carpentry and tailoring. Reverend Scott, who ran the Blantyre Mission for 30 years from 1881, said that 'Africa for the Africans has been our policy from the first'. And it is true that many of the graduates of the mission schools at Blantyre and Livingstonia played a significant role in the eventual rise of Malawian nationalism, as well as in the struggles for equality in Zambia, Zimbabwe and South Africa. Banda himself once referred to Livingstonia as the 'seed-bed' of his Malawi Congress Party.

Livingstone's prediction that legitimate trade might slow the slave trade encouraged two Scottish brothers, John and Frederick Muir, to form the African Lakes Corporation (ALC) in 1878. The ALC not only provided an important source of materials for the missions, but it rapidly became a major trading force on Lake Malawi and the Shire River, and was to prove instrumental in controlling and eventually killing **Mlozi**, the sultan of a vast slaving empire around Karonga.

The so-called '**Scramble for Africa**' (1885–95) was precipitated by Germany's unexpected claim to a vast portion of eastern Africa, firstly Tanganyika (what is now mainland Tanzania) and then parts of Malawi, Uganda, Kenya and Zanzibar. In 1890, Germany relinquished all its claims (except for Tanganyika) in exchange for Heligoland, a tiny but strategic North Sea island. In 1891, the vast British territory north of the Zambezi and south of Tanganyika was given the rather unwieldy name of the British Central African Protectorate, and Harry Johnston was appointed as its first commissioner.

Johnston's overriding concern was to stamp out the slave trade, which, despite its abolition on Zanzibar, was still operating between Lake Malawi and Kilwa. In 1891, Fort Johnston was built near the village of the dominant Yao slave trader, Mpondo. Mpondo's village was destroyed and 270 slaves were released from imprisonment. The Yao slave traders hit back several times, but Johnston was eventually able to stop their shipments across the lake. The south of Malawi was finally freed of slave raids when the last two Yao traders were defeated in 1895, and Fort Lister was built near Mulanje to block the last usable route to the coast. In northern Malawi, Johnston persuaded Jumbe, the overlord of Nkhotakota, to give up the slave trade in exchange for British protection. His attempts at negotiating with Mlozi, the self-styled Sultan of Nkondeland (near Karonga), were less successful. After several battles, Mlozi was captured by Johnston in 1895 and sentenced to death.

Twenty-one years after his death, Livingstone was proved to have been correct – Christianity, commerce and colonialism had ended the slave trade. They had also brought inter-tribal peace to Malawi, as the Yao and Ngoni abandoned their spears for the education offered by the Scottish Missions. Colonialism in Malawi was eventually to take on the more nefarious character it did elsewhere in Africa, though never perhaps to the same degree. Again, the paternalistic Scottish missionaries must take much credit for this: in the words of one of the most fondly remembered missionaries, William Johnson, they 'did not come here necessarily to subjugate [but] to protect and instruct'. Ultimately, it is difficult to argue with the assertion that British intervention was the best thing that happened to Malawi in the troubled 19th century.

NYASALAND In 1907, the British Central African Protectorate was divided into two separate territories: Northern Rhodesia (now Zambia) and Nyasaland (the colonial name for Malawi). Throughout the colonial era, there were strong ties between Nyasaland, Northern Rhodesia and Southern Rhodesia (now Zimbabwe), culminating in the **federation** of the three colonies in 1953.

Nyasaland was the least developed of the three colonies, due to the absence of any significant mineral deposits and also because the region was so densely populated that large-scale cash-crop farming was not a realistic option. A coffee boom at the turn of the 20th century turned out to be short-lived when production fell by 95% between 1900 and 1915. Tea was the only settler-dominated agricultural product that really took off, but its production was restricted to the hills around Thyolo and Mulanje.

Together with this lack of development went a low level of alien settlement. By 1953, the settler population, comprising mainly European administrators and Indian traders, numbered little more than 10,000. The indigenous population, on the other hand, had by this time grown to 2.5 million, creating a population density six times greater than that of Southern Rhodesia, and **ten times greater** than that of Northern Rhodesia.

The lack of development had its good and bad sides. At no point in the colonial era was more than 15% of the land under colonial or settler ownership, in large part due to the unusually scrupulous attitude of early governors such as Johnston and his successor Sharpe in ratifying settlers' claims to having 'bought' land from local chiefs. By 1953, a series of government actions had guaranteed that 90% of the land was for the communal use of Africans, while the remaining 10% was protected in forest reserves or occupied by cities or settler farms. This meant that, unlike many other British colonies where most of the good land was used by settlers to produce cash crops, Africans in Nyasaland were in theory free to continue their traditional **subsistence lifestyle.**

The obstacle that prevented theory from becoming reality was the system of taxation introduced by the colonial administration. This was called a poll tax, something of a misnomer as there was no related poll. It was not good enough for the people of Nyasaland merely to subsist; they were forced by the colonial administration to pay for the privilege. A small number of local farmers got around the need to earn money by growing cash crops such as **tobacco** and **cotton**. Far more Africans entered into the **migrant labour** system: they were in effect forced to leave their homes and to work for paltry wages and in miserable conditions in the copper mines of Northern Rhodesia and at the gold and coal reefs of South Africa and Southern Rhodesia. In the 1930s, it was estimated that 20% of the men of Nyasaland spent a part of any given year working outside the country. Villages were thus robbed of their most able workers for months at a stretch, while traditional family structures collapsed under the stress of long periods of separation. Worse still, in 1938, it was estimated that 5% of the men of Nyasaland had been lost permanently to migrant labour – either victims of the filthy living conditions on the mines, or seduced by the big cities.

ETHIOPIANISM AND THE RISE OF NATIONALISM Protest against colonial rule surfaced in Nyasaland even before World War I, in large part due to the influence of Scottish missionaries, notably Dr Robert Laws, who presided over the Livingstonia Mission for half a century, and the Reverend Joseph Booth, a noted denomination-hopper whose outspoken pro-African politics forced him to leave Nyasaland in 1902.

The early protests in Malawi were strongly linked to the **Ethiopianist Churches** which emerged in America and South Africa in the wake of Ethiopia's victory over Italy at Adwa in 1896 (the victory which resulted in Ethiopia remaining independent for all but five years of the colonial era). Ethiopianist Churches attempted to reconcile Christianity with traditional African customs and beliefs, producing a distinctly African brand of religion with a strongly Baptist flavour. By taking a pro-African stance at a time when few people of African descent had political power, Ethiopianism was an inherently political movement, and it became strongly aligned with the '**Africa for the Africans**' philosophy of the Jamaican visionary Marcus Garvey.

The first indigenous Nyasa to challenge colonial rule was Edward Kamwama, a product of Laws's mission school in Bandawe. Kamwama worked in the gold fields of South Africa for several years, where he met Reverend Booth, who introduced him to the Ethiopianist Watch Tower Church. Kamwama returned to his home in Bandawe in 1908, and formed his own Watch Tower Church, organising the first public **protests** to forced taxation. He was driven into exile by the colonial administration, but the Watch Tower Church grew all the same. Growing out of this movement, and with the encouragement of Dr Laws, the first of a number of Native Associations was formed in 1912. In alliance with so-called 'Tribal Councils', the Native Associations made repeated demands to government to improve educational levels and end taxation.

Reverend John Chilembwe is now heralded as Malawi's first fighter against colonial rule and was yet another product of the mission schools. Chilembwe was born near Chiradzulu in 1871 and worked as a kitchen boy for Reverend Joseph Booth for several years. He was baptised by Booth in 1893 and then travelled with him to the USA, to Lynchburg in Virginia. Here he studied in a Baptist seminary and became influenced by Ethiopianism. On his return to Chiradzulu in 1900, Chilembwe bought land close to the original site of the Magomero Mission, where he founded the Provident Industry Mission (PIM). By 1912, over 800 converts lived in the mission grounds.

Adjoining the PIM were the Bruce Estates, owned by the daughter and son-in-law of Dr David Livingstone. One of the estates, Magomero, was managed by another member of the clan, William Jervis Livingstone. Chilembwe had come into conflict with the adjoining estate over the traditional labour laws and what he felt was the oppressive system of *thangata*, or work in lieu of rent. Chilembwe's full indignation at colonial rule was further exacerbated when many African soldiers died in what he saw as the white man's cause of World War I – the Battle of Karonga, northern Malawi, between Britain and Germany. In his final correspondence, which was censored, from the *Nyasaland Times*, Chilembwe asserted:

> Let the rich men, bankers, titled men, storekeepers, farmers and landlords go to war and get shot. Instead we, the poor Africans, who have nothing to own in this present world, who in death, leave only a long line of widows and orphans in utter want and dire distress, are invited to die for a cause which is not theirs.

On 23 January 1915, three armed columns set out from the PIM. One went to Magomero on the Bruce Estate where Chilembwe ordered them to kill all the European men they found. Another column went to the Nguludi Mission and clubbed – nearly to death – Father Svelsen. A third column headed to Blantyre in order to raid the arsenal for weapons.

The raid on the Bruce Estate was fatal, with William Livingstone and two other Scottish men killed. Livingstone was decapitated in front of his wife and small children in his bedroom at 21.00 as they were retiring to bed. Livingstone's wife Kitty, her two lady houseguests and their five children were then captured and forcibly marched off by Chilembwe's men into the night. The raid on Blantyre failed, with the colonial troops descending on the PIM. Kitty Livingstone and the women and children were found alive after a three-day **manhunt** by the **King's African Rifles**. Chilembwe and his rebels were still on the run, but on 3 February he was shot dead near Mulanje, resisting capture. Many of his supporters were jailed or executed and his church was blown up. The PIM, along with several other Ethiopianist Churches, was revived at the end of World War I, but the ensuing decades saw little in the way of organised protest.

After the end of World War II, protests against colonialism in Nyasaland and elsewhere in Africa became more militant. Thousands upon thousands of African conscripts had been shipped around the world to fight for the freedom of their colonisers; those who returned found their own liberty as restricted as ever. The **first major uprising** against colonialism took place in February 1948 in the Gold Coast, when a group of returned war veterans started a riot in Accra. As a result, Britain granted the Gold Coast self-government in 1953 and full independence in 1957, when the country was renamed Ghana.

Kwame Nkrumah, the first president of Ghana, declared the moment of independence to be 'the turning point on the continent' and indeed it was. In 1957, Ghana joined Ethiopia and Liberia as one of only three African countries with black rule. A decade later, this picture had been reversed. By 1968, only three of Africa's 50 countries (those colonised by Portugal) remained European dependencies, and three others (South Africa, South West Africa and UDI Rhodesia) remained under white rule.

HASTINGS KAMUZU BANDA During the heady years from 1953 to 1957, the Ashanti town of Kumasi in the Gold Coast housed the practice of the Nyasa-born Dr Hastings K Banda. In the year that the Gold Coast became Ghana, Banda returned to the land of his birth after more than 40 years abroad; despite being only a year shy of his 60th birthday, he was destined to dominate every aspect of his homeland's politics for nearly four decades.

Hastings Kamuzu Banda was born at Chiwenga near Kasungu. The most likely year of his birth was 1898, a mere three years after the Chewa chief of Kasungu signed a treaty of protectorateship with Britain. Banda was educated in the mission schools; by 1914, he had passed his Standard Three examinations. In 1915, after being accused of cheating in an examination, Banda decided to leave Nyasaland. He **walked** 800km via Mozambique to Southern Rhodesia, where he worked for a year as a sweeper in a hospital at Hartley. He then obtained a contract to work at a colliery in Natal, the only way he could legally gain entrance to South Africa, but after three months he deserted his job to live in Johannesburg.

It was in Johannesburg that Banda first took an interest in politics. Like many educated Africans of his era, he fell under the influence of the Ethiopianists, joining the AME Church in Johannesburg in 1922. In 1925, the AME sent Banda to the USA to receive further education. For three years he studied at the AME's Wilberforce Institute in Ohio. From 1928 to 1929 he studied at the University of Indiana, then in 1930 he moved to the University of Chicago, where he obtained a Bachelor of Philosophy degree. Finally, in 1932, Banda fulfilled his dream by enrolling at the Mihary Medical College in Nashville, Tennessee, where he was awarded his **Doctorate of Medicine** in 1937.

Banda's dream was to return to Nyasaland to serve his compatriots as a doctor; in 1938, he moved to Edinburgh where he studied for a licence to practise medicine in the British Empire. But when, in 1941, he tried to find medical work in Nyasaland, his applications were repeatedly snubbed. The nurses at Livingstonia refused to serve under a black doctor, while the colonial administration in Zomba, after much deliberation, would offer him work only if he agreed not to attempt to seek social contact with white doctors. Banda declined the offer and instead set up in private practice in Liverpool.

In 1945, Banda moved his practice to London. The benevolence of spirit that was noted by his patients in London also stretched back to his homeland. He made generous donations to the Nyasaland African Congress (NAC), and he financed the education of 40 Africans over a period of seven years. His Harlesden home became a meeting ground for African nationalist leaders based in London; regular visitors included Kwame Nkrumah and Jomo Kenyatta, the future leaders of independent Ghana and Kenya respectively. It seems likely that Banda would have stayed in London indefinitely had it not been for the humiliation of being named as the co-respondent in a divorce suit filed by Major French against his wife Margaret. In August 1953, the respected Dr Banda of Harlesden closed his practice, packed his bags, and, at the urging of Nkrumah, the newly installed prime minister of the Gold Coast, Banda and Mrs French moved to Kumasi.

THE FEDERATION SAGA The idea of federating Nyasaland with Northern and Southern Rhodesia surfaced as early as the 1890s and it was raised several times before World War II without ever coming to anything. After the war, however, the **white settlers** of Southern Rhodesia made a more concerted appeal for federation, knowing that it would give them practical sovereignty over the other two colonies in the face of growing African nationalism. The Africans of Nyasaland and Northern Rhodesia were opposed to federation for precisely the same reason that the white settlers favoured it. As Banda pointed out, under a colonial government 'the relationship between [Africans] and the authorities [was] one of ward and warden', but under a government provided by Southern Rhodesia it would become 'one of slaves and masters'.

The issue of federation became the focal point of protest in Nyasaland. The **Nyasaland African Congress** (NAC), formed in 1943, became the most vocal opponent of Rhodesian rule, and in alliance with Banda in London it entered into negotiation with Britain and Southern Rhodesia to prevent federation. Yet, despite the clear opposition of the African people of Nyasaland and Northern Rhodesia, Britain agreed to federation in 1953 (ironically, the same year in which the Gold Coast was granted self-government), thereby placing the future of Nyasaland under the overtly racist and, to all intents and purposes, self-governing settlers of Southern Rhodesia. Banda described this enshrinement of white dominance in central Africa as a 'cold, calculated, callous and cynical betrayal' and he vowed not to return to Nyasaland until the federation was dissolved.

In August and September of 1953, a series of spontaneous protests against federation took place in Nyasaland, starting in Thyolo and spreading to Chiradzulu, Mulanje and Nkhata Bay. Eleven Africans were killed in these protests and a further 72 were injured. The relatively conservative NAC leadership responded to the protests with some ambiguity, and as a result the organisation fell increasingly under the influence of a group of radical young leaders, the most prominent of whom were Henry Chipembere and the Chisiza brothers, Dunduzu and Yatutu. In 1957, Chipembere asked Dr Banda to return to Nyasaland. After some vacillation, Banda agreed.

Chipembere and his cohorts built Banda up as a messianic symbol of resistance. However, they saw him not as the potential leader of an independent Nyasaland, but as the figurehead through which their more radical views could dominate NAC policy.

Banda had rather different ideas. On his return to Nyasaland in 1958, he took over the NAC presidency and urged its 60,000 members to **non-violent protest**. The first official riot took place in Zomba on 20 January 1959, when 400 people spontaneously rushed the police station after an NAC rally. They were fired on with tear gas and forced to disperse, but the incident marked the start of a spate of riots during which 48 Africans were killed in police fire. The most serious of these incidents took place at Nkhata Bay, where 20 rioters were killed by police reservists.

On 3 March 1959, a State of Emergency was declared, and the NAC was banned. Banda and over 1,000 of his most prominent supporters were arrested. Immediately the NAC was banned, one of its more prominent members, Orton Chirwa, founded the Malawi Congress Party (MCP). Banda became MCP president on his release from jail in April 1960. By releasing Banda, Britain had signalled recognition of the need for change. At the Lancaster House conference of August 1960, Britain disregarded the protests of the Southern Rhodesians and allowed Nyasaland greater autonomy within the federation. And significantly, the colonial administration awarded a **selective vote to Africans**, so that in the election of August 1961 the MCP won 94% of the national vote and all but six of the 28 seats in parliament.

In January 1962, Banda became Minister of Natural Resources and Local Government in a government headed by the colonial governor, **Glyn Jones**. In November 1962, at the Marlborough House talks in London, Britain agreed to a two-phase plan for self-government in Nyasaland, and on 19 December the House of Commons announced that Nyasaland could withdraw from the federation. On 1 February 1963, Banda was sworn in as the Prime Minister of Nyasaland; on the final day of the same year, the federation was formally dissolved, and on 6 July 1964, Nyasaland was **granted full independence** and renamed Malawi.

MALAWI UNDER BANDA Even before independence, Banda had demonstrated to his cabinet a reluctance to accept constructive criticism and other people's ideas. His autocratic tendencies were emphasised when, at the Organisation of African Unity (OAU) summit in Cairo exactly three weeks after independence, he announced that Malawi had 'one party, one leader, one government and no nonsense about it'. It was this sort of statement, as well as a sudden reversal on foreign policy (in 1960, Banda had issued a joint statement with the future president of Tanzania, Julius Nyerere, to the effect that both countries would boycott white-ruled African states, but after independence he showed an unexpected enthusiasm to strike a trade deal with Portuguese Mozambique) that prompted the fateful 'Cabinet Crisis' little more than a month after independence.

On 16 August 1964, following Banda's return from the OAU conference, a group of cabinet members, led by Orton Chirwa, confronted Banda regarding his inflexible leadership and foreign policy. Banda offered to resign, but the cabinet asked him to continue as president on the condition that he would consider their grievances. Instead, Banda dismissed Chirwa and two other ministers from his cabinet. Three other ministers resigned in protest, including Henry Chipembere and the surviving Chisiza brother (in 1961, Dunduzu Chisiza, widely regarded as the most intellectually capable and far-sighted politician of his generation, had become the first of many Malawian politicians to die in a suspicious car 'accident'). The highly talented independence cabinet was overnight transformed into a bunch of yes-men.

Banda faced two more challenges to his rule. In February 1965, Henry Chipembere led a **rebellion** which was foiled by the army at Liwonde. Chipembere escaped to America, but many of his supporters were killed. In 1967, Yatutu Chisiza, another of the Cabinet Crisis discards, led several supporters into Malawi from a base in Tanzania. Chisiza was killed by soldiers. Remnants of Chipembere's rebels used guerrilla tactics to destabilise Banda's government for several years, but by the end of 1970 they had all been rounded up. After the Chipembere rebellion, Banda formally declared Malawi to be a one-party state, and on 6 July 1971, he made himself **Life President**.

It is often said that Banda was a benign dictator. True enough, he was not in the murderous class of somebody like Amin; nevertheless, he was entirely ruthless in his quest to obtain and maintain absolute power. It is conservatively estimated that 250,000 Malawians were **detained without trial** during his rule. Prisoners were underfed and in many cases brutally tortured. Banda's perceived political opponents, if they were not killed by the security police in jail, were victims of suspicious car accidents, or else – as Banda was proud of boasting – became '**meat for crocodiles**' in the Shire River. Several exiled Malawians died in explosive blasts strikingly reminiscent of those used by the South African security police.

To say that Banda was intolerant of criticism is an understatement. Critics were jailed, and not just political critics: it was, for instance, a detainable offence to discuss the president's age or his past relationships and medical activities. Gossip was not tolerated regarding his relationship with the MCP's 'Official Hostess', Cecelia Tamanda Kadzamira, who became Banda's mistress in 1958. Other illegal subjects included family planning (Malawi's population tripled under Banda) and, naturally enough, politics of any variety. Jehovah's Witnesses were persecuted (20,000 fled the country and many who remained or returned were detained or tortured to death) and Muslims were only barely tolerated, probably because they were so numerically strong in areas like Mangochi that even Banda wasn't prepared to stoop to the required scale of genocide.

Censorship was rife under Banda. Thousands of films, books and periodicals were banned, often for absurd reasons. Banda's whimsical dictates even covered personal dress – from 1968 to 1993, Malawian women were **banned from wearing miniskirts or trousers**. Perhaps no other episode illustrates the absurd vanity, megalomania and paranoia of Banda as his banning of an innocuous Simon and Garfunkel song: its release coincided with a rocky patch in Banda's love life and the lyrics ('Cecilia, you're breaking my heart…') were more than he could bear.

That Banda was perceived as benign is partly because so little information about Malawi reached the outside world. Most of all, though, it is because it was in Western interests to support the status quo in Malawi. In a climate of socialist-inspired African nationalism, Banda was an arch-conservative, a self-professed Anglophile, and sufficiently cynical to have open dealings with the South African government throughout the apartheid era. Banda was acceptable simply because he was co-operative. As recently as 1989, Margaret Thatcher and Pope John Paul II both visited Malawi, praising Banda's achievements and uttering not one public word of criticism of what had become the **longest-lived dictatorship** of its sort in Africa.

What did Banda achieve during his rule? Peace and stability, for one thing – though it can be argued that his ruthless dictatorship allowed for little else, and that Malawians are not a people given to civil disorder. Economic growth, for another – but again, Malawi was so underdeveloped at the time of independence that the growth rate he achieved (around 5% per annum on average) might easily have occurred under a genuinely benign leadership. Banda built Malawi its new and more centrally positioned capital at Lilongwe – a capital city funded almost entirely by the South African government. He improved the infrastructure and in particular the road system immeasurably – using Western aid given in exchange for his pro-

Western policies. In short, Banda achieved little that might not have been achieved by a more consensual government. And, in 1993, Malawi remained as it had been at the time of independence: one of Africa's poorest countries.

Banda did much to stir latent ethnic conflict in Malawi. His dream was to restore the ideal of the Maravi Empire, to which end he dressed his speeches in traditional Chewa symbolism and made **Chichewa** the official language, despite the fact that less than 30% of Malawians spoke it as their mother tongue. At the same time, he used the messianic build-up to his return to Malawi and the authority which Africans traditionally invest in a man of his age to create a powerful personality cult. He carried with him at all times a fly-whisk, the traditional symbol of the *sangoma* (witch doctor). On his return to Malawi, he insisted on using a name which he had reduced to a middle initial in Britain and Ghana – Hastings K Banda became Kamuzu (meaning 'the little root', roots being the primary source of traditional Malawian medicines). By using this traditional symbolism, and by emphasising his background as a Western doctor, Banda set himself up, especially in the eyes of village elders, as the new Kalonga of a revived Maravi Empire. Banda was a dictator; he was no fool.

THE ROAD TO DEMOCRACY In the last decade or so of his rule, Banda's was increasingly a puppet presidency, largely due to his advanced years (Banda turned 80 in 1978 and he was 95 when he finally relinquished power). From the mid-1980s onwards, Malawi was to all intents and purposes ruled by Banda's shadowy official hostess and her much-reviled uncle, John Tembo.

John Tembo was born in Dedza in 1932. He went to university in Lesotho and worked as a schoolmaster before he was appointed to Banda's cabinet as Finance Secretary in 1963, an appointment which was unpopular with other cabinet members for its strong air of nepotism. In the early years, Tembo played a sycophantic role in parliament, using his position primarily to acquire a personal fortune (by 1990, he was a director of a major firm in practically every business sector that dealt with government, including Malawi's main bank). Tembo came to be seen as Banda's natural successor, and in January 1992 he finally became, in name, the Minister of State in the Office of the President. In effect, John Tembo was appointed the Executive President of Malawi.

One of the reasons why Malawians tolerated Banda for so long was that, for all his failings, he commanded respect, particularly from the rural population. Another was that nobody could have predicted how long he would live: there was always hope that his replacement would have more democratic inclinations. Tembo neither commanded respect (he was widely seen as the mastermind behind Banda's greatest excesses) nor, at 60, was he particularly old, and his appointment in 1992 made it clear that he was Banda's chosen successor.

Even without Tembo, it is probable that Banda's days as Life President of Malawi were numbered. The end of the **Cold War** meant that supporting the West was no longer enough to ensure Banda a good international press and generous aid packages. In 1989, the British prime minister praised Banda for his 'wise leadership'; two years later, Britain made the belated and hypocritical gesture of withdrawing all non-humanitarian aid to Malawi in protest at Banda's abuse of human rights. The neighbourhood, too, was changing. By the end of 1992, Kenya and Zambia had held their first multi-party elections, Tanzania and Uganda were talking about them, South West Africa had become independent Namibia, and in South Africa the previously unthinkable was fast becoming an eventuality. Banda had become a man out of time.

But despite the change in the external climate, Tembo's appointment was probably the main impetus behind the Catholic bishops' galvanising *Lenten Letter*, which documented in graphic detail the failings and **abuses of power** of the Banda administration. The *Lenten Letter* was read aloud simultaneously, in churches across the country, on 3 March 1992, and then faxed to the BBC. Banda's response to the letter was to place the bishops under house arrest. But for once the world was watching. Banda was condemned by governments and Church bodies worldwide, and within Malawi, for the first time since independence, there was a climate of open dissent. May 1992 saw Malawi gripped by strikes and protests, culminating in the **Lilongwe Riot** of 7 May in which 40 people were shot dead by police. In October 1992, Orton Chirwa, the founder of the MCP and a leading member of the short-lived independence cabinet, died in suspicious circumstances in the Zomba Prison where he had been detained since 1981.

Banda's growing unpopularity left him with little option but to announce a referendum on the question of a **multi-party election**. The referendum took place in March 1993, and it drew an overwhelming majority of votes in favour of change, a popular pro-referendum slogan being 'Votey smarty, votey multi-party'. Two new parties of note emerged: AFORD and the UDF, the latter led by Bakili Muluzi, a Muslim businessman who had once briefly served in Banda's cabinet before resigning.

Polling took place on 17 March 1994. The election was declared substantially free and fair, which in the strict sense it probably was, though the final results were a reflection less of policies and popularity than of regional and ethnic differences. The MCP won by a landslide in the Central Region, AFORD achieved a similar result in the Northern Region, and the UDF won overwhelmingly in the south. The Southern Region being the most populous part of Malawi, the overall election was won by the UDF. **Bakili Muluzi** was made the second President of Malawi.

The general election of 1999 was again won by the UDF and Dr Muluzi was installed for a second presidential term. Although Muluzi proved to be a democratic ruler, in 2002, he and his party attempted to alter the constitution to allow him a third term as president, a move that caused controversy and dissent. Freedom of speech is still a reality, as is a free press, and many Malawians were openly critical of Muluzi's leadership, something that would never have been allowed under Banda.

Banda himself died of natural causes in 1997, aged somewhere between 97 and 101, depending on which of the several possible dates given for his birth you believe. In 1995, the former life president was tried for the alleged murder of three cabinet ministers and an MP who died in a 'car accident' near Mwanza in 1983. Both he and his co-defendants, John Tembo and Mama Cecelia, were acquitted on all charges. This alone says much about the new Malawi: a legal trial was a privilege given to few opponents in the despotic days of Banda and Tembo.

THE NEW MILLENNIUM

Based partly on text supplied for the fourth edition by Nicholas Wright
Gwanda Chakuamba, who had surprised John Tembo and the rest of Malawi by being chosen by Banda to succeed him as leader of the MCP, was declared the close second in the much-disputed 1999 general election won by Dr Muluzi. Whereas Muluzi's first term might be interpreted in terms of the consolidation of Malawian democracy and constitutionalism, his second, which followed this election, was very seriously compromised by **high-level corruption** and the intimidation of political opposition by the UDF Youth Wing, the Young Democrats. Such was the hold Muluzi had established over Malawian politics that, although he narrowly

failed to have the constitution altered to allow himself a third term, he managed, in 2004, to impose upon a reluctant UDF and a suspicious electorate, a presidential candidate heartily disliked by the one and virtually unknown to the other. This was Bingu wa Mutharika, President of Malawi from May 2004 until his unexpected death in April 2012.

Mutharika transformed Malawian politics in February 2005 with his **resignation** from the UDF, ostensibly because his anti-corruption policies not only lacked support from within the party, but had also initiated an alleged assassination plot against him by party members the month before. Mutharika then formed his own party, the Democratic Progressive Party (DPP), which retained a minority in the National Assembly for the rest of his first presidential term (Presidential and National Assembly elections, though held concurrently, are separate ballots). However, Mutharika and the DPP both dominated the May 2009 elections, which also saw the return to prominence of Banda's old crony John Tembo as the MCP presidential candidate with the backing of Muluzi. Mutharika took 66% of the presidential vote, as opposed to Tembo's 30%, and the DPP was even more dominant in the National Assembly vote, securing 114 of the 193 seats, with the next-highest number (30) going to independents, while the MCP and UDF managed a mere 26 and 17 seats respectively.

The Mutharika government was for a time characterised by **vigorous anti-corruption rhetoric**, which inevitably targeted the old UDF bigwigs, including Muluzi, who was briefly arrested in March 2006 on charges of fraud and corruption that were subsequently dropped. Muluzi was arrested again in February 2009 and bailed out within hours, but still stands to face possible charges of 86 counts of corruption and abuse of office, including the alleged diversion of more than US$10 million of donor money into his personal account. The case was still winding its way through the courts in 2012.

A populist feature of the Mutharika era was the lionisation of former president Hastings Banda, whose nickname 'Kamuzu' has been restored to several roads and institutions from which it had been stripped under Muluzi – for instance the national stadium, central hospital and international airport serving Lilongwe. Mutharika was the main mover behind the construction of the new Banda Mausoleum in Malawi, at a cost of US$600,000, and his policies unabashedly harkened back to the **'old-fashioned values'** of the Banda era. At its best, this manifested itself in a certain personal integrity, but Mutharika also shared Banda's intolerance for criticism, and during his second term he became deeply suspicious of certain institutions associated with Malawi's budding democracy – the extraordinarily free press, for instance, and the extremely rowdy National Assembly.

A RETURN TO AUTOCRACY This drift back towards authoritarianism and a poisonous culture of secretiveness was hinted at early in Mutharika's rule when Vice President Cassim Chilumpha was arrested in 2006 for his alleged involvement in a plot to assassinate the president. Autocratic tendencies notwithstanding, the first term of Mutharika's presidency was largely successful – maize and tobacco harvests were bountiful thanks to a popular programme of government fertilizer subsidies (along with good rains), and since Malawi is so heavily tobacco-dependent, **economic growth** reached a stunning 9.7% in 2008.

It was not to last, however. The demand of the International Monetary Fund (IMF) to devalue the kwacha was roundly refused, and donor relations began a long downward spiral in 2010 when, in a highly-publicised trial, two gay men were tried, convicted and sentenced to 14 years imprisonment under anti-sodomy laws.

Amid the international outcry, it took the intervention of UN secretary general Ban Ki-moon to secure a presidential pardon from Mutharika. Later in the year, the purchase of an £8 million presidential jet prompted Britain to reduce annual aid by £3 million, contributing to what quickly turned into acute **forex shortages**. As basic goods and fuel became scarce, the wider social and political environment in Malawi soured as well. Newspapers critical of government were threatened with closure, opposition figures were intimidated and jailed without charge – some dying in mysterious circumstances – and in April 2011 Chancellor College in Zomba was forcibly closed after a row erupted over a professor who drew parallels between Malawi and the Arab Spring countries.

It was into this environment that **Wikileaks** revealed a communiqué from the British high commissioner describing Mutharika as 'ever more autocratic and intolerant of criticism'. Lilongwe wasted no time in expelling the ambassador, and Britain replied with a further suspension of some £550 million in aid over four years. By mid 2011, the majority of Malawi's other major donors had suspended funding as well, rendering foreign currency for vital imports of food and fuel nearly inaccessible. Days-long queues suddenly became the norm, and a rising tide of discontent culminated in the June 2011 **street protests** where security forces gunned down at least 18 demonstrators in Mzuzu and Karonga.

Mutharika was unrepentant in his response to the killings, pledging to would-be demonstrators that 'if you go back to the streets, I will smoke you out'. For the next year Malawians lived under increasingly crippling shortages of the most basic goods and watched as their country's recent democratic and economic gains crumbled.

DIVINE INTERVENTION It was into this menacing atmosphere that the ever-unpredictable hand of fate made its presence known. Bingu had been preparing his brother and education minister, Peter Mutharika, to take over the presidency in 2014, and had all but officially frozen out his vice president, **Joyce Banda**, from anything but a ceremonial role in government. Kept from governing and treated as little more than an observer, she left the ruling DPP and formed her own party, the People's Party (PP), to little fanfare.

In April 2012, with the country on the precipice of dynastic dictatorship, President Bingu wa Mutharika unexpectedly suffered a **fatal cardiac arrest**. Upon Bingu's death, Peter Mutharika was in all but name the acting vice president and anointed successor, but constitutionally speaking he had no legal claim to the presidency. That claim belonged to the long-sidelined Joyce Banda who, during several anxious days of official government silence and furious backroom horse-trading, deftly negotiated the power vacuum, receiving a pledge of support from the army which enabled her to step in and claim the presidency.

Sworn in on 7 April 2012, she became **Africa's second female head of state** after Ellen Johnson Sirleaf of Liberia. Her first priority has been to rebuild the donor relationships destroyed under the previous administration, and she has been largely successful in doing so. Donors are back on board, the British ambassador is once again in Lilongwe, goods are back in stores, and the sense of relief across the country is profound. Since taking office, Banda has sold the controversial presidential jet and taken a series of high-profile actions to rein in the worst excesses of the Mutharika regime. Becoming a darling of the West has come at a price, however, and her move to **devalue the kwacha** in accordance with the IMF has been deeply unpopular; it could derail her chances of winning the 2014 election, should she contest it. Whoever wins the next election will inherit a country still reeling, brought back by the whims of fate from what had become a very dangerous brink.

GOVERNMENT AND ADMINISTRATION

Malawi is a democratic republic, with elections every five years. In 1970, Hastings Kamuzu Banda, Malawi's president since independence in 1964, amended the constitution to declare himself Life President, a position he retained until 1994. During these years Malawi was a one-party state, and the only people who were allowed to stand for election were members of Banda's Malawi Congress Party (MCP). The first truly democratic election took place in May 1994, bringing the United Democratic Front (UDF) to power, with Dr Bakili Muluzi as president. Re-elected in 1999, President Muluzi attempted to change Malawi's constitution to allow him to seek re-election for a third term but prior to the election of May 2004 he installed Dr Bingu wa Mutharika as the UDF presidential candidate. As President of Malawi, Mutharika established a new party, the Democratic Progressive Party, in March 2005, and this became the official ruling party after Mutharika was returned to power in the 2009 elections. Upon Mutharika's death in April 2012, Vice-president Joyce Banda assumed the presidency and, with that, her newly established People's Party was thrust into government after less than one year in existence.

ADMINISTRATIVE REGIONS Malawi is divided into three main administrative regions: Southern, Central and Northern, the capitals of which are respectively Blantyre, Lilongwe and Mzuzu. There are 28 administrative districts, of which Dedza, Dowa, Kasungu, Lilongwe, Mchinji, Nkhotakota, Ntcheu, Ntchisi and Salima lie in Central Region, while Chitipa, Karonga, Likoma, Mzimba, Nkhata Bay and Rumphi fall within Northern Region, and Balaka, Blantyre, Chikwawa, Chiradzulu, Machinga, Mangochi, Mulanje, Mwanza, Nsanje, Phalombe, Thyolo, Zomba and the recently created Neno are all in Southern Region.

ECONOMY

The economy is essentially agricultural. At least 80% of the population is rural, and agriculture accounts for almost 40% of the GDP, 90% of export revenue, and 80% of the workforce. The most important crop in economic terms is tobacco, which accounts for up to 70% of export revenue, depending on annual output and world prices, which have been in decline for some years. Malawi is the second-largest tobacco producer in Africa and the ninth-largest globally, with an annual yield of up to 110,000 tonnes. Other important export crops are sugarcane, which grows in the Shire Valley and on parts of the lakeshore, and tea and coffee, which are associated with highland areas such as Misuku Hills, Thyolo and Mulanje.

Until the 1980s, Malawi was always self-sufficient in staple foods such as maize, beans, rice and cassava, and it regularly exported an excess to neighbouring countries. Periodic drought and rapid population growth mean that this is no longer the case, and the country has experienced several cumulative dry-season famines in recent years, most critically in 2005 when a shortfall of two million tonnes of maize prompted President Mutharika to declare a National Disaster. In 2006, the government initiated a programme of fertiliser subsidies that has done much to boost crop production.

Malawi is heavily dependent on foreign aid, so much so that the development budget dropped by more than 75% when the IMF and other donors placed a moratorium on aid disbursements in 2001, citing the high level of corruption in the Muluzi government. Aid was once again frozen under the late President Mutharika, to disastrous results. Despite the donors who have been enticed to return under

The life, colours and contours of Malawi lend themselves to painting. Sometimes everywhere you look there is another picture.

I rarely travel anywhere without a sketchbook, pencil and watercolours, even if I have a camera in my bag, too. The most rewarding times I have had in Malawi have been when painting – it causes an interaction that is seldom found between tourists and Malawians. It's also thoroughly absorbing and addictive. Trying to record a sunset or a market scene in colour, or a moving elephant in line can be the most intense experience as you observe and allow the feeling of the environment to combine into image through your hand onto paper.

If you don't want to create art yourself, you can buy it. The art scene in Malawi is not limited to the stylised paintings that you will be tempted to buy on the beaches and streets. Among the street art are paintings, batiks and drawings that encapsulate some of the wit, striking looks and movements of many Malawians.

Malawi has very few internationally recognised artists. Among them are two who straddle the Western world and Malawi. Both are based in the UK, and have work that reflects both halves of their lives. The 'new contemporary', Samson Kambalu, is currently winning awards for his conceptual work, while painter David Kelly uses his deep knowledge and understanding of the African bush to make canvases come alive with the wildlife of the national parks.

In Blantyre, artists to look out for include Aaron Banda and David Matoto (highly collectable for birds and village scenes respectively) as well as Brian Hara, Jomwe, Innocent Willinga, Lovemore Kankhwani, Ellis Singanu and Boston Mbale, all of whom exhibit at La Caverna at Mandala House. Artists also exhibit at Central Africana Bookshop in Uta Waleza Shopping Centre.

Lilongwe's galleries include Mtendere Art Gallery in Mbico House along Chilambula Road, Arthouse Africa, behind the Hong Kong Restaurant in Capital City as well as La Galeria in Old Town Mall. La Galeria champions all the top names including Nyangu Chodola, William Mwale, Elson Kambalu, Peter Mtungi, Hughson Mbawa, Noel Bisai, Nixon Malamulo and Peter Chikondi. The highlight of the visual arts calendar is without doubt the Wildlife Society Art Fest in Lilongwe each November, where over 300 artists and craftspeople exhibit.

Malawi has long been famous for its hardwood carvings, which have been exported all over the world. Very few of Malawi's carvers have been credited by name, but through Mua Mission and a couple of the galleries, including African Habit and La Caverna, some of the master carvers are now achieving a recognised status of excellence.

Pottery and ceramics are less common now that plastic has arrived, but clay pots of all sizes are still made in many areas. Dedza and Nkhotakota potteries are the key places to buy glazed stoneware and where traditional clay-pot and ceramics workshops take place.

Malawi attracts more than its share of artistic visitors through Art Safari, a unique travel company which lays an equal emphasis on art and travel, with adventurous itineraries combining art tuition and safari guiding. Many of Malawi's artists have also benefited from its artist-in-residence scheme (e *info@artsafari.co.uk; www.artsafari.co.uk*).

Joyce Banda's leadership, Malawi remains one of the poorest countries in the world, with a GDP of US$14.5 billion in 2012 and an annual per-capita income of US$900. Around 53% of the population lives below the poverty line and nearly a quarter are categorised as ultra-poor according to the National Statistic Office/World Bank. Major long-term concerns are the high rate of population growth, which is expected to push the population above 20 million by 2015, a rapidly growing HIV/AIDS problem and resultant population of orphans, and ongoing deforestation outside protected areas.

PEOPLE AND CULTURE

POPULATION The population of Malawi is estimated to stand at 16.3 million. This represents a massive increase since the 1998 census, which recorded a population of 9,934,000, and a fourfold increase since independence in 1964, when the population was estimated at 3.75 million. Malawi was ranked the seventh most densely populated country in mainland Africa in 2002, with 90 people/km², and that figure now stands at around 137 people/km². Despite this, most of the population lives in rural areas. The most populous city in Malawi is Lilongwe, followed by Blantyre, Mzuzu, Zomba, Kasungu, Mangochi, Karonga, Salima, Nkhotakota and Liwonde.

LANGUAGES The official language of Malawi is English and the national language is Chichewa. The indigenous languages of Malawi all belong to the Bantu group. The most widely spoken of these, especially in the Southern and Central regions, and the joint official language until 1994, is Chichewa. In the north, the most widely spoken language is Chitumbuka. There are many other linguistic groups in the country, some of the more important being Yao, Ngoni and Nyanja.

RELIGION Organised religion has played a major role in the history of Malawi. Its influence started with the slave-trading Yao tribe that settled in southern Malawi after being converted to Islam by Zanzibari Arabs, and picked up when the Christian Portuguese arrived on the scene in the first half of the 19th century to share in the spoils of this evil trade. The arrival of the Scottish explorer, Dr David Livingstone, in 1859, was the catalyst that put an end to the slave trade and the string of mission stations that followed opened up the country for trade and colonisation. The missionaries were a strict bunch and offered a high standard of education to all, a tradition which, to this day, ensures that Malawians are well educated and well disciplined.

The modern Malawian government allows freedom of religion and believes in co-operation between the state and religious organisations for assistance in the socio-economic uplifting of the people – the missions are still very involved in education. It is estimated that about 80% of the country's population is Christian and 13% Islamic; various other faiths and sects make up the remaining few per cent. There is a high degree of religious tolerance between all religions, which contributes to the generally peaceful state of affairs in Malawi.

CULTURE With about eleven different ethnic groups in the country, Malawi has a mosaic of cultural norms and practices. Unique traditional dances and rituals as well as arts and crafts identify the groups. The Museum of Malawi recognises the importance of these traditions, and promotes appropriate activities in schools and other public places. Mua Mission's KuNgoni Art Centre and Museum has embraced the cultures and religions of the Central Region, which is also seen clearly in the

MALAWI MUSIC SCENE: BELIEVE IT

Updated from text supplied for the fourth edition by Harry Gibbs

Malawi music is currently enjoying an explosion of styles and genres which are showcased in bars, clubs and taverns throughout the country every weekend.

Whether it be a traditional band with homemade instruments or a budding Hip Hop or Ragga artist, the standards of music have noticeably improved over the past decade.

Bands such as Wambali Mkandawire and Manyasa and the Black Missionaries have impressed audiences across southern Africa. Lucius Banda, Wendy Harawa, Joseph Tembo and others have toured as far afield as England, France, Australia and Nigeria.

A relative newcomer is John Chibade, who sold over 100,000 copies of his first album within Malawi, while Billy Kaunda and Ben Mankhamba (previously Ben Michael) have maintained their standing with strong recent album releases.

One of the most exciting Malawian acts out today is The Very Best, though they are much better known in the west than within Malawi itself. Fronted by Lilongwe-based singer Esau Mwamwaya and produced by London DJ Johan Hugo, this cross-continental duo is putting together some seriously innovative music, combining frenetic electronic beats with irresistible Afro-pop melodies, and it's all sung in Chichewa. For a sure-fire dance party, check out their cheekily christened 2012 album *MTMTMK*, or *More To Malawi Than Madonna's Kids*.

In Blantyre, the Blue Elephant hosts several bands and Lilongwe's live music scene has been prominent at Chameleon Bar. No mention of Lilongwe would be complete without Chez Ntemba, the pinnacle of Malawi nightlife – a night at Chez Ntemba will often give you the opportunity to watch the sun rise. In Mzuzu, Mzoozoozoo is a pub and place to stay with great character and is also home to Souls of the Ghetto, acoustic winners of the 2005 Kuche Kuche Music Awards.

The major festival in Malawi is Lake of Stars (*www.lakeofstars.org*), which has been held at one or other location along the lakeshore every September since 2004, and has hosted such giants as Andy Cato from Groove Armada and Felix B of Basement Jaxx.

Local radio stations play a vast amount of music from all over the world and also do their part to showcase Malawian musical talent. So when in Malawi, turn on the radio, buy a tape or CD (MP3s are everywhere as well) and go out to the clubs and bars to see what is happening.

approach to the mission's work. Above all though, it is the tradition of hospitality, friendship and courtesy that permeates the entire country and warrants Malawi's epithet 'The Warm Heart of Africa'.

Malawi

Need advice and information?
Our award-winning UK tourist office is *the* source for all your Malawi travel queries, and our website is the top ranked site on Malawi. Provided directly by members of Malawi's Tourist Industry.

tel (UK): 0115 9727250
Email: enquiries@malawitourism.com
www.malawitourism.com

Malawi
Travel Marketing
Consortium

2

Flora and Fauna

By comparison with most of its eastern and southern African neighbours, Malawi is a small country, and too densely populated to support the immense areas of untamed wilderness associated with Tanzania, Zambia and other leading safari destinations. Nevertheless, Malawi is a land of thrilling topographic variety, dominated by the towering escarpments and partially submerged floor of the Great Rift Valley, with habitats that range from the muggy low-lying Lower Shire Valley to the montane grasslands and forests of the Nyika, Mulanje and other such massifs. Significant tracts of indigenous vegetation are protected within a well-managed network of national parks, wildlife reserves and forest reserves, and if Malawi doesn't quite make the premiership league of African safari destinations, it remains highly rewarding to wildlife enthusiasts. Furthermore, unlike many of the continent's premier wildlife destinations, Malawi's top natural attractions – the forested mountaintops, rich birdlife, dazzling fish diversity of Lake Malawi, and wildlife sanctuaries such as Liwonde, Majete and Vwaza Marsh – remain accessible to travellers on a low-to-moderate budget.

VEGETATION

The dominant vegetation type, Brachystegia (or *miombo*) woodland naturally covers around 70% of Malawi's surface area, but has been replaced by cultivation or otherwise degraded over much of this range. As the name suggests, this woodland is dominated by trees of the genus Brachystegia, which tend to be very fire-resistant, and are technically deciduous, losing their leaves over September and October. Brachystegia woodland is found at altitudes up to 1,500m, usually in areas with an average annual rainfall above 1,000mm. In areas of high rainfall, such as the Viphya Mountains, tall Brachystegia trees form a closed canopy, whereas the trees tend to be more stunted and the canopy more open in lower rainfall areas.

Several other woodland types (again named after the most common type of tree) occur in Malawi, mostly at altitudes below 500m. Mopane woodland is dominant in the Liwonde area, while *terminalia* woodland is common in the area east of Zomba and west of Lake Chilwa. The mixed woodland of the Lower Shire Valley and Lilongwe area holds trees of the Brachystegia, Acacia, Combretum and Bauhinia families.

The unmistakable baobab tree (*Adansonia digitalia*) is a characteristic feature of low-lying parts of Malawi, particularly the Lake Malawi shore and the Shire Valley. The unusual, bulbous shape of the baobab tree makes it one of the most photogenic features of the African landscape, and it has given rise to the belief in many parts of Africa that the tree was planted upside down by God. It is thought that some baobab trees grow to be over 3,000 years old. The spongy wood of the baobab (it is related to the balsa tree) is rich in calcium, making it an important food source for elephants in times of drought.

Palm trees are characteristic of low-lying and well-watered parts of Malawi, and together with the baobabs they give places like Liwonde National Park and the Elephant Marsh much of their character. Four types of palm occur naturally in Malawi. The borassus palm (*Borassus aethiopum*) is a tall tree growing up to 20m in height, and is characterised by a distinctive swelling halfway up its stem, and by fan-shaped leaves. It is common along rivers in northern Malawi, such as in Vwaza Marsh Wildlife Reserve, and on the southern lakeshore around Salima and Monkey Bay.

The doum palm (*Hyphaene benguallensis*) grows to a similar height as the borassus, but it has a thinner stem without a swelling, and more frond-like leaves. Doum palms are common on the Lake Malawi shore and in the Shire Valley, particularly in Liwonde National Park and around the Elephant Marsh.

The much smaller wild date palm (*Phoenix relinata*) occurs along rivers, where it may take one of two forms: that of a dense bush, or of a tree hanging over the water. The wild date palm can be recognised by its feathery fronds. It is common along the Shire River (you'll see plenty in Liwonde National Park) and in highland areas such as Thyolo, Viphya and Nyika.

The raffia palm is noted for its large leaves: at up to 18m in length, they are the largest found on any plant in the world. The raffia may have a stem of up to 10m in height, or its leaves may grow straight out of the ground in a cluster. Raffia palms are generally found along streams to an altitude of 1,500m; they are common in the Shire Highlands and in Nkhotakota Wildlife Reserve.

Evergreen forests, though they cover a mere 1% of the country's surface area, provide Malawi's most biodiverse habitat in terms of plants, birds and insects. Evergreen forest is distinguished from woodland by its high interlocking canopy and a predominance of non-deciduous trees. What evergreen forest still occurs in Malawi is confined to remnant pockets in montane areas. Among the more accessible areas of evergreen forest are those on Ntchisi, Mulanje, Viphya, Nyika, Dedza and Zomba mountains.

Semi-evergreen forest covers around 2% of Malawi's surface area. The canopy of this forest is generally formed by *Brachystegia spiciformis* trees, underneath which lies a dense undergrowth of herbs and shrubs. Forest of this type is found on the slopes of Mulanje and Zomba mountains, as well as in the Thyolo and Nkhata Bay areas. It is also common along some rivers.

The most common type of forest in Malawi consists of exotic pine and eucalyptus plantations. These plantations play an important role in providing timber and firewood, and their existence arguably helps protect what indigenous forest remains from being chopped down. In addition, plantations are often interspersed with ribbons of indigenous riverine forest and fringing scrub, which can be very rewarding for seeing wildlife. However, the plantations generally support a very restricted fauna and they tend to be more thirsty than indigenous trees, lowering highland water tables and causing streams that provide vital sustenance to communities living below the watershed to dry up.

Montane grassland and moorland covers about 5% of Malawi's surface area. It is the predominant vegetation type on the plateaux of Nyika, Mulanje and Viphya mountains. These plateaux support a mixture of grasses, heathers and heaths, and are particularly rich in wild flowers, especially after the rains.

A notable feature of Malawi's flora is the high number of orchid species. Around 280 terrestrial and 120 epiphytic orchid species have been recorded in Malawi, with the greatest variety to be found in Nyika National Park and on Mulanje and Zomba mountains. The best time for seeing orchids in bloom is between November and March, though exact flowering times vary from year to year and area to area, depending on local rainfall.

CONSERVATION AREAS

NATIONAL PARKS AND WILDLIFE RESERVES Malawi has five national parks and four wildlife reserves; all except Majete fall under the jurisdiction of the Department of National Parks and Wildlife.

Nyika National Park The country's largest protected area, and the most northerly, centred upon the vast Nyika Plateau, which is deliciously cool when the rest of the country is hot. Primarily a scenic reserve, it also offers some good game viewing, and can be explored from Chelinda Camp. Access is difficult without private transport.

Vwaza Marsh Wildlife Reserve A short way south of Nyika, where it offers easy access to a self-catering camp known for its excellent game viewing (particularly elephant) – a budget traveller's dream come true.

Kasungu National Park On the Zambian border, two hours north of Lilongwe, Kasungu is the largest 'bush' reserve in the country, but wildlife numbers are somewhat depleted and game viewing is highly seasonal. The newly refurbished Lifupa Conservation Lodge offers accommodation to all budgets.

Nkhotakota Wildlife Reserve The country's oldest reserve, supporting a wide variety of game species, including lion and elephant. Lacking in facilities for many years, two newly established hostelries, Bua River Lodge and Tongole Wilderness Lodge, have opened up access to this underrated reserve.

Lake Malawi National Park Established at Cape Maclear in 1980, this is the oldest freshwater national park in Africa, and was declared a UNESCO World Heritage Site in 1984. The park is mostly of interest for its diverse fish and birdlife, is highly accessible to independent travellers and has plenty of accommodation.

Liwonde National Park Along the atmospheric Upper Shire River, this is the country's top destination for big game such as hippo, buffalo and elephant, and the birdlife is simply fantastic. The upmarket Mvuu Camp and Lodge lies in the heart of the park, while the more southerly Liwonde Safari Camp & Bushman's Baobabs Lodge are suited to budget travellers.

Majete Wildlife Reserve Once a victim of heavy poaching, but now restocked with 3,000 head of wildlife and experiencing a new lease of life under the African Parks Foundation, this is rapidly becoming Malawi's top safari destination. Set on the Lower Shire River, this has a good mid-range camp and is also home to the luxurious Mkulumadzi Lodge.

Lengwe National Park In the Lower Shire Valley, where it offers good but limited game viewing (highlights are large herds of buffalo and nyala) and superb birding. There's good accommodation at Nyala Lodge near the entrance gate.

Mwabvi Wildlife Reserve In the far south of the country there were plans for this reserve to be redeveloped, but the concessionaire has since pulled out of the project. Facilities are limited, but it is a fine destination for self-sufficient campers who enjoy hiking with a fair chance of exciting animal encounters.

FOREST RESERVES The Department of Forestry oversees a network of about 65 forest reserves, most of which are dominated by plantation forest, but which also play an important conservation role by preserving what remains of the country's evergreen and semi-evergreen forests interspersed between the plantations. Entrance to forest reserves is free and there are no restrictions on where you walk. In addition, several reserves have accommodation in the form of privatised forest lodges and forestry resthouses, which usually allow camping in their grounds. Animals characteristic of the forest reserves include leopard and various nocturnal small predators, bushpig, samango and vervet monkey, baboon, bushbuck, klipspringer, and red, blue and grey duikers. A few forest reserves still support elephants and attract the occasional vagrant lion from across the border in Mozambique. The forests are also notable for insects (most visibly butterflies) and support a wealth of localised forest birds.

Traditionally, the most popular forest reserves with travellers are Zomba and Mulanje, which protect the eponymous mountains. More recently, the immense Viphya Forest Reserve has gained in popularity due to the excellent Luwawa Forest Lodge, and there are also very good forest lodges in Ntchisi, Dzalanyama, Namizimu and Chongoni forest reserves, the last the focal point of the Chongoni

THE CONSERVATION CHALLENGE

Carl Bruessow, Mount Mulanje Conservation Trust

With a landscape that varies from as low as 35m rising to over 3,000m above sea level, and that includes large freshwater bodies and high mountain plateaux, Malawi has a diverse range of ecological habitats and a rich plant and animal biodiversity. To conserve these habitats and wildlife, the country has proclaimed five national parks, four wildlife reserves and about 65 forest reserves – an impressive commitment of over 20% of the total land area. An indication of the valuable natural heritage here is the 1,000-plus cichlid fish species in Lake Malawi and over 500 plant and animal montane species, all of which are unique to Malawi.

The large mammals of the national parks and wildlife reserves have experienced a continued serious threat to survival over the past 30 years. An underfunded government management authority has battled to carry out its responsibilities and the current status of each protected area reflects the level of involvement of other support agencies. Big mammals have been hunted illegally for their meat and other traditional products ever since these conservation areas were set up and this conflict continues, even where law-enforcement efforts are adequate. All the conservation areas have tourist accommodation, while facilities in the national parks are concessioned out to commercial operations and are of a high standard. There is little doubt that tourists have a direct benefit on the status of wildlife as their presence acts as a deterrent to poachers, and the income generated from tourism supports both local management and community-improvement activities.

Donor assistance to support the country's parks and reserves, and the environment in general, has waned over the past decade as there is a widespread perception that caring for the nation's wildlife and natural resources is a low

Rock Art Area UNESCO World Heritage Site. Other accessible forest reserves covered in the regional part of this guide include Thuma, Dedza Mountain, Mua-Livulezi, Michuru Mountain, Thyolo Mountain, Kalwe, Nkuwadzi and Mughese in the Misuku Hills.

OTHER CONSERVATION AREAS Other places of interest for wildlife and birds include Lilongwe Nature Sanctuary, the Elephant Marsh, Nyala Park, Game Haven, Kuti Wildlife Reserve and Lake Chilwa.

WILDLIFE

MAMMALS Several useful field guides to African mammals are available for the purpose of identification. What most such guides lack is detailed distribution details for individual countries, so the following notes should be seen as a Malawi-specific supplement to a regional or continental field guide.

Predators The **lion** (*Panthera leo*) is the largest African cat, and the animal that every visitor to Africa hopes to see. Lions are sociable animals which live in family prides of up to 15 individuals. They tend to hunt by night, favouring large and medium-sized antelopes. By day, lions generally do little but find a shady spot and sleep the hours away. In Malawi, lions are now extremely rare. They are resident in Nkhotakota Wildlife Reserve, have recently been reintroduced to Majete, and there are plans to reintroduce a resident population to Liwonde in 2013. Vagrants

political priority. In this desperate situation, a number of concerned organisations and individuals have rallied to raise support in a variety of ways. The Wildlife & Environmental Society of Malawi, the original conservation agency formed in 1947, continues to maintain an essential advocacy and support role in the country. Since then a number of other trusts have been established specifically to support activities across most of these parks and this broader public interest is slowly waking up the government. The most significant improvement has been the private sector management takeover by the philanthropic African Parks organisation, which is making a major investment to reinvigorate the Majete Wildlife Reserve.

Malawi's environment and natural resources face an immense sustainability challenge. The majority of Malawians are smallholder farmers but most available arable land is now intensely farmed and the need for local natural resources for livelihood use and sale has also sharpened. The recent increase in the country's already high population has intensified this problem to the point where conservation areas are being encroached in a bid to find more land and forest products. Many of the forest reserves in the southern region originally established for watershed protection have now been completely deforested and opened up for growing crops. The fish stocks of the lakes are depleted and many of the beautiful endemic cichlid fish are threatened by illegal fishing around their island habitats. Motivating a broad public response to reverse this degradation through the adoption of improved approaches and practices is now an essential part of much of the project work being spearheaded by the many local and international non-governmental organisations working in Malawi.

are recorded from time to time in Kasungu, Vwaza Marsh, Nyika, Mwabvi and Liwonde.

Leopards (*Panthera pardus*) are compact cats, marked with rosette-like spots, whose favoured habitats are forests and rocky hills. Leopards are still widespread in Malawi: they live in all the national parks and game reserves, most forest reserves and even in some hilly or wooded regions outside conservation areas. The success of leopards in modern Africa is due largely to their secretive, solitary nature; they are very rarely seen even where they are common. Nyika National Park is said to have the greatest concentration of leopards in central Africa, and sightings are quite commonplace in the vicinity of Chelinda Camp.

Leopard

Cheetahs (*Acynonix jubatus*) are creatures of the open plains, normally seen either on their own or in small family groups. They are superficially similar in appearance to leopards, but easily distinguished by their more streamlined build, the black 'tear marks' running down their face, and their simple (as opposed to rosette) spots. Cheetahs were resident in Kasungu National Park until the late 1970s, but are now probably extinct in Malawi, though plans exist to reintroduce them to Majete.

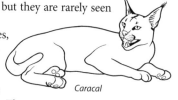

Cheetah

Several smaller species of cat, such as **caracal** (*Felis caracal*), **serval** (*Felis serval*) and **African wild cat** (*Felis silvestris*), occur in Malawi, but they are rarely seen on account of their nocturnal habits.

The largest indigenous canine species, the **African wild dog** (*Lycaon pictus*), is unmistakable on account of its cryptic black, brown and cream coat. Hunting dogs live and hunt in packs, normally about ten animals strong. The

Caracal

African wild dog

introduction to Africa of canine diseases such as rabies has caused a severe decline in hunting dog numbers in recent years, and this endangered species has been on the IUCN Red List of Threatened Animals since 1984. It is no longer resident in Malawi but occasional sightings are reported from reserves on the Zambian border, such as Vwaza Marsh and Kasungu.

Jackals are lightly built dogs, mostly nocturnal in habit and generally solitary by nature. Several species are recognised, but only one – the **side-striped jackal** (*Canis adustus*)– is present in Malawi, and can be recognised by its grey or sometimes yellowish coat, indistinct black side stripe, and white-tipped tail. The side-striped jackal has been recorded in Nyika, Liwonde and Lengwe national parks, and in Vwaza Marsh and Nkhotakota wildlife reserves.

The **spotted hyena** (*Crocuta crocuta*) is a large, bulky predator with a sloping back, black-on-brown lightly spotted coat and dog-like face. Contrary to popular myth, hyenas are not a type of dog; nor are they exclusively scavengers or hermaphroditic. These opportunistic feeders have a complex social structure and innate curiosity that makes them among the most fascinating creatures to watch in the wild. Spotted hyenas are widespread throughout Africa, often living near human habitation, and can be found in all of Malawi's national parks and wildlife reserves, as well as in many forest reserves and even outside conservation areas. The spotted hyena is nocturnal in habit, but because it is not

Spotted hyena

as retiring as most night hunters, it is often seen around dusk and dawn. Probably because the Old and New towns are separated by a wildlife sanctuary, Lilongwe is probably the only African capital where you can regularly hear hyena at night.

The Viverridae is a group of small predators that includes **mongooses** and the cat-like **civets** and **genets**. At least nine mongoose species have been recorded in Malawi, most of which can be readily observed in the right habitat. The **African civet** (*Civettictis civetta*), **tree civet** (*Nandinia binotata*) and **large-spotted genet** (*Genetta tigrina*) are all present in Malawi, but they are rarely seen because of their nocturnal habits. The best chance of seeing these animals is on a night game drive in Liwonde National Park, and campers on Domwe Island in Lake Malawi National Park may spot them as well.

Four representatives of the Mustelidae occur in Malawi: the **honey badger** (*Mellivora capensis*), **Cape clawless otter** (*Aonyx capensis*), **spotted-necked otter** (*Hydrictis maculicollis*) and **striped polecat** (*Ictonyx striatus*). Otters are occasionally seen at Otter Point in Lake Malawi National Park.

Primates The most common primate in Malawi is probably the **vervet monkey** (*Chlorocebus pygerythrus*), a small, grey animal with a black face and, in the male, blue genitals. Vervet monkeys live in large troops in most habitats except desert and evergreen forest. They are frequently seen outside reserves. The closely related **samango** or **blue monkey** (*Cercopithecus mitis*) is a less common species, with a darker, more cryptic coat. Samango monkeys are always associated with evergreen and well-developed riverine forests and are highly vocal. They are commonly found in Zomba, Mulanje and Majete.

Vervet monkey

Blue monkey

The **yellow baboon** (*Papio cynocephalus*) is common throughout Malawi. Like vervet monkeys, baboons are highly sociable animals with a wide habitat tolerance. They are most frequently seen in the vicinity of rocky hills. The greyer **chacma baboon** (*Papio ursinus*) exists alongside the yellow baboon south of Lake Malawi. The unmistakable **black-and-white colobus** (*Colobus angolensis*) is a spectacular equatorial forest monkey whose range nudges into the far north of Malawi, where it occurs sparsely in forest reserves in the Misuku Hills and around Karonga.

The nocturnal bushbabies (or galagos) are small arboreal primates more often heard than seen. The **thick-tailed bushbaby** (*Otolemur crassicaudatus*) generally occurs in true forest, and it can be distinguished from the **lesser**

Lesser bushbaby

bushbaby (*Galago moholi*), a species of woodland and savannah habitats, by its much larger size and bushy tail. The best way to see a bushbaby is to follow its distinctive, piercing call to a tree and then shine a torch to find its large eyes.

Antelope

Large antelope All the antelope described below have an average shoulder height of above 120cm, roughly the same height as a zebra.

Eland

The **common eland** (*Taurotragus oryx*) is Africa's largest antelope, with a lightly striped fawn-brown coat, short spiral horns and a slightly bovine appearance accentuated by its large dewlap. In Malawi, eland are most likely to be seen on the Nyika Plateau, where they are seasonally common, but they occur in most reserves and parks.

Greater kudu

The **greater kudu** (*Tragelaphus strepsiceros*) is another very large antelope, with a greyish coat marked by thin, white stripes and large pink ears. The small dewlap and immense spiralling horns of the male render it unmistakable. Generally found in small groups in woodland habitats, it is present in all Malawi's national parks and wildlife reserves.

The male **sable antelope** (*Hippotragus niger*) is unmistakable with its large, backward-curving horns and black coat. The equally graceful female has smaller horns and is chestnut-brown in colour. Both

Sable antelope

sexes have a well-defined white belly and rump. The sable antelope is now thriving in large herds in Liwonde National Park, and it has been recorded in all Malawi's national parks and wildlife reserves.

The related **roan antelope** (*Hippotragus equinus*) is an equally handsome animal, with a uniform reddish-brown coat and short backward-curving horns.

Roan antelope

It is the most common large antelope on the Nyika Plateau, and it also occurs in Liwonde, Majete, Kasungu, Vwaza Marsh and Nkhotakota.

The **common waterbuck** (*Kobus ellipsiprymnus*) has a shaggy coat and a distinctive white horseshoe on its rump. It is always associated with water, and is particularly common along the Shire River in Liwonde National Park. It also occurs in Kasungu, Majete, Vwaza Marsh and Nkhotakota.

Lichtenstein's hartebeest (*Alcelaphus lichtensteinii*) is an ungainly antelope, closely related to the wildebeest (which, incidentally, does not occur naturally in Malawi, though it has been introduced to Nyala Park and Game Haven), with a red-yellow coat and short stubby horns. It is seen occasionally on the Nyika Plateau and is doing well in the Rhino Sanctuary in Liwonde National Park. It can sometimes be seen in Kasungu and more frequently in Vwaza Marsh, and has been successfully reintroduced to Majete as well.

Medium-sized antelope All the antelope described below have a shoulder height of between 75cm and 95cm, except for the male nyala, which has a shoulder height of slightly over 1m.

The most widespread medium-sized antelope in Malawi is the **bushbuck** (*Tragelaphus scriptus*). The male bushbuck has a dark chestnut coat marked with white stripes and spots, while the female is lighter with similar markings, giving it an appearance much like a European deer. Shy and mostly nocturnal, it occurs singly or in pairs in most forested habitats and riverine woodland in all wildlife reserves and national parks, as well as in many forest reserves.

Bushbuck

The closely related **nyala** (*Nyala angasii*) is a southern African species that reaches the northern extreme of its range in Mwabvi, Majete Wildlife Reserve and Lengwe National Park, where it is common. The nyala can easily be confused with the bushbuck, though the exceptionally handsome male is much larger and shaggier in appearance, with a distinctive white crest running along its spine, and elegant curving horns.

Impala

The most successful breeder of all Malawi's antelopes, the **impala** (*Aepyceros melampus*) is a highly gregarious and photogenic resident of most woodland habitats. It has a bright chestnut coat, distinctive white and black stripes on its rump, and the male has large lyre-shaped horns. The impala has acute hearing and other animals often stay with impala herds so they can listen for the loud snort alarm call. In the mating season males fight (sometimes to the death) to take a herd of females, with the losers rejoining the bachelor groups. The impala is present in Vwaza Marsh, Liwonde, Lengwe, Majete, Mwabvi and Kasungu.

The **southern reedbuck** (*Redunca arundinum*) is a lightly coloured, rather nondescript antelope almost always associated with water. It is present in small numbers in most of Malawi's reserves and national parks, as well as on other mountain plateaux, but it is only common in Kasungu and Nyika national parks.

The related **puku** (*Kobus vardonii*), a woolly golden-brown antelope with no distinguishing features, is found in marshy habitats. Similar in size to the impala it differs in its habits and likes to sit in the sun to chew the cud. It is essentially an animal of Zambia and southern Democratic Republic of Congo, but it occasionally strays into those Malawian reserves which border Zambia, and is more common in Kasungu than the impala.

Reedbuck

Small antelope All the antelope described below have a shoulder height of below 60cm.

The **klipspringer** (*Oreotragus oreotragus*) has a grey, bristly coat which gives it a mildly speckled appearance. Klipspringers live on rocky outcrops and have adapted to the habitat by an ability to jump and climb up almost vertical rock faces. They are seldom seen on account of their size and colouring, and are normally found in pairs. They occur throughout Malawi wherever there are

Klipspringer

suitable habitats, including all the national parks and wildlife reserves except Lengwe, and most rocky mountains outside national parks.

The **oribi** (*Ourebia ourebi*) is a tan-coloured antelope with a white belly, black tail and a diagnostic black patch beneath its ears. It generally occurs in open woodland and grassland, but it is rare, swift and secretive in Malawi, where it has been recorded only in Kasungu and Liwonde national parks.

Sharpe's grysbok (*Raphicerus sharpei*) is widespread in Malawi, occurring in all national parks and wildlife reserves, but it is rarely seen owing to its retiring

DANGEROUS ANIMALS

The dangers associated with Africa's wild animals have frequently been overstated since the days of the so-called Great White Hunters – who did, after all, rather intensify the risk by making a habit of shooting at animals that might turn nasty when wounded. Contrary to the fanciful notions conjured up by images of rampaging elephants, man-eating lions and psychotic snakes, most wild animals fear us more than we fear them, and their normal response to human contact is to flee. That said, while the likelihood of a tourist being attacked by an animal is very low, it can and does happen on occasion, and a number of fatalities have been caused by such incidents in southern Africa.

The need for caution is greatest near water, particularly around dusk and dawn, when hippos are out grazing. Hippos are responsible for more human fatalities than any other large mammal, not because they are aggressive but because they tend to panic when something comes between them and the safety of the water. If you happen to be that something, then you're unlikely to live to tell the tale. Never consciously walk between a hippo and water, and never walk along riverbanks or through reed beds, especially in overcast weather or at dusk or dawn, unless you are certain that no hippos are present. Watch out, too, for crocodiles. Only a very large crocodile is likely to attack a person, and then only in the water or right on the shore. Near towns and other settlements, you can be fairly sure that any such crocodile will have been consigned to its maker by its potential human prey, so the risk is greatest away from human habitation. It is also near water that you are most likely to unwittingly corner a normally placid terrestrial animal – the bushbuck has a reputation as the most dangerous African antelope when cornered.

There are areas where hikers might still stumble across an elephant or a buffalo, the most dangerous of Africa's terrestrial herbivores. Elephants almost invariably mock charge and indulge in some hair-raising trumpeting before they attack in earnest. Provided that you back off at the first sign of unease, they are most unlikely to take further notice of you. If you see them before they see you, give them a wide berth, bearing in mind they are most likely to attack if surprised at close proximity. If an animal charges you, the safest course of action is to head for the nearest tree and climb it. Black rhinos are prone to charging without apparent provocation, but they're too rare in Malawi to be a cause for concern. Elephants are the only animals to pose a potential danger to a vehicle, and much the same advice applies – if an elephant evidently doesn't want you to pass, then back off and wait until it has crossed the road or moved further away before you try again. In general, it's a good idea to leave your engine running when you are close to an elephant, and you should avoid letting yourself be boxed in between an elephant and another vehicle.

nature and nocturnal habits. It is similar in overall appearance to an oribi, though it lacks any distinctive features and is considerably smaller. Sharpe's grysbok occurs in thicket and scrub rather than open grassland.

Livingstone's suni (*Neotragus moschatus*) is a tiny and rather nondescript grey antelope, which in Malawi occurs only in Lengwe and other reserves in the Shire Valley south of Blantyre. In this area, it is likely to be confused only with the significantly larger and more robust grey or common duiker, which can be found in woodland areas.

There are campsites in Malawi where vervet monkeys and baboons have become pests. Feeding these animals is highly irresponsible, since it encourages them to scavenge and may eventually lead to them being shot. Vervet monkeys are too small to progress much beyond being a nuisance, but baboons are very dangerous and have often killed children and maimed adults with their vicious teeth. Do not tease or underestimate them. If primates are hanging around a campsite, and you wander off leaving fruit in your tent, don't expect the tent to be standing when you return.

The dangers associated with large predators are often exaggerated. Most predators stay clear of humans and are only likely to kill accidentally or in self-defence. Lions are arguably the exception, but it is unusual for a lion to attack a human without cause. Should you encounter one on foot, the important thing is not to run, since this is likely to trigger the instinct to give chase. Of the other cats, cheetahs represent no threat and leopards generally attack only when they are cornered. Hyenas are often associated with human settlements, and are potentially very dangerous, but in practice they aren't aggressive towards people and are most likely to slink off into the shadows when disturbed. A slight but real danger when sleeping in the bush without a tent is that a passing hyena or lion might investigate a hairy object sticking out of a sleeping bag, and you might be decapitated through predatorial curiosity. In areas where large predators are still reasonably common, sleeping in a sealed tent practically guarantees your safety – but don't sleep with your head sticking out and don't at any point put meat in the tent.

All manner of venomous snakes occur in Malawi, but they are unlikely to be encountered since they generally slither away when they sense the seismic vibrations made by a walking person. You should be most alert to snakes on rocky slopes and cliffs, particularly where you risk putting your hand on a ledge that you can't see. Rocky areas are the favoured habitat of the puff adder, which is not an especially venomous snake, but is potentially lethal and unusual in that it won't always move off in response to human foot treads. Wearing good boots when walking in the bush will protect against the 50% of snake bites that occur below the ankle, and long trousers will help deflect bites higher up on the leg, reducing the quantity of venom injected. Lethal snake bites are a rarity (in South Africa, which boasts almost as many venomous snakes as Malawi, more people are killed by lightning than by snake bites) but some discussion of treatment is included in the section on *Health*, page 85.

When all is said and done, the most dangerous animal in Africa, exponentially a greater threat than everything mentioned above, is the *Anopheles* mosquito, which carries the malaria parasite. Humans – particularly when behind a steering wheel – run them a close second!

Three duiker species occur in Malawi. The most widespread is the **grey** or **common duiker** (*Sylvicapra grimmia*), a greyish antelope with a white belly and a tuft between its small horns. The grey duiker is common in almost all woodland habitats. The other two duiker species are forest animals and are thus very rarely seen. The **Natal red duiker** (*Cephalophus natalensis*) is a tiny antelope with a reddish coat and no distinguishing markings. The even tinier **blue duiker** (*Cephalophus monticola*), one of the smallest antelope found in southern Africa, is grey with a white tail.

Common duiker

Other herbivores

Back with animals you're unlikely to have much trouble identifying, **elephants** (*Loxodonta africana*), despite the heavy poaching of the 1980s, are still reasonably common in many of Malawi's reserves. Elephants occur naturally in Liwonde, Kasungu, Nyika, Nkhotakota and Vwaza Marsh, and some 200 have been reintroduced to Majete.

Black rhinoceros (*Diceros bicornis*), too, are easy enough to identify – if you can find one. The last indigenous black rhinos were poached from Mwabvi in 1992, and not long before they were a common sight in Kasungu. Black rhino from South Africa were reintroduced into Liwonde National Park's Rhino Sanctuary in 1997, and are breeding successfully. To date, eight individuals have been transferred to Majete, and there are plans to relocate at least a dozen more.

Black rhinoceros

Hippos (*Hippopotamus amphibius*) have also suffered from poaching. Over the past 15 years numbers have dropped dramatically, as they are killed by more efficiently armed villagers affected by famine or protecting their crops or by meat traders. Nonetheless, hippo are still common on most major rivers and lakes, particularly on the part of the Shire River that runs through Liwonde National Park, where well over 1,000 individuals are present. Outside reserves, hippo can be seen in the Salima area, in the Elephant Marsh, and in the Shire River near Nchalo Sugar Estate.

Another unmistakable large animal is the **African buffalo** (*Syncerus caffer*), which occurs in all Malawi's wildlife reserves and national parks except for Lake Malawi.

Burchell's zebra (*Equus quagga burchellii*) is the only equine species found in Malawi. It is common in Nyika National Park. Many survive in Kasungu despite poaching. Herds translocated from Kasungu to Liwonde and Majete are doing very well. Zebra occur in small numbers in all the wildlife reserves except Mwabvi.

African buffalo

Two swine species occur in Malawi. The **warthog** (*Phacochoerus africanus*) is a diurnal swine with a uniform bristly grey coat and the distinctive habit of holding its tail erect when it runs. Warthogs are normally seen in pairs or family groups in savannah and woodland habitats. They are common in all Malawi's wildlife reserves and national parks. The nocturnal **bushpig** (*Potamochoerus larvatus*) has a red-brown coat and a hairier appearance than that of the warthog. It is widespread in forest and riverine woodland, and occurs in all Malawi's

Warthog

national parks and wildlife and forest reserves, but it is very rarely seen owing to its retiring nature.

Several other nocturnal animals are widespread in Malawi, but unlikely to be seen by tourists. The **porcupine**, for instance, occurs in every national park and wildlife reserve and most forests, but the most you are likely to see of a porcupine is a discarded quill on a forest path. The insectivorous **aardvark** (*Orycteropus afer*) occurs in most reserves and national parks, but if you see one you can rank yourself among the luckiest people on the planet.

Hyraxes (dassies) are small mammals which have a guinea pig-like appearance, though they are considered to be more closely related to elephants than any other living animal. The rock hyrax (*Procavia capensis*) is commonly seen on koppies (small hills) and other rocky areas throughout Malawi. The tree hyrax (*Dendrohyrax arboreus*) is a less common animal, and strictly nocturnal. It is more likely to be heard than seen – it has a quite outrageous shrieking call.

Rock hyrax

One characteristic African mammal which was never indigenous to Malawi is the **giraffe** (*Giraffa camelopardalis*). It is not the policy of the wildlife authorities to introduce animals into areas where they have never been recorded. The only record of wild giraffe in Malawi within living memory was when an individual strayed over the Zambian border in Karonga District, where it was killed by terrified villagers. However, herds of **Thornicroft's giraffe** (*Giraffa camelopardalis thornicrofti*) from the Luangwa Valley in Zambia have been translocated into three private reserves in Malawi: Nyala Park, Kuti Wildlife Reserve and Game Haven.

BIRDS The exact number of birds recorded in Malawi is open to debate, with various sources listing between 650 and 750 species, a discrepancy attributable to various controversial taxonomic splits as well as one's acceptance of certain vagrant and uncorroborated records. Either way, it is a highly impressive total for a country smaller than England. The definitive resource for visiting birdwatchers is Francoise Dowsett-Lemaire and Robert J Dowsett's *The Birds of Malawi: An Atlas and Handbook*, but this is best supplemented by a good field guide (see *Appendix 2, Further information*, page 335), and useful checklists can be found online at www.birdlist.org/malawi.htm and http://avibase.bsc-eoc.org/checklist.jsp?region=mw&list=howardmoore.

Roughly 10% of the species recorded in Malawi are not found on the southern African list, making Malawi a particularly rewarding destination for South African birdwatchers. In addition, many species that appear on the southern African list as vagrants or rarities are easily seen in Malawi – African skimmer, racquet-tailed roller, Boehm's bee-eater, wattled crane, Livingstone's flycatcher, spur-winged plover and green-headed oriole being obvious examples.

National parks and wildlife reserves are the best places to see a good variety of birds. Liwonde National Park in particular is excellent – the birdlife along the river is stunning, and guided morning walks from Mvuu Camp almost always yield a few localised species. The forests in Nyika National Park are probably the best place to see birds which occur in Malawi but not in southern Africa: many East African species extend their range no further south than Nyika, Vwaza or the nearby Viphya Plateau.

Evergreen forest is a particularly rich bird habitat, and, unlike game reserves, many of Malawi's forest reserves can be explored on foot. Among the more accessible forest habitats in Malawi are the Viphya and Zomba plateaus, Mulanje Massif, and Ntchisi, Chiradzulu and Thyolo mountains.

Placed by some authorities in the same family as the closely related sparrows, the weavers of the family Ploceidae are a quintessential part of Africa's natural landscape, common and highly visible in virtually every habitat from rainforest to desert. The name of the family derives from the intricate and elaborate nests built by the dextrous males of most species – typically but not always a roughly oval ball of dried grass, reeds and twigs.

It can be fascinating to watch a male weaver at work. First, a nest site is chosen, usually at the end of a thin hanging branch or frond, which is immediately stripped of leaves to protect against snakes. The weaver then flies back and forth to the site, carrying the building material blade by blade in its heavy beak, first using a few thick strands to hang a skeletal nest from the end of a branch, then gradually completing the structure by interweaving numerous thinner blades of grass into the main frame. Once completed, the nest is subjected to the attention of his chosen partner, who will tear it apart if the result is less than satisfactory, and so the process starts all over again.

All but 12 of the 113 described weaver species are resident on the African mainland or associated islands, with at least 25 represented within Malawi. A full 11 of these Malawian species are placed in the genus *Ploceus* (true weavers), which is surely the most characteristic of all African bird genera. Most of the *Ploceus* weavers are slightly larger than a sparrow, and display a strong sexual dimorphism. Females are with few exceptions drab buff- or olive-brown birds, with some streaking on the back, and perhaps a hint of yellow on the belly.

Many males of the various *Ploceus* species conform to the basic colour pattern of the 'masked weaver' – predominantly yellow, with streaky back and wings, and a distinct black facial mask, often bordered with orange. Five Malawian weaver species fit this masked weaver prototype more or less absolutely, and several others approximate it less exactly. Identification of the masked weavers can be tricky without experience – useful clues are the exact shape of the mask, the presence and extent of the fringing orange, and the colour of the eye and the back.

The golden weavers, of which only two species are present in Malawi, are also brilliant yellow and/or light orange with some light streaking on the back, but

Brachystegia woodland also holds several characteristic birds, many of which are found in no other type of woodland, for instance **Stierling's woodpecker** (*Dendropicos stierlingi), *miombo* pied barbet* (*Tricholaema frontata*), **white-winged starling** (*Neocichla gutturalis*), **red-and-blue sunbird** (*Anthreptes anchietae*), **pale-billed hornbill** (*Tockus pallidirostris*) and **chestnut-mantled sparrow weaver** (*Plocepasser rufoscapulatus*). As Brachystegia woodland is the dominant vegetation type in Malawi, most Brachystegia birds are widespread in Malawi.

Malawi boasts an exceptional range of water habitats. Lake Malawi can impress with its kingfishers, cormorants and fish eagles, while Lake Chilwa has a far greater number of birds. The marshes that form around several rivers during the rainy season (known in Malawi as *dambos*) are also excellent for birds – one of the best and most accessible is Mpatsanjoka Dambo near Salima. For waterbirds in general, few places I've visited compare to the Elephant Marsh in southern Malawi, where you're likely to see such unusual species as **purple heron** (*Ardea purpurea*), **African skimmer** (*Rynchops flavirostris*) and **pygmy goose** (*Nettapus auritus*).

they lack a mask or any other strong distinguishing features. Forest-associated *Ploceus* weavers, by contrast, tend to have quite different and very striking colour patterns, and although sexually dimorphic, the female is often as boldly marked as the male.

Among the more conspicuous *Ploceus* species in Malawi are the masked, lesser masked and black-headed weavers – for the most part gregarious breeders forming single- or mixed-species colonies of hundreds, sometimes thousands, of pairs, often in reed beds and waterside vegetation. Most weavers don't have a distinctive song, but they compensate with a rowdy jumble of harsh swizzles, rattles and nasal notes that can reach deafening proportions near large colonies. One more cohesive song you will often hear seasonally around weaver colonies is a cyclic 'dee-dee-dee-Diederik', often accelerating to a hysterical crescendo when several birds call at once. This is the call of the Diederik cuckoo, a handsome green-and-white cuckoo that lays its eggs in weaver nests.

Most of the colonial weavers, perhaps relying on safety in numbers, build relatively plain nests with a roughly oval shape and an unadorned entrance hole. The nests of certain more solitary weavers, by contrast, are far more elaborate. Several weavers, for instance, protect their nests from egg-eating invaders by attaching tubular entrance tunnels to the base – in the case of the spectacled weaver, sometimes twice as long as the nest itself. The thick-billed weaver (a peculiar larger-than-average, brown-and-white weaver of reed beds, distinguished by its outsized bill and placed in the monospecific genus *Amblyospiza*) constructs a large and distinctive domed nest, which is supported by a pair of reeds, and woven as precisely as the finest basketwork, with a neat raised entrance hole at the front.

Really, though, in a country as rich in birdlife as Malawi, almost anywhere is likely to prove rewarding to birdwatchers. Don't ignore the obvious – even a morning walk through Lilongwe Nature Sanctuary can throw up a variety of robins, kingfishers and the gorgeous Schalow's turaco, while, over a ten-year period, more than 100 species were recorded in one garden in Blantyre.

REPTILES The order Crocodilia dates back at least 150 million years, and fossil forms that lived contemporaneously with dinosaurs are remarkably unchanged from their modern counterparts, of which the Nile crocodile is the largest living reptile, regularly growing to lengths of up to 6m. Widespread throughout Africa, the **Nile crocodile** (*Crocodylus niloticus*) was once common in most large rivers and lakes, but it has been exterminated in many areas in the past century – hunted professionally for its skin as well as by vengeful local villagers. Contrary to popular legend, Nile crocodiles generally feed mostly on fish, at least where densities are sufficient. They will also prey on drinking or swimming mammals where the opportunity presents itself, dragging their victim under water until it drowns, then

Common and widespread, but not easily seen unless they are actively searched for, chameleons are arguably the most intriguing of African reptiles. True chameleons of the family Chamaeleontidae are confined to the Old World, with the most important centre of speciation being the island of Madagascar, to which about half of the world's 120 recognised species are endemic. Aside from two species of chameleon apiece in Asia and Europe, the remainder are distributed across mainland Africa.

Chameleons are best known for their capacity to change colour, a trait that has often been exaggerated in popular literature, and which is generally influenced by mood more than the colour of the background. Some chameleons are more adept at changing colour than others, with the most variable being the **common chameleon** (*Chamaeleo chamaeleon*) of the Mediterranean region, with more than 100 colour and pattern variations recorded. Many African chameleons are typically green in colour but will gradually take on a browner hue when they descend from the foliage in more exposed terrain, for instance while crossing a road. Several change colour and pattern far more dramatically when they feel threatened or are confronted by a rival of the same species. Different chameleon species also vary greatly in size, with the largest being **Oustalet's chameleon** (*Furcifer oustaleti*) of Madagascar, known to reach a length of almost 80cm.

A remarkable physiological feature common to all true chameleons is their protuberant round eyes, which offer a potential 180° vision on both sides and are able to swivel around independently of each other. Only when one of them isolates a suitably juicy-looking insect will the two eyes focus in the same direction as the chameleon stalks slowly forward until it is close enough to use the other unique weapon in its armoury. This is its sticky-tipped tongue, which is typically about the same length as its body and remains coiled up within its mouth most of the time, to be unleashed in a sudden, blink-and-you'll-miss-it lunge to zap a selected item of prey. In addition to their unique eyes and tongues, many chameleons are adorned with an array of facial casques, flaps, horns and crests that enhance their already somewhat fearsome prehistoric appearance.

storing it under a submerged log or tree until it has decomposed sufficiently for them to eat. A large crocodile is capable of killing a lion or wildebeest, or an adult human for that matter, and in certain areas outside Malawi large mammals do form their main prey. Today, large crocodiles are mostly confined to protected areas, and large specimens are especially common along the Shire River as it flows through Liwonde National Park and Majete Wildlife Reserve.

A wide variety of **snakes** occurs in Malawi, though – fortunately, most would agree – they are typically very shy and unlikely to be seen unless actively sought. One of the snakes most likely to be seen on safari is Africa's largest, the **rock python** (*Python sebae*), which has a gold-on-black mottled skin and regularly grows to lengths exceeding 5m. Non-venomous, pythons kill their prey by strangulation, wrapping their muscular bodies around it until it cannot breathe, then swallowing it whole and dozing off for a couple of months while it is digested. Pythons feed mainly on small antelopes, large rodents and similar. They are generally harmless to adult humans, but could conceivably kill a small child.

Of the venomous snakes, one of the most commonly encountered is the puff adder, a large, thick resident of savannah and rocky habitats. Although it feeds mainly on rodents, the puff adder will strike when threatened, and it is rightly considered the

In Malawi, you're most likely to come across a chameleon by chance when it is crossing a road, in which case it should be easy to take a closer look at it, since most chameleons move painfully slowly and deliberately. Chameleons are also often seen on night game drives, when their ghostly nocturnal colouring shows up clearly under a spotlight – as well as making it pretty clear why these strange creatures are regarded with both fear and awe in many local African cultures. More actively, you could ask your guide if they know where to find a chameleon – a few individuals will be resident in most lodge grounds.

Of seven species recorded in Malawi, the **flap-necked chameleon** (*Chamaeleo dilepis*) is the most regularly observed. Associated with savannah and woodland habitats and often seen crossing roads, the flap-necked chameleon is generally around 15cm long and bright green in colour with few distinctive markings, but individuals might be up to 30cm in length and will turn tan or brown under the right conditions. Another closely related and widespread savannah and woodland species is the similarly sized **graceful chameleon** (*Chamaeleo gracilis*), which is generally yellow-green in colour and often has a white horizontal stripe along its flanks.

Characteristic of East African montane forests, **horned chameleons** form a closely allied species cluster of some taxonomic uncertainty. Typically darker than the savannah chameleons and around 20cm in length, the males of all taxa within this cluster are distinguished by up to three long nasal horns that project forward from their face. The only member of this group to occur in Malawi is **Meller's giant chameleon** (*Trioceros melleri*), a bulky dark-green creature with yellow stripes and a small solitary horn, mainly associated with the forests, where it feeds on small reptiles (including snakes) as well as insects. It can grow up to 55cm long, making it the largest chameleon known from mainland Africa. At the other end of the size spectrum, two dwarf species whose range is restricted to Malawi are the **Mulanje mountain chameleon** (*Nadzikambia mlanjensis*) and **Malawi stumptail chameleon** (*Rhampholeon platyceps*).

most dangerous of African snakes, not because it is especially venomous or aggressive, but because its sluggish disposition means it is more often disturbed than other snakes. Several cobra species are present, most with characteristic hoods that they raise when about to strike, though they are all very seldom seen. Another widespread family is the mambas, of which the **black mamba** (*Dendroaspis polylepis*) – which will attack only when cornered, despite an unfounded reputation for unprovoked aggression – is the largest venomous snake in Africa, measuring up to 3.5m long. Theoretically, the most toxic of Africa's snakes is the **boomslang** (*Dispholidus typus*), a variably coloured and largely arboreal snake, but it is back-fanged and very passive, and the only human fatalities recorded involve snake handlers.

Most snakes are non-venomous and harmless to any living creature much bigger than a rat. One common species is the **green tree snake** (sometimes mistaken for a boomslang, though the latter is never as green and more often brown), which feeds mostly on amphibians. The **mole snake** is a common and widespread grey-brown savannah resident that grows up to 2m long, and feeds on moles and other rodents. The remarkable **egg-eating snake** lives exclusively on bird eggs, dislocating its jaws to swallow the egg whole, then eventually regurgitating the crushed shell in a neat little package. Many snakes will take eggs opportunistically, for which reason large-scale agitation among birds in a tree is often a good indication that a snake (or small bird of prey) is around.

All African **lizards** are harmless to humans, with the arguable exception of the giant **monitor lizards**, which could in theory inflict a nasty bite if cornered. Two species occur in Malawi: the **water** (*Varanus niloticus*) and the **savannah monitor** (*Varanus exanthematicus*), the latter growing up to 2.2m long and occasionally seen in the vicinity of termite mounds, the former slightly smaller but far more regularly observed by tourists. Their size alone might make it possible to fleetingly mistake a monitor for a small crocodile, but their more colourful yellow-dappled skin precludes sustained confusion. Both species are predatory, feeding on anything from bird eggs to smaller reptiles and mammals, but will also eat carrion opportunistically.

The **common house gecko** (*Hemidactylus frenatus*) is an endearing bug-eyed, translucent white lizard that inhabits most houses as well as lodge rooms, scampering up walls and upside down on the ceiling in pursuit of pesky insects attracted to the lights. Also very common in some areas are various agama species, distinguished from other common lizards by their relatively large size of around 20–25cm, basking habits, and almost plastic-looking scaling – depending on the species, a combination of blue, purple, orange or red, with the flattened head generally a different colour from the torso. Another common family are the skinks: small, long-tailed lizards, most of which are quite dark and have a few thin black stripes running from head to tail.

Tortoises and terrapins are peculiar reptiles, unique in being protected by a prototypal suit of armour formed by their heavy exoskeleton. The most common of the terrestrial tortoises in the region is the **leopard tortoise** (*Stigmochelys pardalis*), which is named after its gold-and-black mottled shell, can weigh up to 30kg, and has been known to live for more than 50 years in captivity. It is often seen motoring along in the slow lane of game-reserve roads. Three species of terrapin – essentially the freshwater equivalent of turtles – are resident in Malawi, all somewhat flatter in shape than the tortoises, and generally with a plainer brown shell. They might be seen sunning on rocks close to water or peering out from roadside puddles.

FISH Each of Africa's three great lakes (Victoria, Tanganyika and Malawi) contains more species of fish than any other lake in the world. It is not yet known which of the three lakes is home to the greatest number of species, because more species are discovered every year and large parts of all three lakes have still to be explored. The most conservative estimate for the number of fish species in Lake Malawi is 850 – a greater number of freshwater species than are found in Europe and North America combined – and the real total may well exceed 1,000. No less remarkable is the fact that only a handful of fish species are known to occur in all three of the great lakes – most of them are endemic to one particular lake.

The vast majority of Lake Malawi's fish belong to the cichlid group, one of the few types of fish that care for their offspring – all but one of Malawi's cichlids are mouth-brooders, meaning that the eggs and fry are held in the mother's mouth until they are large enough to fend for themselves. The best known of these cichlids are the brightly coloured, algae-eating *mbuna*, which formed the subject of Dr Geoffrey Fryer's classic study of adaptive radiation in the 1950s – see box *Cichlids of the Great Lakes*, page 142. A group of *ncheni* **cichlids**, belonging to the *Oreochromis* genus of tilapia, are known collectively in Malawi as *chambo*, and are regarded as the finest eating fish to be found in the lake. However, while cichlids are by far the most important fish in the lake, both in terms of species and actual fish tonnage, several other fish families occur.

The ***usipa*** is a small sardine-like fish that occurs in large shoals, and which forms the backbone of the local fishing industry. Dried *usipa* are sold in bulk at practically every market in Malawi.

The carp family is well represented in Lake Malawi. The ***ngumbo***, a type of barbel, is a large silvery fish reaching up to 60cm in length and occurring in shoals on rocky stretches of shore such as Otter Point at Cape Maclear. Another well-known carp is the ***mpasa*** or 'lake salmon', which is common in the northern part of the lake, where it is an important source of food.

The **African catfish** (*Clarias gariepinus*) is probably the most widespread fish in Africa. It occurs in practically all freshwater habits, largely because of its ability to move across land during wet conditions. The African catfish is common in Lake Malawi. The genus of catfish known collectively as ***Bombe*** or ***Sapuwa*** are all evolved from the African catfish but, since they have lost the ability to cross land, they are endemic to the lake. The *Bombe* catfish are the largest fish found in the lake, measuring up to 1.5m in length and weighing up to 30kg. Belonging to a separate genus of catfish, the predatory ***kampango*** is a popular eating fish throughout Malawi.

Overfishing in Lake Malawi is becoming a major problem. Fish like ***chambo***, once plentiful and a crucial source of food, are now becoming scarce. In addition, overfishing is thought to be responsible for the presence of bilharzia in the lake. For treatment of bilharzia, see *Chapter 4, Health*, page 83.

Inspiring holidays worldwide

Ask Bradt guide book author Mary-Anne Bartlett of Art Safari & Close Encounters Africa to book your tour to Malawi.

Close Encounters Africa arrange bespoke safari's in Africa, Asia & The Polar Regions and will organise your dream tour to Malawi using Malawi's best operators and lodges.

Art Safari runs specialist painting trips to Malawi and worldwide, for adventurous artists and photographers of all standards with exceptional wildlife & landscapes.

Non-painting partners welcome.

Tel: 01394 382235
www.closeencountersafrica.com
www.artsafari.co.uk

THE

RESPONSIBLE SAFARI

CO.

*Specialising in group travel to Malawi
Independent Travel, School Groups, Charity
Challenges, Corporte and Development Travel*

- ABOUT US -

Based in Malawi

5% of RSC income is donated to
community projects in Malawi

Book accommodation online:
www.explore-malawi.com

- NEW FOR 2013 -

The Responsible Safari Co. Africa
Tailor Made Itineraries to Malawi,
Zambia, Mozambique, Tanzania,
Zimbabwe and Indian Ocean

- CONTACT US -

info@responsiblesafaricompany.com
www.responsiblesafaricompany.com
Tel UK: +44 (0)208 133 8611
Tel Malawi: +265 (0)1602 407
Skype: responsible.safari.company

BAREFOOT SAFARIS & Adventure Tours

Discover the Africa of your dreams on a Barefoot Safaris Adventure

Tailor Made Safaris to Botswana, Malawi, Mozambique, Namibia, South Africa,
Swaziland. Tanzania, Zambia & Zimbabwe

www.barefoot-safaris.com

Tel: +27 7346 29232   Email: enquiries@barefoot-safaris.com

3

Practical Information

WHEN TO VISIT

Malawi can be visited throughout the year, but for those with flexible schedules, a few seasonal factors merit consideration. Climatically, the most pleasant time to travel is during the southern hemisphere winter, from May to October, which is characterised by warm to hot days and temperate to cool nights, depending greatly on altitude. Winter is also the dry season, so rain is unlikely to cause road damage or otherwise disrupt your travel plans, the risk of contracting malaria is greatly reduced, and game viewing is at its best as the vegetation dies back, increasing visibility, and animals congregate on perennial water sources.

An advantage of travelling during the summer months of November to April is that rain transforms the parched winter landscape to a lush paradise alive with green foliage, colourful wild flowers and a wealth of fresh fruits and vegetables. Climatically, while the lakeshore can be oppressively hot and humid in summer, the higher-lying areas are balmier, remaining warm at night. A special-interest group for whom summer is the optimum time to be in Malawi is birdwatchers: between November and April, resident species are boosted by a variety of Palaearctic and intra-African migrants, and many species shed their dowdy winter plumage for brighter breeding colours.

ITINERARIES

Itineraries reproduced in travel guides tend to be somewhat restrictive, since there are so many variables for which they cannot allow, for instance means of transport, special interests, budget, season and available time. So, Malawi being a relatively compact country, the best starting point in planning an itinerary is to go through this book picking out a few potential highlights, then work out a rough route that connects them, fleshing it out with other activities or stops *en route*. If you are working with a reputable tour operator, they will be able to advise you as to what is and isn't realistic, and to tailor an itinerary to your requirements. If you'll be travelling independently, there's a lot to be said for picking out a rough circuit but retaining the flexibility to adjust it as you go along, travelling at a pace dictated by events.

You'll have a more relaxing holiday if you settle on a relatively compact itinerary rather than trying to cram in the whole country over two weeks. This particularly applies to travellers using public transport, unless they want their predominant memory of Malawi to be waiting for buses or sitting on them. As a rule of thumb, try to allow at least one day 'off' between travelling days. And when it comes to lakeshore resorts, better perhaps to spend a few days at one resort and settle in there than to visit two or three resorts for a night or two each.

If you have a special interest, it might be worth considering any of the following events that take place in Malawi during the year:

JUNE
Luwawa International Charity Mountain Bike Marathon (see page 251) A 42km race through the South Viphya Forest Reserve on good dirt roads.

JULY
Lake Malawi International Yachting Marathon (see page 160)
Mulanje Porters' Race (see page 223) An international event in which Mulanje porters and other participants race up and down 25km of steep mountain.

SEPTEMBER
Lake of Stars Festival (see page 25) Combines the best of UK and African live acts and DJs for a three-day charity event, raising money for Children in the Wilderness.

NOVEMBER
Wildlife Society Art Fest (see page 23) A mammoth exhibition of the visual arts, held in Lilongwe each November in aid of the Wildlife & Environmental Society of Malawi.

What follows is not a suggested itinerary, then, but an annotated list of some of Malawi's most alluring spots, some well known, others more obscure, all of them worth visiting.

CAPE MACLEAR (see page 144) The most popular resort on the southern lakeshore, centred on the relaxed fishing village of Chembe, and great for snorkelling, diving and kayaking in the cichlid-rich waters of Lake Malawi National Park.

CHINTHECHE AND KANDE (see pages 267 and 264) The long white sands and rocky bays of the northern lakeshore might make you stop longer than you'd planned. There's accommodation for all budgets and activities for all tastes.

CHONGONI ROCK ART AREA (see page 131) Easily explored out of Dedza Town, the prehistoric rock art of Malawi's only terrestrial UNESCO World Heritage Site ties in with dances still performed in Chewa villages today.

DZALANYAMA FOREST RESERVE (see page 113) An excellent weekend trip out of Lilongwe, with some of the most rewarding birdlife in Malawi, and plentiful walking opportunities.

ELEPHANT MARSH (see page 238) Inexpensive, little-visited, atmospheric, with prolific waterbirds – ideal for adventurous backpackers with some days to spare to achieve the journey there.

KASUNGU NATIONAL PARK (see page 248) Seasonal game viewing, a majestic lodge and good camping facilities for those heading north on the M1 from Lilongwe.

LAKE CHILWA (see page 187) A great and surprisingly accessible off-the-beaten-track excursion for backpackers on a tight budget.

LIKOMA ISLAND (see page 273) A good place to get away from it all, with a friendly atmosphere, attractive scenery and some historical interest.

LIVINGSTONIA (see page 315) Site of a turn-of-the-20th-century mission on the Rift Valley Escarpment, overlooking the lake and close to the beautiful Manchewe Falls.

LIWONDE NATIONAL PARK (see page 168) The best game viewing in Malawi, stunning birds, a wonderful atmosphere, and excellent facilities, ranging from campsites to one of the country's finest game lodges.

MAJETE WILDLIFE RESERVE (see page 228) This once-obscure reserve has been the subject of an intensive programme of reintroductions, and it's now one of the country's best game-viewing areas, with a range of facilities including an impressive new luxury safari lodge. It's an excellent excursion from Blantyre in private transport.

MUA MISSION (see page 136) The finest ethnographic museum in Malawi lies on the site of this rustic mission at the Rift Valley base near Dedza and Salima.

MULANJE MASSIF (see page 218) The best montane hiking in Malawi, accessible and affordable to those on a limited budget.

MWABVI WILDLIFE RESERVE (see page 236) This is wonderful hiking country, with very few roads through an unspoilt wilderness.

NKHATA BAY (see page 279) A thriving backpackers' scene, cheap dive courses and a habit of transforming short visits into extended stays.

NKHOTAKOTA (see page 255) An area ready for discovery, with the idyllic combination of lakeside lodges and a large wildlife reserve home to two brand new tourist lodges.

NKOPOLA (see page 156) Here you'll find the major cluster of tourist-class hotels on the southern lakeshore.

NYIKA NATIONAL PARK (see page 301) Malawi's largest national park, offering plentiful hiking opportunities in fantastic scenery. Good game viewing, too.

SENGA BAY (see page 119) The closest lakeshore resort to Lilongwe boasts a clutch of stylish hotels, hippo pools and breeding colonies of birds.

VIPHYA PLATEAU (see page 250) The hiking and birding are not as good as in some other montane areas, but it's still a lovely spot, and Luwawa Forest Lodge is great for mountain biking and other adventure activities.

VWAZA MARSH WILDLIFE RESERVE (see page 307) The most underrated game reserve in the country – plenty of animals, very accessible and reasonably affordable.

ZOMBA PLATEAU (see page 183) The most accessible of Malawi's large mountains, with good walking, camping facilities, horseriding and views that stretch to the edge of the world.

TOURIST INFORMATION

The official source of tourist information is the **Ministry of Tourism, Wildlife and Culture** (\ *01 775702/499;* e *info@visitmalawi.mw; www.visitmalawi.mw*). It has a useful website and offices in Lilongwe and Blantyre, and can also be contacted through any Malawian high commission or other diplomatic mission abroad. You could also look at various websites offering information, such as www.malawitourism.com, www.go2malawi.com, www.guide2malawi.com, www.malawi-tourism-association. org.mw, www.explore-malawi.com and any of the safari companies listed in this book. Another great source of information is the quarterly magazine *The Eye*, which contains detailed listings and lots of tourist-related ads – check out their website www.theeyemw.com. Finally, don't forget to check out our own interactive update website http://bradtmalawiupdate.wordpress.com – we'll be posting regular updates here, and readers are welcome to do the same!

TOUR OPERATORS

A selection of international operators specialising in Malawi is listed below. Note, however, that many excellent safari companies operate out of Lilongwe and/or Blantyre, some with more than 20 years' on-the-ground experience, and these companies are listed in the respective chapters on these cities.

For details of tour operators in Malawi, see *Chapter 5, Lilongwe*, page 96, and *Chapter 12, Blantyre*, page 195.

UK

Aardvark Safaris \ 01980 849160; e mail@ aardvarksafaris.com; www.aardvarksafaris.co.uk. Tailored trips using small, owner-run properties with emphasis on wildlife & scenery.

Art Safari \ 01394 382235; m 07780 927560; e info@artsafari.co.uk; www.artsafari.co.uk; see also advert on page 45. Painting trips led by professional artist (& updater of 4th edition) Mary-Anne Bartlett, ideal for creative travellers of all ages.

Cazenove & Loyd \ 020 7384 2332; e info@ cazloyd.com; www.cazloyd.com. Specialists in private travel in Africa & the Indian Ocean.

Expert Africa \ 020 8232 9777; e info@ expertafrica.com; www.expertafrica.com. Managed by the highly experienced author of the Bradt guides to Zambia, Botswana, Namibia & Zanzibar, this award-winning company arranges flexible trips for all travellers, & is particularly strong on combination safaris with Zambia.

Gane & Marshall \ 01822 600600; e info@ ganeandmarshall.com; www.ganeandmarshall. co.uk. Itineraries include cycling trips.

Okavango Tours & Safaris \ 020 8347 4030; e info@okavango.com; www.okavango.com. Small, friendly company based in north London.

Safari Consultants Ltd \ 01787 888590; e bill@ safariconsultantsuk.com; www.safari-consultants. co.uk. Established in 1983, a specialised safari company dealing with tailor-made & small group departures to east & South Africa.

Wildlife Worldwide \ 0845 130 6982; e sales@ wildlifeworldwide.com; www.wildlifeworldwide. com. Specialising in tailor-made & small group wildlife holidays worldwide.

Zambezi Safari & Travel \ 01548 830059; e info@zambezi.com; www.zambezi.com

GERMANY

Livingstone Tours \ (+49) 07123 920943; e info@livingstone-tours.de; www.livingstone-tours.de. A German-based company specialising in set-departure 2- & 3-week camping tours for small groups of German-speakers. The owner has worked in Malawi for several years & leads the tour himself.

SOUTH AFRICA

Animaltracks (+27) 11 454 0543; e info@
animaltracks.co.za; www.animaltracks.co.za
Pulse Africa (+27) 11 325 2290; e info@
pulseafrica.com; www.pulseafrica.com. Specialises

in tailor-made safaris/holidays to Lake Malawi's
mountains, lakes & national parks.
Touraco Travel Services (+27) 12 803 8585;
e travel@touraco.co.za; www.touraco.co.za

ECOTOURISM AND COMMUNITY INVOLVEMENT

John Douglas, Malawi Travel Marketing Consortium (www.malawitourism.com)
Both the government and the private sector in Malawi are committed to the
principles of ecotourism. The intention is that tourism developments shall
be sustainable, with an avoidance of problems which tourism might impose
on the environment or on socio-cultural aspects of the country. Tourism
resources are to be preserved so that they satisfy the current demands but
are also maintained for the future.

Malawi has the advantage that it has no mass tourism; it is small scale and
intimate. Most of the lodges, whether on the lakeshore, in the game parks
or in the forest reserves, are, by regional standards, modest in size. A great
deal of care has been taken to avoid visual intrusion. Outside Lilongwe,
Blantyre and Mzuzu it is rare to see tourist buildings that rise above a single
storey and none is more than two storeys. Even where there is something of
a concentration of lodges and hotels, as along the southern shore of Lake
Malawi, it is virtually impossible to see one lodge from its nearest neighbour
which might be no more than 1km away. It is hoped that some plans currently
being mooted for substantial hotel construction at Cape Maclear remain
unrealised in favour of small-scale developments.

Seclusion is considered to be an asset worth preserving, with most lodges
blending with their surroundings. A majority are built from local materials
by local labour and care has been taken to reduce environmental impact
to a minimum. For example, Nkwichi Lodge, which has won international
awards for its eco-friendly policies, rightly claims that if it closed, the area
would easily be returned to its natural state in a matter of months. In Vwaza
Wildlife Reserve, Kazuni Safari Camp could be closed down and dismantled
in days and there would be little evidence of its previous existence. Outside
the cities, electricity is often the product of solar power or backup generators.
Attention is paid to sewage disposal and water conservation.

None of this commendable attention to ecotourism tenets would be
possible without an established working relationship with local communities.
Tourism in Malawi means far more than a source of employment. In a country
with one of the world's highest unemployment rates and a desperate over-
reliance on agriculture, it is estimated that for every worker in the tourism
sector there are another dozen reliant on the income achieved. But there
is more to it than a revenue source. Very many of the lodges are active in
supporting their neighbouring villages by purchasing foodstuffs, by assisting
with school building, developing health clinics or establishing charities
which help, for example, the appalling number of AIDS orphans.

The particularly good community relations of members of the private
sector Travel Marketing Consortium enable many lodges to offer their tourists
visits to local villages and, in some cases, overnight stays.

For Malawi, the future of tourism is not only bright, it is green.

RED TAPE

A valid passport is required, with an expiry date at least six months after you intend to depart Malawi. At the time of writing, visas are not required for stays of less than 90 days for holders of US, UK and most, but not all Commonwealth and EU passports (a full list is available at www.foreignaffairs.gov.mw). If you fall into one of these categories, as almost all tourists do, you'll get a free 30-day visitor's pass on entry, extendable at any immigration office for Mk5,000 (about US$16 at the time of writing) per 30 days to a maximum of 90 days. Such rulings are subject to change, however, so it's best to confirm this with one of the embassies listed below before you embark.

Arriving overland in your own vehicle, you need to show registration documents at the border, and must buy a Temporary Import Permit (TIP) and insurance for one month (neither is very expensive). If the vehicle isn't registered in your name, you also need an official letter giving you permission to cross borders with it. For details of diplomatic missions in Malawi, see *Chapter 5, Lilongwe*, page 110, and *Chapter 12, Blantyre*, page 205.

Malawi has an embassy or high commission in the following countries:

ⓔ Belgium 46 Av Hermann-Debroux, Brussels; ☎(+32) 2 231 0980; e embassy.malawi@skynet. be; www.embassymalawi.be

ⓔ Egypt 44 Road 254, Maadi, Cairo; ☎(+20) 2 2519 7381 / 2 2519 7184; e malawi@link.net; www.malawiembcairo.com

ⓔ Ethiopia Woreda 23, Kebele 13, House No 1021, Addis Ababa; ☎(+251) 11 371 1280; e malemb@ethionet.et or malemb@telecom.net.et.

ⓔ Germany 86 Westfälische Str, Berlin; ☎(+49) (0) 30 843 1540; e malawiberlin@aol.com; www. malawiembassy.de

ⓔ Ireland (honorary consul) 21 Leeson Park, Dublin; ☎(+353) 01 496 0888; e padraigom@ yahoo.co.uk

ⓔ Japan Takanawa Kaisei Bldg, 7th Floor, 3-4-1 Minato-ku, Tokyo; ☎(+81) (0) 3 3449 3010/47; e malawi@luck.ocn.ne.jp; www.malawiembassy. org

ⓔ Mozambique 75 Kenneth Kaunda Av, Maputo; ☎(+258) 21 492676; e malawmoz@ virconn.com

ⓔ South Africa 770 Government Av, Arcadia, Pretoria; ☎(+27) 12 430 9900/342 0146; e highcommalai@telkomsa.net

ⓔ Tanzania 1st Floor, Zambia House, Ohio and Sokoine Drive, Dar es Salaam; ☎(+255) 22 2136951/2124623; e mhc@cats-net.com

ⓔ UK 36 John Street, Holborn, London; ☎(+44) (0) 20 7421 6010; e malawihighcommission@ btconnect.com; www.malawihighcommission. co.uk

ⓔ USA 2408 Massachusetts Ave NW, Washington, DC; ☎(+1) 202 721 0270; e malawidc@aol.com, www.malawiembassy-dc.org

ⓔ Zambia 31 Bishop Road, Kabulonga, Lusaka; ☎(+260) 211 265768; e mhcomm@iwayafrica. com; www.malawimissionlusaka.info

ⓔ Zimbabwe 9–11 Duthie Rd, Alexandra Park, Harare; ☎(+263) 4 798584/7; e malahigh@ africaonline.co.zw

GETTING THERE AND AWAY

BY AIR There are no direct flights to Malawi from outside Africa, but connecting inter-African flights are operated by Ethiopian Airlines (*www.ethiopianairlines. com*), Kenya Airways (*www.kenya-airways.com*), South African Airways (*www. flysaa.com*) and Air Malawi (*www.flyairmalawi.com*), though Air Malawi ceased operations in early 2013 pending liquidation and restructuring in partnership with Ethiopian Airlines. Most international flights land at Kamuzu International Airport, 26km from Lilongwe, but Ethiopian Airlines and South African Airways both run services several times weekly to Chileka Airport, 16km north of Blantyre. International and domestic airport taxes are included in the ticket price. Good deals are often available through the individual carrier websites listed opposite, but flight specialists still have a part to play. Below is a list of operators who give good service at a reasonable price. Getting the lowest price will require several calls and may result in some rather complicated routing.

Flight specialists

From the UK

Flight Centre ☏0844 800 8660; www. flightcentre.co.uk. Offices in the UK, Australia, New Zealand, South Africa & Canada. An independent travel retailer with more than 1,200 outlets worldwide. The UK head office is located in New Malden, Surrey.

STA Travel ☏0333 321 0099; e enquiries@ statravel.co.uk; www.statravel.co.uk. STA has 12 branches in London & 25 or so around the country & at university sites. Also has several branches & associate organisations around the world.

Trailfinders ☏020 7368 1200; www.trailfinders. com. Provides a one-stop travel service including

visa & passport service, travel clinic & foreign exchange.

Travel Bag ☏0871 703 4698; www.travelbag. co.uk. 7 UK offices, offering flights, holidays & travel services.

From the USA

Airtech ☏(+1) 212 219 7000; e fly@airtech. com; www.airtech.com. Standby seat broker that also deals in consolidator fares, courier flights & a host of other travel-related services.

STA Travel ☏(+1) 800 781 4040; www.statravel. com

OVERLAND Malawi is a popular fixture on the overland and backpackers' trail between eastern and southern Africa, and as many tourists arrive in Malawi overland as by air. Many such people travel independently, but an increasingly popular choice for first-time visitors is an overland truck trip, which allows you to compress several countries into a limited period. Some of the overland companies include Absolute Africa (*www.absoluteafrica.com*), African Overland (*www.africanoverland.co.za*), African Trails (*www.africantrails.co.uk*), Bukima (*www.bukima.com*), Dragoman (*www.dragoman.com*), Drifters (*www.drifters.co.za*), Exodus (*www.exodus.co.uk*), Kumuka (*www.kumuka.com*) and Which Way Adventure Company (*www.which-way.com*). For independent travellers, the main border crossings are as follows:

To/from South Africa Most people travelling between South Africa and Malawi take a bit of time over the trip, passing through a combination of other southern African countries, including Botswana, Namibia and Zimbabwe, as well as those covered individually below. However, if you literally want to travel between Johannesburg and Malawi as quickly as possible, direct coaches cover the route via Harare and Tete, which involves three border crossings and takes 24 hours if all goes smoothly. A recommended operator is KJ Transport, which has offices on the corner of Smit and Mellie streets in Johannesburg (☏ *(+27) 73 722 7874/72 339 2385*) and in the Blantyre Lodge opposite the main bus station in Blantyre (☏*01 877797/914017*). Coaches depart from Johannesburg at 10.30 on Wednesday and Saturday, and from Blantyre at 08.30 on Tuesday and Saturday. Flyover (m *088 1921001/099 322146*) is another operator, offering coaches departing from Blantyre to Johannesburg on Wednesday and Saturday for US$70. Intercape (m *099 9403398; www.intercape.co.za*) is the most upmarket service, with four buses/week at US$76 or the rand equivalent and offering online booking. Note that if you plan on breaking the journey in Tete or Harare, Intercape passengers *cannot* disembark in Zimbabwe or Mozambique.

To/from Zambia The most frequently used border is Mchinji, on the main road between Lusaka and Lilongwe. Several buses now do this 15–18-hour run directly, including KOBS (m *099 9610581/9938704*) and Ronsil Transport (m *099 9405340/1165236*). Buses depart at 06.00 almost daily and tickets cost US$31. You can also do the trip in stages. Regular buses run from Lusaka to Chipata, 30km from Mchinji, where at least 5km divides the Zambian and Malawian border posts. Once you cross into Malawi, it's only a few minutes' walk to Mchinji Town, where there are several basic resthouses if you arrive too late to catch a minibus to Lilongwe, 90km to the east.

To/from Mozambique Malawi and Mozambique share a long border. Indeed, the large wedge of Malawi to the south of Lilongwe is surrounded by Mozambique on all sides. So there are a great many possible border crossings, though only a few are used regularly by travellers. A remote but enjoyable possibility between northwest Mozambique and Malawi is via Likoma Island. Local fishing boats regularly cross from Likoma to Cobue in Mozambique, and the MV *Ilala* calls in at the Mozambican port of Metangula (see page 271 for timetable); there's a good hostel and campsite in Cobue, but it's easier to get road transport out of Metangula.

Of the various northern road crossings, the one between Mangochi and Mandimba is quite straightforward. Regular transport to the border leaves Mangochi from the main bus station, stopping *en route* at Namwera, a small town with plenty of resthouses. If you can't get a lift along the 7km road between the two border posts, your options are either walking or hiring a bicycle-taxi – and if you opt for the latter you won't regret splashing out on a separate bike for your luggage.

Also worth considering, at least when it's working, is the train service connecting Liwonde to Cuamba via the Nayuchi border. When in service, trains to Nayuchi leave Liwonde at 06.00 Monday to Friday and take about three hours. In Interlagos on the Mozambican side of the border there's a restaurant and resthouse, though if everything runs to schedule you should pick up the train to Cuamba on the same day, a four-hour trip which might take twice as long on a bad day.

The Muloza/Milanje border between Mulanje and Mocuba is worth considering only if you're determined to visit Quelimane. It's easy to get a bus from Blantyre or Mulanje to Muloza, where there's basic accommodation on both sides of the border, but transport from Milanje on to Mocuba is erratic.

The Marka/Villa Nova da Frontiera crossing in Malawi's extreme south should only be considered by those with their own 4x4 transport, or those who are prepared for a long wait on the Mozambique side. Mozambican insurance and visas are not issued here either, so arrange in advance.

Coming from southern Mozambique (or Zimbabwe), most people use the Mwanza/Zobue border post between Blantyre and the Tete Corridor (named after the Mozambican town of Tete). Regular buses with Malasha (m *01 11612314;* m *088 4460946*) and several other companies run between Harare and Blantyre, stopping at Tete, and minibuses also cover this route, though you'll need to change vehicles at Mwanza/Zobue, where the respective border posts are just under 6km apart. Driving up this way from southern Africa, be warned that officials along the Tete Corridor have a reputation for fining drivers for transgressing a variety of obscure or non-existent road regulations, but the road itself is in excellent condition.

To/from Tanzania The only viable road route from East Africa to Malawi connects Mbeya (in the southern Tanzanian highlands) to Karonga via the Songwe border post. Most people cross in stages. From Mbeya, there are plenty of minibuses through to Kyela, the closest town to the border, but you could also break the trip at the beautifully positioned town of Tukuyu, below the forested Mount Rungwe. Either way, ask to be dropped at the turn-off to the Songwe border, a few kilometres before Kyela. From the turn-off, walk the 6km to the border post, or hire a bicycle-taxi. If you need to overnight here, the only accommodation is on the Tanzanian side. However, plenty of minibuses run from here to Karonga, so unless you arrive ridiculously late in the day, the chance of getting stuck at the border is minimal. It is also possible to travel directly between Lilongwe and Mbeya or Dar es Salaam with the Taqwa or EasyBus services, which share an office on Devil Street in Lilongwe (m 099 9334299/538) and between them run every day except Thursday and Friday, leaving Lilongwe at 19.00 and taking about 15 hours to Mbeya (US$28), 27 hours to Dar es Salaam (US$47) and 48 hours to Nairobi (US$88).

For more information on overland travel including Malawi, see Bradt's *Africa Overland* by Siân Pritchard-Jones and Bob Gibbons.

SAFETY

CRIME It is difficult to strike the right balance when discussing crime in a country such as Malawi. An analytical understanding of how and where you are most likely to become a victim of crime will not only help prevent such an experience, but it will also allow you to relax in situations where it isn't a serious concern. African cultures are inherently honest, more so perhaps than ours, and to the average Malawian theft is unspeakably wrong, to the extent that petty thieves are regularly killed by mob justice. Because of this, small-town and rural Malawi remains very safe for travel, because Malawians in general wouldn't think of robbing a tourist, or anybody else for that matter.

On the other hand, crime abounds in the cities, where petty thieves often work the markets and bus stations targeting any likely victim, and tourists are easily identified as such. Even so, there is no significant risk attached to walking around the city centres by day, though the market area of Lilongwe is very dodgy after dark. Elsewhere, don't tempt fate by wandering alone along unlit streets at night, or going out with more money than you need. If you need to carry your money on your person, use a *hidden* money-belt. To avoid revealing its location in public, keep whatever spare cash you are likely to need elsewhere. Don't wear jewellery of financial or sentimental value, and if you can, leave that give-away daypack in your hotel room. Finally, when in doubt, *use a taxi* – they are very cheap in the cities.

Many travellers routinely carry their money-belt on their person, even walking around a city at night. Anecdotal evidence gathered over years of African travel suggests this is not a good idea, as muggings, snatchings and pickpocketings are far more common occurrences than a locked room being broken into. Obviously, an element of judgement comes into this: if a room feels insecure or a hotel has a bad reputation, don't leave anything of importance in it. And when you do leave stuff in a room, check that the windows are sealed and the door is properly locked. One factor to be considered is that some travellers' cheque companies will not refund cheques stolen from a room.

In Malawi, crime against tourists occurs mostly in a few particular 'trouble spots' in the cities and along the lakeshore. The pattern appears to be a sudden outbreak of mugging and snatch thefts in one particular resort, followed by a quiet period, indicating that these robberies are largely the work of one particular gang which is eventually arrested or moves on. Lilongwe, Blantyre, Nkhata Bay, Cape Maclear and

Salima have all experienced problems of this sort in the past, so your best course of action is to be cautious when you first arrive at one of these places, and to ask local advice once you are settled in. Camping wild on parts of the lakeshore is no longer advisable anywhere in Malawi, and we've heard of several instances of tents being broken into at 'proper' campsites.

Be cautious of people who befriend you on buses and offer you food or drink, because it appears that the practice of doping travellers in this manner has spread into Malawi. It's worth noting that con tricks are most likely to be perpetrated by

NOTES FOR DISABLED TRAVELLERS

Gordon Rattray (www.able-travel.com)

Malawi is known for its Great Rift Valley mountains and sandy beaches. It sounds therefore like a thoroughly unattractive destination for somebody with mobility problems. However, the truth is that with enough preparation in advance and the ability to 'rough it' if need be, a trip through Africa's warm heart is quite feasible. The Malawians' innate friendliness, coupled with the ability of Africans to improvise, should ensure that you have as varied and rewarding an itinerary as an able-bodied traveller.

ACCOMMODATION In general, it is not easy to find disabled-friendly accommodation in Malawi. Only top-of-the-range lodges and hotels will have 'accessible' rooms and even then, I've yet to hear of anywhere sporting grab handles, roll-under sinks and a roll-in shower. Occasionally (more by accident than through design) bathrooms are wheelchair accessible, but where this is not the case, you should be prepared to be lifted, or do your ablutions in the bedroom.

TRANSPORT

By road Distances are great and roads are often bumpy, so if you are prone to skin damage you may need to take extra care. I know of no company providing cars adapted for disabled drivers. If you're not sticking to the main roads, you may need to use a 4x4 vehicle, which will be higher than a normal car, therefore making transfers more difficult. Drivers/guides are normally happy to help, but are not trained in this skill, so you must thoroughly explain your needs and always stay in control of the situation.

There is no effective legislation in Malawi to facilitate disabled travellers' journeys by public transport. You will need to ask for help from fellow passengers to lift you to your seat, it will often be crowded and it is unlikely that there will be an accessible toilet. If you can cope with these difficulties, then travelling by bus is feasible and is a much more affordable option than hiring a car.

By air If you need assistance then let the airline know in advance and arrive early for your departure. During the flight, anyone who uses a pressure-relieving wheelchair cushion should consider using it instead of or on top of the fitted seat cushion. I flew with Air Malawi into Blantyre and found the disabled assistance service to be slow, but relatively well managed in comparison with some other African airlines. Blantyre Airport has an aisle chair, allowing a dignified exit from the plane for non-ambulant travellers, and although there is no designated disabled toilet, the rest of the building is level and accessible. As with vehicle transfers, explain your preferred method of transfer carefully beforehand.

a smartly dressed, smooth-talking guy who can easily build up a rapport with a traveller.

For all the above, Malawi remains a remarkably friendly and honest country. What most often gets travellers into trouble is one moment of recklessness – walking around Nkhata Bay at night with a money-belt on, wandering around Lilongwe market with a daypack dangling off your shoulder, dithering in a city bus station with a map in your hand and puzzled expression on your face, arriving in a city at night and not using a taxi to get to a hotel. Focus your energy on recognising

HEALTH AND INSURANCE Malawian hospitals and pharmacies can be basic, so if possible, take all essential medication and equipment with you. It is advisable to pack this in your hand luggage during flights in case your main bags don't arrive immediately. Doctors will know about 'everyday' illnesses, but you must understand and be able to explain your own particular medical requirements. Depending on the season it can be hot; if this is a problem for you then try to book accommodation and vehicles with fans or air conditioning, and a useful cooling aid is a plant-spray bottle.

Travel insurance can be purchased in the UK from Age Concern (\ *0800 169 2700; www.ageconcern.org.uk*), who have no upper age limit, and Free Spirit (\ *0845 230 5000; www.free-spirit.com*), who cater for people with pre-existing medical conditions. Most insurance companies will insure disabled travellers, but it is essential that they are made aware of your disability.

SECURITY For anyone following the usual security precautions (see page 55) the chances of robbery are greatly reduced. In fact, as a disabled person I often feel more 'noticed', and therefore a less attractive target for thieves. But the opposite may also apply, so do stay aware of where your bags are and who is around you, especially during car transfers and similar activities.

SPECIALIST OPERATORS There are currently no disability-specialised operators running trips to Malawi, but several operate in neighbouring countries so I expect this will change. Most mainstream travel companies will listen to your needs and try to create an itinerary that suits.

FURTHER INFORMATION
Books Bradt Travel Guides' *Access Africa: Safaris for People with Limited Mobility* is packed with useful advice and resources for disabled adventure travellers.

Online
www.able-travel.com A regularly updated website with both worldwide and country-specific information.
www.globalaccessnews.com A searchable database of disability travel information.
www.rollingrains.com A searchable website advocating disability travel.
www.youreable.com A UK-based general resource for disability information, with an active forum.
www.apparelyzed.com A site dedicated to spinal injury, but containing information that other disabilities will also find useful. It also hosts a hugely popular forum.

high-risk situations, and do all you can to avoid them. The rest of the time, so long as you conduct yourself sensibly, you have little to fear in terms of crime!

BARGAINING AND OVERCHARGING Tourists to Africa may sometimes need to bargain over prices, but this need is often exaggerated by guidebooks and travellers. Hotels, restaurants, supermarkets and buses charge fixed prices, and cases of overcharging are too unusual for it to be worth challenging a price unless it is blatantly ridiculous. That said, many Malawian hotels have a resident rate, non-resident rate and in-between rate for residents of other African countries, all of which may be negotiable if the hotel is quiet.

It is normal for Africans to negotiate prices for market produce, though less so in Malawi than in most African countries. My experience in markets outside Lilongwe and Blantyre is that I was normally asked the going rate straight off. This doesn't mean you can't bargain prices down a little, but I would query whether it is really worth the effort – the general mentality in Malawi (unlike that in some other African countries) is not to overcharge tourists, and it seems appropriate to respond to this by being reasonably trusting.

The main instance where bargaining is essential is when buying curios. What should be understood, however, is that the fact a curio seller is open to negotiation does not mean that you were initially being overcharged or ripped off. Curio sellers will generally quote a price knowing full well that you are going to bargain it down – they'd probably be startled if you didn't – and it is not necessary to respond aggressively or in an accusatory manner. It is impossible to say by how much you should bargain the initial price down (some people say that you should offer half the asking price and be prepared to settle at around two-thirds, but my experience is that curio sellers are far more whimsical than such advice suggests). The sensible approach, if you want to get a feel for prices, is to ask the price of similar items at a few different stalls before you actually contemplate buying anything. And even when buying curios, it is possible to take bargaining too far – especially when dealing with individuals as opposed to large curio stalls, I don't think it hurts to see the situation for what it is (somebody trying to scrape a living in difficult circumstances) and to be a little generous in your dealings.

BRIBERY Although bribery is often a way of life for local businessmen, it seldom poses a problem for travellers. The biggest risk in some countries is police roadblocks, where self-drivers might be asked to pay arbitrary fines for crimes they never committed, but this seldom if ever happens in Malawi, despite the proliferation of roadblocks.

BUREAUCRACY The tendency to portray African bureaucrats as difficult and inefficient in their dealings with tourists probably says more about Western prejudices that it does about Malawi. Sure, you come across the odd unhelpful official, but such is the nature of the beast everywhere. Far more commonly, government officials in Malawi are remarkably courteous and helpful in their dealings with tourists, often to a degree that is almost embarrassing – and a far cry from the treatment African visitors to Europe or the USA can expect from officialdom. That said, a decisive factor in determining the response you receive from African officials will be your own attitude. Walk into every official encounter with an aggressive, paranoid approach, and you are quite likely to come across as arrogant and to be treated as such. Instead, smile, try to be friendly and patient, and recognise that the officials do not speak English as a first language and may have difficulty following you. In short, treat officials with respect, and they'll tend to treat you in the same way.

LEGAL MATTERS The simple truth about the law in Malawi is that travellers who don't break it are highly unlikely to fall foul of it. It should be emphasised, however, that it is unequivocally illegal to possess or to smoke marijuana (*chamba*), and that the government has been known to raid backpacker hostels in the recent past, and to have police informants pose as dealers. Travellers caught in the act or in possession risk paying a hefty fine or facing deportation, or at worst being prosecuted and jailed. Any traveller who carries marijuana across an international border, no matter how small the amount, is legally speaking a drug smuggler, and likely to be treated as such if caught. It is also worth noting that homosexuality is officially illegal in Malawi, though it would probably require an act of overt exhibitionism for it ever to become an issue for travellers.

WOMEN TRAVELLERS

Sub-equatorial Africa is probably one of the safest places in the world for women to travel solo, and Malawi poses few risks specific to female travellers who apply the same common sense they would at home. Unwanted flirtation and the odd direct sexual proposition are a possibility, especially if you mingle with Malawians in bars, but a firm 'no' should defuse any potentially unpleasant situation. Men in Malawi probably constitute less of a sexual hassle than men in many Western countries, and for that matter than other male travellers.

Most Malawians have better things to worry about than how female tourists choose to dress, especially in established resort areas. That said, it would be insensitive to wear shorts or a revealing top in areas with a strong Islamic presence, or in villages where tourists are still relatively unusual. Unlike during the Banda era, however, it is no longer illegal or even unusual for women to wear trousers as opposed to a skirt.

Any female (or, for that matter, male) readers concerned about travelling alone in Malawi, but unable to find a travel companion, might be reassured by the thought that there are plenty of places in Malawi where it will be easy to meet with kindred spirits, and there's a lot to be said for hooking up with people along the way – better, by far, than making an advance commitment to travelling with somebody who you don't know well enough to be sure they'll be a suitable travel companion.

WHAT TO TAKE

LUGGAGE If you intend using public transport or doing much hiking, it's best to carry your luggage on your back. There are three ways of doing this: with a purpose-made backpack, with a suitcase that converts to a rucksack or with a large daypack. The choice between a convertible suitcase or a purpose-built backpack rests mainly on your style of travel. If you intend doing a lot of hiking, you're definitely best off with a proper backpack. However, if you carry everything in a smaller 35–45-litre daypack, the advantages are manifold on public transport and in terms of overall mobility.

CAMPING GEAR Accommodation in Malawi isn't as cheap as it used to be, so you can make a significant saving by carrying camping gear – a lightweight tent, a bedroll and a sleeping bag. For most purposes, a light sheet sleeping bag is as useful as the real thing, performing the important role of enclosing and insulating your body, and your tent should be as light as possible. Camping gear probably won't squeeze into a daypack, in which case a sensible compromise is to carry a large daypack in your rucksack. That way, you can carry a tent and other camping equipment when you need it, but at other times you can reduce your luggage to fit into a daypack and leave what you're not using in storage.

MONEY-BELT It is advisable to carry all your hard currency and credit cards, as well as your passport and other important documentation, in a money-belt. The ideal money-belt for Africa can be hidden beneath your clothing, as externally worn money-belts are as good as telling thieves that all your valuables are there for the taking. Use a money-belt made of cotton or another natural fabric, though bearing in mind that such fabrics tend to soak up a lot of sweat you will need to wrap plastic around everything inside.

MAPS The best and most current roadmap is Macmillan's 1:150,000 Malawi Road Map (*www.macmillan-africa.com*), which also has loads of town plans and maps of game reserves, and is available at most bookshops in Lilongwe and Blantyre. There's also an adequate ITMB 1:90,000 map, but it is less accurate and user-friendly. The map sales offices in Lilongwe and Blantyre sell 1:50,000 and 1:25,000 survey maps covering the whole country at US$10 per sheet. Good town plans of Blantyre, Lilongwe, Mzuzu and Zomba can be bought for the same price.

CLOTHING If you're carrying your luggage on your back, restrict your clothes to the minimum, ie: one or two pairs of trousers and/or skirts, one pair of shorts, three shirts or T-shirts, at least one sweater (or similar), depending on when and where you are visiting.

Ideally, bring light cotton or microfibre trousers. Jeans are also great for durability, but they can be uncomfortable in hot weather and slow to dry after washing. Skirts, like trousers, are best made of a light fabric, and should reach below the knee for reasons of protocol (short skirts will cause needless offence to many Malawians and may be perceived as provocative in some quarters). Chitenje cloth can be bought at any market to wear over shorts or trousers as a skirt, or as a sarong on the beach. Any fast-drying, lightweight shirts are good, but pack at least one with long sleeves for sun protection. For general purposes, one warm sweater or fleece should be adequate in Malawi, but you'll need more serious cool-weather gear for places like Mulanje and Nyika, especially in the southern winter. During the rainy season, it's worth carrying a light waterproof jacket or an umbrella.

Socks and underwear *must* be made from natural fabrics, and bear in mind that re-using them when sweaty will encourage fungal infections such as athlete's foot, as well as prickly heat in the groin region. Socks and underpants are light and compact enough to make it worth bringing a week's supply. As for shoes, bulky hiking boots are probably over the top for most people, but a good pair of walking shoes, preferably with some ankle support, is recommended. It's also useful to carry sandals, flip-flops or other light shoes.

OTHER USEFUL ITEMS A mobile phone (unlocked or get it unlocked in any city) will be useful. You can buy a local SIM card for next to nothing and top-up cards are readily available and inexpensive. This also doubles as your alarm clock for any early starts.

Binoculars are essential for close-up views of wildlife, especially birds. Compact binoculars are more backpack-friendly, but their restricted field of vision as compared with traditional binoculars can make it difficult to pick up animals in thick bush. For most purposes, 7x magnification is fine, but birdwatchers might find a 10x magnification more useful.

If you stay in local hotels, carry a padlock, as many places don't supply them. You should also carry a towel, soap, shampoo, toilet paper and any other toiletries you need (all of which are now available in Shoprite and some other supermarkets, including tampons). A torch is essential as electricity is never a guarantee. Another perennial favourite is the Swiss knife or multi-purpose tool.

Even in the cities you'll find the range of fiction books is limited and very expensive, though some cheaper secondhand books are available in Lilongwe, Blantyre and Mzuzu, but it's a good idea to bring a few reading books with you.

If travelling in your own vehicle, make sure you have a good set of tools, a selection of wire, string and rope, your driver's licence and the vehicle's registration papers (and a letter of permission to use the vehicle if it's not registered in your name). Depending on how far, where and when you're driving, you might also consider spare engine oil, a jerrycan for fuel, a fan belt, spare fuses and a fluorescent light that plugs into the cigarette lighter.

Medical kits and other health-related subjects are discussed in *Chapter 4, Health*, but do note that contact-lens solutions may not be available, so bring enough to last the whole trip and bring glasses in case the intense sun and dry African climate irritates your eyes.

ELECTRICITY

Malawi uses the British three square-pin plug and a 240-volt supply, so take adapters and transformers if necessary.

MONEY AND BANKING

The unit of currency is the Malawi kwacha, divided into 100 tambala. Notes are printed in denominations of Mk1,000, 500, 200, 100, 50, and 20, while smaller denominations are coins, which are seldom used. Foreign currency can be converted to kwachas at any branch of Standard, First Merchant, NBS or National Bank, as well as at many upmarket hotels and at any of several private bureaux de change (generally called forex bureaux) in Lilongwe or Blantyre. Banks are open 08.00–15.00 Monday–Friday and 08.00–11.00 Saturday; they are closed on Sundays and public holidays. Private forex bureaux normally keep longer hours, and some might open on Sunday.

The most widely recognised currency is the US dollar, followed by the euro, the pound sterling and the South African rand. If you are from any of the countries that use these currencies, it is probably best to travel with that currency.

In May 2013 the rate of exchange stood at approximately US$1=Mk400, £1=Mk620, €1=Mk525 and ZAR1=Mk45. The best exchange rates are generally available in Lilongwe and Blantyre, but there is no longer a significant difference between the rates available at banks and those offered at private forex bureaux.

Changing money is generally a reasonably swift and straightforward transaction in Lilongwe, Blantyre and other large towns. Banking facilities and ATMs have mushroomed in Malawi recently, but there are still a number of popular tourist spots (including Cape Maclear) without foreign exchange or ATM facilities, so it's advisable to change what you expect you'll need while you're still in a large town. There are scarcely any black-market street touts in Malawi, and even upmarket hotels may be reluctant to change money for non-residents, so plan your finances carefully.

CASH, CARD OR TRAVELLERS' CHEQUE? The safest way to carry hard currency is in the form of travellers' cheques, which can be refunded if they are lost or stolen, but do note that relatively few outlets actually take travellers' cheques these days, and that you cannot use them at private forex bureaux. Some banks may also require you to show proof of purchase before they will change your travellers' cheques, so carry that document with you, but never in the same place as the actual cheques.

More convenient than travellers' cheques are credit cards. There are now ATMs in all major cities (usually at the Standard, National, FMB or NBS bank) where you can withdraw up to Mk20,000 (some ATMs will allow up to Mk40,000) per transaction against foreign Visa and in some cases MasterCard or Maestro. You can also use your Visa at the foreign-exchange desks of most banks, though this can be time-consuming.

Furthermore, while things have improved greatly in recent years, card usage remains somewhat limited in Malawi as compared with more Westernised countries. For one, credit cards are not always readily accepted in shops, hotels and restaurants (though some places in Blantyre and Lilongwe will take them) and they are near useless outside major cities, except at selected upmarket game lodges and resorts. And those places that do accept credit cards generally take Visa only; other less well-known cards are not recognised, nor are the likes of American Express and Diners Club. An additional downside to paying with credit cards is that handling fees are often added. Finally, if the card is lost or damaged, you are unlikely to be able to arrange a replacement or an alternative source of funds very easily.

In essence, then, cash is king! It is accepted at all forex outlets, as well as by private traders outside banking hours, and you'll get far more kwachas for your dollar than with travellers' cheques or cards. The only drawback is that cash is also eminently stealable, and all but untraceable, and while theft is not a huge problem in Malawi, it does happen. The choice is yours. But whatever you do, note that US$100 notes issued before 2002 are not accepted by many forex outlets owing to the large number of forgeries in circulation, and notes of US$20 or less generally fetch a poorer rate than higher-denomination bills.

BUDGETING A budget is a personal thing, dependent on how much time you are spending in the country, what you are doing while you are there and how much money you can afford to spend. Even if you use facilities that are mainly geared to locals, Malawi is now a relatively expensive country. You can generally find a very basic room in a local hotel for up to US$10, and a simple meal for US$2–3. Buses are cheap, as are drinks. Rigidly budget-conscious travellers can probably keep costs down to US$35 per day, travelling solo, or US$40 for a couple. A budget of US$55–65 per person per day would be a lot more flexible for day-to-day costs, but if you want to indulge in activities such as horseriding, safari, climbing, trekking, kayaking or diving in Lake Malawi – experiences that will make your time in Malawi even more special – you might want to set aside US$400–800 for these. At the other end of the budget scale, a no-expense-spared upmarket safari using the very best lodges might easily work out at US$500 per person per day.

PRICES QUOTED IN THIS BOOK All prices were collected on the ground in late 2012, and will almost certainly be subject to inflation during the lifespan of this edition. The rate of exchange was approximately US$1=Mk325 at the time of research, but it has continued to slide rather dramatically and it remains unclear if and when the kwacha will stabilise. The real value of goods and services has remained relatively stable, however, and because of this we have converted all prices (save nominal amounts) into US dollars. This way, even if the kwacha continues to lose value, the prices listed in dollars will still reflect the actual cost of goods and services when converted back into kwacha at the current rate. Because of the long-term instability of the kwacha, many lodges and other institutions already quote rates in US dollars, or more occasionally euros or sterling. Despite the rates being quoted in hard currency, almost everything in Malawi, from national park fees to meals in upmarket restaurants, can be paid for in kwachas. For rough on-the-spot conversion purposes, Mk1,000 is worth about US$2.50, £1.60, €1.90 or ZAR22 as of May 2013.

GETTING AROUND

INTERNAL FLIGHTS Air Malawi (*www.flyairmalawi.com*) entered liquidation during early 2013, but it is widely expected to return to service in partnership with Ethiopian Airlines later in the year. When they do resume services, their routes will likely include domestic flights connecting Lilongwe to Blantyre, Karonga, Mzuzu and Makokola Retreat on the southern Lake Malawi shore. A more reliable option is Ulendo Airlink (*www.flyulendo.com*), which offers daily services to Likoma Island, Chelinda (Nyika National Park), and Mfuwe (Zambia). Private charters are also offered by Nyassa Air Taxi (*www.nyassa.mw*), and all are easily arranged through a reliable tour operator such as Wilderness, Land & Lake or Ulendo. There is a US$7 departure tax on all domestic flights, payable in cash at the airport.

SELF-DRIVE Malawi is easy to drive around. Speed limits on main roads are 80km/h for big trucks, 90–100km/h for other vehicles, and 60km/h in towns. As in most former British colonies, and all neighbouring countries, driving is on the left side of the road, requiring an additional adjustment for visitors from North America and mainland Europe. Petrol is blended with ethanol and has a low octane rating, and diesel is now higher in price than petrol. The crippling fuel shortages that struck Malawi during 2010–2012 have thankfully gone, but smaller-scale shortages still occur, so it's wise to always fuel up when you have the chance.

Many car-hire companies operate out of Blantyre and Lilongwe, and some of the more reputable firms are listed in the respective chapters on these cities. If you decide to rent a vehicle, take a good look under the bonnet before you drive off, and check the state of all tyres including the spare. You should also be provided with two reflective triangles and a fire extinguisher, as you are legally required to carry these and police may ask for them at checkpoints. One reader has recommended you bring an aerosol puncture-repair kit with you, for added security should you have to drive on your spare tyre on a poor road.

If arriving with your own vehicle, you've probably made sure it's tough and well kitted out, as driving *to* Malawi is worse than driving *around* Malawi. You don't need a 4x4, especially in the dry season, but a robust vehicle with high ground clearance is best.

The state of the roads in 2012 was generally very good, with good new tar on many of the main arteries. The worst trunk road in the country is probably the southern M1 between Nchalo and Bangula. The road up to Livingstonia will challenge most vehicles, even though its many hairpin bends are partially concreted. The Rumphi S103 back road to Livingstonia, though stunning, is impassable in the rainy season. Much of the M3 between Zomba and Blantyre is currently undergoing expansion, as it has long been too narrow and uneven for the volume of traffic using it.

Remember though that roads can deteriorate fast – good tarred roads develop horrendous pot-holes with no maintenance and dirt roads become impassable if not graded regularly. Rain washes roads and bridges away, causing delays and worry even if recent repairs and emergency bridges have not taken too long to complete (only days or weeks, not months or years as in the past). This is Africa, not Europe or the States, and it's what you came for. So take care and, if in doubt, ask local advice.

Those who have never before driven in rural Africa will need to adjust their driving style for Malawi. Basically, this means driving more slowly than you might on a similar road in a Western country, and slowing down when you approach pedestrians or cyclists on the road or livestock on the verge. Drunken driving is a serious problem in Malawi, and minibus drivers tend to drive as if they might be drunk even when 'sober. Be extra alert to vehicles overtaking in tight situations, driving on the wrong side of the road (especially where there are pot-holes), pulling out behind you without warning, and generally behaving as if it's their last day on earth. The police now have speed cameras as well, which are often positioned on blind curves or hills. The fine for speeding is a flat Mk5,000 (about US$16 at the time of writing), which is payable on the spot, but be sure to ask for a receipt. Don't drive at night – night driving is extremely hazardous, largely because so many vehicles in Malawi don't have functional headlights.

One final tip – generally Malawians expect everyone to be driving from south to north, and position all signs to lodges and places of interest to face south. Frustrating if you're coming from the north.

AXA COACH From its foundation in 1947 to its collapse precisely 60 years later, the parastatal Shire Bus Lines was the dominant public transport provider in Malawi. Fortunately, a private company called Axa, founded in December 2006 with just three coaches to its name, has stepped capably into the breach, providing superior coach and bus connections to most corners of the country with a fleet of 40 modern vehicles. Other bus services are available, but Axa's reputation for safety, reliability and comfort make it a clear first choice wherever possible.

Full details of the expanding routes, as well as fares and timetables, are (sometimes) available on the website www.agmamalawi.com or via email (e *agma@malawi.net or ampex@axamalawi.com*), and you can also contact their local booking offices in Blantyre (*Kamuzu Highway, next to the Chichiri Centre & just off Glyn Jones Rd in central Blantyre;* \01 820100/876000/874254), Lilongwe (*Old Town, next to Immigration & behind Lilongwe City Mall;* \01 755233/921571; m 099 9220901), Mzuzu (*near Tutla's Supermarket;* \01 931207/310785/930933), Karonga (\01 362767) or Salima (m 099 9048456). A brief summary of services follows.

Executive Coach The premier service runs non-stop between Blantyre and Lilongwe thrice-daily, leaving at 06.30, 12.00 and 16.00, taking four hours in either direction. The service offers personalised air conditioning and reading lights, ample legroom, on-board toilet and snacks, reclining seats, and television and DVD facilities. It costs US$22 one-way.

Deluxe Coach Similar in standard to the Executive Coach, but lacking the on-board toilet, this consists of two separate services running once daily between Blantyre and Mzuzu (leaving at 07.00), and another running once daily between Mzuzu and Chitipa (leaving at 06.00). The number of stops is strictly limited and includes Dedza, Ntcheu, Lilongwe, Kasungu, Jenda, Mzimba, Mzuzu, Karonga and Chitipa. It reaches Lilongwe after six hours, Mzuzu after about 12 hours, and it's another six hours to Karonga. Because of the schedules, those looking to take this route all the way through will have to spend a night in Mzuzu between buses. Sample fares are US$16 Blantyre–Lilongwe, US$22 Blantyre–Mzuzu and US$5.50 Mzuzu–Karonga.

Country Commuter Similar to the old country buses run by Shire Bus Lines, though of a much higher quality, these cover several different routes, ie: Blantyre to Dwambazi via Balaka; Blantyre to Santhe via Lilongwe; Blantyre to Mzuzu via Mangochi, Salima, Nkhotakota and Nkhata Bay; Muloza to Lilongwe via Mulanje and Blantyre; Lilongwe to Mzuzu via Nkhotakota and Nkhata Bay; and Lilongwe to Mzuzu via Kasungu and Mzimba. They stop at all towns and villages *en route*, so offer access to more places than the Deluxe Coach, and are cheaper, but also tend to take a lot longer for inter-city runs such as Lilongwe to Mzuzu.

CYCLING IN MALAWI   *Taken from a letter by Wim van Hoom*

We found that most parts of Malawi are very suitable for riding a bicycle. Since one of our bikes didn't arrive in Malawi, we had to buy a local mountain bike. This wasn't up to the standard of a European or American bike, but it was adequate and very cheap at around US$100. Generally, a mountain bike will cost a bit more than this (around US$120–150 including rear pannier and mudguards) and you will be able to arrange to sell it back to the shopkeeper at the end of your trip, so there's a good case for buying your bike after you arrive rather than flying one over to Malawi.

For long hauls, bicycles can easily be transported on the roof of a bus or minibus for a small fee, but you can expect minor damage to the paintwork, and should ask for help when you load and unload them. Suitable straps are available in the main bus stations, and we preferred to let a Malawian fasten the bike, because they are more aware of the dos and don'ts of handling baggage.

We did some cycling on surfaced roads, but we preferred not to, especially in the vicinity of large towns, because they can be very busy and some people drive like madmen. Drivers in Malawi expect a cyclist to make way for them by pulling over to the verge, a reflex we hadn't developed, and a habit that wastes time when you are trying to cover a lot of distance.

The dust roads were more interesting and enjoyable, and allow you to explore areas inaccessible to travellers dependent on public transport. We passed through many small villages where travellers are a relative novelty, and were always met with great enthusiasm and hospitality. It was always easy to organise somewhere to pitch a tent, and often local people would help us find food. We normally paid the villagers the equivalent to what we would have paid for a room or meal in a basic local resthouse. The small resthouses along the way were also an unforgettable experience (not least because we regularly bumped our heads against the low door frames!).

The 1:250,000 maps we bought in Lilongwe and Blantyre proved to be excellent for route finding. Contrary to what we had been told (and to our own experiences in other countries), we were never pointed in the wrong direction by somebody who didn't want to 'disappoint' us. It happened more than once that somebody we stopped to ask for directions walked with us to show us a good short cut. The only navigational problem we had was that some village names are incorrect on the maps, but asking for another village in the same direction always solved this.

OTHER BUSES AND MINIBUSES Several buses other than Axa operate main routes through Malawi, with **National Bus Company** (↳*01 985981/238, 971451/2, 611380;* e *nationalbuscompany@africa-online.net*) the foremost among them. National runs scheduled services on all main routes between Blantyre and Mzuzu up to five times daily, covering both the M1 via Lilongwe and the M5 lakeshore via Mangochi. Blantyre–Mzuzu will cost about US$12.50.

Beyond Axa and National, an interchangeable assortment of bus companies plies Malawi's roads, but they are generally far slower than Country Commuters, and serious delays and breakdowns are frequent. More popular with travellers are the innumerable *matola* minibuses (shared taxis) that cover most conceivable routes. These have the advantage of speed (assuming that you take an express minibus) and flexibility (they leave when full rather than adhering to a strict timetable), but they are often in poor repair and driven with reckless abandon by drunken lunatics. *Matola* lifts may also come from private individuals who want to make a bit of extra cash from a journey that they're undertaking anyway. In both cases, there is normally a fixed fare for *matola* rides along any given route, and on routes where there are buses, this is generally the same as the bus fare, or slightly cheaper – expect fares to work out around US$3.25 per 100km, though this will depend on road conditions and the popularity of the route.

HITCHING Hitchhiking is generally slow in Malawi and not advisable on main routes. In any case, many of the lifts you will be offered will expect payment, which is the accepted custom. On minor roads, where the line between hitching and *matola* rides is at best blurred, the sensible policy is to flag down whatever vehicle passes your way, take the odd free lift when fortune favours you, but otherwise be prepared to pay.

FERRY AND RAIL The MV *Ilala* ferry is a popular means of travelling around the lake and to Likoma and Chizumulu islands; see *Chapter 18, The Lake Ferry and the islands,* page 270, for details. The only railway lines in Malawi connect Lilongwe to Blantyre via Salima, Blantyre to Nsanje (near the Mozambican border in the south of the country) via Luchenza, and Liwonde to Nayuchi (on the Mozambican border northeast of Blantyre). Services are very slow, overcrowded and erratic, and offer no practical advantages over road transport.

ACCOMMODATION

Detailed accommodation listings for specific places of interest are given in the regional part of the guide and each establishment is placed in one of five categories: exclusive/luxury, upmarket, moderate, budget and shoestring. The purpose of this categorisation is twofold: to break up long hotel listings that span a wide price range, and to help readers isolate the range of hotels that will best suit their budget and taste. The application of categories is not rigid. Aside from an inevitable element of subjectivity, it is based as much on the feel of a hotel as its rates (which are quoted anyway) and placement is also sometimes influenced by the standard of other accommodation options in the same place.

EXCLUSIVE/LUXURY This category embraces a handful of international four- and five-star luxury hotels, as well as a few select smaller lodges and resorts notable less for their luxury than for offering a genuinely exclusive experience. Rates are typically upwards of US$300 for a double room. This is the category to look at if you want the best and/or most characterful accommodation and have few financial restrictions.

UPMARKET This category includes most Western-style hotels, lodges and resorts that cater mainly to international tourist or business travellers but lack the special something that might elevate them into the luxury or exclusive category. Hotels in this range would typically be accorded a two- to three-star ranking elsewhere, and they offer smart en-suite accommodation with a good selection of facilities. Rates are typically around US$100–200 for a double, dependent on quality and location. Most package tours and privately booked safaris use accommodation in this range.

MODERATE In Malawi, as in many African countries, there is often a wide gap in price and standard between the cheapest hotels geared primarily towards tourists and the best hotels geared primarily towards local and budget travellers. For this reason, moderate is the most nebulous of the categories, essentially consisting of hotels which, for one or other reason, couldn't really be classified as upmarket, but are also a notch or two above the budget category in terms of price and/or quality. Expect unpretentious en-suite accommodation with hot water and possibly television, a decent restaurant and efficient English-speaking staff. Prices for moderate city and beach hotels are generally in the US$50–80 range for a double. This is the category to look at if you are travelling privately on a limited or low budget and expect a reasonably high but not luxurious standard of accommodation.

BUDGET Accommodation in this category falls into two broad types. There are hotels aimed largely at the local market that don't approach international standards, but are still reasonably clean and comfortable, with a decent restaurant attached, and en-suite rooms with running cold or possibly hot water. Then there are the more Westernised but equally affordable backpacker hostels and beach resorts that form the accommodation mainstay for many independent travellers to Malawi. Expect to pay around US$20–50 for a double, depending on the location, or less to pitch a tent or stay in a dorm. This is the category to look at if you are on a limited budget, but want to avoid total squalor!

In this guide, prices don't include breakfast unless otherwise stated within the listing.

SHOESTRING This is the very bottom end of the market, usually small local guesthouses with simple rooms and common showers and toilets. Running the gamut from pleasantly clean to decidedly squalid, hotels in this category typically cost around US$10–20 for a room. It is the category for those for whom keeping down costs is the main imperative.

CAMPING Almost every national park, backpackers' hostel and lakeshore resort in Malawi allows camping, typically at a cost of around US$3–5 per person. Campsites are split across the accommodation categories but would most often be associated with the budget range.

EATING AND DRINKING

The staple diet in Malawi is *nsima*, a stiff porridge made from pounded maize meal boiled in water. Most local people do not feel they have eaten unless they have had a couple of lumps of *nsima*. *Nsima* will be familiar to visitors from East Africa under the name of *ugali*, and to people from southern Africa as *mieliemeal*. Few travellers develop a taste for *nsima*, so it is fortunate that most local restaurants also serve rice and potato chips (or occasionally cassava or sweet potato chips).

RESTAURANTS At tourist-class hotels and restaurants in the major towns, you can eat food to international standards at a very reasonable price – there are few upmarket restaurants in Malawi where you can't eat well for under US$10 for a main course (though better restaurants in Lilongwe and Blantyre might be more like US$15). Local restaurants tend to serve a predictable and somewhat dull menu of beef (*nyama ngombe*), chicken (*mkuku*) or fish (*nsomba*) with chips or rice or *nsima*, but are very reasonably priced at anything from US$2–4 for a starch-heaped plate, often accompanied by a sharp-tasting dollop of stewed cassava or pumpkin leaves (*chisisito*), or a heap of stewed beans. Popular fish include *chambo* (a type of tilapia), *kampango* (a type of catfish) and *mpasa* (a large cichlid with dark flesh that is often referred to as lake salmon). The most widely available fish in Malawi is *usipa*, a tiny fish that is generally sun-dried after it is caught.

COOKING FOR YOURSELF If you want to put together your own meal, you'll find that the variety of foodstuffs available varies from season to season and from town to town, and sudden shortages of commonplace items are to be expected. In most towns, you can buy fresh bread at the People's Superette or other supermarkets, or at a bakery. Supermarkets also normally stock a variety of spreads and packaged food such as yoghurt, potato crisps, biscuits and sometimes cheese and cold meat. Fruits and vegetables are best bought at markets, where they are very cheap, as is fresh meat. Potatoes, onions, tomatoes, bananas, sugarcane and some citrus fruits are available in most markets around the country. In larger towns and in agricultural areas a much wider selection of fruits and vegetables might include avocados, peas and beans, paw-paws, mangoes, coconuts and pineapples. For hikers, packet soups are about the only dehydrated meals available throughout Malawi. Dried staples such as rice, maize meal and pasta can be bought in supermarkets and markets.

DRINKS Brand-name soft drinks such as Pepsi, Coca-Cola and Fanta are widely available in Malawi and cheap by international standards. If the fizzy stuff doesn't appeal, you can buy imported South African fruit juices at most large supermarkets. Frozen fruit squashes are sold everywhere in Malawi for a few kwacha; they're very sweet but otherwise quite refreshing on long walks and bus trips. Tap water is generally safe to drink in towns, providing the chlorine hasn't run out, but bottled mineral water is available if you prefer not to take the risk.

Traditional African beer is made of fermented maize or millet. It is brewed in villages for private consumption, and also brewed commercially to be sold in litre cartons. The most popular brand of traditional beer is the wonderfully titled Chibuku Shake-Shake (the latter half of the name refers to the need to shake the carton before opening), and special Chibuku bars can be found in most towns and villages. A carton of Chibuku is very cheap and, despite its gruel-like texture, surprisingly rich in nutrients when compared with most alcoholic drinks. Unfortunately, African beer is something of an acquired taste: most travellers can't stand it.

Carlsberg enjoys a near-total beer monopoly in Malawi, and their flagship product, 'Green', is the most popular alcoholic drink in the country (after Chibuku) and all the Carlsberg beers are inexpensive. Most visitors settle on a Green as first choice (named, naturally, after the colour of its label), a light lager with 5% alcoholic content or the stronger Special Brew. A Carlsberg beer which is proving popular is called Kuche Kuche (which means 'all night long'). It has a lower alcohol content of 3.7%, is sold in 500ml bottles and is cheaper than Green.

There is now also Carlsberg Light at only 2.4%. Other visitors prefer the richer Carlsberg Stout.

Wines are widely available in hotels, bars and supermarkets at high import prices. Spirits such as cane, brandy and gin are manufactured locally, while a good variety of imported spirits is available in supermarkets and better bars. The Malawi Gin is well-loved, so much so that the manufacturers can't always keep up with demand, and bars will periodically run short of it. It may not be quite what you're used to, but is well worth trying, and closing the day at least once with a sunset and an MGT – Malawi Gin & Tonic, that is – is practically mandatory.

PUBLIC HOLIDAYS

Banks, government offices and many shops and businesses close on public holidays. When a holiday falls on a Saturday or Sunday it is taken on the subsequent Monday. Malawi's relatively small Muslim population celebrates the Islamic holidays, but this has no significant practical effect on travellers. In addition to Easter, which falls on a different date every year, the following public holidays are taken in Malawi:

New Year's Day	1 January
John Chilembwe Day	15 January
Martyrs' Day	3 March
Labour Day	1 May
Kamuzu Day	14 May
Freedom Day	14 June
Independence Day	6 July
Mother's Day	15 October
Christmas Day	25 December
Boxing Day	26 December

For details of particular events taking place in Malawi during the year, see *Annual events* box, page 48.

SHOPPING

Malawi is a good place to buy curios, both in terms of price and quality, and cheap surface mail makes shipping your purchases home a viable prospect. Malawi is best known for hardwood carvings and wooden chairs, but bear in mind that every such purchase contributes to the demise of a rare hardwood tree. The Mulanje cedar, endemic to the high-altitude plateaux of Mulanje, is used to make cedar boxes renowned for their distinctive pleasant smell and light colour – but these items will weigh heavy on the rucksack (and on the conscience of ecologically conscious travellers). Other popular items include polished soapstone carvings, malachite jewellery and a wide range of basketwork and pottery items.

Curios are inexpensive throughout, but are generally cheapest away from Blantyre, Lilongwe and the more popular lakeshore resorts. Three places recommended as good value are the woodcarving stalls at the Mangochi turn-off 3km from Liwonde Town, the long line of stalls at Salima, and the stalls 1km from Machinga towards Liwonde, which are good for chairs. There are also good stalls at Nkopola and Nkhata Bay and near to Mua Mission on the Monkey Bay turn-off. Wherever you shop, expect to bargain over prices, and be aware that many curio sellers will be as happy to barter their wares against used clothing.

MEDIA AND COMMUNICATIONS

TELEPHONE The telephone service is efficient by African standards, and lines are generally clear, though the rains can wreak havoc with landlines. If you are spending a while in Malawi and have your own mobile (cell) phone, a local SIM card is cheap and airtime can be bought from street vendors and many shops. Otherwise, official phone booths stand outside most post offices, though the private 'one lady and her phone' stalls that line many urban roads are more likely to work.

All landline numbers share an area code of 01 followed by six other digits. TNM and Airtel are the two dominant mobile providers, and both have good service nationwide, but certain remote areas are still sometimes covered by one network and not the other. Airtel numbers all begin with 099, and TNM with 088, and both are then followed by seven digits. The international dialling code

PHOTOGRAPHIC TIPS   *Ariadne Van Zandbergen*

EQUIPMENT Although with some thought and an eye for composition you can take reasonable photos with a 'point-and-shoot' camera, you need an SLR camera if you are at all serious about photography. Modern SLRs tend to be very clever, with automatic programmes for almost every possible situation, but remember that these programmes are limited in the sense that the camera cannot think, but only makes calculations. Every starting amateur photographer should read a photographic manual for beginners and get to grips with such basics as the relationship between aperture and shutter speed.

Always buy the best lens you can afford. The lens determines the quality of your photo more than the camera body. Fixed fast lenses are ideal, but very costly. A zoom lens makes it easier to change composition without changing lenses the whole time. If you carry only one lens, a 28–70mm (digital 17–55mm) or similar zoom should be ideal. For a second lens, a lightweight telephoto zoom will be excellent for candid shots and varying your composition. Wildlife photography will be very frustrating if you don't have at least a 300mm lens. For a small loss of quality, tele-converters are a cheap and compact way to increase magnification: a 300mm lens with a 1.4x converter becomes 420mm, and with a 2x it becomes 600mm. Note, however, that 1.4x and 2x tele-converters reduce the speed of your lens by 1.4 and 2 stops respectively.

For wildlife photography from a safari vehicle, a solid beanbag, which you can make yourself very cheaply, will be necessary to avoid blurred images, and is more useful than a tripod. A clamp with a tripod head screwed onto it can be attached to the vehicle as well. Modern dedicated flash units are easy to use; aside from the obvious need to flash when you photograph at night, you can improve a lot of photos in difficult 'high contrast' or very dull light with some fill-in flash. It pays to have a proper flash unit as opposed to a built-in camera flash.

DIGITAL/FILM Digital photography is now the preference of most amateur and professional photographers, with the resolution of digital cameras improving the whole time. For ordinary prints a 6 megapixel camera is fine. For better results and the possibility to enlarge images and for professional reproduction, higher resolution is available up to 24 megapixels.

Memory space is important. The number of pictures you can fit on a memory card depends on the quality you choose. Calculate in advance how many pictures for Malawi is +265, with the leading zero being dropped afterwards when calling from abroad.

Where possible, listings in this book include landline and mobile numbers. Generally, it will be easier to get through to a mobile, but these numbers are by their very nature more changeable than landlines, especially as in many cases it is simply the mobile of a receptionist or manager. Landlines are less reliable in telephonic terms, but far more likely to be attached to the same institution a few years down the line.

INTERNET AND EMAIL Fast broadband or satellite internet facilities are readily available in cities and larger towns, as well as at many resort areas and smaller villages. Internet cafés in cities and large towns generally charge Mk5–10 per minute but rates are higher at upmarket hotels and in more remote areas. For those carrying their own laptop, Skyband has established Wi-Fi hotspots in several cafés,

you can fit on a card and either take enough cards to last for your trip, or take a storage drive or memory stick onto which you can download the content. A laptop gives the advantage that you can see your pictures properly at the end of each day and edit and delete rejects, but a storage device is lighter and less bulky.

Bear in mind that digital camera batteries, computers and other storage devices need charging, so make sure you have all the chargers, cables and converters with you. Most hotels have charging points, but do enquire about this in advance. When camping you might have to rely on charging from the car battery; a spare battery is invaluable.

DUST AND HEAT Dust and heat are often a problem. Keep your equipment in a sealed bag, stow films in an airtight container (eg: a small cooler bag) and avoid exposing equipment to the sun. Digital cameras are prone to collecting dust particles on the sensor which results in spots on the image. The dirt mostly enters the camera when changing lenses, so be careful when doing this. To some extent photos can be 'cleaned' up afterwards in Photoshop, but this is time-consuming. You can have your camera sensor professionally cleaned, or you can do this yourself with special brushes and swabs made for the purpose, but note that touching the sensor might cause damage and should only be done with the greatest care.

LIGHT The most striking outdoor photographs are often taken during the hour or two of 'golden light', after dawn and before sunset. Shooting in low light may enforce the use of very low shutter speeds, in which case a tripod will be required to avoid camera shake.

With careful handling, side lighting and back lighting can produce stunning effects, especially in soft light and at sunrise or sunset. Generally, however, it is best to shoot with the sun behind you. When photographing animals or people in the harsh midday sun, images taken in light but even shade are likely to be more effective than those taken in direct sunlight or patchy shade, since the latter conditions create too much contrast.

Ariadne Van Zandbergen is a professional travel and wildlife photographer specialising in Africa. She runs The Africa Image Library. For photo requests, visit www. africaimagelibrary.com or contact her by email at e ariadne@hixnet.co.za.

restaurants and lodges in Lilongwe and Blantyre, as well as at selected resorts and hotels countrywide (including all units in the Sunbird chain), and airtime cards are available for the same outlets – see the website www.skyband.mw for full details of hotspots and cards.

MY GAP YEAR AT ST THERESA PRIVATE SCHOOL
Pete Bexton

I was sent to Malawi by a gap-year organisation called Project Trust, which specialises in 12-month placements. I was working as a volunteer teacher at St Theresa Primary School in Chiwembe, a township on the outskirts of Blantyre. The school was set up by Mrs Kotokwa, a local Malawian, in 1994. Initially she rented a single room in a decrepit government building, where she had three pupils in different classes and only two teachers – herself and one other. As can be imagined, this was a task in itself; however, after much dedication, she now owns her own land and buildings. Over 300 pupils attend the school and she has 20 trained teachers working alongside her. Although incomplete owing to lack of funds, St Theresa is improving greatly because of the dedication and perseverance of both Mrs Kotokwa and the teachers.

Government schools in Malawi are free, but the standard of education is very poor and classes are grossly overcrowded. Classes may consist of up to 150 pupils, with a maximum of two teachers in charge. At present the school day lasts from 07.30 to 15.00, and consists of nine lessons, a morning break and a lunch break. St Theresa is a private school, and classes range from nursery to Standard 8, equivalent to an English primary school. Children's ages range from three years up to 16 or 17; this is because children have to resit classes if they fail. Occasionally a child will miss a year's schooling to help support his or her family. As with an English school, St Theresa's pupils study English, mathematics, French, religious education, general studies, science and drawing. Although the national language is Chichewa, all subjects are taught in English. Since Malawi is such a poor country, and the school has very limited funds, the children have no bought toys. Sports equipment is non-existent and textbooks are old, incomplete and few and far between. However, the children are used to their lack of resources and are able to make games using both balls and rope made out of plastic bags. Although their games are simple, they find great enjoyment in them, and they are very innovative when they need a new pastime.

In Malawi, the next stage of education after primary school is secondary school. To get to secondary school, the children must pass the General Certificate of Education (GCE) at the end of Standard 8. Children who do not pass the GCE have either to pay fees and go to a private school, or stop their education. Because of this there are a large number of children in Malawi who do not continue their education after about the age of 13.

My role at St Theresa was the same as that of any other teacher. I had a full timetable every day of the week, and I had my roster of break and lunch duties. This is one of the things that made my year even more enjoyable, as I was on the same level as all the other teachers, and was able to make friends with them as an equal. I was also able to give the teachers a Western perspective on teaching methods, and help with timetabling the school day. It was a great privilege working alongside the Malawians, and I learnt more in this year than I ever could have hoped.

STUFF YOUR RUCKSACK – AND MAKE A DIFFERENCE

www.stuffyourrucksack.com is a website set up by TV's Kate Humble which enables travellers to give direct help to small charities, schools or other organisations in the country they are visiting. Maybe a local school needs books, a map or pencils, or an orphanage needs children's clothes or toys – all things that can easily be 'stuffed in a rucksack' before departure. The charities get exactly what they need and travellers have the chance to meet local people and see how and where their gifts will be used.

The website describes organisations that need your help and lists the items they most need. Check what's needed in Malawi, contact the organisation to say you're coming and bring not only the much-needed goods but an extra dimension to your travels and the knowledge that in a small way you have made a difference.

POST AND COURIER International post is slow and unreliable: allow at least three weeks for it to get through. Surface mail out of Malawi is very cheap, which makes it an excellent place from where to post curios. For express courier and parcel services, DHL is well represented.

NEWSPAPERS Malawi has a free press, and a number of English-language newspapers and magazines are available, offering fascinating coverage of local news, politics and local sport. The main newspapers are *The Nation* and *The Daily Times*, both also available online at www.mwnation.com and www.bnltimes.com, respectively.

TELEVISION AND RADIO The erratic state television service MTV is supplemented in many homes and most hotels by DSTV, a South African satellite broadcast service that includes BBC News, CNN and several sports and entertainment channels. There are a variety of private radio stations; Capital FM (*www.capitalradiomalawi. com*) is among the most influential, broadcasting popular African music and news in larger cities nationwide.

CULTURAL ETIQUETTE

Most Malawian etiquette is very easy to pick up. There are many spots in Malawi that are thoroughly modernised, but the villages remain very traditional and some areas of the cities and resorts will treat you with more respect if you adhere to Malawian cultural etiquette. Markets and bus stations are also curiously old-fashioned. I have noted a few guidelines here to reinforce those already mentioned elsewhere in this guide; none are essential but they will help the way people accept you:

- Always use the formal greetings of 'hello, how are you?' and plenty of 'thank you's too.
- Women should wear a *chitenje* or a skirt in the villages.
- People may find too much physical contact between men and women offensive.
- If you want to camp in a village, always ask the permission of the chief.
- Pay for lifts if you choose to hitch.
- Respect other people for the job they have been trained to do.

Kate Webb, Responsible Safari Company (*01 602407;* e *info@ responsiblesafaricompany.com; www.responsiblesafaricompany.com)*

When visiting any destination we should all be looking to travel more responsibly and visiting local communities is one way you can do this. Malawians are renowned for their warm welcome and with tourism still in its infancy it remains very easy to head off the tourist trail and experience rural Africa.

The Responsible Safari Company offers eco-tourism day visits in Blantyre, Thyolo, Mulanje, Zomba, Mangochi and Cape Maclear to ensure the benefits of tourism reach local communities in these areas. These visits offer the chance to interact with local Malawians, learn more about rural village life, cook Malawian food and join in some traditional dancing! Visits can range from one hour to overnight stays and longer skilled volunteer placements can also be arranged.

When visiting any local community, keep these guidelines in mind to ensure your visit makes a positive impact:

- Do make time to visit local communities. These experiences are often the most memorable of your time in Malawi.
- Don't hand out money direct to the community; this causes problems between community members and encourages a begging culture.
- Do support local sustainable organisations, to ensure your benefit is shared by the whole community.
- Don't hand out sweets. Dental healthcare is not accessible for most people in Malawi.
- Do donate locally bought resources, pens, papers, books etc to local schools and projects.
- Don't take photographs without asking. Do email or send your pictures back to the community when you return home.
- Do learn a few words of Chichewa, a smile and a local greeting will make you friends very quickly!
- Do respect local customs by wearing conservative clothing when visiting local communities.
- Do buy locally made handicrafts as this helps to support the local economy.

For more information about how you can get involved during your time in Malawi contact The Responsible Safari Company, based in Blantyre, Malawi

4

Health

with Dr Felicity Nicholson and Dr Jane Wilson-Howarth

People new to Africa often worry about tropical diseases, but if you take the appropriate precautions, it is accidents that are more likely to carry you off. Road accidents are very common in many parts of Malawi, so be aware and do what you can to reduce risks: try to travel during daylight hours and refuse to be driven by a drunk. Listen to local advice about areas where violent crime is rife, too.

BEFORE YOU GO

IMMUNISATION Preparations to ensure a healthy trip to Malawi require checks on your immunisation status: it is wise to be up to date on tetanus, polio and diphtheria (now given as an all-in-one vaccine, Revaxis, which lasts for ten years), typhoid and hepatitis A. Immunisations against rabies and hepatitis B may also be recommended. Proof of vaccination against yellow fever is needed for entry into Malawi if you are coming from a yellow fever endemic area. Immunisation against cholera may be recommended for Malawi, especially if there is a known outbreak.

Hepatitis A vaccine (eg: Havrix Monodose or Avaxim) comprises two injections given about a year apart. The course costs about £100 but may be available on the NHS, protects for 25 years and can be administered even close to the time of departure. Hepatitis B vaccination should be considered for longer trips (two months or more) or for those working with children or in situations where contact with blood is likely. Three injections are needed for the best protection and can be given over a three-week period if time is short for those aged 16 or over. Longer schedules give more sustained protection and are therefore preferred if time allows and have to be used for those under 16. Hepatitis A vaccine can also be given as a combination with hepatitis B as 'Twinrix', though two doses are needed at least seven days apart to be effective for the hepatitis A component, and three doses are needed for the hepatitis B. Again this schedule is only suitable for those aged 16 or over.

The newer injectable typhoid vaccines (eg: Typhim Vi) last for three years and are about 85% effective. Oral capsules (Vivotif) may also be available for those aged six and over. Three capsules over five days lasts for approximately three years but may be less effective than the injectable forms depending on how they are absorbed. Typhoid vaccination should be encouraged unless the traveller is leaving within a few days for a trip of a week or less, when the vaccine would not be effective in time. Vaccinations for rabies are ideally advised for everyone, but are very important for travellers visiting more remote areas, especially if you are more than 24 hours from medical help and definitely if you will be working with animals (see *Rabies*, page 85).

Experts differ over whether a BCG vaccination against tuberculosis (TB) is useful in adults: discuss this with your travel clinic.

Along with road accidents, malaria poses the single biggest serious threat to the health of travellers in most parts of tropical Africa, Malawi included. It is unwise to travel in malarial parts of Africa while pregnant or with children unless it is absolutely necessary: the risk of malaria in many parts is considerable and these travellers are likely to succumb rapidly to the disease. The risk of malaria more than 1,800m above sea level is low.

MALARIA IN MALAWI The *Anopheles* mosquito which transmits the malaria parasite is most abundant near marshes and still water, where it breeds, and the parasite is most prolific at low altitudes. Parts of Malawi lying at an altitude of 2,000m or higher (Zomba, Nyika and Mulanje plateaux) are regarded to be free of malaria. In mid-altitude locations such as Lilongwe, Blantyre and Mzuzu, malaria is largely but not entirely seasonal, with the highest risk of transmission occurring during the hot, wet summer months of November to April. The low-lying Lake Malawi hinterland and Shire Valley are high risk throughout the year, but the danger is greatest during the summer months. This localised breakdown might influence what foreigners working in Malawi do about malaria prevention, but since tourist activity in Malawi is focused around the lake, all travellers to Malawi must assume that they will be exposed to malaria and should take precautions throughout their trip (see below).

MALARIA PREVENTION There is not yet a vaccine against malaria that gives enough protection to be useful for travellers, but there are other ways to avoid it; since most of Africa is very high risk for malaria, travellers must plan their malaria protection properly. Seek current advice on the best antimalarials to take: usually mefloquine, Malarone or doxycycline. If mefloquine (Lariam) is suggested, start this 2½ weeks (three doses) before departure to check that it suits you; stop it immediately if it seems to cause depression or anxiety, visual or hearing disturbances, severe headaches, fits or changes in heart rhythm. Side effects such as nightmares or dizziness are not medical reasons for stopping unless they are sufficiently debilitating or annoying. Anyone who has been treated for depression or psychiatric problems, has diabetes controlled by oral therapy or who is epileptic (or who has suffered fits in the past) or has a close blood relative who is epileptic, should probably avoid mefloquine.

In the past doctors were nervous about prescribing mefloquine to pregnant women, but experience has shown that it is relatively safe and certainly safer than the risk of malaria. That said, there are other issues, so if you are travelling to Malawi while pregnant, seek expert advice before departure.

Malarone (proguanil and atovaquone) is as effective as mefloquine. It has the advantage of having few side effects and need only be continued for one week after returning. However, it is expensive and because of this tends to be reserved for shorter trips. Malarone may not be suitable for everybody, so advice should be taken from a doctor. The licence in the UK has been extended for up to three months' use and a paediatric form of tablet is also available, prescribed on a weight basis.

Another alternative is the antibiotic doxycycline (100mg daily). Like Malarone it can be started one day before arrival. Unlike mefloquine, it may also be used in travellers with epilepsy, although certain anti-epileptic medication may make it less effective. In perhaps 1–3% of people there is the possibility of allergic skin reactions developing in sunlight; the drug should be stopped if this happens and an alternative sought. It is also unsuitable in pregnancy or for children under 12 years.

Chloroquine and proguanil are no longer considered to be effective enough for Malawi but may be considered as a last resort if nothing else is deemed suitable.

All tablets should be taken with or after the evening meal, washed down with plenty of fluid and, with the exception of Malarone (see opposite), continued for four weeks after leaving Malawi.

Despite all these precautions, it is important to be aware that no antimalarial drug is 100% protective, although those on prophylactics who are unlucky enough to catch malaria are less likely to get rapidly into serious trouble. In addition to taking antimalarials, it is therefore important to avoid mosquito bites between dusk and dawn (see *Avoiding insect bites* box, overleaf).

There is unfortunately the occasional traveller who prefers to 'acquire resistance' to malaria rather than take preventive tablets, or who takes homeopathic prophylactics thinking these are effective against killer disease. Homeopathy theory dictates treating like with like so there is no place for prophylaxis or immunisation in a well person; bona fide homeopathists do not advocate it. It takes at least 18 months residing in a holoendemic area for someone to get some immunity to malaria, so travellers to Africa will not acquire any effective resistance to malaria. The best way is to prevent mosquito bites in the first place and to take a suitable prophylactic agent.

MALARIA DIAGNOSIS AND TREATMENT Even those who take their malaria tablets meticulously and do everything possible to avoid mosquito bites may contract a strain of malaria that is resistant to prophylactic drugs. Untreated malaria is likely to be fatal, but even strains resistant to prophylaxis respond well to prompt treatment. Because of this, your immediate priority upon displaying possible malaria symptoms – including a rapid rise in temperature (over 38°C), and any combination of a headache, flu-like aches and pains, a general sense of disorientation, and possibly even nausea and diarrhoea – is to establish whether you have malaria, ideally by visiting a clinic.

Diagnosing malaria is not easy, which is why consulting a doctor is sensible: there are other dangerous causes of fever in Africa, which require different treatments. Even if you test negative, it would be wise to stay within reach of a laboratory until the symptoms clear up, and to test again after a day or two if they don't. It's worth noting that if you have a fever and the malaria test is negative, you may have typhoid or paratyphoid, which should also receive immediate treatment.

Travellers to far-flung parts of Malawi – for instance some of the more remote lakeshore resorts, and in national parks and montane areas – would be wise to carry a course of treatment to cure malaria, and a rapid test kit. With malaria, it is normal enough to go from feeling healthy to having a high fever in the space of a few hours (and it is possible to die from falciparum malaria within 24 hours of the first symptoms). In such circumstances, assume that you have malaria and act accordingly. Experts differ on the costs and benefits of self-treatment, but some say that it leads to over-treatment and to many people taking drugs they do not need; yet treatment may save your life. There is also some division about the best treatment for malaria, but either Malarone or Coarthemeter are the current treatments of choice. Discuss your trip with a specialist either at home or in Malawi.

For information on other insect borne diseases, see page 81.

As the sun is going down, don long clothes and apply repellent on any exposed flesh. Pack a DEET-based insect repellent ideally containing between 50–55% of the chemical DEET. You also need either a permethrin-impregnated bed-net or a permethrin spray so that you can 'treat' bed-nets in hotels. Permethrin treatment makes even very tatty nets protective and prevents mosquitoes from biting through the impregnated net when you roll against it; it also deters other biters. Otherwise retire to an air-conditioned room or burn mosquito coils (which are widely available and cheap in Malawi), or sleep under a fan. Coils and fans reduce rather than eliminate bites. Travel clinics usually sell a good range of nets, treatment kits and repellents.

Mosquitoes and many other insects are attracted to light. If you are camping, never put a lamp near the opening of your tent, or you will have a swarm of biters waiting to join you when you retire. In hotel rooms, be aware that the longer your light is on, the greater the number of insects will be sharing your accommodation.

Aside from avoiding mosquito bites between dusk and dawn, which will protect you from elephantiasis and a range of nasty insect-borne viruses, as well as malaria (see page 76), it is important to take precautions against other insect bites. During the day it is wise to wear long, loose (preferably 100% cotton) clothes if you are pushing through scrubby country; this will keep off ticks and also tsetse and day-biting *Aedes* mosquitoes which may spread viral fevers. Putting on **socks** and **long clothes** (including long-sleeved shirts or blouses) at dusk reduces the risk of bites and the amount of repellent needed. Be aware, however, that malaria mosquitoes usually hunt at ankle level and their bite can penetrate through socks, so apply repellent to your feet and ankles whether you wear socks or not.

Tsetse flies hurt when they bite and it is said that they are attracted to the colour blue; locals will advise on where they are a problem and where they transmit sleeping sickness.

Minute, pestilential, biting **blackflies** spread river blindness in some parts of Africa between190°N and 170°S. The disease is caught close to fast-flowing rivers since flies breed there and the larvae live in rapids. The flies bite during the day but long trousers tucked into socks will help keep them off. Citronella-based natural repellents (eg: Mosi-guard) do not work against them.

Tumbu flies or *putsi*, often called mango flies in Malawi, are a problem where the climate is hot and humid. The adult fly lays her eggs on the soil or on drying laundry and when the eggs come into contact with human flesh (when you put on clothes or lie on a bed) they hatch and the larvae bury themselves under the skin. Here they form a crop of 'boils' each with a maggot inside. Smear a little Vaseline over the hole, and they will push their noses out to breathe. It may be possible to squeeze them out but it depends if they are ready to do so as the larvae have spines that help them to hold on.

In *putsi* areas either dry your clothes and sheets within a screened house, or dry them in direct sunshine until they are crisp, or iron them.

Jiggers or **sandfleas** can be best avoided by wearing shoes. They latch on if you walk barefoot in contaminated places, and set up home under the skin of the foot, usually at the side of a toenail where they cause a painful, boil-like swelling. They need picking out by a local expert.

In addition to the various vaccinations recommended, it is important that travellers should be properly protected against malaria. For detailed advice, see pages 76–7.

Ideally you should visit your own doctor or a specialist travel clinic (see below) to discuss your requirements if possible at least eight weeks before you plan to travel.

TRAVEL INSURANCE Don't think about travelling without a comprehensive medical travel insurance policy, specifically one that will fly you home in an emergency. There are innumerable policies available, and many travel clinics sell their own versions, so do shop around for the best deal for you.

PROTECTION FROM THE SUN Give some thought to packing suncream. The incidence of skin cancer is rocketing as Caucasians are travelling more and spending more time exposing themselves to the sun. Keep out of the sun during the middle of the day and, if you must expose yourself to the sun, build up gradually from 20 minutes per day. Be especially careful of exposure in the middle of the day and of sun reflected off water, and wear a T-shirt and lots of waterproof suncream (at least SPF15) when swimming. Sun exposure ages the skin, makes people prematurely wrinkly, and increases the risk of skin cancer. Cover up with long, loose clothes and wear a hat when you can. The glare and the dust can be hard on the eyes, too, so bring UV-protecting sunglasses and, perhaps, a soothing eyebath.

TRAVEL CLINICS AND HEALTH INFORMATION A full list of current travel clinic websites worldwide is available on www.istm.org. For other journey preparation information, consult www.nathnac.org/ds/map_world.aspx (UK) or wwwnc.cdc. gov/travel (US). Information about various medications may be found on www. netdoctor.co.uk/travel. All advice found online should be used in conjunction with expert advice received prior to or during travel.

PERSONAL FIRST-AID KIT A minimal kit contains:

- A good drying antiseptic, eg: iodine or potassium permanganate (don't take antiseptic cream)
- A few small dressings (Band-Aids)
- Suncream
- Insect repellent; antimalarial tablets; impregnated bed-net or permethrin spray
- Aspirin or paracetamol
- Antifungal cream (eg: Canesten)
- Ciprofloxacin or norfloxacin, for severe diarrhoea
- Tinidazole for giardia or amoebic dysentery (see box text, *Treating travellers' diarrhoea*, page 82)
- Antibiotic eye drops, for sore, 'gritty', stuck-together eyes (conjunctivitis)
- A pair of fine-pointed tweezers (to remove hairy caterpillar hairs, thorns, splinters, coral, etc)
- Alcohol-based hand rub or a bar of soap in a plastic box
- Condoms or femidoms
- A digital thermometer
- Sterile syringe

MEDICAL FACILITIES Private clinics, hospitals and pharmacies can be found in most large towns, and doctors generally speak fluent English. Consultation fees and laboratory tests are remarkably inexpensive when compared with most Western countries, so if you do fall sick it would be absurd to let financial considerations dissuade you from seeking medical help. Commonly required medicines such as broad spectrum antibiotics and Flagyl are widely available and cheap throughout the region, as are malaria cures and prophylactics. Fansidar and quinine tablets are best bought in advance – in fact it's advisable to carry all malaria-related tablets on you, and only rely on their availability locally if you need to restock your supplies.

If you are on any medication prior to departure, or you have specific needs relating to a known medical condition (for instance if you are allergic to bee stings

LONG-HAUL FLIGHTS, CLOTS AND DVT

Any prolonged immobility, including travel by land or air, can result in deep vein thrombosis (DVT) with the risk of embolus to the lungs. Certain factors can increase the risk and these include:

- Previous clot or close relative with a history
- Being over 40, with an increased risk over 80 years of age
- Recent major operation or varicose veins surgery
- Cancer
- Stroke
- Heart disease
- Obesity
- Pregnancy
- Hormone therapy
- Heavy smoking
- Severe varicose veins
- Being very tall (over 6ft/1.8m) or short (under 5ft/1.5m)

A DVT causes painful swelling and redness of the calf or sometimes the thigh. It is dangerous only if a clot travels to the lungs (pulmonary embolus). Symptoms of a pulmonary embolus (PE) include chest pain, shortness of breath, and sometimes coughing up small amounts of blood and commonly start three to ten days after a long flight. Anyone who thinks that they might have a DVT needs to see a doctor immediately.

PREVENTION OF DVT
- Keep mobile before and during the flight; move around every couple of hours
- Drink plenty of fluids during the flight
- Avoid taking sleeping pills and excessive tea, coffee and alcohol
- Consider wearing flight socks or support stockings (see *www.legshealth. com*)

If you think you are at increased risk of a clot, ask your doctor if it is safe to travel.

QUICK TICK REMOVAL   *Dr Jane Wilson-Howarth*

African ticks are not the prolific disease transmitters they are in the Americas, but they may spread Lyme disease, tick-bite fever and a few rarities. Tick-bite fever is a non-serious, flu-like illness, but still worth avoiding and is treatable with doxycycline. If you get the tick off whole and promptly, the chances of disease transmission are reduced to a minimum. Tick removers are now available (eg: Tick Twister) which remove the tick without damaging the mouthparts. If you do not have one then the next best thing is to manoeuvre your finger and thumb so that you can pinch the tick's mouthparts, as close to your skin as possible, and slowly and steadily pull away at right angles to your skin. This often hurts. Jerking or twisting will increase the chances of damaging the tick, which in turn increases the chances of disease transmission, as well as leaving the mouthparts behind. Once the tick is off, dowse the little wound with alcohol (local spirit, whisky or similar are excellent) or iodine. An area of spreading redness around the bite site, or a rash or fever coming on a few days or more after the bite, should stimulate a trip to a doctor.

or you are prone to attacks of asthma), then you are strongly advised to bring any related drugs and devices with you.

COMMON MEDICAL PROBLEMS

Travellers' diarrhoea Travelling in Malawi carries a fairly high risk of getting a dose of travellers' diarrhoea; perhaps half of all visitors will suffer and the newer you are to exotic travel, the more likely you will be to suffer. By taking precautions against travellers' diarrhoea you will also avoid typhoid, cholera, hepatitis, dysentery, worms, etc. Travellers' diarrhoea and the other faecal-oral diseases come from getting other people's faeces in your mouth. This most often happens from cooks not washing their hands after a trip to the toilet, but even if the restaurant cook does not understand basic hygiene, you will be safe if your food has been properly cooked and arrives piping hot. The maxim to remind you what you can safely eat is:

PEEL IT, BOIL IT, COOK IT OR FORGET IT.

This means that fruit you have washed and peeled yourself, and hot foods, should be safe but raw foods, cold cooked foods, salads, fruit salads which have been prepared by others, ice cream and ice are all risky. And foods kept lukewarm in hotel buffets are often dangerous. If you are struck, see the box overleaf for treatment.

It is much rarer to get sick from drinking contaminated water but it happens, so try to drink from safe sources. Water should have been brought to the boil (even at altitude it only needs to be brought to the boil), or passed through a good bacteriological filter or purified with chlorine dioxide. Mineral water has been found to be contaminated in Malawi but should be safer than contaminated tap water.

Insect-borne diseases Malaria is by no means the only insect-borne disease to which the traveller may succumb (for advice on preventing and treating malaria, see box on page 76). Others include sleeping sickness and river blindness (see *Avoiding* *insect bites* box, page 78). Dengue fever is becoming more common in Malawi but there are many other similar arboviruses. These mosquito-borne diseases may mimic malaria but there is no prophylactic medication against them. The mosquitoes that carry dengue fever viruses bite during the daytime, so it is worth applying repellent if you see any mosquitoes around. Symptoms include strong headaches, rashes and excruciating joint and muscle pains and high fever. Viral fevers usually last about a week or so and are not usually fatal. Complete rest and paracetamol are the usual treatment; plenty of fluids also help. Some patients are given an intravenous drip to keep them from dehydrating. It is especially important to protect yourself if you have had dengue fever before, since a second infection with a different strain can result in the potentially fatal dengue haemorrhagic fever. For advice on sleeping sickness, see page 84.

Skin infections Any mosquito bite or small nick in the skin gives an opportunity for bacteria to foil the body's usually excellent defences; it will surprise many travellers how quickly skin infections start in warm humid climates and it is essential to clean and cover even the slightest wound. Creams are not as effective as a good drying antiseptic such as dilute iodine, potassium permanganate (a few crystals in half a cup of water), or crystal (or gentian) violet. One of these should be available in most towns. If the wound starts to throb, or becomes red and the redness starts to spread, or the wound oozes, and especially if you develop a fever, antibiotics will probably be needed: flucloxacillin (250mg four times a day) or cloxacillin (500mg four times a day). For those allergic to penicillin, erythromycin (500mg twice a day) for five days should help. See a doctor if the symptoms do not start to improve in 48 hours.

TREATING TRAVELLERS' DIARRHOEA *Dr Jane Wilson-Howarth*

It is dehydration which makes you feel awful during a bout of diarrhoea and the most important part of treatment is drinking lots of clear fluids. Sachets of oral rehydration salts give the perfect biochemical mix to replace all that is pouring out of your bottom but other recipes taste nicer. Any dilute mixture of sugar and salt in water will do you good: try Coke or orange squash with a three-finger pinch of salt added to each glass (if you are salt-depleted you won't taste the salt). Otherwise make a solution of a four-finger scoop of sugar with a three-finger pinch of salt in a 500ml glass of water. Or add eight level teaspoons of sugar (18g) and one level teaspoon of salt (3g) to one litre (five cups) of safe water. A squeeze of lemon or orange juice improves the taste and adds potassium, which is also lost in diarrhoea. Drink two large glasses after every bowel action, and more if you are thirsty. These solutions are still absorbed well if you are vomiting, but you will need to take sips at a time. If you are not eating you need to drink three litres a day plus whatever amount is pouring into the toilet. If you feel like eating, take a bland, high-carbohydrate diet. Heavy greasy foods will probably give you cramps.

If the diarrhoea is bad, or you are passing blood or slime, or you have a fever, you will probably need antibiotics in addition to fluid replacement. A single dose of ciprofloxacin (500mg) repeated after 12 hours may be appropriate. If the diarrhoea is greasy and bulky and is accompanied by sulphurous (eggy) burps, the likely cause is giardia. This is best treated with tinidazole (four x 500mg in one dose, repeated seven days later if symptoms persist).

Fungal infections also get a hold easily in hot moist climates so wear 100% cotton socks and underwear and shower frequently. An itchy rash in the groin or flaking between the toes is likely to be a fungal infection. This needs treatment with an antifungal cream such as Canesten (clotrimazole); if this is not available try Whitfield's ointment (compound benzoic acid ointment) or crystal violet (although this will turn you purple!).

Eye problems Bacterial conjunctivitis (pink eye) is a common infection in Malawi; people who wear contact lenses are most open to this irritating problem. The eyes feel sore and gritty and they will often be stuck together in the mornings. They will need treatment with antibiotic drops or ointment. Lesser eye irritation should settle with bathing in salt water and keeping the eyes shaded. If an insect flies into your eye, extract it with great care, ensuring you do not crush or damage it otherwise you may get a nastily inflamed eye from toxins secreted by the creature.

Prickly heat A fine pimply rash on the trunk is likely to be heat rash; cool showers, dabbing (not rubbing) dry, and talc will help. Treat the problem by slowing down to a relaxed schedule, wearing only loose, baggy, 100% cotton clothes and sleeping naked under a fan; if it's bad you may need to check into an air-conditioned hotel room for a while.

OTHER DISEASES
Bilharzia or schistosomiasis
With thanks to Dr Vaughan Southgate of the Natural History Museum, London, and Dr Dick Stockley, The Surgery, Kampala
Bilharzia or schistosomiasis is a disease that commonly afflicts the rural poor of the tropics. Two types exist in sub-Saharan Africa – *Schistosoma mansoni* and *Schistosoma haematobium*. It is an unpleasant problem that is worth avoiding, though it can be treated if you do get it. This parasite is common in almost all water sources in Malawi, even places advertised as 'bilharzia free'. The most risky shores will be close to places where infected people use water, wash clothes, etc.

It is easier to understand how to diagnose it, treat it and prevent it if you know a little about the life cycle. Contaminated faeces are washed into the lake, the eggs hatch and the larva infects certain species of snail. The snails then produce about 10,000 cercariae a day for the rest of their lives. The parasites can digest their way through your skin when you wade or bathe in infested fresh water.

Winds disperse the snails and cercariae. The snails in particular can drift a long way, especially on windblown weed, so nowhere is really safe. However, deep water and running water are safer, while shallow water presents the greatest risk. The cercariae penetrate intact skin, and find their way to the liver. There male and female meet and spend the rest of their lives in permanent copulation. No wonder you feel tired! Most finish up in the wall of the lower bowel, but others can get lost and can cause damage to many different organs. *Schistosoma haematobium* goes mostly to the bladder.

Although the adults do not cause any harm in themselves, after about four–six weeks they start to lay eggs, which cause an intense but usually ineffective immune reaction, including fever, cough, abdominal pain, and a fleeting, itching rash called 'safari itch'. The absence of early symptoms does not necessarily mean there is no infection. Later symptoms can be more localised and more severe, but the general symptoms settle down fairly quickly and eventually you are just tired. 'Tired all the time' is one of the most common symptoms among expats in Africa, and bilharzia, giardia, amoeba and intestinal yeast are the most common culprits.

Although bilharzia is difficult to diagnose, it can be tested at specialist travel clinics. Ideally tests need to be done at least six weeks after likely exposure and will determine whether you need treatment. Fortunately it is easy to treat at present.

Avoiding bilharzia If you are bathing, swimming, paddling or wading in fresh water which you think may carry a bilharzia risk, try to get out of the water within ten minutes.

- Avoid bathing or paddling on shores within 200m of villages or places where people use the water a great deal, especially reedy shores or where there is lots of water weed.
- Dry off thoroughly with a towel; rub vigorously.
- If your bathing water comes from a risky source try to ensure that the water is taken from the lake in the early morning and stored snail-free, otherwise it should be filtered or Dettol or Cresol added.
- Bathing early in the morning is safer than bathing in the last half of the day.
- Cover yourself with DEET insect repellent before swimming: it may offer some protection.

HIV/AIDS The risks of sexually transmitted infection are extremely high in Malawi, whether you sleep with fellow travellers or locals. About 80% of HIV infections in British heterosexuals are acquired abroad. If you must indulge, use condoms or femidoms, which help reduce the risk of transmission. If you notice any genital ulcers or discharge, get treatment promptly since these increase the risk of acquiring HIV. If you do have unprotected sex, visit a clinic as soon as possible; this should be within 24 hours, or no later than 72 hours, for post-exposure prophylaxis.

Sleeping sickness African trypanosomiasis, or sleeping sickness, is a parasitic infection caused by *Trypanosoma brucei*, transmitted by the tsetse fly. There are two sub-species; one predominates in East Africa and usually causes an acute infection, whereas the other predominates in Central and West Africa and causes a slower progressive, chronic infection. In the UK, travel-associated cases are rare but those that have been reported have usually been associated with travel to the game parks of East Africa.

The parasite is transmitted by the bite of an infected tsetse fly. Tsetse flies are around the size of a honey bee. In East Africa, the main reservoirs for the parasites are domestic and wild animals such as antelope and cattle. The tsetse flies here tend to inhabit savannah and woodland areas. One bite from an infected tsetse fly is enough for a human to become infected. Trypanosomiasis cannot be spread directly from person to person.

How long can you have the infection before developing symptoms? For East African trypanosomiasis, first symptoms (skin lesion around the bite with lymph node enlargement) will occur 5–15 days after the bite, with fever occurring after one to three weeks. For West African trypanosomiasis, symptoms may not present for some weeks after the infective bite. East African trypanosomiasis is a much faster progressing disease than the West African form, which can progress over a number of years.

How can you avoid getting sleeping sickness? There is no vaccine or drug to prevent sleeping sickness. The only way to prevent it is to avoid tsetse fly bites and be aware of the risk. Tsetse flies are attracted by movement and dark colours, particularly blue. They have been known to follow moving vehicles, therefore windows should remain closed when driving through endemic areas. Travellers are advised to wear insecticide-treated close weave and loose-fitting clothing and use a good repellent containing N, N-diethylmetatoluamide (DEET) on exposed skin. Insect repellents are not as effective against tsetse flies as they are against mosquitoes but are better than nothing. If sunscreen is also being used, repellent must be applied after sunscreen. More information about the disease is available from the NaTHNaC website.

ANIMALS

Rabies Rabies is carried by all warm-blooded mammals (beware the village dogs and small monkeys that are used to being fed in the parks) and is passed on to man through a bite, scratch or a lick of an open wound. You must always assume any animal is rabid as they can often look well but can still be infectious. Have a low threshold for seeking medical help as soon as possible after any potential exposure. Meanwhile scrub the wound with soap under a running tap or while pouring water from a jug for a good 10–15 minutes. The source of the water is not important at this stage but if you do have antiseptic to hand then put this on afterwards. The soap helps stop the rabies virus entering the body and along with an antiseptic will guard against wound infections, including tetanus.

Pre-exposure vaccination for rabies is ideally advised for everyone, but is particularly important if you intend to have contact with animals and/or are likely to be more than 24 hours away from medical help. Ideally three doses should be taken over a minimum of 21 days.

All three doses are needed in order to change the treatment needed following an exposure.

If you are bitten, scratched or licked over an open wound by a sick animal, then post-exposure prophylaxis should be given as soon as possible, though it is never too late to seek help, as the incubation period for rabies can be very long. Those who have not been immunised before will need four to five doses of rabies vaccine given over 28–30 days and should also receive a product called Rabies Immunoglobulin (RIG), either human or horse. The RIG is injected round the wound to try to neutralise any rabies virus present and is a pivotal part of the treatment if you have not had pre-exposure vaccine. RIG is expensive and may not be readily available so it is important to insist on getting to a place that has it. Another reason for having good insurance.

Tell the doctor if you have had pre-exposure vaccine, as this will change the treatment you receive. You will no longer need to have RIG and will only need a couple of doses of vaccine, ideally given three days apart. And remember that, if you do contract rabies, mortality is 100% and death from rabies is probably one of the worst ways to go.

Snake bite Snakes rarely attack unless provoked, and bites in travellers are unusual. You are less likely to get bitten if you wear stout shoes and long trousers when in the bush. Most snakes are harmless and even venomous species will dispense venom in only about half of their bites. If bitten, then, you are unlikely to have received venom; keeping this fact in mind may help you to stay calm. Many so-called first-aid techniques do more harm than good: cutting into the wound is harmful; tourniquets are dangerous; suction and electrical inactivation devices do not work. The only treatment is antivenom. In case of a bite which you fear may have been from a venomous snake:

- Try to keep calm – it is likely that no venom has been dispensed.
- Prevent movement of the bitten limb by applying a splint.
- Keep the bitten limb BELOW heart height to slow the spread of any venom.
- If you have a crêpe bandage, bind up as much of the bitten limb as you can, but release the bandage every half-hour.
- Evacuate to a hospital which has antivenom.

And remember:

- NEVER give aspirin; you may offer paracetamol, which is safe.
- NEVER cut or suck the wound.
- DO NOT apply ice packs.
- DO NOT apply potassium permanganate.

If the offending snake can be captured without risk of someone else being bitten, take this to the doctor – but beware since even a decapitated head is able to bite.

travel magazine

Since 1993, we've been helping travellers escape the crowds and seek out the most unique cultures, wildlife and activities around the globe.

Wanderlust offers a unique mix of inspiration and practical advice, making it the ultimate magazine for independent-minded, curious travellers.

For more about *Wanderlust* and for travel inspiration visit www.wanderlust.co.uk

Hot on Africa
Just some of the destinations we cover...

Bradt

Available from bookshops or
www.bradtguides.com

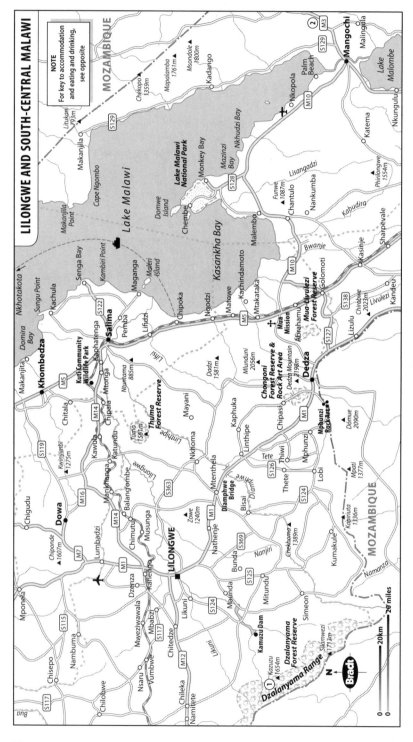

LILONGWE AND SOUTH-CENTRAL MALAWI

NOTE
For key to accommodation and eating and drinking, see opposite

MOZAMBIQUE

Lake Malawi

Lake Malombe

Mangochi

Malingula

Nkungulu

Katema

Palm Beach

Nkopola

Msondole ▲1800m

Kadango

Mapalamba ▲1761m

Chekopo ▲1359m

Lithkani ▲793m

Makanjila

Makanjila Point

Cape Ngombo

Monkey Bay

Lake Malawi National Park

Domwe Island

Chembe

Mazinzi Bay

Nkhudzi Bay

Phirilongwe ▲1554m

Sharpevale

Kasinje

Kobudira

Nankumba

Chantulo

Lisangadzi

Funwé ▲1087m

Malembo

Bwanje

Solomoti

Kasankha Bay

Kachindamoto

Matowe

Ngodzi

Mtakataka

Mua-Livulezi Forest Reserve

Mua Mission

Abrahams

Lizulu

Chirobwe ▲2023m

Kandeu

Livulezi

Maganga

Kambiri Point

Maléri Island

Chipoka

Senga Bay

Sungu Point

Kachula

Domira Bay

Makanjita

Nkhotakota

Khombedza

Kaphatenga

Salima

Pemba

Lifidzi

Lifidzi

Mtonga

Kuti Community Wildlife Park

Chipala

Ntumtama ▲885m

Dodzi ▲1581m

Mlunduni ▲2056m

Chongoni Forest Reserve & Rock Art Area

Dedza Mountain ▲2198m

Dedza

Chipasi

Mphunzi Rock Art

Dómue ▲2090m

Mpati ▲1377m

Lobi

Thuma Forest Reserve

Tuma ▲1561m

Kwinjimbi ▲1275m

Chitala

Kawuka

Katundu

Menkhaaga

Linthipe

Lilongwe

Mayani

Nkhoma

Kaphuka

Linthipe

Mtenthela

Tete

Thiwi

Thete

Mphunzi

Dowa

Chiponde ▲1607m

Chigudu

Balang'ombe

Musunga

Chimutu

Lumbadzi

Kanengo

Dzenza

Namanzi

Kapinuta ▲1336m

Kumakule

Chekhama ▲1389m

Nanjiri

Bunda

Madinda

Mitundu

Simeon

Nathenje

Bisai

Djamphwe Bridge

Zowe ▲1240m

LILONGWE

Mponela

Chisepo

Nambuma

Mponela

Nsaru

Vumbwe

Mbabzi

Mwezimwala

Chitedze

Likuni

Likuni

Kamuzu Dam

Kazuzu ▲654m

Dzalanyama Forest Reserve

Silamuwzi ▲1713m

Chileka

Namitete

Chilobwe

Dzalanyama Range

MOZAMBIQUE

N

Bradt

0   20km
0   20 miles

png

S129 · M3 · S129 · M10 · S128 · M10 · M5 · S138 · S127 · S122 · M5 · M14 · S119 · M16 · M14 · M7 · M1 · S363 · S126 · S124 · S124 · S125 · S369 · S117 · S115 · S117 · M12 · ②· ①

Part Two

LILONGWE AND
SOUTH-CENTRAL MALAWI

OVERVIEW OF PART TWO

The five chapters that follow cover the city of Lilongwe, the southern part of Lake Malawi from Senga Bay in the north to Mangochi in the south, and the part of the western highlands that fall, between the same latitudes.

Chapter 5 concentrates on Lilongwe, which is not only the capital and largest city in Malawi, but also forms the main gateway to the country for travellers arriving by air or overland from Zambia. Also included in this chapter are a handful of sites dotted around Lilongwe, most significantly the bird-rich Dzalanyama Forest Reserve to the southwest.

Chapter 6 covers Senga Bay, the closest part of the lakeshore to Lilongwe, along with associated sites such as the town of Salima and the under-publicised Thuma Forest Reserve and Kuti Wildlife Reserve.

Inland and uphill, *Chapter 7* focuses on sleepy Dedza, the highest town in the country, and a host of nearby cultural sites, most significantly the superb KuNgoni Museum in the Mua Mission, and the mysterious Chongoni Rock Art Area, recently inscribed as a UNESCO World Heritage Site.

The stunning Lake Malawi National Park, the country's only other UNESCO World Heritage Site, is the subject of *Chapter 8*. Renowned for its wealth of aquatic life, this park is the site of the legendary resort village of Chambe on Cape Maclear, while Monkey Bay is the former southern terminus of the lake ferry MV *Ilala*.

Chapter 9 follows the lakeshore south of Monkey Bay, an area studded with upmarket resorts, including the venerable Makokola Retreat and Nkopola Lodge. The southernmost tip of the lake is also the outlet for the Upper Shire River, which flows towards Lake Malombe via the town of Mangochi, also covered in this chapter.

Land & Lake Safaris

Your Malawi & Zambia Specialist Tour Operator

Classic scheduled safaris, Tailor made tours, Day trips, Reservations, Car hire, Weekend excursions, Information office & more …
TEL: + 265 (0)1 757 120 / FAX: + 265 (0)1 754 560
We have been operating in Lilongwe for 25 Years

www . landlake. net

Land & Lake Safaris
Malawi & Zambia

5

Lilongwe

Lilongwe is not the most imposing of African cities. More than three decades after being proclaimed capital of Malawi, it still comes across as something of a work in progress: a scattered and incohesive patchwork of commercial hubs, administrative and ambassadorial zones, leafy upmarket residential suburbs and village-like suburban shanty towns that sprawl unconvincingly between grassy fields and large tracts of indigenous woodland and plantations.

The city has two main focal points, Old Town and Capital City, both very different in character, but neither exactly over-endowed with personality. Most travellers end up in Old Town, which is the main centre of commerce, boasting an energetic market and bus station, a sprinkling of shiny new malls and all manner of slightly anachronistic Indian retail stores. The Old Town has witnessed rapid expansion in recent years, yet it still has the feel of a southern African everytown, similar in mood and appearance to any number of medium-sized regional urban centres south of the Zambezi.

Capital City, by contrast, is a true original. Custom-built during the Banda era, it still feels tangibly contrived, an open-air huddle of semi-skyscraping office blocks, freshly painted banking houses, leaf-shrouded embassies, warehouse-like supermarkets and half-full car parks whose distinguishing feature is a kind of collective capacity to cancel each other out. From whatever angle you approach Capital City, and no matter how often, it is difficult to shake off the feeling that it ended before it began and you somehow blinked at the wrong moment!

So it's not Dakar or Timbuktu, but Lilongwe could scarcely be a more equable or manageable introduction to urban Africa. The climate is comfortable, getting in and out of town is simplicity itself, accommodation is abundant and conveniently situated, and shops and markets are well stocked. In some ways, Lilongwe feels like a microcosm of the country it governs – small but deceptively densely populated, friendly and personal, dusty and colourfully chaotic, and full of contrasts. Behind the houses and offices, within eyeshot of parliament, people still grow maize in their gardens. Villagers cycle miles from outlying areas to sell produce at the country's largest market, weaving between the buses that form jerking, hooting, belching queues in the Old Town centre. And as night falls, the familiar urban rumble is punctuated by sounds eerily evocative of Lilongwe's African setting – the wild whooping of spotted hyenas and chilling cries of bushbabies, both of which haunt the nature sanctuary bisected by the main trunk road between Old Town and Capital City.

HISTORY

Lilongwe was founded in 1906 on the banks of the Lilongwe River, initially as a settlement for Asian traders, though its pleasant climate rapidly attracted European

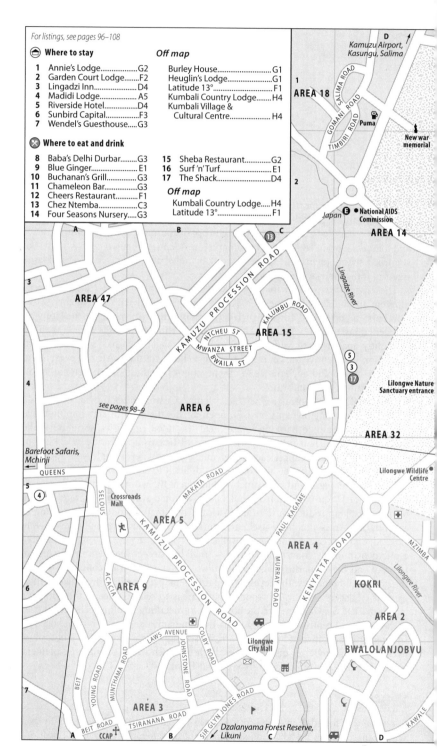

For listings, see pages 96–108

⌂ Where to stay

1	Annie's Lodge	G2
2	Garden Court Lodge	F2
3	Lingadzi Inn	D4
4	Madidi Lodge	A5
5	Riverside Hotel	D4
6	Sunbird Capital	F3
7	Wendel's Guesthouse	G3

Off map

Burley House	G1
Heuglin's Lodge	G1
Latitude 13°	F1
Kumbali Country Lodge	H4
Kumbali Village & Cultural Centre	H4

✖ Where to eat and drink

8	Baba's Delhi Durbar	G3
9	Blue Ginger	E1
10	Buchanan's Grill	G3
11	Chameleon Bar	G3
12	Cheers Restaurant	F1
13	Chez Ntemba	C3
14	Four Seasons Nursery	G3
15	Sheba Restaurant	G2
16	Surf 'n' Turf	E1
17	The Shack	D4

Off map

| Kumbali Country Lodge | H4 |
| Latitude 13° | F1 |

Kamuzu Airport,
Kasungu, Salima

AREA 18

Puma

New war memorial

Japan **National AIDS Commission**

AREA 14

AREA 47

KAMUZU PROCESSION ROAD

KALUMBU ROAD

NTCHEU ST
MWANZA STREET
BWAILA ST

AREA 15

Lingadze River

Lilongwe Nature Sanctuary entrance

AREA 6

see pages 98–9

AREA 32

Barefoot Safaris,
Mchinji

QUEENS

Lilongwe Wildlife Centre

SELOUS

Crossroads Mall

AREA 5

MAKATA ROAD

KAMUZU PROCESSION ROAD

PAUL KAGAME

AREA 4

KENYATTA ROAD

MZIMBA

KOKRI

Lilongwe River

ACACIA

AREA 9

MURRAY ROAD

AREA 2

LAWS AVENUE

JOHNSTONE ROAD

COLBY ROAD

Lilongwe City Mall

BWALOLANJOBVU

BEIT

YOUNG ROAD

MUNTHAMA ROAD

AREA 3

TSIRANANA ROAD

SIR GLYN JONES ROAD

BEIT ROAD
CCAP

Dzalanyama Forest Reserve,
Likuni

KAWALE

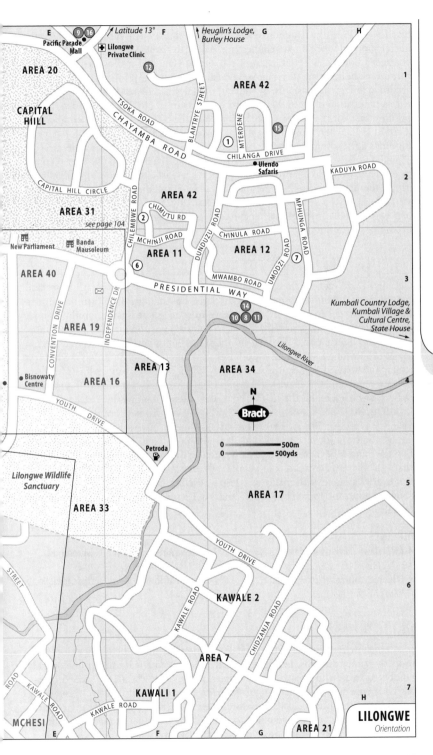

E   9 16   ↗ Latitude 13°   F   ↗ Heuglin's Lodge,   G   H

Pacific Parade
Mall

✚ Lilongwe
Private Clinic

Burley House

AREA 20   AREA 42

TSOKA ROAD

CHAYAMBA ROAD

BLANTRYE STREET

MTERDENE

12

CAPITAL
HIILL

1

CHILANGA DRIVE

1

15

•Ulendo
Safaris

KADUYA ROAD

2

CAPITAL HILL CIRCLE

CHILEMBWE ROAD

AREA 42

CHIMUTU RD

AREA 31

see page 104

2

MCHINJI ROAD

DUNDUZU ROAD

CHINULA ROAD

MPHUNGA ROAD

⊞   ⊞ Banda
New Parliament   Mausoleum

AREA 11

AREA 12

UMODZI ROAD

7

6

AREA 40

MWAMBO ROAD

PRESIDENTIAL   WAY

CONVENTION DRIVE

INDEPENDENCE DR

✉

AREA 19

Kumbali Country Lodge,
Kumbali Village &
Cultural Centre,
State House →

3

14
10 8 11

•Bisnowaty
Centre

AREA 16

AREA 13

AREA 34

Lilongwe River

YOUTH   DRIVE

4

N

Bradt

Petroda

0 ══════ 500m
0 ══════ 500yds

Lilongwe Wildlife
Sanctuary

AREA 17

5

AREA 33

STREET

6

YOUTH DRIVE

KAWALE ROAD

KAWALE 2

CHIDZANJA ROAD

AREA 7

ROAD

KAWALE ROAD

KAWALI 1

KAWALE ROAD

H

7

MCHESI

E   F   G   AREA 21

LILONGWE
Orientation

business. In 1909, the fledgling township's future status was assured when it became the terminus of the first road connecting Malawi to Zambia. By the 1930s, Lilongwe boasted a hotel, a hospital, a European sports club, and a mosque and Muslim sports club built by the thriving Asian business community. In 1947, Lilongwe was accorded full township status. By the time of Malawi's independence, Lilongwe was, with a population of around 20,000, second only in size to Blantyre, and its central position made it the obvious choice to replace the colonial capital of Zomba. This it did in 1975, when Capital City was purpose built (with the help of South African funding) a few kilometres north of the established Old Town. Since it became the capital, Lilongwe's population has soared dramatically: it passed the 100,000 mark in 1980 and overtook Blantyre as the country's largest city when it topped 500,000 c2000, though this status is something of a debate, and the answer differs based on statistical sources used. Common estimates in 2012 placed Lilongwe's population between 782,000 and 821,000, and recent trends suggest it's well on its way to exceeding one million.

GETTING THERE AND AWAY

Getting in and out of Lilongwe couldn't be more straightforward. All buses and minibuses to Lilongwe terminate at the large bus station [99 F7] in Old Town. Buses to most destinations in Malawi leave from the same bus station throughout the morning through to mid-afternoon, so there is no reason for rushed early starts.

Kamuzu International Airport [off map] lies 26km north of the city centre on the M1 to Kasungu. Although most buses travelling north or south on the M1 will stop at the turn-off to the airport, they may not drive all the way in. Taxis between the city centre and the airport cost around US$25–28 and take about 30 minutes.

Several buses make the 15–18-hour run from Lilongwe to Lusaka directly, including **KOBS** (m *099 9610581/9938704*) and **Ronsil Transport** (m *099 9405340/1165236*). Buses depart from just outside the main station [99 F7] at 06.00 almost daily and tickets cost US$31. It is also possible to travel directly between Lilongwe and Mbeya or Dar es Salaam with the **Taqwa** or **EasyBus** services, which share an office on Devil Street in Lilongwe (m *099 9334299/538*) and between them run every day except Thursday and Friday, leaving Lilongwe at 19.00 and taking about 15 hours to Mbeya (*US$28*), 27 hours to Dar es Salaam (*US$47*) and 48 hours to Nairobi (*US$88*).

AIRLINES
✈ **Air Malawi** Sunbird Capital Hotel; ☏01 772132/773680

✈ **Ethiopian Airlines** Bisnowaty Centre; ☏01 771002/771308

✈ **Kenya Airways** ADL Hse, Independence Dr; ☏01 774227/774330

✈ **South African Airways** Sunbird Capital Hotel; ☏01 772242

ORIENTATION

It is somehow emblematic of the capital's functionality that, where other cities have properly named suburbs, Lilongwe is divided up into a few dozen chronologically numbered areas, with Area 1 being the oldest part of town, Area 2 the second-oldest, etc (and house numbers, where they exist, follow the same confusing logic). Navigating around this patchwork city is therefore often more about spatial awareness than remembering road names and numbers of buildings. Fortunately, public transport is easy to master, making travel around and out of town very simple.

Most visitors end up staying in Areas 1–4, which collectively comprise the Old Town, to all intents and purposes Lilongwe as it was prior to the construction of Capital City on Areas 16, 19 and 40. Other important areas in tourist terms include the recently developed Areas 5 and 9, site of the Crossroads Mall [98 A2] and several hotels and eateries, and the prettier residential Areas 10, 42 and 43 northwest of the Capital City.

The main commercial centre of the Old Town is bisected by Kamuzu Procession, site of such landmarks as the Sunbird Lilongwe Hotel [98 C4], the Standard [98 D4] and National [98 C4] banks, the main post office [98 D5] and half a dozen restaurants. The most important intersection on Kamuzu Procession, flanked by the new Lilongwe City Mall/Nico Centre [98 D4] and Shoprite Centre [98 D4] , is with Kenyatta Avenue, the most direct road from the Old Town to Capital City. There is a minibus rank [98 D4] where you can pick up transport to Capital City on Kenyatta Avenue about 100m from the intersection in front of Shoprite.

About 100m south of the post office, Kamuzu Procession forms a large roundabout with Glyn Jones Road at the north end of the golf course. From this roundabout, Kamuzu Procession continues across a bridge over the Lilongwe River to the east, where it climbs through the old Indian trading quarter. About 500m past the bridge, before the two mosques, traffic lights mark the intersection with Malangalanga Road, which is where you'll find the bus station [99 F7], market [99 F7] and the majority of cheap private resthouses.

Capital City lies 5km from the Old Town along Kenyatta Avenue. The two parts of town are separated by the Brachystegia woodland of Lilongwe Nature Sanctuary and blue-gum plantations planted to fuel the city. Aside from housing most of the embassies and airline offices, as well as the British Council, it offers few urgent reasons why visitors might want to visit Capital City.

GETTING AROUND

During daylight hours, minibuses run back and forth pretty much non-stop between the Old Town and Capital City. The best place to pick these up in the Old Town is near the main bus station, opposite the Engen Garage [99 F7] and also from in front of Shoprite [98 D4]. The fare is nominal and tourists are not overcharged.

There are plenty of taxi cabs in Lilongwe, and fares are low by international standards. Main taxi ranks in the Old Town are opposite the bus station, then also next to Shoprite [98 D4], in front of the post office [98 D5], and in the grounds of the Sunbird Lilongwe Hotel [98 C4]. In Capital City, you will find taxis in the grounds of the Sunbird Capital Hotel [104 D1]. Taxis are also available at the airport.

CAR HIRE The only international car-hire firm operating out of Lilongwe is **Avis** (e *reservations@avis.co.mw; www.avis.com/car-rental/location/mw*). The main office is near the Old Town centre on Paul Kagame Road (✆ *01 756105*) but there are also branches in the Sunbird Capital Hotel [104 D1] (✆ *01 776670*) and at the airport (✆ *01 700223*). There are plenty of other local car-hire companies operating out of Lilongwe, including:

🚗 **Apex Rent A Car** off Paul Kagame Rd; ✆ 01 754610; m 099 9950707; e apexcars@globemw. net; www.apexrentacarmw.com; see advert on page 116.

🚗 **Crossroads Car Hire** Crossroads Hotel; ✆ 01 750333; m 099 9127777/9824561; www. crossroadscarhire.com

🚗 **Countrywide Car Hire** Aquarius House, off Convention Dr; ☏ 01 770080/854/044; m 099 9510951; e info@countrywidemw.com; www.countrywidemw.com

🚗 **Sputnik Rent A Car** Kassam House, Paul Kagame Rd; ☏ 01 758253/6; e sputnik@sdnp.org.mw; www.sputnik-car-hire.mw

🚗 **SS Rent A Car** [98 C4] Kamuzu Procession Rd; ☏ 01 751478/750112; m 099 9010070; e info@ssrentacar.com; www.ssrentacar.com; see also advert on page 190.

TOURIST INFORMATION

The official source of tourist information is the **Ministry of Tourism, Wildlife and Culture** (☏ *01 772702/775499*; e *info@visitmalawi.mw; www.visitmalawi.mw*), whose headquarters [104 B4] is on the nameless road running parallel to Convention Drive in Capital City. They also have a new office in the Lilongwe City Mall [98 D4] near Game. In practice, your best bet is often other travellers or safari company offices.

TOUR OPERATORS AND SAFARI COMPANIES

The following upmarket operators are all well established and share excellent reputations for safaris in Malawi and into neighbouring Zambia:

African Nomad Safaris [98 B2] Post Dot Net Box 183, Crossroads; m 088 8575338/8723964; e info@africannomadsafaris.com; www.africannomadsafaris.com. Small independent operator specialising in affordable tailor-made camping safaris.

Barefoot Safaris [98 A2] Mchinji Rd; ☏ (+27) 7346 29232; e enquiries@barefoot-safaris.com; www.barefoot-safaris.com; see also advert on page 46. A small owner-managed safari company concentrating on conservation & ecology, offering bespoke safaris in Malawi and southern Africa.

Kiboko Safaris [98 C5] Lister Rd; ☏ 01 751226; m 099 9838485; e enquiries@kiboko-safaris.com; www.kiboko-safaris.com; see also advert on page 117. Located in the Kiboko Town Hotel, this company offers fixed-departure budget safaris around Malawi & to Zambia's South Luangwa National Park.

Land & Lake Safaris [98 B4] Laws Rd; ☏ 01 757120/01 754 560; e info@landlake.net; www.landlake.net; see also advert on page 90. Another very reputable company, with 25 years' experience

in Malawi & Zambia, Land & Lake also operates Dzalanyama Forest Retreat.

Malawian Style m 99 996 9075; e info@malawianstyle.com; www.malawianstyle.com; see also advert on inside front cover. Specialist tour operator offering adventure packed, small group tour packages in & around Malawi, Zambia & Mozambique.

Ulendo Safaris [93 G2] Chilanga Dr; ☏ 01 794555; e info@ulendo.net; see also advert on page viii of colour section. Now boasting its own large building in Area 10, Ulendo is a fast-growing safari operator & booking agent that offers safaris & accommodation in all corners of Malawi.

Wilderness Safaris Malawi [104 A6] Bisnowaty Centre; ☏ 01 771153; e reservations@wilderness.mw; www.wilderness-safaris.com. Wilderness Safaris is one of southern Africa's most highly regarded operators, & its Malawian representative is no exception. It is the concessionaire for Chelinda & Mvuu lodges in Nyika & Liwonde national parks, & Chintheche Inn on the northern lakeshore.

 WHERE TO STAY *See map, pages 98–9 unless otherwise stated.*

Lilongwe has accommodation options to suit most tastes and budgets. At the upper end of the price scale, Latitude 13 is the most luxurious place in town, while popular business hotels include the Sunbird Capital, Sunbird Lilongwe and newer Crossroads Hotel, but tourists seeking an overtly African setting are pointed to the Madonna-sanctioned Kumbali Country Lodge and equally rustic Sanctuary

Lodge, both of which rank among the most exclusive and charming hostelries in the country. Recent years have seen a boom in small owner-managed bed-and-breakfast-type establishments, of which Wendel's Guesthouse and Madidi Lodge stand out, while the contrasting picks of the more moderately priced options are the couldn't-be-more-central Kiboko Town Hotel and delightfully remote Barefoot Safari Lodge. Dropping further in price, Korea Gardens is a very reasonably priced set-up spanning the budget and moderate categories, the long-serving Mabuya Camp and newer Mufasa Lodge are both very popular with backpackers, and the most peaceful place to pitch a tent is Sanctuary Lodge Campground.

EXCLUSIVE AND LUXURY

Heuglin's Lodge [map page 93] (6 rooms) 01 771153/393; m 088 8822398; e reservations@wilderness.mw or heuglins@globemalawi.net; www.wilderness-safaris.com. Set on Blantyre St to the north of Capital City, this homely lodge, operated by Wilderness Safaris, is set in palm-shaded gardens with plenty of bird activity & a swimming pool. There's also a large bar & dining area, broadband internet, & comfortable rooms, most of which are en suite. It feels a bit overpriced, though significant discounts are offered to African residents. *US$210/320 sgl/dbl inc dinner, B&B.*

Kumbali Country Lodge [map page 93] (16 rooms) m 099 9963402/088 8963402; e kumbali@kumbalilodge.com; www.kumbalilodge.com. Situated on a working farm 6km east of the city centre, past State House, Kumbali is the smartest & most exclusive lodge in Lilongwe following extensive renovations in early 2009. It is also Madonna's residence of choice when visiting the country. Combining English country homeliness with earthy African décor, the main building is a 2-storey construction with thatched roof, terracotta tile floors, & wood & wrought-iron furnishings. The continental food is ranked among the best in Malawi, with most ingredients coming straight from the farm. The lodge also has superb & very spacious chalets, every detail of which is lovingly designed & made with exceptional craftsmanship, & they all come with walk-in netting over the beds, DSTV, Wi-Fi & cable internet, writing desk, wall & ceiling fan, en-suite tub & shower, & a balcony overlooking the lovely gardens. There's no swimming pool, nor much in the way of prescribed activities, but the farm includes 250ha of indigenous woodland to explore, & you can also visit the nearby cultural village. It's very competitively priced for what you get. *US$180/220 sgl/dbl B&B, US$210/250 suite, US$20 pp for 3-course dinners.*

Latitude 13° [map page 93] (9 rooms) m 099 6403159/088 2200849; e reservations@thelatitudehotels.com; www.thelatitudehotels.com. Since opening in 2012, this stunning property has arguably become the most fashionable hotel in all of Lilongwe. The dazzling rooms are boldly decorated in shocks of black, white, & grey, & all feature open floor plans with sizeable beds, lounge areas, rainfall showers, bathtubs, flatscreen DSTV, & Wi-Fi. The 90m² multi-levelled garden suites have floor-to-ceiling windows, while house suites enjoy balconies overlooking the black swimming pool & modernistic statuary in the palm-fringed courtyard. It's urban, chic & cosmopolitan, providing a dramatic counterpoint to the usual safari-styled luxury experience. The bar & lounge is decked out with modern art & wouldn't be out of place in Cape Town, & the indoor or alfresco dining is some of the best in the country. *US$220/274 sgl/dbl B&B.*

Presidential Hotel & Bingu wa Mutharika Conference Centre [map page 104] Known around Lilongwe as the 'five-star' hotel, this government-owned (& Chinese-funded) behemoth opposite the Sunbird Capital was built under the Mutharika administration to host the since-aborted African Union summit in 2012. It's been named to commemorate the late president who spearheaded the project, but there's no operator as of yet & it stands empty outside of special events & summits.

Sanctuary Lodge [map page 104] (10 rooms) 01 775200/1/2; e enquiries@thesanctuarylodge.net; www.thesanctuarylodge.net. Bordering Lilongwe Wildlife Centre, this fabulous new lodge is a genuine nature lover's paradise, set in 8ha of indigenous woodland alongside the Lilongwe River, yet conveniently located within walking distance of Capital City, alongside a main minibus route to the Old Town. The comfortable chalets are spaced widely through the Brachystegia woodland, & come

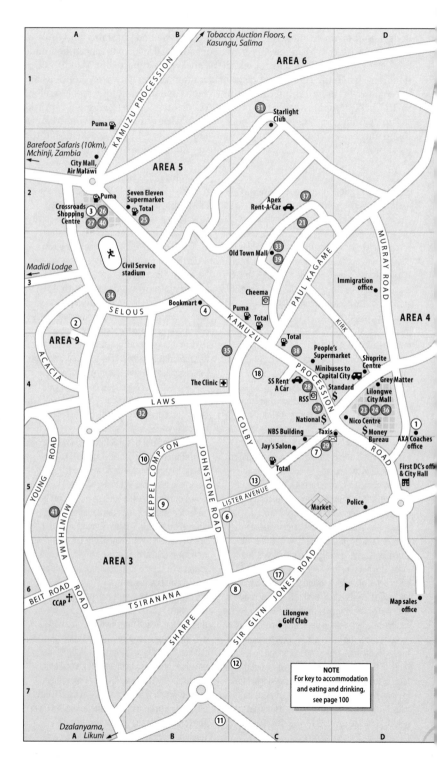

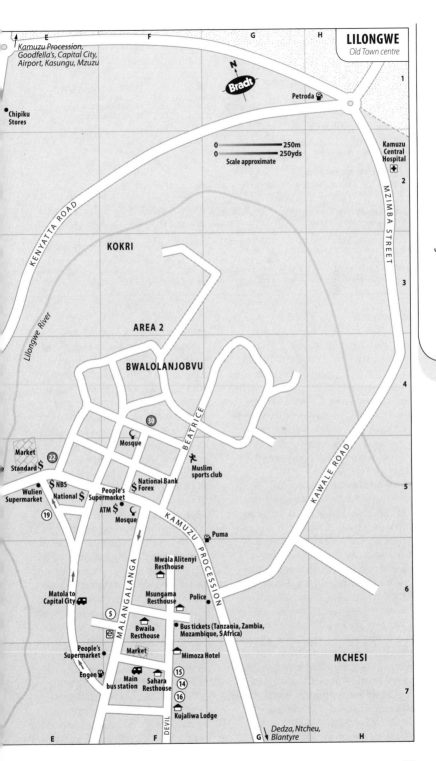

LILONGWE
Old Town centre

Kamuzu Procession,
Goodfella's, Capital City,
Airport, Kasungu, Mzuzu

Chipiku
Stores

Petroda

Kamuzu
Central
Hospital

0 — 250m
0 — 250yds
Scale approximate

KENYATTA ROAD

MZIMBA STREET

Lilongwe River

KOKRI

AREA 2

BWALOLANJOBVU

BEATRICE

KAWALE ROAD

30

Mosque

Muslim
sports club

Market

Standard

22

NBS

Wulien
Supermarket

National

People's
Supermarket

ATM

National Bank
Forex

Mosque

19

KAMUZU PROCESSION

Puma

Mwala Alitenyi
Resthouse

MALANGALANGA

Matola to
Capital City

Msungama
Resthouse

Police

5

Bwaila
Resthouse

Bus tickets (Tanzania, Zambia,
Mozambique, S Africa)

People's
Supermarket

Market

Mimoza Hotel

MCHESI

Engen

Main
bus station

Sahara
Resthouse

15

14

16

Kujaliwa Lodge

DEVIL

Dedza, Ntcheu,
Blantyre

with twin, ¾ or a king-size bed, fridge, tea/coffee making, writing desk, AC & quality wrought-iron, cane & dark-wood furnishings. Despite its centrality, you're too far from the road to hear any traffic at night, especially when the insects are on song. You're also sure to hear the nocturnal wailing of bushbabies, & with luck you might see one of these engaging bug-eyed critters emerge from a tree hollow at dusk. The highly regarded restaurant has a wide balcony overlooking the swimming pool. Highly recommended. *US$145/175 sgl/dbl B&B.*

🛏 **Sunbird Capital** [map page 104] (182 rooms) ☎01 773388; e capitalres@sunbirdmalawi.com; www.sunbirdmalawi.com. In contrasting style to the personalised rustic lodges listed above, this flagship hotel in the countrywide Sunbird chain is an efficient & well-run multi-storey monolith geared towards international business travellers. It is located in large gardens on Capital Hill, within easy walking distance of Capital City. The large carpeted rooms all come with king-size or twin beds, safe, AC, DSTV, tea/coffee making, & other facilities include a large swimming pool, a business centre, representative offices of several airlines, & a bookshop & salon in the foyer. There is a well-regarded upmarket restaurant in the hotel, as well as a good snack bar. A wide selection of rooms is available. *US$213/237 standard sgl/dbl, US$224/249 deluxe, US$274/298 executive, US$334/358 suite, all rates B&B.*

UPMARKET

🛏 **Burley House** [map page 93] (9 rooms) ☎01 794555/645; e reservations@ulendo.net; www.ulendo.net. Situated off Ufulu Rd in the upmarket residential Area 43, this comfortable & quiet lodge, managed by the Ulendo Travel Group, lies in green gardens about 2km north of Capital City. The standard rooms have private (but not en-suite) bathrooms, & the executive rooms & suites are all en suite. All rooms are carpeted & come with AC, DSTV, nets & broadband & Wi-Fi connectivity, & facilities include a bar, dining room & lounge with pool table. *US$100 dbl, US$200 4-bed family room, all rates B&B.*

🛏 **Cluny Lodge** (7 rooms) ☎01 751633; m 088 8764805; e bev.taale@africa-online.net; www.clunylodge.net. This cosy owner-managed lodge is in green gardens on a quiet cul-de-sac in Area 9, within walking distance of the Crossroads Mall & the Old Town centre. It offers a choice of brightly furnished standard rooms with private (but not en-suite) bathrooms, or en-suite executive rooms, all with a dbl bed, net, DSTV, AC, Wi-Fi, writing desk, modern pine furniture, & some have lounge areas. Dinner is served by request. Long-term apartments are also available. *US$100/125 standard sgl/dbl, US$160/185 executive, US$160/185 suite, all rates B&B.*

🛏 **Crossroads Hotel** (101 rooms) ☎01 750333/444; e crossroadshotel@malawi.net or reservations@crossroadshotel.net; www.crossroadshotel.net. This smart business hotel near the Kamuzu Procession/Mchinji Rd roundabout is an extension to the Crossroads Mall, & for anybody who has been in Malawi a while, stepping into the foyer – complete with piped music & AC – can feel like a holiday in itself. As might be expected, it's less strong on character than on facilities, which include a gym, swimming pool, spa, jacuzzi, business centre & top-notch Asian restaurant, as well as access to all the amenities & shops at the adjacent mall. The carpeted rooms have a bright contemporary feel, & come with twin, queen- or king-sized beds, AC, safe, flat-screen DSTV, tea/coffee making, internet access & en-suite tub & shower. *US$145/170/205 sgl/dbl/suite, US$185/210/300 deluxe, all rates B&B.*

🏠 **Madidi Lodge** [map page 92] (10 rooms) 📞 01 752661/920901; m 088 8607169; e info@ madidilodge.com; www.madidilodge.com. Tucked away in a quiet corner of Area 9, this likeable lodge, converted from a large sprawling house within walking distance of the Crossroads Mall, is the closest thing in Lilongwe to a boutique hotel. Decorated with colour & flair, each of the 8 spacious rooms & 2 apts is different in shape & size, but all share a contemporary African feel, & have a dbl bed with walk-in netting, DSTV, Wi-Fi, fridge, tea/coffee station & safe. The owner-managers live on the property & go out of their way to make guests feel at home. The restaurant has tasty snacks & meals in the US$4–7 range as well as a different 3-course dinner every day. This is a great set-up for business travellers seeking a small & more personalised alternative to the usual bland international hotels. There's a stylish new black swimming pool to lounge around, gym with personal trainer available, & they offer rejuvenating spa treatments including aromatherapy & massage. There are budget rooms with shared facilities as well. *US$60/90 sgl/dbl, US$75/105 deluxe sgl/dbl, US$98/128 executive sgl/dbl, US$20/33 backpacker sgl/dbl, all rates B&B.*

🏠 **Mafumu** (30 rooms) 📞 01 750594/982; m 088 8957500; e info@mafumu.com; www. mafumu.com. Located in trim gardens near the Lilongwe Golf Club, this new lodge offers gleaming tiled rooms handsomely appointed in dark wood & marble. All rooms have a king-sized bed, AC, flatscreen DSTV, writing desk, computer with internet, kitchen facilities including minibar & microwave, phone, safe, private terrace, tea/coffee facilities & bathtub. The classy restaurant offers a wide menu including steaks & a variety of pastas for

US$6–9. There are no pool or gym facilities, but it's still excellent value. *US$130/150 sgl/dbl, all rates B&B.*

🏠 **Pacific Hotel** [map page 104] (48 rooms) 📞 01 773166/1666; e reservations@ pacifichotelsmw.com; www.pacifichotelsmw. com. This characterless converted office block has a convenient but otherwise uninspiring location overlooking a minibus station in Capital City. The en-suite rooms with AC & DTSV are pleasant & reasonable value, & there is a decent restaurant & gym, but no alcohol is served. *US$100/120 standard sgl/dbl, US$120/145 deluxe, all rates B&B.*

🏠 **Sunbird Lilongwe Hotel** (94 rooms) 📞 01 756333; e lilongwehotel@sunbirdmalawi.com; www.sunbirdmalawi.com. This is a well-known & conveniently central landmark in the Old Town, not as slick as its Sunbird counterpart in the Capital City, but a lot cheaper & with a location that has more to offer explorative tourists. Dating back to the colonial era, it retains a slightly old-fashioned feel, & lies in large wooded gardens boasting an attractive swimming pool area & a popular patio restaurant. The large, comfortable rooms have king-size or twin beds with walk-in nets, DTSV, AC, writing desk & en-suite tub & shower. Good value. *US$189/214 sgl/dbl, US$213/237 superior sgl/dbl, US$230/255 studio sgl/dbl; all rates B&B.*

🏠 **Wendel's Guesthouse** [map page 93] (7 rooms) 📞 01 770237/771771; m 099 9940167/9964167; e wendels@africa-online. net; www.wendelslodge.com. Founded in the mid-1990s, this owner-managed guesthouse lies in attractive residential grounds with a swimming pool about 1km east of Capital City. The bright rooms have dbl or twin beds with net, fan, writing desk & tea/coffee station & en-suite tub & shower. There's a residents' lounge with a good library, Wi-Fi, DSTV & DVD facilities, & the owner is a qualified German chef who can prepare a varied selection of 3-course dinners. A small office has a computer with internet, colour printer & scanner. Overall, it's highly recommended, especially to German-speakers & business visitors needing a homely environment. *US$95/140 sgl/dbl B&B.*

MODERATE

🏠 **Annie's Lodge** [map page 93] (8 rooms) 📞 01 794572; m 099 9253399; e annieslodge@ gmail.com; www.annieslodge.com. Set in quiet evergreen gardens in Area 10 about 500m north of Capital City, this well-established lodge is popular with regular business visitors, & the large rooms with twin or king-size beds, nets, AC, fan, Wi-Fi, DSTV & en-suite tub & shower seem like exceptional value at the price. There are suites with self-catering facilities, & the lodge also prepares meals by request. *US$70/80 sgl/dbl, US$80/90 executive suite, all rates B&B.*

🏠 **Barefoot Safari Lodge** (6 chalets) ☎01 707346/7; m 088 8788769/8333936 e enquiries@ barefoot-safaris.com; www.barefoot-safaris. com; see advert on page 117. Situated 10km from Lilongwe along the Mchinji Rd, this attractive lodge, the HQ of Barefoot Safaris, lies in 8ha of landscaped gardens & makes for a refreshing 'bush' alternative to staying in town. The thatched self-catering chalets have twin beds with fitted nets, en-suite showers, & a likeable African ambience. There are also 5 walk-in tents with beds & bedding, a campsite for pitching your own tent, & a communal ablution block with hot water. The Nightjar Bar & Restaurant is well stocked with drinks & serves full meals for US$15. *US$60/110/145 sgl/dbl/trpl chalet B&B, US$15/25 sgl/dbl fitted tent, US$10 pp camping, US$5 pp b/fast.*

🏠 **Crown Hotel** (43 rooms) ☎01 751560; m 088 8313679; e crownhotell@gmail.com. This unremarkable multi-storey hotel has a conveniently central location & reasonably priced rooms with twin or dbl bed, nets, AC, DSTV, Wi-Fi, fridge & a private balcony. Ask for a room facing away from the street. *US$46/55 sgl/dbl, US$59 executive dbl.*

🏠 **Kiboko Town Hotel** (12 rooms) ☎01 751226; m 099 9838485; e reservations@kiboko-safaris. com; www.kibokohotel.com; see advert on page 117. On the top floor of a colonial-style 1940s building in a convenient location next to the post office, with Don Brioni's Restaurant & the rest of the Old Town only a step outside the door. The en-suite rooms, small but neat & clean, come with Wi-Fi, DSTV, fan & nets, there's a very pleasant residents' bar with indoor & outdoor seating, & funky African décor. *US$59/69 standard sgl/dbl, US$69/79 luxury sgl/twin, US$78/98/108 executive sgl/dbl/trpl, all rates B&B.*

🏠 **Kumbali Village & Cultural Centre** [map page 93] (12 rooms) m 099 9963402/088 8963402; e kumbali@kumbalilodge.com; www. kumbalilodge.com. Situated on the same farm as the Kumbali Country Lodge, this lower-key lodge is one of the most intriguing around Lilongwe, offering something close to a genuine village experience, though it's not to everybody's tastes,

& is difficult to access without private transport. Accommodation is in simple mud, wood & thatch huts (with mattresses & nets) scattered in a patch of Brachystegia woodland, while meals & drinks are served in an uncluttered traditional boma – a great set-up for stargazing, bush walks to the nearby Lilongwe River, or getting to watch local craftsmen at work. *US$30 pp B&B.*

🏠 **Lingadzi Inn** [map page 92] (36 rooms) ☎01 754166/1754129; e info@lingadziinn.mit. mw; www.mit.mw. Managed as a training hotel by the Malawi Institute of Tourism, this is an adequate, affordable & rather old-fashioned lodge on Paul Kagame Rd north of the Old Town. It has neat, pretty grounds bordering Lilongwe Nature Sanctuary, & hyenas are often heard at night. Standard rooms have 2 dbl beds, nets, fan, DSTV & en-suite shower. The restaurant serves a decent but unimaginative selection of mains in the US$5–7 range, & there's an outdoor dining area. *US$47/70 sgl/dbl.*

🏠 **Riverside Hotel** [map page 92] (40 rooms) ☎01 750511/772; m 099 2771914/088 8822222; e riverside@malawi.net; www.riversidehotelmalawi. com. On Paul Kagame Rd next to Lingadzi Inn, this efficient but characterless modern hotel has smart rooms with tiled floors, DSTV, AC, fan, writing desk, tea/coffee station, plenty of cupboard space, & en-suite hot shower. The restaurant serves a varied selection of Western, Indian & Chinese dishes for US$5–8, & vegetarians are well catered for. Good value. *US$54/60 sgl/dbl, US$120 full apt.*

BUDGET AND CAMPING

🏠 **Akulenje Inn** (15 rooms) ☎01 753695. This lodge has a conveniently central location in the Old Town, in the same compound as offices for Axa Coach. Rooms are adequate but unexceptional, with carpets, DSTV, AC & en-suite tub or shower. Fair value. *US$22/27 sgl/twin.*

🏠 **Garden Court Lodge** [map page 93] (12 rooms) ☎01 773083. Tucked away in suburban grounds behind the Sunbird Capital Hotel, this seems a very clean & pleasant set-up, & good value too. All rooms have a fan & the en suites come with DSTV, fridge & AC. *US$20 dbl sharing bathroom, US$40 en-suite dbl.*

🏠 **Golden Peacock Hotel** (14 rooms) ☎01 756632; m 088 8824532; e goldenpeacock@ globemw.net. In Area 3 around the corner from Korea Gardens, this is a simple, no-frills place with manifestly outmoded décor offering accommodation in dbl rooms with nets & fans. There's a Chinese restaurant attached. *US$9.50 pp using communal showers, US$22 en-suite dbl.*

⌂ **Korea Garden Lodge** (45 rooms) ⍾01 753467/757854; **e** info@kglodge.net; www. kglodge.net. In quiet gardens behind St Peter's Resthouse, only 5mins' walk from the Old Town centre, this comfortable & very reasonably priced lodge has a swimming pool next to the restaurant, which has free Wi-Fi access & serves excellent Korean food. The clean, modern rooms are brightly decorated & have a wood or carpeted floor, pine furniture, nets & fans. *US$28.60/30.80 sgl/dbl using shared bathrooms, US$45.10/57.20 en suite, US$57.20/66 en suite with DSTV, US$80.30/85.30 with AC, all rates B&B.*

⌂ **Longonot Guesthouse** (17 rooms, 6 under construction) ⍾01 750132; **m** 088 8385131; **e** info@longonot.net; www.longonot.net. This quiet little guesthouse in Area 3 has pleasant rooms with rather old-fashioned décor but good facilities, including Wi-Fi, AC, fan, nets & en-suite tub or shower. Meals are available on request, & there are economy rooms as well. *US$27–38 depending on room size & sgl or dbl occupancy, US$12.50/17 en-suite economy room.*

⌂ **Mabuya Camp** (14 rooms) ⍾01 754978; **m** 099 9746239/9664651; **e** info@mabuyacamp. com; www.mabuyacamp.com; see also advert on page 290. This welcoming spot has long been the most popular backpacker haunt in Lilongwe, & the dynamic owner-managers see to it that it stays that way. It's set in sprawling green gardens about 1km south of the Old Town centre off Glyn Jones Rd, & has a lively feel & good range of facilities, including a swimming pool, pool table, internet café & Wi-Fi access, book-exchange service, useful noticeboard, busy bar, & snacks & meals in the US$3–7 range. Accommodation is in new en-suite dbl rooms, thatched A-frames, standing tents or a dorm, & there are separate campsites for overland trucks & independent travellers. *US$45 en-suite dbl, US$25 dbl A-frame, US$10 pp dorm bed, US$6 pp standing tent with bedding/camping.*

⌂ **Mufasa Backpacker Lodge** (6 rooms, 4 dorms) ⍾01 923126; **m** 099 9071665; **e** info@ mufasamalawi.com; www.mufasamalawi.com. This superior new backpackers' lodge, on Lister Avenue in Area 3, boasts a convenient central location, good facilities, Wi-Fi, cosy outdoor residents' bar (which regularly hosts live music),

& bright décor, epitomised by the collection of masks that lines the walls. The rooms are very clean, all beds are netted, & you can order from the in-house menu or eat at any of several restaurants in the neighbourhood. Bed space is limited so best to book. (Note that, as of May 2013, the Mufasa Backpacker Lodge (Lilongwe) was closed and showed no sign of reopening.) *US$42 executive dbl, US$33 en-suite dbl or twin, US$8–11 pp dorm bed, US$5 pp camping; all except camping B&B.*

Å **Sanctuary Lodge Campground** [map page 104] (10 rooms) ⍾01 775200/1/2; **e** enquiries@ thesanctuarylodge.net; www.thesanctuarylodge. net. Situated in a pristine patch of Brachystegia next to Sanctuary Lodge, this is by far the nicest place to camp in Lilongwe, both for the bush setting & for the facilities, which include a self-catering kitchen, access to the lodge restaurant, ablution blocks with hot water, & a dormitory. *US$9 pp camping or dorm bed.*

SHOESTRING

⌂ **Crystal Lodge** (35 rooms) ⍾01 724867. This is an acceptable local guesthouse on the 1st floor of a building practically opposite the bus station in the Old Town. Rooms are basic but quite clean, & have nets & fans. *US$4.75/5.75 sgl/dbl sharing bathroom, US$8.75 en-suite dbl, US$9.50 with TV.*

⌂ **Kwasakwasa Lodge** (4 rooms) **m** 088 8873769/099 5271174; **e** info@kwasakwasa.be; www.kwasakwasa.be. In suburban Area 3, not too far from the Old Town centre, this small lodge is affiliated to the eponymous Belgian NGO, details of which are on its website. A bit of a work in progress, it serves Lilongwe's only Belgian waffles, as well as full meals for US$5, & it has four rather basic but comfortable rooms in a house surrounded by vegetable gardens, as well as camping space. *US$9.50/15.75 sgl/dbl, US$3.25 per tent camping.*

⌂ **St Peter's Resthouse** (6 rooms) **m** 099 5299364. In Area 3, opposite the golf club, this place has been popular with travellers for some years. It has 3 dbl rooms, 1 trpl, & 2 4-bed dorms, all with nets, but best to ring in advance to check availability. *US$3.25 pp dorm bed, US$6.25 dbl.*

⌂ **Sabina Central Lodge** (12 rooms) **m** 088 8373172/099 9336491. Set back from the bus station, this seems surprisingly quiet & well kept. *US$12.50 en-suite dbl with net & fan.*

⌂ **SAS Executive Lodge** **m** 088 4426898. Just opposite the bus station, this small place has clean

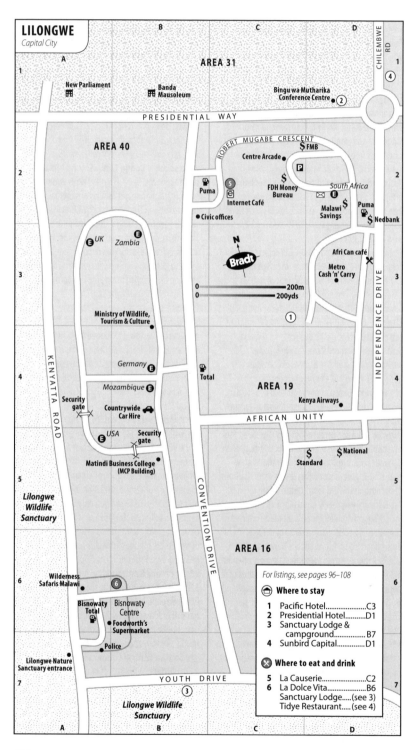

LILONGWE
Capital City

AREA 31

New Parliament

Banda Mausoleum

Bingu wa Mutharika Conference Centre (2)

CHILEMBWE RD

(4)

PRESIDENTIAL WAY

AREA 40

ROBERT MUGABE CRESCENT

$ FMB

Centre Arcade

P

Puma

Internet Café

FDH Money Bureau

South Africa

Malawi Savings $

Puma

$ Nedbank

Civic offices

UK

Zambia

Bradt

N

Afri Can café ✕

Metro Cash 'n' Carry

INDEPENDENCE DRIVE

0 _____ 200m
0 _____ 200yds

(1)

Ministry of Wildlife, Tourism & Culture

Germany

Mozambique

Total

AREA 19

Kenya Airways

AFRICAN UNITY

Security gate

Countrywide Car Hire

KENYATTA ROAD

USA

Security gate

Matindi Business College (MCP Building)

$ National
Standard $

CONVENTION DRIVE

Lilongwe Wildlife Sanctuary

AREA 16

Wilderness Safaris Malawi

(6)

Bisnowaty Total

Bisnowaty Centre

Foodworth's Supermarket

Police

Lilongwe Nature Sanctuary entrance

YOUTH DRIVE

(3)

Lilongwe Wildlife Sanctuary

For listings, see pages 96–108

🏠 **Where to stay**
1 Pacific Hotel.....................C3
2 Presidential Hotel...........D1
3 Sanctuary Lodge & campground................B7
4 Sunbird Capital...............D1

✕ **Where to eat and drink**
5 La Causerie.......................C2
6 La Dolce Vita....................B6
   Sanctuary Lodge.....(see 3)
   Tidye Restaurant.....(see 4)

en-suite rooms & food available on site. *US$14 dbl room with TV.*

🏠 **Sosi Lodge** (12 rooms) m 099 9062426. One of the better cheapies around the bus station, this has clean rooms & a friendly welcome. *US$5.50 sgl, US$8.50 en suite with ¾ bed.*

🏠 **Sunset Lodge** (18 rooms) ✆ 01 724770/718; m 088 8183239; e sunsetlodge@globemw.net.

Situated on Malangalanga Rd, this is the pick of the lodges close to the bus station, with far nicer rooms & a quieter location than most of the competition. The clean rooms all have a net & fan, but best ask for Rooms 13–18, which face the river rather than the street. *US$11/12.5 en-suite sgl/dbl, US$14/15.50 with DSTV.*

✗ WHERE TO EAT

The main concentration of restaurants is in the Old Town, along or close to the south end of Kamuzu Procession, between the junctions with Colby and Glyn Jones roads. There is also a good selection in and around the Crossroads Mall, at the junction of Kamuzu Procession and the Mchinji Road. The central part of Capital City is poorly endowed when it comes to restaurants, but some of the best places in Lilongwe are dotted around the posh residential northern suburbs bordering it. The cheapest places to eat are the stalls and small local restaurants around the bus station, which serve filling formulaic local fare for around US$2 per plate.

OLD TOWN *See map, pages 98–9.*
South end of Kamuzu Procession (Area 3)

✗ **Ali Baba Restaurant & Take-Away** Kamuzu Procession; ✆ 01 755224; m 088 8955555; ⊕ 08.00–21.00 daily. A cheaper option, this serves Lebanese dishes, along with burgers, steaks & the like. Generous portions are in the US$3–5 range.

✗ **Augusto's Ristorante** m 088 8908625; ⊕ 08.00–23.00 daily. Inside the new Lilongwe City Mall, this constantly busy café keeps long hours & makes an impressive selection of authentic Italian pastas & pizzas for US$6–7.

✗ **Bombay Palace** m 088 8202202; ⊕ 12.00–14.00 Tue–Sun, 18.00–22.00 daily. In the same complex as Game & Spar, this tastefully decorated Indian restaurant is a new branch of the long-serving Blantyre favourite. The menus are identical, offering an extensive selection of meat & vegetarian dishes in the US$6.50–8 range.

✗ **Don Brioni's Bistro** Lister Av; m 099 9933627/9967482; e donbrionismw@hotmail.com; ⊕ 17.00–late daily. Situated below Kiboko Town Hotel, this long-serving favourite has a comfortable aura of faded chic, indoor & outdoor seating, a varied international menu with a slight emphasis on Italian dishes (though pizzas are no longer available) & a well-stocked bar that stays open until the last customer leaves or collapses. Most meat & fish dishes cost around US$9–11.

✗ **Kiboko Brasserie** Lister Av; ✆ 01 751226; www.kiboko-safaris.com; ⊕ 07.00–17.00 daily. In the courtyard of the Kiboko Town Hotel, this is a great spot for a light alfresco lunch, serving a variety of salads, sandwiches, filled pancakes & other dishes for US$5–6.

✗ **Korea Garden Lodge** Tsiranana Rd; ✆ 01 753467; ⊕ b/fast, lunch & dinner daily. The poolside restaurant in this popular hotel is highly rated for Korean food, with prices in the US$8–10 range. There's a plush bar & lounge to unwind in too.

✗ **Land & Lake Café** ✆ 01 757120/754303; www.landlake.com; ⊕ lunch Mon–Sat. Worth the uphill walk, this tranquil café offers a lip-smacking selection of wraps, toasted sandwiches & salads for US$6, along with coffee, iced rooibos tea, cakes, muffins, & even milkshakes. Just blocks from the centre, the leafy grounds feel miles away.

✗ **Mamma Mia** Off Paul Kagame Rd; ✆ 01 758362; e mammamia@globemw.net; ⊕ 11.00–13.30 & 17.00–21.30 Tue–Sun. This popular upmarket trattoria in Old Town Mall serves crusty pizzas & other Italian food. From the gleaming stainless-steel kitchen to cosy corners & the shaded patio, the place exudes quality. Pizzas cost US$6.50–9.50 & pastas & other mains are US$8–10.

✗ **Noble Chinese Restaurant** Colby Rd; ✆ 01 750075; ⊕ 11.30–14.30, 17.30–22.30 daily. This busy, newly remodelled place opposite the Sunbird Lilongwe has some of the best Chinese food in

Lilongwe, & it's great value at US$6.50 for a 'small' portion (sufficient for 1 person) or US$9.50 for a large portion (serves 2).

✘ **Papaya** m 099 1800900; ⏰ 07.30–18.00 Tue–Sat, 10.00–18.00 Sun. Once again in the new Lilongwe City Mall, this cheerful café is an excellent quick option for those wanting something a bit fresher & healthier than the usual offerings. Generous wraps, fruit smoothies, quesadillas, & stir-fries are all here for US$3–4.

✘ **Sana Food Centre** 01 753510; m 099 9355677; ⏰ 08.30–22.00 daily. A one-stop shop for fast food in the centre, this popular spot offers a menu of pizzas, curries, burgers & everything in between for US$4–5. No alcohol, but there is DSTV, usually tuned to football or cricket.

✘ **Serendipity Lifestyle Café** Off Paul Kagame Rd; m 099 4448444; www.serendipity.mw; ⏰ 08.00–22.00 daily. Tucked inside the Old Town Mall, this relaxed café offers excellent breakfasts, sandwiches, salads & cappuccinos, along with meat & fish mains for US$6.25. There's a full bar, & it gets busy in the evenings.

✘ **Tranquility Tea Garden** 01 972482; m 088 8134361; ⏰ 08.00–18.30 daily (until 17.00 in winter). Down a quiet road in suburban Area 3, you could hardly say this café hasn't earned its name. Seating is in the primrose garden, & meals include wraps, sandwiches & salads at around US$7. Numerous teas & coffees are of course on offer, & homemade cookies, cakes & milkshakes round out the desserts.

Near the market/bus station (Area 1)

✘ **Annie's Coffee Pot** This Old Town stalwart has seen better days. It no longer has accommodation, the once-varied menu has been whittled down to a few local staples for around US$2.25, & coffee is of the instant variety. No alcohol.

✘ **Gazebo Restaurant** 01 727130; ⏰ 08.00–21.00 daily. This unpretentious eatery on the backstreets north of Glyn Jones Rd has a varied menu of burgers & sandwiches for US$2.50–3, while full meals & pizzas cost US$6.25. There's indoor & outdoor seating. No alcohol.

Crossroads Mall and environs (Areas 5 and 9)

✘ **Café Delight** Kamuzu Procession; ⏰ 07.30–20.30 daily. Popular with locals, this

diner opposite the Crossroads Mall scores heavily when it comes to variety, portion sizes & prices, serving everything from stews & grills to pizzas & burgers, mostly at US$3–4. Western palates may find the food a touch greasy, & it's no place for vegetarians. No alcohol.

✘ **Copper Pot** Crossroads Mall; 01 750333/444; ⏰ 12.00–14.30 daily & 18.30–22.00 Tue–Sun. Part of the Crossroads Hotel, this classy restaurant specialises in Chinese & Indian dishes, with plenty of choice for vegetarians, but it also has a good selection of continental fare & a great wine list. Mains US$6–9.

✘ **Cappuccino's Café** Crossroads Mall; m 099 9872287; ⏰ 08.00–17.00 Mon–Sat. This easy-going modern café is a Skyband Wi-Fi hotspot with indoor & outdoor seating, good filter coffee, & tasty salads, sandwiches & other snacks for US$6–8. There's a Portuguese-style lunch on Saturdays. No alcohol.

✘ **Mo's Club** Selous Rd; m 02 11951424; ⏰ 11.00–23.00 daily. The swimming pool complex at the Portuguese Club charges day membership of US$3 to swimmers, but there's no fee for using the chilled poolside bar & restaurant, though there's nothing discernibly Portuguese about it & it serves the usual fare for US$4–5.

✘ **Steers & Pizza Inn** Crossroads Mall; ⏰ 09.30–21.30 Mon–Thu, 09.30–23.00 Fri & Sat, 10.00–22.00 Sun. Homesick fast-food junkies will want to make a beeline for these South African franchises, which specialise in burgers/grills for US$4.50–5.50 & pizzas for US$5, & share a modern premises with indoor & outdoor eating. No alcohol.

CAPITAL CITY AND NORTHERN SUBURBS See map, page 104.
Capital City (Areas 40 and 19)

✘ **La Causerie** Behind Centre Hse; 01 773828; m 088 8644905; ⏰ 12.00–15.00 Mon–Fri. Incredibly, this is the only proper restaurant within the main cluster of offices & banks in Capital City. Fortunately, it's very good, with excellent service, & a cosmopolitan menu of meat & seafood dishes (plus a few vegetarian options), mostly in the US$8–10 range.

✘ **La Dolce Vita** Kenyatta Rd; 01 776538; e ladolcevita@nyassa.mw; ⏰ 07.45–17.30 Mon–Thu & Sat, 07.45–22.00 Fri. In the Bisnowaty Centre behind Wilderness Safaris, this relaxed Italian eatery serves pizzas, pastas & salads for around US$8, to take away or to eat in the small courtyard, & it also has exceptional ice cream.

✗ **Sanctuary Lodge** ☎01 775200/1/2; www.thesanctuarylodge.net; ⏲ 08.00–21.30 daily. There's no better place in Lilongwe for a relaxed sundowner than the balcony of this lovely bush lodge on Youth Drive, & the cuisine is also superb, with most items on the short but imaginative menu falling in the US$12–17 range.

✗ **Tidye Restaurant** Chilembwe Rd; ☎01 773388; ⏲ 18.30–22.00 daily. The refined contemporary African restaurant in the Sunbird Capital Hotel is one of the most highly regarded & prestigious places to eat in Lilongwe, & also one of the priciest, with most dishes costing upwards of US$13.

Presidential Way and beyond (Areas 34 and 44) *See map, pages 92–3.*

✗ **Baba's Delhi Durbar** Presidential Way; ☎01 926421; m 088 8795780; ⏲ 11.00–14.00 & 18.00–23.00 daily. In the Four Seasons Nursery, this excellent Indian restaurant, like its counterpart in Blantyre, serves a varied selection of meat & vegetarian dishes in the US$7–10 range.

✗ **Buchanan's Grill** Presidential Way; ☎01 772859; ⏲ 10.00–14.30 Mon–Sat & 17.00–21.30 daily. Named after a 19th-century settler John Buchanan, this highly rated restaurant lies in the Four Seasons Nursery about 1km east of Capital City. There's a stylish dining room, or you can eat out on a shady deck overlooking a tree-fringed rock pool. It specialises in seafood & meat grills, with a continental touch, for around US$10–15.

✗ **Kumbali Country Lodge** m 099 9963402; www.kumbalilodge.com; ⏲ lunch & dinner daily. Widely thought to offer the top culinary experience in Lilongwe, this beautiful lodge serves 3-course set menus for US$20 pp, & it has a great wine list, too. Seating is limited & it's 6km out of town, so best to book in advance.

North of Capital City (Areas 42 and 20) *See map, pages 92–3.*

✗ **Blue Ginger** Mphonongo Rd; ☎01 795225; m 088 8214444; ⏲ 11.00–14.00 & 20.00–23.00 Mon–Sat. In the Pacific Parade Mall, this stylish & highly regarded restaurant has a well-stocked bar & an extensive Chinese & Indian menu, with vegetarian dishes at around US$6.75 & meat & chicken at US$8–10.

✗ **Cheers Restaurant** Off Blantyre Rd; m 088 8510812; ⏲ 10.00–22.00 daily. This aptly named Chinese restaurant in Area 24 has indoor & garden seating, as well as private rooms, & serves a long list of meat & vegetarian dishes for US$7.50–10.50.

✗ **Latitude 13°** Mphonongo Rd; m 099 6403159/088 2200849; www.thelatitudehotels.com. This most stylish of Lilongwe restaurants is attached to the hotel of the same name, & offers a fine dining experience among the best in Lilongwe. Dishes are Malawi-inspired, but combine influences from the Mediterranean & Asia. The rotating mains include steaks, pork & fish for around US$12–15, & there's always a vegetarian option. The wine list is extensive, & the bar stocks an impressive variety of imported spirits.

✗ **Surf 'n' Turf** Mphonongo Rd; m 088 8669944; ⏲ 12.00–14.00 & 18.00–23.00 daily. This superior grill in the Pacific Parade Mall specialises in sumptuous steaks & seafood, with mains mostly around US$10, & a good wine list.

✗ **Sheba Restaurant** Mtendere Rd; ☎01 794829; ⏲ 12.00–14.30 Mon–Sat, 13.00–14.30 Sun & 18.00–22.00 daily. One of the best-value eateries in Lilongwe, & probably the most unusual to Western palates, this Ethiopian restaurant lies in a suburban garden around the corner from Ulendo Safaris & serves set menus of 3–4 fiery Ethiopian dishes for 2–3 people at around US$19–22, or stand-alone mains for US$3.75–4.75.

ENTERTAINMENT AND NIGHTLIFE

See map, pages 98–9 unless otherwise stated.
Most of the bars also serve good food, with more limited menus perhaps but always good value. All except Chameleon and Chez Ntemba are in Old Town on or close to Paul Kagame Road.

♀**Alexzander's Pub** This lively local bar on Paul Kagame Rd has DSTV (making it very popular during crunch international football matches), pool tables & a welcoming atmosphere.

♀**Chameleon Bar** [map page 93] m 088 8833114; e millercalcon@malawi.net. Part of the Four Seasons Nursery on Presidential Way, this popular pub attracts a mixture of locals, expats & tourists. It's a good place for a quiet drink in the early evening, but if you are looking for a party then best to head there after 22.00. It has regular karaoke & live music nights, including Sunday afternoon jazz.

☆ **Chez Ntemba** [map page 92] m 099 9207588; www.chez-ntemba.com; ⊕ 18.00–late daily. With indoor & outdoor dance floors, pumping music & flashing lights, this out-of-the-way venue in Area 47 is where many revellers finish their nights (or mornings). It's part of the pan-African Chez Ntemba chain, which has more than 15 nightclubs dotted around the continent. There are nightly discos supplemented by occasional live music.

♀**Diplomats Pub** One of the best new bars in Lilongwe, the modern, centrally located Diplomats is a hub for expats & Lilongwe's trendy set. The dance floor is always busy, the bar is well-stocked, & there are comfortable booths if you need a rest.

Thursday nights have Salsa dancing & it's simply the place to be on weekends.

♀**Harry's Bar** ☎01 757979 m 088 8878888. Relocated, but still tucked away in an industrial area off Paul Kagame Rd, this cosy small bar has warm décor, a good selection of drinks, & an interesting collection of contemporary African & Western music, making it a very popular rendezvous with young volunteers & residents. On a lively night you'll be impressed by the swiftness of the bar staff, as well as the quality of the music – with dancing if you stay late enough. Pub grub is served in the evenings.

☆ **Pirates' Casino** ☎01 751254. Situated off Paul Kagame Rd, this tends to be more of a late-night drinking, gambling & dancing place, full of fun & quite some style.

♀**The Shack** [map page 92] On Paul Kagame Rd next to Lingadzi Inn, this is a great pub-cum-social club that was started by the Round Table & is supported by most of Lilongwe's younger expats. With volleyball outside on Wed evenings & Happy Hour on Fri, it's a good place to make sporting & social contacts.

SHOPPING

There are now several shopping malls in Lilongwe. The most central are the **Shoprite Centre** [98 D4] and the newly built **Lilongwe City Mall** [98 D4], which face each other at the junction of Kamuzu Procession and Kenyatta Road, hosting the South African Spar and Game chains. The **Shoprite Supermarket** in the eponymous mall has long been the best in the city centre, but **Spar** and **Game** are both comparable. Smaller but almost as central, and with several shops geared to tourists, is the **Old Town Mall** [98 C3] off Paul Kagame Road. Then there's the large **Crossroads Mall** [98 A2] at the junction of Kamuzu Procession and the Mchinji Road, which has recently been joined by the (ingeniously named) **City Mall** [98 A2], with a Mr Price clothes shop, on the opposite side of the Mchinji Road.

Closer to Capital City, the **Bisnowaty Centre** [104 B6] opposite the entrance to Lilongwe Nature Sanctuary [104 A7], is the site of the peerless **Foodworths Supermarket**, a Total filling station, the head office of Wilderness Safaris, and a top-notch DVD shop. The **Pacific Parade Mall** [93 E1] northwest of Capital City also has a good selection of shops but fewer that are likely to be of interest to tourists.

The **central market** [99 F7], next to the bus station, is the best place to buy fresh fruit and vegetables. It is also a good place to buy cheap clothes, music, most notably from Malawi, South Africa and the Congo, and practically anything else you can think of, from curtains, televisions and coal irons to chickens, pots, baskets and shoes.

BOOKS AND MAPS The newly opened **Grey Matter** [98 D4] ☏ *01755411/920788;* ⊕ *08.00–17.30 Mon–Sat*) bookshop is far and away the best in the country, with a wide selection of new and classic titles. **Central Africana Bookshop** [98 C3] ☏ *01 756317; www.centralafricana.com;* ⊕ *07.30–17.00 Mon–Fri, 09.00–12.30*

Sat) in Old Town Mall has a fabulous selection of new and antiquarian books, including some very valuable Africana. Relocated to the ground floor of an arcade on Kamuzu Procession uphill from the Sunbird Lilongwe Hotel, **Bookmart** [98 B3] (⏱ *09.00–16.45 Mon–Fri, 09.00–12.00 Sat*) has the best choice of secondhand novels in Malawi, selling for US$1.50–2.50. The Department of Surveys' **map sales office** [98 D6] sells 1:50,000 and 1:250,000 sheets covering most of Malawi for Mk1,500. The office is in the Old Town on a side road that radiates southward from the Glyn Jones Road/Kamuzu Procession roundabout.

CRAFTS AND CURIOS The main cluster of curio sellers is outside the post office [98 D5] in Old Town, where hard bargaining is the order of the day. There are also quite a few curios on sale in the main car park [104 C2] on Independence Drive in Capital City. Or if you prefer, visit one of the following shops, which generally offer better-quality goods and higher non-negotiable prices:

🏠 **African Habitat** [98 C3] ☎ 01 752363; e africanhabitat@malawi.net. In the Old Town Mall, this is a beautiful craft & curio shop selling high-quality carvings, furniture & textiles.
🏠 **La Galleria** [98 C3] ☎ 01 757742; e lacaverna@malawi.net. The sister shop to La Caverna in Blantyre, this gallery in the Old Town

Mall exhibits paintings, sculpture & textiles by the top Malawian artists.
🏠 **Things of Africa** [98 C5] m 088 8964779; e thingsofafrica@africa-online.net. This excellent shop below the Kiboko Town Hotel is packed with art & handicrafts work from the whole region.

SUPERMARKETS If you want to self-cater, there's a good range of fruit and vegetables on sale at the market. Most supermarkets sell a fair range of foodstuffs, the largest and best being the **Shoprite** [98 D4] at the intersection of Kenyatta Road and Kamuzu Procession – when it opened a few years ago, everyone walked around it with their mouths open in amazement. Just as good are **Spar** and **Game** [98 D4], directly across the street in the Lilongwe City Mall. Better still for imported goods and delicatessen items is the **Foodworths Supermarket** [104 B6] in the Bisnowaty Centre, and **Bowers** [98 C3] in the Old Town Mall. Also very good are the **Seven-Eleven** [98 A2] and **Foodzone** [98 A2] opposite and in the Crossroads Centre, and the various **People's Supermarkets** studded around the Old Town.

SPORTS AND SWIMMING

If you're into sport, then a trip to the **Lilongwe Golf Club** [98 C6] (☎ *01 753118/598* m *099 5604096*) would soon find you playing golf, tennis, squash or swimming, with partners, caddies and ball boys all ready to take part too. A day's membership costs US$7.50, there's a green fee of US$6.25 for 18 holes or US$3.75 for nine holes, a caddy fee of US$3.25 for 18 holes or US$1.50 for nine holes, and clubs for rent. Day members must pay an additional US$1 to use the golf club's swimming pool; a far cheaper option is the **Portuguese Club** [98 A3] on Selous Road, where a US$3 day membership gives you access to the pool. Sporting campers can take advantage of the pleasant and well-equipped campground, however, and with it get full use of the facilities and restaurant for the camping fee of US$5 per person per night.

OTHER PRACTICALITIES

BANKING AND FOREIGN EXCHANGE The main cluster of banks in the Old Town is along Kamuzu Procession near the junction with Kenyatta Road, where the

Standard Bank [98 D4] and **NBS** [99 E5] both have full foreign-exchange facilities and ATMs where local currency can be drawn against international Visa, Maestro and MasterCards. There are even more banks in Capital City, several of them clustered among the office blocks immediately south of Presidential Way, but the most useful to tourists are the Standard Bank [104 D5] and National Bank [104 D5] on African Unity Drive, which also have forex bureaux and international ATMs. Elsewhere there are international ATMs in Crossroads Mall and on the south side of Glyn Jones Road near the junction with Malangalanga Road. Most of the **private forex bureaux** have yet to recover from a government-ordered shutdown in 2009, but a notable exception is the **Victoria Forex Bureau** [98 D4] (⊕ *08.00–16.00 Mon–Fri, 08.00–12.00 Sat)* located in the Shoprite Centre. Forex facilities are available at Kamuzu Airport to tie in with all international flights.

DIPLOMATIC MISSIONS Most foreign high commissions and embassies are in Capital City, and several – including those of the USA, UK, France, Germany, Mozambique and Zambia – stand along the interior of an anonymous loop road on the west side of Convention Drive. Note, however, that the Austrian and Dutch embassies are both in Blantyre rather than Lilongwe.

🕀 **Belgian honorary consulate** Bougainvillea Cl; ✆01 710358; e consubel@malawi.net

🕀 **Chinese embassy** Off Convention Dr; ✆01 794751; e chinaemb_mw@mfa.gov.cn

🕀 **Danish embassy** Chilembwe Hse; ✆01 784825; e denmal@malawi.net

🕀 **Finnish honorary consulate** Ufulu Rd; ✆01 795398; e outifincon@africa-online.net

🕀 **German embassy** [104 B4] Off Convention Dr; ✆01 770250; e info@lilongwe.diplo.de; www.lilongwe.diplo.de

🕀 **Irish embassy** 3rd Fl, Arwa Hse; ✆01 776405/408; e lilongweemdiplomats@dfa.ie

🕀 **Mozambican high commission** [104 B4] Off Convention Dr; ✆01 784100; e mozambique@malawi.net

🕀 **Norwegian embassy** Arwa Hse; ✆01 774211; e emb.lilongwe@mfa.no

🕀 **South African embassy** 3rd Fl, Kang'ombe Hse; ✆01 773722; e sahc@malawi.net

🕀 **UK high commission** [104 A3] Off Convention Dr; ✆01 772400; e bhclilongwe@fco.gov.uk; http://ukinmalawi.fco.gov.uk

🕀 **US embassy** [104 A5] Off Convention Dr; ✆01 773166; e ConsularLilongwe@state.gov; www.lilongwe.usembassy.gov

🕀 **Zambian high commission** [104 B3] Off Convention Dr; ✆01 772635

🕀 **Zimbabwean high commission** 7th Fl, Gemini Hse, Capital City; ✆01 733988; e zimhighcomllw@malawi.net

HAIR AND BEAUTY TREATMENT There are many good hairdressers and beauticians in Lilongwe, able to cut men's and women's hair equally well, and several will do hair treatments and colouring at a fraction of Western prices. Recommended salons include **Jay's** [98 C5] (*in the Old Town opposite the Bohemian Café;* ✆ *01 758041)*, **Lifestyle Hair & Beauty** [104 B6] (*Bisnowaty Centre;* ✆*01 775834)* and **Salon Mystic** [98 A2] (*Crossroads Mall;* ✆*01 920235)*. Of these, Lifestyle has been recommended as the best salon in the country, and it uses the Dermalogica product range.

HEALTH The **Medicare Laboratory** [98 C5] (✆ *01 750152)* in the NBS Building in the Old Town opposite the Kiboko Town Hotel [98 C5] is the best place to go for tests of any sort. A malaria test, for instance, takes ten minutes to produce and costs a few dollars. **Likuni Mission Hospital** [98 A7] (✆ *01 766602)*, a few kilometres out of town on the Likuni road, is regarded as the best in the Lilongwe area, though the **Kamuzu Central Hospital** [99 H2] (✆ *01 753555/721555)* off Mzimba Road is more central for simple routine checks. There are also three pharmacies in the

Nico Centre, one next to Shoprite [98 D4], and one next to Kiboko Town Hotel [98 C5]. There is a good dentist in Old Town Mall [98 C3]. **AC Opticals** (01 756161/770493; e a.c.opticals@malawi-net) in Plaza House and the Old Town Mall [98 C3] has a full range of optical goods.

IMMIGRATION The **immigration office** [98 D3] (01 754297) is a short way off Paul Kagame Road – the route is signposted from the Sunbird Lilongwe Hotel. Visa and visitor's pass renewals are processed here in a matter of minutes. When you know it's so easy, it's really not worth the hassle of overstaying your visitor's permit.

INTERNET There are email facilities in any number of small internet cafés in Old Town and also at the business centre in the foyer of the Sunbird Capital Hotel [104 D1], as well as at the Centre Arcade [104 C2] in Capital City, and in the Crossroads Mall [98 A2]. Most charge a fairly uniform rate of Mk5–10 per minute, though some charge only for the time you use, while others sell prepaid time from 15 minutes upwards. Most internet cafés operate from around 08.00 to 17.00 on weekdays and several close on Saturday afternoons and Sundays, but those inside hotels keep longer hours. Skyband has more than 40 Wi-Fi hotspots dotted around Lilongwe, and anyone can obtain access using a prepaid Access Card (voucher). For more information contact Skyband (01 756558; e lilongwe@skyband.mw; www.skyband.mw).

WHAT TO SEE AND DO

LILONGWE NATURE SANCTUARY [104 A7] (01 771271; ⊕ 07.30–18.00 daily; entrance US$1) Extending over 150ha of Brachystegia woodland between the Old Town and Capital City, this attractive suburban sanctuary has been split into two roughly equal halves, with the sector to the east of Kenyatta Road now utilised by the Lilongwe Wildlife Centre (covered separately below). However, the old nature sanctuary remains a thoroughly worthwhile goal for keen walkers and birders, with a chance of seeing a few large mammals. It's also very affordable and accessible, as the entrance gate lies on the west side of Kenyatta Road opposite Bisnowaty Centre, only 100m from the main minibus route between the Old Town and Capital City.

Fortunately, the rather depressing zoo that once stood close to the entrance has closed, and its former inhabitants have been relocated to the wildlife centre on the other side of the road. But the sanctuary's small network of trails, passing through pristine Brachystegia woodland and the riparian forest lining the Lingadzi River, is well worth exploring over an hour or two. The main point of interest is birds, with more than 200 species recorded, and the riverine paths are especially rewarding, offering a good chance of seeing the colourful Hueglin's robin and Schalow's turaco, raptors such as brown snake eagle and black sparrowhawk, the elusive African finfoot, and a variety of kingfishers, weavers and finches. Secretive mammals that occur here naturally include spotted hyena, otter, porcupine, bushpig and grey duiker, and there's a good chance of seeing vervet monkeys, bushbucks and crocodiles along the river. When you've finished exploring the reserve, you might want to stop for a meal or drink at the restaurant outside the gate.

LILONGWE WILDLIFE CENTRE [104 A5] (01 757120; m 099 3800289; e wildlife@ llwc.org; www.lilongwewildlife.org; ⊕ 08.00–17.00 daily; entrance US$5/3 foreigner adult/child, US$4/2 resident/child, US$1.50 Malawians/child) Comprising the part of Lilongwe Nature Sanctuary on the east side of Kenyatta Road, this award-winning centre opened in July 2007 to provide shelter of international standard to rescued, confiscated, orphaned and injured wild animals, to rehabilitate such animals for controlled release into the wild where feasible, and as an interactive conservation educational centre for local Malawians. (The majority of their visitors are Malawian children on school trips.) Funded by entrance fees and donations, the centre's large fenced enclosures now house a varied menagerie of over 200 permanent residents, including a lioness and small troop of samango monkeys rescued from captivity in Europe, and a leopard transported from the old zoo across the road, along with rescued blue monkeys, crocodiles and numerous other species who have been rescued in Malawi and elsewhere. The centre has also nurtured then overseen the release of several troops of vervet monkey in Kasungu National Park and three bushbabies to Lake Malawi National Park, and there are ongoing release programmes with their partner organisation, Kuti Wildlife Reserve near Salima (see page 124). Guided tours run on the hour and take about 60 minutes, and visitors can also explore the 4km network of unguided walking trails along the Lingadzi River. There's a gift shop and outdoor bar, and as of 2013 a new restaurant. Long-term (from two weeks to several months) volunteer opportunities are also available; check the website for details.

BANDA MAUSOLEUM AND WAR MEMORIAL Recent years have seen a spate of monument construction north of Capital City, most strikingly perhaps the mausoleum of former president His Excellency Dr Hastings Kamuzu Banda, which was formally opened in 2006 by former President Bingu wa Mutharika. The mausoleum [104 B1] is easy to spot on Presidential Way, a short distance west of the T-junction with Kenyatta Avenue, next to the newly completed Parliament Building. There are theoretically plans to open an information centre and museum next to the mausoleum, but these seem to be a long way off. Don't bother with the 'guides' at the mausoleum, as they won't tell you much about the mausoleum that isn't immediately apparent already.

The former war memorial next to the Banda Mausoleum has been torn down and replaced by the ostentatious **Presidential Hotel & Bingu wa Mutharika Conference Centre** [104 D1], which was originally intended to host the aborted African Union summit in 2012, but today sits largely empty. Before the hotel was built, the old memorial had already been usurped in stature by a grandiose new war memorial [92 D1] inaugurated by former President Mutharika in November 2007. Also difficult to miss, the memorial stands tall and obelisk-like, surrounded by its very own car park, on the right side of the Salima road 800m north of the Kamuzu Procession/Presidential Way roundabout. The monument is dedicated to the King's African Rifles and other Malawian troops who fell in the two world wars, as well as in more recent battles, with pride of place going to a statue of the autocratic President Banda, who died in hospital aged somewhere between 97 and 101.

PARLIAMENT [104 A1] (✆ 01 773566/773208; www.malawi.gov.mw) Completed in 2010, the enormous new Chinese-built Parliament building (helpfully labelled 'Parliament Building' on the entry arch) is an impressively showy structure, adding a new twist to the already surreal architectural grab bag that is Capital City. Engineering fans and political junkies are free to take a guided tour or even observe parliamentary proceedings, but it requires a bit of advance planning. Head to the entry gate, where you complete a visitor's form on which you have to specify when (date and time) you'd like to come and take the tour. They require 48–72 hours' notice, so if you do want to visit, it makes sense to stop here when you first get into town. Inside the grounds you'll find a Malawi-shaped fountain and portraits of all the former presidents, while the tour itself takes you into the tiled and colonnaded entry hall, followed by the 104-seat chamber's gallery, and a resource library for parliamentarians. You're not allowed onto the chamber floor, and the whole tour will likely take less than an hour.

TOBACCO AUCTION FLOORS [98 B1] An eye-opening visit is to go early morning to the tobacco auction floors, out on the Salima road, where guided visits can be booked in advance from April to September through the safari companies. With three types of tobacco sold in over 10,000 bales from the floor each morning, it is a mesmerising sight, as the buyers, sellers and auctioneers walk up and down the rows of carefully numbered 100kg bags. The warehouse stores over 80,000 bales of tobacco at any one time.

SKYDIVING The **Malawi Parachute Association** (m *099 9926230;* e *skydive@ nyassa.mw; www.skydive.mw*), in partnership with Nyassa Air Taxi (*www.nyassa. mw*) offers a variety of skydiving packages from Kamuzu Airport, starting at US$340 for a beginner's tandem jump. It's best to book at least a week in advance, and for information on upcoming jumps, check www.facebook.com/skydivemalawi.

SHORT TRIPS FROM LILONGWE

Several short trips are possible from Lilongwe, though most are of more interest to residents looking for a weekend break than to tourists. Useful details of places of interest around Lilongwe (including areas like Dedza, Salima and Ntchisi, which are covered elsewhere in this guide) are contained in the sadly now out-of-print 60-page booklet *Day Outings from Lilongwe* (Judy Carter, Wildlife Society of Malawi, 1991).

KAMUZU DAM Named after the late President Banda, the two Kamuzu dams lie about half an hour's drive south of Lilongwe, along the road between Likuni towards Dzalanyama. The dams have created a huge artificial lake, Lilongwe's main water supply, and Kamuzu Dam II is also the site of the Lilongwe Sailing Club, where it's usually possible to hire dinghies, and there's plenty of birdlife on the shore.

Getting there and away Follow the Likuni road south of town for 21km, through the trading centres of Likuni and Tanga, then turn left into a side road signposted for Kamuzu Dam II. After 4km you'll reach the entrance gate to the official viewing platform over the dam (*nominal entrance & vehicle fee*), where a turn to the right leads straight to the entrance of the sailing club.

Where to stay
Lilongwe Sailing Club Cottage (3 rooms) 01 707213; m 088 8621430; e nordin@ eomw.net; www.lilongwesailing.com; US$3.50 day membership. Consisting of 1 dbl & 2 twin rooms, this self-catering cottage in the sailing club grounds comes with a gas stove, cooking utensils, flush toilet & solar-heated hot shower. *It is rented out at US$24 for the 1st night & US$10 for additional nights.*

DZALANYAMA FOREST RESERVE Gazetted as a forest reserve in 1922, Dzalanyama – Chichewa for 'Place of Animals' – extends over 990km² on the Mozambican border, about 60km southwest of Lilongwe. The reserve's dominant feature is the Dzalanyama Hills, whose steep slopes form a 70km watershed between Malawi and Mozambique, and it protects extensive areas of indigenous Brachystegia woodland studded with large granite boulders. Some large wildlife remains, most visibly vervet monkey, chacma baboon and bush duiker, but a small herd of sable antelope is resident, leopard and samango still haunt the forests, and spotted hyena are often heard at night.

Dzalanyama is renowned among birdwatchers for its checklist of 300-plus species, and it is generally regarded to be the most diverse and best site in the country for Brachystegia-associated birds. As is often the case in this habitat, many birds tend to move around in mixed bird parties, which means you might go long periods seeing very little then suddenly be confronted by a flurry of multi-species activity. A good walk entails following the main logging road south from the forest lodge towards the waterfall. The boulders to the right are a good site for the boulder-chat, a Zimbabwean near-endemic recorded nowhere else in Malawi. And mixed bird parties might include the likes of *miombo* pied barbet, Stierling's woodpecker, cinnamon-breasted tit, Arnot's chat, white-tailed blue flycatcher, yellow-bellied eremomela and Stierling's barred warbler. The *dambo* about 2km from the forest lodge supports a good selection of sunbirds, finches and seedeaters alongside Whyte's barbet and the dashing little bee-eater. Other more scarce Dzalanyama specials include pale-billed hornbill, Souza's shrike, Boehm's flycatcher, Anchieta's sunbird and olive-headed weaver.

Getting there and away Transport can be arranged with Land and Lake Safaris, or any other operator for that matter, or you can drive there yourself, following the Likuni road out of Lilongwe as for the Lilongwe Sailing Club, but continuing straight past the turn-off to Kamuzu Dam II. The access road sometimes becomes impassable after rain, and even at the best of times, the 60km drive will probably

SOUTH LUANGWA NATIONAL PARK, ZAMBIA

This low-lying park, which covers an area of 9,050km^2 in Zambia's Luangwa River Valley, is widely regarded as one of the finest wildlife reserves anywhere in Africa. The reserve harbours innumerable elephant, buffalo and hippo, as well as a wide variety of antelope and other ungulates, substantial numbers of lion, leopard and spotted hyena, and smaller numbers of cheetah and wild dog. The entrance to South Luangwa and its main cluster of lodges lies little more than 100km from Mchinji on the Malawian–Zambian border west of Lilongwe, and since Malawi itself lacks any reserve comparable in size or in game viewing, South Luangwa is visited from Malawi with increasing frequency.

Any of the Lilongwe-based tour operators listed on page 96 can organise an excursion to South Luangwa, either as part of a longer tour of Malawi or else as a self-contained trip out of Lilongwe. The cost of such an excursion will depend greatly on whether you camp at one of the cheaper sites or stay at an upmarket lodge. Kiboko Safaris is the best first port of call for budget camping safaris, while the other operators are aimed more at the middle and upper price ranges. For visitors needing a Malawian visa, remember to get a double-entry one, so as to be able to return after your side trip to South Luangwa. Zambia also requires a yellow-fever certificate, which may be asked for at the border and a fine imposed if it cannot be produced. The best months to visit are from June to September, though game viewing is excellent throughout the year.

More extensive details on South Luangwa (and travel elsewhere in Zambia) are to be found in Bradt's *Zambia* guide, written by Chris McIntyre.

take the best part of two hours, paying close attention to the map supplied to all self-drive guests upon booking.

Where to stay

Dzalanyama Forest Retreat [map page 88] (4 rooms) 01 757120/754303; e info@landlake.net; www.landlake.net. Formerly run by the Department of Forestry, this wonderfully isolated self-catering cottage is now managed privately by Land & Lake Safaris. Idyllically positioned above the fast-flowing Makata Stream, it has 4 twin rooms using a common toilet & hot

shower, as well as a lounge, dining area, balcony & kitchen. It is staffed with a chef, & contains all necessary equipment, including refrigerator & cooking facilities, but guests must bring their own food unless other arrangements have been made. Advance booking is necessary. *US$30/50 sgl/dbl per room, US$160 whole house.*

BUNDA MOUNTAIN AND DAM A large granite dome rising to 1,410m southwest of Lilongwe, scenic Bunda Mountain is the site of an important Chewa rain shrine (where traditional rain ceremonies are still performed twice annually) and home to rock-nesting raptors such as black eagle and augur buzzard. Below the mountain, Bunda Dam, part of the Bunda College of Agriculture, is fringed by marshes that regularly host crowned crane, pelicans and various waterfowl, herons and waders.

Getting there and away Follow the M1 south of Lilongwe for 10km, then turn right towards the Bunda College of Agriculture, the entrance gate of which lies about 20km from the M1. The dam lies 5km from the entrance gate; turn into the gate and ask directions from there. To get to the base of the mountain, continue past the gate for 500m, then turn left onto a track that follows the edge of a plantation forest, and then turn right at the first T-junction.

NKOMA MOUNTAIN East of the M1 between Lilongwe and Dedza, this Brachystegia-covered mountain rises to an elevation of 1,784m, and offers some rewarding walking and views over the surrounding plains. Near its base, the Nkoma Mission is known for its stunning Dutch Cape architecture. To reach it, follow the M1 south of Lilongwe for 35km, from where it is 16km to the mission grounds. Saturday is market day in Nkoma Town, so there's direct transport there from Dedza. On other days, at least one bus runs daily between Lilongwe and Nkoma. There is an inexpensive and clean resthouse in the mission grounds, and more basic local accommodation can be found in town, near to the market. You could also ask at the mission about the rustic hut that lies halfway up the mountain. The ascent from the mission to the rocky summit is quite steep (550m over 2km), and the staff will be able to point you along the right path.

apexrent-a-car

The only company that specialises in 4x4's

"We go the extra mile!"

Tel: 01 754610/612/615
Cell: 099 9950707, 088 8859776/65617
Fax: 01 751430
Email: apexcars@globemw.net

www.apexrentacarmw.com

KIBOKO TOWN HOTEL
LILONGWE

Tel: +265 (0)1751226
+265 (0)999838485

reservations@kiboko-safaris.com

Book your room online!

WWW.KIBOKOHOTEL.COM

KIBOKO
SAFARIS

WWW.KIBOKO-SAFARIS.COM

BOOK YOUR SAFARI ONLINE!

Tel: +265 (0)1751226
+265 (0)999838485

enquiries@kiboko-safaris.com

BAREFOOT SAFARI LODGE
LILONGWE

www.barefoot-safaris.com

Barefoot Safari Lodge and Camping Ground situated just 10kms from the centre of Malawi's capital, is ideally located for access to the airport and as a base for Safari's in Malawi and beyond. For more information email us or visit our website

Tel: +27 7346 29232   Email: enquiries@barefoot-safaris.com

117

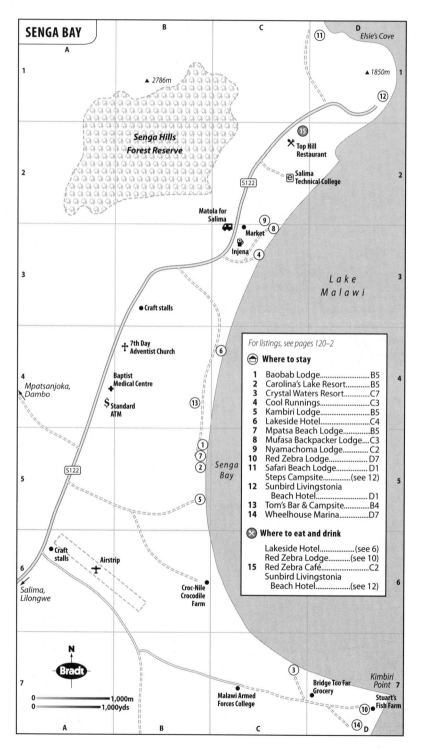

SENGA BAY

A B C D

Senga Hills Forest Reserve

▲ 2786m

▲ 1850m

Elsie's Cove

⑪

⑫

⑮
✕ Top Hill Restaurant

🏛 Salima Technical College

S122

Matola for Salima 🚐

Market

⑨

⑧

Injena 🛏

④

● Craft stalls

L a k e M a l a w i

✝ 7th Day Adventist Church

⑥

✚ Baptist Medical Centre

$ Standard ATM

⑬

Mpatsanjoka, Dambo

①

⑦

②

Senga Bay

S122

⑤

● Craft stalls

Airstrip ✚

↙ *Salima, Lilongwe*

Croc-Nile Crocodile Farm ●

For listings, see pages 120–2

⬡ **Where to stay**

1 Baobab Lodge.....................B5
2 Carolina's Lake Resort.........B5
3 Crystal Waters Resort..........C7
4 Cool Runnings.....................C3
5 Kambiri Lodge.....................B5
6 Lakeside Hotel.....................C4
7 Mpatsa Beach Lodge...........B5
8 Mufasa Backpacker Lodge....C3
9 Nyamachoma Lodge.............C2
10 Red Zebra Lodge.................D7
11 Safari Beach Lodge..............D1
   Steps Campsite..............(see 12)
12 Sunbird Livingstonia
   Beach Hotel.....................D1
13 Tom's Bar & Campsite..........B4
14 Wheelhouse Marina.............D7

⊗ **Where to eat and drink**

   Lakeside Hotel................(see 6)
   Red Zebra Lodge............(see 10)
15 Red Zebra Café...................C2
   Sunbird Livingstonia
   Beach Hotel.................(see 12)

N

Bradt

0 _____ 1,000m
0 _____ 1,000yds

③

Bridge Too Far Grocery ●

Kimbiri Point

Stuart's Fish Farm ●

Malawi Armed Forces College ●

⑩

⑭

6

Senga Bay and Surrounds

Senga Bay is the closest Lake Malawi resort to Lilongwe, situated 120km to the east by road, and as such it has become a popular weekend retreat and conference venue for residents of the capital. It also makes a useful first or last port of call for fly-in tourists to Malawi, with a dozen or more beach resorts that collectively cater to most tastes and budgets slung along the 8km of sandy beach that runs south from Senga village to Kambiri Point.

Senga Bay isn't as scenically dramatic as Cape Maclear or the northern lakeshore, and it's probably fair to say that the main reason for its popularity is simply its proximity to Lilongwe. Nevertheless, the long sandy beach is everything you could hope for, and the surrounding area is relatively rich in wildlife, making it a worthwhile place to settle into for a few days. The main points of interest are the Mpatsanjoka River (excellent birding and resident hippo), Lizard Island and the tropical fish and crocodile farms near Kambiri Point.

Socially, Senga Bay lacks the easy-going traveller scene associated with Nkhata Bay or Cape Maclear. Indeed, the larger lakeshore hotels at Senga now function primarily as conference venues, and although a handful of more low-key resorts still cater to families and motorised travellers, the backpacker-oriented camps that once scattered the village seem to be a thing of the past. Gone, too, are the persistent touts who once haunted Senga Bay, and with them, thankfully, a former reputation as something of a hotspot for crime against tourists.

Senga Bay is often referred to as Salima, the name of the nearest town and the administrative district in which it lies. All roads in and out of Senga Bay do in fact converge at Salima, which is a bustling junction town situated 20km west of the lake, and has many facilities absent from Senga Bay itself. For those with private transport, the private Kuti Wildlife Reserve on the outskirts of Salima is worth a look, as is the nearby Thuma Forest Reserve. Further south, Mua Mission (see page 136) offers fascinating insights into the cultures and tribes of the central region, and it is easily visited as a day trip from Senga Bay.

GETTING THERE AND AROUND

The gateway to Senga Bay is Salima, connected to Lilongwe by the surfaced M14; to Cape Maclear, Mangochi, Zomba and Blantyre by the M5 south, which branches from the M14 about 2km west of central Salima; and to Nkhotakota, Nkhata Bay and Mzuzu by the M5 north, which branches from the M14 another 5km to the west. The drive from Lilongwe to Senga Bay via Salima takes about 90 minutes in a private vehicle (allow two hours if traffic is heavy outside Lilongwe).

Using public transport, regular minibuses connect Lilongwe to Salima, costing US$2.50. Coming from elsewhere, there are plenty of direct minibuses from

Mangochi and Nkhotakota, and all buses along the M5 north and south will stop at Salima to drop and pick up passengers.

Once in Salima, a steady stream of minibuses and *matola* pick-up trucks run along the good surfaced road between the bus station and the market in Senga village for about US$1. From the market, it's about 2.5km along the tar road to the Livingstonia Beach Hotel and Steps Campsite, 3km to Safari Beach, about 1km to Cool Runnings and nearby lodges, and 1.5km to the Lakeside Hotel.

Resorts closer to Kambiri Point can be accessed from the tarred Salima–Senga Bay road by a series of signposted side roads. Most of these resorts lie about 3–5km from the main road. On foot, the best way to reach any of these resorts is to take transport from Salima towards Senga Bay, hop off at the appropriate turn-off, and then walk or hitch to the lakeshore. The alternative is to go through to Senga Bay, and continue along the tar road to the Sunbird Livingstonia Beach Hotel [118 D1], then to turn left onto the beach and follow it southwards. In terms of distance, there's not much in it, but walking along the beach will be tiring and slower, especially if you have a heavy pack.

 ## WHERE TO STAY *See map, page 118.*

UPMARKET
⌂ **Crystal Waters Resort** (55 rooms) m 088 8607311; e superior@globemw.net. Not in the same class as any of the hotels in this category, this large resort caters almost exclusively to the conference market & has an appropriately sterile aesthetic, characterised by manicured gardens & tiled interiors. It lies on a pleasant stretch of beach near Kambiri Point about 5.5km from the main road, & facilities include a swimming pool. *US$28 standard dbl with DSTV, fan, phone & en-suite bathroom with combination tub/shower, US$38 deluxe dbl with AC, US$50 dbl executive or family room, all rates B&B.*

⌂ **Kambiri Lodge** (50 rooms) ✆01 263352; e kambiri.manager@gmail.com; www. alexanderhotels.net. The best-value conference venue in Senga Bay, this isolated low-rise lodge has an attractive lakeside location 3km from the main road near the crocodile farm. The spacious & brightly decorated rooms have wood ceilings, dbl bed with net, fan, fridge, tea/coffee facilities, TV & a private balcony. Facilities include a business centre, good swimming beach, restaurant with buffet & 2 bars. *US$30/40 sgl/dbl, US$57 family room.*

⌂ **Safari Beach Lodge** (10 rooms) ✆01 263143/002; m 099 3265538; e info@ safaribeachlodge.net; www.safaribeachlodge.net. In Senga Hills Forest Reserve, this popular lodge is reached via a 900m dirt road signposted to the left outside the gates of the Livingstonia Beach Hotel. Upgraded in 2008, the lodge is aptly named,

with an aesthetic more akin to a bush lodge than a typical beach resort, & a wildly attractive setting on a wooded cliff overlooking the lakeshore. The 4 en-suite dbl rooms in the main building (a former forestry resthouse) have AC & TV, & are ideal for less mobile visitors. More characterful are the 4 dbl & 2 5-bed family en-suite chalets strung along a cliffside path, all with private balcony & lake views, but no AC or TV. A restaurant with indoor & outdoor seating serves burgers, fish & other continental dishes for US$6–10, & the serene platform bar nestled between boulders overlooking the lake is simply stunning. There is a large swimming pool, a private beach, some 10ha of forest to ramble through, snorkelling gear & canoes for exploring the lake, fragrant gardens & a fair amount of small wildlife in the immediate vicinity. The lodge can organise safaris into Thuma Forest Reserve (see page 125). *US$110/140 sgl/dbl, an additional US$55 pp for family chalets, all rates B&B.*

⌂ **Sunbird Livingstonia Beach Hotel** (35 rooms) ✆01 263222/444; e livingstonia@ sunbirdmalawi.com; www.sunbirdmalawi.com. The oldest hotel on Lake Malawi, built in the 1930s, was originally known as the Grand Beach Hotel, & its layout is instantly recognisable today from old photos in the public areas. Boasting compact flowering grounds, a beautiful private beach, comfortable rooms, & a whitewash & creosote exterior reminiscent of the Cape Dutch style, it is one of the country's most attractive lakeside hotels, though some character has been sacrificed as its core market has shifted from tourism to conferences. Facilities include watersports, gym, canoe- & snorkelling-equipment hire, a swimming pool & tennis court, & a good 1st-floor restaurant, & the front desk can arrange a variety of local excursions. The checklist of birds recorded in the grounds, available from reception, includes several interesting species. All rooms are en suite with DSTV, fridge, AC & private balcony. Non-guests can use the pool for US$2. *US$145/175 sgl/dbl, US$155/185 chalet, US$180/210 suite, US$230 family room (sleeps up to 4), all rates B&B.*

MODERATE

⌂ **Baobab Lodge** (14 rooms) ☏ 01 263495; m 099 9375574. This low-key lodge, in a small lakeshore compound next to Carolina's, has cramped but clean & well-maintained thatched rooms with DSTV, fan & en-suite shower & toilet. The attached restaurant offers the usual fare for US$4–6. Fair value. *US$19/22 sgl/dbl, US$38 family room, all rates B&B.*

⌂ **Carolina's Lake Resort** (27 rooms) ☏ 01 263320; m 088 8361635; e carolina.malawi@gmail.com. This is the oldest of a cluster of small lodges set on the lakeshore almost 3km from the main road (past the Lakeside Hotel), & it looks it. Some sock-pulling is required if it's to re-establish itself as one of the more appealing options in this range. *US$8 dorm bed, US$11/17.50 sgl/dbl using common shower, US$18/20.50 en-suite or chalet sgl/dbl, all rates B&B.*

⌂ **Lakeside Hotel** (17 rooms) ☏ 01 263400; e lakesidemalawi@yahoo.com. Situated 1km from the main road *en route* to Carolina's, this place is a bit short on character, but otherwise it's a great choice, with a fine lakeside location, an excellent Indian/Chinese restaurant, & reasonably priced modern rooms with tiled floor, fridge, DSTV, AC, fan & large en-suite bathroom. Rooms 1–6 have private balconies with clear lake views. *US$31/41 sgl/dbl, US$41 executive dbl, US$50 family room.*

⌂ **Mpatsa Beach Lodge** (16 rooms) m 099 3046980; e mpatsabeachlodge@gmail.com. This newer hotel next to Carolina's is very slick & modern from the outside. The rooms have good facilities including DSTV, AC & net, but they are also rather awkwardly shaped. Rates have come down thanks to devaluation, but they remain on the steep side. *US$41/50/56.50 sgl/dbl/trpl B&B.*

⌂ **Red Zebra Lodge** (8 rooms) ☏ 01 263064/165; m 099 9913630/3716276; e esther@lakemalawi.com; www.lakemalawi.com. This popular & well-established small lodge forms part of the tropical fish farm owned by cichlid specialist Stuart Grant. Accommodation is in spacious comfortable rooms with dbl bed, net, writing desk, tall wooden ceiling, DSTV, & whimsically piscine en-suite hot shower. There's a good restaurant, & boat excursions (including sundowner cruises) & other day trips range from US$70 to US$274 per party, & you can also take a tour of the fish farm. Very good value. *US$36/62 sgl/dbl B&B.*

BUDGET AND CAMPING

⌂ **Cool Runnings** (3 rooms) ☏ 01 263398; m 099 9915173; e coolrunnings@malawi.net. Presided over by an energetic owner-manager involved in several local community projects, this easy-going lakeside resort is in green gardens studded with impressive trees that attract a variety of bird species & harbour a resident genet family. Total accommodation & camping space is limited to around 20 people, so ring before you walk the 1km from the main road. Assuming you do find space, the food is among the best in Senga Bay, & the vibe is very relaxed & sociable. Facilities include kayaks & windsurfers to rent, & excursions to Lizard Island & other sites can be arranged. *US$5 pp camping, US$8 pp standing tent, US$10 pp 2-bed dorm in garden, US$35 dbl en-suite room with net, fan.*

⌂ **Mufasa Backpacker Lodge** (4 rooms, 2 dorms) m 099 6618114/088 8919098; e info@mufasamalawi.com; www.mufasamalawi.com. Recently taken over by Mufasa Backpackers, this is their newest property & was still undergoing improvements at the time of writing. Located about 1km from the main road, it is relatively accessible by foot & the rooms are simple, comfortable & clean. Ask for a room with AC, as they are the same price as those without. The beachfront restaurant serves the usual fare & makes for a relaxed place to watch the waves roll in. Kayaks are available for hire. *US$36 en-suite dbl, US$34 dbl/twin using common shower, US$8 dorm bed, US$4 pp camping, all rates exclude b/fast.*

⌂ **Nyamachoma Lodge** (9 rooms, 3 under construction) ☏ 01 263105; m 099 5879918. This simple locally owned lodge has a convenient location in Senga village, within easy walking distance of the beach, & the en-suite dbl or twin rooms with net & fan are more than adequate at the price. *US$14 dbl B&B.*

⚑ Steps Campsite For contact details see Sunbird Livingstonia Beach Hotel, page 120. This spacious site has a great position next to the Livingstonia Beach Hotel & is under the same management. Facilities include a bar with DSTV, laundry, hot showers, credit-card facilities & electricity. The bar serves snacks, & campers are welcome to eat at the neighbouring hotel, provided they adhere to the relatively formal dress code (no shorts or flip-flops). *US$5 pp camping.*

⌂ Wheelhouse Marina (9 rooms) ☎01 263139; m 099 9963345; e wheelhouse@africa-online.net. The closest accommodation to Kambiri Point is named after its trademark wheel-shaped stilted wood bar, which has long since collapsed. (It has since been replaced by a simple thatched bar on the sand.) Set in wonderful wooded grounds, this is an ideal spot for campers, & there are also several simply furnished self-catering cottages (often full so advance booking is necessary), as well as 6 chalets & a 7-bed dorm. Rates lower on w/days. *US$4 pp camping, US$7.50 pp dorm bed, US$50 en-suite dbl with fridge & kettle, US$150 large family cottage.*

SHOESTRING

⌂ Tom's Bar (4 rooms) ☎01 263017; m 099 5522504. On the opposite side of the road to the lake, halfway between the Lakeside Hotel & Carolina's, this is a friendly local set-up offering basic accommodation and a large campsite. *US$9.50 twin, US$1.50 pp camping.*

✗ WHERE TO EAT   *See map, page 118.*

Most of the lodges and hotels listed above serve adequate to good food. The following stand out, and are all open for breakfast, lunch and dinner:

✗ Lakeside Hotel The place to head for when you tire of the predictable fare served at most other hotels & restaurants, this is also the best option for vegetarians, with a dauntingly varied menu of Chinese, Indian & other dishes at around US$6.50. No alcohol served, but it's fine to bring your own.

✗ Red Zebra Café m 099 9212823. Affiliated to the eponymous lodge, this is the only stand-alone eatery of note in Senga Bay, set in large gardens about 1.5km from the village near the entrance to the Livingstonia Beach Hotel. You can sit indoors or on the shady balcony, & enjoy a variety of fish & other main dishes for around US$3–5, or snack on banana pancakes & waffles.

✗ Red Zebra Lodge The thatched bar/restaurant at this lodge near Kambiri Point has DSTV, serves a varied menu of continental meals in the US$5–7 range, & also has snacks for around US$2.50. Fish is the speciality.

✗ Sunbird Livingstonia Beach Hotel Ostensibly the most upmarket restaurant in the area, the 1st-floor restaurant here is open to non-residents of the hotel provided that they dress reasonably smartly. Mains are in the US$7–9 range; it also serves a selection of substantial snacks for around US$4, & you have the option of eating alfresco in the wooded gardens or around the pool.

SHOPPING

If you're cooking for yourself, Senga village has a basic market [118 C3], but you'd be better off stocking up in Salima, which has several supermarkets, including a People's Superette, and a large market spilling over with fresh produce. The **craft stalls** that once lined the main road through Senga Bay have relocated to two sites along the Salima road: the closest is 1km past the **central market** and the other one lies 3km further towards Salima at the junction for Red Zebra Lodge.

OTHER PRACTICALITIES

BANKING AND FOREIGN EXCHANGE Standard Bank operates the sole ATM in Senga Bay; it accepts Visa and is located on the main road south of the village.

Smarter hotels will usually exchange limited amounts of foreign currency for residents as well. There are several banks with forex facilities and ATMs accepting Visa in Salima, including National Bank (between the post office and police station), NBS and First Merchant Bank.

INTERNET The Sunbird Livingstonia Beach Hotel [118 D1] is a Wi-Fi hotspot and sells Skyband cards, and Safari Beach Lodge has Wi-Fi at a comparable rate. There is no bona fide internet café in Senga Bay itself; the closest is at Salima Technical College [118 C2], but the hours of operation and connection may be erratic. In Salima, your best bet is Tamamu Internet Café, which charges Mk5/min and sits opposite the Engen filling station on the Senga Bay road.

WHAT TO SEE AND DO

Lazing around on the beach, or perhaps hiring some watersports equipment, will be enough to occupy many people's time at Salima. There are, however, quite a few options for those who want to explore.

LIZARD ISLAND This small rocky island, which lies just off the beach in front of the Livingstonia Beach Hotel [118 D1], is known for its dense population of monitor lizards, and also as the breeding ground for large numbers of white-breasted cormorants. It's easy enough to organise a day trip to the island (inclusive of a fish barbecue) with guides in Senga Bay village, and several of the lodges also organise cruises there. Red Zebra Lodge [118 D7] operates the best and most comfortable boats in the area.

MPATSANJOKA DAMBO The lush and seasonally marshy Mpatsanjoka River runs in an arc north of Senga Hill, before emptying into Lake Malawi about 2km north of Senga Bay. The river is home to a small resident population of hippos, crocodiles and water monitors, and is also noted for its prolific birdlife. The simplest way to reach the hippo pools is to adopt a local child as your guide (ask around in the village), and you may find beach touts who will offer to escort you, though it's not too difficult to find your own way there. Take the path crossing the hill from the road to Safari Beach Lodge [118 D1], then descend to the beach and follow it through the reed fishing village northwards for a good 30 minutes to the river mouth. From here, it's about 3km upriver to the area where you're most likely to see hippos (you know you have gone far enough when you connect with a dirt road that bridges the river).

Seeing the hippos requires a little luck, and it would be wise to be very cautious, especially in the morning, since people have been killed by hippos in this area. If you don't see the hippos, you can be certain of seeing plenty of birds, including a good variety of hornbills, kingfishers, weavers and finches. It's a good place to see the colourful Boehm's bee-eater, as well as the secretive and very localised rufous-bellied heron. In the wet season, you could cross the bridge and continue north along the road for about 2km to an area of rice cultivation, where several unusual birds (including crowned crane and common pratincole) are regulars.

TROPICAL FISH FARM [118 D7] (\ *01 263165/407; www.lakemalawi.com; nominal entrance fee*) This farm near Kambiri Point was established by Stuart Grant to breed lake cichlids for the European tropical fish market, and as a holding point for fish being exported from the lake. A huge variety of cichlids can be seen in the tanks, including several rare species, and visitors are welcome.

CROC-NILE CROCODILE FARM [118 B6] (🕐 08.00–16.30; entrance US$1.50/1 adult/child) Situated about 3km from the main road along the same side road as Kambiri Lodge, this place breeds crocodiles mainly for their skins, and the breeding tanks hold specimens of all sizes.

SALIMA With a population estimated at 43,000, Salima, only 20km from Senga Bay, is the eighth-largest town in Malawi. The northern terminus of the original railway to Blantyre laid in the 1930s, it thrived commercially as a funnel for agricultural produce from the north until the 1970s, when the railway was extended past Lilongwe to Mchinji. Salima's strategic location at the junction of several trunk roads ensures that all visitors to Senga Bay pass through *en route*. Using public transport, you'll have to disembark at the bus station to pick up a *matola* to Senga Bay. The only motivations for exploring this rather nondescript and sprawling town beyond the bus station are practical: it has several banks, a post office, a bustling market, internet and a couple of well-stocked supermarkets.

⌂ WHERE TO STAY

⌂ **Mwambiya Lodge** 📞 01 262314; m 099 9647799; e mwambiyalodges@gmail.com. This local guesthouse, 1km down the Senga Bay road, has simple en-suite rooms with hot water, bed nets & fan. It's probably the best place in town, but their motto of 'why be anywhere else?' might be a bit of a stretch. The attached restaurant/bar serves Malawian staples for around US$3. If you want to look further, a few adequate resthouses are dotted around the bus station as well. *US$8/11.50 sgl/dbl B&B.*

KUTI WILDLIFE RESERVE (📞 021 19151256; m 099 3800289; kuti.malawi@gmail.com; www.kuti-malawi.org; entrance US$1.50 for a vehicle, US$1.50/1 adult/child) This 3,000ha community-owned reserve protects an area of grassy Brachystegia woodland that has been restocked with game after having been decommissioned as a government cattle ranch in the 1990s. Operated in partnership with the Lilongwe Wildlife Centre, the main stakeholders in the reserve are the 11 villages that border the former ranch, housing a total of around 30,000 people. Some 50% of revenues raised by entrance and other fees helps fund community projects, ranging from the rehabilitation of boreholes and clinics to tree planting and seedling production. The park also houses an environmental education centre for local schoolchildren, and it is hoped that once wildlife volumes increase, excess animals can also be sold. These projects are volunteer-supported, and there are ongoing placements available for interested individuals or groups.

The most striking area in Kuti is a large swamp-like lake covered in water lilies and papyrus. Local fishermen use small balsa-wood coracles to punt through the marshland and the area is teeming with birds. The park also supports an increasingly varied selection of mammals. Naturally occurring species such as greater kudu, duiker, bushbuck, genet, civet and bushpig have fared well since the park was protected, while the likes of giraffe, zebra, nyala, sable, impala and warthog have been introduced and now roam freely within the reserve. Kuti is also the primary destination for rehabilitated animals from the Lilongwe Wildlife Centre that are ready for release into the wild. Game viewing is best during the dry season, especially over July–September.

Kuti lies about 8km from Salima by road and can easily be accessed in a private vehicle, though a 4x4 may be required after rain. The entrance, reached via a 4km dirt road, is signposted along the north side of the M14 to Lilongwe some 4km west of the main junction with the M5 South and about 2km east of the junction with the M5 North. Those taking public transport can be dropped off at the Kuti turn-off and walk the remaining 4km, or taxis and bicycle taxis are readily available in Salima. There are two campsites with ablutions and barbecue facilities, and self-catering accommodation is available at Senga Camp, 2km past the entrance gate. Camping costs US$10 per person, and there are four five-bed A-frame huts available at US$20/70 per person/per unit. Additionally, six-person private villas with full kitchen are available at US$100–120, while new waterfront chalets overlooking the lake are currently under construction. Activities include day and night game drives, game walks and cycling, and all can be either self-guided or accompanied.

THUMA FOREST RESERVE (\ *01 972649;* e *thuma@wag-malawi.org; www.wag-malawi.org; entrance US$2/5 Malawians/foreigners plus US$5 per car*) This 197km² forest reserve, gazetted in 1926, lies due east of Lilongwe, where it spans a stretch of the Rift Valley Escarpment rising from a basal altitude of 575m to the 1,564m peak of Thuma Mountain. Bounded by the Lilongwe River to the north and the Linthipe River to the south, it protects a wide variety of habitats, including Brachystegia woodland, bamboo forest and evergreen forest, and it forms the most northerly component in a complex of protected areas stretching south to Mua-Livulezi. Until recently, Thuma had seen little scientific exploration and even less tourist development, and poaching was a major problem. Then, in 1996, conservation management was handed over to a small NGO called the Wildlife Action Group (WAG), which has managed to control poaching with the co-operation of local villagers, making Thuma something of a flagship reserve for its linked goals of protecting some of Malawi's lesser-known wilderness areas and opening them up to revenue-generating tourism.

Characterised by rugged escarpment scenery and an untrammelled wilderness atmosphere, Thuma offers the opportunity to track a wide variety of large mammals on foot. Some 40-odd large mammal species have been recorded, including significant populations of elephant and buffalo, both on the increase according to data collected in 2007, as well as leopard, spotted hyena, baboon, vervet monkey, bushbuck, greater kudu, klipspringer, Sharpe's grysbok, common duiker and various small predators. The bird checklist, though still incomplete, includes more than 170 species, including the first Malawian record for Natal francolin. There's plenty more information about the reserve, including full checklists, on the website listed above.

Tourist development remains very low key, but is ideal for genuine outdoor enthusiasts. The attractive campsite costs US$5 per person and it has basic cooking, shower and toilet facilities, but visitors must bring their own camping equipment, food and drinks. Unguided walking is forbidden, owing to the presence of elephant and buffalo, but guided hikes are available at US$10 per person.

Getting there and away From Salima, follow the M14 towards Lilongwe for 6.5km past the junction with the M5 to Nkhotakota, and the turn-off to Thuma Forest Reserve is signposted to the left shortly before a roadside baobab tree (if you pass an electric power station on the right, you've missed the turn-off). Follow this road for 4.5km, crossing the Lilongwe River *en route*, then turn right into the village of Nkangayawala, and after another 6.5km you'll see another baobab to the right with a sign for Thuma painted on it. Turn right here, and you'll enter the forest reserve after 500m and reach the campsite after another 10km.

DEDZA

For listings, see pages 128-9

Where to stay
1 Dedza Pottery Lodge
2 Golden Dish Catering & Resthouse
3 Lumbili Resthouse
4 Mapiri Country Golf Lodge
5 Panjira Lodge
6 Rainbow Resthouse

Where to eat and drink
7 Boiz Club
Dedza Coffee Shop (see 1)
Panjira Lodge (see 5)
Mapiri Country Golf Lodge (see 4)

Dedza Mountain

Chongoni Forest Reserve

Lilongwe

Sawmill

Daiman's Stall
Mpira Showroom
Dedza Handmade Art Gallery

Dedza Teacher Development Centre

Catholic church

Golf course (closed)

Energem

Hospital
Market
Baker's Pride
Woza Woza Bar

Step by Step Restaurant
Police block
Puma

Mozambique

Blantyre

M1

500m
500yds

Central Dedza

Boma (1947)
Forestry office

Africa Muslim Centre
Police
Office block
Bus station
Stadium
AY Business Centre
CCAP church
Frotia Entertainment Centre
Halaal Restaurant
Mosque
Malawi Savings
Standard
Metro Cash 'n' Carry

Asangalale Rest House
Raheel Superette
NBS Total
Chipiku Stores FMB

Njati

200m
200yds

126

7

Dedza and Surrounds

Dedza is a moderately substantial town that runs along a short bypass loop 85km southeast of Lilongwe and 230km north of Blantyre. It's a pleasant but inherently unremarkable place, best known within Malawi for its relatively cool highland climate and as the home of Dedza Pottery. The surrounding countryside, by contrast, is of great scenic interest, characterised as it is by massive granite inselbergs that erupt above the Rift Valley Escarpment, many of which are protected within the Dedza Mountain, Chongoni and Mua-Livulezi forest reserves.

The area around Dedza holds considerable allure for walkers, birdwatchers and other outdoor enthusiasts. But it is especially noteworthy for its wealth of archaeological and cultural sites. Foremost among these is the little-known Chongoni Rock Art Area, inscribed as Malawi's first terrestrial UNESCO World Heritage Site in 2006, and readily explored from Dedza Town. Also of interest is the cultural tourism programme at Mpalale, 10km outside Dedza, and the Mua Mission's superb KuNgoni Centre for Arts and Culture, nestled at the escarpment base about 20km further east as the crow flies.

DEDZA

The eponymous capital of Dedza District is a neat and relaxed town of around 20,000 people, situated about 1km northeast of the M1 between Lilongwe and Blantyre, and not much further from the border with Mozambique. It is the highest town in Malawi, set at an altitude of 1,590m at the southern foot of Dedza Mountain, and the climate is correspondingly chilly, especially in the early morning and evening during the winter months of June to August. The town is mainly of interest as a base for exploring the mountains, forests and rock-art sites that dot the surrounding countryside.

Dedza straddles a 5km surfaced loop road running northeast of the M1. The town centre starts about 3km along this loop road coming from the direction of Lilongwe, while the hospital and main market lie another 1km south towards Blantyre. The north end of the town centre boasts a few minor architectural landmarks, ranging from a colonial-era boma built in 1947 to the well-tended bus station. Further out of town, Dedza Pottery is the best known of several worthwhile handicraft enterprises that line the road towards the WICO Sawmill.

GETTING THERE AND AWAY Dedza lies about 85km southeast of Lilongwe along the surfaced M1. This is the most direct route between Malawi's two largest cities, so it carries a relatively heavy traffic flow. In a private vehicle, the drive should take 60–90 minutes, depending greatly on traffic conditions as you leave Lilongwe. For people driving on towards Lake Malawi National Park, it's worth noting that the once-tortuous S127, which branches east from the M1 at Masasa about 20km south of Dedza, is now surfaced and undulates its way down the escarpment for 30km to Golomoti, from where a new surfaced extension of the S127 connects with the M10 to Monkey Bay.

All buses that travel between Lilongwe and Blantyre on the M1 stop at Dedza, express buses included. The bus journey from Lilongwe to Dedza takes less than two hours. Direct minibuses to Dedza leave regularly from in front of the bus station in Lilongwe and cost Mk1000. If you're heading between Dedza and Blantyre, the main town you'll pass through on the M1 is the vegetable growers' market town of Ntcheu. All you need to know about Ntcheu is that it is on the Mozambican border, it's thoroughly dull and scruffy, it has several resthouses, a good supermarket and a couple of banks, and you're unlikely to get stuck there unless you want to.

TOURIST INFORMATION Dedza Pottery and Panjira Lodge are both helpful when it comes to local information, and they can help arrange guided and/or motorised day trips to the Chongoni Rock Art Area. You could also talk to the forestry office opposite the boma. A highly informative website (*www.visitdedza.com*) is maintained by the Norwich-Dedza Partnership, a British charity that supports various education, health, agriculture, tourism development and public-sector projects by providing volunteer workers, supplying computers and other materials, and offering small-scale funding.

WHERE TO STAY *See map, page 126.*
Moderate
🏠 **Dedza Pottery Lodge** (6 rooms) \01 223069/131; m 0888 853425; e dedzapottery@ africa-online.net; www.nyasalodges.com. Situated

1.4km along the Chongoni road, which branches north from the tarred loop road about 250m northeast of the junction with the M1, Dedza Pottery has long hosted the finest restaurant in this

DIAMPWE BRIDGE

When travelling between Dedza and Lilongwe, look out for the Diampwe Bridge, the oldest such structure in Malawi. It crosses the Diampwe River about 40km out of Lilongwe, about halfway between the villages of Mtenthele and Linthipe. The original bridge was built in 1923 and it was once a vital link to Blantyre and points further south for the growing outpost of Lilongwe. An arched brick structure, it was restored as a footbridge in 1991, in tribute to a new public awareness of heritage in Malawi.

If you stop here, reflect on the account of Colonel Colville, who 'marched to the point where the Diampwe river crosses the Dedza–Lilongwe high road' in late 1908, and described his wildlife encounters there in his 1911 publication *1,000 Miles in a Machilla*:

> While at breakfast, we were suddenly told that elephants were in sight, and, running up to the top of a small hill … we saw a large herd about two miles off walking quietly along …. There were about 50 in all, mostly cows and calves, with at least two fine old bulls amongst them, one enormous looking beast towering above the others. Our camp that evening was well situated on high ground overlooking the Diampwe river; here a fair-sized stream, with low marshy banks… we saw hartebeest and sable; eland were reported, and reedbuck we could see from our tent, so that I think we should have done well to have remained two or three days in the neighbourhood; but push on was the order.

part of Malawi, & it now offers accommodation to a similar standard. The smart & spacious superior rooms have wheelchair ramps, powerful en-suite hot shower, DSTV, Globe Wi-Fi, minibar, safe, nets, electric mosquito killers, heaters, fans, private balcony with seating, & complimentary tea/coffee. The adjacent pottery shop sells useful & colourful mementos of Malawi. It also offers pottery courses, & arranges guided day trips to the various rock-art sites in the vicinity for US$19/26 sgl/dbl (your vehicle) or US$57/66 (their vehicle). Guided walks on Dedza Mountain are available for around US$7–15. *US$32/44/48 sgl/dbl/trpl, US$40/54/60 superior sgl/dbl/trpl, US$4 pp camping, all rates exclude b/fast.*

🏠 **Mapiri Country Golf Lodge** (10 rooms) \01 223411/422/401; m 088 8724348; e mapirilodge@gmail.com. Tucked away on wooded grounds behind the (currently defunct) golf course, this trim, newly renovated lodge is short on golf but long on comfort. The en-suite rooms are bright & airy & feature dbl beds, AC, large nets, DSTV, fridge, coffee/tea facilities, writing desk & phone. Suites have a full kitchen & lounge area. The inviting restaurant/bar serves a good variety of continental & Malawian mains, & makes for a relaxed place to catch up on the latest international football. *US$34/43 standard sgl/dbl, US$42/53 deluxe sgl/dbl, US$59/68 suite sgl/dbl, all rates B&B.*

🏠 **Panjira Lodge** (14 rooms) \01 223822; m 099 5271797; e panjira@yahoo.com. This well-organised local lodge lies in a large green compound on the outskirts of the town centre, about 10mins' walk from the bus station past the boma. The spacious standard rooms come with

a dbl bed, net & en-suite hot shower, & superior rooms also have DTSV, but are otherwise not significantly better value than standard rooms. The restaurant is good, the staff are a helpful source of information about local rock-art sites, & they can also arrange transport with local drivers at negotiable rates. *US$25/35 standard sgl/dbl, US$30/46 superior sgl/dbl, all rates B&B.*

Budget
🏠 **Rainbow Resthouse** (31 rooms) \01 223062. Comfortably the pick of the cheap local lodges scattered around the town centre, this long-serving resthouse offers the choice of budget rooms with en-suite facilities, nets & cold showers at the back of the large compound, or smarter & larger superior dbls with en-suite hot showers & DSTV in the front. An acceptable restaurant & popular bar are attached. Good value. *US$6.50/9.50 sgl/twin, US$16 superior dbl, all rates exclude b/fast.*

Shoestring
🏠 **Golden Dish Catering & Resthouse** (17 rooms) \01 900470; m 099 9000006. This offers clean but basic accommodation with nets & cold showers. The on-site nightclub is potentially noisy at w/ends. A restaurant serves adequate meals in the US$2–3 range. *US$3.25/5/6.25 sgl/dbl/trpl, US$9.50 en-suite dbl/trpl.*

🏠 **Lumbili Resthouse** (6 rooms) m 099 5796967. The rooms here are nothing special, but they are very cheap & the large green compound has a quiet but convenient location opposite the CCAP church. *US$2.50 sgl.*

✖ **WHERE TO EAT AND DRINK** *See map, page 126.*

🍸 **Boiz Club** ⊕ 12.00–late daily. This popular sports bar has been under the same management for longer than a decade. Drinks are affordable & there's DSTV, a pool table & a dartboard. Packet snacks available.

✖ **Dedza Coffee Shop** \01 223069/131; m 0888 853425; ⊕ 06.00–22.00 daily. Even if you don't stay at Dedza Pottery, it's well worth the walk out of town to enjoy a lazy afternoon tea at the associated coffee shop. Sit indoors or under a thatched gazebo to sample the excellent filter coffee, lemonade, lasagne, quiches, scones or their trademark cheesecake. There's also a varied selection of mains at around US$6–7.

✖ **Mapiri Country Golf Lodge** \01 223411/422/401; m 088 8724348; ⊕ 06.00–22.00 daily. The attractive new restaurant & bar at Mapiri boasts a broad menu of chicken, steaks, fish, pizza & pasta in the US$4–6 range. Major sporting events are shown on a flat-screen TV in the comfortable, African-inspired lounge.

✖ **Panjira Lodge** \01 223822 m 099 5271797; ⊕ 07.00–22.00 daily. Among the better choices in the town centre, Panjira Lodge offers a reasonably varied menu of tasty meat, chicken & vegetarian dishes in the US$4–5 range, but what's available on a given day is typically a bit more limited.

SHOPPING If you are hiking in the area, best stock up in Lilongwe. Failing that, the **Metro Cash 'n' Carry** both stock packaged goods, as does the **Raheel Superette** opposite. There is a good **market** at the south end of the town centre, and fresh bread is available from the **Baker's Pride**, just south of the market.

OTHER PRACTICALITIES
Banks and foreign exchange The **NBS, Standard Bank** and **FMB** on the main road all have ATMs taking Visa cards, and the Standard Bank also accepts MasterCard and Maestro. There are no dedicated forex bureaux, but the banks can change hard currency cash at bank rates.

Crafts Dedza is known for its varied range of craft shops and stalls, all of which lie out of town along the left side of the Chongoni road. Best known is **Dedza Pottery** (✆ *01 223069/131;* ⏱ *07.30–18.00 daily*), which specialises in handcrafted ceramic tableware, figurines and other statues, and also stocks a very good range of books and maps about Malawi. Closer to town, **Daiman's Stall** (m *099 5244523;* ⏱ *07.30–18.00 daily*) sells detailed wooden models of cars and bicycles, often with moving parts, as well as masks and jewellery. The **Mpira Showroom** (✆ *01 11622553;* ⏱ *07.30–16.00 daily*) next door is owned by a carver trained at the Mua Mission, and it sells a variety of paintings, woodcarvings and wooden tableware. Finally, the commendable **Dedza Handmade Art Gallery** (m *099 3243674;* e *dedza.hmag@gmail.com; www.dedzahandmadeart.com;* ⏱ *06.00–18.00 Mon–Sat, 13.30–18.00 Sun*) at the base of the road sells homemade paintings, bags, jewellery, journals, Malawi-style toy dolls and numerous items made from recycled paper (including the figurines!).

Internet In the town centre, your best bet is the **AY Business Café** (m *099 3070061;* ⏱ *06.00–20.00 Mon–Sat, 12.00–17.00 Sun*) which charges Mk5 per minute for fast broadband access. Heading out of town towards Dedza Pottery, the **Dedza Teacher Development Centre** (✆ *01 223368;* ⏱ *07.30–16.30 Mon–Fri, 09.00–14.00 Sat*) has a fast connection on newer computers for Mk5 per minute.

Maps If you plan on exploring on foot, you'd do well to get hold of the 1:50,000 map of Dedza (sheet 1434A4) for Dedza Mountain and Chongoni Forest Reserve. This can usually be bought at the map sales offices in Lilongwe or Blantyre. If it's not available, the Monkey Bay map (sheet 7) in the Malawi 1:250,000 series is also useful.

WHAT TO SEE AND DO
Dedza Mountain This impressive mountain, its upper slopes protected within the Dedza Mountain Forest Reserve, rises to 2,198m on the northern outskirts of Dedza Town. The mountain is largely covered in plantation forest, but there are still remnant patches of evergreen and riverine forest on the upper slopes, supporting typical forest animals such as samango monkey, bushpig, baboon and even leopard. The indigenous forest is also notable for birds and epiphytic orchids, while more open areas are rich in wild flowers after the rains.

The mountain can be climbed as a day trip from town, starting from behind Mapiri Country Golf Lodge and using any of several converging and diverging routes that head in the rough direction of the (frequently visible) communications antennae on the upper slopes. It takes two–three hours to reach the communications antennae on foot, or you can drive along a reasonably well-maintained road. The guards who look after the antennae can give you directions to good vantage points, offering views as far as Lake Malawi on clear days. To reach the summit from here, you need to continue for another 3km along the ridge. Guided walks can also be organised through Dedza Pottery.

Mpalale village Situated about 11km from the town centre off the road between Dedza Pottery and the junction for the Chongoni Forest College, this small village bordering Chongoni Forest Reserve has established a community-tourism programme offering an opportunity to engage with traditional Chewa culture. Best booked two days in advance (and reconfirmed the morning of), a lively programme of traditional dances and songs includes the festive Chimtali and funereal Gule Wamkulu, the latter boasting a strong link to some of the figures depicted at rock-art sites around Dedza, as well as the oddball Mganda, with its clear colonial military influences. The programme costs US$16 for the first six people and US$2 for each additional person, and you can ring through a booking to the Mpalale headman (m *099 9589639*), Chembekezo (m *099 9684276*) or Caiphas (m *088 8350193*). Proceeds are used towards projects and improvements in Mpalale.

Bembeke Cathedral Established as a Catholic sanatorium in 1903, Bembeke became a White Fathers mission station in 1910, and the impressive face-brick church there was built by Fr Jean-Louis Lesueur over 1915–19. Its most notable feature is the powerful frescoes that adorn the interior, which depict typical religious scenes with African protagonists, and were by the local artist Michael Kapalamula. The cathedral is open to casual visitors when there are no services, or you can ring ↖099 9291914 to arrange a guided tour in advance. To get to the cathedral, follow the M1 southeast of Dedza for 7km, then turn left at Mwalawankhondo trading centre and follow the dirt road for 7km via Kanchito.

CHONGONI ROCK ART AREA

Stretching northwest of Dedza for about 25km, the Chongoni Rock Art Area is one of Malawi's most neglected national treasures, containing 127 rock faces and shelters that represent an ancient painting tradition dating back at least 2,000 years. Despite being inscribed as the country's second UNESCO World Heritage Site (the other being Lake Malawi National Park) in 2006, the area has seen little formal tourist development. Despite this lack of development, several panels can still be visited with reasonable ease by interested travellers, most notably those at Chencherere, Namzeze and Mphunzi.

At the core of the 126km^2 UNESCO-inscribed rock-art area, the Chongoni Forest Reserve lies immediately east of the M1 north of Dedza, and is also the site of the Chongoni Forestry College and associated Kazela Forestry Resthouse. Two-thirds of the painted panels lie within the forest reserve, including Chencherere and Namzeze, but the rock-art area also extends southwest from the M1 as far as Mphunzi Mountain, where a cluster of eight panels forms the most worthwhile goal in the area for those with time to visit one site only.

Rock paintings aside, this is a very scenic part of Malawi, studded with dozens of massive granite inselbergs, and ideal for casual rambling, whether you're based in Dedza Town or the resthouse at Chongoni Forestry College. The forest reserve supports a mixture of plantation forest and Brachystegia woodland, as well as small patches of evergreen forest on some of the hills. Baboon, vervet monkey, rock hyrax, grey duiker and klipspringer are quite common, leopard and samango monkey are

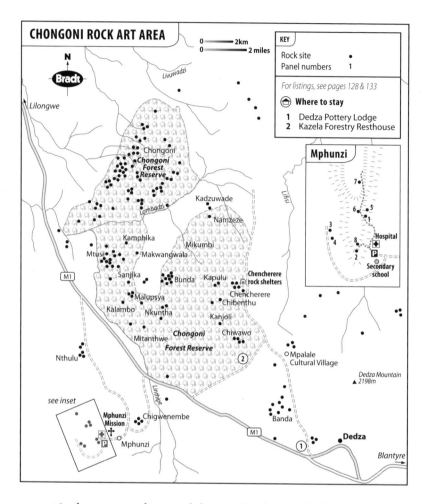

CHONGONI ROCK ART AREA

KEY

Rock site •
Panel numbers 1

For listings, see pages 128 & 133

Where to stay
1 Dedza Pottery Lodge
2 Kazela Forestry Resthouse

Mphunzi

present in the evergreen forest, and the varied avifauna includes a similar range of Brachystegia-associated species as Dzalanyama, as well as a limited selection of forest species.

GETTING THERE AND AWAY There are two main routes to Chongoni Forest Reserve. Coming from Dedza, the most straightforward option is the dirt road past Dedza Pottery towards Linthipe trading centre. The signposted turn-off to the Forestry College is about 10km past Dedza Pottery, and it's another 1.5km to the resthouse. For motorists coming from Lilongwe, the most direct approach to Chongoni is from the M1, following a dirt road signposted 'Forestry College and National Monument' on the east side of the road 9km northwest of Dedza. It's 5.5km from the junction to the resthouse. Chencherere National Monument stands on the left side of the Linthipe road another 4km north of the junction for the Forestry College. Namzeze is almost impossible to find without a guide; the junction from the Linthipe road is about 2km north of Chencherere and from there it's another 30-minute drive and 15-minute walk to the unsignposted shelter. There is no public transport on any of these roads (apart from the M1).

Mphunzi falls outside the forest reserve, about 8km southwest of the M1. It can be reached directly from Dedza by following the M1 towards Lilongwe for 13km, then taking an unsignposted dirt road to the left. The junction is easy enough to locate next to a minibus stage 4.3km northwest of the turn-off to Chongoni Forestry College and 500m past 'Linthipe 3 Bridge' (the first bridge you'll cross coming from Dedza). Follow the dirt road for 5.8km, with Mphunzi Mountain and its quartet of granite domes clearly visible ahead, until you reach a T-junction, where you need to turn left. After 600m, turn right into Mphunzi trading centre at the signpost for Mphunzi Secondary School, then after another 400m take the fork to the right. It's 500m from here to the old mission church and another 800m to the small Mphunzi Hospital at the eastern base of the mountain, where a faded metal signboard has a diagrammatic map of the mountain and rock-art sites. The dirt road to Mphunzi is usually in fair shape and most vehicles will get through without a problem. There is no formal public transport to the trading centre, but you could walk there from the M1 in under two hours, or pick up a bicycle-taxi at the junction. Alternatively, the occasional *matola* vehicle runs from the junction on the M1 to the trading centre, which is only 15 minutes' walk from the eastern base of the mountain. Another option is to arrange a car and driver from Dedza Town, either through Dedza Pottery or Panjira Lodge.

⌂ WHERE TO STAY *See map, opposite.*

⌂ **Kazela Forestry Resthouse** (8 rooms) m 099 9232434/088 1598424. Part of the Chongoni Forestry College, this refurbished resthouse is good value and makes for a great rural alternative to Dedza itself. It stands in a patch of Brachystegia woodland at the base of the impressive granite dome of Chiwawa Hill. There are standard & en-suite twins & dbls, the latter complete with hot bath, heater, dressing table & mirror. You can also camp in the resthouse compound. Facilities include a well-equipped kitchen, a communal dining room & lounge, & Ed's Bar, which has DSTV & cold beers, & prepares simple meals for around US$3–4. It does occasionally fill up with forestry people, so ring ahead before you head out here. *US$6.50 sgl, US$11/13 en-suite twin/dbl, all rates exclude b/fast.*

WHAT TO SEE AND DO

Chencherere National Monument At least four painted shelters are dotted around this small but steep hill in the Chongoni Forest Reserve. The most important is Mwana wa Chencherere (literally 'Child of Chencherere') II, set in a southwest-facing recess beneath a large granite boulder next to the much larger main hill. The shelter's existence was first reported in the 1930s, and when it was subjected to formal archaeological studies in the 1970s, it ranked among the finest examples anywhere of the late white style, especially rich in the spreadeagled anthropomorphic figures associated with the *nyau* society. Today, sadly, the defaced paintings are in a terrible state, obscured beneath more recent half-witted scrawling of the 'Fred was here' variety, and rock-art enthusiasts will find the sites at Namzeze and Mphunzi far more rewarding.

Namzeze Recently cleared of scrub and formally considered open to tourists, the solitary rock panel at Namzeze is reputedly the best single example of late white paintings within the forest reserve now that Chencherere has been defaced, but it is unsignposted, almost impossible to locate without a guide, and lacks the combined stylistic variety of the eight Mphunzi shelters. The figures here are zoomorphic and depict a menagerie of real and fantastic mammals (as well as one bird), and are mostly side-on rather than spreadeagled. Unless this is signposted by the time you reach the Dedza area, you will need a guide to find it.

Mphunzi The most rewarding of the three Chongoni rock-art sites open to tourists is Mphunzi Mountain, where eight different panels – most undemanding to reach – are scattered around the base of a steep and distinctively shaped mountain capped by four granite domes. Mphunzi is of more recent historic interest, too: Dr Livingstone once set camp at the mountain's western base, while the eastern base was chosen as the site of a Dutch Reformed Church mission in 1903, and still houses a rundown brick-face church built in the early 20th century. Rock paintings aside, Mphunzi makes for a lovely excursion from Dedza, set amid a dramatic boulderscape that supports a wealth of wild flowers and birds, plentiful baboons, and a relict population of spotted hyenas that emerge from the caves after dark.

Panels 1, 2 and 5–8 are all on the eastern slopes of Mphunzi and are accessible on foot from the car park. There are no formal guides, but you should have no problem finding a volunteer to show you the sites (known locally as 'Akafula writing') for a tip. Panels 2 and 8, situated at the base of the mountain no more than five minutes' walk from the hospital, are easily located along a short footpath directly behind the signpost. Panel 2 consists of a few red schematic paintings while Panel 8 has only late white paintings, with the dominant figure being a large elephant, but both panels are rather faded and significantly inferior to the others at Mphunzi.

BACKGROUND TO THE CHONGONI ROCK ART

The rock art of Chongoni falls into two distinct schools. The more ancient of these comprises schematic paintings executed in red oxide pigments and usually associated with large boulders and shelters suitable for habitation. These red schematic paintings are attributed to the Akafula hunter-gatherers who lived here for at least two millennia prior to the arrival of the Bantu-speaking precursors of the Chewa about 500 years ago. The Akafula were related to the Pygmoid people known elsewhere in Africa as Batwa and Bushmen, and their slight build and short stature is alluded to in the Chewa nickname Mwandionera Pati (literally 'Where did you first see me?'). Akafula men, evidently sensitive about their height, habitually directed this question at a taller by-passer, and if the interrogator felt that the answer implied he was too short to be seen from a distance, he would fire a poison arrow at the insulter.

The red oxide paint used by the Akafula was similar to that employed by the renowned Bushmen artists whose work adorns the uKhahlamba-Drakensberg and many other rock-art sites south of the Zambezi. However, where the more prolific southern rock art mostly comprises naturalistic images of animals, people and mythic creatures, the panels at Chongoni are dominated by schematic geometric designs and patterns. The precise intent behind these abstract images died out with its creators, but it is likely that they represent climatic and celestial phenomena and were linked to rainmaking and/or fertility cults. Overall, these red schematic paintings are less engaging to the uninitiated than their more naturalistic southern counterparts, but Chongoni is probably the largest cluster in this style anywhere in Africa.

The more modern school comprises the so-called late white paintings, which are less finely executed and more naturalistic than the red schematics they frequently overlay. The late whites typically depict animals or zoomorphic figures, often in a spreadeagled pose. Reptiles are strongly favoured, and while many figures quite clearly show a real animal, others are more fantastic and presumably represent a legendary creature. Painted in clay, the late whites are associated with

The better-preserved Panels 1 and 5 also lie at the base of the mountain, a few hundred metres further north, and are reasonably easy to find along a footpath that skirts the field closest to the mountain then forks left to a cluster of large boulders. Panel 1 consists of several very detailed and well-preserved red schematic paintings, while Panel 5, just around the corner, consists of a single tall painting, partially water-damaged and somewhat schematic, which most probably represents a giraffe. About 10m to the right of this, a set of well-preserved zoomorphic figures can be seen at head height. Panel 6, another poorly preserved red schematic, is on the slopes above this and difficult to locate without a guide.

Somewhat less accessible but emphatically worth the effort, Panel 7 is possibly the most interesting set of paintings anywhere in the World Heritage Site. It consists of a large overhang a steep 20–30 minutes' walk uphill of Panel 5, and would be nigh impossible to find without a guide. The black-and-white zoomorphic figures here are very well preserved and mostly reptilian in form – chameleons, other lizards and crocodiles – though there are also some more humanlike creatures, and some are spotted. The views from this shelter encompass layers of mountains running deep into Mozambique, and you are almost certain to see baboons on the way.

the agriculturalist Chewa, and they form part of a living tradition insofar as the most recent ones date to the early 20th century and the sites are still used by the local Chewa for initiation and rainmaking rituals.

Despite the contrast in style, the red schematic and late white paintings evidently form a cultural continuum. The Chewa lived alongside the Akafula until the mid 19th century, and openly admit to having learned their rainmaking traditions from the skilful hunter-gatherers who they eventually displaced entirely. The Chewa rainmakers living around Chongoni are mostly women, and many of the zoomorphic paintings are secret symbols linked to female initiation ceremonies. The more anthropomorphic figures observed in some shelters are masked characters associated with the clandestine *nyau* society of masked funereal dancers, which went underground during the 19th and early 20th centuries in response to the incursion of the Ngoni invaders, Christian missions and colonial government. Indeed, masked figures similar to those seen in the rock paintings still dance in traditional ceremonies around Chongoni today, creating a dynamic link between the rock art of Chongoni and the dancing performances given by the cultural tourism programme at the bordering village of Mpalale.

This sense of continuity played a large role in the inscription of Chongoni as a UNESCO World Heritage Site, as noted in the committee's document of nomination in 2006:

> The dense and extensive collection of rock art shelters reflects a remarkable persistence of cultural traditions over many centuries ... in the Chewa agricultural society. The strong association between the rock art images and contemporary traditions of initiation and of the nyau secret society, and the extensive evidence for those traditions within the painted images over many centuries, together make the Chongoni landscape a powerful force in Chewa society and a significant place for the whole of southern Africa.

Also exceptionally well preserved, Panels 3 and 4 are at the western base of Mphunzi, and can be approached within 200m by road. To reach them from the hospital grounds, take the road back towards the church for about 300m, then turn right. Follow this road, which skirts the southern base of the mountain, through a small village of attractively painted houses for 1.7km, until you see a pair of conspicuous boulders lying about 200m apart on your right. The first of these is Panel 4, said to be a site where Livingstone once set camp, and also known as the Bull Site, though most of the zoomorphic white figures here looked more reptilian than bovine to this observer. The next shelter houses the superb Panel 3, where one hollow depicts a 1.2m-high lizard and snake alongside three football-sized circles, and the other shows a menagerie of humanlike and reptilian figures.

MUA MISSION AND SURROUNDS

About 20km east of Dedza as the crow flies, Mua Mission is one of the oldest Catholic outposts in Malawi, established at the base of the Rift Valley Escarpment by the so-called White Fathers in 1902. It is also now one of the key points on the tourist map of south-central Malawi, largely because of the superb Chamare Museum, which forms part of the KuNgoni Centre for Arts & Culture founded by Fr Claude Boucher Chisale in 1976. The mission is also a well-known training centre for woodcarving: it's possible to visit the workshop, and to buy the carvings at a shop attached to the museum. Other attractions include a peaceful botanical garden and the nearby KuNgoni Falls. In addition to welcoming day and overnight visitors, the mission takes advance bookings for courses, seminars and retreats for interested individuals or groups wishing to explore more detailed aspects of the local culture and its interaction with Christianity.

GETTING THERE AND AWAY Mua Mission lies 1km west of the M5 between Salima and Blantyre, some 45km south of Salima and 20km north of the junctions with the newly surfaced S127 to Dedza and Lilongwe, and the S127 to Monkey Bay and Mangochi along the main tar road to Balaka. The dirt turn-off to the mission is clearly signposted 'Mua Parish'. There is plenty of public transport along the M5 but not to the mission itself.

 WHERE TO STAY

Pantondo Chalets (10 rooms) ☎ 01 262706; m 099 9511884; e admin@kungoni.org; www. kungoni.org. Set in attractive (though recently reported to be somewhat unkempt) gardens on a rock opposite Mua Mission, with the Nadzipokwe River clefting its way in between, these well appointed & comfortable en-suite twin rondavels are decorated in traditional style & have walk-in nets, lamps & hot water. Meals are available at US$8 & camping is permitted. *US$31/42 sgl/dbl B&B, US$8 per tent camping.*

WHAT TO SEE AND DO

Around the mission The **Chamare Museum** (*contact details as for Pantondo Chalets;* ⊕ *07.30–16.00 Mon–Sat; entrance US$3*) is the centrepiece of the KuNgoni Centre for Arts & Culture. It's also the finest ethnographic museum in Malawi, and a source of endless information about the three main tribes of the central region, the Yao, Chewa and Ngoni. Opened in 1999, the museum is worth at least two–three hours of your time, starting with a circle around the outside walls, which are covered in murals giving a pictorial history of Malawi. Inside, the displays focus on the living Malawian culture as much as the past, with particular reference to the interaction between local people and Islamic and Christian settlers and missionaries who arrived in the 19th century.

The highlight of the museum, elaborated on at the Namalikhate village on the edge of the mission, is the world's largest collection of Gule Wamkulu masks, around 400 in total. The Gule Wamkulu is the most important traditional Chewa dance, a colourful and thrilling masquerade that depicts multiple facets of human behaviour and is usually reserved for VIP funerals. The masks depict a wide range of characters who collectively enact a series of morality plays – there's the rhinoceros-like sexually aroused Gandali whose resistant wife Namalocha breaks a pot over his head to humiliate him, the crocodile-meets-bull chiefly figure of Chimbano whose abstinence unlocks the fertility of newly initiated teenage girls, the thieving genital-baring Dzimwe who prowls the night like a hyena, the wise old owl Chinkhombe, the ancient spiritualist Chadzunda, and many others. This well-constructed Gule Wamkulu display ties in with and illuminates several other attractions described in this chapter: the same dance is performed by the community project at Mpalale near Dedza, and the masked figures associated with Gule Wamkulu are the central theme for some of the late white rock panels in Chongoni.

Other attractions close to the museum include the impressive seminary and church, the latter decorated with interesting semi-traditional religious art, several mission buildings dating to the early 20th century, and the well-stocked art gallery, which charges an entrance fee of US$1. For nature-lovers, the Nadzipokwe River below the museum and KuNgoni Falls a short distance upstream provide a peaceful spot for a walk, as does the lush botanical garden. Behind the museum, dating to the earliest years of the mission, is the carpentry shop, where the carvers use their feet to hold the wood they are working on, while they carve intricately, and a cemetery with the graves of several early missionaries. The remains of what was a well-intentioned but rather dreary animal orphanage remain on site, but the animals themselves have thankfully been relocated to more hospitable climes at the superbly capable Lilongwe Wildlife Centre.

Mua-Livulezi Forest Reserve This sizeable forest reserve, which lies at an altitude of around 800m below the Bembeke Escarpment, protects medium-altitude Brachystegia and bamboo woodland rather than the plantation and evergreen forest more typically found at higher altitudes. Little information about the fauna of the reserve is available, but it offers some good birding, and the predominantly indigenous vegetation may still support a few mammals, most probably vervet monkey, duiker, leopard and hyena. There are also good views, and the clear, babbling Namkokwe River is a nice place for a dip, and (although I can give no guarantees) probably too rocky and fast flowing for bilharzia to be a realistic cause for concern. From the Mua Mission, a roughly 25km road leading to Mganja on the S127 between Masasa and Golomoti passes through the reserve for several kilometres, offering stunning scenery the whole way. With an early start, you could hike between Mua and Mganja in a day, and it would make an excellent route for cyclists.

Balaka This market town lies on the M8, just south of the intersection with the Blantyre road, and is on most bus routes between the north and the south. The only point of interest is the huge Catholic church at the Balaka Mission on the edge of the town and home to the Montfort Press, which publishes a range of books and magazines. An interesting by-product of the press is **Chifundo Artisans Network** (m *088 8365960; www.facebook.com/chifundoartisansnetwork;* ⊕ *08.00–17.00 daily*), where you can see paper being made by hand and textiles being dyed and made into clothing. This was originally a Peace Corps programme which has developed into a sound business and a welcome tourist attraction, complete with a café serving cold drinks, Italian coffee, muffins, cakes and more. The paper-making, tie-dyeing and finishing workshops can be visited on weekdays, signposted behind the mission church towards the Montfort Press and about 3km along dirt roads. Another attraction in Balaka, attached to the mission, is the Chapel of Reconciliation, which was built so that people leaving Malawi's prisons could go to church without community disapproval, a first step to re-integration, and features murals made at Mua. If you need accommodation here, try the moderate Mlambe Motel or cheaper Zembani Lodge.

Explore Africa in your own home...

If you are planning a trip to Africa, or just like to learn more about it, *Travel Africa* magazine is the ideal read for you. Published in the UK, each edition comprises at least 120 pages of travel ideas, practical information and features on Africa's attractions, wildlife and cultures.

SPECIAL OFFER! Subscribe for four issues (one year) and we'll give you an extra issue **FREE!** Phone, fax or email us or subscribe online using our secure server. Quote BRADT in the gift voucher box to make sure you get your free issue...

www.travelafricamag.com tel: 01844 278883
email: subs@travelafricamag.com   4 Rycote Lane Farm, Milton Common, OX9 2NZ, UK

CAPE MAC LODGE

Enjoy your stay with a breathtaking view of the
3 islands and our various activities:
Swimming pool, 8 seater jacuzzi, Windsurfing, Table tennis,
Volleyball, Hoby-cat, Pedal boating, Canoeing,
TV and Internet sky band hot spot in the bar.
All rooms are air conditioned and equipped with fridges,
TVs for USB and DVD, Massages available

Tel: +265 999 621 279
Email: rogerl@africa-online.net   www.capemaclodge.com

8

Lake Malawi National Park

Gazetted in 1980 and inscribed as a UNESCO World Heritage Site four years later, Lake Malawi National Park (LMNP) extends over some 95km² of land and water at the southern end of the lake. The park covers much of the Nankumba Peninsula, a tapering sliver of mountainous land that juts northward towards Cape Maclear, and it also includes the surrounding lake waters and nine rocky offshore islands. The park was set aside for its unique diversity of fish, the evolutionary significance of which has been compared to the finches of the Galapagos Islands. LMNP is also perhaps the country's most popular snorkelling and diving destination, with the islands in particular offering the opportunity to see dozens of different cichlid species swirling colourfully around the rocks, a wildlife encounter as memorable as anything Malawi has to offer on land.

The mountainous interior of Nankumba Peninsula is practically uninhabited, a rugged landscape of steep, densely vegetated slopes that rise from the 500m lakeshore to the 1,143m Nkhunguni Peak in the west and the 963m Dzimwe Peak in the east. By contrast, the flatter parts of the shoreline are quite heavily settled, for which reason several fishing villages still exist as low-rise urban enclaves, not officially part of LMNP but surrounded by it on all sides. The best known of these villages is Chembe on Cape Maclear, which vies with Nkhata Bay and Senga Bay as the most developed resort village anywhere on the lake. Also situated on the Nankumba Peninsula, about 1km east of the national park boundary, the small port town of Monkey Bay forms the main gateway for road public transport to LMNP and Cape Maclear.

MONKEY BAY

Overlooking a sheltered harbour 1km outside the park boundary, Monkey Bay is the largest settlement on the Nankumba Peninsula, with a population estimated at 15,000, and the main gateway to LMNP and Cape Maclear for those using public transport. The ferry harbour at Monkey Bay is (as of May 2013) no longer called upon by the MV *Ilala*, but the small town remains the main bus and minibus terminus servicing the peninsula. For this reason, many travellers pass through Monkey Bay, but very few do more than head straight on to Cape Maclear. Historically, this is largely due to the vastly better accommodation options elsewhere on the peninsula, so it is worth noting that Monkey Bay does now boast a couple of very decent options with the potential to attract budget-conscious backpackers away from the increasingly upmarket Cape Maclear. Languid at the best of times, Monkey Bay is feeling practically somnambulant these days as *Ilala* route changes have deprived the town of its most obvious raison d'être.

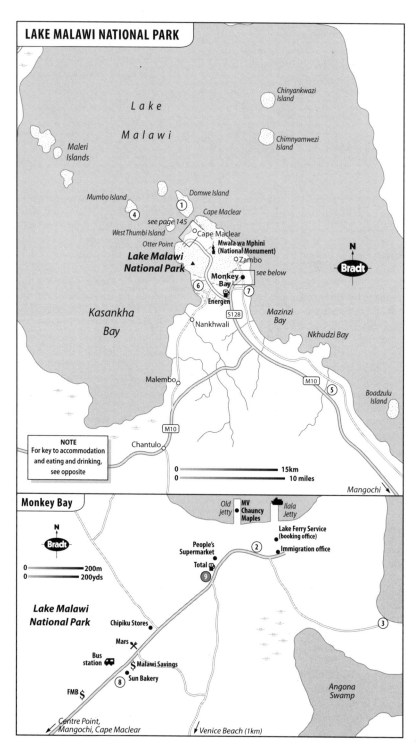

LAKE MALAWI NATIONAL PARK

L a k e

M a l a w i

Chinyankwazi Island

Chimnyamwezi Island

Maleri Islands

Mumbo Island

Domwe Island

(1)

Cape Maclear

(4)

see page 145

West Thumbi Island

○ *Cape Maclear*

○ *Otter Point*

Mwala wa Mphini (National Monument)

○ *Zambo*

see below

Lake Malawi National Park

Monkey Bay

(6)

(7)

N

Bradt

Energen

S128

Kasankha Bay

○ *Nankhwali*

Mazinzi Bay

Nkhudzi Bay

○ *Malembo*

M10

(5)

Boadzulu Island

M10

○ *Chantulo*

NOTE
For key to accommodation
and eating and drinking,
see opposite

0	15km
0	10 miles

Mangochi

Monkey Bay

N

Bradt

Old jetty

MV Chauncy Maples

Ilala Jetty

Lake Ferry Service (booking office)

People's Supermarket

(2)

Immigration office

Total

(9)

0	200m
0	200yds

Lake Malawi National Park

Chipiku Stores

Mars

Bus station

(3)

Malawi Savings

Sun Bakery

(8)

FMB

Centre Point, Mangochi, Cape Maclear

Venice Beach (1km)

Angona Swamp

LAKE MALAWI NATIONAL PARK
For listings, see pages 144 & 150–1

🛏 **Where to stay**
1 Domwe Island Camp
2 Ilala Village Lodge
3 Mufasa Rustic Backpackers Camp
4 Mumbo Island Camp
5 Norman Carr Cottage
6 Pumulani Lodge
7 Venice Beach Backpackers
8 Zawadi Resthouse

✖ **Where to eat and drink**
9 Lake End Restaurant
   Mufasa Rustic Backpackers
   Camp (see 3)

Off map
Centre Point

GETTING THERE AND AWAY Monkey Bay Harbour, at the north end of the small town centre, is no longer an embarkation point for the MV *Ilala*, but the **Malawi Shipping Company** (📞 01 587361/411/221/203, 01 773738/9; e *ilala@malawi.net or ilala.lake. malawi@gmail.com*) still maintains an office here. Long the southernmost port of call for the *Ilala*, Monkey Bay was somewhat surprisingly removed from the itinerary in May 2013 making the relatively little-known Chipoka the new southernmost terminus. As this book went to print, the *Ilala* was just

MV *CHAUNCY MAPLES*

Docked inauspiciously in Monkey Bay Harbour, the MV *Chauncy Maples* is the oldest ship in Africa, built in Scotland by Alley & McLean for the UMCA in 1899, then shipped in 3,480 pieces to Quelimane on the coast of present-day Mozambique. From Quelimane, the boat's 11-ton boiler was transported inland intact on a wheeled carriage hauled by some 450 Ngoni porters, an exercise that took more than three months, while the other parts were towed by barge up the Zambezi to be reassembled on the Upper Shire River near Mangochi and launched on 6 June 1901.

Named in memory of the first bishop of Likoma, who drowned when his boat capsized in a storm in 1896, the MV *Chauncy Maples* initially served as a floating school and hospital, while also carrying supplies from the mainland to the UMCA headquarters on Likoma. Seconded to the colonial government during World War I, it was used as a troop carrier and to support the gunship HMS *Gwendolyn*'s attack on the German ship *Hermann Von Wessman*, but after the war it was returned to the UMCA and once again administered education and medical assistance to remote lakeshore communities.

In 1953, the high cost of maintenance persuaded the UMCA to sell the MV *Chauncy Maples* to the government, and it was used as a passenger ship by Nyasaland Railways. Following independence, the boat was taken over by the government of Malawi, refitted and remodelled as a more stylish passenger ship in 1967 and again in 1971, and it continued to ply the lake up and down several times a month until 1992, when its licence was withdrawn after it nearly capsized in a storm. However, formal inspections at the time revealed the riveted steel hull to be in excellent condition, and following a dry-dock inspection at Monkey Bay in 2009, the marine engineer Pieter Volschenk concluded that the boat was in better condition than many modern ships are after 20 years at sea.

As a result, the Malawian government, supported by various local and British donors, is in the process of resurrecting the MV *Chauncy Maples* as a hospital ship, which will travel the lake administering free medical treatment, maternity care, dentistry, immunisation for babies and family planning to lakeshore communities. For further information, see the website www. chauncymaples.org.

returning to service after a nearly year-long renovation, so this could potentially change again. For updates on the *Ilala*, visit http://updates.bradtguides.com/malawi. For further details of the itinerary and ticket prices, see page 271).

Coming by road, Monkey Bay lies about 10km from the M10 between Salima and Mangochi, along a good surfaced feeder road branching north at Chirombo junction. The quickest and best road route from Lilongwe, still not shown on most maps of Malawi, entails following the M1 through Dedza to Masasa, then the newly surfaced S127 to Golomoti, then the M5 south for about 1km before turning left into a new extension of the S216 that connects with the M10 *en route* to Chirombo

CICHLIDS OF THE GREAT LAKES

The staggering diversity of Africa's terrestrial fauna is old news, but few people are aware that the continent also harbours the greatest freshwater fish diversity of any continent. And nowhere does this diversity reach such heights as in Lake Malawi, whose 850 described fish species – with more awaiting formal discovery – exceeds the number of freshwater species known from Europe and North America combined.

Lake Malawi's fish diversity is the product of the most dramatic incidence of explosive speciation known to evolutionists. The majority of these fish species are cichlids – pronounced 'sicklids' – members of a perch-like family of freshwater fish called Cichlidae that ranges through the Middle East, Madagascar, Asia and South and Central America. It is in Africa's three largest lakes, however, that this widespread family has undergone an unprecedented explosion of evolutionarily recent speciation that has resulted in it constituting an estimated 5% of the world's vertebrate species!

The cichlids of Africa's great lakes are generally divided into a few major groupings, often referred to by scientists by their local Malawian names, such as the small plankton-eating *utaka*, the large, pike-like and generally predatory *ncheni*, the bottom-feeding *chisawasawa*, and the algae-eating *mbuna*. People who have travelled in any part of Africa close to a lake will almost certainly have dined on one or other of the *tilapia* (or closely related *oreochromis*) cichlids, large *ncheni* that make excellent eating and are known in Malawi as *chambo*. To aquarium keepers, snorkellers and scuba divers, however, the most noteworthy African cichlids are the *mbuna*, a spectacularly colourful group of small fish of which some 300 species are known from Lake Malawi alone.

The *mbuna* of Lake Malawi first attracted scientific interest in the 1950s, when they formed the subject of Dr Geoffrey Fryer's classic study of adaptive radiation. This term is used to describe the explosion of a single stock species into a variety of closely related forms, each of which evolves specialised modifications that allow it to exploit an ecological niche quite different from that exploited by the common ancestral stock. This phenomenon is most likely to occur when an adaptable species colonises an environment where several food sources are going unused, for instance on a newly formed volcanic island or lake. The most celebrated incidence of adaptive radiation – the one that led Charles Darwin to propose the theory of evolution through natural selection – occurred on the Galapagos Islands, where a variety of finch species evolved from one common seed-eating ancestor to fill several very different ecological niches.

The explosive speciation that has occurred among Africa's cichlids is like Darwin's finches amplified a hundredfold. The many hundreds of cichlid species and Monkey Bay. There are also good road connections to Monkey Bay from Salima, Mangochi and Blantyre.

There is plenty of public transport in all directions, including daily National coaches to/from Blantyre that leave at around 11.00 daily from Limbe. Alternatively, take a bus to Salima, Golomoti or Mangochi and catch a minibus from there rather than trying to take a bus the whole way through. Minibuses from Mangochi or Golomoti cost around US$3.50 and those from Salima cost US$6. There is no public transport along the 18km road between Monkey Bay and Cape Maclear, so you will either have to hitch or else wait for a *matola* ride, which costs around US$2.

present in Lake Tanganyika and Lake Nyasa-Malawi are evolved from a handful of river cichlids that entered the lakes when they formed about two–three million years ago. (No less remarkable is the probability that the 200 or so cichlids in Lake Victoria are all evolved from a few common ancestors over the 10,000–15,000 years since the lake last dried up.) In all three lakes, specialised cichlid species have evolved to exploit practically every conceivable food source: algae, plankton, insects, fish and molluscs. Somewhat macabrely, the so-called kiss-of-death cichlids feed by sucking eggs and hatchlings from the mouths of mouth-brooding cichlids! No less striking is the diverse array in size, coloration and mating behaviour displayed across different species. In addition to being a case study in adaptive radiation, the cichlids of the great lakes are routinely cited as a classic example of parallel evolution – in other words, many similar adaptations appear to have occurred independently in all three lakes.

Not only have cichlids undergone several independent radial explosions in all three of Africa's great lakes, but the same thing has happened in microcosm in many smaller lakes throughout the continent. Uganda's Lake Nabugabo, for instance, harbours five endemic cichlid species, all of which must have evolved since the lake was separated from Lake Victoria by a sandbar less than 4,000 years ago. Why cichlids and not any of several other fish families is a question that is likely to keep ichthyologists occupied for decades to come. One factor is that cichlids are exceptionally quick to mature, and are thus characterised by a very rapid turnover of generations. They also appear to have an unusually genetically malleable anatomy, with skull, body, tooth and gut structures readily modifying over a relatively small number of generations.

This capacity to colonise new freshwater habitats is boosted by a degree of parental care rare in other fish – the mouth-brooders, which include all but one of the cichlid species of Lake Malawi, hold their eggs and fry in their mouths until they are large enough to fend for themselves. Most fascinating, bearing in mind that the separation of breeding populations lies at the core of speciation, there is mounting evidence to suggest that cichlids have a unique capacity to erect non-physical barriers between emergent species – possibly linked to a correlation between colour morphs and food preferences in diverging populations.

Africa's lake cichlids are never likely to rival its terrestrial wildlife as a tourist attraction. All the same, snorkelling and diving in LMNP – which may host as many as half the lake's cichlid species within its relatively compact area – is both thrilling in itself, and a wonderfully humbling introduction to what has justifiably been described as a 'unique evolutionary showcase'.

WHERE TO STAY *See map, page 140.*

Budget

⌂ **Ilala Village Lodge** (15 rooms) \01 587359; m 099 9767084; e ilala@malawi.net. Closed when the *Ilala* was taken out of service in 2012, it's unclear if they will reopen since the *Ilala* will now bypass Monkey Bay entirely. Situated right alongside the harbour administrative buildings & operated by the Malawi Shipping Company, this is a pleasant & comfortable little lodge, & was once very convenient for catching the MV *Ilala*. The clean, cool, tiled rooms have 2 beds, nets, fan & basin, & though they are not en suite, the bathrooms with hot shower are shared between 2 rooms only. The restaurant serves meals for around US$4 & has DSTV. *US$10/17 sgl/dbl.*

⌂ **Mufasa Rustic Backpackers Camp** (8 rooms) m 099 3080057; e info@ mufasamalawi.com; www.mufasamalawi.com. This backpackers' camp is a flagship location of the growing Mufasa chain & operates to a similar standard as their other properties. It has a great location, on a quiet sandy beach on the isolated Ungunda Bay, overlooking a small island & next to a swamp frequented by hippos & crocs, yet it is only 500m from the ferry harbour. It has a restaurant & bar, & offers good birding, boat rides & snorkelling gear, with regular beach bonfires to light up the evenings. *US$20/25 sgl/dbl or twin, US$9 pp dorm bed, US$5 pp camping.*

⌂ **Venice Beach Backpackers** (23 rooms) m 099 9319453. About 30mins' walk from the town centre, this pretty backpackers' place lies on a wide sandy beach alongside a rustic fishing village. It has a decent restaurant & offers limited watersports, but has a reputation for being disorganised. *US$14 dbl using common showers, US$17.50 en-suite dbl, US$6.25 pp dorm bed, US$3.25 pp camping.*

Shoestring

⌂ **Zawadi Resthouse** (16 rooms) m 099 9427323. The best of a few basic local resthouses in Monkey Bay, this has adequately clean dbl & twin rooms & a central location near the bus station. *US$3.25 pp using common showers, US$8 en suite dbl.*

✗ WHERE TO EAT AND DRINK *See map, page 140.*

✗ **Lake End Restaurant** m 099 2266482; ⊙ 07.30–24.00 daily. This lively central eatery & bar offers pool, darts & DSTV sporting events with indoor & outdoor seating. They whip up the usual Malawian staples for US$2–3.

✗ **Mufasa Rustic Backpackers Camp** m 099 3080057. The beachside restaurant & bar here serves burgers & other backpacker fare for US$4–6, & the view is undoubtedly the best in town.

♀ **Centre Point** Just over 1km out of town on the main road to the M10, this outdoor bar lacks a lake view but is pleasant enough, & basic meals are sometimes available.

CAPE MACLEAR (CHEMBE)

Situated in a 6km² enclave of unprotected land within LMNP, the second-largest settlement on the Nankumba Peninsula is the fishing village known to locals as Chembe but to most outsiders as Cape Maclear. It's a beautiful spot, enclosed by tall forested mountains and lush rocky islands, and one that has long enchanted overseas visitors.

David Livingstone visited here in 1861 and named the cape after his friend Sir Thomas Maclear, the then Astronomer Royal at the Cape of Good Hope, and his enthusiasm for the setting led to it being chosen as the original site of the Livingstonia Mission (1875–81). In 1949, Cape Maclear was chosen as the site of an overnight stop on the BOAC Flying Boat Service in 1949–50, and 30 years later it emerged as the hippest and most chilled-out travel crossroads in Malawi, if not anywhere on the emergent backpackers' trail between Nairobi and Victoria Falls. Indeed, back in its early 1990s heyday, Cape Maclear was frequently touted as sub-Saharan Africa's answer to Kathmandu or Marrakech, legendary for its relaxed vibe and party atmosphere.

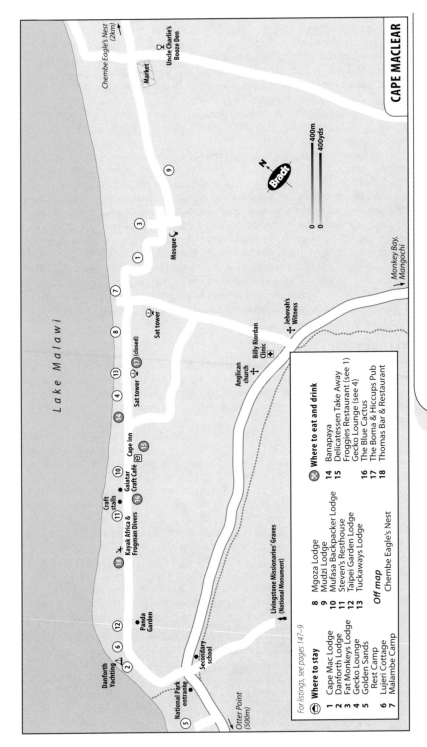

CAPE MACLEAR

For listings, see pages 147–9

Where to stay

1 Cape Mac Lodge
2 Danforth Lodge
3 Fat Monkeys Lodge
4 Gecko Lounge
5 Golden Sands
6 Lujeri Cottage
7 Malambe Camp
8 Mgoza Lodge
9 Mudzi Lodge
10 Mufasa Backpacker Lodge
11 Steven's Resthouse
12 Taipei Garden Lodge
13 Tuckaways Lodge

Off map

Chembe Eagle's Nest

Where to eat and drink

14 Banapaya
15 Delicatessen Take Away
   Froggies Restaurant (see 1)
   Gecko Lounge (see 4)
16 The Blue Cactus
17 The Boma & Hiccups Pub
18 Thomas Bar & Restaurant

Lake Malawi

Chembe Eagle's Nest (2km)

Uncle Charlie's Booze Den

Market

Mosque

Sat tower

Sat tower

Sat tower

17 (closed)

Cape Inn

Gaiatar Craft Café

Craft stalls

Kayak Africa & Frogman Divers

Panda Garden

Danforth Yachting

National Park entrance

Otter Point (500m)

Secondary school

Livingstone Missionaries' Graves (National Monument)

Billy Riordan Clinic

Anglican church

Jehovah's Witness

Monkey Bay, Mangochi

8

145

Cape Maclear experienced a slump in fortunes in the late 1990s, when the party moved northward to Kande and Nkhata Bay, a shift that was exacerbated by post-millennial political developments in Zimbabwe (and more recently right here in Malawi), which diverted travellers and overland trucks away from the Tete Corridor between Harare and Blantyre in favour of the more northerly route through Zambia. Today, however, Cape Maclear is experiencing a strong revival in fortunes, having adapted its mood to changed circumstances by offering a greater choice of mid-range and upmarket facilities, aimed at residents and volunteers as much as passing backpackers.

In addition to having the broadest range of accommodation options anywhere on the lake, Cape Maclear offers a peerless range of aquatic activities, from snorkelling and diving to kayaking and motorised lake excursions. The notoriously assertive beach-boy and tout culture that once characterised the village has been diffused, thanks to the adoption of a rota system that assigns a specific guide to a specific lodge for a specific period. And yet there remains a gratifyingly integrated feeling to tourist development in Chembe, with most lodges lying right in the heart of the village, so that visitors are exposed to everyday African life in an unforced manner very different from any other lakeside resort in Malawi. Furthermore, Chembe is one of the few accessible parts of the Malawian lakeshore to face northwest, which not only ensures some protection from the fierce winds that sometimes rise on the lake, but also means it is perfectly positioned for spectacular sunsets.

GETTING THERE AND AWAY The turn-off to Cape Maclear is next to the Energem filling station on the west side of the 10km feeder road to Monkey Bay, about 5km north of Chirombo junction on the M10. An array of signs to the various lodges renders it difficult to miss. The road is partially surfaced and should be passable in most vehicles, but heavy corrugations on the untarred sections can make for a spine-jarring 18km drive.

Using public transport, you must first head to Monkey Bay. There's no formal public transport from here to Cape Maclear, but one dedicated pick-up serves as a sardine-tin-on-wheels *matola* between the two, running backwards and forwards a few times daily for US$2 per person. There is no schedule as such, and unless you phone the driver (m *099 9214699*) to make another arrangement, best wait in Monkey Bay as the vehicle is often full by the time it reaches the junction. Leaving Cape Maclear, you can either phone the driver to check his movements, or just listen out for the horn. Hitching is also a possibility, in which case it's best to stop off at the junction, but you could be in for a long wait.

Coming from Lilongwe or Salima/Senga Bay, it may also be possible to arrange a private motorboat transfer, which takes about three hours in decent weather. As the road network has improved this option has become less popular, but Cool Runnings in Senga Bay and Gecko Lounge at Cape Maclear may be able to arrange a boat for around US$200 for up to six people, and you could also try Kayak Africa or Danforth Yachting. Another possibility if you want to get somewhere quickly is the private pick-up truck owned by Reggie at Gecko Lounge (m *099 9935598*); his rates of US$35 one-way to/from Monkey Bay, US$85 to/from Mangochi or US$210 to/from Blantyre or Lilongwe cover as many people as fit in the vehicle. Oddly, when headed to Lilongwe it is often cheaper to hire a driver from there to fetch you in Cape Maclear than it is to arrange a ride locally. A recommended Lilongwe-based driver is Mr Mavuto (m *099 9801449*), who will transfer a carload of passengers to Lilongwe for US$125.

WATERSPORTS OPERATORS Cape Maclear is a haven for watersports enthusiasts, offering excellent opportunities for scuba diving, snorkelling, kayaking, yachting and various motorised activities. Any lodge can make arrangements, and the village is so small that it is easy to make your own enquiries, but the following companies stand out:

Danforth Yachting m 099 9960077/770; e info@danforthyachting.com; www. danforthyachting.com. This company charters a fully equipped & crewed 38ft ocean-going 8-bed catamaran called Mufasa for day excursions as well as longer sailing safaris from 2 nights to 2 weeks' duration, all detailed on their website. The dive school also offers PADI courses & casual dives for US$50.

Kayak Africa & Frogman Divers m 099 9942661/9952488; e letsgo@kayakafrica.com; www.kayakafrica.com. This long-serving kayaking & diving centre can organise outings to their tented camps on the islands off Cape Maclear, as well as stand-alone kayaking, snorkelling & diving excursions. A PADI open-water diver qualifying course here costs US$375, while a casual dive (qualified divers) costs US$40 (pp, parties of two or more) & casual snorkelling US$15.

WHERE TO STAY *See map, page 145.*
Upmarket
Cape Mac Lodge (12 rooms) m 099 9621279; e rogerl@africa-online.net or capemaclodge@ yahoo.com; www.capemaclodge.com; see also advert on page 138. This impressive lodge opened in 2005 at the west end of the village. It has leafy private gardens leading right onto the beach, a swimming pool & jacuzzi, & a wide range of activities on offer, including snorkelling, kayaking, table tennis & catamaran excursions, all included in the room rate. The fine French restaurant serves some of the best fresh fish you will find anywhere in Malawi, as well as excellent steaks & meat dishes. The lodge buildings are architect designed, with high thatched roofs coming down almost to the ground, & all rooms have AC, nets, DSTV & en-suite showers. *US$115/165 sgl/dbl, US$210 family room, all rates B&B.*

Chembe Eagle's Nest (11 rooms) m 099 9966507; e enquiries@chembenest.com; www. chembenest.com. The most remote lodge in Cape Maclear, this has a fantastic location below tall hills on the northeast edge of the bay about 3km out of the village. The thatched en-suite dbl or twin chalets are earthily decorated & have nets, fan, hot shower & private balcony facing the beach. The restaurant serves an eclectic menu with quiches & wraps, & is worth a trip from town. The beach is attractive & there are some massive rocks for sunset views, with sundowner catamaran cruises also offered at US$15pp. Campers will find the best facilities in town, including hot showers & plug points. *US$85 pp inc b/fast & dinner, US$10 pp camping.*

Danforth Lodge (8 rooms) m 099 9960077/770; e info@danforthyachting.com; www.danforthyachting.com. The most exclusive retreat in Chembe, situated at the west end of the village, Danforth is a quiet owner-managed lodge with its own yacht charter company & PADI dive school. Various other aquatic activities are on offer, including wakeboarding, waterskiing & kayaking, as well as mountain biking. It is set in large lakeshore gardens centred on an infinity swimming pool & trampoline for the kids, & has a highly regarded restaurant with indoor & outdoor seating for lodge guests only. The swish & spacious tiled rooms have AC, net, fan, tea/coffee, Wi-Fi & en-suite hot shower & tub. Family rooms are available. *US$150/190 pp FB low/high season.*

Lujeri Cottage (4 rooms) \01 460277/266/243; m 099 9960344; e lujerilodge@ lujeri.com. Owned by Lujeri Tea Estate, this private self-catering cottage next to Danforth Yachting is rented out as a unit sleeping up to 9 people in 2 en-suite bedrooms & 2 rooms sharing a bathroom, all with nets, fan & solar-heated water. It has a large deep-freeze, fridge, gas stove & cooking utensils, & there is a cook, but guests must bring all food supplies. It's good value for groups. *US$170 for the whole house*

Moderate
Gecko Lounge (4 rooms, 1 dorm) \01 11955783; m 099 9787322/9833856; e kitemalawi@gmail.com or ndalamalawi@ gmail.com; www.geckolounge.net. This bright &

colourful place comes with a matching attitude, thanks to the dynamic management & enthusiastic staff. There's the choice of en-suite twin rooms with net, fan, lockbox & hot shower, larger self-catering double chalets that also have fridge, hotplate, safe & private veranda, or small 2–4-bed reed-partitioned dorms with nets & lock-boxes. The bar has DSTV for those who want to catch up on their sport, the restaurant is excellent in its own right, & the good-sized garden is on the beachfront. An exhaustive selection of services includes all the usual aquatic activities (including waterskiing), guided day trips to most local points of interest, Skyband Wi-Fi, a BBQ area, about 300 DVDs (& player), book exchange, laundry & an endless supply of filtered drinking water courtesy of the Chembe Water Project (*www.chembewaterproject.org*) sponsored by the lodge. *US$80 dbl, US$110 dbl chalet with kitchen, US$15 pp dorm bed.*

⌂ **Mgoza Lodge** (7 rooms) m 099 5632105; e kay@mgozalodge.com or alan@mgozalodge.com; www.mgozalodge.com. Named after the *mgoza* trees that shade the beachfront lawn, this lovely new lodge features imaginatively designed beachfront rooms with king-size beds, nets & en-suite tub or shower, as well as a breezy 1st-floor dorm above the excellent restaurant. The effervescent manager is a trove of information on the area, & can arrange most village & aquatic activities. There's a relaxed bar with one of the widest playlists in town. *US$55 dbl or twin, US$5 dorm bed, discounts for residents.*

Budget

⌂ **Fat Monkeys Lodge** (8 rooms, 2 dorms) ☏ 01 11955777; m 099 9948501; e fatmonkeys@africa-online.net. At the northeast end of the village, this lively & spaciously laid-out beachfront lodge is a good compromise between comfort & cost, & many backpackers wind up here as a result. The bright en-suite rooms are large & have 3–4 beds with nets, Skyband Wi-Fi is on offer, & the restaurant serves a limited selection of meals for around US$5.50. There's a good beach, an equally good feel about the place, & all the usual aquatic activities are on offer or can be arranged. *US$55 en-suite trpl, US$60 en-suite 4-bed room, US$75 en-suite 4-bed cottage, US$10 pp in 6-bed dorm, US$6 pp camping.*

⌂ **Mufasa Backpacker Lodge** (10 rooms, 1 dorm) m 099 1557940; e info@mufasamalawi.

com; www.mufasamalawi.com. Set in a large shady beachfront garden in the heart of the village, this has a pleasant, relaxed ambience, small rooms decorated with colourful tapestries, & popular meals with burgers, spaghetti & more for around US$4–5. The standard aquatic activities are available, & this is a good spot to sit back & watch the village hustle & bustle by day, & enjoy a beachside bonfire by night. *US$22 dbl or twin, US$25 trpl, US$8 pp in 6-bed dorm, US$5 pp camping.*

⌂ **Taipei Garden Lodge** (11 rooms, 1 dorm) m 088 1466586/4421776; e taipeigardenlodge@yahoo.com. Formerly known as 'Cedar House' because of the aromatic wooden furnishings in each room, this unassuming lodge offers clean & simple rooms centred around a sandy courtyard along the beach. All rooms have nets, fans & use shared ablutions. The restaurant tries some Asian recipes you won't find elsewhere in Cape Maclear. *US$12.5/22 sgl/dbl B&B, US$4.75 dorm bed, camping US$2.5 excluding b/fast.*

⌂ **Tuckaways Lodge** (6 rooms) ☏ 099 9833856/3405681; e tuckawaysmw@gmail.com; www.tuckawaysmw.com. Owned by the same people as Gecko Lounge, this lodge lies 100m further down the beach & offers accommodation in stilted reed dbl & twin chalets on wooden decks with private verandas overlooking the lake. Ablution facilities are in a separate block. *US$65 dbl, US$100 family room.*

Shoestring

⌂ **Malambe Camp** (5 rooms, 1 dorm) m 099 9258959; e malambe_camp@btinternet.com. This camp feels like a real throwback to Cape Maclear as it was 10 years ago, offering accommodation in naturally ventilated no-frills reed huts with twin beds & nets. It arranges a wide range of boat trips & tours, & an open-air restaurant/bar serves curries for around US$4. A bit quiet on last inspection, but it seems like a well-priced & chilled set-up. *US$6.25/9.50 sgl/dbl, US$3.25 pp in 14-bed dorm, US$3 pp standing tent, US$2 pp camping.*

⌂ **Mudzi Lodge** (10 rooms, 4 under construction) m 099 9943256/088 2860221. On the northeast side of the village a short walk from the beach, this spotless new budget lodge doesn't waste time on finery & decoration, but it has bright, clean rooms with big nets & shared bathrooms set around a spick & span courtyard. *US$9.50/19 sgl/dbl.*

🏠 **Steven's Resthouse** (12 rooms) m 099 9927755. This Cape Maclear institution, run by the same Malawian family for the best part of 3 decades, was for years the very pulse of the local backpacker scene. Sadly, it hasn't really kept up with changing times, & although it's pretty much the same as it always was in terms of facilities, if not better, the ownership seems to have little appetite to compete with its newer & funkier neighbours. No longer signposted, you can find it across from Blue Cactus restaurant. There's a no-frills restaurant, & the sporadically rowdy bar still operates opposite. *US$8 dbl.*

✖ WHERE TO EAT AND DRINK *See map, page 145.*

✖ **Banapaya** m 088 2134778; ☕ restaurant 07.00–21.30 daily, bar until 00.30, later on weekends. This musical hangout promises bonfires & drumming after dark, with the possibility of lessons as well. The restaurant offers a respectable variety of mains including duck(!), curries, chicken & fish , all in the range of US$3–5.

✖ **Delicatessen Take Away** m 099 5397798. This unassuming set-up just off the main drag comes highly recommended & features a daily rotating menu; expect to find pastas, pies, samosas & the usual Malawian staples for US$2–3. They even occasionally bake cookies!

✖ **Froggies Restaurant** m 099 9621279; ☕ 08.00–09.30, 12.00–13.30 & 19.00–21.30 daily. Part of Cape Mac Lodge, this thatched open-sided restaurant is probably Cape Maclear's finest dining venue, with a diverse continental menu (& tongue-in-cheek name) that reflects the nationality of its owners. Lunchtime pastas, salads, burgers & other snacks are in the US$3–5 range, but this place really comes into its own in the evening, with a great selection of fish, steak & other mains at US$6–8 & yummy desserts.

✖ **Gecko Lounge** ☎ 01 599188; ☕ restaurant 07.30–21.00 daily, bar stays open later on Fri & Sat. The stilted veranda bar/restaurant here is one of the most attractive in the village, with contemporary décor & a lake view, & it serves great pizzas (around US$10) & an imaginative daily selection of fish, vegetarian & meat dishes for around US$7.50. The resident tea-taster has moved on, but they still serve a fine cuppa. The well-stocked bar has a varied cocktail menu, there are regular DJ parties, & a large-screen TV shows major sporting events & the occasional DVD movie night.

✖ **The Blue Cactus** m 099 9157690; ☕ restaurant 07.00–21.00, bar until 00.00. Malawian staples, burgers, curries & drinks are dished up at this low-key local spot near Steven's for about US$3.

✖ **The Boma & Hiccups Pub** m 099 5483823; ☕ bar 08.30–late Tue–Sun. In an unfortunate turn of events, The Boma was gutted by a fire in late 2012 just as it seemed to be hitting its stride. The owners plan to rebuild & should be back up & running during the life of this edition. Expect grilled meat & fish dishes (speciality *kampango*) for around US$5–6, weekend BBQs & long hours. A pool table, lounge with DSTV, & DJ booth with dance floor will all hopefully keep the party going once again in the near future.

✖ **Thomas Bar & Restaurant** m 099 9709581; 07.30–21.00 daily. Situated next to Kayak Africa, this unpretentious restaurant serves simple but tasty fare in the US$2.25–3.25 range (try the chicken curry) & the attached bar, serving inexpensive beers, is a good place to meet locals.

SHOPPING A few small grocery shops along the main drag sell a limited selection of groceries, but a far better selection of goods is available at the **People's Supermarket** in Monkey Bay. The eco-conscious **Gaiatar Craft Café** (m 099 9300559; ☕ 09.00–12.00, 13.30–17.00 *Tue–Sun*) sells locally made handicrafts, many of which are produced through a Cape Maclear women's co-op. They serve Malawian tea and coffee on their tranquil outdoor terrace, and you can buy some to take home as well. Plenty of **craft stalls** are studded around town, including a cluster facing Steven's Resthouse.

OTHER PRACTICALITIES

Banking and foreign exchange There's nothing of the sort in Cape Maclear, but Monkey Bay has ATMs from **FMB** and **Malawi Savings Bank**, both accepting

Visa. Some of the smarter lodges will accept hard currency payments and can probably trade small amounts for local currency, while travellers with Mastercard/Maestro will have to head down the road to Mangochi.

Internet The only bespoke internet café is **The Cape Inn** (m *099 1585502;* e *elisabeth@thecapeinn.com;* ⊕ *07.30–19.00 daily)* which has laptops and dongles for use at Mk10/min. Another option is Gecko Lounge, a Wi-Fi hotspot that sells Skyband cards and has a computer to use them on.

INSIDE LAKE MALAWI NATIONAL PARK

The main tourist focal points on the Nankumba Peninsula are Chembe/Cape Maclear, and to a lesser extent Monkey Bay, both of which make a useful base from which to explore the clear cichlid-rich waters and hilly interior of LMNP. However, there are also several isolated accommodation options and points of interest within the park proper, not least of which are the contrastingly superb and equally exclusive Pumulani Lodge and Mumbo Island Camp. Other sites of interest include a trio of very different national monuments and the snorkelling and diving havens formed by the rocky shores of islands such as Domwe and West Thumbi. And while it's the aquatic wildlife such as fish, hippo and otters that rightly attracts the most attention, the rugged interior of LMNP also hosts a fair amount of terrestrial wildlife, most visibly yellow baboon, rock hyrax, monitor lizards, and more than 200 bird species, but also more elusive creatures such as greater kudu, bushbuck, zebra, klipspringer, impala, grysbok, grey duiker, leopard, serval and bushpig, and even the occasional stray elephant from the Mangochi area.

WHERE TO STAY *See map, page 140.*
Exclusive

🏠 **Mumbo Island Camp** (7 rooms) ✆021 7831955 m 099 9942661/9952488; e letsgo@ kayakafrica.com; www.kayakafrica.com. This exclusive but down-to-earth retreat on hilly Mumbo Island is one of the most romantic spots in the country, set miles away from anything, amid tall boulders overlooking the lake, to generate a real 'Robinson Crusoe' feel. Built entirely with timber, thatch & canvas, accommodation is in comfortably furnished tents with shaded balconies, hammocks, hot bucket showers & 'eco-loos', & the communal dining area offers simple buffets of home-style cooking & a well-stocked bar. You can kayak there from Cape Maclear, or take the twice-daily motorboat transfer. Snorkelling in the rocky bay in front of the camp is fantastic, not only for the profusion of colourful cichlids but also for the near certainty of close-up otter sightings. You can also kayak around the island, take the magical sundowner cruise, or follow any of several footpaths to the upper slopes. Scuba diving is also available. *US$225 pp inc all meals, & kayak & snorkelling gear, with a significant discount for residents.*

🏠 **Pumulani Lodge** (10 rooms) ✆(+260) 216 246090/1/2; e info@pumulani.com; www. pumulani.com. This stunning luxury lodge on the southeast slopes of the Nankumba Peninsula is in a class of its own, marrying the stylish exclusivity of southern Africa's finest bush lodges with a serene lakeshore location. It's run by the highly regarded Robin Pope Safaris & was designed as a place to chill out after a safari in this Zambian operator's stronghold of South Luangwa National Park. Set within a tiny enclave of private land surrounded by LMNP on 3 sides, it has a magnificent location high on the slopes, & accommodation is in exquisitely decorated architect-designed 125–175m² private villas with 4-poster king-size bed, walk-in netting, AC, large sitting area with a selection of books about Malawi, minibar, large bathroom with tub & shower. The private beach is ideal for lazing around, but optional activities range from kayaking & bird walks (with a good chance of specials such as Livingstone's flycatcher & Pel's fishing owl) to sundowner dhow trips, & snorkelling & diving excursions near the islands. The dining area offers panoramic views over the lake & the food is world class. *US$465 pp all-inclusive, US$190 pp FB for residents, low season discounts may apply.*

Moderate

⌂ **Domwe Island Camp** (3 rooms) ☏021 7831955 m 099 9942661/9952488; e letsgo@kayakafrica.com; www.kayakafrica.com. Run by the same company as Mumbo Island, this shares many features with its more upmarket cousin, but is geared more towards self-caterers. There are 3 fully furnished safari tents, as well as 2 camping spots, a fully equipped kitchen with fridge, & a chef to prepare food, which guests must supply themselves. There is good snorkelling & kayaking

but the gear must be arranged in advance. *US$60 pp, US$25 pp camping.*

Budget

⌂ **Golden Sands Rest Camp** Situated a few hundred metres inside the entrance gate to LMNP, this basic self-catering resthouse has few facilities & plenty of derelict buildings, but it's by far the most peaceful budget option near Cape Maclear, with a great position on the beach below Otter Point, & monkeys & birds in abundance. There's a fridge, stove & cook. *US$4.75 pp en-suite room, US$1 pp camping, additional US$10 park entrance fee.*

WHAT TO SEE

Otter Point This national monument is the best mainland snorkelling site, situated about 2km from Chembe village and 1km inside the entrance gate to LMNP. The clear water here is teeming with cichlids of several colours: blue, orange and yellow. On land you should see rock hyrax, baboons, a variety of lizards and, if you're lucky, even a klipspringer or grysbok. Spotted-necked otters are common in the area. Entrance to the national park costs US$10 per person for non-residents. You can hire snorkelling equipment in the village.

West Thumbi Island The islands of LMNP offer perhaps the finest snorkelling on the lake, and West Thumbi is no exception, with Mitande Point in particular boasting one of the lake's most diverse cichlid communities, making it a popular site with day trippers from Cape Maclear. Inexpensive snorkelling trips can be arranged through the guide assigned to your hotel, and are usually inclusive of a fish barbecue, snorkelling equipment and transport by boat (you may have to bargain).

Mission graves Little remains today of the original Livingstonia Mission established at Cape Maclear by Lt E D Young on 17 October 1875. The high incidence of malaria here led to the mission being relocated in 1881, and the settlement was abandoned entirely in 1896. However, the mission cemetery, now preserved as a national monument, can still be seen below the boulders about 1km from central Chembe and 300m uphill of the entrance gate to LMNP.

Mwala wa Mphini The third and least publicised of LMNP's national monuments, this bizarre 10m-high rock lies 4km from Cape Maclear on the east side of the dirt feeder road from Monkey Bay. As its name (literally 'Rock of Tribal Face Scars') suggests, the front of the rock is covered with a criss-cross pattern of deep etchings that looks to be of human origin. In fact, the incisions are a natural geological phenomenon, created by the uneven weathering of an exposed crystalline rock.

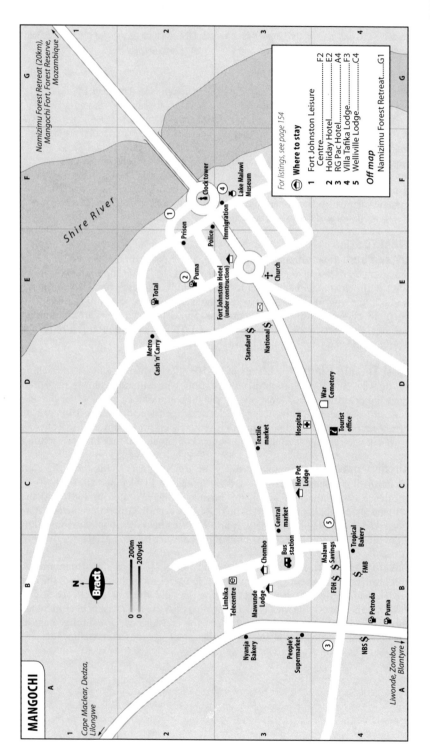

MANGOCHI

*Cape Maclear, Dedza,
Lilongwe*

*Namizimu Forest Retreat (20km),
Mangochi Fort, Forest Reserve,
Mozambique*

N
Bradt

0   200m
0   200yds

Shire River

Clock tower ⚑
①
● Prison
Police ●
Immigration ⬛
② Puma 🅿
🅿 Total
Lake Malawi
Museum ⚑ ④

● Metro
Cash 'n' Carry

Fort Johnston Hotel
(under construction)
⬛
Church ✝

Standard $
National $

● Textile
market

Hospital ✚
Tourist
office ℹ

War
Cemetery ⬜

Hot Pot
Lodge ⬛

Central
market ●

Chombo ⬛
Bus
station ⬛
⑤
Malawi
Savings $

Limbika
Telecentre ℮
Mawunde
Lodge ⬛

FDH $ $
● Tropical
Bakery
$ FMB

Petroda 🅿
Puma 🅿

Nyanja ●
Bakery

People's ●
Supermarket

③
NBS $

*Liwonde, Zomba,
Blantyre*

ⓘ **Where to stay**
For listings, see page 154

1 Fort Johnston Leisure
   Centre...............................F2
2 Holiday Hotel..................E2
3 RG Pac Hotel..................A4
4 Villa Tafika Lodge...........F3
5 Welliville Lodge..............C4

Off map
   Namizimu Forest Retreat......G1

9

Mangochi and
the Southern Lakeshore

Few travellers visit Mangochi, but it is among the more historic and characterful towns in Malawi, and worth the slight diversion from the M5 for its pretty riverside location, minor historical monuments and moderately interesting museum. A more popular attraction, starting about 10km north of Mangochi, is the row of resorts that line the southern Lake Malawi shore, among them the legendary Makokola Retreat and Nkopola Lodge. Mangochi is the closest large town to Cape Maclear, with good banking and foreign-exchange facilities, and it also has a plethora of markets and supermarkets where travellers heading to the likes of Liwonde National Park can stock up. The nearby forest reserves are almost entirely undeveloped for tourism, with the exception of the superb Namizimu Forest Retreat about 20km east of Mangochi.

MANGOCHI

Originally called Fort Johnston, Mangochi is one of the oldest towns in Malawi, and the sixth largest, with a population currently estimated at 55,000. The Old Town centre, on the west bank of the Shire River as it flows between lakes Malawi and Malombe, has a tangible Islamic influence dating to the slaving era, and its faded whitewashed buildings and sticky tropical ambience recall some of the more rundown towns along the Swahili coast.

Wide avenues lined with jacarandas, borassus palms and thick fruit trees testify to the Old Town's former importance, as does the row of old colonial buildings and monuments lining the Shire waterfront. At first glance, the somewhat rundown condition of many of these buildings appears to indicate a more recent decline in fortunes. Like so many Malawian towns, however, Mangochi has two discrete parts, and any notion of economic torpor will be dispelled by a visit to the bustling modern commercial centre, 1.5km west of the Shire River between the bus station and the main road to Blantyre.

HISTORY The short stretch of the Shire River that separates Lake Malawi from Lake Malombe is far easier to cross by boat than the vast lakes to its north and south, and as such it became an important route funnel for mid 19th-century Yao slave caravans heading to the Mozambican coast. The original Fort Johnston (named after Sir Harry Johnston, the first British Consul General of Nyasaland) was established in 1891 on the east bank of the river to restrict the Yao slave trade by plugging this gap. The fort was relocated to the west bank of the river in 1897, and at the same a time a second British fort was established in the Mangochi Hills about 30km to the east. In 1899, Fort Johnston was designated as a township by the colonial authorities, and it remained a river port and naval centre of some importance throughout the colonial era. Shortly after Malawi's independence, the town was renamed Mangochi.

GETTING THERE AND AWAY Mangochi lies about 65km from Monkey Bay at the southern end of the M10 and 75km north of Liwonde along the M3. The Old Town centre lies about 1km east of the main road between Monkey Bay and Liwonde and it can easily be bypassed if you so choose. Mangochi is an important public transport hub, and there is no shortage of bus and minibus transport to Monkey Bay, Lilongwe, Liwonde, Zomba and Blantyre.

WHERE TO STAY AND EAT *See map, page 152.*

Moderate

RG Pac Hotel (32 rooms) ⎷01 593607; m 088 8717960. Situated alongside the main junction with the Blantyre road, this modern dbl-storey hotel is set around a sandy central courtyard & has a good restaurant with indoor & outdoor seating serving Malawian staples & a few more exotic dishes in the US$2–3 range. The en-suite rooms have tiled floors, nets, DSTV & hot showers. *US$9.50/11 sgl/dbl B&B.*

Villa Tafika Lodge (21 rooms) ⎷01 593544/609740; m 088 1961707/099 9957805; e info@villatafika.com; www.villatafika.com. The oldest building in Mangochi, Villa Tafika was built in 1891 &, prior to falling into an advanced state of disrepair in recent decades, it served variously as the Hotel Fort Johnston, European Club, home of World War I hero Captain Rhoades, & the District Commissioner's residence. Fully restored with a wide balcony, thatched roof & a new wing at the back, it reopened as a hotel in 2007, & now stands out as the most attractive place to stay in Mangochi, even if the potentially lovely riverside setting is blocked by a tall wall. The restaurant serves a good selection of local & international dishes for around US$4. All rooms are en suite with DSTV, net, fan & hot water. *US$19 standard room with dbl bed, US$25 classic room with king-size bed, US$37.50–45 suite, all rates B&B.*

Budget

Holiday Hotel (35 rooms) ⎷01 594789; m 099 9635410. This is a pleasant hotel in the backstreets of the Old Town, with a restaurant serving local meals for US$2–3. The standard twin rooms have nets & use common showers, while the en-suite rooms have nets, fans & hot showers. *US$2.50/5 sgl/dbl exc b/fast, US$9.50/11 standard/executive en-suite twin, B&B (for 1).*

Welliville Lodge (10 rooms) ⎷01 594600; m 088 8660865; e welliville@gmail.com. This local lodge is conveniently located on the main road through town, & offers a warm welcome & comfortable en-suite rooms with TV, nets & fan. You can order meals on site, or pop next door to The Canoe Ice Cream Den & Restaurant where you'll definitely find chapattis & Malawian staples for US$2–3, &, if you're lucky, ice cream. *US$9.50/12.50 standard/executive dbl.*

Shoestring

Fort Johnston Leisure Centre (4 rooms) ⎷01 593264; m 088 8330071. A far more attractive option than the innumerable cheapies dotted around the bus station, this riverfront lodge & bar has a great location opposite Villa Tafika, & the slightly rundown en-suite rooms all have a dbl bed & net. *US$8 dbl.*

SHOPPING There is a well-stocked **People's Supermarket** [152 B3] on the main Blantyre road, and the town has a busy **fruit and vegetable market** [152 C3] near the bus station [152 B3].

OTHER PRACTICALITIES

Banks and foreign exchange
The **National** [152 E3] and **Standard** [152 E3] banks stand alongside each other opposite the post office in the old part of town. Both have foreign-exchange facilities and an ATM that accepts international Visa and MasterCard. On the new side of town, **FMB**, **FDH**, **NBS** & **Malawi Savings Bank** [152 B4] are all represented with ATMs and forex facilities. **National Bank** also has an ATM at People's Supermarket.

Immigration The **immigration office** [152 F3] near the clock tower roundabout takes a few minutes to process visitors' pass extensions for Mk5,000 (about US$16 at the time of writing) per extra 30 days.

Internet The best (and currently only) option is the air-conditioned **Limbika Telecentre** [152 B3] (m *099 9655800; ⊕ 08.00–20.00 Mon–Sat),* which has new computers and a fast connection at Mk5/min. There is irregular Wi-Fi at Villa Tafika for those with laptops.

WHAT TO SEE AND DO

Lake Malawi Museum [152 F3] (✆*01 584346; ⊕ 07.30–12.00, 13.00–17.00 daily; entrance US$0.75)* Housed in the colonial-era Gymkhana Clubhouse, the Lake Malawi Museum, established in 1971, focuses on the history and ecology of the lake, and the lifestyle of the lakeshore peoples. There is also a good display on lake transport featuring old monochrome photos of the MV *Chauncy Maples* and the original MV *Ilala.*

Around town The **Queen Victoria Clock Tower** is a prominent red-brick clock tower set within the main traffic circle in the Old Town. Built in 1903 in memory of Queen Victoria, it was subsequently dedicated to the 143 people who drowned when the MV *Viphya* sank on Lake Malawi in 1946. Nearby is the cannon from HMS *Gwendolyn*, used by Captain Rhoades to sink the German *Hermann Von Wessman* at Liuli in 1914. Immediately east of the clock tower, the Mangochi Bridge [152 F2] across the Shire River was built with Japanese funding and officially opened in January 2002. The **Commonwealth War Cemetery** [152 D4], which lies on the south side of the main road between the new and old parts of town, contains the graves of about 40 colonial officers and soldiers killed in World War I.

Mangochi Fort and Forest Reserve Extending over some 325km², Mangochi Forest Reserve is one of the largest in Malawi, protecting the prominent Mangochi Hills, which rise to an altitude of 1,742m about 20km east of Mangochi Town. Rising from the 500m lake littoral, the reserve is notable for its varied altitudinal range, and it supports a diverse flɔra, with Brachystegia woodland dominant up to around 1,400m, and a combination of open grassland and montane forest at higher altitudes. Relatively untrammelled and remote, the reserve is still visited seasonally by elephants from Liwonde National Park, and it may also still support a small population of lions, alongside various antelope and more than 150 bird species.

Set at an elevation of 1,370m on the northern slopes of the hills, the best-known landmark in the forest reserve is Mangochi Fort, which was built by the British in 1897 to curb the slave trade to Mozambique, and served for 30 years prior to being abandoned in 1928. It was built on the original stockade of Chief Jalasi, the Yao leader who controlled the slave trade in this part of Malawi prior to his capture in 1895. The vast fort originally housed a garrison of 40 British soldiers, and it later served as a training camp for the King's African Rifles during World War I. Several of the thick stone walls are still standing today, making it the most substantial surviving relic of the slave-trading era, and it was declared a national monument in 1967. The fort can be reached from the M3 east of Mangochi Town, but getting there involves a steep 650m ascent on foot. The views from the top are fantastic.

9

Where to stay *See map, page 88.*

⌂ **Namizimu Forest Retreat** (10 rooms)
m 099 7225300; e tara@namizimu.com; www.
namizimu.com.On a steep hillside 20km east of
Mangochi in the even lesser-known Namizimu
Forest Reserve to the north of the M3, this
exceptionally tranquil colonial-era estate is
the only accommodation in either reserve. The
exceedingly warm owner-managers can help
arrange any number of hikes & excursions through
this secluded corner of Malawi, & there are
motorbikes & kayaks available for hire. The serene,
forested grounds host a spring-fed plunge pool
& hot tub, colonial home with fireplace & wide
veranda, & a number of breathtaking outdoor

showers improbably tucked away on secluded
rocks. All rooms are en suite with solar lighting &
showers, double beds, nets, & private verandas.
Organic meals are provided on a full-board basis &
there is a simply stocked honesty bar. The lodge is
at the end of a steep 1.5km track best approached
in a 4x4, but parking is available in Chowe village
at the base of the hill. They also operate a self-
catering camp on the remote eastern shore of
Lake Malawi, contact above for details. Advance
booking essential. *US$80–100 pp FB. (Lake Camp:
US$50 family room, US$15 dorm bed, US$10
camping.)*

FROM MANGOCHI TO MONKEY BAY

About 10km north of Mangochi, the Shire River flows from the southern heel of
Lake Malawi. This far southern part of the lake consists of a roughly 15km-wide
sliver of water which extends for about 50km up to Monkey Bay and the Cape
Maclear Peninsula. Accessed via the surfaced M10, this area is generally known
as the Southern Lakeshore, and it is prime resort country, hosting two of the lake's
longest-serving upmarket properties in the form of Makokola Retreat and Nkopola
Lodge, as well as the newer Norman Carr Cottage and a plethora of smaller and
cheaper options.

WHERE TO STAY *See map opposite.*
Upmarket

⌂ **Madzi Kuwala** (6 rooms) 01 794555;
e reservations@ulendo.net; www.ulendo.net.
This secluded beachside cottage lies just south
of the Norman Carr Cottage along the same dirt
road, branching east from the M10 about 2.5km
south of Chirombo junction. It sleeps up to 13 in
six bedrooms with nets & fans & features an open
layout with lounge & dining area, covered patio,
DSTV, fully equipped kitchen & plunge pool. There
are staff on site who can help prepare meals, but
guests must bring all food themselves. *US$200
whole house w/day, US$250 whole house w/end.*

⌂ **Makokola Retreat** (48 rooms) 01
580244/445/469; e enquiries@makokola.
com; www.makokola.com. About 2km north of
Nkopola, the rebranded 'Club Mak' is still the best
known of Malawi's lakeshore hotels, & extensive
renovations & refurbishments have ensured it
maintains its high standards. The en-suite rooms
with AC are spacious & beautifully furnished with
hardwoods & ethnic textiles, & the gardens with
large baobab trees are immaculately maintained.

A neatly kept 9-hole golf course, a good selection
of watersports & a huge 30m swimming pool
make this a favourite holiday destination, though
relatively pricey. *US$264/406 superior sgl/dbl,
US$294/452 suite, US$323/524 executive suite, all
rates all-inclusive.*

⌂ **Nkopola Lodge** (55 rooms) 01 5804444;
m 088 8965123; e Nkopola@sunbirdmalawi.com;
www.sunbirdmalawi.com. Part of the national
Sunbird chain, this well-patronised but impersonal
beach lodge is the focal point of Nkopola village,
22km north of Mangochi Town. Reached via a 1.3km
surfaced side road, the lodge has an attractive layout
& wonderful position at the base of a rocky & thickly
wooded hill. The birdlife here is fantastic, & vervet
monkeys inhabit the grounds. Other attractions are
the large swimming pool, excellent watersports
facilities (mostly free to hotel residents), & the
string of good curio stalls lining the road outside the
lodge grounds. The food here is also very good, with
mains in the US$6.50–9 range & cheaper snacks
available, too. The large en-suite rooms in the main
hotel all come with twin or king-size beds, walk-in

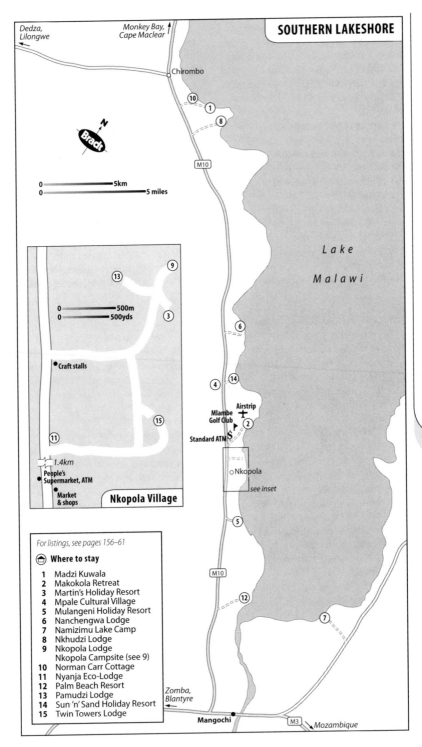

SOUTHERN LAKESHORE

Dedza, Lilongwe

Monkey Bay, Cape Maclear

Chirombo

10
1
8

M10

Lake Malawi

6

4 14

Airstrip

Mlambe Golf Club
2

Standard ATM

Nkopola

see inset

5

M10

12

7

Zomba, Blantyre

Mangochi   M3   *Mozambique*

Nkopola Village inset

9

13

500m
500yds

3

Craft stalls

15

11

1.4km

People's Supermarket, ATM

Market & shops

Nkopola Village

For listings, see pages 156–61

Where to stay

1 Madzi Kuwala
2 Makokola Retreat
3 Martin's Holiday Resort
4 Mpale Cultural Village
5 Mulangeni Holiday Resort
6 Nanchengwa Lodge
7 Namizimu Lake Camp
8 Nkhudzi Lodge
9 Nkopola Lodge
   Nkopola Campsite (see 9)
10 Norman Carr Cottage
11 Nyanja Eco-Lodge
12 Palm Beach Resort
13 Pamudzi Lodge
14 Sun 'n' Sand Holiday Resort
15 Twin Towers Lodge

157

nets, DSTV, fan, AC, minibar & tea-/coffee-making facilities, & there are more basic en-suite twin rooms with AC at the adjacent campsite (covered on page 160). The hotel is a Skyband Wi-Fi zone & there is an NBS Bank ATM on site. *US$177/201 standard sgl/dbl, US$194/218 superior sgl/dbl, US$267 family room, all rates B&B.*

🏠 **Norman Carr Cottage** (6 rooms, 1 family cottage) m 099 9207506/088 355357; e taffy@ africa-online.net; www.normancarrcottage.com. The most northerly resort on this stretch of coast, this welcoming & flexible owner-managed place lies along a 1.8km dirt road branching east from the M10 about 2.5km south of Chirombo junction. Formerly the lakeshore retreat of the renowned Zambian conservationist Norman Carr, it now offers homely accommodation & good food on a beautiful wooded bay with a fine swimming beach. Large & airy beach-facing suites have king-

size 4-poster beds with walk-in nets, & open-air showers in a private atrium. There's plenty of indoor & outdoor seating, & a large lounge with a good library for rainy days. *US$165/270 sgl/dbl, US$145/240 courtyard sgl/dbl, all rooms FB, inc boat trips, snorkelling gear, kayaks & other non-motorised watersports.*

🏠 **Palm Beach Resort** (10 rooms) m 099 9912726/9943050; e palmbeach@africa-online. net; www.palmbeach-mw.com. The most southerly resort anywhere on the lake, this owner-managed set-up lies 1.8km from the M10 via a signposted turn-off 11km north of Mangochi & 2km from the Shire River outlet. The large grounds are very attractive & dotted with tall palm trees, but the resort as a whole seems slightly unfocused. Accommodation is in tall thatched en-suite chalets with net, fan & attractive ethnic décor. There is also a bar & a good restaurant. *US$35 pp B&B, US$50*

THE ELEPHANTS OF PHIRILONGWE

Some 40km west of Mangochi, Phirilongwe Forest Reserve recently became the setting for the sort of irresolvable conflict between wildlife and humans that seems inevitable in the context of Malawi's rapid population growth. Named after the 1,554m-high Mount Phirilongwe, this forest reserve was until recently the core territory of one of Malawi's last free-ranging herds of elephant, estimated to be anything from 60 to 100 strong, based on a 2007 aerial survey in which 57 individuals were counted.

The Ndowa Hills surrounding Phirilongwe support a rapidly growing human population of around 3,000 subsistence farmers, split between 30 villages. As a result, the forest reserve has been subject to repeated encroachment over the years, and competition for resources between people and elephants is intense. The elephants cannot survive off the fruits of the forest alone, so they have taken to raiding surrounding agricultural land, regularly destroying crops and killing at least ten people. And the angry villagers have responded by using nail-embedded planks, guns, arrows, snares and poison to maim or kill any elephants that threaten their crops – of eight individual elephants darted to fit radio collars in 2007, three had partially amputated trunks and another two were scarred with bullet wounds.

The seemingly irresolvable conflict came to a head in 2009 when the International Fund for Animal Welfare (IFAW), African Parks Foundation (APF) and Department of National Parks and Wildlife (DNPW) signed an agreement to translocate the Phirilongwe elephants 250km to Majete Wildlife Reserve in the Shire Valley. This plan met with widespread support from local villagers and chiefs, but shortly after the translocations started in June 2009, a court injunction was placed on proceedings at the application of a local businessman, Ismail Khan, and his organisation Friends of Phirilongwe (FOP), which demanded that an Environmental Impact Assessment be conducted before the elephants were relocated.

pp FB, US$100 self-catering chalet sleeping up to 5, US$7 pp camping.

🏠 **Sun 'n' Sand Holiday Resort** (150 rooms) ☏01 598069/150; m 088 8864919; e info@ sunnsandmw.com; www.sunnsandmw.com. Geared more to the conference market than to tourists, this is a large & impersonal hotel with great facilities & a nice beach location but a rather packaged feel. Situated 5km north of Makokola Retreat, it has a conference centre, large swimming pool, a restaurant serving good Indian & Western cuisine, a selection of sports & even a small supermarket, & there are ostriches in the grounds. The en-suite rooms are pretty good value, though, & they all come with king-size or twin bed with nets, tiled or wooden floor, DSTV, AC & minibar. *US$45.50/62.50 sgl/dbl, US$52/73.50 superior sgl/ dbl, US$73.50/86 suite sgl/dbl, US$266 chalet, all rates B&B.*

Moderate

🏠 **Mpale Cultural Village** (12 rooms) ☏01 11957663; m 099 5244108; e mcsl@mcslmw. com or balakasibaiton@gmail.com; www. mpaleculturalvillage.com. Set just west of the M10 atop Mpale Hill, this admirable community tourism project seeks to preserve & promote Yao culture, & proceeds go towards a variety of community development projects. They offer comfortable accommodation in en-suite thatched chalets with TV, AC, four-poster beds, nets & locally made décor, as well as traditional mud huts with woven bedding for those seeking a true village experience. Offerings include Yao music & dance performances, craft workshops, oral histories, a good restaurant, & an on-site museum featuring traditional Yao instruments, hunting implements & other artefacts. *US$35/52 sgl/dbl chalet, B&B.*

According to FOP, the elephants had great potential to develop as a key tourist attraction in Mangochi District, they also played an important role as protectors of the forest reserve against further human encroachment, and the human conflict could be resolved simply by fencing Phirilongwe as a wildlife reserve. A spokesperson for the DNPW agreed that in principle this would be 'the ideal scenario' but pointed out that 'there is no finance and there is no suitable area … the only solution is to move them out to an existing reserve that's properly fenced … because at this stage these elephants are very aggressive: they hate people, the people hate them'. Meanwhile Chief Nankumba, spokesman for the Traditional Chiefs of Mangochi, threatened to lead a march on the District Commissioner's office if the injunction wasn't lifted, stating: 'We have lost human lives, crops and property to elephant stampedes … The elephants must go to Majete now.'

The injunction was duly lifted, and by 4 July, when the operation ended, a total of 83 elephants had been captured and released into Majete. Jason Bell-Leask of IFAW reported that '12 of the 14 groups of elephants captured and relocated included individuals that had suffered injuries caused by human intervention – seven of the elephants had trunk amputations caused by snares, one had a deformed foot from a gin trap injury, actual snares had to be removed from three of the elephants, one elephant was blind in one eye from a gun shot wound, and a number of others bore scars from bullet wounds and snares'. It would be difficult to take issue with Bell-Leask's assertion that 'moving the elephants was, without argument, the only solution to a terrible situation for both the elephants and the community … this is a victory for both elephants and people'. In the big picture, however, there is a certain hollowness to the victory. Yes, the elephants are safely fenced away at Majete, the people of Phirilongwe can breathe more freely in their absence, and we should be glad for that. But somehow the victory feels like one minor subsidiary battle won in the course of a ceaseless campaign to tame the world's diminishing wildernesses.

LAKE MALAWI YACHTING MARATHON

The longest freshwater yachting race held in Africa, the Lake Malawi Yachting Marathon 500 International has taken place annually in July since 1984. An eight-day 560km race, it has traditionally been operated as a benefit event, raising funds for lakeshore communities and wildlife projects. All classes of boat are eligible. A challenging and sometimes dangerous race, it starts at Makokola Retreat or Nkopola Lodge and then runs in stages, with a slightly different route each year, with overnight stops at Cape Maclear, Senga Bay, Nkhotakota, Dwangwa and Likoma Island, before finishing up at Chintheche Inn. Entry fees are US$350 per person and US$100 per yacht and include camping fees, catering and transport. They say it's one long party! For further details, check the website www.sailing.org.za.

⌂ **Nanchengwa Lodge** (7 rooms, 2 dorms) m 099 9274696/5825697; e ryan@nanchengwa. com; www.nanchengwa.com. This friendly family-run set-up is one of the longest-serving lodges on this part of the lakeshore, with a delightful beachfront location, a relaxed & welcoming atmosphere, friendly dogs & fabulous home cooking with produce from their own farm. It lies 2km from the M10 along a dirt road signposted 19km south of Chirombo. In terms of accommodation, there's the choice between en-suite twin or dbl rooms in the main house, thatched A-frame beach houses sleeping up to 4, or new dbl tree houses. The owners are working on several school & community projects in the local village & welcome enquiries from aspirant volunteers. *US$50/80 sgl/dbl in the main house B&B, US$25 pp beach house; US$15 pp tree house, US$10 pp dorm bed, US$6 pp camping.*

⌂ **Nkhudzi Lodge** (8 rooms) m 099 9386669; e nkhudzilodge@webmail.co.za; www.nkhudzilodge.com. Situated 3km from the M10 along a turn-off signposted 5km south of Chirombo junction, this is a comfortable lodge with soft lawns stretching under trees on the bank above the beach. Standing tents that sleep 4–8 are available, & it offers a swimming pool & watersports, as well as badminton & volleyball; there are also inner tubes for mucking around in the water. There's a restaurant serving meals for around US$3.50. *US$23.50–30 dbl B&B, US9.50– 12.50 standing tents, US$4.75 per tent camping.*

⌂ **Nkopola Campsite** (7 rooms) Contact details as for Nkopola Lodge. This annex to Nkopola Lodge, also under the same management, has pleasant but more basic rooms than its more

upmarket neighbour (but still with AC) & a large shady campground. *US$31.50 twin, US$6.50 per tent camping.*

Budget

⌂ **Martin's Holiday Resort** (7 rooms) m 099 4254382. Situated around the corner from Nkopola Lodge & offering indirect access to the same beach, this is one of the best-value options in this part of Malawi, despite looking a bit ramshackle at first glance. The large en-suite dbl rooms are very clean & have a cold shower & private balcony with a distant lake view. There is no restaurant but you can eat at the nearby lodge or elsewhere in Nkopola village. *US$15.75/17.25 sgl/dbl B&B.*

⌂ **Pamudzi Lodge** (19 rooms) \ 01 580770; m 088 8309566. Also set back from the lake in Nkopola village, this place has clean, newly remodelled en-suite rooms with net, fan & DSTV. Ask for a new room, as they're smarter & cost the same. *US$20.50/23.50 sgl/dbl.*

⌂ **Twin Towers Lodge** (16 rooms) m 099 5718131/9553129; e alikopaga@yahoo.co.uk. Also in Nkopola village, this place offers a variety of clean & comfortable dbl rooms & suites, all with fan, net & en-suite hot shower, & while the accommodation is fine at the price, the cramped compound & relative distance from the beach count against it. The attached restaurant/bar serves the usual staples. *US$14 twin, US$20.50 dbl, US$25 suite with AC.*

Shoestring

⌂ **Mulangeni Holiday Resort** (26 rooms) \ 01 580698/200/201; e mulangeni@globemw. net. Only 800m from the M10 & 20km north of

Mangochi, this attractively located resort looks a little shabby & neglected. The en-suite rooms come with fan, net & hot bath, & Rooms 10–17 are right on the beach, but they feel a touch overpriced for what you get. By contrast, the twin standing tents, though simple, are protected by thatch shelters & seem like excellent value in the shoestring range. You can also camp cheaply. *US$26.50/34.50 sgl/dbl, US$6.25 twin standing tent, US$1.50 pp camping.*

⌂ **Nyanja Eco-Lodge** (12 rooms) m 099 1580114; e nelson@nyanjalodges.com; www.nyanjalodges.com. The website for this local lodge offers up a thought-provoking introduction: 'Earth is a planet among nine other planets. And Nyanja Lodges are lodges among others located on planet earth.' Metaphysicians can ponder away, but those of a more terrestrial persuasion will be glad to know that this earthly lodge sits directly along the M10 in Nkopola village. While there's nothing particularly 'eco' or interplanetary about it, it does feature freshly painted double rooms with ceiling fans, nets, DSTV & en-suite hot showers, with a restaurant & lively bar attached. *US$16 dbl.*

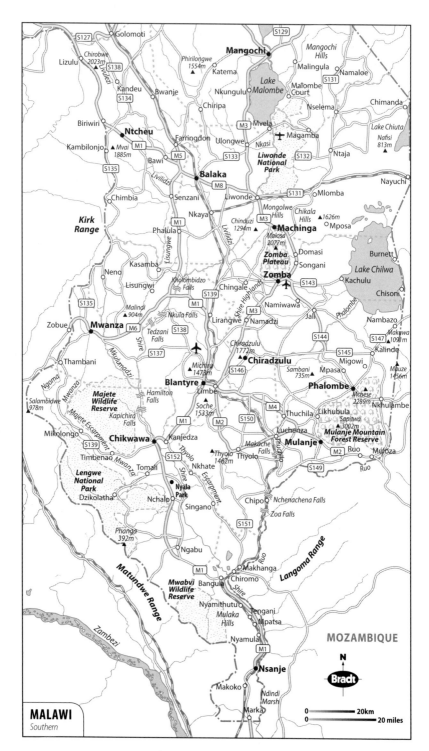

Part Three

SOUTHERN MALAWI

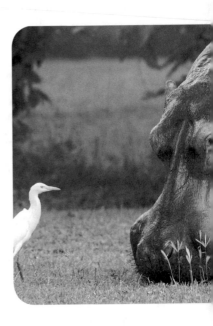

OVERVIEW OF PART THREE

The next five chapters cover the densely populated southern part of the country below lakes Malawi and Malombe. This area is quite different from the rest of Malawi in geographic terms, most obviously in that the Rift Valley south of Malombe is not submerged by a lake but run through by the Shire River, and also insofar as it now moves towards the country's western border, which means that the southern highlands around Zomba, Blantyre, Thyolo and Mulanje all lie along the eastern rather than the western escarpment.

Starting in the north of the region, pretty much where the last chapter left off, *Chapter 10* follows the Shire River south from Lake Malombe to the town of Liwonde, passing *en route* through the stunning Liwonde National Park.

South of Liwonde, the M5 ascends east from the Rift Valley floor to the pretty former capital of Zomba, which forms the main subject of *Chapter 11*, along with the adjacent hikers' paradise that is Zomba Plateau, and nearby Lake Chilwa, the country's only Ramsar wetland.

Chapter 12 covers Blantyre, the country's second-largest city, and the main transport hub and route focus in the south. *Chapter 13* heads southeast from Blantyre to the magnificent Mulanje Massif, the tallest peak in central Africa and perhaps the top hiking destination anywhere in Malawi.

The remote and low-lying Lower Shire Valley is the subject of *Chapter 14*, which includes coverage of four important wildlife destinations: the newly resurgent Majete Wildlife Reserve, Lengwe National Park, Mwabvi Wildlife Reserve and the bird-rich Elephant Marsh.

LIWONDE SAFARI CAMP

- INSIDE Malawi's Top National Park
- Free Town Pick-Up
- Nightly Campfires
- Sleep Amongst Wildlife!

AFFORDABLE SAFARI PARADISE

+265 (0)88 1813240
liwondesafaricamp@gmail.com
www.liwondesafaricamp.com

10

Liwonde

The influential Yao chief Liwonde has lent his name not only to Malawi's tenth-largest town, situated at the juncture of the M3 and the Shire River south of Lake Malombe, but also to the country's finest safari destination, Liwonde National Park. Both the town and the national park are dominated by the captivating tropical aura of the Shire River, but while the town is otherwise a somewhat humdrum affair, the national park is a true gem, one that ranks highly on any 'to do' list for Malawi. True, when it comes to Big Five game viewing, Liwonde National Park doesn't compare to the best on offer in neighbouring Zambia or Tanzania (though there's plenty of wildlife around, notably dense concentrations of elephant, hippo and crocs). But it is undoubtedly one of the prettiest game reserves in central Africa, the opportunity to explore the magnificent palm-fringed river by boat is not to be missed, and the birdlife is astounding.

LIWONDE TOWN

Gateway to the eponymous national park, Liwonde is a more substantial town than first appearances might suggest, with a population estimated at 31,000. It straddles the Shire River about 40km south of the outlet from Lake Malombe, and only 5km from where it flows out of the southern boundary of the national park. Like so many Malawian towns, Liwonde comprises two discrete parts. The compact Old Town centre, which lies about 1km southeast of the Shire River immediately north of the M3 between Mangochi and Zomba, is quieter but more developed in terms of urban facilities, housing a large hospital and organised market. On the northwest side of the road barrage across the river, by contrast, is the satellite town referred to as Liwonde Barrage, a scruffier and livelier settlement that grew organically around the police block and bus stop on the M3.

Even those in transit, with no intention of visiting the national park, might want to stop at Liwonde Barrage to soak up the archetypal tropical African river scene: low-wooded hills in the background, fishermen punting past in traditional dugouts, hippos grunting and snorting, and thick reed beds rustling with birdlife, all to the background of market and street noises. Better still, take a lunch break at one of the several hotels that line the river on either side, or leave yourself time to spend a night on the riverfront, and maybe take a boat trip a short way upriver to look for hippos, birds and other wildlife.

GETTING THERE AND AWAY Liwonde is a major route focus, situated alongside the M3 about 100km north of Blantyre, 50km north of Zomba and 75km south of Mangochi. Branching west from the M3 a few kilometres north of town, the M8 leads via Balaka to the M5 northward to Salima and the M12 to Dedza and Lilongwe,

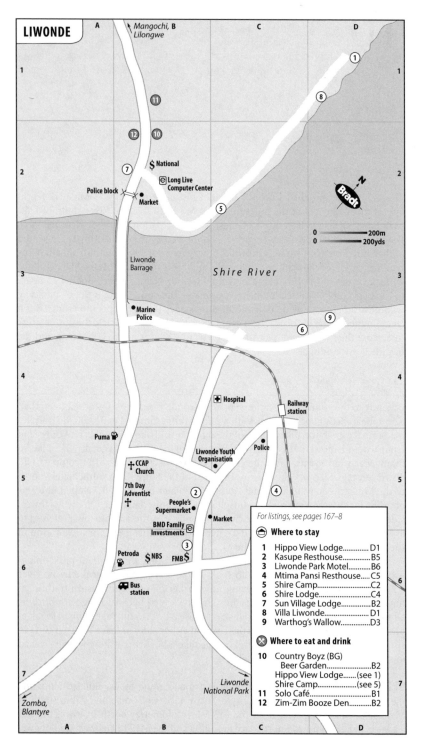

LIWONDE

Mangochi, B
Lilongwe

National

Long Live
Computer Center

Police block
Market

Liwonde
Barrage

Shire River

N
Bradt

| 0 | 200m |
| 0 | 200yds |

Marine
Police

Hospital

Railway
station

Puma

Liwonde Youth
Organisation

Police

CCAP
Church

7th Day
Adventist

People's
Supermarket

Market

BMD Family
Investments

Petroda

NBS

FMB

Bus
station

Liwonde
National Park

Zomba,
Blantyre

For listings, see pages 167–8

Where to stay

1   Hippo View Lodge..............D1
2   Kasupe Resthouse.............B5
3   Liwonde Park Motel............B6
4   Mtima Pansi Resthouse.....C5
5   Shire Camp.........................C2
6   Shire Lodge.........................C4
7   Sun Village Lodge...............B2
8   Villa Liwonde......................D1
9   Warthog's Wallow...............D3

Where to eat and drink

10 Country Boyz (BG)
      Beer Garden......................B2
      Hippo View Lodge.......(see 1)
      Shire Camp.....................(see 5)
11 Solo Café............................B1
12 Zim-Zim Booze Den...........B2

which is 220km away. All these roads are surfaced and in good condition, but taking traffic into account, allow 90 minutes to drive from Blantyre in a private vehicle, and three–four hours from Lilongwe. There are regular buses in every direction, though many don't actually go into town but stop at Liwonde Barrage and the turn-off to the Old Town centre. By contrast, minibuses out of Liwonde mostly leave from the station [166 B6] in the Old Town centre. Liwonde is also the best place to board the train to Nayuchi on the Mozambican border, at least when it's in service.

WHERE TO STAY *See map, opposite.*

Upmarket

Hippo View Lodge (96 rooms) 01 542822/225; e hippo@hippoviewlodge. com; www.hippoviewlodge.com. This large & impersonal business-class monolith is on the northwest bank of the Shire River about 1.5km upstream of the M3. Set in manicured 2ha lawns where hippo regularly come to graze, it caters mainly to the conference market, but it's also well equipped for tourists. Facilities include a business centre, good Indian restaurant & gift shop, & boat trips on the Shire (around US$60/hr for up to 12 people). Before you reach the swimming pool there are crocodile warnings against swimming in the river. The rooms are comfortable but at best uninspired & in some cases quite gloomy, though the standard rooms were mid-renovation when we visited & are likely to improve. Standard twins are carpeted with DSTV, phone, nets & en-suite hot shower, & superior rooms also have AC, which is quite an asset in this sticky climate. *US$47/73 sgl/dbl, US$57/95 superior, US$70/110 deluxe, US$79/126 suite, all rates B&B.*

Shire Lodge (52 rooms) 01 542277; e shirelodge@globemw.net. On the southeast bank of the river, this glossy institutional behemoth is aimed squarely at the conference market, but the modern tiled rooms with AC, DSTV, phone, nets, coffee/tea facilities & en-suite hot shower will appeal to tourists as well. Entirely rebuilt in 2012, the green riverside compound features geometric gardens, a good restaurant/bar & shaded terraces with views over the Shire. There are also plans for a swimming pool. Skyband Wi-Fi is available for those with laptops, but computer use in the business centre is overpriced. *US$63/82 sgl/dbl, B&B.*

Moderate

Villa Liwonde (5 rooms) 099 9957805/9400402; e villaliwonde@yahoo.com; www.villatafika.com/villaliwonde.htm. On the

west bank of the river about 500m before Hippo View, this mostly self-catering lodge consists of a Mediterranean-style house set in a spacious garden with a balcony from where you can spot hippos & birds during b/fast. Rooms are all en suite & there is a fully equipped kitchen with a cook, DSTV, generator, BBQ, landing-bay for boats, a jacuzzi & access to the swimming pool at Hippo View. There is also a staffed bar with pool table & meals are available on request for US$4. *The house sleeps up to 12 & can be rented in its entirety for US$145, but rooms are also available separately at US$25 dbl or US$44 for a 4-bed room, all rates B&B.*

Budget

Liwonde Park Motel (12 rooms) 01 542338; m 088 8824196. Set in a well-tended leafy compound, this is the smartest lodge in the Old Town centre. It offers en-suite accommodation with DSTV, net, fan & hot showers in all rooms, plus AC in superior ones. *US$15.75/20.50 ordinary/ superior dbl B&B.*

Shire Camp (4 rooms) m 088 8594304; e shirecamp@gmail.com. This place has a lovely & convenient location on the northwest bank of the Shire only 400m from the M3. There are 4 reed chalets with dbl beds & en-suite hot showers & camping is also permitted. They can arrange a variety of services including car hire & boat safaris starting at US$75. The friendly bar & restaurant has good food & fantastic river views. *US$11 dbl B&B, US$3.50 pp camping.*

Sun Village Lodge (20 rooms) 01 11570861. This is a decent little hotel situated at Liwonde Barrage right next to the police block, but the basic en-suite rooms seem overpriced. *US$12/22.50 sgl/dbl.*

Warthog's Wallow (10 rooms, 4 under construction) m 099 1452345. Though it looks a bit forlorn compared with its newer, sharper neighbours, this is still a serviceable budget option, in an attractive patch of fever tree forest on the

10

southeast bank of the river next to Shire Lodge. The thatched rooms are clean & cool, & come with twin or dbl bed, nets, writing desk, en-suite hot shower & fan or AC. The swimming pool was parched on our last visit, but this could theoretically change. Meals are prepared by request at a flat fee of US$4 pp per sitting. *US$12.50 small dbl, US$19 standard dbl/twin, exc b/fast.*

Shoestring

⌂ **Kasupe Resthouse** (19 rooms) m 099 9117199. This central lodge has very basic rooms, pungently aromatic common showers & toilets, & the sole merit of being very cheap. *US$2/2.50 sgl/dbl.*

⌂ **Mtima Pansi Resthouse** (51 rooms) ✆01 542231; m 088 8724956. Clear favourite among the real cheapies, this large local resthouse sprawls in green gardens a block away from the Old Town centre & bus station. En-suite rooms in the new wing have cold showers, 1 or 2 dbl beds, nets & in some cases a fan, & the old wing has basic rooms without shower. *US$3.25–6.25 dbl (old wing), US$4.50–9.50 en-suite dbl (new wing).*

✗ WHERE TO EAT AND DRINK *See map, page 166.*

✗ **Hippo View Lodge** ✆01 542822/225; ⊕ 12.00–22.00 daily. The large open-sided restaurant at this upmarket hotel seats 150 people, & it has a great view of the river. It specialises in Indian cuisines, with vegetarian selections at US$6 & meat & fish dishes up to US$12.

✗ **Shire Camp** m 088 8594304; ⊕ 06.00–22.00 daily. Another good spot for a riverside meal, this locally run restaurant is also the best place to catch sporting events on DSTV. It serves a limited menu of fish & other dishes for around US$3. The food is good, especially at the price, but service can be slow, so eat elsewhere if you are in a hurry.

✗ **Solo Café** ✆01 542095; m 099 9488711; ⊕ 06.00–22.00 daily. Though it lacks a river view, this is a great little café with indoor & outdoor seating on the M3 close to the barrage. It has efficient service & a varied menu, with b/fasts, meat, fish & vegetarian dishes at US$2.75 & burgers & snacks for US$1.50.

♀ **Country Boyz (BG) Beer Garden & Zim-Zim Booze Den** Facing each other on opposite sides of the M3, these local hangouts compete daily for the honour of having the loudest tunes (& best names) in Liwonde Barrage.

SHOPPING The large **market** [166 B2] at the Mangochi turn-off is an excellent place to buy curios. Under the purpose-built market area is a wide range of highly polished woodcarvings, including an army of straw-hatted fishermen carrying fish. The **central market** [166 C5] and **People's Supermarket** [166 B5] opposite are the places to stock up on processed goods for those camping in the national park.

OTHER PRACTICALITIES

Banking and foreign exchange The **National Bank** [166 B2] at Liwonde Barrage and **NBS** and **FMB** branches [166 B6] in the Old Town centre all have ATMs accepting Visa cards and can exchange hard currency during banking hours.

Internet In Liwonde Barrage, the closet-sized **Long Live Computer Center** [166 B2] (m *088 8714342;* ⊕ *08.00–17.00 Mon–Sat*) only has one computer, but offers internet access at Mk10 per minute. A better bet is **BMD Family Investments** [166 B5] (m *099 1536971;* ⊕ *08.00–20.00 daily)* which charges Mk8/min at its first-storey location overlooking the old town market. For Skyband Wi-Fi, head to Shire Lodge.

LIWONDE NATIONAL PARK

(⊕ *Early–18.00 daily (entrance gate); entrance US$10/7 pp per day for foreigners/ residents. Self-drivers must also pay US$3 per car per day.*) Dominated by the sluggish Shire River and its lush fringing vegetation, Liwonde National Park

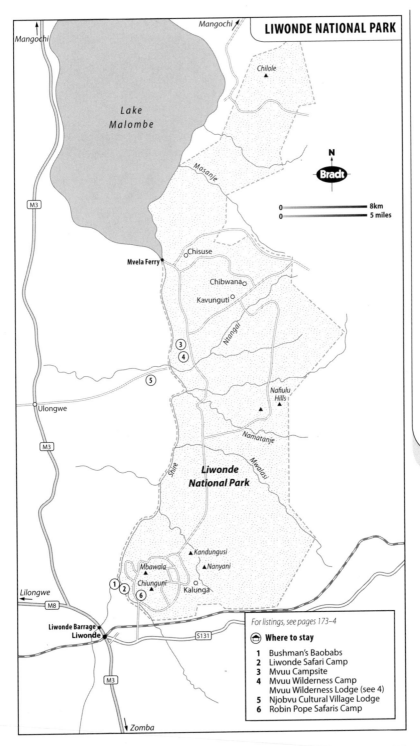

LIWONDE NATIONAL PARK

Mangochi

Mangochi

Chilole ▲

Lake
Malombe

Masanje

N
Bradt

0 ———————— 8km
0 ———————— 5 miles

M3

○ Chisuse

Mvela Ferry

Chibwana ○

Kavunguti ○

Ntangai

③
④

⑤

Nafiulu
Hills
▲

○ Ulongwe

Namatanje

M3

Shire

**Liwonde
National
Park**

Mwalasi

▲ Kandungusi

Mbawala
▲   ▲ Nanyani

Chiunguni
▲

① ②

⑥   ○
Kalunga

Lilongwe
←
M8

Liwonde Barrage ✕
Liwonde ●

S131

M3

Zomba

For listings, see pages 173–4

⊛ **Where to stay**

1 Bushman's Baobabs
2 Liwonde Safari Camp
3 Mvuu Campsite
4 Mvuu Wilderness Camp
   Mvuu Wilderness Lodge (see 4)
5 Njobvu Cultural Village Lodge
6 Robin Pope Safaris Camp

evokes every romantic notion of untrammelled Africa, especially at night, when the air resonates with the uninhibited chirruping of frogs and grunting of hippos. And while this 548km² reserve has to rank as a second-string safari destination compared with the continent's finest, it does offer the finest wildlife viewing and birdwatching in Malawi, and its aesthetic merits – this is the quintessential African river scene – elevate it close to being one of Africa's truly great game reserves.

Liwonde is a relatively small park, only 50km long and nowhere more than 15km wide, and an estimated 100,000 people live within 5km of its unfenced boundaries, where they attempt to scrape a living in what is technically a marginal agricultural area. As a result, there has been a long history of conflict between wildlife and local villagers, and poaching is an ongoing problem, one that has resulted in the local extinction of several large mammal species, including lion and African wild dog (see box below), though there is talk of reintroducing the former during the lifespan of this edition. Regardless, there is still plenty of wildlife to be seen in Liwonde, and sightings here feel very genuine, wild and pristine.

Mvuu is the park's most-established lodge, and is involved community projects that attempt to bring local people into contact with the park in a positive way. Operated by Wilderness Safaris, who manage Mvuu, Children in the Wilderness

BACKGROUND TO LIWONDE NATIONAL PARK

The earliest written account of the Liwonde area dates to 1868, when Captain Henry Faulkner passed this way on an expedition to search for Livingstone. Faulkner described Chikalogwe, at the southern end of the park, as 'an extensive plain [where] waterbuck, impala, reedbuck and gazelle [sable antelope] might be seen wherever I looked, as far as the eye could reach … The glasses showed me that there were many hartebeest, and there seemed to be at least a hundred buffalo … I never saw such quantities of game.'

Faulkner's report is echoed by many who followed in his footsteps. In 1894, O'Neill proclaimed the Liwonde area to be 'unquestionably the best game country I have passed'. Henry Drummond, who passed through in 1902, reported seeing immense herds of zebra in the area, while Vaughn-Kirby wrote in 1899 that spotted hyenas were 'to be met with in astonishing numbers' and the *Nyasaland Handbook* of 1908 declared that 'eland … can be seen in herds of 40 to 50 animals.' Meanwhile, in 1890, Harry Johnston regarded hippos in the Upper Shire to be so abundant and hazardous that 'they should be mercilessly exterminated'.

Unfortunately as is so often the case, the arrival of Europeans initiated the demise of these great animals. For two decades starting in the 1870s, ivory hunters visited the area regularly, exporting thousands of tons annually. And by the 1890s, the area had been established as a favoured recreational hunting ground for administrators and settlers based in Zomba, only 50km to the south. In 1932, Stephen Murray's *Handbook to Nyasaland* stated that 'some years ago big game was very numerous' in the vicinity of Liwonde, but 'there is now very little game left and what there is is very scattered'. Indeed, the nyala antelope, regularly shot by hunters in the first decade of the 20th century, were most likely extinct by that time, while wildebeest, once common in the area, were last seen in 1926, and black rhino were also probably hunted out in the same decade.

The situation deteriorated further in the post-war era. African wild dog, still 'very numerous' in 1932 according to Murray, were last seen in 1975. Eland became (*www.childreninthewilderness.com*) has implemented a life-skills programme for orphans living around the park. Kids come on summer camp to learn everything from first aid, human rights, democracy and nutrition to information about HIV/AIDS. The newly opened Bushman's Baobabs lodge operates the Mchire Children's Centre in conjunction with the International Fund for Animal Welfare (*www.ifaw.org*), offering a variety of educational programmes for local children.

VEGETATION Liwonde National Park supports a range of habitats that belies its small size, with more than 1,000 vascular plant species recorded. Ecologists recognise seven main vegetation plant communities within the park. Roughly three-quarters of the park supports a monotonous cover of mopane woodland, dominated by the mopane trees that form a 12m-high canopy, but also supporting stands of *Candelabra euphorbia*, mesmerising python vines and countless baobabs' scarred where people have removed bark for cloth making. Elsewhere, there is reed swamp and marshland along the Shire River and southeast shore of Lake Malombe, floodplain grassland in the south, mixed woodland on all the hills, tall grass tree savannah along the narrow floodplains of seasonal streams, small pockets of dry deciduous thicket riverine, and semi-deciduous riverine forest. Wild flowers are seasonally plentiful during the rains, and include brightly coloured flowers, lilies

extinct during the colonial era, while the last naturally occurring Lichtenstein's hartebeest, buffalo and zebra were recorded in 1960, 1970 and 1971 respectively. In order to protect the remaining wildlife, a Controlled Hunting Area was proclaimed in 1962 and partially fenced two years later to prevent elephants from raiding crops in bordering villages (a move that met with limited success, as wire from the fence was removed and used to make snares by the villagers it was intended to protect!). Liwonde was upgraded to become a game reserve in 1969, largely at the initiative of the Yao chief for whom it is named, and it became a national park in 1973.

Since 1973, the park's mammals have experienced mixed fortunes. Hippos are more numerous even than in Johnston's day, thanks to an increase in suitable habitat following the construction of Liwonde Barrage downstream, and elephant numbers have increased from an estimated 200 in 1977 to around 900 today. Other species have proved to be more vulnerable to land pressure exerted on this small park by surrounding villages. Lions, for instance, were once abundant in the area, and they remained resident in Liwonde until the late 1990s, since when occasional vagrants have pitched up and soon after vanished, most likely poisoned or shot by cattle herders living around the park.

In 1992, the Malawi-based J&B Circle, with sponsorship from the famous whisky group, implemented a programme to reintroduce black rhino, which became extinct in Malawi in the late 1980s, to Liwonde National Park. The first pair of black rhinos was airlifted from South Africa to a specially fenced and guarded sanctuary within the park in 1993. Since then, two more have been brought in and numbers have grown steadily. There are now nine rhinos in Liwonde and another four have been translocated to Majete Wildlife Reserve. The rhino sanctuary is also a stronghold for recently reintroduced populations of buffalo, eland, hartebeest, roan antelope and zebra.

10

and ground orchids, while the stumpy impala lily bursts into striking pink bloom during the dry season.

WILDLIFE The most prominent large mammals are elephant and hippo. An estimated 900 elephant are resident, and it is quite normal to see three or four herds coming to drink at the river in the course of a day. Even more impressive is the hippo population. Some 2,000 hippos live along the 40km stretch of the Shire River which runs through the reserve (more than one every 20m!), surely one of the densest hippo populations on the African continent. Crocodiles, too, are ridiculously common – and, in many cases, quite terrifyingly large. Antelope are well represented, with impala and waterbuck being conspicuous along the river, while the denser mopane woodland supports several hundred sable antelope. Other common mammals include bushbuck, warthog, vervet monkey and yellow baboon.

Predators are relatively scarce. Spotted hyenas are seldom seen but frequently heard at night, whooping or cackling above the grunts of the hippos and shriek of Pel's fishing owl. African wild dog and lions have been hunted out as vermin, though the latter do occasionally pass through, and a small pride was resident for several months as recently as 2002. Leopards are present but very seldom seen, while smaller nocturnal hunters include serval, genet and side-striped jackal. It is hoped that if prey numbers increase, then predators might return in larger numbers from thinly populated parts of Mozambique.

BIRDS Liwonde is one of the top sites in Malawi for birdwatching, with a very different species composition from most of the country's other avian hotspots. More than 400 species have been recorded, and a recent ornithological tour counted more than 250 in two days! For casual visitors, it's the water-associated birds that tend to make the biggest impression, most notably perhaps the striking and vociferous African fish eagle, the abundant pied kingfisher, and, if you are lucky enough to see them, the outsized saddle-billed stork and goliath heron.

Liwonde is one of the best places anywhere to seek out a few rarer water-associated birds, among them Pel's fishing owl, red-necked falcon (which often perches in the canopy of borassus palms), palm-nut vulture, rufous-bellied heron and white-backed night heron. It is the only site in Malawi for spur-winged lapwing, a species that had never been recorded in the country until a vagrant pair pitched up near Mvuu in the late 1990s, since when it has established itself along the river in substantial numbers.

Away from the water, birds of prey are very well represented, including the likes of bateleur, martial eagle and all three snake eagles, and it is one of the few places in Malawi where the striking southern ground hornbill remains quite common. Liwonde is home to several localised woodland species, many of which are of particular interest to southern African birdwatchers, a list that includes the locally common brown-breasted barbet, Boehm's bee-eater, Lilian's lovebird, Livingstone's flycatcher, collared palm thrush and green twinspot along with more sparsely distributed mopane specialists such as racket-tailed roller and pale-billed hornbill.

GETTING THERE AND AWAY The park can be visited as part of an organised safari out of Lilongwe (in which case the operator will make all arrangements to get you there), but it can also be reached independently in a private vehicle, or by catching public transport as far as Liwonde Town and then arranging a private transfer. However you visit, there is a choice of three access points: by boat from Liwonde Town along the Shire River, by road from Liwonde Town, or by road via Ulongwe to a car park on the west bank of the river directly opposite Mvuu. There is also an airstrip in the park, should you be in a position to charter a flight.

Many self-drive visitors to Mvuu use the Ulongwe route. This entails following the M3 between Liwonde Town and Mangochi to the village of Ulongwe (about 25km north of the barrage) then heading east along a side road signposted for Mvuu Camp. This road passes through the entrance gate after 14km, then it's another 1km to the river, car park and jetty, where Mvuu will collect you by boat. Although this is the easiest way to drive to Mvuu, it has one major disadvantage in that you'll effectively be without a vehicle and will need to do all your drives in camp vehicles. This route cannot be used to get to Liwonde Safari Camp or Bushman's Baobabs.

If you prefer to have your own vehicle, or you'll be staying at Liwonde Safari Camp/Bushman's Baobabs, then you should head towards the main entrance to the national park, which is 6km from Liwonde Town along the surfaced D221, and clearly signposted. Liwonde Safari Camp & Bushman's Baobabs are located on a side road *prior* to reaching the main entrance, while the yet-to-be-named Robin Pope Safaris camp lies just 2km past the main entrance, and Mvuu is about 30km further in. The roads are usually fine in any vehicle with reasonable clearance in the dry season, and you should normally get through in a 4x4 at any time of year, but the internal roads are sometimes closed or impassable during the rainy season, so check road conditions in advance with your camp.

For travellers dependent on public transport, the most straightforward and cost-effective option is to catch a bus or minibus to Liwonde Town, where Liwonde Safari Camp will collect you free of charge by prior arrangement. Bushman's Baobabs offers the same service for US$5.

Because it is deeper into the park and more expensive, Mvuu is less popular with travellers on a budget. However, the camp can arrange a motorboat transfer between Liwonde Town and Mvuu, a fantastic trip, but also a rather costly one at US$80 per person for a minimum of two people. You could also ask around in Liwonde Town, where prices are negotiable, but you're probably looking at more than US$100 per party. Another option would be to bus to Ulongwe and then hire a bicycle-taxi to navigate the 15km to the jetty opposite Mvuu Camp, where a boat will fetch you.

WHERE TO STAY *See map, page 169.*
Exclusive

 Mvuu Wilderness Lodge (8 rooms) `\`01 771153/393; m (24hrs) 088 8822398; e info@wilderness.mw; www.wilderness-safaris.com. Possibly the most exclusive safari lodge anywhere in Malawi, this lies about 200m from the larger Mvuu Wilderness Camp, but operates as an entirely separate entity. The luxurious dbl tents are in the classic safari style & private balconies overlook a small, marshy pool on the bank of the river. Mvuu Lodge holds its own with the best luxury tented camps in southern Africa, blending a high level of comfort & tasteful décor with a wonderful bush atmosphere. The raised communal deck offers excellent mammal & birdwatching (hippos sometimes graze metres away at night, a blessing if you happen to be a noisy eater!) & there is a telescope & a library of field guides with which to amuse yourself. Activities include guided game walks, game drives & boat trips, as described in greater detail later in the chapter. There is also a rock swimming pool reserved for the use of lodge guests. *US$565/890 sgl/dbl mid-Jun–mid-Nov, US$485/730 other months, rates inc all meals & activities, services of the private rangers allocated to the lodge, but exc drinks.*

Robin Pope Safaris Camp `\`01 794491/5483; e info@robinpopesafaris.com; www.robinpopesafaris.com. Scheduled to open in early 2014, this as yet unnamed camp will be run by the highly regarded Robin Pope Safaris, which also runs Pumulani in Lake Malawi National Park & Mkulumadzi in Majete Wildlife Reserve. It will offer intimate, upmarket tented accommodation nestled in the saddle of Chinguni Mountain & Mbawala Hill, only a short distance from the main gate in the south of the park. Rates will be comparable with other Robin Pope lodges & will include meals, game drives & other activities.

Upmarket

🏠 **Mvuu Wilderness Camp** (12 rooms)
📞 01 771153/393; m (24hrs) 088 8822398; e info@wilderness.mw; www.wilderness-safaris. com. Though not as luxuriously exclusive as the eponymous lodge, this superb safari camp shares a similarly memorable setting on the east bank of the Shire about 30km north of Liwonde Barrage, & offers the same range of activities. It stands amid a cluster of immense baobab trees, facing a dense reed bed & a borassus palm forest. Warthogs graze the lawns by day, hippos by night, while elephants regularly come to drink on the bank opposite & are discouraged from visiting the camp at night. Both the river & surrounding bush are alive with birds. Accommodation is in very comfortable en-suite standing tents or stone chalets, all with a private balcony facing the river, & a campsite aimed at independent visitors is attached. Facilities include a swimming pool & gift shop. *US$360/520 sgl/dbl mid-Jun—mid-Nov, US$330/460 other months, rates incl all meals & 2 activities daily, but exc drinks.*

Moderate

🏠 **Bushman's Baobabs** (17 rooms, 2 dorms)
m 099 5453324; e bushmansbaobabs@africa-online.net; www.bushmansbaobabs.com. Nestled between the Shire River & the park boundary, this new lodge opened in 2010 under the same management as the former Chinguni Hills Lodge. Set in a thoroughly baobab-studded courtyard, the en-suite thatched chalets & standing tents are extremely attractive & feature warm, African-style décor & verandas with seating. There is a large & welcoming honesty bar & lounge area with a selection of guidebooks, & meals are available at the restaurant for between US$10—20. The 20-bed dorm & associated shower complex does feel a bit institutional, though. Activities include game walks & drives (*US$20/25 pp*), canoe safaris (*US$20 pp*), boat safaris (*US$45 pp*), village walks (*US$15 pp*), & they offer pickup from Liwonde town for US$5. *US$60 pp dbl/twin en-suite chalet, US$45 pp dbl/twin en-suite standing tent, US$25 pp dbl/ twin standing tent, US$15pp dorm bed, US$7.50 camping, all rates excluding b/fast.*

Budget and camping

🏠 **Liwonde Safari Camp** (5 rooms, 1 dorm)
m 088 1813240; e liwondesafaricamp@gmail. com; www.liwondesafaricamp.com; see also advert on page 164. This supremely relaxed camp is by far the best choice for backpackers seeking a true wilderness experience without the frills of an upmarket safari lodge. Platform tents are scattered around the densely vegetated grounds & linked to the observation deck, luxurious showers, dorms & cosy restaurant/bar by a set of short paths. Casual hikes, pickup from Liwonde, & coffee/tea are all offered free of charge, while a variety of game drives, boat safaris & walking safaris are available from US$25—65. Nights are spent around the campfire or by candlelight at the bar, where elephants & others pay the occasional unscheduled visit. *US$30/45 sgl/dbl standing tent, US$10 dorm bed, US$7.50 camping, all rates excluding b/fast.*

🛖 **Mvuu Campsite** Contact details as for Mvuu Wilderness Camp. This well-organised campsite stands adjacent to Mvuu Wilderness Camp & has a similarly wonderful riverside setting. A self-catering kitchen with a freezer & cooking utensils is available to those bringing their own food, & a cook can be arranged by request. Alternatively meals can be taken in the camp at US$15 for b/ fast, US$20 for lunch & US$25 for dinner. *Camping US$15 pp.*

🏠 **Njobvu Cultural Village Lodge**
m 088 8623530; e info@njobvuvillage.org or enochchidothi@yahoo.com; www.njobvuvillage. org. Initiated several years ago by Wilderness Safaris, & still closely affiliated to Mvuu Wilderness Camp, this is a community-tourism project based in the village of Ligwangwa, immediately outside the western boundary of the national park. Sleeping arrangements here are completely authentic – a mat laid on the floor of a mud hut, with or without a mattress as you like – & visitors are exposed to the realities of Malawian village life through a range of activities, from village walks & visits to a traditional doctor or village headman, to local-style village cooking & traditional dances around the campfire. The village lies 11km along the road connecting Ulongwe to the west-bank jetty for Mvuu, just outside the entrance gate, & can be reached by bicycle-taxi from Ulongwe for around US$6 pp. It can also be visited as a day or overnight trip from Mvuu. *US$16 pp B&B, US$6 per meal, US$8—10 pp activities, US$50 all-inclusive.*

ACTIVITIES AND WILDLIFE VIEWING The areas immediately around the lodges are rewarding to explore, both for the wildlife and the interesting changes in habitat. All the camps offer an excellent choice of game-viewing activities, including boat safaris, game drives and walking safaris, with the standard of guiding at Mvuu being particularly high. At Mvuu, these activities are included in the standard room rate, but campers and day visitors can also partake at a cost of US$30 per person for boat safaris and game drives, and US$20 for walking safaris.

Game walks Best undertaken in the early morning, these offer the wonderful experience of exploring the African bush on foot. You're not likely to see a great number of mammals on these walks (warthog, impala and hippo are most likely to be encountered near the camps, and feel relieved if you haven't met a herd of elephant), but this is compensated for by the prolific birds. Mvuu Wilderness Camp and Lodge organise walks around Mvuu, which offer a good chance of seeing several special birds, while a walk from Bushman's Baobabs, Liwonde Safari Camp, or the new Robin Pope Safaris camp will give you a different view of the park, and the opportunity to see striking birds such as racket-tailed roller and the Narina trogon.

Boat trips Motorised launch trips along the Shire River leave Mvuu every morning after breakfast and from the other camps by arrangement. The vegetation along the river is splendid: thick stands of borassus and wild date palms, ghostly baobab trees, yellow fever trees and dense beds of papyrus. Close encounters with hippos are guaranteed, you can be confident of seeing elephants, waterbuck, impala, crocodile and vervet monkeys, and there is a fair chance of seeing sable antelope from the boat. Birds are everywhere: among the more common species are fish eagle, jacana, white-breasted cormorant (these breed along the river profusely in the dry season), darter, long-toed lapwing, African skimmer, and a variety of kingfishers and herons.

Night boat safaris from Mvuu Lodge are a must for serious birders as they offer an excellent chance of spotting Pel's fishing owl in action, as well as the nocturnal white-backed night heron. You'll be amazed at how closely the boat is able to approach roosting birds such as giant and malachite kingfishers (the latter nothing short of dazzling in the spotlight), as well as huddled flocks of colourful little bee-eaters.

Only offered by Bushman's Baobabs, canoe trips through the marshland out onto the river are an unforgettable experience, stomach-lurching when you're near to a large animal and totally serene when you're not.

Game drives Organised game drives with the lodges have the advantage of being in heavy-duty 4x4s that allow off-road exploration on the tracks along the river. But visitors with private transport have a number of dirt roads to explore. The best game viewing is along the river near Mvuu, and there is also a fair amount to be seen on the floodplain in front of the new Robin Pope Safaris camp, but the roads between the two camps pass through thick mopane woodland where wildlife is very sparse. Of particular interest is the road following the Shire River north from Mvuu to where it exits Lake Malombe, as several tracks lead down to the river. A large hollow baobab at Mvera Ferry in the far north of the park is used as a shelter during the rains when people wait for the ferry; it has room for at least 20 people inside. It also has two types of strangler fig growing on it. The tree is mentioned by Livingstone in his journals as one of their campsites.

Chinguni Hill, encircled by a rough dirt road, is the most prominent landmark in the south, a Brachystegia-covered hill that offers exceptional panoramic views of the Shire lagoons beyond the Chikalogwe Plain and is interesting for its localised wildlife as well as being popular with elephant, kudu, sable and buffalo. At the foot of Chinguni Hill is a hollow baobab tree, containing human skeletons thrown there, thought to be of leprosy sufferers. Another baobab tree along the Riverside Drive is probably over 4,000 years old, over 21m high and almost 18m in girth. The Chikalogwe Floodplain below Chinguni Hill is an open area of swamp and reeds that's much loved by elephants, which often submerge themselves entirely, belied only by the egrets taking off from their backs. In the reeds are clusters of palm trees and the occasional termite mound. Waterbuck and impala usually laze on the sands in front of the reeds.

Rhino sanctuary Only accessible as part of an organised game drive from Mvuu, this 49km² fenced enclosure is where the J&B Circle have successfully reintroduced breeding pairs of black rhinoceros, as well as providing a safe haven for other species such as sable, buffalo, eland, hartebeest, roan antelope and zebra, all now numerous there. Rhino spotting is never easy as these guys are very shy. Elephants crash through the electric fences occasionally, but mostly this is an elephant-free zone, which is noticeable in the dense vegetation. It is a beautiful area. The ultimate aim is to drop the fences and release game into greater Liwonde Park. It will be a pleasure to see rhino at the river's edge again, but I guess this will happen only if poaching is completely stamped out.

Around camp There's plenty of wildlife to be seen in the camps, especially at Mvuu, where hippos and crocodiles are a permanent presence on the river only metres from your tents, as is a large variety of waterbirds, while elephants come down to drink most days and gigantic monitor lizards can be seen basking on the riverbank. The woodland around the camp offers some great birding, with a good chance of picking up several Liwonde specials, including brown-breasted barbet (often seen near the jetty), Lilian's lovebird, Livingstone's flycatcher, collared palm thrush, eastern bearded scrub robin, African fish eagle and Boehm's bee-eater (these perch openly around the car park). The localised bat hawk can be seen near the river on most evenings. People staying at the lodge are likely to see a greater variety of animals coming to drink at the pool: bushbuck and impala are regular visitors, leopards are seen on occasion, and the birdlife is outstanding.

11

Zomba and Surrounds

The leafy and relaxed town of Zomba, former capital of Malawi, is 65km north of Blantyre. Often claimed to have been the most beautiful capital anywhere in the British Empire, the town also forms the gateway to several of the country's most striking natural features. These are the Zomba Plateau, an isolated igneous massif that rises to an altitude of 2,085m immediately west of town, the low-lying Lake Chilwa, a vast expanse of marsh and open water listed as the only Ramsar wetland site in Malawi, and the weathered sandstone pinnacles of the Chikala Pillars. In touristic terms, the biggest attraction is undoubtedly the Zomba Plateau, which is serviced by a pair of highly regarded upmarket lodges, and offers some fine highland walking opportunities, limited wildlife viewing, and several memorable viewpoints. By contrast, Lake Chilwa is poorly developed for tourism, despite offering some of the finest aquatic birdwatching in the country. The Chikala Pillars remain an insider's destination, hidden away and entirely undeveloped, though the Zomba branch of the Wildlife & Environmental Society of Malawi offers excellent guided excursions to both the pillars and Lake Chilwa.

ZOMBA TOWN

Zomba was founded in 1891 as the capital of the British Central African Protectorate, a role it retained throughout the colonial era and for a decade after independence until 1975, when it was usurped by the more centrally located Lilongwe. Zomba remained the seat of parliament until 1994, and it still houses several important institutions, including the National Archives and main campus of the University of Malawi. It is the fourth-largest town in the country, with a population that rose from around 20,000 at the time of independence to an estimated 105,000 in 2009.

From a visitor's perspective, Zomba is probably the most immediately appealing of Malawi's larger towns. Admittedly, this isn't saying much, but the modern town exudes a rustic peacefulness (belying its sometimes bloody past), and it also has in its favour a wonderful setting at the base of the eponymous mountain, and a distinctive architectural character determined by the many ostentatious colonial relics that line the leafy avenues between the main road and the mountain's wooded footslopes.

A small town in comparison with Lilongwe or Blantyre, Zomba has two distinct parts. The original administrative centre, with its plentiful British colonial buildings, is centred upon the Mulunguzi River, while the more bustling modern town centre, which seems to have taken shape in the 1950s and boasts several interesting buildings of Indian design, straddles the main road about 1.5km to the southwest. Also of note is the central market, which has as good a selection of fresh produce

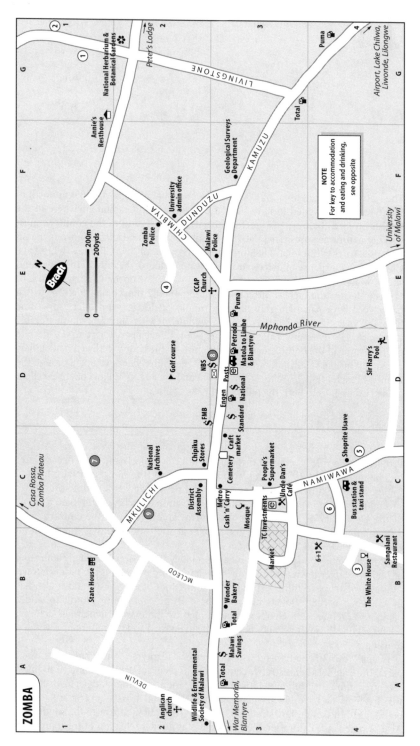

ZOMBA

as you'll find in Malawi, and the lovely golf course and National Herbarium. For all that, Zomba's charms can be exhausted within a few hours, and its main attraction for travellers is the proximity to Zomba Mountain.

HISTORY Dr David Livingstone's Zambezi Expedition undertook the first recorded exploration of the Zomba area in early 1859. Livingstone and his companion John Kirk climbed Zomba Mountain, summiting close to the site of the present-day Ku Chawe Inn. Livingstone is also credited as the first European to reach Chilwa, though in reality, this lake – like many of Livingstone's 'discoveries' in Malawi – was most probably already known to Portuguese traders from Mozambique. In 1859, the Manganja agriculturists of Zomba were suffering greatly at the hands of Yao slave raiders. The Zambezi Expedition became indirectly involved in the Yao–Manganja war when, in August 1861, Bishop Mackenzie, together with a handful of British soldiers and over 1,000 Manganja warriors, marched from Magomero Mission onto the slopes of Zomba Mountain and razed several Yao slaving villages.

Livingstone had been impressed by the fertility of the Zomba area, which made it the obvious site for the Church of Scotland's pioneering mission in the Shire Highlands, established in 1876. However, the ferocity of the local slave trade counted against the location, as did the density of wild animals, and the missionaries instead settled further south, at what is now Blantyre. Ten years later, Captain Haimes bought 500ha of land below Zomba Mountain from Chief Malemia, a site chosen for its strategic location to fight the Yao slave traders. In 1889, the agriculturist John Buchanan, then Acting British Consul, erected a sugar mill alongside the Mulunguzi River where it flows through present-day Zomba; two years later his effective successor Sir Harry Johnston, Commissioner of British Central Africa, established his residence close by, and proclaimed Zomba as the protectorate's capital.

GETTING THERE AND AWAY Zomba flanks the surfaced M3 about 65km north of Blantyre (via Limbe) and 55km south of Liwonde Barrage. The road is in good condition, and the drive in either direction shouldn't take longer than 45 minutes in a private vehicle. The M3 to Blantyre was undergoing expansion as of early 2013, so expect delays until road works are complete. Many buses between Blantyre and points north (such as Lilongwe and Mzuzu) take the M1 bypassing Zomba, but all buses to/from Blantyre and Liwonde, Mangochi or Monkey Bay will stop at Zomba. In addition, regular minibuses connect Zomba to most other major centres in southern Malawi. Fares are US$3.25 to Limbe/Blantyre or Liwonde, US$6.50 to Monkey Bay, and US$7.50 to Lilongwe. Most minibuses leave from the central bus station [178 C4] near the market, but you can also pick up transport to Limbe/Blantyre along the M3 opposite NBS Bank [178 D3].

TOURIST INFORMATION There's no tourist information office as such, but the **Wildlife & Environmental Society of Malawi (WESM)** [178 A2] (☏ *01 526212;* m *099 9241375* e *wesm-za@sdnp.org.mw*) sets up day trips to Lake Chilwa and the Chikala Pillars and also stocks a very useful map of Zomba Plateau and booklet about Chilwa's birdlife, both inexpensive. You can also reach the WESM's birder-in-chief, Tiwonge Gawa, at e birdsmalawi@gmail.com. Another good option is **African Heritage** (⊕ *08.30–16.30 Mon–Sat, 10.30–16.30 Sun;* ☏ *01 11955900;* m *099 9235823;* e *info@africanheritage.mw; www.africanheritage.mw*), a new organisation with offices and a small café at the Zomba Golf Club [178 C2], from where they organise cultural tours of Zomba and beyond.

 WHERE TO STAY *See map, page 178.*
Although there is a growing selection of quality accommodation dotted around Zomba Town, tourists on an upmarket budget will probably prefer to stay at the Ku Chawe Inn or Zomba Forest Lodge (see page 185) on the Zomba Plateau.

Upmarket

🏠 **Hotel Masongola** (41 rooms) ☏ 01 524688; e hotel2001@gmail.com. This is Zomba's most historic & smartest lodge, with a splendid location on the well-wooded slopes near the Botanical Gardens & Mulunguzi River. It is the oldest building in town, with foundations laid by Captain Haimes in 1886, & it was the residence of Sir Harry Johnston from 1899 to 1901, when construction of State House was completed. After that, this fine building, with its spire-like green roof, served as a temporary residence for senior colonial officials, before being converted to a government hostel in 1949 & privatised in 2001. The bright, tiled en-suite rooms all have a roof fan, DSTV & netting, & the larger executive rooms have fridge & tea/coffee-making facilities. There's a good & reasonably priced restaurant & bar in the original main building, whose veranda overlooks the green surrounds. It has a private generator to combat Zomba's regular power outages. *US$33/48 sgl/ twin, US$38/52 executive sgl/dbl, all rates B&B.*

Moderate

🏠 **Annie's Lodge** (47 rooms) ☏ 01 527002; m 099 9957608; e annieslodge@gmail.com; www.annieslodge.com. In the historic quarter of town below the Masongola, this popular business hotel opened in 2005 in a converted 1920s building that served as a members' bar for the neighbouring parliament prior to its relocation to Lilongwe. A variety of en-suite room types is available, all with DSTV, fan, carpet & dbl or twin bed; it's worth noting that high-ceilinged standard rooms in the old building possess far

more charm than some of the newer & pricier options, & that rooms at the anonymous annex around the corner are very inferior & rather poor value. A popular restaurant/bar is attached. *US$30/36 standard sgl/dbl, US$37–79 superior rooms & flats, all rates B&B.*

🏠 **Peter's Lodge** (16 rooms) ☏ 01 525884 m 099 5671596. Situated about 2km from the town centre & inconvenient for non-motorised travellers, this quiet suburban lodge offers decent accommodation in tiled rooms or chalets with dbl bed, net, DSTV, writing desk & en-suite bathroom with tub. There's a residents' bar & small restaurant serving meals in the US$4 range, with pizzas at US$5–6. *US$20/25 standard sgl/dbl, US$22/30 executive sgl/dbl with AC, all rates B&B.*

Budget

🏠 **Casa Rossa** (2 rooms, 2 dorms) m 088 1366126/099 1184211; e info@casarossamw. com; www.casarossamw.com. Run by a charming & culinarily gifted Italian couple, this new lodge & campsite sits in a lovingly restored colonial home about 1½km up the plateau road from central Zomba. Rooms are simple & thoughtfully appointed, & the wrap-around veranda makes for one of the most relaxed spots in all of Zomba. Standing tents & campsites are sprinkled throughout the leafy gardens, all featuring plug points & *braai* facilities. The stellar restaurant serves a wide variety of homemade Italian dishes & is rapidly becoming a destination in itself. Accommodation space is limited, so ring before you walk up from town. *US$10–15 pp dorm bed, US$20/40 sgl/twin using shared bathroom, US$45* *en-suite dbl, US$20/25 standing tent twin/dbl, US$5 pp camping.*

☐ **Pakachere Backpackers** (2 rooms, 3 dorms) m 099 4685934/088 1675454; e info@pakachere.com; www.pakachere.com. This bright & colourful oasis behind the golf course is a hugely welcome addition to Zomba's somnolescent backpacker scene, offering cheerful dorms, airy en-suite dbl rooms, a spacious lounge, internet, kitchen facilities, book exchange & a family-size dining tables that encourage making friends & easy conversation. The restaurant/bar offers up a backpacker-friendly menu of curries, pizzas, pastas & a tempting selection of baked goods including apple pie. Breakfast & lunch go for about US$3, while dinners are US$5. *US$10 pp dorm bed, US$35 en-suite dbl, US$4 pp camping, US$5 pp hired tent, all rates excluding b/fast.*

☐ **Spar Lodge** (10 rooms) ✆01 526700; m 088 8309347. Perched on the 1st floor directly opposite the bus station, this local lodge is a surprisingly pleasant option for those who want to stay in the centre. Rooms are clean & airy, & all come with en-suite hot shower, fan, net & DSTV. Meals are available for US$2–3. *US$14/19 sgl/dbl.*

Shoestring

☐ **Ndindeya Motel** (46 rooms) ✆01 525558. This venerable motel behind the bus station has long been the pick of the rather dismal selection of cheapies dotted around central Zomba. All rooms are en suite & a decent restaurant/bar is attached. *US$7/8.50 sgl/dbl, US$11 executive dbl.*

☐ **Zomba City Assembly Resthouse** (36 rooms) Under the same ownership as the more upmarket Peter's Lodge, this no-frills lodge opposite the main bus station couldn't be more conveniently located, & the cell-like rooms come with nets & are reasonably clean, but it's potentially noisy & has few virtues other than cheapness. *US$3.75 dbl, US$5.50 en-suite dbl.*

✗ WHERE TO EAT AND DRINK *See map, page 178.*

For a town of its size, Zomba boasts an unexpectedly good and varied selection of eateries, some associated with hotels, others not:

✗ **Annie's Restaurant** ✆01 527002; ☺ 06.30–22.00 daily. In the 1920s main building of Annie's Lodge, this place has plenty of ambience, & there's the option of sitting indoors or on the shaded balcony. The varied selection of continental meat, fish & vegetarian dishes falls in the US$4–6 range, & a full b/fast costs US$5.

✗ **Casa Rossa** m 088 1366126/099 1184211; www.casarossamw.com. ☺ 08.00–21.00 Tue–Sun. Home-style Italian food, reasonable prices (*mains US$4.50–6.50*) & a commanding view over Zomba town make Casa Rossa a true gustatory delight. The relaxed ambiance belies the sophisticated menu; you'll find a cheese platter including fresh mozzarella, dessert crepes & an impressive list of homemade pastas including gnocchi, tortelloni, tagliatelle, mezzelune & more. The full bar includes some Italian selections as well.

✗ **Domino Café** ✆01 525305; ☺ 07.30–22.00 daily. More of a bar than a restaurant, Domino's tends to be especially busy when major international football matches are shown on the big-screen DSTV, but it also has comfortable outdoor seating & a reputation for good pizzas (& typical Malawian meals) in the US$2–6 range.

✗ **Hotel Masongola** ✆01 524688; ☺ b/fast, lunch & dinner daily. The characterful indoor restaurant (with breezy terrace) at this historic hotel serves a varied selection of salads & snacks for US$2.50–4.50, pizzas for around US$5 & other mains in the US$5–7 range. It's a popular meeting place among Zomba's business set.

✗ **Ndindeya Motel** ✆01 525558; ☺ 06.30–22.00 daily. This place serves tasty local staples (chicken, beef or *chambo* with rice or chips) for around US$1–2.50. Somewhat surprisingly, it also features a full bar.

✗ **Tasty Bites** ✆01 525487; ☺ 09.00–20.00 Mon–Sat, 10.00–20.00 Sun. A popular lunchtime venue with volunteers & local office workers, this Indian-owned restaurant serves a selection of curries for US$5, burgers & fried meals in the US$2–4 range, pizzas at about US$6 & it's a good choice for vegetarians. No alcohol served.

✗ **Zomba Golf Club** ✆01 525660; ☺ lunch & dinner daily. Centrally located opposite the golf course, this serves decent if unadventurous meals for around US$2.50 per main, though you need to pay day membership (*US$3*) to partake. They do sometimes waive the membership fee for diners though, so it's worth checking. The African Heritage café is also here, serving baked goods & coffee/tea in a casual outdoor setting.

SHOPPING The supermarkets in Zomba are very well stocked by Malawian standards, especially the **Metro Cash 'n' Carry** [178 C3] on the junction of Kamuzu and Namiwawa, which has an in-house butchery and bakery, and **People's Supermarket** [178 C3] on Namiwawa Road. The **central market** [178 B3] in Zomba is not, as is sometimes claimed, one of the largest in Africa, but it is one of the friendliest and does stock a better-than-average selection of fresh fruit and vegetables. The **Wonder Bakery** [178 B3] produces fresh bread several times daily, and does a very good brown loaf. Strawberries and raspberries grown on the plateau can be bought from the vendors who lurk in front of the Metro Cash 'n' Carry [178 C3]. The main cluster of **craft stalls** is on Kamuzu Highway next to the cemetery [178 C3], and **African Heritage** at the Zomba Golf Club [178 C2] stocks an excellent selection of crafts and books about Malawi.

OTHER PRACTICALITIES

Banks and foreign exchange All the major banks stand in line along the Kamuzu Highway. The **Standard Bank** [178 D3] has an ATM where local currency can be drawn against international Visa, MasterCard and Maestro, and Visa can also be used at the **National Bank, NBS,** or **FMB** ATMs [178 D3]. After a government-ordered shutdown in 2009, Malawi's private forex bureaux are slowly reopening, but there were still none in Zomba at the time of writing.

Car rental The **Eagle Car Hire** firm (m *099 4575770/088 1506566*) at the Petroda Filling Station rents out saloon cars (*US$19/day & Mk45/km*) and minibuses or 4x4s (*US$22/day & Mk50/km*) – possibly worth looking at for a day trip to Lake Chilwa or a safari to nearby Liwonde National Park.

Internet The best internet cafés are **Posts** [178 D3] (m *01 525399; ⊕ 07.00–17.00 Mon–Fri, 09.00–12.00 Sat*), charging Mk5/min next to the National Bank and **TC Investments** [178 C3] opposite the central market, which is more expensive at Mk10/min. For those with their own laptop, Globe Wi-Fi cards can be used at Tasty Bites [178 D3] and Skyband cards can be used at the Ku Chawe Inn on Zomba Plateau.

Sports You'd scarcely think so today, but the central Gymkhana Club, built in 1923, formed the hub of Zomba's social activity in the colonial era. Now, renamed as the **Zomba Golf Club** [178 C2] (m *01 525660*), it possesses a rather timeworn and neglected atmosphere, but day members are welcomed (*US$3 daily*) and the nine-hole golf course remains highly attractive to enthusiasts, who must pay an additional US$1.50 course fees, US$1.50 caddy fees and US$3 to hire a set of clubs. The club also has tennis and squash courts, and it serves decent meals. The **Harry Johnston Primary School** (m *01 525280*) has an outdoor swimming pool open to day visitors for US$2.50, and if you're in town on a Sunday, they also host informal volleyball or football matches starting at around 16.00; they're a good place to meet volunteers and locals.

Taxis The main taxi stand is next to the bus station. Fares are negotiable but expect to pay around US$5 for a ride within town and up to US$25 for a one-way transfer to Zomba Plateau.

above The impressive St Michael and All Angels' Church is the second oldest building in Blantyre, built by Scottish missionaries between 1888 and 1891 (I/A) page 206

below Mua Mission is one of the oldest Catholic outposts in Malawi, established at the base of the Rift Valley Escarpment by the so-called White Fathers in 1902 (WS) page 136

above   **Female bushbuck (*Tragelaphus scriptus*) with calf** (MU) page 35

left   **Rainbow skink (*Trachylepis margaritifera*)** (MU) page 44

below left **Giraffe (*Giraffa camelopardalis*)** (AZ) page 39

below   **Yellow baboon (*Papio cynocephalus*)** (AZ) page 33

right **Spotted hyena (*Crocuta crocuta*)** (WS) page 32

below left **Warthog (*Phacochoerus africanus*)** (WS) page 38

below right **Golden cichlid (*Melanochromis auratus*)** (DH/FLPA) page 142

bottom **Flap-necked chameleon (*Chamaeleo dilepis*)** (SS) page 43

above left The weaver is a quintessential part of Africa's natural landscape. Pictured, Eastern golden weaver (*Ploceus subaureus*) (MU) page 40

above right The often solitary Denham's bustard (*Neotis denhami*) can be spotted in the grasslands of the Nyika Plateau (MU) page 303

below left Look out for the vociferous African fish eagle (*Haliaeetus vocifer*) in the Liwonde National Park (RPS) page 172

below right The bearded scrub-robin (*Erythropygia quadrivirgata*) can be spotted in the Lengwe National Parks (AZ) page 232

bottom Malachite kingfishers (*Alcedo cristata*) are commonly seen near slow moving water (WS) page 239

above With the reintroduction of lions (rounding out the 'Big Five') in 2012, Majete Wildlife Reserve has arguably distinguished itself as Malawi's premier game-viewing destination (AZ) page 228

below left The southern part of Elephant Marsh is thick with hyacinths and white lilies (AZ) page 238

below right Water rushes 125m down the breathtaking Manchewe Falls, near Livingstonia (AZ) page 320

above Featuring rich birdlife and stunning viewpoints, the Zomba Plateau is a wonderful place to explore on horseback (JWLP/A) page 186

left Cape Maclear is a perfect spot for kayaking. Most people choose to paddle across to the tropical Mumbo Island (KA) page 147

below Cycling is a great way to explore Malawi's towns and countryside alike. Pictured, cyclists in the Nyika National Park (WS) page 65

above Motorised boat trips along the Shire River offer excellent wildlife-viewing opportunities in Liwonde National Park. Close encounters with hippos, elephants and crocodiles are all likely (WS) page 175

below Guided walking safaris are a great way of viewing large mammals such as roan antelope and zebra around Chelinda Camp (WS) page 305

visit mount
mulanje

Come and hike up the mountain
Swim in the cool river pools
Stay in our cosy warm log cottages
Enjoy our delicious fruits and vegetables
Drink the original African tea
Be fascinated by all the unique plants and animals
in the rainforests and cedar cloud forests
Enjoy the spectacular vistas
And, be awed by the nightly star-scapes!

For all information and reservations, contact InfoMulanje:
Situated above Mulanje Pepper Pizza, in Chitakale
Call us on +265 (0)1 466 466
Mail us on infomulanje@sdnp.org.mw
Visit our website www.mountmulanje.org.mw

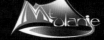

WHAT TO SEE AND DO It's definitely worth lounging around at the **National Herbarium and Botanic Gardens** [178 G2] (↴ *01 523388;* e *nhbgm@malawi.net; www.sdnp.org.mw/enviro/herb*) for a few hours, and close inspection of the labels on the trees will give you more botanical information than you are likely to remember. It's a thoroughly peaceful park where students sit on the grass reading or discussing their subjects, and church groups gather to act out Bible scenes and sing gospel songs on Sundays.

The oldest building in town is the **Hotel Masongola** [178 G1] (see page 181), whose bar and restaurant form an obvious focal point for a stroll through the old part of town, which is studded with buildings dating to the early 20th century. Probably the most architecturally interesting old building in Zomba is **State House** [178 B1], which dates from 1901, but is inaccessible to casual passers-by. Other local landmarks within walking distance of the town centre are the **War Memorial** to the King's African Rifles, which lies about 1km back along the M3 towards Blantyre, the nearby **Catholic church**, and the **University of Malawi** south of the M3.

Further out of town, **Mikuyu Prison**, along the road towards Lake Chilwa, is the site of one of the darker moments in Malawi's recent history. During the Banda years, this is where an estimated 3,000 people – mostly political prisoners – were incarcerated (usually without trial) in crammed and appalling conditions. The prison closed in the 1990s and reopened a few years later as the darkly interesting Prison Museum, but it reverted to its original function as a prison in 2005 and is no longer open to tourists. The award-winning poetry of Jack Mapanje, a Malawian now based in the UK, evokes the futility of his incarceration at Mikuyu with an eloquence that the bare cells of the museum lacked (see *The Chattering Wagtails of Mikuyu Prison*, Heinemann, 1993, and *Skipping without Ropes*, 1998). His newest book is the searing *And Crocodiles Are Hungry at Night* (2011), a poignant memoir of his years at Mikuyu.

ZOMBA PLATEAU

Rising to the immediate northeast of the eponymous town, the Zomba Plateau is an isolated syenite protrusion that extends over around 130km² and reaches an altitude of 2,087m at Malumbe Peak in the southwest. The plateau's northwest rim forms the southern escarpment of the Upper Shire Valley, and is characterised by sheer drops of up to 1,200m, offering spectacular views over the plains below. Much of the plateau is protected in Malawi's oldest forest reserve (gazetted in 1913), and while much of the indigenous vegetation has made way for pine plantations, it also supports significant patches of indigenous riverine and montane forest, as well as areas of tangled scrub and Brachystegia woodland. A large dam was constructed in 1999 in the bowl of the mountain, but this does little to interrupt the natural feel.

Though it is less spectacular and wild than the larger Mulanje and Nyika plateaux, the upper reaches of Zomba are considerably more accessible, and a vast network of footpaths makes it one of the most popular areas in Malawi for rambling and hiking. For most visitors, Zomba's scenery is undoubtedly its main attraction, but the mountain also supports a rich birdlife, while mammal species present include elusive populations of leopard, serval cat and mongooses. Antelope present on the mountain include bushbuck, klipspringer and red duiker, vervet monkey and yellow baboon are reasonably common, and the lovely samango monkey is seen in indigenous forests, particularly around Chingwe's Hole and Zomba Forest Lodge.

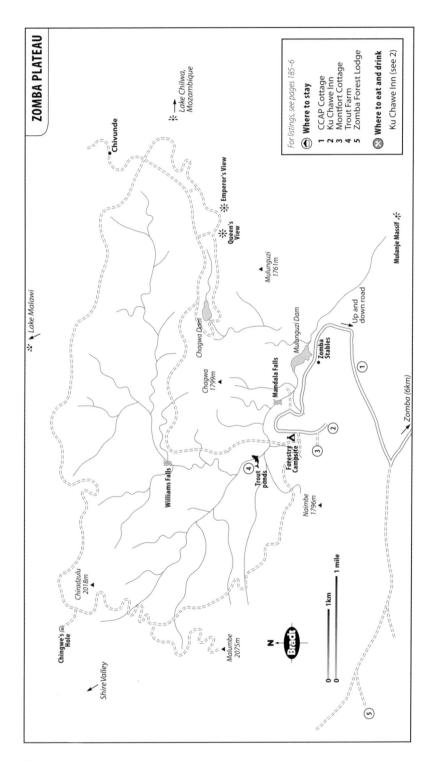

ZOMBA PLATEAU

For listings, see pages 185–6

Where to stay
1 CCAP Cottage
2 Ku Chawe Inn
3 Montfort Cottage
4 Trout Farm
5 Zomba Forest Lodge

Where to eat and drink
Ku Chawe Inn (see 2)

Lake Malawi

Lake Chilwa, Mozambique

Chivunde

Emperor's View

Queen's View

Mulunguzi 1761m

Chagwa Dam

Mulunguzi Dam

Chagwa 1799m

Mandala Falls

Zomba Stables

Up and down road

Williams Falls

Trout ponds

Forestry Campsite

Naimbe 1796m

Chingwe's Hole

Chiradzulu 2018m

Shire Valley

Malumbe 2075m

Zomba (6km)

Mulanje Massif

N

Bradt

0   1km
0   1 mile

GETTING THERE AND AWAY The 10km road from Zomba Town to the top of the plateau used to split about halfway up into a separate up-road and down-road, but it is now surfaced in its entirety and carries two-way traffic all the way to the top. The Ku Chawe Inn, forestry campsite and other private cottages are all clustered near the edge of the escarpment at the end of the road. To get to them, follow the road signposted for Ku Chawe Inn from the centre of Zomba Town opposite the supermarket.

There is no public transport to the top of the mountain. If you are in a hurry, the best thing to do is organise a private taxi at Zomba bus station. This will cost around US$25, possibly a little less if you bargain. If you're lucky (and start early enough) you might catch a lift. The alternative is to walk, which is perfectly feasible, though steep-going towards the end. If you want to walk down the mountain, then take the 'Potato Path', which is signposted from near the Ku Chawe Inn and takes about an hour to walk when dry – but is dangerously slippery and steep in wet conditions.

If you want to stay at Zomba Forest Lodge, you need to go straight on at the barrier up the old up-road, then take the second left turning. It's about 4km from the turn-off on a well-maintained road along the contour of the mountain.

WHERE TO STAY *See map, opposite.*

Exclusive
Zomba Forest Lodge (4 rooms) m 099 2802702; e zombaforestlodge@gmail.com. Recently reopened under new owner-managers, this artfully restored former forestry resthouse lies in a remote & densely forested area about halfway up the mountain (see directions above). An idyllic & restful retreat, it has no electricity, a warm & cosy open hearth & handmade artwork on the walls. Food is a focus here, & the owners delight in sharing their craft with guests. Plenty of wildlife, including a semi-resident troop of 35 samango monkeys, passes through the gardens, which also offer views to Mount Mulanje & the Shire Valley. Birders have a good chance of spotting local specialities such as white-winged & yellow-throated apalis, white-tailed crested flycatcher, Livingstone's turaco & starred robin. *Approx US$75 pp, inc full b/fast & 3-course dinner.*

Upmarket
Sunbird Ku Chawe Inn (40 rooms) `01 514211; e kuchawe@sunbirdmalawi.com; www. sunbirdmalawi.com. One of Malawi's flagship hotels, the venerable Ku Chawe Inn is set in attractive wooded grounds offering a commanding position from the edge of the escarpment to Lake Chilwa. All rooms are en suite with twin or king-size beds, combination tub/shower, fridge, heater or log fire, tea/coffee-making facilities & flat-screen DSTV. The restaurant is very good, with most mains falling in the US$7–10 range, though cheaper snacks are available. Bookings

can be made online or by contacting the hotel directly. *US$214/238 sgl/dbl, US$237/261 superior, US$260/285 deluxe, US$304/328 suite, all rates inc excellent buffet b/fast.*

Budget and camping
CCAP Cottage (3 rooms) m 088 8375972; www.blantyresynod.org. Situated on the edge of the plateau & boasting views of Mulanje & beyond, this is a comfortable self-catering set-up that can host up to eight people. Rooms include an en-suite dbl, as well as a twin room & 4-bed dorm using shared ablutions. The kitchen is fully equipped & the living room has a large fireplace just asking to be gathered around. Book ahead. *US$8 pp.*

Montfort Cottage `01 524565; m 099 0307833. Another pleasant self-catering option, Montfort Cottage is within walking distance of Ku Chawe & features a sunny terrace, comfortable rooms & a fireplace to ward off the evening chill. Cooking staff are on hand should you require a meal, but ingredients have to be brought from town. Advance bookings are necessary because the keys are kept in town. Don't forget to pick them up before you head up the mountain! *US$8 pp.*

Trout Farm (5 rooms, more under construction) m 088 8638524. Looking a little rundown & no longer very active on the trout-rearing front, this is still the most convenient budget option on the plateau, about 500m from the main road from town. It is essentially a self-catering set-up, but meals can usually be prepared on request & there was a restaurant in the works on our last visit. Barring that, you could always walk the 1km to Ku Chawe Inn for a meal. A large block of new rooms was under construction in early 2013. When completed, expect a new en-suite twin or dbl to go for around US$22. *US$6.25 pp twin, US$9.50 pp en-suite twin, US$22 4-bed cottage, US$2 pp camping.*

✖ WHERE TO EAT Unless you are staying at Zomba Forest Lodge, the only reliable restaurant is at the **Ku Chawe Inn**. If you're not prepared to pay that sort of price, bring all the food you need from Zomba Town. Remarkably, Himalayan raspberries grow all over on the plateau; you can buy a generous portion from the vendors outside Ku Chawe for around US$1. There are also strawberries at most times of year, grown in fields around the villages lower down.

EXPLORING ZOMBA PLATEAU The plateau is mostly of interest to ramblers and hikers, though its major points of interest can be seen from a vehicle by following the road that encircles the plateau. There are trout in most of the streams and in the dam, but it's not easy to get a permit. If you've had your fill of driving or rambling, the **Plateau Stables** (m *088 8714443/099 1557101*; e *parsons@ewimax.mw; www. plateaustables.com*) offer horseback rides from one hour to all day. They are an enchanting way to explore the mountain and cost US$35/hour.

A short nature trail runs from past **Mulunguzi Dam** along the forested banks of the Mulunguzi River and the **Mandala Falls**. This is a good area to see mammals (most commonly bushbuck and vervet monkey). Birds which are likely to be seen include black saw-wing swallow, mountain wagtail, Bertram's weaver, Livingstone's turaco and white-tailed crested flycatcher. From here, you can follow the road past the trout farm to the **Williams Falls**, upstream along the same river. This takes about an hour in either direction, longer if you start to explore the many relict forest patches for birds.

Many day visitors to the plateau will visit **Chingwe's Hole**, a natural hole that lies about two hours' walk from the Ku Chawe Inn and which can be reached by car. Hidden within a tiny copse of moss-draped trees, Chingwe's Hole is only about 8m in diameter, but locals reckon it is at least 60m deep and some claim it reaches the base of the Rift Valley (though recent explorations suggest it may be only 20m deep). There is a tradition that chiefs in the old days threw their enemies into 'bottomless' Chingwe's Hole, and a rumour persists that Banda's regime revived this tradition.

A few amiably lonesome vendors lurk around the car park at Chingwe's Hole, in the hope of selling the occasional passing tourist one of the fantastic crystalline rocks collected in the vicinity. The views across the Shire Valley are fantastic, and stretch all the way to distant Lake Malawi on a clear day. A 3km circular nature trail leads from the hole past some excellent viewpoints (views to Lake Malombe) and into a patch of montane forest where samango monkeys are seen with regularity, and a variety of forest birds (starred robin, Schalow's turaco, a variety of bulbuls and warblers, as well as the very localised Thyolo alethe) is present.

With a 4x4 vehicle, you can follow the outer escarpment around the plateau edge to the eastern escarpment, where the **Emperor's** and **Queen's viewpoints** (respectively named after Emperor Haile Selassie of Ethiopia and the Queen Mother of Great Britain, both of whom visited the plateau in the 1950s) offer wonderful views towards Lake Chilwa.

Further information An extensive network of signposted roads and footpaths means that the walking opportunities on the Zomba Plateau are practically limitless.

The relief model of the plateau in the forestry compound is useful for getting your bearings. Dedicated walkers are pointed to the excellent 36-page booklet *Zomba Mountain: A Walker's Guide* by Martyn and Kittie Cundy, which covers 15 walking routes, and includes several maps. If you can't locate that book, the fold-out *Guide to Zomba Plateau* sold for Mk100 by the WESM office in Zomba has a very useful map and several hiking recommendations.

LAKE CHILWA

The second-largest and most southerly of Malawi's major lakes, Chilwa couldn't contrast more in atmosphere with Lake Malawi. Surrounded by flat plains and isolated hills, Chilwa's shallow, slimy, reed-lined and mildly saline waters extend over 650km², though they are subject to great fluctuations in water level, and are nowhere more than 3m deep. Only a century ago, Chilwa covered around 1,750km² and its shore extended close to the bases of Mulanje and Zomba mountains (both now 20–30km distant), while in 1968, a severe local drought caused the lake to dry up altogether, and it came close to doing the same thing over 1995–96. This is because Chilwa is a vast but very shallow sump with no known outlet, so its size is almost totally dependent on recent run-off from Zomba and Mulanje.

There is a definite atmosphere about Chilwa, remote and otherworldly. At dusk, with only Mulanje and Zomba mountains punctuating the open horizon, the pink- and orange-tinged sky is the picture of serenity. The well-vegetated and in parts rather marshy shore is a birdwatchers' paradise, supporting a great variety of herons, waders and other shorebirds (glossy ibis are often common), while the baobabs on Chisi Island host the likes of trumpeter hornbill and various snake eagles. Offbeat local beliefs flourish in this environment: one oft-related legend concerns a small python-infested island that mysteriously disappeared all at once.

In 1997, Lake Chilwa was designated a Ramsar wetland of international importance, the first and only such site in Malawi, and it now receives international funding towards conservation. Following the drought of 1995–96, water levels are up again and the lake now produces 20% of Malawi's fish requirements, with some 35 villages with a combined 60,000 inhabitants pulling in more than 17,000 metric tons annually. In addition, Chilwa offers arguably the best aquatic-bird viewing in Malawi, supporting large populations of waterfowl of international importance, including estimated populations of around 500,000 lesser moorhen, 200,000 lesser gallinule, 100,000 black crake and fulvous whistling duck and 5,000 glossy ibis.

Unfortunately, Chilwa's avian wealth is increasingly threatened by subsistence hunting. Some experts estimate that up to one million birds were snared or shot annually in the late 1990s, and several once-common species of large waterbird are now thought to be locally extinct, among them the spectacular saddle-billed stork, wattled crane, and grey-crowned crane. A recent development, funded by Danish aid, has been the establishment of 20 bird-hunting clubs at villages around Lake Chilwa – not, as you might think, to encourage the hunting of birds, but to manage it sustainably and to provide local hunters with alternative sources of income. One such club, at Khanda, 25km from Zomba, recently started offering birding tours of the lake in conjunction with the Wildlife & Environmental Society of Malawi (WESM).

GETTING THERE AND AROUND
Organised trips The easiest way to see Lake Chilwa is to make advance arrangements to do a day trip with the WESM (for contact details, see page 180) for about US$10. They no longer have a vehicle of their own, but you may be able

11

to negotiate a motorcycle or other vehicle to Khanda with them (or hire one for the day in Zomba), ideally departing before sunrise to be at the lake in time for the best birding. Here, a local guide belonging to the Khanda Bird Hunting Club will walk you to the harbour (about 15 minutes) and take you out on a plank boat to a densely vegetated part of the lake where the likes of African jacana, black crake, squacco heron, whiskered tern and various ducks are common. The boat trip costs US$3 per person. Note that during the rainy season the area can be muddy and it is therefore advisable to bring a raincoat or an umbrella and wear gumboots (the latter can be borrowed at Khanda upon request).

Independent visits Using public transport, and for overnight stays, the best access to the lake is at a fishing village called **Kachulu**, which lies on the western shore, roughly 30km by road from Zomba Town. It's a lovely spot, and Kachulu is the sort of small, friendly, workaday African village that too few visitors to Africa ever get to experience. No buses run to Kachulu, but inexpensive minibuses and *matolas* leave when full from Zomba, or the turn-off just north of Zomba. Guides from the WESM (for contact details, see page 180) will accompany you on a day trip using public transport for about US$4.

From Kachulu, you can organise a boat to punt you across to Chisi Island, which consists of a couple of semi-submerged hills. There are some huge flocks of birds on Chisi's shore, while the baobab-studded hills are home to monkeys and hyenas. There are several small villages on Chisi and it could well be a rewarding place for self-sufficient campers to pitch a tent for a day or two. It's easy to organise a boat across to Chisi, and the ride takes about 30 minutes each way. Bear in mind that dense reed beds pose a navigational hazard to inexperienced rowers, so don't hire a boat without a local fisherman to take you around.

During the dry season mobile stilted fishing villages are set up on Lake Chilwa; these would certainly be worth visiting – ask at Kachulu Fishery Station of their whereabouts, and be prepared for a long journey to visit them.

The northern part of Lake Chilwa is very marshy, particularly during the rains, and it is rated as one of the best birdwatching areas in Malawi, with large flocks everywhere, notably greater and lesser flamingoes, pelicans and the localised black egret. With your own 4x4 vehicle, you could explore the area by driving along the D221 east of Liwonde Town, then (at Nsarama) turning left onto the dirt road T393 to Mphonde village, 8km from the Mozambican border. The best time to visit Mphonde is between September and December.

An interesting and challenging travel route would be to hop aboard one of the large motorised boats that service the villages on and around the lake from Kachulu and get off on the Mozambican side at Sombe.

🏠 **WHERE TO STAY** There are two basic resthouses in Kachulu, both of which have a few inexpensive single rooms. The **private resthouse** seems better than the **council resthouse**; the long-drop toilets are reasonably clean, and the obliging staff will boil up hot water for an open-air shower. If you have thoughts of exploring the lake beyond Kachulu, you'll probably need a tent.

✖ **WHERE TO EAT** There are a few restaurants in Kachulu, but you would be well advised to bring your own food from Zomba. If you're stuck, you'll probably be able to find some bread and tomatoes or bananas at one of the kiosks in the distinctly underwhelming market (which sells mostly fish). If you want to explore beyond Kachulu, you should definitely aim to be self-sufficient in food.

FURTHER INFORMATION The University of Malawi's *Lake Chilwa Co-ordinated Research Project: Decline and Recovery of a Lake*, edited by Margaret Kalk, might be of interest to some readers, though it was published in 1970 and is out of print. A newer publication is the annotated and illustrated bird checklist for Lake Chilwa sold at the WESM office in Zomba. If you do explore Lake Chilwa beyond Kachulu and Khanda, it would be useful to have the appropriate 1:50,000 or 1:250,000 map (the detail on the latter is pretty good).

CHIKALA PILLARS   With thanks to Lindsey Macdonald of WESM.

A series of eroded sandstone pinnacles located deep in the forests and farmland outside Zomba, the Chikala Pillars remain wholly undeveloped as a tourist attraction; it's likely you'll have the place to yourself. These tortured rock formations are evocative of the Marafa Depression in Kenya, rising at least 8m from the canyon floor in an assortment of walls and stand-alone towers. The stratified spires form a series of canyons and serene 'chapels', appropriately named since, at first glance, the pillars look like a series of earthen church steeples, all jostling for space in reach for the heavens. Others spread their ever-eroding tendrils into the valley, a geological strangler fig of sorts, slowly being reabsorbed into the surrounding earth. It's great rambling territory, and birders here may encounter owls, as they are known to roost in the area's many hollows and crevices.

GETTING THERE AND AWAY The easiest way to reach the Chikala Pillars (⊕ S15.096528°, E35.361944°) is to arrange a day trip with the WESM in Zomba, who can arrange for a guide to accompany you for as little as US$4. They are not feasibly reached via public transport, and a 4x4 is recommended for self-drivers. From Zomba, take the M3 north towards Liwonde. After 30 minutes or so, you will reach Malosa village, where you turn right at the hard-to-miss signpost for Lake Chilwa/Ramsar wetland. Continuing along this road for approximately 15 minutes, you approach a trading centre where the road forks and heads to the right – stay left at this fork. Follow this road through several villages until you reach the forestry station, where you will take another left fork, eventually leading to an army post where you can park your car. From here it's a 30-minute hike and you can ask a soldier for directions, or one will likely guide you for a small fee. The trail passes through brachystegia woodland, crossing a stream that has to be waded before you reach the pillars. Only for the intrepid!

RENT-A-CAR

Cars • Trucks • Busses • Offroad • Motorbikes

BLANTYRE (Head Office):

20 Glyn Jones Road
PO Box 2282
Blantyre, Malawi
Tel: +265 (0) 1-822836/822882
Fax: +265(0)1-825074
Email: info@ssrentacar.com

LILONGWE:

Kamuzu Procession Road
Old Town
PO Box 997
Lilongwe, Malawi
Tel: +265 (0) 1-751478/750112
Fax: +265(0)1-751529
Email: lilongwe@ssrentacar.com

"The largest, oldest and most reliable car rental company in Malawi"

www.ssrentacar.com

12

Blantyre

Malawi's oldest city and main commercial centre, Blantyre comes across as positively bustling by comparison with anywhere else in this most laidback of countries. Emanating from a compact central business district (CBD) bristling with people, traffic and commerce, it also seems a lot more cohesive – more obviously a proper city – than the capital Lilongwe. Blantyre has a pleasant midlands climate, set at an altitude of around 1,000m in a well-watered valley ringed by low hills, the largest of which are Michuru (1,473m), Soche (1,533m) and Ndirande (1,612m), and the CBD is surrounded by mature green suburbs dotted with hotels and restaurants.

Blantyre has evolved greatly in recent years, in particular the city centre, where an outbreak of multi-storey office blocks house numerous banks and other financial institutions (including the Stock Exchange of Malawi, which opened in 1998). Recent years have also seen a general diffusion of upmarket shopping, eating and nightlife facilities from the city centre to the suburbs, a trend epitomised by the glistening new Chichiri Mall, the country's largest shopping centre and home to its only cinema complex. Despite this, when it comes to accommodation and eating out, Blantyre offers significantly better value for money than the capital, presumably because it attracts a more inherently stringent business-oriented clientele than the free-spending governmental/aid/NGO industries that prop up the hospitality industry in Lilongwe.

An important regional transport hub, Blantyre forms the northeast terminus of the so-called Tete Corridor connecting Zimbabwe to Malawi via western Mozambique. Formerly the most popular transit route for travellers crossing between South Africa and East Africa, the Tete Corridor has diminished in importance over the past decade as a result of the ongoing crisis in Zimbabwe, combined with Malawi's own troubles in recent years, which means that relatively few travellers pass through Blantyre these days. For those who do, however, Blantyre – though not really a tourist attraction in itself – is a stimulating yet very manageable city, with enough going on to keep you busy for a day or two, and it also forms a good springboard for exploring more remote areas such as Mulanje and the Lower Shire Valley.

HISTORY

Blantyre is not only the oldest European settlement in Malawi, but also one of the oldest anywhere in the region, pre-dating the likes of Nairobi, Harare, Lusaka and Johannesburg. It started life in October 1876 as a mission station, founded by Henry Henderson for the Established Church of Scotland, and is named after the small Scottish village where David Livingstone was born. The original mission was sited between the Likabula and Nasalo rivers, on a patch of fertile land granted to the Church by Chief Kapeni, who hoped that its presence would protect his people from Ngoni raids. Unfortunately, however, the mission's first leader, Reverend Duff

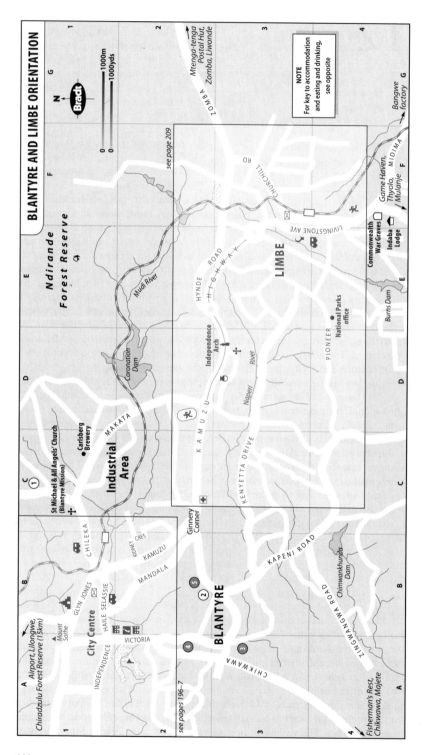

BLANTYRE AND LIMBE ORIENTATION

NOTE
For key to accommodation and eating and drinking, see opposite

Ndirande Forest Reserve

Industrial Area

City Centre

BLANTYRE

LIMBE

Airport, Lilongwe, Chiradzulu Forest Reserve (15km)

Fisherman's Rest, Chikwawa, Majete

Mtenga-tenga Postal Hut, Zomba, Liwonde

Bangwe factory

Game Haven, Thyolo, Mulanje

Commonwealth War Graves

Indaba Lodge

National Parks office

Independence Arch

Ginnery Corner

St Michael & All Angels' Church (Blantyre Mission)

Carlsberg Brewery

Coronation Dam

Mudi River

Burns Dam

Napeti River

Chimwankhunda Dam

Mount Sothe

see page 209

see pages 196–7

CHILEKA

GLYN JONES

HAILE SELASSIE

VICTORIA

INDEPENDENCE

KIDNEY CRES

KAMUZU

MANDALA

MAKATA

KAMUZU

HYNDE ROAD

HIGHWAY

PIONEER

KENYETTA DRIVE

CHIKWAWA

KAPENI ROAD

ZINGWANGWA ROAD

LIVINGSTONE AVE

CHURCHILL RD

MIDIMA

ZOMBA

1000m
1000yds
0
0

192

BLANTYRE AND LIMBE Orientation
For listings, see pages 195–204

⊖ **Where to stay**
1 Grace Bandawe Hostel.....C1
2 Leslie Lodge.........................B2

Off map
  Fisherman's Rest................A4
  Game Haven.......................F4

⊗ **Where to eat and drink**
3 Club Mustang Sally............A3
4 Colony Club Casino............A2
5 TJ's Bar..................................B2

Macdonald, ruled over the surrounding hills with a despotic cruelty, flogging and killing suspected thieves and murderers without even the pretence of a trial. The behaviour of the early Blantyre missionaries caused a scandal in the British press, forcing many of them to retire. In 1881, Reverend Clement Scott succeeded Macdonald, initiating a period of improved relations between the missionaries and Chief Kapeni's subjects.

The healthy, fertile climate around Blantyre proved attractive to European settlers, and the mission's strategic position served as an excellent communication centre for trade between Lake Malawi and the Zambezi Valley. In 1878, the Scottish brothers John and Frederick Moir chose the area called Mandala, immediately south of the present-day city centre, as the headquarters of the African Lakes Corporation, thereby initiating Blantyre's rise as the country's major commercial centre. In 1882, the Moir brothers constructed the double-storey Mandala House, now the oldest building in the country. Blantyre became a British consular location in 1883 and attained municipality status by 1895. By 1905, the fledgling city had started to take recognisable shape, though urban development was confined to the mission, Mandala and an administrative and commercial centre bounded by present-day Haile Selassie Road, Glyn Jones Road and Hannover Avenue.

Following the arrival of the railway there in 1906, the Shire Highlands Railways Company established the discrete township of Limbe, about 6km east of Blantyre, as its headquarters and repair centre. By 1910, Limbe had outgrown Blantyre in terms of population, thanks to the establishment of an Imperial Tobacco Group packaging and grading factory, and an influx of Indian retailers. In 1956, Limbe was formally incorporated into Blantyre, and the amalgamated city is sometimes referred to as Blantyre/Limbe. It remains the most important commercial centre in the country, and it was the most populous city throughout the 20th century, with some 478,000 residents (as opposed to Lilongwe's 435,000) recorded in the official 1998 census. Since then, however, Blantyre seems to have slipped behind Lilongwe into second place, though this varies depending on your source of statistics. Common estimates in 2012 placed Blantyre's population between 728,000 and 856,000.

GETTING THERE AND AWAY

Blantyre is the largest transport hub in southern Malawi. Buses and minibuses come and go regularly in every direction from the Wenela bus station [197 G4] on Chileka Road. Buses coming to Blantyre from the direction of Zomba or Mulanje stop in Limbe bus station [209 A4] before proceeding to Blantyre itself. Minibuses will sometimes terminate at the Mibawa bus station [197 F5] in central Blantyre rather than Wenela, and this is also where to get rides to/from Limbe. Sample minibus fares are US$3 to Mulanje, US$3.25 to Zomba, US$5.75 to Liwonde and US$8 to Lilongwe.

Travellers heading directly between Blantyre and Lilongwe (or points further north) will probably want to take advantage of the various express services operated by **Axa Coaches**. Full details of these services are on page 291, and there are two

Blantyre GETTING THERE AND AWAY

12

Blantyre offices, one on Kamuzu Highway next to the Chichiri Shopping Centre [209 B1], and the other just off Glyn Jones Road near the centre [197 F5]. **National Bus Company** (✆ *01 611380*) also runs nearly a dozen buses daily from the Wenela station, including routes to Lilongwe, Mzuzu, Mulanje and others.

For travel to/from Zimbabwe and South Africa, you have several options. **Intercape** (*www.intercape.co.za;* m *099 9403398*) is the most upmarket service, with four buses/week at US$76 departing from Blantyre Lodge [197 G5], and you can book online. Note that this service is to Johannesburg only, and Intercape passengers *cannot* disembark in Zimbabwe or Mozambique. **KJ Transport** (✆ *01 877797/914017*) runs two coaches weekly, leaving Blantyre at 08.30 on Tuesday and Saturday, and Johannesburg at 10.30 on Wednesday and Saturday, taking about 24 hours. Bookings and departures are also from Blantyre Lodge [197 G5], opposite the main (Wenela) bus station and the Johannesburg contact numbers are +27 (0)73 7227874/(0)72 3392385. **Flyover** (m *088 1921001/099 322146*) is another operator, offering coaches departing from Wenela station to Johannesburg on Wednesday and Saturday for US$70. For those headed to Harare or Tete, **Malasha** (✆ *01 11612314;* m *088 4460946*) runs at least twice weekly between the Wenela bus station and Harare for US$30. Minibuses to the Mozambican border at Mwanza/Zobue depart throughout the day from the Mibawa bus station [197 F5] and cost US$4.50.

Blantyre – or more accurately Limbe – is also the centre of Malawi's limited, intermittent and little-used **rail** network. The only route of interest for adventurous travellers is from Blantyre to Nayuchi on the eastern border, where it connects with the Mozambique rail service. It is supposed to run Mondays to Fridays, though often only runs once a week (if that), and entails a change at Nkaya, but it would probably be better starting in Liwonde. Cheap, but not for the faint-hearted.

Chileka International Airport (✆ *01 692231/254*) lies 19km from the city centre. It is the oldest airport in Malawi, but it receives fewer international flights than Lilongwe's Kamuzu Airport. South African Airways flies twice a week from Johannesburg, and Ethiopian Airlines connects to Addis Ababa thrice-weekly. Air Malawi entered liquidation in early 2013, but it is expected to resume offering domestic and regional connections in partnership with Ethiopian Airlines later in the year. Taxis to the airport cost around US$27.

AIRLINES Major airlines represented in Blantyre include:

✈ **Air Malawi** [196 A4] 4 Robin's Rd; ✆ 01 820811/ 030

✈ **Ethiopian Airlines** Finance Hse, Victoria Av; ✆ 01 834676/833048

✈ **Kenya Airways** Mount Soche Hotel; ✆ 01 820877

✈ **South African Airways** Livingstone Towers, Glyn Jones Rd; ✆ 01 820629/617

ORIENTATION AND GETTING AROUND

Blantyre's compact CBD is roughly triangular in shape, bounded by Glyn Jones Road to the north, Haile Selassie Road to the south and Hannover Avenue to the west. The main north–south thoroughfare, a block east of Hannover Avenue, is Victoria Avenue, where you'll find the tourist and map sales office, a People's Supermarket [196 B6], and several banks and forex bureaux. The Mount Soche Hotel [196 B4], on the junction of Victoria Avenue and Glyn Jones Road, is perhaps the best-known landmark in the city centre.

Immediately east of the city centre, Glyn Jones Road and Haile Selassie Road converge at a roundabout to become the Kamuzu Highway. About 200m east of this roundabout is the clock tower roundabout where Chileka Road branches from Kamuzu Highway to the northeast. The main bus station (often called 'Wenela' after the area it's located in) [197 G4] is 500m along Chileka Road; around it lies most of Blantyre's budget accommodation.

Kamuzu Highway connects Blantyre to the satellite town of Limbe, 6km to the east. Though part of the same municipality, Limbe now functions as a separate town to Blantyre in most respects, with its own main road, market [209 E3] and bus station [209 A4]. Regular minibuses connect Blantyre and Limbe via the Kamuzu Highway; the conductors shout 'Highway … Limbe' or 'Highway … Blantyre' depending on which direction they are going. The Chichiri Shopping Centre [209 B2] lies along the Kamuzu Highway towards Limbe, as does the Museum of Malawi [209 C2] and Axa Coach terminus [209 B1].

Car hire

🚗 **Avis Car Hire** Main office: Makata Rd, also at Chileka International Airport; ✆ 01 871495/870230/622719; m 088 8868700; e reservations@avis.co.mw; www.avis.com/car-rental/location/mw
🚗 **Countrywide Car Hire** [196 B6] Plantation House; ✆ 01 822434/854/232; m 099 9954759; e info@countrywidemw.com; www.countrywidemw.com

🚗 **Silver Line Car Hire** Axa Complex on Glyn Jones Rd; ✆ 01 832551/602870; m 099 9270200/9470691; e info@silverlinecarhire.com; www.silverlinecarhire.com
🚗 **SS Rent-A-Car** [196 C5] 20 Glyn Jones Rd; ✆ 01 822836/821597; m 088 8829322; e info@ssrentacar.com; www.ssrentacar.com

TOURIST INFORMATION

The **tourist office** [196 B7] (✆ 01 820300) on the bottom end of Victoria Avenue is reasonably helpful when open, and stocks a good range of pamphlets and books.

TOUR OPERATORS AND SAFARI COMPANIES

Many tour operators are based in Blantyre or have offices there, making it easy to organise travel and accommodation around the country and into neighbouring countries:

Jambo Africa [196 C4] SS Rent-A-Car Building, Glyn Jones Rd; ✆ 01 835356/823709; m 088 8202420/8902421; e jamboafrica@africa-online.net; www.jambo-africa.com
Responsible Safari Company ✆ 01 602407/0208 133 8611 (UK); m 099 9306631; e info@responsiblesafaricompany.com; www.

responsiblesafaricompany.com; see also advert on page 46
Wilderness Safaris Malawi [196 A4] Protea Hotel Ryall's; ✆ 01 836961; m 088 8204946; e reservations@wilderness.mw; www.wilderness-safaris.com

🏠 **WHERE TO STAY** See map, pages 196–7 unless otherwise stated.

EXCLUSIVE
🏠 **Game Haven** [map page 192] (5 rooms, 20 under construction) m 099 9971287/8; e info@gamehavenmw.com; www.gamehavenmw.com.

Situated 14km from Limbe along the Thyolo road, this owner-managed lodge lies in a 900ha private game sanctuary stocked with zebra, wildebeest, sable antelope, nyala & other African wildlife. The

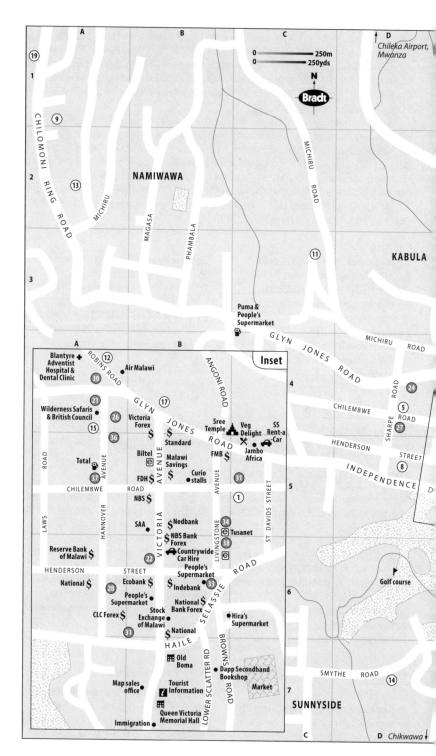

NAMIWAWA

KABULA

Chileka Airport,
Mwanza

0 ——— 250m
0 ——— 250yds

Puma &
People's
Supermarket

GLYN JONES ROAD

MICHIRU ROAD

Inset

Blantyre
Adventist
Hospital &
Dental Clinic

Air Malawi

Wilderness Safaris
& British Council

Victoria
Forex

CHILEMBWE ROAD

Sree
Temple

Veg
Delight

SS
Rent-a-
Car

Jambo
Africa

Standard

FMB

Biltel

Malawi
Savings

Total

Curio
stalls

FDH

NBS

SAA

Nedbank

Tusanet

NBS Bank
Forex

Countrywide
Car Hire

People's
Supermarket

Reserve Bank
of Malawi

National

Ecobank

Indebank

People's
Supermarket

National
Bank Forex

CLC Forex

Stock
Exchange
of Malawi

Hira's
Supermarket

National

HAILE SELASSIE ROAD

Old
Boma

Golf course

Map sales
office

Tourist
Information

Dapp Secondhand
Bookshop

Market

SMYTHE ROAD

SUNNYSIDE

Queen Victoria
Memorial Hall

Immigration

D Chikwawa ↓

196

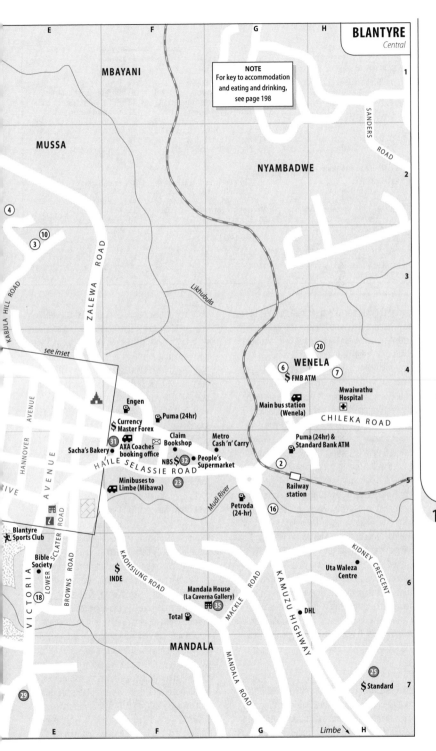

MBAYANI

NOTE
For key to accommodation
and eating and drinking,
see page 198

MUSSA

NYAMBADWE

SANDERS ROAD

ZALEWA ROAD

KABULA HILL ROAD

Likhubula

see inset

WENELA

20

6    $ FMB ATM   7

Main bus station
(Wenela)

Mwaiwathu
Hospital

CHILEKA ROAD

Engen

$ Currency
Master Forex

Puma (24hr)

Claim
Bookshop

Metro
Cash 'n' Carry

Puma (24hr) &
Standard Bank ATM

Sacha's Bakery   AXA Coaches
booking office

31

NBS $ 32

People's
Supermarket

HAILE SELASSIE ROAD

Minibuses to
Limbe (Mibawa)

23

2

Railway
station

Mudi River

Petroda
(24-hr)

16

Blantyre
Sports Club

Bible
Society

$
INDE

KAOHSIUNG ROAD

Mandala House
(La Caverna Gallery)

35

Total

MACKLE ROAD

KAMUZU HIGHWAY

KIDNEY CRESCENT

Uta Waleza
Centre

DHL

MANDALA

MANDALA ROAD

25

$ Standard

18

HANNOVER AVENUE

AVENUE

SCLATER ROAD

BROWNS ROAD

LOWER

VICTORIA

RIVE

29

E   F   G   H

Limbe

BLANTYRE Central
For listings, see pages 195–204

⌂ Where to stay

1 Big Brother's Guesthouse....................C5	8 Henderson Street Guesthouse.................D5	14 Pedro's Lodge..............D7
2 Blantyre Lodge..................G5	9 Hostellerie de France....A1	15 Protea Hotel Ryall's....A4
3 Casa Mia............................E3	10 House Five Guest House.............................E3	16 Royal Palm Hotel........G5
4 Chez Maky..........................E2		17 Sunbird Mount Soche Hotel...............B4
5 Chilembwe Lodge...........D4	11 Kabula Lodge..................C3	18 Victoria Hotel..............E6
6 Doogle's..............................G4	12 Malawi Sun Hotel...........A4	19 Villa 33.........................A1
7 Family Lodge.....................H4	13 Namiwawa Lodge..........A2	20 Wenela Lodge...........H4

✖ Where to eat and drink

21 21 Grill...............................A4	Chez Maky.................(see 4)	33 Krazy Grills & Sizzlers......................B6
22 Alem Ethiopian Restaurant...................B6	28 Chez Ntemba............. A6	34 Leah's Kitchen.............B5
	Doogles.....................(see 6)	35 Mandala Café..............G6
23 Ali Baba Restaurant & Take-Away.................. F5	29 Gelato Carnival............E7	36 Mibawa Café.................A5
24 Baba's Delhi Durbar......D4	30 Hong Kong Restaurant....................A4	Michiru Restaurant.......(see 17)
25 Blue Elephant................H7	Hostellerie de	Quarter Bistro....(see 10)
26 Bombay Palace.............A4	France.....................(see 9)	37 Steers & Debonairs Pizza...........................A5
Café 33.....................(see 19)	31 Kips.......................C5, F5, B6	
Casa Mia...................(see 3)	32 KFC..................................... F5	38 Super Snax.................B6
27 Casablanca...................D4		

closest thing to a bush retreat in the greater Blantyre area, it offers accommodation in spacious cottages with 4-poster queen- or king-size beds, sitting room with fireplace, optional DSTV & fridge, & a large bathroom with tub & shower. The excellent Ambrosia Restaurant serves an extensive menu of seafood, poultry, meat & venison dishes in the US$7–17 range, & all meals are accompanied by home-grown organic vegetables. There is a professionally-designed 9-hole golf course & driving range, & other activities include guided game drives, guided walks, fishing & lazing around the well-appointed swimming pool. *US$70/120 sgl/dbl B&B.*

⌂ **House Five Guest House** (6 rooms) `02 12953053`; m 088 8901762; e housefive@africa-online.net or hostaria@africa-online.net; www.ulendo-collection.com. This breezy place on Kabula Hill was the 1st boutique lodge in Blantyre & is housed in the former US consulate. It offers great views to the surrounding hills, yet is only a few mins' walk from the CBD. Rooms are bright, smartly decorated & come with twin or king-size beds, writing desk, walk-in nets, fan, tea/coffee facilities, Wi-Fi & DSTV. There's a swimming pool as well. *US$100/120 sgl/dbl B&B.*

UPMARKET

⌂ **Casa Mia** (10 rooms) m 01 11915559; m 099 9965851; e casamia@africa-online.net; www.blantyreaccommodation.com. Located on Kabula Hill behind the eponymous restaurant, this

stylish boutique lodge offers bright & thoughtfully appointed en-suite rooms surrounding a courtyard with swimming pool & exercise equipment. Rooms have wrought-iron 4-poster queen beds, terracotta tiles, tea/coffee facilities, writing desk, lounge area, AC, DSTV, & Skyband Wi-Fi. It's attached to one of the best restaurants in town, & is a short walk from the CBD. *US$70/85 sgl/dbl, US$85/100 superior sgl/dbl, all rates B&B.*

⌂ **Fisherman's Rest** [map page 192] `+44 (0)1437 711 038 (UK);` m 088 8836753; e enquiries@fishermansrest.net; www.fishermansrest.net; see also advert on inside back cover. Situated 20km from Blantyre along the Chikwawa road, this family-run lodge sits in a 20ha private reserve on the edge of a dizzying escarpment, offering spectacular views of the Great Rift Valley below. There's a variety of accommodation on offer, including self-catering houses, but the most compelling has to be the bush hides with private balcony & outdoor shower, from where you can hope to see any of the numerous antelope resident in the grounds. Community projects are a priority here (many with a religious affiliation), & visitors are welcome to participate, or you can have a dip in the pool & try the exhilarating bike ride down the escarpment. No alcohol is served, but it's acceptable to bring your own. *US$80/115 bush hide or cottage sgl/dbl, US$230 2-bedroom cottage, US$375 4-bedroom cottage, US$25 pp standing tents, all rates B&B.*

⌂ Malawi Sun Hotel (32 rooms) ☎01 824808/822969; **e** info@malawisunhotel.com; www.malawisunhotel.com. This modern hotel, on Robin Rd around the corner from the Mount Soche, has large grounds offering lovely views towards Mount Ndirande. Spacious & contemporarily styled rooms come with terracotta tiles, uncluttered wooden furnishings, net, AC, safe, fridge, tea/coffee facilities, DSTV, Wi-Fi & a private balcony with seating. There's a swimming pool, video game arcade, & several restaurants are attached, but no alcohol is served. Decent value. *US$125/156 sgl/dbl B&B.*

⌂ Protea Hotel Ryall's (120 rooms) ☎01 820955; **e** ryalls@proteamalawi.com; www.proteahotels.com. Established by Louise Stratton in 1921 & named after her husband Frank Ryall, this 4-star member of the South African Protea chain stands at the top end of Hannover Av, around the corner from the Mount Soche Hotel. Despite being the oldest hotel in town, numerous renovations & expansions have rendered it somewhat characterless, & there is no garden. The rooms are large & comfortable, with DSTV, AC & en-suite hot shower, & facilities include a swimming pool, gym, business centre, Wi-Fi, disabled access, 2 good restaurants & 2 bars. *Rates vary with demand, starting at US$180/215 sgl/dbl & topping out at US$220/255 B&B.*

⌂ Sunbird Mount Soche Hotel (136 rooms) ☎01 820588/071; **e** mountsocheres@sunbirdmalawi.com; www.sunbirdmalawi.com. A flagship of the government-owned Sunbird Group, this is the smartest address in Blantyre, offering a range of accommodation from standard rooms to superior suites. Centrally situated at the junction of Glyn Jones Rd & Victoria Av, it stands in expansive green gardens with a large swimming pool & views to the surrounding mountains. The refurbished rooms all have DSTV, AC, fan, minibar, en-suite combined tub/shower & 24hr room service – ask for one facing the gardens rather than the road – & there's free broadband at the business centre. The plush Michuru Restaurant is on the 5th floor & the mid-range Gypsy Restaurant on the ground floor. There is a quiet cocktail bar in the main building, while the livelier Sportsman's Bar has a separate entrance. *US$224/249 sgl/dbl, US$310/334 sgl/dbl executive, all rates B&B.*

⌂ Victoria Hotel (84 rooms) ☎01 823500/822669; **m** 099 9957645; **e** reservations@hotelvictoriamw.com; www.hotelvictoriamw.com. At the bottom of Victoria Av about 5mins' walk from the city centre, this is significantly improved with the addition of a new wing. The older standard rooms are somewhat dowdy & cramped & come with DTSV, safe, minibar, Wi-Fi & AC, while deluxe rooms in the new wing are considerably more sleek & spacious, with flatscreen TV & contemporary bathrooms. The grounds are small & the location on a busy trunk road is potentially noisy, but the deluxe rooms are decent value for the price. Facilities include a restaurant & swimming pool. *US$76/91 superior sgl/dbl, US$106/122 deluxe sgl/dbl, US$152 suite B&B.*

MODERATE

⌂ Chez Maky (8 rooms) ☎01 833764; **m** 099 9203029/9945308; **e** chezmakymw@gmail.com. Owner-managed by an amiable & welcoming Cameroonian expat, this is a great place to stay, a few hundred metres along Kabula Hill Rd (signposted to the right up from the Mount Soche Hotel). It's a converted old house with a very chilled-out atmosphere, a new hillside swimming pool & incredible views over Ndirande Mountain. Rooms & apts vary in size, most are en suite, & all are comfortable & come with DSTV, Wi-Fi & nets. An excellent restaurant spills onto the balcony & the constantly evolving menu has a strong Franco–African flavour. *A negotiable US$40–100 per room, depending on room size & sgl/dbl occupancy, inc meals & laundry.*

⌂ Chilembwe Lodge (35 rooms) ☎01 824649/88. This unpretentious hotel has a quiet suburban setting on Chilembwe Rd but is only a couple of blocks' stroll from the city centre & plentiful restaurants on Hannover Av. Standard sgl rooms have a tiled floor, 3/4 bed, fan, net & DSTV, superior rooms have a dbl bed & fridge, while deluxe rooms have a king-size bed, walk-in netting & AC. All rooms have Skyband Wi-Fi. It's nothing special, but convenient & reasonably priced. *US$50 sgl, US$55/65 superior sgl/dbl, US$70/80 deluxe, all rates B&B.*

⌂ Hostellerie de France (20 rooms) ☎01 669626/668397; **m** 088 8833586; **e** hostfrance@globemw.net; www.hostellerie-de-france.com. Boasting a scenic location in suburban Namiwawa, this idiosyncratic pension lies about 3km from the city centre at the corner of Chilomoni Ring Rd & Kazuni Close. The rooms, studios & apts are clean, & some have DSTV, fridge, nets &/or private balcony. Facilities include a jacuzzi & swimming pool, & the restaurant serves delicious French food, optionally accompanied by a connoisseur selection of French wines & Cuban cigars. This place will appeal greatly to gourmands, French-speakers & those who value characterful accommodation (a rare commodity in Blantyre), but we've also had negative feedback about the omnipresence of the owner-manager. *Most rooms are in the US$50–70 range, some at US$25–30, best US$100–130.*

🏠 **Leslie Lodge** [map page 192] (7 rooms) 📞01 871671; m 099 9828929/4317; e finch@ africa-online.net; www.leslielodge.com. This is another small & popular owner-managed lodge, situated south of the city centre at the junction of Mahatma Gandhi & Leslie Rd, opposite a Petroda filling station. The spacious dbl & twin rooms have contemporary décor, DSTV & minibar, & some have AC, private balcony &/or self-catering facilities. Evening meals are available by request. Contact the lodge for rates.

🏠 **Pedro's Lodge** (8 rooms) 📞01 833430; m 088 8842670; e pedros@globemw.net or pedros@africa-online.net; www.pedroslodge.com. This comfortable owner-managed lodge lies on Smythe Rd, off Victoria Av below the sports club, & has twin & dbl rooms with DSTV, Wi-Fi, fan, netting & complimentary tea & coffee. A good restaurant/ bar with DTSV & Wi-Fi is attached, & there's a swimming pool. *US$60/70/80 sgl/dbl/twin B&B, inc laundry.*

🏠 **Royal Palm Hotel** m 099 5138905; e royalpalmhotel@sikumw.com. Set in a modestly green compound along Kamuzu Highway, this Cape Dutch-inspired hotel has the feel of an old mansion, replete with big stuffed chairs, fireplaces, wooden accents & domed ceilings. The rooms are drab compared with the common areas, but they have AC, DSTV, ceiling fan & Wi-Fi. The restaurant serves mostly Indian mains with lots of vegetarian options at US$4.50, & meat dishes for US$8. *US$62.50/78.50 sgl/dbl B&B.*

🏠 **Shire Highlands Hotel** [map page 209] (40 rooms) 📞01 840243/847464; e marketing@ alexanderhotels.net; www.alexanderhotels.net. On Churchill Av in central Limbe, this dbl-storey colonial relic had become a bit rundown prior to a change of ownership, but subsequent renovation has restored plenty of character to the common areas. The old-fashioned but well-maintained en-suite rooms have dbl bed, DSTV & AC. Upstairs rooms have tubs, those downstairs have showers, & executive rooms have a separate lounge. Facilities include a swimming pool, business centre, gift shop & 2 bars, while the Naperi Restaurant serves Malawian & international cuisine. Cultural evenings with traditional dancing are held on occasional Fridays. *US$40/55 sgl/dbl, US$45/58 sgl/dbl executive, additional 20% premium for non-residents seldom enforced, all rates B&B.*

🏠 **Villa 33** (9 rooms) m 099 9960231; e reservations@thevilla.mw; www.thevilla.mw; see also advert on page 210. Set in large gardens at 33 Chilomoni Ring Rd, this new owner-managed lodge offers accommodation in spacious & airy tiled en-suite rooms with queen-size beds, DSTV, fan, safe, Wi-Fi & attractively modern furnishings. It's a nice quiet setting, there's a lovely terrace well-suited to savouring an espresso, & the excellent Café 33 in the same compound is home to what must be Blantyre's only *tapas* menu. Self-catering apartments are available for both short & long-term rental, & there's a free laundry service. *US$70/80 sgl/dbl B&B.*

BUDGET

🏠 **Blantyre Lodge** (52 rooms) 📞01 834460. Right opposite the bus station, this might be a good option for late arrivals or early departures, & the spacious rooms are adequately comfortable. Intercape & KJ Transport buses depart from here. *US$25 dbl using shared facilities, US$35/50 en-suite sgl/dbl, rates inc b/fast for 1 person.*

🏠 **Chichiri Lodge** [map page 209] (16 rooms) 📞01 1604482; m 088 8866893. This is an unpretentious but clean & comfortable lodge on Kamuzu Highway a few mins' walk from Chichiri Mall. The en-suite twins have 1 ¾ & 1 sgl bed, DSTV, net, fan & fridge, & a restaurant serves decent meals for US$4.75. *US$19/23 sgl/dbl B&B.*

🏠 **Comfort Inn** [map page 209] (8 rooms) 📞01 870424; m 088 1100404; e stellaliabunya@ yahoo.com. A few doors down from Chichiri Lodge, this is an equally convenient & secure small lodge, & the dbl or twin rooms are equipped with net, fan, fridge, DSTV, en-suite hot shower & ample cupboard space. Good value. *US$20.50/25 sgl/dbl, US$25/30 executive sgl/dbl.*

🏠 **Grace Bandawe Hostel** [map page 192](42 rooms) 📞01 830305/981056; m 088 8833523; e gracebandawehotel@gmail.com; www.blantyresynod.org. On Chileka Rd, 500m out of town from the bus station, this Church-run hostel lies in peaceful green gardens opposite the original Blantyre Mission, & its clean & brightly decorated twin rooms have an en-suite hot shower. The atmosphere is somewhat institutional & it is quite a distance from any bars & restaurants, though an on-site restaurant serves canteen-like grub (but no alcohol). *US$30/42 sgl/dbl, US$36/50 suite sgl/dbl.*

🏠 **Henderson Street Guesthouse** (6 rooms) 📞 01 823474; m 099 9238967; e hsghblantyre@ gmail.com. With views of the National Bank HQ from the wrap-around porch, this affable budget lodge has a serene & convenient location in a wooded suburban garden on Henderson St, less than 500m from the city centre. The cosy tiled rooms with cane furniture all come with a dbl bed, walk-in netting, DSTV & en-suite hot shower, & it's within easy walking distance of most facilities, from internet & forex bureaux to half a dozen restaurants. Meals are also available for guests at US$2.50. A hidden gem. *US$17.25 dbl, US$27 family room, all rates B&B.*

🏠 **Kabula Lodge** 📞 01 821216; m 099 9950361; e kabulalodge@africa-online.net; www.kabulalodge.co.mw. Well-loved by local volunteers, this unassuming lodge has simple but comfortable accommodation & lovely views of the surrounding hills. Rooms have Skyband Wi-Fi, writing desk, nets, fans & hot showers. There's a balcony restaurant/bar serving Malawian staples. Long-term rates are negotiable. *US$15 pp twin, US$30/50 sgl/dbl self-contained.*

🏠 **Namiwawa Lodge** (22 rooms) 📞 01 667394/11919454; m 088 4373804/8630272. Situated off Magasa Rd in the upmarket suburb of Namiwawa, this modern lodge offers new tiled executive rooms with wooden-beam ceilings, DSTV, fan, net, writing desk & en-suite hot shower. A decent restaurant is attached. There are also rooms with self-catering facilities, & it's good value overall. *US$20.50/23.50 sgl/dbl, US$47/56.50 executive sgl/dbl, all rates B&B.*

🏠 **Wenela Lodge** (9 rooms) m 099 4475655; e wenelalodge@gmail.com. This convenient family-run lodge consists of a converted homestead set in a green garden less than 5mins' walk from the main bus station. The high-ceilinged twin & dbl rooms are light & airy, & some are en suite, & there are nets but most don't have fans. Meals are available for US$2.75. *US$12.50/17.25 sgl/dbl, US$14/19 en suite, all rates B&B.*

SHOESTRING

🏠 **Big Brother's Guesthouse** (11 rooms) 📞 01 833815; m 099 9919235. The most central shoestring option is this small & welcoming local lodge, which has clean tiled rooms with net & fan, some en suite. Good value. *US$9.50/12.50 sgl/dbl, US$11/15.75 en-suite sgl/dbl.*

🏠 **Doogle's** (8 rooms, 4 dorms) 📞 01 602710; m 088 8837615; e doogles@africa-online.net. About 100m from the main bus station, this large hostel has been the most popular shoestring option in Blantyre for the best part of 2 decades, & it remains the pick in this price range. In addition to clean accommodation, it has a lively bar with pool table, a swimming pool, a good noticeboard, a lounge with DSTV & DVD player, hot showers, luggage storage, internet access & good meals for US$3–4. There's live music on Thursday nights, & a FMB ATM right next door. *US$25/40 sgl/dbl, US$25 chalet, US$10 pp dorm bed, US$5 pp camping.*

🏠 **Family Lodge** (7 rooms) 📞 01 833170; m 099 9934277. This likeable lodge lies in a pleasant garden just around the corner from Doogle's & the bus station, & it offers the choice of basic but clean sgls with ¾ bed & net in an outdoor annex using shared showers, or twin/ dbl rooms with fan & net in the main building, 2 of which are en-suite baths, while the other 2 share a bathroom. Good value & a warm welcome. *US$6.25/9.50 sgl/dbl, US$12.50 en-suite dbl.*

✕ WHERE TO EAT *See map, pages 196–7 unless otherwise stated.*

Blantyre is endowed with restaurants to suit most tastes and budgets. Being so close to the trade routes from the Mozambique coast, it is known for seafood, especially prawns, but a good range of European, African and Asian foods is represented. There are at least a dozen worthwhile restaurants in the city centre, many concentrated on Hannover Avenue, and a similar number scattered around the suburbs. For convenience, the listings overleaf are arranged by location, rather than by price or type of cuisine.

CITY CENTRE
Hannover Avenue

✕ **21 Grill** ✆01 820955; ⊕ 11.00–15.00 & 18.00–23.30 Mon–Fri, 18.00–23.30 Sat–Sun. An annex to Protea Hotel Ryall's, this is the smartest eatery in Blantyre, enforcing a strict dress code (no T-shirts, caps or shorts) & a veto on under-18s Mon–Fri. The chef has built up a phenomenal reputation for the imaginative fusion cuisine, which infuses continental-style dishes with African, Asian & Latin American flavours. Mains are mostly in the US$11–13 range, & there's live music on Fridays & Saturdays.

✕ **Bombay Palace** ✆01 821153; m 088 8200200; ⊕ 12.00–14.00 Tue–Sun, 18.00–22.00 daily. This smart licensed Indian restaurant has been a favourite for years, & it remains great value, with an extensive menu of meat & vegetarian dishes in the US$6.50–8 range, excluding rice/bread.

✕ **Hong Kong Restaurant** ✆01 624467; ⊕ 12.00–13.30 & 18.00–22.00 Tue–Sun. At the top of Hannover Av, on the junction with Glyn Jones & Robins roads, this is an unpretentious, affordable & very good Chinese restaurant with a varied menu catering to carnivores & vegetarians alike. Small portions, sufficient to feed 1 person, cost around US$4.50, while large portions (enough for 2) are US$7.50, with rice an additional US$2.50. Drinks are also reasonably priced by Blantyre standards.

✕ **Steers & Debonairs Pizza** ✆01 610611; m 099 5660441 ⊕ 08.30–22.00 Mon–Thu, 08.30–23.00 Fri–Sat. These two South African chains are newly represented in Blantyre, & hugely popular. Burgers, grills, sandwiches & pizzas are the order of the day, with combos starting around US$5. There's also free delivery.

East of Hannover Avenue

✕ **Alem Ethiopian Restaurant** Victoria Av; ✆01 823455; m 088 8660444; ⊕ 07.00–20.30 Mon–Sat. A welcome surprise to those travellers who've already visited Ethiopia, this is an excellent place for neophytes to sample Africa's most unusual cuisine. Spicy Ethiopian dishes are mostly around US$6 & it also serves traditional Ethiopian coffee, & blander local fare in the US$2.50–4 range. No alcohol served.

✕ **KFC** ⊕ 09.00–21.00 Sun–Thu, 09.00–22.30 Fri–Sat. Those with a craving for American-style fast food & fried chicken need look no further than Blantyre's very own KFC. Meals start at about

US$4.50, with combos going for closer to US$8. They're open holidays as well.

✕ **Kips Snacks** ✆02 12911237; m 088 8856811/099 9856811; ⊕ 07.00–midnight daily. This popular Indian-owned eatery has an eclectic menu of pizzas, burgers, toasted sandwiches, Western-style grills & Indian dishes, mostly under US$6. There's the choice of indoor or outdoor seating, & good ice cream to follow up. They've even got hubbly-bubbly pipes for those who fancy a puff.

✕ **Krazy Grills & Sizzlers** Cnr Henderson & Haile Selassie rds; m 02 12952387; ⊕ 08.30–21.00 Mon–Thu, 08.30–22.00 Fri–Sat. Formerly a branch of the popular South African Nando's but now on its third name change, this still serves a similar selection of Portuguese-style peri-peri chicken dishes along with burgers, kebabs & fish, mostly for under US$6.50. No alcohol served.

✕ **Leah's Kitchen** Livingstone Av; ⊕ 07.30–20.00 Mon–Sat. A take-away with limited seating, this place dishes up burgers, fried chicken, pizzas & other fast food in the US$2–3 range. No alcohol served.

✕ **Michiru Restaurant** Glyn Jones Rd; ✆01 820588; ⊕ 12.00–14.30 & 16.00–22.00 daily. On the 5th floor of the Mount Soche Hotel, this is one of the most prestigious eateries in Blantyre, notable as much for the panoramic views over the city bowl & surrounding hills as for the superb continental & fusion cuisine, with mains in the US$12–20 range. If it's too pricey, Gypsy's on the ground floor of the same hotel is also very good but more affordable.

✕ **Super Snax** Livingstone Av; m 099 4472765; ⊕ 09.00–19.00 Mon–Fri, 10.00–20.00 Sat. This neat & clean locally run restaurant serves unimaginative but filling Malawian fare for around US$2 per plate. No alcohol.

SUBURBAN BLANTYRE
Kabula

✕ **Baba's Delhi Durbar** m 099 9888985/2121606; ⊕ 10.00–14.00 & 18.00–22.00 daily. A newer branch of its popular Lilongwe namesake, this reliable Indian restaurant charges around US$5.50 for vegetarian dishes, US$6.50 for meat & chicken & US$9.50 for prawns & fish. It's on Glyn Jones Rd, only a block or 2 west of Hannover Av.

✕ **Casa Mia** Kabula Hill Rd; ✆01 915559; m 099 9110269; www.blantyreaccommodation.com; ⊕ 06.00–11.00, 12.00–16.00, 18.00–22.00

daily. Among the smartest eateries in Blantyre, this Kabula Hill restaurant offers fine dining in a Mediterranean atmosphere, complete with archways, a wall-sized wine rack & a shady outdoor dining area. Their speciality is beef, which is all sourced & aged locally, but duck, lamb, fish, chicken, prawns, butternut squash ravioli & tiramisu also grace the lengthy menu. Chicken & vegetable dishes start at US$8, with steaks going for US$12.

✗ Chez Maky ☎01 833764; m 099 9203029/9945308; e chezmakymw@gmail.com; ⏰ 08.00–24.00 daily. One of the best-loved establishments in town, the restaurant here serves a regularly changing menu of tasty African & Western dishes, with a strong French & West African influence. Mains are around US$6.50. Open late, there's live music every other Friday, & it's a great place to chill out any night of the week.

✗ Quarter Bistro Kabula Hill Rd; ☎02 12953053; m 088 8901762; ⏰ 12.00–21.00 Wed–Mon. This artistic spot is set around a small courtyard in the grounds of House Five on Kabula Hill, & offers relaxed indoor & alfresco dining. Cosy & warmly decorated, they serve steaks for about US$9, pastas, kebabs & salads for US$3.50–5, & there's a good selection of wine & cocktails at the bar.

Namiwawa

✗ Café 33 Chilomoni Ring Rd; m 099 9960231. Sharing premises with Villa 33 but under separate management, this new restaurant/bar serves a unique menu of Spanish-style *tapas*, as well as a creative variety of Mediterranean-inspired dishes, including hummus & pita bread, roasted vegetables, lasagne, fish cakes & pesto. There's good music, lively décor, the choice of indoor or garden seating, & excellent coffees & desserts.

✗ Hostellerie de France Chilomoni Ring Rd; ☎01 669626; m 088 8833586; e hostfrance@ globemw.net; www.hostellerie-de-france.com; ⏰ 10.00–22.00 daily. This relaxed little hotel is renowned for serving the best French cuisine in Blantyre, with mains in the US$6.50–8 range & full menus for around US$13.50. The owner takes visible pride in the extensive French wine list & selection of Cuban cigars.

Mandala

✗ L'Hostaria Kidney Crescent; m 088 8282828; ⏰ 12.00–14.00 & 18.30–22.45

daily. In the Uta Weleza Centre, off Kamuzu Highway, this smart Italian restaurant is deservedly popular for lunch & dinner, offering the winning combination of great food & a relaxed, individualistic atmosphere. The pizzas are reasonably priced at US$8–10, while pasta & meat dishes are a little pricier.

✗ Mandala Café Mandala Road; ☎01 871952/671932; m 099 9917181; e lacaverna@ malawi.net; ⏰ 08.00–16.30 Mon–Fri, 08.00–13.00 Sat. Situated alongside La Caverna Art Gallery in Blantyre's oldest building, this is a great place for a light lunch, with seating in the shady gardens & a selection of Thai & Italian dishes for US$8–9, as well as fresh coffee & cake. Serves house wines, beers including Peroni, Italian grappa & liqueurs. It's also a skyband Wi-Fi hotspot.

Sunnyside

✗ Gelato Carnival ☎01 1612441/633444; ⏰ 07.00–21.00 Mon–Thu, 07.00–22.00 Fri–Sun. In addition to its namesake gelato, this family-friendly complex of restaurants just south of the CBD boasts an enormous menu that runs the gamut from sushi to smoothies, with burgers, grills, Asian mains & Middle Eastern dishes as well. There's a playground & you can either eat inside or on a comfortable semi-enclosed deck. Most mains come in at about US$5, with burgers slightly less & pizzas at US$6.50.

Chichiri Shopping Mall *See map, page 209.*

✗ Café Rouge ☎01 878795; m 088 8821795; ⏰ 08.00–19.00 Mon–Thu, 08.00–22.00 Fri–Sat, 09.00–22.00 Sun. Filter & speciality coffees, along with a vast selection of sandwiches, burgers, grills & all-day b/fasts in the US$4–5 range, are on offer at this busy café, which has plenty of indoor & outdoor seating.

✗ Curry Inn ☎01 622327; m 099 9425435; ⏰ 10.00–19.30 Mon–Sat. The smartest eatery in the Chichiri Mall, this serves a good selection of Indian meat & vegetarian dishes for around US$8.

✗ Jungle Pepper m 088 8826229/099 9926229; ⏰ 08.30–20.30 daily. This serves good pizzas & other dishes at US$6–8, & though it is strongly geared to the take-away market, it does have limited seating.

ENTERTAINMENT AND NIGHTLIFE

See map, pages 196–7 unless otherwise stated.

Blantyre doesn't have the most thriving nocturnal scene in Africa, but there are several venues worth checking out, whether you are seeking a few sociable drinks, live music, a cultural fix or the latest movies.

Blue Elephant m 099 9955242; e casamia@africa-online.net; ⏰ 10.00–24.00 Mon–Thu, 10.00–04.00 Fri & Sat, 12.00–22.00 Sun. Just up the road from L'Hostaria on Kidney Crescent, this perennially popular sports bar serves unimaginative but good steak & chips & other pub grub ranging from US$2 to US$6. There's usually sport on the TV by day & music by night, with live bands performing from around 20.00 on Wed & Sat.

Casablanca Across from Chilembwe Lodge, this relaxed local spot has a pool table, football on DSTV, cold drinks & lots of reggae.

Doogle's m 088 8837615; e doogles@africa-online.net. This legendary backpackers' hostel has a lively bar that often attracts a friendly expat crowd & encourages easy mingling. There's also good cheap food, an eclectic music selection with live music on Thursdays, & a pool table.

Mibawa Café m 099 6282711; ⏰ 09.00–02.00 Wed–Sun, 09.00–23.00 Mon–Tue. On Hanover Ave across from Ryall's, this new club is the best place in town for live music, with a rotating group of bands playing five nights a week. There are three separate bars inside, a well-equipped main stage, & DSTV sports at the snack bar outside. There's a US$2 cover on nights with live music.

TJ's Bar [map page 192] 01 985588; m 099 9951 207; ⏰ daily until late. This sports bar opposite the College of Medicine in Mount Pleasant is rated the best in town. It also serves great grilled chicken at reasonable prices.

☆ **Chez Ntemba** m 099 9207588; www.chez-ntemba.com; ⏰ 18.00–late daily. Fully adorned in mirrors, disco balls & flashing lights, this lively venue is now part of the pan-African Chez Ntemba chain, which has more than 15 nightclubs dotted around the continent. There

are nightly discos supplemented by occasional live music.

☆ **Club Mustang Sally** [map page 192] m 099 5812156; ⏰ 24/7. This infamous joint is where Blantyre goes when it's looking to party. There's a laser light show, big screen TVs, DJs every night & a swimming pool in the middle of the club. It's open all the time, but the party may not get going until late.

☆ **Colony Club Casino** 01 823283/831140; e colonyclubcasino@kairointernational.com; www.kairointernational.com; ⏰ 16.00–04.00 daily. The only casino in Blantyre opened on Victoria Av, south of the sports club, in 2002. It has more than 40 gaming machines, 7 poker & other tables, a restaurant & a bar.

☆ **French Cultural Centre** 01 871250; e direction@ccfmw.org; www.ambafrance-zm.org. In sprawling grounds on the junction of Moi Rd & Kasungu Cres, this is the only such cultural centre in Blantyre, & while it's currently not open on a daily basis, it does regularly host quality live music, theatre & poetry. Look out for posters or leaflets advertising evening events.

☆ **Shire Highlands Hotel** [map page 209] 01 840243/847464. This pleasant hotel in Limbe hosts Fri 'cultural evenings' featuring traditional music & dancing – well worth a look! (But be sure to call ahead & check if the performance is actually taking place.)

Cine City 01 912873; ⏰ screenings 17.30 & 20.00 Wed–Mon, also at 14.30 Fri–Sun. This 4-screen cinema complex lies below the Game Store in Chichiri Mall & shows reasonably recent Hollywood movies, supplemented by the odd Bollywood product. Tickets normally cost US$6–7, while budget shows on Mon, Wed, & Thu cost US$3.75.

SHOPPING

BOOKS AND MAPS The best general bookshop in Blantyre is the **Central Bookshop** (01 872094; ⏰ 09.00–18.30 Mon–Fri, 09.00–17.00 Sat, 10.00–13.00 Sun) in the Chichiri Shopping Centre [209 B1]. This stocks a fair range of novels, as well as many books published in Malawi and a variety of imported field guides and travel guides.

Opposite L'Hostaria in the Uta Waleza Shopping Centre [197 H6] on Kidney Crescent off Kamuzu Highway is the **Central Africana Bookshop** (↖ *01 876110; e centralafricana@africa-online.net; www.centralafricana.com;* ☉ *07.30–17.00 Mon–Fri, 09.00–12.30 Sat*), which stocks the best selection of current books about Malawi, as well as a good range of obscure and out-of-print African titles. If you're looking for something specific in this line, you can contact them in advance. There is a well-stocked **map sales office** (↖ *01 623722;* ☉ *08.00–17.00 Mon–Fri*) in the Department of Surveys' office [196 B7] on the southern end of Victoria Avenue. A 1:16,000 map of Blantyre and Limbe can be bought at any map sales office in the country.

CRAFTS AND CURIOS Meccas include **La Caverna** [197 G6] (*Old Manager's Hse, Mandala Rd*) (see overleaf) and **African Habitat** [197 H6] (*Uta Waleza Shopping Centre next to L'Hostaria on Kidney Cres;* ↖ *01 873642;* m *088 8832705*). Both stock an eye-opening range of high-quality African art, sculpture and handicrafts. The main area for curio street shopping is Chilembwe Road at Victoria Avenue, though the traders may be re-located to a covered area soon. The **Wildlife & Environmental Society of Malawi** (↖ *01 843502; e wesm-hq@africa-online.net; www.wildlifemalawi.org*) has a small shop [209 G2] with books, art and craft work at their office in Limbe near to the Shire Highlands Hotel.

SUPERMARKETS The new Chichiri Mall [209 B1] at the traffic circle on Kamuzu Highway between Blantyre and Limbe has revolutionised shopping in this part of Malawi. With a huge, well-stocked **Shoprite Supermarket** and **Game** as its main tenants, the mall also boasts fashion shops, banks, a pharmacy, a bookshop, restaurants and cafés, and a Postnet agency for phone, internet, copying and DHL. Open until late and over weekends, this makes a welcome change from the smaller supermarkets dotted around the city.

OTHER PRACTICALITIES

BANKING AND FOREIGN EXCHANGE Most of the large banks are clustered on and around Victoria Avenue, and many also have branches in Limbe CBD. There are foreign-exchange facilities at most of these banks, as well as several forex bureaux dotted around the city centre, including **Victoria Forex** [196 B4] on Victoria Avenue. Outside banking hours, most of the upmarket hotels will exchange money for hotel residents. The ATMs outside the **National Bank** [196 B6], **NBS Bank** [196 B5] and **Standard Bank** [196 B5] on Victoria Avenue accept international Visa and MasterCard, as do the same banks' branches on Churchill Road in Limbe, and there is also a Standard Bank ATM in the Chichiri Shopping Centre [209 B1].

DIPLOMATIC MISSIONS Most are in Lilongwe rather than Blantyre, but two notable exceptions are listed below:

❸ **Austrian consulate** Livingstone Hse, Livingstone Av; ↖ 01 638476; e austria@nyassa.mw

❸ **Dutch consulate** Metcalfe Dr, Kabula Hill; ↖ 01 635268; e dutchconsulate@malawi.net

HOSPITAL The **Mwaiwathu Hospital** [197 H4] in Chileka Road, just above the bus station and Doogle's, offers a comprehensive medical service and is open all hours (↖ *01 822999/834989*). The best place currently for malaria tests is the **Blantyre Adventist Hospital** [196 A4] (↖ *01 820399; e bah@malawi.net*) on Robins Road behind the Mount Soche Hotel [196 B4]. **Queen Elizabeth Hospital** [209 A1] (✆ *01 874333*) is the huge hospital on Ginnery Corner and is the best place for accident and emergency.

IMMIGRATION Visitors' passes and visas can be renewed at the immigration office [196 B7] on Victoria Avenue (✆ *01 823777*).

INTERNET Myriad internet cafés are dotted around the city centre. Most offer a reasonably fast and reliable broadband service, and browsing starts at around Mk5 per minute. They all offer much the same service, but **Biltel Internet** [196 B5] on Victoria Avenue is worth highlighting, for its unusually long opening hours (⏰ *08.00–20.00 daily*). There are also a few internet cafés in Limbe, and in the Chichiri Mall [209 B1]. For travellers carrying a laptop, Skyband has more than 40 Wi-Fi hotspots dotted around Blantyre, and anyone can obtain access using a prepaid Access Card (voucher). For more information, contact Skyband (✆ *01 824255;* e *blantyre@skyband.mw; www.skyband.com*).

WHAT TO SEE AND DO

HISTORIC BLANTYRE It may be one of the oldest cities in the southern African interior, but Blantyre has little to show for it in the way of historical landmarks. Within the city centre, the main cluster of old buildings is at the south end of Victoria Avenue, which was named in 1897, Queen Victoria's 60th jubilee. The oldest building here, the plain tin-roofed **Old Boma** [196 B7] was constructed in 1900 as a courthouse and administrative centre, and is practically unchanged in layout a century later. The kink in Victoria Avenue a block further south accommodates the **Queen Victoria Memorial Hall** [196 B7], a much grander building that formally opened in 1903, two years after the death of its matriarch namesake, and became the town hall in 1933.

Outside the city centre, Chileka Road is the site of the original Blantyre Mission, which lies about 500m north of the bus station, just before the Grace Bandawe Hostel. Here, the **St Michael and All Angels' Church** [192 C1] is the second-oldest building in Blantyre, built by Scottish missionaries between 1888 and 1891. It's an impressive piece of Victorian architecture, and well worth a visit, especially on Sundays when it holds emotive services in English and Chichewa.

Malawi's oldest standing building, on Mandala Road about 1km southeast of the city centre, is **Mandala House** [197 G6], which was constructed with grass, mud and bricks by the African Lakes Corporation (ALC) in 1882. Enclosed by wide balconies on all four sides, this double-storey building, also known as the Old Manager's House, is still instantly recognisable from photos dating to the late 19th century. The first managers of the ALC, John and Frederick Moir, originally lived in the first floor of the building, and used the ground floor as an office. Various outbuildings were used as storehouses and as defence against the Yao and Ngoni raids, but these are all gone now.

Historical interest aside, Mandala House is also the site of **La Caverna Art Gallery** (✆ *01 871952/671932;* m *099 9917181;* e *lacaverna@malawi.net;* ⏰ *08.00–16.30 Mon–Fri, 08.00–13.00 Sat*). This is the finest art gallery in the country, displaying hundreds of pieces in a wide variety of styles, ranging from wildlife portraits to contemporary African fine art. In addition, the building is home to the **Historical Society of Malawi** (✆ *01 872617; www.societyofmalawi. org;* ⏰ *09.00–12.00 Mon–Fri, & 18.00–19.30 Thu*), which was founded in 1946, and whose library now contains the country's most extensive collection of Africana books, covering every imaginable subject, with the main focus being Malawi. Finally, the excellent **Mandala Café** (see page 203) overlooking the leafy gardens is a great spot for lunch or a coffee.

OTHER PLACES OF INTEREST

Museum of Malawi [209 C2] (m *088 8896213;* e *mikemiggondwe@yahoo.com;* ⏰ *10.00–16.00 Tue–Sun; entrance US$1*) This small museum is sandwiched between Kasungu Avenue and Kamuzu Highway, about halfway between Blantyre and Limbe, and immediately beside Blantyre Civic Centre. The formal entrance is on Kasungu Avenue, and somewhat inconveniently for those using public transport, it is unsignposted on the Kamuzu Highway side, from where it is recognisable by the vintage rail carriages in the grounds, and accessible via a stiff inauspicious gate. The entrance hall houses a lamentable natural history display comprising a few stuffed and mounted animals from Lengwe and Liwonde national parks. Exhibits in the main hall include the Machinga Meteorite, a 93kg ball of metallic stone that fell to ground in Machinga District in 1981, crashing 1m deep into the earth in a collision that was audible up to 13km away. This hall also houses a fascinating ethnographic section displaying life-sized Chewa masks and dancing outfits, including the devilish Kwaweni Kulihe Mkuwe, who enforces local customs on visitors, the 'spoilt child' Chisenga, the amorous Kang'wang'wi, and a menagerie of semi-mythical beasts. Outside the main building, a few open-air exhibits document early 20th-century transport in Malawi.

Carlsberg Brewery Tours [192 C1] (☏ *01 870222*) Malawi's most famous brewery, which opened in Blantyre in 1968, offers popular free day tours every Wednesday at 14.30, though it's doubtful whether the attraction lies so much in the brewing process as in the complimentary beer-swilling session at the end of the tour. It is best to arrange a tour a day in advance and to gather together a group of people at somewhere like Doogle's to split the taxi fare.

Skydiving The Malawi Parachute Association (m *099 9926230;* e *skydive@nyassa. mw; www.skydive.mw*), in partnership with Nyassa Air Taxi (*www.nyassa.mw*) offers a variety of skydiving packages from Chileka Airport, starting at US$340 for a beginner's tandem jump. It's best to book at least a week in advance, and for information on upcoming jumps, check www.facebook.com/skydivemalawi.

Sports and swimming If skydiving seems like a bit much, terrestrial and aquatic activities are on offer at the Blantyre Sports Club [197 E6] (☏ *01 821173/835095;* e *btsportsclub@africa-online.net; www.blantyresportsclub.com*), founded in 1894 – well before there were even planes to jump out of! Today the club offers squash, tennis, swimming, darts, snooker, workout facilities and a nine-hole golf course. Day membership costs US$6.25, and golfers also have to pay US$2.50 greens fees, US$2.50 for a caddy, and US$6.25 for club rental. Swimming, squash and tennis all have nominal fees associated with them as well. The Khonde Restaurant & Bar (⏰ *07.30–22.00*) sits on a large balcony overlooking the main pitch, and indoors there's AC and DSTV. There's a Sunday buffet for US$6.25, but you still have to pay day membership.

Bangwe Factory (☏ *01 918951/912762;* e *macoha_bangwefactory@yahoo.com; www.macoha.wix.com/macoha;* ⏰ *07.30–17.00 Mon–Fri, 08.00–12.00 Sat*) Situated on the M4 in Limbe, the Bangwe Factory was founded in 1976 as a project of the Malawi Council for the Handicapped (MACOHA), with the aim of providing training and employment in spinning and weaving to disabled individuals. Today, it has a staff of more than 100 people, of which over 85% are disabled, and it produces a number of items including T-shirts, bags, rugs and wall hangings. Tours are given daily for a US$1 donation, and there is a factory store where the employees' handiwork is available for purchase – great for souvenirs. It's probably best to ring in advance and let them know you're coming, and they can advise you on the best route to take. (You'll want a minibus headed for Namiyango/Bangwe from the Limbe bus station; ask to be dropped at the MACOHA factory.)

Limbe Town (see map, opposite) With a discrete CBD centred on the parallel Churchill Road and Livingstone Avenue (which run one-way in opposite directions), Limbe feels more like the centre of a medium-sized town than a suburb of a large city, even though it was amalgamated with Blantyre back in 1956. Vibrant, bustling and well worth exploring, central Limbe is relatively unaccustomed to tourists – indeed, it's very rare to see a *muzungu* here – and the lack of high-rise buildings means it still boasts plenty of old colonial and Indian façades dating to its pre-amalgamation heyday. From April to September tourists are welcome to visit the **tobacco-auctioning floor** [209 F3] (01 840377) on Churchill Road near the Shire Highlands Hotel. Though not as large as its counterpart in Lilongwe, it's still highly impressive and an organisational feat. The nearby **Limbe Sports Club** [209 E4] (01 641022/145) offers the usual assortment of sports and golf, and you can enquire about camping on the grounds as well.

Michiru Mountain Conservation Area The closest conservation area to Blantyre, 8km northeast of the city centre, Michiru Mountain faces enormous pressure from local people needing firewood, but it still protects a variety of habitats including plantation forest, indigenous woodland and open grassland. Naturally occurring wildlife includes spotted hyena, leopard, serval, genet, bushpig, vervet monkey, baboon, bushbaby, bushbuck, grey duiker, klipspringer and reedbuck, and more than 200 bird species. Facilities include a basic campsite, and three well-defined walking trails of between 2km and 5km in length. It is permitted to walk in the reserve at night, when a variety of nocturnal animals may be seen.

To get to Michiru, follow Glyn Jones Road west from the Mount Soche Hotel for roughly 200m, then turn right into Kabula Hill Road and then left into Michiru Avenue. About 2km along Michiru Avenue the tarmac ends; a further 6km along the road you come to a turn-off where a green stone reads 'Michiru Conservation Area'. Ignore this and the next two turn-offs, and turn into the road marked 'Car Park and Nature Trails'. If you don't have private transport, you could catch a taxi to the entrance gate, and then walk or hitch back to town. Alternatively, you could camp in the reserve. For further details, contact the Chief Forester's office (01 635921).

Chiradzulu Forest Reserve Chiradzulu Mountain, 15km north of Blantyre, supports the most accessible evergreen forest in the Blantyre area, a small patch of 200ha set above the 1,500m contour, some of which was destroyed by fire in the late 1990s. The mountain is of particular interest to birdwatchers, as many unusual forest species are present, including Thyolo alethe, a variety of robins, bulbuls and crowned eagle, and the green-headed oriole, a specimen of which was captured here in 1896. Mammals include vervet and samango monkeys, baboon, spotted hyena, red duiker and bushbuck.

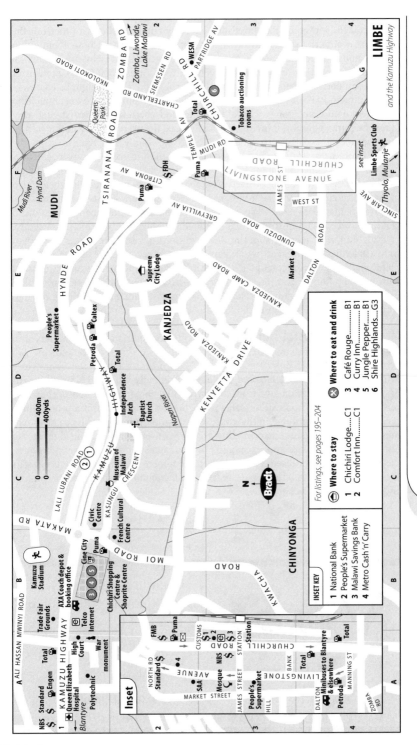

LIMBE
and the Kamuzu Highway

Zomba, Liwonde,
Lake Malawi

● WESM

Tobacco auctioning
rooms

Limbe Sports Club
Thyolo, Mulanje

● Market

Supreme
City Lodge

People's
Supermarket

Independence
Arch

Baptist
Church

Museum of
Malawi

Civic
Centre

French Cultural
Centre

Cine City

Chichiri Shopping
Centre &
Shoprite centre

AXA Coach depot &
booking office

Telco
Internet

War
monument

High
Court

Trade Fair
Grounds

Kamuzu
Stadium

Queen Elizabeth
Hospital

Polytechnic

Blantyre

NBS   Standard

Total

Engen

For listings, see pages 195–204

Where to stay

1 Chichiri Lodge.....C1
2 Comfort Inn.........C1

Where to eat and drink

Café Rouge............B1
Curry Inn...............B1
Jungle Pepper.......B1
Shire Highlands....G3

3
5
6

INSET KEY

1 National Bank
2 People's Supermarket
3 Malawi Savings Bank
4 Metro Cash 'n' Carry

Inset

FMB

Puma

Standard

SAI

Mosque

People's
Supermarket

NBS

Total

Petroda

Minibuses to Blantyre
& elsewhere

Station

12

Chiradzulu Mountain can be visited as a day trip from Blantyre or from the small town of Chiradzulu, which lies at the mountain's eastern base about 20km from Limbe, is connected to it by regular minibuses and has at least one basic local guesthouse. To get there in your own vehicle, follow the M3 towards Zomba for about 4km, and then branch left onto the tarred S146. The (unsignposted) turn-off to Chiradzulu Forest Reserve lies a few kilometres before the town, about 1km south of a dam immediately west of the S146, and you reach the forest edge after 4km. The indigenous forest is easily explored along the firebreaks separating it from the surrounding eucalyptus plantations.

The Chiradzulu area has played a prominent role in Malawian history. It was near the base of the mountain that Livingstone helped Bishop Mackenzie found the Church of Scotland's short-lived Magomero Mission in 1861. The largest farm in the Chiradzulu area was later bought by one Mr Bruce, a stepson of Livingstone, and was managed by another member of the clan, William Livingstone – who would be decapitated in front of his family during the 1915 rebellion initiated by Chiradzulu's most famous son, the Reverend John Chilembwe. The Providential Industrial Mission founded by Chilembwe was forced to close after the above-mentioned incident, but it reopened ten years later, and it remains an active mission with several points of historical interest. It lies near Mbombwe trading centre, 5km east of the Limbe–Chiradzulu road, along a signposted dirt road starting close to Chiradzulu Secondary School.

Mtenga-tenga Postal Hut Museum (✆ 01 534306) This low-key museum, known locally as Mtokoma (telecommunication), is on the west side of the M3 between Blantyre and Zomba at Namaka, 33km north of Limbe and 5km before Namadzi. It consists of a restored postal hut originally built in 1927 with burnt bricks transported manually from Blantyre. The name *mtenga-tenga* ('carrier') was first applied to the 169,000 Malawians who served as ammunitions and stores carriers in World War I, but in this context it refers to the runners who carried mail on foot in those days. Situated roughly midway between Blantyre and Zomba, the hut was a resting place and exchange point for mail carriers operating between the two towns. The museum charts the development of early postal services in Nyasaland, and it also houses an impressive collection of stamps from the colonial and post-independence eras.

Villa 33

Blantyre

Lodge & Restaurant

www.thevilla.mw

**Ensuite Rooms and
Self-Catering Apartments
Tranquil Gardens
Free Laundry
Free Internet Access**

T: +265 9999 60 231
reservations@thevilla.mw

13

Mulanje and Surrounds

Towering above the Mozambican border east of Blantyre, Mulanje is the tallest mountain in south-central Africa, a rugged island in the sky that erupts in dramatic isolation from the gently undulating countryside of Mulanje, Phalombe and Thyolo districts. A granite outcrop of quite staggering proportions, the Mulanje Massif reaches a peak altitude of 3,002m, some 2km higher than the towns that stand at its base. The upper plateau, serviced by ten well-maintained huts, offers some of the most rewarding hiking opportunities in the country, while the peaks are renowned for their rock climbing.

Tourism to this part of Malawi is inevitably, and rightly, centred upon Mulanje, but the mountain also overlooks what is reputedly the oldest tea-growing area in Africa, centred on the small town of Thyolo midway between Mulanje and Blantyre. This is a verdant landscape of breezy, rolling hills, swathed in orderly tea plantations, and interspersed with relict patches of indigenous forest – most famously, the biologically rich mahogany forest on the upper slopes of Thyolo Mountain, which lies within the privately owned but very accessible Satemwa Tea Estate.

MULANJE TOWN

Sedate, spacious and green, the small trading centre of Mulanje, population 21,000, is one of the most picturesque towns in all of Malawi, set amid tea estates at the southwest base of the towering Mulanje Massif. In touristic terms, Mulanje serves primarily as a springboard for hikes on the eponymous mountain, and it is well organised and well equipped in this regard, boasting a good selection of budget hotels and eateries, a helpful tourist office, and a local tour operator specialising in affordable organised climbs. In addition to being a hiking base, Mulanje is also gaining popularity with Blantyre residents for day visits to its restaurants and the nearby Likhubula Pools. The town is also an important gateway for overland travel to/from Mozambique, situated about 16km from the Muloza/Milanje border post at the southeast base of the Mulanje Massif.

Mulanje Town started life as Fort Anderson, one of two British forts built in the region to control the Yao slave trade to Mozambique via the Fort Lister Gap. The original Fort Anderson was actually built in 1893 about 20km away from the present-day town, but it was relocated there after three years, though so far as we are aware no traces of it remain. Fort Anderson was renamed Mlanje in 1907 and this was later corrected to the more accurate spelling Mulanje.

Today, the town comprises two discrete parts. Coming from the direction of Blantyre, you arrive first at Chitakale, which is the main commercial centre, hosting a People's Supermarket, a well-stocked vegetable market, a few basic resthouses and the tourist information centre. Chitakale stands at the junction for the road north

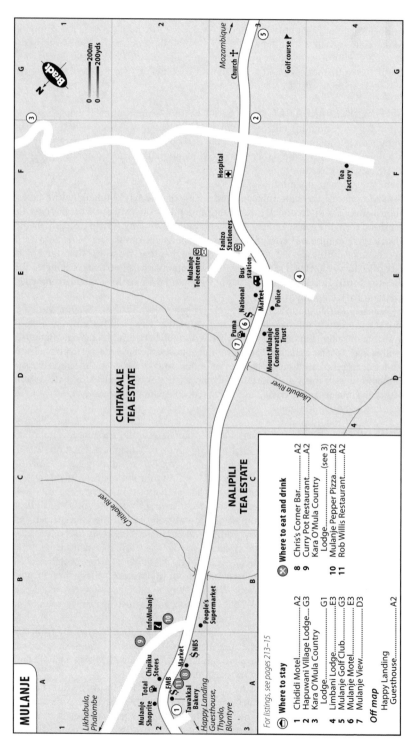

MULANJE

Likhabula,
Phalombe

Chitkale River

Chitkale River

CHITAKALE
TEA ESTATE

NALIPILI
TEA ESTATE

Likbulula River

Mozambique
Church ✝

Golf course ▶

Hospital ✚

Tea
factory ●

Mulanje
Telecentre

Fanizo
Stationers

Bus
station

National

Market

Police

Mount Mulanje
Conservation
Trust

Puma

InfoMulanje

Mulanje
Shoprite Total

Chipiku
Stores

FMB

Tawaktal
Bakery

Market

NBS

People's
Supermarket

Happy Landing
Guesthouse,
Thyolo,
Blantyre

Bradt

N

0 ——— 200m
0 ——— 200yds

For listings, see pages 213–15

Where to stay

1 Chididi Motel.....................A2
2 Hapuwani Village Lodge....G3
3 Kara O'Mula Country
   Lodge..............................G1
4 Limbani Lodge..................E3
5 Mulanje Golf Club............G3
6 Mulanje Motel..................E3
7 Mulanje View...................D3

Off map
   Happy Landing
   Guesthouse.....................A2

☒ Where to eat and drink

8   Chris's Corner Bar.............A2
9   Curry Pot Restaurant.........A2
    Kara O'Mula Country
    Lodge........................(see 3)
10 Mulanje Pepper Pizza.......B2
11 Rob Willis Restaurant........A2

212

to Phalombe via Likhubula Forestry Station, the most popular base for climbing Mulanje, so travellers heading directly to the mountain normally disembark there. The older administrative part of Mulanje, home to most of its smarter hotels, lies about 1.2km further east, and it is reached by following a flame-tree-lined stretch of the M2 that bisects Chitakale Tea Estate.

GETTING THERE AND AWAY Mulanje is 65km from Blantyre along the surfaced M4, a journey that shouldn't take longer than 40 minutes in a private vehicle. Regular minibuses to Mulanje run throughout the day, cost US$3, mostly depart from the minibus station in Limbe rather than from Blantyre itself, and generally continue all the way east to Muloza on the border with Mozambique. There are no villages along the M4 so many minibuses use the older M2, which adds about 30km to the distance, passing through Thyolo exactly halfway between Blantyre and Mulanje. Depending on how frequently the minibus stops, this longer route can take up to two hours. There are also regular direct minibuses from Thyolo to Mulanje, costing US$2, while minibuses between Mulanje and Chitakale cost US$0.30.

TOURIST INFORMATION Situated above Mulanje Pepper Pizza in Chitakale, the well-organised **InfoMulanje** [212 B2] (✆ *01 466466/506;* m *088 8122645;* e *mmct@ mountmulanje.org.mw or infomulanje@sdnp.org.mw; www.mountmulanje.org.mw;* ⊕ *08.00–17.00 Mon–Sat*; see also advert on page xvi of colour section) is the place to contact when planning a hiking trip to Mulanje. The staff will give up-to-date information about the state of the paths, make mountain-hut bookings, organise guides and porters and can also make lodge accommodation reservations. They have a comprehensive list of places to visit, catering to all budgets, and also organise field and factory tours around the nearby tea estates. It is affiliated to the **Mount Mulanje Conservation Trust** [212 D3], an NGO that focuses mainly on ecological matters relating to Mulanje, and that has an office opposite the Mulanje View Hotel [212 D3] in the administrative part of town. If the tourist information office is closed when you hit town, InfoMulanje also maintains a very useful noticeboard in the Mulanje Golf Club [212 G3].

TOUR OPERATOR One locally based company offering professional guided hikes on Mulanje is **Tiyende Pamodzi Adventures** (✆ *01 467737;* m *099 9313851;* e *hikemulanje@africa-online.net*), also contactable through InfoMulanje. This reputable operation offers a variety of all-inclusive tailored hikes and packages, from day hikes (*US$45 per person*) and overnight ascents (*US$195 pp sharing or US$283 single*) to a seven-day traverse (*US$705 pp sharing or US$1,025 single*). The newly opened **Mulanje Outlook Travel** (✆ *01 11942119;* m *088 8178014/099 9798795;* e *mulanjeoutlook@gmail.com; www.mulanjeoutlooktravel.com*) is also locally owned, and offers a range of similar services which are detailed on their website.

⌂ **WHERE TO STAY** *See map, opposite.*

Moderate

⌂ **Hapuwani Village Lodge** (40 rooms) m 088 8873005/099 9873005. Still under construction when we visited, this colonnaded new lodge looks to be aimed squarely at the conference market, but will likely have some of the smarter rooms in town when completed. Expect tiled en-suite rooms with a full complement of

facilities, including swimming pool, AC, restaurant/ bar & DSTV. *Call for rates.*

⌂ **Kara O'Mula Country Lodge** (27 rooms) ✆ 01 466515; m 099 9286423/212 234506; e reservations@karaomula.com; www.karaomula. com; see also advert on page 226. On the slopes above town, 1.5km uphill from the post office, this stylishly rustic lodge has been converted from a former District Commissioner's residence built in 1905. It offers the choice of simply decorated standard en-suite rooms with 1 dbl & 1 ¾ bed in the main building, or slightly costlier but much nicer executive rooms in stand-alone cottages containing a dbl bed with frame & net, terracotta tiled floor, private balcony & wood & bamboo furniture. Amenities include a swimming pool (*US$2 for non-guests*), a pool table, a lounge with DSTV & Wi-Fi, a wide balcony overlooking plantation & indigenous forest, & one of the best restaurants in town. The lodge is also the starting point for the Boma Path to Lichenya Hut, & safe parking is available here. Standard rooms seem overpriced; executive rooms are better value. *US$50/65 sgl/dbl standard rooms, US$65/75 executive, US$7 pp camping, all rooms B&B.*

Budget

⌂ **Limbani Lodge** (38 rooms) ☏ 01 466390. Centrally located near the police station, this has the same owner as the Mulanje Motel, & it's ostensibly more upmarket, though the rooms all look a little scruffy & the lack of a bar or restaurant underscores the slightly moribund aura of neglect. Still, it is pretty good value. *US$8 en-suite dbl with hot shower, US$11 dbl VIP room with TV & kitchenette.*

⌂ **Mulanje Motel** (19 rooms) ☏ 01 466245. A couple of doors up from the Mulanje View, this seems like better value, & it also has a livelier bar & restaurant (serving adequate Malawian staples

for around US$2.50), which isn't necessarily a good thing for those seeking a restful night before climbing the mountain. *US$8 twin using common shower, US$10 smart new en-suite twin.*

⌂ **Mulanje View Hotel** (37 rooms) ☏ 01 466348; m 099 9191600. This is one of the better options in the town centre, set in reasonably attractive gardens with a view of the mountain. The gardens are a far nicer place to eat than the rather cheerless & institutional restaurant. *US$5/8 sgl/twin with shared shower, US$11 en-suite twin.*

Shoestring

⌂ **Chididi Motel** (22 rooms) m 088 8105230/099 2225235. The pick of an indifferent selection of cheapies in Chitakale, this friendly place lies in a big garden & has clean rooms with nets, fans & basins. There is a lively restaurant/bar on site. Good value. *US$2/2.50 sgl/dbl, US$3.50/5 en suite.*

⌂ **Happy Landing Guesthouse** (18 rooms) m 099 7211451/2/0. Slightly outside of town, this is another option for those on a rock-bottom budget. *US$1.75 dbl with nets & common showers.*

Camping

⋏ **Mulanje Golf Club** ☏ 01 466260; m 099 9672304. This offers secure & secluded camping around the swimming pool & the overnight rate includes access to sports facilities, including the swimming pool. *US$7 pp camping.*

✕ WHERE TO EAT AND DRINK See map, page 212.

✕ **Curry Pot Restaurant** m 099 9718205; ⊕ 08.00–20.00 daily. Despite the name, this place serves the standard bland Malawian fare of beef/chicken with chips/rice for US$1.50.

✕ **Kara O'Mula Country Lodge** ☏ 01 466515; ⊕ 07.30–21.00 daily. Another great place to eat, this has good views from the balcony seats, but also indoor seating for chillier days, & it serves a cosmopolitan menu of mostly meat & chicken dishes in the US$4.50–6.50 range, with fresh vegetables grown in their own hillside garden.

✕ **Mulanje Golf Club** m 099 9764398/9672304; restaurant ⊕ 12.00–13.30 & 18.00–19.30 daily. A short walk east from the town centre, this has a great veranda with a view over green tea fields to the flanks of Mulanje Mountain. It serves a variety of steaks, curries, pizzas & pies

for US$3–4, though day visitors must pay day membership of US$3.25 pp too.

✕ **Mulanje Pepper Pizza** m 088 8878830/099 9826229; www.junglepepperpizza.com; ⊕ 09.00–16.30 Mon–Thu, 09.00–21.00 Fri–Sat, 09.00–1800 Sun. Situated in Chitakale at the turn-off to Likhubula, this pizza mainstay was recently taken over & remodelled by the Blantyre-based Jungle Pepper. It's still the smartest restaurant in town & an excellent spot for some post-hike refreshment. There's a genuine pizza oven & outdoor seating on a delightful shaded portico. Pizza & pasta dishes are mostly around US$7 & cheaper snacks are available.

✕ **Rob Willis Restaurant** m 099 8373451; ⊕ 08.00–midnight daily. This pleasant & affordable restaurant has indoor & outdoor seating, a full bar & a varied menu of sandwiches & burgers for US$1.25–2.25 & full meals for US$2.25–3.25.

♀ **Chris's Corner Bar** This lively & well-stocked bar has a pool table, a good music system & a dance floor.

SHOPPING If you're heading to the Mulanje Massif, you can stock up at the People's Supermarket [212 B2] opposite the Likhubula junction in Chitakale. This doesn't have anything like the range of goods available in nearby Blantyre, but it does stock frozen sausages, fresh bread and the usual tinned goods. The **market** in Chitakale [212 E3] has as good a range of vegetables as any in Malawi, and there is also a good **market** [212 A2] in Mulanje proper.

OTHER PRACTICALITIES
Banks and foreign exchange The **National Bank** [212 E3] next to the Mulanje Motel has a forex bureau and an ATM that accepts international Visa cards, while **NBS** and **FMB** [212 A2] are represented in Chitakale with ATMs and forex facilities. There is no private forex bureau, but if the banks are closed you could try at the nearby Mozambican border.

Internet The best options are in Mulanje town: **Mulanje Telecentre** [212 E2] (☺ 07.30–12.00, 13.00–16.30 Mon–Fri, 09.00–12.00 Sat) is behind the post office and charges Mk5/min. Alternatively, **Fanizo Stationeries** is just across the road.

Sports The **Mulanje Sports Club** [212 G3] (☏ 01 466260; m 099 9672304) charges US$3.25 per person for day membership, which gives you access to the nine-hole golf course, as well as tennis, squash, badminton, snooker, darts and the bar/restaurant. Use of the swimming pool is an extra US$1.25 per person.

THE MULANJE RING ROAD

The roughly circular road that loops around the Mulanje Massif provides access to all the ascent routes up the mountain, as described in greater detail below, as well as being an interesting drive in its own right. It also offers a range of accommodation options more interesting than most of what is available in Mulanje Town, whether it is the upmarket self-catering lodges on the Lujeri Tea Estate, the more moderate lodges at Likhubula Forestry Station or the budget options at Phalombe and the Fort Lister Forestry Office.

Coming from Blantyre, the loop effectively starts at Chitakale, where a dirt road veers northward towards Likhubula opposite the People's Supermarket. About 6km north of Chitakale, the road passes through Likhubula, where the eponymous forestry station forms the most popular and accessible starting point for Mulanje hikes. Another 28km further northeast, the small town of Phalombe is the most northerly point on the ring road, and where you need to take a right turn for the 14km road across the Lister Pass to Nkhulambe trading centre. A 30km dirt road leads south from here to the Mozambican border town of Muloza, where you reconnect with the tar some 16km east of Mulanje Town and Chitakale.

GETTING AROUND The full loop road covers about 90km, and is unsurfaced in its entirety, with the exception of the 16km stretch between Chitakale and Muloza. The road between Chitakale and Phalombe is regularly graded and can generally be taken at around 60km/h in any vehicle, though this can easily change after rain, so check locally. The Lister Pass can be rough going in parts, while stretches of the road between Nkhulambe and Muloza are very sandy, so good clearance is a prerequisite for self-drive visits, and a 4x4 would be a good idea in the rainy season.

Using public transport, at least one bus and several minibuses connect Chitakale and Phalombe daily, stopping at Likhubula village, and it's easy enough to find a *matola* ride. There is also plenty of public transport between Chitakale, Mulanje Town and Muloza. However, no public transport crosses the Lister Pass between Phalombe and Nkhulambe, and there is very little between Nkhulambe and Muloza.

From Phalombe, a 10km road leads north to the friendly but totally nondescript trading centre of Migowi, which has a few adequate guesthouses, and forms a potential springboard for a couple of *very* off-the-beaten-track explorations. These are the back routes along little-used dirt roads to Chiradzulu Mountain and Blantyre, and a road running northward via Kalinde and Nambazo to the remote, marshy southern shore of Lake Chilwa. The S144 from Phalombe to Zomba town via Mpasa and Jali will make a good shortcut when the (seemingly abandoned) roadworks are completed, but as things stand the tarmac only begins near Jali, and it's a very rough road before that.

These routes are all best approached in a sturdy pick-up truck or 4x4, and there is no public transport.

LIKHUBULA The normal springboard for Mulanje hikes, Likhubula Forestry Station lies about 6km north of Chitakale, and 1km east of Likhubula trading centre along a turn-off signposted some 50m past the bridge across the Likhubula River. It is the starting point for the popular Skyline and Chapaluka paths to Chambe Hut, as well as the Lichenya path to Lichenya Hut and CCAP Hope Rest Cottage, and a good place to organise DIY hikes of Mulanje (see page 223). Likhubula Forest Lodge is also the home of Tiyende Pamodzi Adventures, the only local operator offering organised climbs (see page 213).

Likhubula is a good goal for day trippers wanting to explore the lower slopes of Mulanje. It's a beautiful area, swathed in plantation and indigenous forest, and the rock pools along the Likhubula River immediately south of the forestry station are great for a refreshing dip on a hot day. A 45-minute footpath runs from the forestry station uphill along the same river to an attractive waterfall that plunges into the 60m-deep **Dziwe la Nkhalamba** (literally 'Old People's Pool', in possible reference to the ancient spirits associated with Mulanje). The waterfall can be difficult to find without a guide.

Where to stay *See map, page 220.*

Moderate

CCAP Likhubula House (4 chalets, several dorms) 01 980611; m 088 8868139/ 099 9496638; e likhubula@malawi.net; www. blantyresynod.org. Recently renovated with a grant from the Scottish government, this Church-run hostel, established in the 1960s, now consists of 2 4-bed chalets & 2 twin chalets, as well as several 4–10-bed dormitories. The chalets each have a lounge, a veranda, a private garden & a fully equipped self-catering kitchen, though meals can be supplied by request. Facilities include a swimming pool. Income from the accommodation is used to fund

programmes for orphans & vulnerable children in the local community. *US$47–76 sgl/dbl for 4 people in 4-bed chalet, US$11 pp dorm, US$5 pp camping.*

Likhubula Forest Lodge (5 rooms) m 099 9220560/088 4079890; e likhubula@africa-online. net; www.cholemalawi.com. This privatised & renovated forestry lodge is near the forestry office in Likhubula. There are 4 rooms in the main building, 1 of which is en suite, & there is an additional en-suite room in a self-standing annex. It has a well-equipped self-catering kitchen, but self-caterers need to bring their own food, & it is also possible for the staff to provide meals by prior arrangement (*b/fast US$10, lunch US$6 & dinner US$12). US$34/50/66 sgl/dbl/trpl, US$40/56/72 en* suite, *camping US$6 pp, all rooms B&B. The whole lodge can be booked as a unit for US$245 per party.*

PHALOMBE Situated 34km northeast of Chitakale, Phalombe is an overgrown village (population 3,000) that sprawls around a staggered four-way junction and serves as the administrative capital of the eponymous district. It has a scenic location at the base of the Fort Lister Gap, one that renders it vulnerable to flash floods, most devastatingly on 10 March 1991, when hundreds of people died in a rock avalanche and mudslide, a tragedy commemorated in a memorial opposite the municipal offices. The Phalombe Catholic Mission, 5km out of town, is the site of an impressive colonial-era church and a large hospital built in the early 1960s. The main local point of interest, however, is Fort Lister Pass, which is reached by turning right at the junction immediately before the police station.

Where to stay and eat

Shoestring

🏠 **Haest Lodge** (12 rooms) m 088 8518435. This unexpectedly comfortable lodge lies in a well-maintained compound on the left side of the road immediately north of the main junction. It has a very popular restaurant that serves tasty & filling local staples (beef/chicken with chips/*nsima*/rice) for US$2–3. There are basic rooms using common showers, & musty but otherwise very decent en-suite rooms with net, fan & hot shower. *US$3.50/7 sgl/dbl, US$13.50 en-suite dbl, all rates B&B.*

FORT LISTER GAP The 14km road running east from Phalombe to Nkhulambe crosses the Fort Lister Gap, a mid-altitude saddle that separates Mulanje from its smaller, more northerly neighbour, Mount Mchese. Known locally as Mpata – The Gap – this was an important slave caravan route in the 19th century, used by the Yao traders based close to present-day Blantyre to transport captives to Quelimane on the coast of Mozambique. In 1893, the British colonial administration established Fort Lister (named after Sir Villiers Lister, a strong opponent of slavery) at the western ascent of the pass, in order to curb the Yao slave trade with Mozambique. By the turn of the century, Fort Lister also served as the base for the local district officer, and it also served as a post office prior to 1903, when the actual fort was abandoned in favour of present-day Phalombe (which was known as Fort Lister until 1934).

If you are interested in visiting the original site of the fort, look out for a small faded blue signpost hidden in the grass on the right side of the road some 3.5km out of Phalombe, and follow the rough motorable track for 600m until it terminates at a small car park. From here, it's another 500m or so on foot to the site of the old fort, crossing a river on the way, but it is very difficult to locate without a guide. Assuming you do find the right footpath, the outer defences of the fort are still easily discerned, and you can also see the ruins of several outbuildings. A small cemetery within the old fortifications houses the grave of Gilbert Stevenson, cousin to the author Robert Louis Stevenson.

Minor historical interest aside, the Fort Lister Pass is a very scenic road, with Mulanje dominating the southern skyline, and the sheer granitic cliffs of Mount Mchese towering to the north. The road passes through three small villages, but otherwise most of the surrounding landscape is protected within a forest reserve, and plenty of indigenous Brachystegia remains. Some 7.5km out of Phalombe, a 400m branch road to the right leads to the Fort Lister Forestry Office, which offers basic accommodation and forms the trailhead for what is widely regarded to be the easiest ascent of Mulanje, since it starts at a significantly higher altitude than the others. The 6.5km descent from the forestry office to Nkhulambe is if anything even more stunning than the ascent, passing through dense Brachystegia woodland, patches of bamboo forest and riparian forest with the two mighty peaks towering on either side.

 Where to stay and eat *See map, page 220.*

Shoestring

🏠 **Fort Lister Forestry Resthouse** (3 rooms) The little-used resthouse here is aimed at hikers, offering beds & mattresses but no bedding. A self-catering kitchen with utensils is available, but it's best to bring all food. *US$5 pp.*

MULOZA TO NKHULAMBE The 30km stretch of road running south through the tiny ribbon of lowland Malawi that separates the Mulanje Massif from Mozambique is far rougher and sandier than its western counterpart. It passes through what feels like one long continuous village, and you'll find yourself dodging between the people, livestock and bicycles milling around nonchalantly, making it unsafe to travel much faster than 25–30km/h. There's not much in the way of public transport or accommodation along this road, at least not until you reach Muloza itself, a typically bustling border town that boasts several small resthouses, and is connected to Mulanje Town – and for that matter Limbe and Blantyre – by a good surfaced road and a steady stream of minibuses.

LUJERI TEA ESTATE Tucked away in a crescent of Mulanje Mountain between Mulanje Town and Muloza, this beautiful tea estate lies right at the southern base of the massif, and its slopes are covered in neat tea plantations interspersed with rivers, lakes, patches of lush indigenous forest and tall stands of bamboo. The two lodges on the estate form the most upmarket bases for exploring the Mulanje foothills, and the estate offers some wonderful walking opportunities, as well as being the trailhead for a four- to five-hour hike to Madzeka Hut on the southern edge of the Mulanje Plateau – or just a great place to relax after a few days' hiking. In season, tea-factory tours can be arranged for US$10 per person for people staying at the estate, or US$15 per person for outsiders, ideally by prior arrangement using the contact details below.

 Where to stay and eat *See map, page 220.*

Upmarket

🏠 **Lujeri Guesthouse** (5 rooms) 📞01 460277; 📱 099 9960344; e lujerilodge@lujeri.com. The estate guesthouse, set in attractive gardens just a stroll away from the lodge, has a homely living area & sleeps 10 people. *US$190 self-catering for the whole house & cook's services.*

🏠 **Lujeri Lodge** (4 rooms) 📞01 460277; 📱 099 9960344; e lujerilodge@lujeri.com. A converted tea planter's home right in the heart of lush tea fields, this self-catering lodge retains a winningly anachronistic atmosphere, with its Edwardian furnishings, wide wraparound balcony, magnificent & lovingly maintained gardens & attentive house staff. 10 people can sleep here comfortably & live in quite some style, & there's also a swimming pool & mini tennis, but self-caterers must bring all their own food. *US$200 for the whole house (self-catering, inc the services of a cook), an additional US$40 pp for dinner, lunch & b/fast.*

MULANJE MASSIF

Mulanje is a spectacular 650km² granite inselberg that rises in dramatic isolation above the Phalombe Plains southeast of Blantyre. The massif consists of a plateau of rolling grassland set at an average elevation of 2,000m, but this is incised by several thickly wooded ravines, and studded with 20 peaks of 2,500m or higher, including Sapitwa, the highest point in central Africa at 3,002m. By contrast, the plains below Mulanje have a mean altitude of 650m, though the northern slopes are linked to the discrete 2,289m Mount Mchese by the Fort Lister Gap, a mid-altitude saddle with an average elevation of around 950m. Both Mulanje and Mchese are protected within the Mount Mulanje Forest Reserve, which was proclaimed in 1927 and is managed by the Mount Mulanje Conservation Trust (MMCT).

Less than an hour's drive from Blantyre, Mulanje has long been the country's premier hiking and rock-climbing destination, popular with residents and tourists alike for its dramatic scenery and well-organised and inexpensive facilities. Indeed, Mulanje is the main focal point of the Mountain Club of Malawi (MCM), which was founded as the Mlanje Mountain Club in 1952 and adopted its present name in 1980. There are innumerable hiking routes from the base to the plateau, the most popular being the Skyline Path to the Chambe Basin and the Lichenya Path to the Lichenya Plateau, both of which start at Likhubula Forestry Station some 8km from Mulanje Town. On the plateau itself there are ten mountain huts, one owned by the CCAP, and the remainder maintained by the MMCT and MCM in collaboration with the Forestry Department. These huts are connected to each other by well-marked trails ranging from three to six hours' walking duration, and the peaks and valleys of Mulanje offer enough walking and climbing possibilities to keep anybody busy for at least a month. In addition, many of the streams on Mulanje are stocked with trout, and fishing permits are issued by the forestry office at Likhubula.

GEOLOGY AND VEGETATION Mulanje is composed of hard metamorphic rock such as granite and syenite, formed by an extrusion of magma about 130 million years ago, and gradually exposed as the elements eroded away the softer surrounding rocks. In this respect, Mulanje is very similar to the granite koppies that are such a characteristic feature of the central African landscape, for instance in the vicinity of Dedza, but on a far grander scale. And unlike most koppies, Mulanje is sufficiently large and tall to induce the formation of rainclouds, which means that its southern and eastern slopes receive unusually high levels of precipitation, and the massif is the headwater for almost every river that runs through this part of Malawi.

Several different vegetation types cover Mulanje. The lower slopes of the massif, where they have not been planted with exotic pines and eucalyptus, are covered in closed-canopy Brachystegia woodland. The main vegetation type of the plateau is not dissimilar in appearance to the alpine moorland found on East Africa's larger mountains: a combination of heathers, heaths and grasses. The moorland is notable for supporting a wide array of wild flowers, including various helichrysums, irises, lobelias and aloes, a large number of which are endemic to the mountain.

Evergreen woodland and forest is largely restricted to ravines and watercourses. The most notable forest tree on Mulanje is the endemic Mulanje cedar *Widdringtonia whytei*, a magnificent timber tree which can reach a height of over 40m. Mulanje's cedars have been depleted in the last century owing to timber felling, but several impressive stands remain, the most accessible of which lies in the saddle southeast of the Chambe Basin and includes many trees that are thought to be over 300 years old.

Although Mulanje has been officially protected since 1927, much of the surrounding countryside was cleared for tea cultivation in the early 20th century, and the forest reserve is among the most ecologically compromised in the country. The wholesale destruction of natural cover started in the colonial era, when extensive plantation forests were established within the reserve. Post-independence

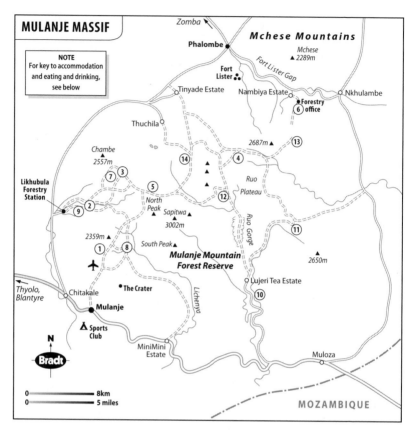

MULANJE MASSIF

For listings, see pages 216–18 & 221–3

Where to stay

1 CCAP Hope Rest Cottage
2 CCAP Likhubula House
3 Chambe Hut
4 Chinzama Hut
5 Chisepo Hut
6 Fort Lister Forestry Resthouse
7 France's Cottage
8 Lichenya Hut
9 Likhubula Forest Lodge
10 Lujeri Guesthouse & Lodge
11 Madzeka Hut
12 Minunu Hut
13 Sombani Hut
14 Thuchila Hut

human encroachment has also been extensive, partly because the vast tea estates outside the reserve have inadvertently deprived locals of arable land, and partly because of the influx of refugees to the region during the Mozambican civil war. Indeed, as recently as the mid-1970s, the southeast slopes around Chisongeli supported the country's largest single block of rainforest, extending over some 40km², but this was almost totally destroyed in the 1980s as a result of illegal felling and land clearing. Today, the total amount of indigenous forest amounts to perhaps 50km², most of it on the upper slopes and plateaux, and the forest on Mchese is generally in better shape than on Mulanje itself.

WILDLIFE The earliest recorded visitors to Mulanje encountered vast herds of eland on the grassy plateau, and sable and other woodland antelopes in the foothills. Today, the only mammals seen with any regularity in the open highlands are klipspringer, rock hyrax, red rock hare and vole. In the woodlands of the lower slopes and in forested areas, there is a good chance of seeing vervet and (in the Chambe Basin) samango monkeys. Red duiker, bushbuck, leopard, bushpig and porcupine are present but seldom encountered in wooded habitats.

The selection of birds recorded on the grasslands of the plateau is not great; species of interest include Shelly's and Hildebrandt's francolin, wailing cisticola and a variety of swifts and swallows, including the localised blue swallow from October to March. The upper slopes also provide an ideal habitat for raptors such as auger buzzard, black eagle, lanner and peregrine falcon, and rock kestrel. Of more interest to serious birdwatchers are birds found in the forest and woodland, among them bar-tailed trogon, Thyolo alethe, spotted ground thrush, green-headed oriole, white-winged apalis and an endemic race of olive-flanked robin-chat. Also endemic to Mulanje are five species of lizard (including a dwarf chameleon) and one squeaker frog.

 WHERE TO STAY *See map, opposite.*
There are ten huts on the mountain, nine run by the Forestry Department in conjunction with the MCM and MMCT, and one by the CCAP. They all cost US$6 per person. Firewood, cooking fireplaces and water are provided at all the huts, but you must bring your own food, and kitchen equipment and bedding are provided only at the CCAP hut. The nine forestry huts can be booked at Likhubula Forestry Station or through the InfoMulanje office in Chitakale, and the CCAP hut is bookable through CCAP Likhubula House. Staff at the huts cut firewood and light cooking fires. For Mountain Club members, pots and pans are available, but take your own candles. Camping is permitted at US$3 per person, but only around the huts.

The most frequently used huts are Chambe Hut, Lichenya Hut, the CCAP hut and the smarter France's Cottage, all of which lie on the eastern side of the massif, within a day's walk of Likhubula Forestry Station. Full details of all huts, including photographs and Google Earth waypoints, are available on the MCM website (*www.mcm.org.mw*), but a brief overview is provided below.

CCAP Hope Rest Cottage *(1,981m;* ⊕ *S15.96968° E35.53508°)* Constructed in 1899, & making extensive use of Mulanje cedar, this private cottage sleeps 8 people in 3 bedrooms with bedding provided, & it has basic kitchen utensils & an outside pit-latrine toilet. It lies 4hrs' walk from Likhubula Forestry Station, Mulanje Town or Chambe Hut, & 1hr from Lichenya Hut. There are natural swimming pools a 15-min walk away.

Chambe Hut *(1,860m;* ⊕ *S15.90875° E35.54304°)* This popular hut lies in the Chambe Basin 3–4hrs' walk from Likhubula along the Skyline Path, & it offers a spectacular view of the 2,557m Chambe Peak. It can sleep 16 people in 2 large rooms & an outdoor covered veranda. There's drinking water on tap, & pit-latrine toilets.

Chinzama Hut *(2,139m;* ⊕ *S15.89776° E35.65341°)* This is beautifully situated in the Ruo Basin on the north of the plateau, 3hrs' walk from Sombani or Thuchila huts. It sleeps up to 12 people in 2 rooms. It has long-drop toilets & there are natural swimming pools only 5mins away.

Chisepo Hut *(2,219m;* ⊕ *S15.93363° E35.58273°)* This is the newest hut, especially built for those who want to climb Sapitwa, a 5–6hr return trip. It is about 3hrs' walk from Chambe or Thuchila Hut, sleeps 15 people, & has pit-latrine toilets.

France's Cottage *(1,843m;* ⊕ *S15.90863° E35.53514°)* This colonial forestry cottage, renovated in 2005, was the home of forester Freddie France, who died during a crossing of the flooded Ruo River during Laurens van der Post's famous expedition to Mulanje (recounted in the book *Venture into the Interior*). Situated just 200m from Chambe Hut, it is the best furnished of the forestry huts, sleeping 6 people in 2 bedrooms, & has piped water & a pit-latrine toilet.

Lichenya Hut *(1,840m;* ⊕ *S15.97369° E35.55133°)* After the original burnt down a few years ago, Lichenya Hut was rebuilt to sleep more than 20 people in 3 large rooms. There is a bucket shower & pit-latrine toilets, & a natural swimming pool is 5mins away. It stands on the Lichenya Plateau 4–5hrs' walk from Likhubula, Mulanje Town or Chambe Hut, & 1hr from the CCAP Cottage.

🏠 **Madzeka Hut** (1,820m; ✪ S15.95535° E35.68799°) Situated on the southeast of Mulanje, 4–5hrs' walk from the Lujeri Tea Estate, this wooden hut was built in 1966 above a set of rocky rapids. It sleeps 12 people in 2 rooms, & is well placed for hiking several of the southern peaks.

🏠 **Minunu Hut** (2,015m; ✪ S15.92478° E35.63857°) This small rickety hut sleeps 6

people in 1 room. Set above a stream with natural swimming pools, it offers views of the Ruo Gorge & access to the 2,964m Nakodzwe Peak.

🏠 **Sombani Hut** (2,070m; ✪ S15.89298° E35.69800°) Rebuilt in the 1960s after the original hut was destroyed by fire, Sombani is the most accessible hut coming from Fort Lister, lying 3–4hrs' walk from the forestry station. It is about 3hrs from Chinzama & Madzeka huts. It sleeps 10 people in 2 rooms & is convenient for ascents of the northern peaks of Namasile, Matambale & Chinzama, all of which are around 2,650m high.

MULANJE IN LEGEND

No other geographic landmark in Malawi is quite so shrouded in myth and legend as Mulanje, unsurprisingly perhaps when you consider the extent to which its forbidding silhouette dominates the skyline for miles around. Several legends pertaining to the mountain might be grounded in fact, among them persistent whisperings that it still harbours a secretive population of 'little people', possibly Batwa hunter-gatherers, who act as its spiritual protectors. Of course, this is highly unlikely, taken in the most literal sense, but it does seem likely that the upper slopes of Mulanje formed the last Malawian refuge to the Batwa, recently enough that they live on in the folk memory as spirits.

Several other spirits are associated with the mountain. One such entity is Napolo, a serpentine creature who reputedly moves between Mulanje and Mchese, generating the misty *chiperone* conditions that frequently enclose the upper slopes. Napolo is also blamed for thunderstorms and other destructive weather conditions, and some believe he induced the tragic flash flood that claimed so many lives at Phalombe in March 1991. Other legends describe a humanlike one-eyed, one-legged, one-armed creature that floats slowly in the air, waiting to lure anybody who looks at it up the mountain to disappear forever.

Local beliefs about Mulanje are reflected in the Chichewa name of its highest peak. Sapitwa is variously said to be derived from the phrases 'musapite' and 'sapitidwa', which respectively translate as 'do not go there' and 'the place you cannot reach' – the first suggesting that the peak is considered to be out of bounds for spiritual reasons, the second simply that it is difficult to reach. To an extent, both interpretations are true, and either way, anybody planning to climb Sapitwa would be wise to treat it with respect – at least two tourists have died while attempting a solo summit in the past decade.

A more recent legend pertaining to Mulanje is that Tolkien climbed it shortly before he wrote *The Hobbit* and based several aspects of the book on the trip, going so far as to name the homeland of its protagonists after the nearby Shire River. So far as we can ascertain, Tolkien did indeed visit Malawi at some point, but not Mulanje itself, and aside from the Shire coincidence, it seems more likely that the Hogsback Mountains in the Eastern Cape province of South Africa, which he visited as a child, inspired the landscapes described in the book.

If you're in the area around mid-July, ask about the Mulanje Porters' Race – now an international event – organised by the MCM. The Mulanje porters and other entrants race up and down 25km of steep mountain in one of Africa's maddest and most daunting fitness challenges, taking in the heights of the Skyline Path to Chambe. You're unlikely to win, but the prizes have included a bicycle, a plane ride and a night of luxury in a posh hotel. The event is open to men and women, and further details can be obtained through InfoMulanje or the MCM or MMCT.

🏠 **Thuchila Hut** (*2,303m*; ✪ *S15.89563° E35.60960°*) Built in 1901, this is the oldest of the non-CCAP huts on Mulanje, & the highest, set below a formation known as the Elephant's Head. It sleeps 16 people in 4 rooms & is well suited for ascents of 6 different peaks, including Sapitwa. A natural swimming pool lies 15mins away.

HIKING PRACTICALITIES Organising a hike up Mulanje is a straightforward procedure, either through InfoMulanje or through Likhubula Forestry Station, where you can book mountain huts and arrange porters and guides as required. A guide is strongly recommended, as is a porter, at least for your first day – the ascent of Mulanje is *very* steep. Expenses are minimal. The entrance fee is under US$1 per day, huts only cost US$6 per person per night, camping costs US$3, and the official rates for porters and guides are US$12 and US$15 respectively – so you are looking at a maximum outlay of around US$25 per person per day.

Guides and porters can be hired from all accessible paths around the mountain as they have positioned themselves at the start of all popular paths. It is mandatory to hire porters through the forestry office when climbing from Likhubula and Fort Lister because they are on a rotation schedule in order to provide them all with the basic amount of income, and not least because it will make your hike more enjoyable. On other paths, the chairman of the local porters' group can be asked for advice on whose turn it is next to go up. Most of the guides and porters have been trained to assist tourists.

It is worth paring down your luggage to the bare minimum before tackling Mulanje; spare gear can be left at the forestry station or at Doogle's in Blantyre. What you do need is a sleeping bag or thick blanket, and plenty of warm clothing for the chilly highland nights. There are mattresses for visitors in each hut, but for those without sleeping bags it may be possible to book bedding (check with InfoMulanje, see page 213). You must also bring all the food you will need. The ideal place to stock up is in Blantyre, but there is a People's Supermarket in Chitakale opposite the turn-off to Likhubula and, a few hundred metres away, a well-stocked vegetable market.

A week or so would be required to do a full circuit of the huts, and you could spend considerably longer than a week on Mulanje if you so chose, but most visitors settle for two or three days, a day each for the ascent and descent, and one day for exploring part of the plateau. There are at least half a dozen different ascent/descent routes. Most popular by far is the Skyline Path from Likhubula Forestry Station to Chambe Hut or France's Cottage, which takes three to four hours one-way. Also popular and accessible is the Boma Path, which leads from Mulanje Town (past Kara O'Mula Country Lodge) to the CCAP and Lichenya huts, a steep four– to five-hour ascent that can be treacherously slippery after rain. A good option for those with three days is to ascend using the Skyline Path on day one, cross between

Chambe Hut/France's Cottage and CCAP Cottage/Lichenya Hut on day two, then descend via the Boma Path on the third day. The three-hour ascent from Fort Lister to Sombani Hut is regarded to be the easiest option by locals, but access to Fort Lister can be problematic. Exhaustive coverage of possible ascents and routes between huts is posted on the MCM website.

Mulanje can be climbed at any time of year. The dry, cool months from mid-April to September are generally regarded as the best for hiking, though there is a danger of treacherous mists (called *chiperone*) enveloping the massif between May and July. If you are caught in *chiperone* conditions, you must stay put, as walking is very dangerous, even along marked trails. During the rainy season (November to early April), many paths become slippery and some may be temporarily impassable owing to flooding. The Skyline Path to Chambe is safe at all times of year as it crosses only one river, and there is a bridge.

Mulanje is not high enough for serious altitude-related illness to be a cause for concern, though people arriving directly from sea level may feel some mild effects at higher altitudes. Nevertheless, the mountain should not be underestimated, as attested by the still unexplained disappearance of Dutch tourist Linda Pronk in 2003 and the death due to exposure of Brazilian national Gabriel Buchman in 2009. Be careful, take a guide, or consider hooking up with the MCM, which visits Mulanje, or other mountains, almost every weekend. They have a wealth of local knowledge which can save you money and trouble and enhance the whole Mulanje experience.

FURTHER INFORMATION Frank Eastwood's 150-page *Guide to the Mulanje Massif* (Lorton Communications) has long been considered *the* definitive guide to the mountain. Published in 1979, the guide is now rather dated in some respects, but the route descriptions are still extremely useful to people undertaking lengthy hikes or who intend on climbing the rock faces. Unfortunately, it has long been out of print, and though secondhand copies can be bought through amazon.com, they are quite pricey. The good news is that Frank has written to Bradt to say he is working on a completely updated new edition, so let's hope that sees the light of day soon!

Excellent online sources of information about Mulanje are the websites run by the **MCM** (*www.mcm.org.mw*) and **MMCT** (*www.mountmulanje.org.mw*). For local advice, the InfoMulanje office in Chitakale (see page 213) can discuss the most suitable route options, book mountain huts, organise your guides and porters,

---

MWALANTHUNZI STONE

To the left of the road between Limbe and Thyolo is the Mwalanthunzi Stone, a large meteorite steeped in local beliefs. If you are heading north, this stone will guide you safely on your journey (it doesn't work if you're going south). You must walk around the stone three times using a small stone (normally perched in a crevice at the top of the meteorite) to tap the lucky stone. Should you involuntarily whistle as you walk, then something unexpected will happen to you. When road builders decided to move the stone, its wrath caused floods, destroying the new road. The stone was back in place the next day. When they moved the stone again (a further distance this time), the stone was back in place the next morning. Undeterred, they decided to crush the stone and use it in the road. The next day the stone was back in place. In the end the road builders decided to move the road a little to the right and to leave the magical stone alone.

and make lodge accommodation reservations. The map sales office in Blantyre sells an excellent 1:40,000 contour map of the Mulanje Massif for a few dollars. It was first published in 1995, and shows all footpaths and huts on the plateau.

THYOLO

Situated about halfway between Mulanje and Blantyre, Thyolo – pronounced *Cholo* – is the tea capital of Malawi, and one of the oldest towns in the country. The leafy administrative centre consists of a cluster of colonial-era government offices built around a rather pointless roundabout, and it is separated from the busy market and bus station by a tea field. About 1km back towards Limbe lie a string of shops, among them a PTC Supermarket. As with most Malawian towns, there is nothing much to do here, but it's a pleasant place to hang about. All Saints' Anglican Church behind the Thyolo Sports Club is worth visiting, its unassuming graveyard serving as a reminder of how many Europeans came to settle here. The Thyolo Club itself offers golf, tennis, swimming and squash for a day membership fee of about US$6.50 plus greens fees for golfers. And if you're looking for the chance to limber up your legs before making an assault on Mulanje, the countryside around Thyolo is riddled with dirt roads that make for great rambling.

The main tourist focus in the Thyolo area is Satemwa Tea Estate, which was one of the first European land claims registered in Malawi, dating back to 1874, and has been in the same family since 1923, when it was acquired by Maclean Kay, a rubber planter from Malaya. Satemwa lies on the slopes of the 1,462m Thyolo Mountain, where what little remains of the once-extensive mahogany forest above the 1,100m contour is protected within the 10km² Thyolo Forest Reserve. Sadly, much of the original forest here has been chopped over the past century, initially to make way for tea plantations, and more recently by peasant farmers desperate for farmland and firewood in what is reputedly the district with the densest rural population in Malawi. Today, two lodges on the Satemwa Tea Estate offer the opportunity to explore the remaining forest, with its tall stands of mahogany, flap-leafed dragon trees and attendant birds, including rarities such as green-headed oriole, white-winged apalis, Thyolo alethe, little green bulbul and moustached green tinker barbet.

GETTING THERE AND AWAY Most buses along the M2 between Blantyre and Mulanje stop at Thyolo. Far quicker than buses are the minibuses and other *matola* vehicles that run directly between Limbe bus station and Thyolo, and cost around US$2 per person. The entrance to Satemwa Tea Estate is clearly signposted about 2km from Thyolo town centre along the main road to Blantyre, and it's about 5km from the entrance gate to the accommodation.

WHERE TO STAY

Exclusive

 Huntingdon House (5 rooms) \01 794555; e reservations@ulendo.net; www.ulendo.net. Set in a magnificent garden in the heart of Satemwa Tea Estate, this enchanting lodge is housed in the original family home built by Maclean Kay in 1928. Tastefully renovated & refurbished, it retains a strong period charm yet is also strongly informed by contemporary aesthetics. Accommodation is in 5 large opulent suites, 1 of which was originally the family chapel, & there's a lounge & dining room with log fire & silver-service dining. A wide range of activities includes guided bird walks & picnics on Thyolo Mountain, tours of the estate & tea factory, bass fishing, croquet & lawn bowls, mountain-bike, horseback or quad-bike excursions, & day trips to Mount Mulanje. *US$300/450 sgl/dbl high season, US$225/350 sgl/dbl low season, rates inc all meals & activities.*

Moderate

⌂ **Chawani Bungalow** (4 rooms) ☎ 01 794555; e reservations@ulendo.net; www.ulendo.net. Also within the Satemwa Tea Estate, this small lodge consists of a historic tea planter's homestead set in a lush manicured garden rattling with birdlife, within easy walking distance of the forested Thyolo Mountain & subtropical rainforests on Satemwa Estate. Decorated in rustic Edwardian style, it offers accommodation for up to 10 people in 4 rooms, 2 of which are en suite, & has a comfortable dining room, lounge & veranda. It makes for a wonderful family w/end retreat, & is most often rented out to groups on a serviced self-catering basis (a chef is provided but guests need to bring all food), but meals can be taken at Huntingdon House with prior arrangement. It offers a similar range of activities to Huntingdon House. *US$150–175 for the whole house on a self-catering basis.*

Budget

⌂ **Tione Motel** m 099 5115413. Situated in Thyolo Town about 5 mins' walk from the bus station – anybody will direct you – this place is far better than its faded exterior suggests & has a busy bar & a fair restaurant. *US$2 dbl using communal facilities, US$4/5 en-suite twin/dbl.*

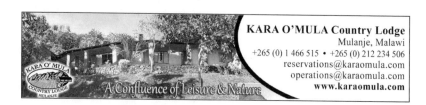

KARA O'MULA Country Lodge
Mulanje, Malawi
+265 (0) 1 466 515 • +265 (0) 212 234 506
reservations@karaomula.com
operations@karaomula.com
www.karaomula.com

A Confluence of Leisure & Nature

14

Lower Shire Valley

Southwest of Blantyre, the M1 snakes and slithers down the Thyolo Escarpment into the steamy lowlands of the Lower Shire Valley, a tapering wedge of Malawian territory surrounded by Mozambique on three sides. It's a dramatic drive, with lurching hairpin bends offering awesome views across the hills of Majete Wildlife Reserve into Mozambique, then finally the meandering Shire River comes into view, flowing southward to its confluence with the Zambezi. This southernmost sliver of Malawi retains the feel of wild, untrammelled Africa: the wide and lush Shire River still supports prodigious numbers of hippo and crocodile, a trio of protected areas harbours a variety of terrestrial wildlife, and urban centres such as Chikwawa, Nsanje and Bangula come across as strikingly un-Westernised by comparison with Blantyre.

This was the first part of Malawi to be documented by Europeans. In January 1859, Livingstone's Zambezi Expedition steamed up the Shire until its path was blocked by the Kapichira Falls, in what is now the Majete Wildlife Reserve. When Livingstone travelled up the Shire again in 1861, to help Bishop Mackenzie establish the first mission in central Africa, the region was controlled indirectly by Portuguese slavers. By 1863, when Livingstone made his final trip here, the slave trade had transformed the Shire into 'literally a river of death', according to his companion Dr Rowley, its banks lined with dead and emaciated Africans. And the malaria associated with this low-lying riverine habitat proved to be equally deadly to several expedition members: Bishop Mackenzie died on a now-submerged island at the confluence of the Ruo and Shire in 1862, and two other clergymen, Reverend Scudamore and Dr Dickinson, died in the Chikwawa area in 1863, along with the 25-year-old geologist Richard Thornton.

The main attractions of the Lower Shire Valley today are the raw beauty of the riverine landscape and a high diversity of mammals and birds. The region supports three officially protected areas, namely Majete Wildlife Reserve, Lengwe National Park and Mwabvi Wildlife Reserve, and there is also the private Nyala Park (in the Nchalo Sugar Estate) and the unprotected Elephant Marsh. Despite this, the Lower Shire Valley doesn't see a great deal of tourism, though successful reintroduction programmes at Majete have turned this once-neglected park into perhaps the finest game-viewing destination in all of Malawi, rivalled only by Liwonde National Park. The reserves are most easily explored in a private vehicle, ideally a 4x4, but the Elephant Marsh is readily accessible to backpackers.

However you visit, be prepared for some serious weather – this is the lowest-lying part of Malawi, dropping to 38m above sea level near Nsanje, and temperatures of 35–40°C are commonplace in summer – and be aware that malaria is rife. The best time to visit on both fronts is from June to August, when the weather is reasonably cool and dry, and this is also the best season for game viewing. Be aware, too, that this part of Malawi is conspicuously lacking in modern facilities such as internet cafés, ATMs and forex bureaux.

GETTING AROUND

The southern extension of the M1 starts at Blantyre and runs all the way through the Shire Valley to the remote Mozambican border, past the towns of Chikwawa, Nchalo, Bangula and Nsanje. The first 39km of this road, as far as Kanjedza, is very steep in parts, and it's not unusual to be trapped behind crawling trucks for long stretches, so allow plenty of time. The M1 is tarred until the small town of Ngabu, and picks up again between Bangula and Nsanje. South of Nsanje and between Ngabu and Bangula the road is unsurfaced or so heavily pot-holed as to make no difference. Plenty of buses and minibuses traverse the M1 between Blantyre and Nsanje, but there is little or no public transport on other roads in the area.

The three official protected areas all lie to the west of the M1 along feeder roads of variable quality, and are best explored in a private 4x4, especially during the rainy season.

CHIKWAWA

Chikwawa is a sprawling town of 12,000 set on the west bank of the Shire 50km south of Blantyre at the junction of the M1 and the feeder road to Majete Wildlife Reserve. The area immediately around Chikwawa is of interest mainly to bird enthusiasts. About 1km out of town, in September, a nesting colony of carmine bee-eaters can be reached by following the dirt road opposite the police station to the west bank of the Shire River. On the M1, about 3km south of the turn-off to Chikwawa, the Kasinthula fish ponds are noted for waterbirds, particularly the large numbers of migrant waders which are attracted to the area between July and December.

 WHERE TO STAY

Matechanga Motel (12 rooms) 01 420313; m 099 9512421/088 4299613; e matechangamotel@yahoo.com. This small hotel has the cleanest rooms in town, & a restaurant serving beef, chicken & burgers in the US$2.50–5 range. It lies about 300m from the main road & is signposted to the left of the feeder road to Majete. *US$2.75/5 sgl/dbl, US$10/15 en-suite with fan, B&B.*

MAJETE WILDLIFE RESERVE

(⏱ *Early–18.00 daily (entrance gate); entrance US$20/10/4 for international visitors/foreign residents/Malawian nationals, 50% discount for all children under 12. Vehicle entrance US$4.*) Gazetted in 1955 and neglected by almost everybody except poachers for its first half-century of existence, Majete Wildlife Reserve is in the midst of a dramatic and encouraging resurgence. With the reintroduction of lions (rounding out the 'Big Five') in 2012, Majete has arguably distinguished itself as Malawi's premier game-viewing destination. The catalyst for this reversal of fortunes is the private African Parks Network (APN), which entered into a 25-year management contract with the government in March 2003, with the twin aims of resuscitating the reserve as a conservation area and as a source of sustainable income for surrounding communities. The APN has since reintroduced more than 3,000 head of game into the reserve, erected fences, improved the road infrastructure, constructed an excellent community-owned tented camp, cultural

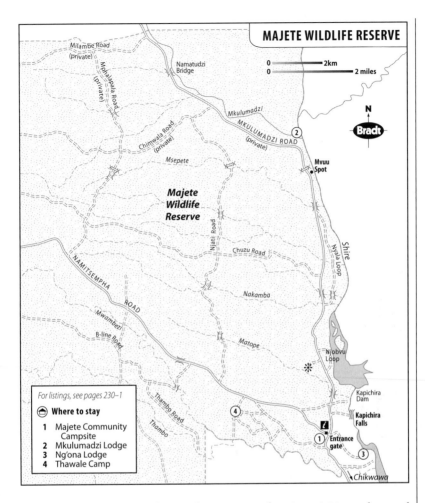

For listings, see pages 230–1

⌂ **Where to stay**

1 Majete Community Campsite
2 Mkulumadzi Lodge
3 Ng'ona Lodge
4 Thawale Camp

centre and campsite, initiated a varied programme of tourist activities, and granted the highly regarded Robin Pope Safaris a private concession for their stunning new five-star luxury lodge, Mkulumadzi.

Protecting a 700km² tract of rocky Brachystegia woodland sloping down to the western bank of the Shire River, Majete naturally supports a wide variety of large mammals, including all of the so-called Big Five, but numbers dwindled in the late 20th century as a result of intensive poaching. In 1988, for instance, the reserve's estimated 200 elephants were targeted by armed ivory poachers and within four years almost none was left. Other species hunted to local extinction by the 1990s include lion, African wild dog, buffalo, sable antelope, eland, zebra and hartebeest, while the likes of hippo, warthog, zebra, greater kudu, bushbuck, waterbuck, grey duiker, klipspringer and spotted hyena were greatly reduced in number. Since the APN took over, populations of naturally occurring large mammals have all started to recover, and their variety and number has been boosted by the reintroduction of large numbers of buffalo, sable antelope, waterbuck, warthog, eland, Lichtenstein's hartebeest, nyala, impala, zebra and elephant, mostly from other protected areas in Malawi, as well as five black rhino from South Africa and one from Liwonde.

Tourist movement is currently restricted to the northeast sector of the reserve, where a temporary 140km² sanctuary, bounded by the Shire River to the east, has been fenced off by the APN on the other three sides. Most of the reintroduced animals are resident within this sanctuary, though some have also been settled outside and the long-term plan is to fence the reserve in its entirety and then break down the temporary sanctuary. A 200km network of dirt roads traverses the sanctuary, allowing visitors with their own vehicle, ideally a 4x4, to explore it at their leisure. It should be noted, however, that roads signposted as 'private' lead to the Robin Pope Safaris concession and are for Mkulumadzi guests only. Both camps offer a range of guided activities including day and night drives, bush walks, boat trips and elephant tracking on foot. Birding is excellent, too, with more than 300 species recorded, including such noisy and conspicuous characters as trumpeter hornbill and black-collared barbet, as well as a good selection of Brachystegia specialists, raptors and (along the river) waterbirds.

Only a few years ago, it would have been misleading to compare Majete to Liwonde National Park, further north along the Shire River – but the improvement in game viewing, infrastructure and accommodation over recent years has placed Majete in direct competition with Liwonde for the honour of being Malawi's premier park. This ongoing development is massively encouraging, and Majete now boasts the greatest antelope diversity in the country, offering a good chance of seeing half a dozen species in the course of a day, including the majestic greater kudu, handsome sable antelope and localised Lichtenstein's hartebeest. The reintroduced elephants are also a highly visible presence, and hippos are plentiful in the Shire River as it flows along the park's eastern boundary. The 600-odd buffalo mostly move in a few large herds, so sightings are somewhat more hit and miss, while black rhinos and leopards are shy and seldom seen. The introduction of three lions in 2012 has been a hugely significant step in Majete's redevelopment, and there are plans for them soon to be joined by at least two others. Today, Majete has definitively come into its own, and can stake a very credible claim as Malawi's top game-viewing destination.

GETTING THERE AND AWAY The entrance gate to Majete lies 20km from the M1 along a feeder road signposted from Chikwawa. Coming from Blantyre, the junction is on your right, about 1km after the M1 crosses a 196m-long bridge across the Shire River. After about 3km, the tar ends and you need to turn left, and from there it's plain sailing. Depending on how much time you spend stuck behind trucks on the descent from Blantyre, the drive might take anything from one to two hours in a private vehicle. There is no public transport between Chikwawa and the entrance gate, but you can arrange a pickup with Thawale Camp for US$19 per person (minimum two).

WHERE TO STAY AND EAT *See map, page 229.*
Exclusive

🏠 **Mkulumadzi Lodge** (8 rooms) ✆ 01 794491/5483; e info@robinpopesafaris. com; www.mkulumadzi.com. This superlative new luxury lodge from Robin Pope Safaris sits overlooking the confluence of the Shire & Mkulumadzi Rivers, deep inside a 7,000ha private concession in the north of the park. Opened in 2011, it raises the bar for luxury lodges in Malawi, & easily ranks among the finest such lodges in southern Africa. There are 8 indulgent open-fronted chalets with living roofs set along the riverbank, all of which are solar powered & open onto wide private balconies with stunning river views. The secluded chalets are light & airy with an open floor plan, walk-in netting, delightful in-net AC, large bathtub, outdoor shower, lounge area, minibar, writing desk & a selection of books about Malawi. There are a range of activities on offer, including morning & night game drives, boat safaris, hikes, sundowners & cultural tours. Game viewing in the private concession is some of the best in the park, & offers the highest chance of encountering the newly reintroduced lions. There's also a swimming pool to lounge around, exceptional food & captivating views from the breezy main lodge & dining area. *US$395 pp all-inclusive, US$185 pp FB for residents, low season discounts may apply.*

Moderate

⚊ Majete Community Campsite Next to a wooded stream about 200m from the entrance gate, this attractive community-run campsite has 2 stilted shelters, hot showers, flush toilets & a dining area with a stocked bar & BBQ facilities, but visitors must bring all food with them. Alternatively, there is a restaurant (⊕ *07.00–18.00 daily*) at the heritage centre serving mains for US$6–8 & cheaper snacks. *US$10 pp camping, an additional US$5 for use of a shelter.*

⌂ Ng'ona Lodge m 099 9216398/9; e ngonalodge@gmail.com. Located 1.6km down a signposted side road opposite the Majete entrance gate, this promising new lodge has a picturesque riverside location, large swimming pool & restaurant with full bar serving meals in the US$8–11 range. There are four self-contained chalets planned, but as of early 2013 only the campground was operational. Regardless, this is still a very attractive set-up & the only option outside of the park proper. *US$15 pp camping.*

⌂ Thawale Camp (6 rooms, 1 luxury chalet) m 099 9521741; e thawale@african-parks.org; www.african-parks.org. Built in 2006, this wonderfully down-to-earth bush camp consists of 6 widely spaced tented chalets set in a tall thicket overlooking a waterhole about 3km inside the entrance gate. All units have an en-suite hot shower, private balcony with seating, twin or dbl bed, & generator-driven light, fan & electric socket. There's also 1 luxury tented chalet with a superb outdoor bathroom. The kitchen serves up unadventurous but tasty home-style cooking, & there is a well-stocked honesty bar. The spotlighted waterhole attracts plenty of wildlife, with elephant & buffalo frequently coming to drink at night, & the trees around camp are often teeming with weavers, warblers & other small birds. All activities mentioned below can be arranged at the camp. This is a genuinely thrilling bush experience, & the camp is good value. *US$150/300 sgl/dbl FB, US$170/340 luxury chalet.*

ORGANISED ACTIVITIES An excellent range of organised activities is on offer. Guided game drives cost US$25 per person, while night drives including sundowners cost US$35 per person and offer the best chance of seeing predators. For a more intimate look at the bush, general bush and birding walks cost US$20. More energetic visitors who want to see the part of the reserve outside the fenced sanctuary might want to organise a hike up Majete Hill, the tallest point in the reserve, for US$40. All these rates are per person with a minimum of two except Majete Hill, which requires a group of at least four. Another possibility is a cultural tour of one of the villages bordering the park, or a traditional dance performance, which costs US$107 for a group of up to six. There is also a gift shop at the small heritage centre at the entrance gate.

SELF-DRIVE GAME DRIVES A good network of roads runs through the sanctuary, though some require a 4x4 or at least a vehicle with very good clearance, and a map is available at the entrance gate. If your time is limited, the best area to concentrate on is the river, which can be explored by following the Mkulumadzi Road north from the entrance gate towards Mvuu Spot, then looping back via Nyala Loop. This is a good place to see vervet monkeys, baboons, nyalas, impalas, greater kudus, zebras and warthogs, and with other water sources in Majete being thin on the ground, elephant and buffalo regularly cross the road to drink, especially in the mid-morning and late afternoon. It's well worth stopping at Mvuu Spot, with its resident hippo and good birding potential.

A highlight of any game drive is Kapichira Falls, reached by a short self-guided footpath from close to the park entrance. Though slightly blemished by the hydroelectric scheme above it, this is a dramatic and very noisy surge of white water, one whose energy seems more lateral than vertical, but too powerful to be dismissed as mere rapids. You can imagine how depressed Livingstone felt when he saw this huge torrent of water, which effectively put an end to his exploration of Malawi by river. If you can persuade a ranger to guide you on a walk, this is exhilarating walking country, with a mass of birds in the riparian forest fringing the riverbanks, and the possibility of visiting the solitary grave of Richard Thornton. The only known Malawian breeding site of the rock pratincole is on a small island near to Kapichira.

Away from the river, the 'view spot' about 1km west of the Mkulumadzi Road offers a great overview of the wild expansive hills of Majete from atop a tall boulder teeming with lizards. Further inland, game viewing is more erratic, but the dense Brachystegia woodland northwest of Thawale Camp is the best place to seek rarer antelope such as sable, eland and Lichtenstein's hartebeest.

LENGWE NATIONAL PARK

(⊕ *Early–18.00 daily (entrance gate); entrance US$10/7 pp per 24hrs for international visitors/residents. Vehicle entrance US$3. A useful map can be bought at the gate for a nominal fee. The park may close mid-Jan–end May during the rains, but this has not been the case for several years.*) Originally set aside as a 120km² game reserve in 1928, Lengwe was elevated to national-park status in 1970, and extended to its present size of 887km² five years later, with the addition of a large tract of non-cultivatable land stretching to the Mozambican border. The reserve was originally created to protect what was then the world's most northerly extant population of nyala antelope (subsequently introduced to the more northerly Majete Wildlife Reserve), and it is thought the park's population of this beautiful antelope now stands at 2,000–3,000. It is also an important refuge for the suni, a small, inconspicuous and very localised thicket-dwelling antelope.

As with the other reserves in the Shire Valley, Lengwe runs along the Mozambican border to the west of the M1, and it is named after an area of thorny and impenetrable scrub in the east of the park. Though relatively arid, with an annual rainfall figure of 600mm, Lengwe is densely vegetated. There is lush riparian woodland along some of the watercourses, and the remainder of the park is covered in wooded savannah and dense thickets interspersed with some impressive stands of baobab and palm trees. Tourist traffic is low, and dense vegetation lends the winding roads a secluded air. With a ranger it is possible to hike all day in this majestic park.

Only a small eastern extension of this vast park has been developed for tourism. Within this small area, however, there is a good network of roads, as well as several viewing hides and an inexpensive camp and campsite. In terms of game viewing, Lengwe can feel a little underwhelming after a day or two in Majete. True, the wildlife here all occurs naturally, unboosted by any reintroduction programme, but the selection of large mammals isn't very varied, and except in a few areas it is less than prolific. On the plus side, what you do see, you tend to see well. Mammals you should see are impala, duiker, bushbuck, warthog, vervet monkey, samango monkey and baboons, and with a bit of luck buffalo, greater kudu and suni. The only large predators in the reserve are spotted hyena and leopard, the former often being very vocal, but neither is often seen.

Birds are aplenty, with more than 330 species recorded. Among the more interesting species likely to be seen are woolly necked stork, trumpeter hornbill, bearded scrub-robin, yellow-spotted nicator and all three species of snake eagle found in Malawi. Dedicated birders will also want to look out for the localised

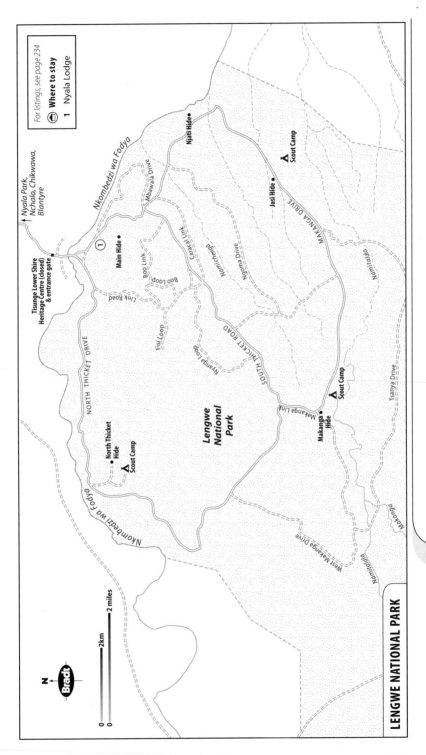

LENGWE NATIONAL PARK

For listings, see page 234
Where to stay
1 Nyala Lodge

racquet-tailed roller and pale-billed hornbill. For the less fanatical, it's always magical to watch a heron fishing for frogs through the grass, a paradise flycatcher flitting through the foliage, or a Boehm's bee-eater hawking for insects.

GETTING THERE AND AWAY The turn-off to Lengwe is on the west side of the M1, about 20km south of Chikwawa and 8km north of Nchalo. From the turn-off, it's a further 9km to the park entrance gate – a straight and uninspiring drive through a busy sugar plantation, which makes it all the more surprising when you suddenly come to the trees of Lengwe National Park. Without transport, you could certainly walk to the gate, or catch a bicycle-taxi, then ring the lodge to see if there is anyone who could collect you. Nyala Lodge and the campsite are only just inside, but you are not allowed to enter the park without a vehicle on account of buffalo and other animals. It's also worth noting here that there is an airstrip at nearby Nchalo Sugar Estate should you wish to charter a plane.

WHERE TO STAY See map, page 233.

🏠 **Nyala Lodge** (11 rooms) \01 823709/835356; m 088 8202420/902421; e jamboafrica@africa-online.net; www.jambo-africa.com. The former national park rest camp has been privatised & completely renovated by Jambo Africa, & it is now a wonderfully sultry & extremely comfortable place to stay. The thatched semi-detached chalets are en suite & very spacious, sleep up to 4 people in 1 dbl & 2 sgl beds, & have netting, fans, electric sockets, & six of the units have AC. Cheaper & more basic chalets using common ablutions can be found at the campsite, or you can pitch your own tent. There is a small swimming pool near the thatched bar/dining area, which overlooks a waterhole that attracts plenty of passing game. There's a hide under construction, & plans to set up waterhole cameras for game viewing at the bar. The restaurant serves toasted sandwiches for US$3 & full meals for US$10, & the Sun BBQ is a full-on meatfest. *US$137.50/259 sgl/dbl FB, US$94/171.50 B&B, US$47 dbl campsite chalet, US$7 pp camping.*

ORGANISED ACTIVITIES Nyala Lodge offers a good selection of organised activities, including game drives for US$23.50 per person and early morning walks for US$14 per person. Further afield, it can also arrange visits to Ndakwera Cultural Village, day trips to Majete, Mwabvi and Nyala Park, fishing trips on the Shire River and motorboat safaris from Nchalo Sports Club to the Elephant Marsh.

SELF-DRIVE GAME DRIVES Maps of the rough road network in the developed eastern sector of the park are available at the entrance gate and at Nyala Lodge. The best game-viewing loop, easily covered in 30 minutes, is a short circuit running northwest along Makanga Drive for 1.3km, stopping at Main Hide *en route*, and then returning via Mbawala Drive. The thick woodland around Main Hide supports a wide variety of birds as well as a troop of the localised samango monkey, while Mbawala Drive runs through a large grassy plain that's enclosed by dense thicket and supports large numbers of impala, nyala, greater kudu, baboon and warthog – you can't help but feel that the cheetahs due for reintroduction in the dense Brachystegia woodland at Majete would be in their element in this open terrain!

A more elaborate route from the intersection of Makanga and Mbawala drives entails continuing northwest for 2.5km to Njati Hide (overlooking New Jasi Pan), then following Makanga Drive in a southerly direction for 11km via Jasi Hide to Makanga Hide, then veering back north for about 8.5km along South Thicket Road and Caracal Link. The open grassland along parts of Makanga Drive supports healthy numbers of buffalo, and it's also a good place to look for the bizarre turkey-like southern ground hornbill and large raptors such as snake eagles and vultures.

The three hides were all constructed or completely renovated in 2009, and it's worth stopping at them all and sitting quietly for 15 minutes to see what wildlife emerges. Allow two to four hours for this drive, depending on how often you stop, and don't attempt it in a vehicle with low clearance.

TISUNGE LOWER SHIRE HERITAGE CENTRE This admirable project was shuttered when we last visited, but it could theoretically reopen during the lifespan of this edition. Situated at the entrance gate to Lengwe, Tisunge (Chichewa for 'Let's Preserve') has been established by the Mlambe Foundation (*www.mlambefoundation.org*) in collaboration with the Department of Antiquities and the Department of National Parks and Wildlife to promote greater awareness of natural and cultural resources through sustainable community tourism. The site has been chosen for historical as well as practical reasons: the entrance of Lengwe has long been the capital of the Lundu dynasty, which ruled over the Lower Shire Valley and parts of Mozambique from the 13th century until the colonial era, and the current Paramount Chief Lundu still resides there today. At present, the main feature of the cultural centre is a craft shop that sells the high-quality products of a local weaving and spinning co-operative involving more than 30 people in six villages surrounding the park. There's also a library here for the use of local villagers.

NCHALO SUGAR ESTATE

The largest employer in the Lower Shire Valley is this vast sugar estate, which extends either side of the M1 from the border of Lengwe National Park to the west bank of the Shire River. From a touristic perspective, there are two main points of interest on the estate: the well-organised Nchalo Sports Club, with its riverside clubhouse and popular golf course, and a tiny but well-stocked game sanctuary called Nyala Park. There's also a small town called Nchalo straddling the M1 at the main entrance gate to the sugar estate, which has a few resthouses should the need arise, a decent supermarket and market if you're stocking up for a visit to Lengwe or elsewhere, and the last reliable opportunity to fuel up the car for those heading further south to Bangula or Mozambique. And if you're in need of a refuel yourself, Arrows Restaurant serves good chicken and chips for US$2.50.

NCHALO SPORTS CLUB (m *01 425357; m 088 8230110; e bfehrenbach@illovo.co.za; rooms US$48/70 sgl/dbl FB*) Overlooking the Shire River about 6km from the main entrance gate, the estate's sports club used to be the smartest place to stay in the immediate vicinity of Lengwe, and the en-suite rooms remain pretty good value. The club lacks the bush atmosphere of Nyala Lodge, however, though a good variety of birds can be seen from the grounds, along with hippos and crocs if you are lucky. It also has a good restaurant, and visitors are welcome, though the day membership fee of US$8 for all but members of affiliated sports clubs in Malawi makes it an expensive option simply for a meal. Tennis, squash, swimming and gym use are covered by the day membership fee, but an additional fee of US$10 plus club hire is charged to play golf on the 18-hole course. Tours of the sugar estate and factory can sometimes be arranged through the human resources manager.

NYALA PARK (m *099 1978716;* ⊕ *06.00–18.00; entrance US$2 pp plus US$3 per vehicle, with guides available at US$1.50. Camping US$3 pp.*) This 350ha game park protects a precious chunk of indigenous woodland, dominated by magnificent fever trees, in the midst of the cane fields that cover the rest of the sugar estate.

It's been stocked with a variety of indigenous wildlife, including nyala and impala, along with several species that don't occur naturally in this part of Malawi, such as wildebeest, giraffe and blesbok. In terms of variety and visibility, it actually offers better game viewing than Lengwe, though in reality it's more like a large zoo than a real wildlife sanctuary, making it a great family excursion. The birding is very good, and because there are no predators, walking is permitted. The park lies about 3km from the M1 and is signposted on the east side of the road directly opposite the turn-off to Lengwe.

MWABVI WILDLIFE RESERVE

(⊕ *Early–18.00 daily (entrance gate); entrance US$10/7 pp per day for foreigners/ residents. Self-drivers must also pay US$3 per car per day.*) This remote, little-known and infrequently visited reserve started life in 1928 as the Thangadzi Game Reserve, set aside to protect an isolated population of nyala antelope. It was expanded in 1953 and renamed after the Mwabvi River, also the local Henga name for the forest ordeal tree *Erythropheleum suaveolens*, which grows along the riverbanks, and whose bark was traditionally used to make a drink that determined a suspect's guilt or innocence. The borders of Mwabvi were further extended in 1975 and it now covers some 340km² of rugged wilderness along the Mozambican border in the far south of Malawi west of the M1.

The reserve supports a mixed cover of dense Brachystegia, mopane and Acacia woodland, and it is studded with scenic rocky outcrops and gorges, which are accessible via a small network of dirt roads and walking trails. It was once an important stronghold for black rhino, with a population estimated at 17 in 1959 and 15–30 in the mid-1970s, but this endangered animal has not been seen in the reserve for more than two decades. Poaching has had a drastic effect on other animals in Mwabvi, and while the likes of lion, leopard, sable antelope and buffalo are still resident or occasional visitors from across the border, you're more likely to see greater kudu, baboon, vervet monkey and impala, and the wildlife is sparsely distributed and skittish. It is of interest to birders for the presence of several species more normally associated with coastal habitats, for instance Rudd's apalis, Woodward's batis and grey sunbird.

The conservation and tourist development of Mwabvi was taken over by an NGO called Project African Wilderness (PAW) in 2007, but they have since folded and as of now the reserve is under Department of National Parks and Wildlife management. Remote, tricky to find, and lacking all but the most basic facilities, Mwabvi comes across as the type of African wilderness that is waiting for the world to begin and the animals to re-enter the stage. As such, it will disappoint anybody seeking a pure game-viewing experience, but it is highly recommended to keen walkers as an opportunity to explore an untrammelled wilderness area that still supports a decent quota of wildlife. Guided walks are in fact the only activity on offer; they cost US$10 per person and can be arranged at the entrance gate.

GETTING THERE AND AWAY Coming from the north, the turn-off to Mwabvi is signposted two times to the right of the M1 approaching the small town of Bangula, roughly 1km and 5km after you cross the bridge over the Thangadzi River. Turn right onto either of these earth roads and follow the signs (and your nose) as you will need to take another right turn and then a left-hand fork. Look out for blank brick signs – the information has been removed, but these are the turning locations. (If you get lost, villagers along the way can usually point you in the right direction.)

This track leads to the entrance gate of the reserve, where you must sign in. Ideally, you want to visit the reserve in a 4x4, though a saloon with high clearance should make it through to the camp in the dry season. Mwabvi is not a practical destination without your own transport. Jambo Safaris (see page 195) offers excursions to Mwabvi from Blantyre or the nearby Lengwe National Park.

 WHERE TO STAY

In addition to the developed sites listed below, there are basic campsites at the entrance to Mwabvi Gorge (11km from the entrance gate), and at Motape (7km from the entrance gate).

 Chipembere Camp 01 11946234. This camp lies about 1km outside the entrance gate & offers the option of a dorm bed or camping. It seems to be nominally operational, but we were unable to roust anyone out on our last inspection. It would be best to ring either one of these places in advance to confirm they are accepting guests. There is an ablution block & cooking facilities. *US$15 pp dorm bed, US$5 pp camping.*

Migudu Camp 01 11946234. This campsite, about 3km inside the entrance gate, is an ideal base from which self-sufficient travellers can explore the park. On a rocky crest, it comprises 6 secluded individual campsites, each with its own fireplace & rubbish bin, as well as a central dbl-storey building with an ablution block & an upstairs viewing platform. The setting is magnificent, the birdlife plentiful, & a small waterhole below the deck attracts sporadic wildlife. Campers must bring all their own provisions. *US$8 pp camping.*

BANGULA

The closest town to Mwabvi, Bangula lies about 50km south of Nchalo, close to the Mozambican border and the confluence of the Ruo and Shire rivers. It's a rather rundown place, consisting of a single dirt road lined with time-worn shops and houses, but it might well gain in significance as and when a planned surfaced road linking Blantyre to the Mozambican town of Caia is completed. Today there is a new tarmac road between Bangula and Nsanje, but judging by the state of the roadworks c2012, the remaining sections won't be finished anytime soon. Bangula used to be the main springboard for visits to the Elephant Marsh, 10km to the northeast, and it still is for travellers without private transport, but the collapse of a bridge outside town in 1998 means it is no longer possible to drive to the marsh from here. There's a People's Supermarket, a few restaurants and plenty of minibus transport to Nchalo and Nsanje, but no filling station.

 WHERE TO STAY AND EAT

Aska Motel (14 rooms) 01 453369; m 088 1846666. This adequate motel lies in large green grounds alongside the main road & has large en-suite rooms with net & fan, & meals available for US$2–2.50. *US$4.75/8 sgl/twin, US$6.50/11 self-contained sgl/dbl.*

P & Partners Restaurant Just north of the main junction, this friendly spot has all the usual staples for around US$2.

NSANJE

Malawi's southernmost town, Nsanje is a steamy, low-lying sprawl just west of the Shire River, hemmed in by the Mozambican border on three sides. Neater, cleaner and a bit more freshly painted than your average small Malawian town, Nsanje boasts a modest assortment of services including an airstrip, guesthouse, Malawi Savings Bank ATM and a filling station. That said, these are likely to be considerably less reliable than their counterparts further north, so it would be best to treat them as a last-gasp fallback. There are regular minibuses to/from Blantyre for US$8.50, and irregular *matolas* to the remote Mozambican border post at Marka/Villa Nova da Frontiera, some 20km south of town. (Note that transport on the Mozambican side is very irregular, and neither visas nor insurance for self-drivers are available at this crossing.) Within Malawi, Nsanje is known primarily for the Nsanje World Inland Port, a white-elephant project built under the Mutharika administration with the intention of opening shipping routes along the Shire and Zambezi rivers to the Indian Ocean. Almost unbelievably, since opening in 2010 the port has yet to receive its first ship. The Malawian authorities failed to negotiate permissions for vessels to transit Mozambican waters, and even the demonstration barge sent to commemorate the ribbon cutting never arrived, as it had been detained by Mozambican authorities for a lack of permits. Today the port sits choked with water hyacinth, unused save for a few fishermen in dugouts and washerwomen on the empty quayside.

WHERE TO STAY

Nsanje Discovery Lodge ℡ 01 456348; e discoverylodgensanje@yahoo.com. In a compound on the west side of the M1, this is more or less the only option in town, offering drab but clean en-suite dbl/twin rooms with nets & fan. The attached restaurant serves Malawian favourites for about US$2. Ignore the adverts around town for Takulandilani Guesthouse; they've closed up shop but no one has bothered to take down the signs. *US$2.75 sgl with shared bathroom, US$8/9.50 self-contained sgl/dbl B&B.*

ELEPHANT MARSH

Extending over 500km², the Elephant Marsh is a vast maze of perennial and seasonal ponds, swamps and channels extending eastward from the banks of the Shire River. Paradoxically, this vast permanent marsh lies in an area of very low rainfall – less than 100mm in poor years – and it is fed almost entirely by the spillover from the Shire and various tributaries rising in the Thyolo Escarpment. The marsh was named by Livingstone, who recorded a herd of around 800 elephants and plentiful hippos here on his first expedition up the Shire. In 1896, the colonial authorities proclaimed it as a game reserve, and hunting was forbidden without a licence, but the elephants had been all shot out by 1910 anyway, and it was de-gazetted as a result.

Today, the Elephant Marsh is not formally protected in any way, but it still supports Malawi's largest population of crocodiles, large numbers of hippos, smaller aquatic mammals such as otters, and a rich aquatic birdlife, spectacular both in numbers and variety. Even if you're not into birds, the Elephant Marsh is a lush and beautiful area with a compelling sense of place. In the south of the marsh, the water is thick with purple-flowered hyacinth and white lilies, and the surrounding area is studded with massive baobab trees and tall palms, while the northern sector is a maze of narrow channels where crocodiles slide sinisterly into the water.

Usually explored from the bordering villages of Makhanga and Mchacha James in the south, this remote and under-publicised marsh is visited by few travellers, but those who do make it invariably regard it as a highlight of their time in Malawi. Gliding silently along the water, surrounded by lush vegetation and with birds in every direction, is sheer visual bliss. And many of the boatmen at Mchacha James, the main launching point for dugout excursions, are articulate and knowledgeable about every aspect of the marsh, and excellent bird guides, likely to generate enthusiasm in the most aviphobic of passengers. Serious bird enthusiasts who also stop regularly *en route* to Mchacha James as well as taking a boat trip can expect to see up to 50 water-associated species, including African fish eagle and African marsh harrier, purple and goliath heron, sacred and glossy ibis, open-billed and yellow-billed stork, malachite and pied kingfisher and – two birds that rank highly on many birders' wish list – the cryptically marked pygmy goose and the aptly named African skimmer.

GETTING THERE AND AWAY Unless you set up an organised safari, the best base for boat trips into the marsh is Mchacha James, a small village that lies on the edge of the marsh about 15km northeast of Bangula via Makhanga. Makhanga and Mchacha James used to be accessible by road from the M1 and Bangula, but not since 1998, when a bridge was washed away during heavy flooding. Bangula still remains the best access point to the Elephant Marsh for travellers without a vehicle, but self-drivers will need to approach it from the east side of the river, following the S152 from Kanjedza or the S151 from Thyolo.

Getting to Makhanga

From Bangula To reach Mchacha James from Bangula, your first goal is the village of Makhanga, which lies about 10km east of the M1 along a road forking out of Bangula town centre 100m or so south of the railway crossing. Walk along this road for a few hundred metres, and you'll come to the tributary of the river where the bridge was washed away in 1998. Small boats now ferry passengers across the river for US$1.50 per person, where a line of bicycle taxis stand waiting, charging US$1 per person to go straight to Makhanga. In wet years, when the marsh practically laps the road, you might prefer to walk. Either way, it's well worth investigating the pair of pools that flank the road only 200m past the river crossing, looking out for African jacana, open-billed storks and various herons, egrets, waterfowl and kingfishers. The abundant birdlife is a good inducement to walk.

From Kanjedza The best road to Makhanga is the dirt S152, which branches southeast from the M1 at the village of Kanjedza, which lies at the base of the escarpment 40km from Blantyre and had a prominent police roadblock at the time of writing. The S152 is a scenic road, running along the base of the Thyolo Escarpment to the east of the Shire River. It is normally in good shape most of the way – a cruising speed of around 50km/h is realistic – and a 4x4 is not really required, though any of the several streams that cross the road might render it temporarily impassable after rain. After 55km the road passes through the small junction town of Muona, where it connects with the S151 from Thyolo. From Muona it's another 15km to Makhanga, though seasonal flooding means that you may need to divert to the left after 8km at the Namiyala Primary School, and follow a rough track for 3km before connecting with the main road. There is limited public transport between Kanjedza and Muona, but nothing along the 15km between Muona and Makhanga.

From Thyolo A 70km road leads to Muona from Thyolo, on the M2 between Blantyre and Mulanje. Descending from the breezy tea plantations atop the Thyolo Escarpment to the sweltering base of the Rift Valley, the road is surfaced as far as Makwasa, 22km out of Thyolo, and it offers stunning views over the Shire River, with the Mulanje Massif visible on the northeast horizon in clear weather. Once you reach Muona, directions to Makhanga are the same as from Kanjedza.

Makhanga to Mchacha James Mchacha James lies on the edge of the marsh about an hour's walk out of Makhanga. To get there, follow the main road towards Muona out of Makhanga for 800m, past the Islamic Cultural Centre, then take the left fork signposted for the Chitsuka and Melewa irrigation schemes. From the turn-off, you'll wander through a sprawling village for about 4km before you reach a large brick-face mosque, from where it is another 500m to a beach where a dozen or so dugouts are lined up. If in doubt, ask directions ('James' is the key word). The rate for boat hire at Mchacha James will depend on how long you want to go out for, and also on your negotiating skills, but the initial asking price is around US$24 for a two- to three-hour trip in a dugout carrying two passengers. You might want to check the stability of the boat before you go out into the crocodile-infested waters!

WHERE TO STAY It is perfectly possible to visit the Elephant Marsh as a day trip using any of the previously mentioned routes, but the most rewarding time to visit is the early morning, so there is a strong case for sleeping closer by. If you decide to do this, the best option is the friendly but rudimentary **Tiyesembo Guesthouse** (m *088 4280894; US$3.50/7 sgl/dbl with a light, a net & very little else*), which is on the left side of the road as you enter Makhanga Town from Bangula. There's also basic accommodation available at the **EM Seven Guesthouse** (℘ *01 459214*) in Muona.

ORGANISED SAFARIS The best way to see the whole marsh is on a motorised boat trip, starting at the jetty at Nchalo Sports Club and following the Shire River from there. The only operator that offers these trips is Jambo Safaris, which operates Nyala Lodge (see *Lengwe National Park, Where to stay,* page 234, for contact details). Their full-day safari to the Elephant Marsh costs US$164.50 per person with a minimum group of two. The trip is dependent on water levels, and it is generally not possible towards the end of the dry season.

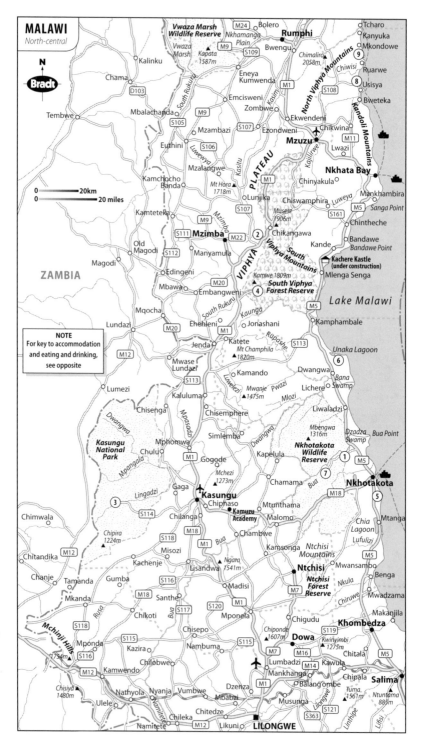

MALAWI
North-central

N

Bradt

0 ———— 20km
0 ———— 20 miles

ZAMBIA

NOTE
For key to accommodation
and eating and drinking,
see opposite

Tcharo
Kanyuka
Mkondowe
⑨
Ruarwe
⑧ Usisya
Bweteka

Bolero
Vwaza Marsh
Wildlife Reserve
M24
Nkhamanga
Plain
M9
S109
Rumphi
Bwengu
Chimaliro
2058m
North Viphya Mountains
Chiwisi

Kalinku

Chama

D103

Tembwe

Mbalachanda
S105
M9

Euthini
S106

Mzalangwe

Kamchocho
Banda

Vwaza
Marsh
Kapata
1587m
Eneya
Kumwenda
M1
Emcisweni
Zombwe
S107
Ezondweni
Mzambazi
Ekwendeni
Chikwina
Mzuzu
Kallirwe
Lwazi
M11

Nkhata Bay

Chinyakula
Mankhambira
Sanga Point
Chiswamphira
Luweya
S161
Chintheche
Musese
1906m
Kande
Bandawe
Bandawe Point
②
Chikangawa
Kamteteka
S107
Mt Hora
1718m
Lunjika
Mzimba
Mzimba
②
PLATEAU
Kasitu
Luwewya
Kondoli Mountains

Old
Magodi
S112
S111
Mzimba
M22
Manyamula

Magodi

Edingeni

Mbawa

Mqocha

Lundazi

Lumezi

Chisenga

Chitandika

Chanje
Tamanda

Mkanda
Gumba
S116

Mchinji Hills
1734m
Mponda
S118
S115
Kazira

Chisiya
1480m
S116
M12
Kamwendo

Ulele
Nathyola
Nyanja
Vumbwe

Chileka

Namitete

Chilobwe

Chikoti
S117

Chisepo
Nambuma
S115

Dzenza

Chitedze

Likuni

LILONGWE
M12
S363
S121

Mbabzi

Musunga

Balang'ombe
M1

Mankhanga
M14
Lumbadzi
M7
Kawula
M16
Kwinyimbi
1275m
Chitala
M5
Chipala
Salima
Tuma
1561m
Ntuntama
885m
Linthipe
Lifisi

Dowa
Chiponde
1607m
S119
Khombedza
Makanjila

Chigudu

Mponela
M1
S120
Chiruwe
Nkula
Benga
Mwadzama

Santhe
M18
Madisi
Lisandwa
Ngara
1541m

Kachenje
S118
M1
Bua
Misozi
M18
Chambwe
Kamsonga
Ntchisi
Mountains
Ntchisi
Ntchisi
Forest
Reserve
Mwansambo
M7

Chipira
1224m
M12

Chilanga
S114
Kamuzu
Academy
Chiphaso
Malomo
Mtunthama
M18

③
Gaga
Kasungu
Mchezi
1273m
Chamama
Bua
⑦
Nkhotakota
⑤
M18
M5

Lingadzi
Gogode
M1
Kapelula

Kasungu
National
Park
Mpangala
Chulu
Mphoma
Simlemba
Dwangwa
Mbengwa
1316m
Nkhotakota
Wildlife
Reserve
Dzadza
Swamp
Bua Point
①
M5

Chisemphere

Kaluluma
Luwezi
Mwanje
1475m
Mlozi
Liwaladzi

Chisenga

Mpasadzi

Kamando

Mwase
Lundazi
S113
Dwangwa
Lichere
Bana
Swamp

Jenda
Katete
Mt Champhila
1820m
S113
Dwangwa
Unaka Lagoon
⑥

Ehehleni
M1
Jonashani
Raposhe
Kamphambale
Chia
Lagoon
Mtanga
Lufulizi
M5

M20
Kaunga
Kamwe 1809m
South Viphya
Forest Reserve
④
M5
Lake Malawi

Embangweni
M20
VIPHYA
South Viphya
Mountains
Mlenga Senga
Kachere Kastle
(under construction)

South Rukuru

Mzimba

M9

Luwewya
Kasitu

242

Part Four

NORTH-CENTRAL MALAWI

OVERVIEW OF PART FOUR

This next five chapters provide coverage of sites located to the north of Lilongwe and south of Mzuzu, an area run through by two main roads, the lakeshore M5 and more westerly highland M1. They include coverage of the lakeshore north of Senga Bay as far as Nkhata Bay, the lake ferry and islands, and various inland sites accessible from the M1.

Chapter 15 covers the land route between Lilongwe and Mzuzu, notably the lovely montane Ntchisi Forest Reserve, the vast Kasungu National Park, and the country's largest forest reserve in the form of South Viphya, site of the popular Luwawa Forest Lodge.

The historic lake port of Nkhotakota is the focal point of *Chapter 16*, which also includes coverage of a cluster of resorts about 10km south of the port itself, and the up-and-coming Nkhotakota Wildlife Reserve, where two excellent new safari lodges have recently opened.

The next three chapters stick to Lake Malawi, with *Chapter 17* following the lakeshore north of Nkhotakota via Dwangwa and Kande to Chintheche. *Chapter 18* provides a detailed overview of the movement of the MV *Ilala* as well as the two islands it services, Likoma and Chizumulu, while *Chapter 19* concentrates on the ever-popular resort village of Nkhata Bay.

15

Inland from Lilongwe to Mzuzu

Although the lakeshore route between Lilongwe and Mzuzu is the more popular option with travellers, the inland route via the M1 is more direct, and in better condition, and it also offers a few worthwhile diversions to nature lovers. The prime attractions are the immense Kasungu National Park on the Zambian border, the more low-key Ntchisi Forest Reserve on the M7 north of Lilongwe, and the vast South Viphya Forest Reserve, where Luwawa Lodge offers perhaps the best selection of terrestrial adventure activities available anywhere in Malawi.

NTCHISI FOREST RESERVE

A highly accessible weekend retreat coming from Lilongwe, the 75km² Ntchisi Forest Reserve protects one of the most extensive patches of montane forest remaining in Malawi. A recently privatised forest lodge at the reserve entrance provides a perfect base for exploring the forest, and it offers unguided and guided hikes along a network of clearly marked walking trails, as well as mountain-biking excursions (indeed, keen cyclists can follow small scenic roads from Ntchisi all the way to the lake).

The main stand of evergreen forest covers the upper slopes of the 1,705m-high Ntchisi Mountain. It is home to a variety of large mammals including samango and vervet monkey, red and blue duiker, bushpig, porcupine and leopard. The occasional elephant used to stray into the forest from the neighbouring Nkhotakota Wildlife Reserve, though this seems unlikely now that local villages and farmland have expanded. The forest also protects a wide variety of forest birds and butterflies, some massive buttressed old trees and colourful orchids (the last are most prolific from November to April), while the lower slopes around the lodge protect characteristic Brachystegia birds.

The best hike for those with limited time leads along a motorable road uphill past the resthouse towards the edge of the evergreen forest. This road passes through moss-covered Brachystegia trees, then through alternating patches of plantation forest, boulder-strewn grassland and isolated stands of indigenous forest until it ends after about 3km. From here, a clear path leads into the forest, past tortuously shaped strangler figs, lush fern-bordered watercourses, trees studded with epiphytic orchids, tangled lianas and mossy rocks – a setting straight out of a Tarzan movie. The variety of habitats along this walk makes for excellent birdwatching – look out for red-throated twinspot, East African swee, starred robin and a variety of greenbuls, canaries and sunbirds, as well as baboons and red squirrels.

GETTING THERE AND AWAY The forest reserve is 120km from Lilongwe by road; a two-hour drive. From Lilongwe, take the M1 north past the airport to Mponela, then turn right onto the surfaced T350, which is signposted for Ntchisi Town. After

35km, shortly after passing Ntchisi Hospital, you reach a T-junction where you need to turn right onto a dirt road signposted for Dowa. After 10km, shortly after passing a radio transmitter, take the left turn signposted for Ntchisi Forest Lodge and follow this for 12km to Chintembwe, where you need to turn right onto a signposted road that brings you to the lodge after 4km. You should get through in a saloon car in the dry season, but a 4x4 might be necessary after rain. There is no public transport to the forest reserve, but the managers can arrange transfers from Lilongwe.

Upon leaving the forest reserve, travellers driving on to Kasungu or Nkhotakota must return to the T350 and continue north along it to the small but well-equipped highland town of Ntchisi. A well-maintained 30km dirt road connects Ntchisi to the M18, a recently surfaced road that runs for 125km between Kasungu (on the M1 between Lilongwe and Mzuzu) and Nkhotakota (on the lakeshore M5 between Salima and Mzuzu).

 WHERE TO STAY

Ntchisi Forest Lodge (5 rooms) m 099 9971748/9741967; e forestlodge@ntchisi.com; www.ntchisi.com. Situated immediately inside the forest reserve entrance near a forestry school, this old colonial homestead was built as a highland holiday retreat for District Commissioner John Canyon in 1914. It was later used as a Department of Forestry resthouse, & is now an idyllic private lodge offering sweeping views across to Lake Malawi. The 4 twin rooms & 1 family room are all en suite, & the stylish décor blends colonial & ethnic styles. The highly praised kitchen serves a mix of African & Western dishes using organic local produce, some of it sourced from the lodge's own permaculture garden. *US$115/190 sgl/dbl inc b/fast & 3-course dinner, with significant discounts for Malawi residents, US$7 pp camping.*

KASUNGU

The fifth-largest urban centre in Malawi, with a population estimated at 60,000, Kasungu is a chaotic one-street town offering anything and everything from the hardware stores and supermarkets that line the main road to the huge dusty market that sprawls behind it. Within Malawi, Kasungu District is best known as the birthplace of Hastings Banda, and the town remains a stronghold for the Malawi Congress Party once led by the former life president. Oddly enough, when former President Bingu wa Mutharika decided to evacuate the presidential palace in Lilongwe in 2005, on the grounds that it was haunted by evil spirits, he reputedly took up residence at Banda's former palace in Kasungu. Today, the M1 between Lilongwe and Mzuzu bypasses Kasungu, and most people drive past the town oblivious to its existence, which frankly is no great loss. However, it is the closest town to the famous Kamuzu Academy and the springboard for safaris into Kasungu National Park.

GETTING THERE AND AWAY Kasungu lies about 130km north of Lilongwe along the M1, 240km south of Mzuzu, and 125km west of the lakeshore port of Nkhotakota along the recently surfaced M18. All these roads are in good condition and the drive from Lilongwe typically takes about 90 minutes in a private vehicle. Most buses between Lilongwe and Mzuzu stop at Kasungu, and there are also direct minibuses costing US$4.50 from Lilongwe and US$7 from Mzuzu. Public transport along the quiet M18 is rather more limited, but a few minibuses run that way daily.

WHERE TO STAY AND EAT *See map, opposite.*

Chikho Hotel (29 rooms) 01 253844/5; m 088 2988440/099 5726124; e chikhohotel@ gmail.com. In finely manicured grounds at the southern junction with the M1, this shiny new

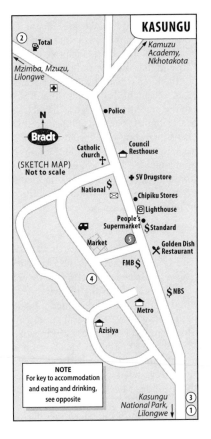

KASUNGU
For listings, see pages 246–7

Where to stay
1 Chikho Hotel
2 Kasungu Inn
3 Kasungu Lodge
4 Teja Resthouse

Where to eat and drink
5 Nyika Bakery

US$48/63 sgl/dbl, US$63/78 executive, all rates B&B.

Kasungu Inn ☎ 01 253306/151; m 099 9148305/088 8833974; e info@kasunguinn. com; www.kasunguinn.com. A short distance out of town along the Mzimba road, this long-serving hotel has large but slightly tired en-suite twin rooms with mosquito nets, DSTV, fan & hot showers. The executive rooms are sharper & have flatscreen TV & tea/coffee facilities. An exceedingly drab restaurant serves tasty meals for US$3.50–5 including the standard steak, chicken & fish. US$27/36 standard sgl/dbl, US$36/49 executive.

Kasungu Lodge ☎ 01 253387; m 099 9286097. Under the same management as Teja & marginally nicer, this place offers self-contained rooms near the southern junction to the M1. US$8/9.50 en-suite sgl/dbl, US$12.50/14 executive sgl/dbl with DSTV.

Teja Resthouse ☎ 01 253387; m 088 8337351. This is about the best of a few cheapies scattered around the bus station area. US$3.25/4.75 sgl/twin using common showers, US$4.75 en-suite dbl.

business-oriented hotel is Kasungu Town's most upmarket accommodation. Amenities include DSTV, Wi-Fi, swimming pool, & executive rooms have AC & jacuzzi tubs. The restaurant serves Indian & Chinese dishes, along with a variety of other mains in the US$4–6 range.

OTHER PRACTICALITIES There are a handful of banks along the main road, including **FMB**, **NBS**, and **Standard Bank**. The ATM at Standard Bank accepts Visa, Mastercard and Maestro, while the others are Visa-only. Ecclesiastically approved internet is available at the **Lighthouse Christian Centre** (⏱ 08.00–17.00 Mon–Fri, 08.00–16.00 Sat) at Mk5/min. **Golden Dish Restaurant** serves up reliable Malawian staples for US$3–4, and those planning to camp in the park can stock up at the well-provisioned **People's Supermarket** and **Nyika Bakery**.

WHAT TO SEE AND DO
Kamuzu Academy (☎ 01 259288/246/264; m 099 9964010; e academic@ka.ac. mw; www.kamuzuacademy.com) The self-styled 'Eton of Africa' may seem like a strange tourist attraction, but this enormous sprawling public school in the middle of nowhere is of considerable interest, not only for its own merits and facilities, but also for the amount of exploring that can be done in the surrounding area. It was

founded by President Banda in 1981, and the students (all Malawian, including scholarship students from remote villages) once wore a bizarre colonial uniform of shorts and a boater, and still learn Latin and Greek. The sports facilities are the best in Malawi, and attract athletes from all around the country, and the academic standard is also exceptional, thanks largely to the long-serving headmaster Frank Cooke, who was awarded an MBE in 2005. A recent birding group found 109 species in the school grounds, thanks partly to the presence of a large artificial lake in front of the main buildings. The school estate supports 6,000–8,000 people, and it even has a working farm, with 1,000 chickens providing eggs for all the pupils' breakfasts. The academy is easy enough to reach by minibus, about 30 minutes out of Kasungu along the M18 towards Nkhotakota. Guided visits to nearby tobacco estates can be arranged, while Chipata Mountain (just into Nkhotakota Game Reserve) is within striking distance by car. A resthouse in the grounds has three affordable en-suite bedrooms. Bookings must be made in advance.

KASUNGU NATIONAL PARK

(⏰ *Early–18.00 daily (entrance gate); entrance US$10 pp per day, US$3 per car*) This 2,316km² national park is the second largest in Malawi, protecting an area of Brachystegia woodland along the Zambian border west of Kasungu Town. It was established as a forest reserve on tsetse-infested land in 1922, designated a game reserve in 1930 and granted full national park status in 1970. Several rivers run through the park, the most significant of which are the Dwangwa and Lingadzi. Kasungu was once the most popular game-viewing destination in Malawi, and it still probably supports a greater variety of large mammals than any of the country's other protected areas, but populations have been devastated by poaching. General game viewing is poor by comparison with Liwonde, Majete, Nyika or Vwaza national parks, though recent clampdowns on poaching give some cause for future optimism, as does the planned opening of a fenced inner sanctuary (similar to those in Majete and Liwonde).

Kasungu was once the best place in Malawi to see black rhinoceros, but these are now locally extinct, along with cheetah. Elephants are still present, but a 2005 survey undertaken by the University of Pretoria suggested the population – once the largest in Malawi, topping the 1,000 mark – has dropped to around 150. And while you might hear the occasional roar of a lion, you will seldom see one. Leopard, genet and civet are more common. Recent sightings of African wild dog in the park are cause for excitement, though you'd be incredibly lucky to spot them. The park is still excellent terrain for elephants, however, with woodlands, grazing areas and Lake Lifupa in front of the lodge, where at least half the population will come down to drink twice a day in the dry season. Relatively common ungulates include Burchell's zebra, warthog, buffalo, puku, sable antelope, roan antelope, kudu, reedbuck and the very localised Lichtenstein's hartebeest.

Kasungu National Park offers a real unspoilt bush experience: it's a place to come and escape the rest of the world, be lulled to sleep by frogs and be woken by fish eagles. However, it's best to arrive without too many expectations of the wildlife, but rather to be content to enjoy the grunting and snorting of hippo, the calm sight of puku sitting in the sun and incredible flowers, including many orchids in the first months of rain. In addition to the wildlife, Kasungu boasts several prehistoric sites, including an iron-smelting kiln, rock paintings, the remains of fortified villages, and more than 300 bird species have been recorded. One of the loveliest views in Kasungu is from Black Rock, a hill to be climbed up where the whole of the park stretches endlessly before you, with hills behind hills as far as the eye can see. Best of all, the park is accessible in price both to backpackers and more comfort-loving creatures.

Lifupa Conservation Lodge runs morning game drives and night drives, the latter – seriously chilly in winter – offering the opportunity to see a variety of nocturnal predators. Activities range from US$6–50, including game drives, fishing, walking safaris, community visits & exploring the rock paintings. With a good map it is quite possible to drive around the park without a guide.

GETTING THERE AND AWAY The entrance gate lies 38km from Kasungu Town along the dirt S114, which is usually navigable in any vehicle. (In fact, the main danger along this road is not getting stuck so much as skidding off it!) Here you can also get a peek at Kamuzu's hillside former palace, but it's not open to the public. From the park entrance gate it's another 22km to Lifupa Conservation Lodge. Without private transport, it's best to take a taxi or moto-taxi from Kasungu Town, which will cost you about US$45 for a taxi or US$16 for a moto, though you will need to bargain. Lifupa Conservation Lodge can help arrange transport as well.

WHERE TO STAY *See map, page 242.*

Lifupa Conservation Lodge (22 rooms, 1 dorm) m 099 9768658; e info@lifupa.com; www.lifupa.com. Kasungu's only lodge has changed hands several times in recent years, but the ebullient new manager has big plans & is hopefully here to stay. Since taking over in 2012, they have lovingly set about restoring one of Malawi's most serene & secluded retreats. The lodge overlooks Kasuni Dam, which supports a number of hippo as well as attracting elephants & other animals coming to drink. The main lodge can sleep 35 people in 16 newly redecorated dbl & trpl thatched chalets, all with en-suite bathrooms & private balconies. There is also plenty of space in the campsite, where a few simple safari tents & bush huts overlook the lake, & there are common hot showers & a self-catering kitchen & dining area. All guests can use the lodge's attractive communal bar & dining area, with its dramatic thatched upper deck. The focus here is on sustainability, & they offer numerous volunteer programmes in conservation & anti-poaching, as well as partnerships with the local community & women's group. It has extremely tasty food, particularly famous for the delicious homemade jams & baked goods, as well as their vegetarian options. Game drives & guided walking safaris are offered, & there is a swimming pool in the works. *US$95 standard dbl B&B, US$155 superior trpl B&B, US$18 pp safari tents/bush hut, US$11 pp dorm bed, US$9 pp camping.*

MZIMBA

Situated at the western base of South Viphya about 100km from Mzuzu by road, Mzimba was the administrative centre of Northern Region in colonial days, but its significance has declined in recent years, following the emergence of Mzuzu as the capital of the north, and the construction of the new M1, which (unlike the old main north–south road) runs 15km to its east. Somewhat isolated today, this town of around 28,000 remains a stronghold of Ngoni culture, and it is still the capital of an eponymous district, the largest in Malawi at 10,430km². The plain around Mzimba, characterised by relatively poor soils and low rainfall, is an important centre of tobacco production, while plywood and other timber products from South Viphya are processed by the Raiply Plywood Company at Chikangawa, 15km to the east. Visited by few travellers, and lacking any obvious points of interest, Mzimba is a well-equipped and pleasant little town, and a potential springboard for public transport to Vwaza Marsh Wildlife Reserve (see page 307).

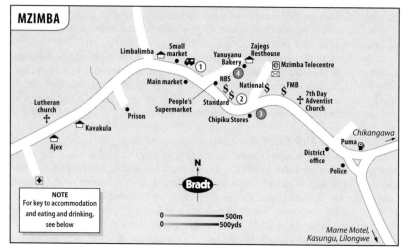

GETTING THERE AND AWAY So far as travel practicalities go, buses between Lilongwe and Mzuzu seldom divert to Mzimba, so it's probably easier to catch a direct minibus, which costs around US$4 from Mzuzu or US$7.25 from Lilongwe. If you are thinking of heading on to Vwaza Marsh, minibuses to Rumphi via Kazuni Camp leave when full in the morning, and there is also a daily bus, departing from Mzimba at about 14.00.

WHERE TO STAY AND EAT First choice has to be the **Mame Motel** (*40 rooms;* \ *01 342453/327*), which lies in attractive gardens about 1.5km from the town centre along the southern feeder road to the M1. It has a variety of rooms ranging from basic singles at US$5 to en-suite executive doubles with DSTV for US$25, and a restaurant serving the usual Malawian meals in the US$2.50–3.50 range. Camping is also possible at a negotiable rate. Cheaper options in the town centre include the **Kanjinga** and **Mbanasi guesthouses**, while good eateries include **Zungu Restaurant** and the **Donald & Tendai Restaurant**.

OTHER PRACTICALITIES There's a well-stocked **People's Supermarket** on the main road, internet for Mk5/min at **Mzimba Telecentre** (⊕ *07.30–17.00 Mon–Fri, 09.00–13.00 Sat*) behind the post office, and several banks with ATMs accepting Visa, including **NBS**, **FMB**, **National Bank** and **Standard Bank**, with the latter also accepting MasterCard and Maestro.

SOUTH VIPHYA FOREST RESERVE

Extending for some 90km south of Mzuzu, South Viphya is Malawi's second most extensive mountain range (after Nyika), including some 800km² of undulating plateau above the 1,600m contour, and with a highest point of 1,954m in the north.

Thinly settled in pre-colonial days, the crisp plateau supports a natural cover of montane grassland interspersed with evergreen forest, though today about 60% of its area is planted with exotic pines – reputedly the largest artificial forest in Africa – used to produce plywood and timber products at Chikangawa. The industry here is very visible, and you can expect to see a significant amount of logging and burning, particularly on the way to & from Mzuzu. Fortunately, an estimated 50km² of indigenous forest still remains, including large tracts of montane rainforest at Nthungwa, Chamambo and Kawandama, and smaller ribbons of riparian forest and mid-altitude forest elsewhere. There are also still expanses of more-or-less pristine montane grassland and marshy drainage channels, while the lower slopes support patches of Brachystegia woodland. The entire complex is protected in the well-managed South Viphya Forest Reserve, the largest such entity in Malawi at 1,150km².

South Viphya is wonderful walking terrain, and perhaps the best area in the country for mountain biking. There are two main bases for exploring: the award-winning Luwawa Forest Lodge, though inaccessible without private transport, is a very well-organised private set-up offering a superb range of amenities and activities, while the newly refurbished forestry resthouses at Kasito are cheaper and more accessible on public transport.

Whichever base you choose, the forests of South Viphya support a varied fauna, including the country's largest population of red duiker, along with yellow baboon, vervet monkey, bushbuck and the more elusive likes of bushpig and leopard. It's also of particular interest to birdwatchers, with more than 280 species recorded, including many localised forest species and several otherwise restricted to Nyika. Key birds associated with South Viphya include Denham's bustard, bar-tailed trogon, moustached green tinkerbird, Whyte's barbet, olive-flanked robin-chat, Fülleborn's boubou, Bertram's weaver, olive-headed weaver and yellow-crowned canary.

GETTING THERE AND AWAY Luwawa Forest Lodge lies to the east of the M1, a 10km drive on a rutted sandy road (in fact there are three access roads off the M1, two clearly signed; the better option depends on which direction you're coming from). With private transport, bank on a three- to four-hour drive from Lilongwe. Without private transport, you might call the lodge to see if there's a lift going, or ask for a bespoke transfer hike (*US$10 per person*) or hike the 8km on the D73 (branching off the M1).

Far more accessible are the resthouse and lodge at Kasito, which lie 500m apart on opposite sides of the M1 about 25km north of the junction for Mzimba and 4km

LUWAWA INTERNATIONAL CHARITY MOUNTAIN BIKE MARATHON

The annual Luwawa International Charity Mountain Bike Marathon has taken place every June since the inaugural event in 2004. The race starts at Kasito Lodge, Chikangawa, and finishes 42km later at Luwawa Forest Lodge. Bikers hurtle along the M1 through the South Viphya Forest Reserve on good dirt roads, passing through pristine indigenous Brachystegia woodland over the Viphya Mountain ridge road to Luwawa Dam. Beautiful scenery lines the well-marked tracks up and down remote hills, taking in the biggest pine forest in Africa. Cyclists are encouraged to enter the race sponsored in aid of local charities and particularly the Luwawa Environmental Trust. The nominal entrance fee includes course marshalling, vehicle backup and first-aid support. For enquiries, contact Luwawa Forest Lodge (*www. luwawaforestlodge.com*).

15

south of Chikangawa. Using public transport, any minibus or country bus running along the M1 towards Mzuzu can drop you at Kasito bus stage, which lies directly opposite Kasito Resthouse and 500m from Kasito Lodge. When you're ready to leave, you may find buses are reluctant to pick up passengers at the Kasito bus stage. It's better to walk about 1km up the M1 towards Mzimba and wait at Macdonald's bus stage (named after a Scottish forestry officer who camped on the site for several years in the colonial era). To pick up an express bus, it's best to walk the 4km to Chikangawa.

 WHERE TO STAY *See map, page 242.*

Moderate and camping

🏠 **Luwawa Forest Lodge** (6 rooms, 1 dorm) 📞01 342333; m 099 9512645; e luwawa@ malawi.net; www.luwawaforestlodge.com. The winner of the 2008 Community Development Work & Sustainable Tourism award, this upgraded forestry resthouse overlooking Luwawa Dam was originally built as a clubhouse for road engineers in 1984 & was privatised under the present owner-manager in 1998. It is a wonderful base for exploring the plateau, with several walking trails in the immediate vicinity & a daunting range of activities on offer, ranging from ecotourist visits to the Tumbuka village of Donija Nkhoma to abseiling, rowing, mountain biking or just relaxing in the sauna (options elaborated upon on the detailed website). The welcome is warm (not only that, there's often a fire in the hearth) & the food is very tasty, with mains costing US$10 & 3-course meals US$20. Accommodation ranges from spacious en-suite chalets with hot bath &

smaller rooms using shared facilities to a 14-bed dorm & a campsite. *US$60 pp B&B en-suite chalet, US$45 pp dbl with shared facilities, US$14 pp dorm, US$7 pp camping.*

Budget

🏠 **Kasito Lodge** (4 rooms) 📞01 11994266; m 099 9377069; e francois.hudson@cplmalawi. com; www.cplmalawi.mw. Set in terraced grounds alongside the main road to Mzuzu, this old-fashioned forestry lodge was in the process of partnering with Citrefine Plantations, an essential oils producer, to take over management of the lodge in early 2013. It's not yet clear what sort of facilities will be on offer, but it's a charming area & there are plenty of walking opportunities in the surrounding hills. Volunteer opportunities with the plantation & a number of social development programmes they sponsor are already available, & there are further details on their informative website.

WHAT TO SEE AND DO Luwawa Forest Lodge is run by outdoor and environmental enthusiasts, so if you stay here you might find yourself doing anything from visiting any of the seven village projects (and taking part) or hiking, abseiling, rock climbing, mountain biking, sailing, canoeing and orienteering (there's suitable equipment for hire). The forest walks and birding are very rewarding and montane grassland is also accessible. Fishing on the dam is permitted in season. Surprisingly there's squash, table tennis, volleyball, sailing, canoeing, forest fitness courses and 4x4 challenges as well. Of all this though, Luwawa is best known for its mountain biking, and the lodge has developed a three-day mountain-bike safari to Lake Malawi (a bit longer by foot). For more details see their website.

It requires more initiative to explore from Kasito, but the possibilities are endless. From the garden of Kasito Lodge, you can follow a clear path to the base of the valley and over a small stream, where, after about 200m, it connects with a disused road. Turn left into this road, and after perhaps 2km, passing through plantation forest and dense undergrowth, rich in butterflies and notable for several immense communal webs built by a type of spider with a bright purple body the size of a thumb, you should come to a five-point junction. Take the first left downhill into a thick patch of indigenous forest which can be extremely good for birds: among the more interesting species I saw here were olive-bellied mountain bulbul, Fülleborn's black boubou and golden weaver. The middle path meanders to Kasito Dam, an attractive spot set in a pine plantation, and reasonably rewarding for birds. It takes about 15 minutes to walk from the junction to the dam, and once there you can follow a track past the dam for another ten minutes or so to reach the M1, where a left turn will take you back to the lodge. Wozi Hill is also off this junction by only a couple of kilometres, from where you will have views over the whole area. Also worth a look is the riverine forest which runs along a stream about 100m west of the M1 towards Chikangawa. There are several side roads off the M1 in this area which you could explore.

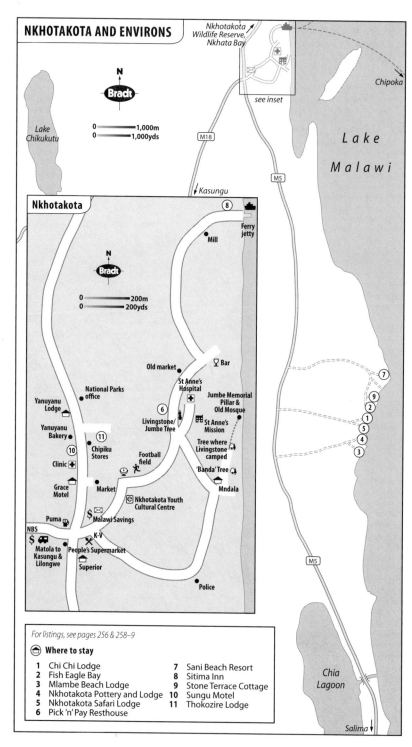

NKHOTAKOTA AND ENVIRONS

N

Bradt

Nkhotakota
Wildlife Reserve,
Nkhata Bay

see inset

Chipoka

*Lake
Chikukutu*

0 — 1,000m
0 — 1,000yds

M18

M5

L a k e

M a l a w i

↓*Kasungu*

Nkhotakota

8

Mill

Ferry
jetty

N

Bradt

0 — 200m
0 — 200yds

Old market

🍷 Bar

St Anne's
Hospital

National Parks
office

6

Jumbe Memorial
Pillar &
Old Mosque

Yanuyanu
Lodge

Livingstone/
Jumbe Tree

St Anne's
Mission

Yanuyanu
Bakery

11

Tree where
Livingstone
camped

10

Chipiku
Stores

Football
field

'Banda' Tree

Clinic

Mndala

Grace
Motel

Market

Nkhotakota Youth
Cultural Centre

Puma

Malawi Savings

NBS

K-V

Matola to
Kasungu &
Lilongwe

People's Supermarket

Superior

Police

M5

7
9
2
1
5
4
3

*Chia
Lagoon*

Salima ↓

For listings, see pages 256 & 258–9

Where to stay

1 Chi Chi Lodge
2 Fish Eagle Bay
3 Mlambe Beach Lodge
4 Nkhotakota Pottery and Lodge
5 Nkhotakota Safari Lodge
6 Pick 'n' Pay Resthouse
7 Sani Beach Resort
8 Sitima Inn
9 Stone Terrace Cottage
10 Sungu Motel
11 Thokozire Lodge

16

Nkhotakota and Surrounds

Nkhotakota is a town of considerable historical note. For much of the 19th century, it was the busiest slave-trading centre on Lake Malawi, presided over by the legendary Jumbe dynasty, and it is still sometimes described as the largest traditional market village in sub-equatorial Africa, a somewhat mysterious label, as the modern market, though well stocked, is thankfully quite unexceptional. An eponymous district capital, Nkhotakota today supports a population of 35,000, making it the ninth-largest town and second-largest port in Malawi. It is also an important transport hub, serviced by the MV *Ilala* and situated at the strategic intersection of the lakeshore M5 and the M18 to Lilongwe and Kasungu.

Like many other settlements in Malawi, Nkhotakota is a town of two halves. The older quarter, close to the lakeshore, is studded with relics of its infamous past, and it retains a strong and ancient Islamic presence, despite housing the old mission church. The main commercial centre of Nkhotakota, which straddles the M5 about 1km further inland, is the site of several lodges, banks and supermarkets, as well as the post office, new market and internet facilities. A tree-shaded avenue, planted in the slaving era, connects the M5 to the old quarter, from where a newly surfaced road leads for 1km to the ferry jetty used by the MV *Ilala*.

Nkhotakota itself is probably less often visited by travellers than the string of excellent resorts that runs along the lakeshore starting about 10km further south. The town also lends its name to Nkhotakota Wildlife Reserve, a little-known tract of mountainous wilderness, now home to two of Malawi's finest wilderness lodges.

HISTORY

The slave trade at Nkhotakota – then known as Kota Kota – was established in the 1840s by Jumbe Salim bin Abdullah, a Zanzibari trader of mixed Arab and African descent. Jumbe settled at Nkhotakota and went on to found an Islamic dynasty that ruled the area for several generations (indeed, one of his descendants still served as the local chief at the end of World War II). And by the 1850s, Nkhotakota had become the main terminus from which as many as 20,000 slaves annually were shipped across the lake from present-day Malawi to the Indian Ocean port of Kilwa Kivinje (in Tanzania).

In 1861, Livingstone became possibly the first European to reach Nkhotakota, and he described the area as 'an abode of lawlessness and bloodshed ... literally strewed with human bones and putrid bodies'. Livingstone returned to Nkhotakota in September 1863, hoping to convince the incumbent Jumbe ruler to abandon the trade in slaves. Though the two men engaged in a lengthy meeting, Livingstone's efforts were in vain, and the slave trade out of Nkhotakota continued into the 1890s, when Commissioner Harry Johnston persuaded the ageing Jumbe to sign a treaty in exchange for British protection.

GETTING THERE AND AWAY

Nkhotakota lies on the surfaced and well-maintained M5 about 200km south of Nkhata Bay and 110km north of Salima. It is connected to Kasungu, 125km to the west, by the recently surfaced M18, which also forms part of the most direct route to Lilongwe, a 200km run along the M7 via Ntchisi, of which only the 30km stretch immediately north of Ntchisi is unsurfaced. There is plenty of public transport in all directions: all buses between Nkhata Bay and Salima stop at Nkhotakota, and there are regular minibuses to Chintheche, Salima, Kasungu and Ntchisi (where you can change for Lilongwe).

Nkhotakota is the last port of call for northbound lake steamers before they cross to Likoma Island; see the schedule on page 271.

TOURIST INFORMATION

The **District Assembly** runs a useful website (*www.nkhotakota.com*). The **National Parks & Wildlife Office** on the M5 north of the main junction is a good source of information about Nkhotakota Wildlife Reserve (◥ *01 292464;* m *099 9921032*).

 ## WHERE TO STAY AND EAT *See map, page 254.*

Accommodation in Nkhotakota Town is generally on the basic side, the exception being the characterful Sitima Inn, and most visitors stay at one of the beach resorts south of town (see page 258).

MODERATE

⌂ **Sitima Inn** (9 rooms) m 099 9260005; e sitimainn@gmail.com; www.sitimainn.com. This inimitable owner-managed lodge, only 100m from the ferry jetty, was built by a district commissioner in the 1960s & has since served as an orphanage, school & government resthouse. Privatised in 2008, it's an intriguing building, boasting an Art Deco façade & an extraordinary assortment of car doors, ship parts & hospital beds built right into the walls. The gloriously breezy upstairs Crow's Nest Bar has a good view over the jetty, & the ground-floor Captain's Table Restaurant serves an eclectic selection of mains – seafood, steaks, vegetarian, sometimes even crocodile meat – for US$4–8. *US$80 en-suite dbl with AC, US$45/60 en-suite sgl/twin with AC, US$30/40 sgl/twin using common showers, US$10 pp 4-bed dorm, all rates excluding b/fast.*

BUDGET

⌂ **Sungu Motel** (12 rooms) m 088 8562684. Situated on the M5, this adequate overpriced hotel has decent en-suite rooms with TV, fan & net, & a bar & restaurant is attached. The nearby **Grace Motel** is similar if it's full. *US$19 dbl.*

⌂ **Thokozire Lodge** (10 rooms) m 099 6609484/088 2348633. Tucked just metres off the M5, this new local lodge is significantly better value than its competitors on the main road. Rooms are freshly painted & clean, with fan, net & en-suite hot shower. There's no restaurant, but you can easily get meals nearby. *US$6.50 en-suite dbl.*

SHOESTRING

⌂ **Pick 'n' Pay Resthouse** (27 rooms) ◥ 01 292359; m 099 1356762/088 1746557. Situated in the old quarter, this stalwart lodge has been popular with travellers for years, & it remains the pick of the cheapies. There is an annex off the M5 near the market. *US$2.25/3.25 sgl/dbl, US$4.75/6.25 en-suite sgl/dbl with net & fan.*

SHOPPING

There is a good **People's Supermarket** on the main junction, and a busy **market** about 300m further north along the M5. The **Yanuyanu Bakery** bakes fresh bread daily. There are no craft shops or stalls.

OTHER PRACTICALITIES

FOREIGN EXCHANGE AND BANKING On opposite sides of the main M5/M18 junction, **Malawi Savings Bank** and **NBS** both have ATMs accepting Visa and forex facilities.

INTERNET The **Nkhotakota Youth Cultural Centre** (✆ 01 292284; m 099 1761365; ⊕ 07.30–18.00 Mon–Fri, 08.00–16.00 Sat, 14.00–17.00 Sun) is on the right of the main road from the M5 to the old quarter, this ambitious community centre runs an internet café charging Mk10 per minute, with proceeds funding music, art, sports, and cultural events for local youth. There are occasional concerts and film screenings, and a newly-opened restaurant. You can keep track of upcoming events at their website, www.facebook.com/NkhotakotaCulturalCentre.

WHAT TO SEE AND DO

Several national monuments are dotted around Nkhotakota, the most significant and easy to find being the **St Anne's Mission** compound in the old quarter of town. The old Anglican church, built in 1894, is still there, hosting services in Chichewa every Sunday morning, and the adjacent **St Anne's Hospital** celebrated its centenary in 2002. The '**magnificent fig tree**' under which Jumbe and Livingstone met is still standing in the mission compound, which is also the burial place of Chauncy Maples, the first bishop of Likoma.

A cluster of more arcane antiquities can be reached by taking the surfaced road that runs southeast from St Anne's for 400m, then instead of following the tar as it veers to the right, continuing straight along a rutted dirt road for about 50m, and turning left immediately after you pass the **Mndala Resthouse**. About 200m further, to the right, stands the **shady tree** under which Dr Hastings Banda held his first convention in 1960. Another 150m will bring you to the tree where, in 1863, according to the plaque, Livingstone 'sailed through Kaweya to meet Chief Malenga Chanzi, and gave him an umbrella'. From here, a 300m footpath leads to the solitary surviving wall of **Bondo Mosque**, part of Chief Jumbe's lakeshore headquarters from 1860 to 1890.

BEACHES SOUTH OF NKHOTAKOTA

A cluster of mid-range and budget lodges and resorts runs along a beautiful stretch of lakeshore 3–5km east of the M5 and accessible from it along a series of junctions that are clearly signposted between 11km and 15km south of Nkhotakota Town. These resorts include the highly regarded Nkhotakota Pottery Lodge and associated Nkhotakota Safari Lodge, the newer Fish Eagle Bay, and a few cheaper options, of which the established Sani Beach Resort stands out. These days, this cluster of resorts is a more important tourist focus than Nkhotakota Town but do note that while the resorts lie within about 2km of each other, they are not all mutually accessible by road, so make sure you take the correct turn off.

16

Another 10km south of the last turn-off to these beach lodges, the M5 crosses a bridge over what must surely be a contender for the world's shortest river. This is the Chia River, a wide papyrus-lined channel that runs for about 700m between Lake Malawi and the Chia Lagoon. About 7km long and 2km wide, the lagoon is an important source of fish locally, and it reputedly supports a dense population of crocodiles. If you're driving, it's worth getting out at the bridge, as there is quite a bit of birdlife around. Good views over the lagoon can also be obtained from the secondary school on the right side of the M5 about 2km before the bridge, coming from Nkhotakota.

WHERE TO STAY   *See map, page 254.*

Moderate

Fish Eagle Bay (10 rooms) m 088 8853962/099 9331134; e fisheaglebay@gmail.com; www.fisheaglebay.com. This smart resort is the archetypal tropical beach idyll, set on a brilliant white palm-fringed stretch of sand some 6km from the M5 along a dirt road signposted from Sani village, 11km south of Nkhotakota. Accommodation is in simple but very attractive rondavels with whitewashed exterior, thatched roof, wooden doors & frames, 1 dbl & 1 sgl bed, nets, en-suite hot showers & natural ventilation supplied by the lake breeze. Meals cost around US$5. A wide range of aquatic activities are on offer, including kayaking, sailing, waterskiing & windsurfing. *US$35/52 sgl/dbl B&B, US$105 self-catering family cottage, US$10 pp camping.*

Mlambe Beach Lodge (10 rooms) ☏ 01 292622; m 099 5124428; e fluxdrikus@yahoo.com. Situated 800m south of Nkhotakota Pottery & reached along the same road, this pleasant but unremarkable lodge offers accommodation in small, neat twin or dbl en-suite rooms with net, fan & handmade Malawian furnishings. There are also several en-suite chalets sleeping up to 8, a campsite & a restaurant that was under renovation when we looked in. Overpriced. *US$28.50/57 sgl/dbl, US$81 deluxe chalet, US$8 pp camping.*

Nkhotakota Pottery and Lodge (13 rooms) ☏ 01 903192; m 099 9380105/088 4581098; e nkhotakotapottery@africa-online.net; www.nyasalodges.com. This well-established lodge is 5mins' walk from the co-managed Nkhotakota Safari Lodge, but 9km by car, along a dirt road signposted from the M5 almost 15km south of Nkhotakota Town. The en-suite rooms have nets, fans, minibar & mains electricity, & there are also 3 basic rooms using common showers. The restaurant & range of excursions are similar to the neighbouring safari lodge, &

you can also use the pottery workshop, which is fully equipped with electric & foot-driven potters' wheels & offers raku & electric-kiln firing. Better still, if you're keen on learning more about pottery, sign up for an all-inclusive w/end. *US$32/44/48 standard sgl/dbl/trpl, US$40/54/60 superior, US$4 pp camping, rates exc b/fast.*

Nkhotakota Safari Lodge (10 rooms) ☏ 01 903192; m 099 9380105/088 4581098; e nkhotakotapottery@africa-online.net; www.nyasalodges.com. Under the same management as the neighbouring Nkhotakota Pottery, this attractive lakeshore lodge has standard thatched rondavels with en-suite hot showers, nets, minibar, mains electricity & safe, & there are larger deluxe chalets with balconies. An excellent lakefront restaurant/bar serves Western-style mains for around US$7–10, as well as snacks & coffee. The main attraction here is the splendid private swimming beach, but the lodge also offers boat rides, guided walking safaris into the nearby Nkhotakota Game Reserve, historical tours of Nkhotakota Town, & pottery courses at the adjacent Nkhotakota Pottery. It lies 3.8km east of the M5 along a dirt road signposted 13km south of Nkhotakota Town. *US$32/44/48 standard sgl/dbl/trpl, US$51/62/75 deluxe, US$4 pp camping, rates exc b/fast.*

Budget and camping

Chi Chi Lodge (8 rooms) m 088 8334440; e chokothobansiley@yahoo.com. This unassuming new lodge is about 13km south of Nkhotakota Town on the same road as Nkhotakota Safari Lodge. It's on a lovely stretch of beach, & has en-suite dbl rooms with AC, DSTV, nets, fans & some really ostentatious headboards. It's a bit sterile but very pleasant, & there's a restaurant/bar on site serving up mains for US$4.50, with burgers & snacks for less. *US$32 dbl.*

Sani Beach Resort (10 rooms, 4 dorms)
m 099 9601482/088 8334454; e sani_beach_
resort@hotmail.com. The owner-managed Sani
Beach Resort has an attractive location on a rocky
peninsula fringed by sandy beaches, about 5km
from the M5 along the same road as Fish Eagle
Bay. It's looking a bit sleepy these days, but is still
the best budget option in this part of Malawi. The
rustic restaurant/bar has a great location atop a
big black rock, but it suffered a fire in late 2012
& was being rebuilt at the time of writing. In the
meantime, simple meals are available on request
for US$4. The accommodation & campsite are
set among a grove of fig trees high on the beach.
The en-suite dbl chalets, twin bungalows using
common showers & 4-bed dorms are all simply
furnished but clean, & come with nets. *US$12.50
twin/dbl, US$19 en-suite twin/dbl, US$6.50 pp
dorm, US$3.25 pp camping.*

Stone Terrace Cottage (8 rooms) m 099
9476755/088 8836854. Situated between Fish
Eagle Bay & Sani Beach, this place has a truly
wonderful setting on a rocky promontory adjacent
to a great swimming beach, & the beach bar
would take full advantage of this, if it were open.
Unfortunately it all seems a bit forlorn these days,
& the accommodation isn't particularly compelling
as the bedrooms are all in the monolithic main
building, lack of any sea view, & the décor is
decidedly outmoded. Still, the staff are warm &
helpful, & they can help prepare meals. Adequate
value. *US$12.50/19 sgl/dbl.*

NKHOTAKOTA WILDLIFE RESERVE

(⊕ *Early–18.00 daily (entrance gate); entrance US$10/7 pp per day for foreigners/
residents. Self-drivers must also pay US$3 per car per day.*) In the scenic well-watered
Rift Valley Escarpment west of Nkhotakota Town, this is the oldest wildlife reserve
in Malawi, and one of the country's largest conservation areas, extending over some
1,800km². The rugged terrain spans altitudes of 500m in the east to 1,638m at the
peak of Mount Chipata, and it is intersected by the Bua, Kaombe and Dwangwa
rivers. The reserve sprawls either side of a 30km stretch of the recently surfaced
M18 between Nkhotakota and Kasungu, and yet it was almost totally undeveloped
for tourism until the opening of two excellent tourist lodges overlooking the Bua
River (see *Where to stay*, overleaf) in 2010.

This pristine bush, with a dominant vegetation cover of Brachystegia woodland,
harbours a rich diversity of mammals, most visibly warthog, bushbuck, vervet
monkey and yellow baboon, but also elephant, buffalo, eland, sable antelope,
greater kudu, lion, leopard and spotted hyena. Indeed, Nkhotakota Wildlife
Reserve probably supports the country's last viable lion population, estimated
to stand at around 45–50, as well as the largest number of elephants, though a
recent game count suggests that this may have dropped from an estimated 1,700
in 1998 to between 1,000 and 1,500 today. The undulating terrain and thick
vegetation of Nkhotakota Wildlife Reserve can make animal spotting difficult, but
it has also probably helped curb poaching in an area that is under constant risk of
encroachment from surrounding villages.

Brachystegia woodland aside, the highlands are dominated by *julbenadia* species,
and the top of Chipata Mountain supports around 44ha of montane forest, where
there are huge 80m-tall trees that ten people with their arms outstretched can scarcely
reach around. Forest mammals include blue and vervet monkeys, and such secretive
nocturnal creatures as leopard and bushpig. At lower altitudes, riverine forests include
the impressive raffia palms and the large *Adina microsofala* and other fruiting trees, as
well as rare epiphytic orchids. Hot springs occur near to the Bua River.

More than 280 bird species have been recorded in the varied habitats of Nkhotakota
Wildlife Reserve, a number that will likely increase with further exploration.
Raptors are especially well represented and include palmnut vulture, martial eagle,
black-breasted snake eagles and gymnogene. It is also an important stronghold for

16

Brachystegia species such as pale-billed hornbill, Whyte's barbet, *miombo* pied barbet, white-headed black chat and olive-headed weaver. The evergreen forest on Mount Chipata protects a variety of unusual birds, notably moustached green tinkerbird, starred robin, yellow-streaked bulbul and grey-olive bulbul.

Aside from the M18, where you are bound to see baboons, and a few other rough tracks, the reserve has a limited road network, and is best explored on foot. Do, however, resist any temptation to get out of your vehicle and walk for miles without a game ranger, as it is both dangerous and illegal. Hitching or cycling along the M18 is also inadvisable; one roadside epitaph tells of the death of a woman taken from her bicycle by a lion. It's far more sensible to visit on a guided walk, as detailed below.

GETTING THERE AND AWAY Access from the lakeside M5 road is via a clearly signposted turn-off 12km north of Nkhotakota Town, and 800m north of Lozi trading centre. From here, it is about 8km to the entrance gate, and a further 2km to Bua River Lodge. For Tongole Wilderness Lodge, continue straight along this dirt road until you come to a junction within the reserve. Turn left here, and after 22km, mostly uphill, you will drive into camp. There are signposts within the reserve, but they're easy to miss. A 4x4 or strong pickup is advisable for both camps, but a saloon car should be able to reach Bua River Lodge in the dry season.

For those without their own transport, both lodges will arrange pickups from Nkhotakota Town, or alternatively you can take a minibus to Lozi trading centre, then hire a bicycle taxi to the entrance gate/Bua River Lodge for about US$2.

Several of the lakeside lodges can organise trips into the reserve, most reliably Nkhotakota Pottery and Lodge, and Nkhotakota Safari Lodge (see page 258). They will arrange for the game rangers from Parks and Wildlife to accompany you. The National Parks and Wildlife office in Nkhotakota will also assist, but they do not have transport (see page 256 for contact details).

Chipata Camp, in the southwest of the reserve, is best accessed from the M18 halfway between Kasungu and Nkhotakota – watch out for the memorial marking the spot where an unfortunate woman was caught and eaten by a lion in 2002. Chipata Camp is 7km from the main road along a rough track.

WHERE TO STAY *See map, page 242.*
Exclusive

🏠 **Tongole Wilderness Lodge** (10 rooms)
📞 (UK) +44 (0) 20 8123 0301; m 099 1337681;
e reservations@tongole.com; www.tongole.com;
see also advert, opposite. Opened in April 2011,
this luxury eco-lodge lies deep within the reserve
at the confluence of the Bua & Kachenga rivers &
has quickly established itself as one of the finest
lodges anywhere in Malawi. Solar-powered & built
from locally sourced materials, this family-run lodge
prides itself on its sustainability & involvement in
a number of community & conservation initiatives.
The open-fronted thatched chalets are tastefully
decorated with wood, marble & wrought iron, &
have king-size beds, walk-in nets, tub, shower &
large private balconies overlooking the river. They
offer a wide range of activities, including walking
safaris, game drives, canoe safaris, fishing trips,

bush dinners, cultural tours & visits to prehistoric
rock-art sites. Guests can eat & relax in the great hall
or any of the staggered balconies surrounding it,
& opportunities for mammal & birdwatching from
the vertigo-inducing observation deck are fantastic.
Staff occasionally put on a refreshingly casual drum
& dance performance & there are nightly campfires.
US$345/275 pp high/low season, all-inclusive.

Upmarket, moderate, budget and camping

🏠 **Bua River Lodge** (6 rooms, 1 under
construction) m 099 5476887; e buariverlodge@
gmail.com; www.buariverlodge.com; see also
advert, opposite. Spanning either side of the
Bua River, this secluded new camp offers superb
safari tent accommodation suited to a variety of
budgets. Connected by a network of paths along

the wooded riverbank, the en-suite tents are all pitched on wooden decks with thatched shades, open-air showers & viewing decks overlooking the river. The spacious luxury tents set on an island mid-river are especially private, while the captivating multi-level restaurant/lounge on the opposite bank is the centrepiece. There are also campsites & backpacker rooms with flush toilets & hot showers, a shaded relaxation deck, plus kitchen & BBQ facilities for self-catering. Activities on offer include game walks & drives, fishing, birding, climbing Chipata Mountain & overnight camping safaris that explore remote & little-visited areas of the reserve. Most room rates are full board, but campers & backpackers are welcome to eat at the restaurant for around US$10–20. *US$125–150 pp island FB, US$85–100 pp standard FB, US$125 6-bed self-catering cottage, US$15 sgl/ dbl backpacker room, US$7.50 pp camping.*

Ă Chipata Camp \01 292464; m 099 9921032. This is a bush campsite with a toilet & shower block but no other facilities. It is refreshing to be somewhere so completely undeveloped & to be completely on your own in the bush with no-one looking after you. For further details & to confirm availability of camping space, talk to the National Parks & Wildlife office in Nkhotakota Town. *US$5 pp.*

BUA RIVER LODGE
NKHOTAKOTA WILDLIFE RESERVE
www.buariverlodge.com

Guided wilderness walking safaris
Overnight fly-camping safaris
Excellent birding and fishing
Relaxation guaranteed

Luxurious, secluded, full-board riverside accommodation
Great food and excellent service
Integral camp site with hot showers
Idyllic location

+265 (0)995476887
buariverlodge@gmail.com

Four Luxury Riverside Rooms

Hiking, Canoeing, Fishing, Camping, & Fly Camping

Breathtaking Miombo Woodland

+265 (0) 99 133 7681
+44 (0) 208 123 0301

INFO@TONGOLE.COM
RESERVATIONS@TONGOLE.COM

WWW.TONGOLE.COM

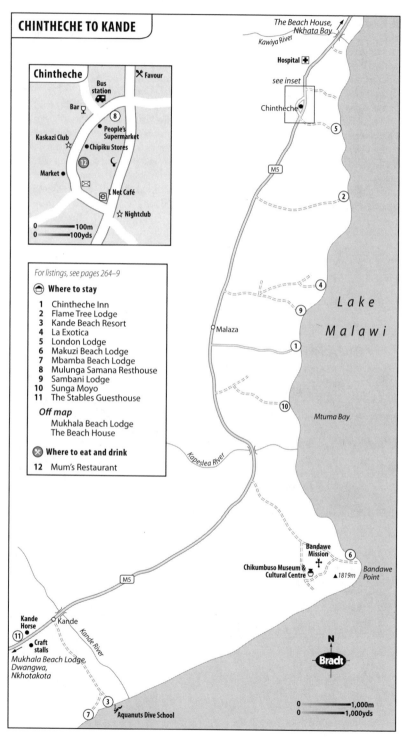

CHINTHECHE TO KANDE

The Beach House,
Nkhata Bay

Kawiya River

Hospital ✚

see inset

Chintheche ●

M5

② ●

Lake

Malawi

Malaza ○

①

⑩

Mtuma Bay

Kapeslea River

Bandawe
Mission ✝ ⑥

Chikumbuso Museum &
Cultural Centre ☖ ▲1819m

Bandawe
Point

M5

Kande
Horse ●
⑪ ○ Kande

● Craft
stalls

Kande River

Mukhala Beach Lodge,
Dwangwa,
Nkhotakota

N

Bradt

0 ————— 1,000m
0 ————— 1,000yds

③ ●
⑦ ○ ● Aquanuts Dive School

Chintheche

✗ Favour

Bus
station 🚌

Bar 🍷

⑧

● People's
Supermarket

Kaskazi Club
☆

● Chipiku Stores

⑫ ☽

Market ●

✉

🖃 ┗ Net Café

☆ Nightclub

0 ————— 100m
0 ————— 100yds

For listings, see pages 264–9

🛏 **Where to stay**

1 Chintheche Inn
2 Flame Tree Lodge
3 Kande Beach Resort
4 La Exotica
5 London Lodge
6 Makuzi Beach Lodge
7 Mbamba Beach Lodge
8 Mulunga Samana Resthouse
9 Sambani Lodge
10 Sunga Moyo
11 The Stables Guesthouse

Off map
   Mukhala Beach Lodge
   The Beach House

✖ **Where to eat and drink**

12 Mum's Restaurant

17

The Lakeshore from Dwangwa to Chintheche

The 198km stretch of the lakeshore M5 between Nkhotakota and Nkhata Bay passes through few towns of note, the most significant being Dwangwa and Chintheche, respectively about 50km north of Nkhotakota and 40km south of Nkhata Bay. But the beaches along this stretch of the lake are close to paradise, with its perfect arcs of white sand punctuated by jagged rocky outcrops, patches of Brachystegia woodland, and even some remnant forest. The area hosts several legendary beach resorts, from the overlanders' Mecca that is Kande Beach Lodge to the more upmarket and sedate likes of Chintheche Inn, Ngala Beach Lodge and Makuzi Beach Lodge. Chintheche and Kande also lie on the widest part of the lake, and here more than anywhere in Malawi, with the Mozambican shore an indistinct blur on the horizon or invisible altogether, it is easy to be lulled into the feeling you are at the ocean.

DWANGWA

The M5 north of Nkhotakota runs parallel to the lakeshore, but seldom in view of it, for about 50km before it skirts the Bana Swamp and crosses the Dwangwa River to reach Dwangwa trading centre. Satellite to the Illovo Sugar Estate that sprawls from it in all directions, Dwangwa is an odd little place, thick with the clinging odour of molasses, and emphatically lacking in aesthetic appeal. In terms of facilities, Dwangwa has ATMs from Standard Bank, FNB and NBS, a few grocery shops and identikit resthouses along the main road, and is the one reliable opportunity to fuel up between Nkhotakota and Chintheche. A more inviting prospect, 15km north of town, is the beautifully renovated Ngala Beach Lodge, now one of the country's top lakeshore resorts. And for self-drivers, the new M5 Restaurant, 20km north of town, is a great place to break for a meal.

 WHERE TO STAY *See map, page 242.*
Upmarket
🏠 **Ngala Beach Lodge** (14 rooms) m 088 8192003/099 9340369; e info@ngalabeach.com; www.ngalabeach.com. On a promontory about halfway between Dwangwa & the Dwambazi River mouth, this attractive lodge lies in flowering gardens flanked by 2 secluded private beaches about 400m from the M5. The owner-managers have recently implemented an extensive programme of upgrades, including a swimming pool & wheelchair-friendly ramps. The stylishly renovated rooms are in semi-detached thatched cottages, have a spacious open-plan split-level layout, & come with twin or king-size beds, wooden furnishings, fan, private balcony & en-suite hot shower. The beach is good for swimming, & the gourmet restaurant in the thatched communal area charges around US$6–10 for mains (Wed is pizza night). The managers can arrange day trips to Kande for horserides or diving, as well as access to the golf course at the sugar estate. It's worth noting that its north-facing location means it is spared the worst of the gales in the windy season. *US$ 100/140 sgl/dbl executive room, US$100/160*

A-frame B&B, discounts for residents, US$5 pp camping in a large lakeshore campsite.

Moderate

🏠 **Kasasa Club** 📞 01 295266. Situated on the Illovo Sugar Estate, this sports club has a golf course, swimming pool & attractive clubhouse with DSTV, bar & restaurant. Although the club is aimed primarily at estate workers, visitors are welcome to stay in one of the pleasant en-suite chalets in the grounds. In theory, you should book in advance, but the chalets are rarely full. To get to the club, take the left turn next to the filling station about 1km south of the town centre, & follow it for 3km. *US$33 pp.*

Budget

🏠 **Kataya Lodge** (24 rooms) 📱 088 8307698/1435750; e info@katayalodge.com; www.katayalodge.com. Situated alongside Ngala, this neat local lodge is on a great swimming beach, with a casual restaurant/bar offering meals between US$4–6. The simple whitewashed rooms all have en-suite hot showers, nets, fans & coffee/tea facilities, while executive rooms have AC & lake views. Good value, but it's worth springing for a beachside executive room. *US$23.50/26.50 sgl/dbl, US$26.50/31.50 executive sgl/dbl, all rates B&B.*

KANDE

On the face of it, there's little to distinguish Kande, which straddles the M5 about 75km north of Dwangwa, from hundreds of other similarly nondescript roadside villages scattered around Malawi. However, the name of this humble village has been immortalised in overland truck circles thanks to the enduring popularity of Kande Beach Resort, situated at the end of a 2.5km dirt road that leads southeast from the M5 to the lakeshore. Since its foundation in the early 1990s, Kande Beach Resort has been Lake Malawi's most consistently busy overland truck stop, on account of its lovely location, hands-on management and easy-going party atmosphere. The Kande area is also a fabulous centre for outdoor enthusiasts, being home to the country's top commercial stable, along with the highly regarded Aquanuts Dive School, which offers a plethora of aquatic activities.

 WHERE TO STAY *See map, page 262.*

Upmarket

🏠 **Kachere Kastle** 📱 099 3809321; e kacherekastle@hotmail.com; www. kacherekastle.com. Though it's not scheduled to open until 2014, this custom-built château will soon boast a fully functioning moat & drawbridge, complete with tower rooms poised above the lakeshore & surrounding villages. Some 12km south of Kande near Mlenga Senga, this owner-managed lodge will offer en-suite rooms, swimming pool, restaurant & swim-up bar, full camping facilities, DSTV & a range of aquatic & terrestrial activities. *US$100–150 expected for a dbl/suite B&B, approx US$10 pp camping.*

🏠 **Mbamba Beach Lodge** (6 rooms) 📱 099 5441278/9; e mbambabeach@hotmail.com; www.mbambabeachmalawi.com. Just metres from Kande Beach Resort but miles away in character, this elegant new owner-managed lodge is a quiet, modern retreat, with a minimalist European style &

graceful African accents. The rooms have king-size beds, nets, Wi-Fi, rainfall showers, private decks & hand-carved furnishings. The beach is excellent for swimming & there's a boat for hire, but there's also a tempting new infinity pool, *braai* facilities, & lounge chairs under shady cashew & flame trees. Indoors, there's a top-notch kitchen, dining area & breezy lounge with fireplace & DSTV. It's not signposted, but take the turn-off for Kande Beach & look for a right fork about 300m before you hit the water. Advance bookings required. *US$75/130 sgl/dbl, US$86/150 deluxe sgl/dbl, B&B. US$100 boat house dbl, US$150 4-bed self-catering cottage, US$500 whole house.*

🏠 **The Stables Guesthouse** (3 rooms) 📱 088 8500416/099 3164271; e info@kandehorse. com; www.kandehorse.com. This attractive owner-managed lodge is a first-rate addition to the highly regarded Kande Horse, which lies in a patch of thick Brachystegia woodland on the northwest side of the M5, about 3km from the lake & 1km from Kande village. The loft-style guest rooms here evoke an Edwardian English country house, with their wooden floors & antique furnishings, & they come with 2 ¾ beds, big private balconies with cane seating, en-suite toilet & private bathroom with combination tub/shower. The relaxed farmyard atmosphere will make horse (& other animal) lovers feel right at home, with the stables right next door, & dogs, cats, ducks & other domestics wandering around freely. For details of horse trails, see *Activities, below. US$65/110 sgl/dbl B&B, US$190/360 sgl/dbl FB & riding package for non-residents, discounts for Malawi residents.*

Moderate ·

🏠 **Mukhala Beach Lodge** (8 rooms) m 099 9075599; e ons@malawi.net. This isolated resort lies about 3km from the M5 along a dirt road branching towards the lakeshore some 5km southwest of Kande. It boasts a superb sandy beach, with a backdrop of fig & other evergreen trees, & accommodation in a large brick-face thatched building set back from the lake. The clean tiled en-suite rooms have a dbl or twin bed & net, & those facing the lake also have an outdoor deck with a 2nd bed upstairs. There's a sleepy air about the place, but the new stone deck & bar built over the water is a stunning spot to unwind. The restaurant serves a good selection of meat, fish & vegetarian dishes, as

well as pizza & pasta, in the US$4–5 range. *US$9.50 standard dbl, US$19 with lake view.*

Budget and camping

🏠 **Kande Beach Resort** (31 rooms) m 088 8263500/099 9863500; e info@kandebeach.com or kandebeach@hotmail.com; www.kandebeach.com. This legendary resort lies 2.5km from the M5 along a turn-off signposted from Kande village, which has a bus stage used by both express & country buses. Positioned on a beautiful stretch of beach, & run with the permission & co-operation of the local chief, Kande has the sort of atmosphere that tempts travellers into staying on for weeks; busy & sociable when a few overland trucks pull in, peaceful & intimate when the trucks are absent, & plenty to do (or not to do) either way. There is a large open Africa-shaped bar, & the Soft Sand Restaurant (☉ 07.00–20.00 daily) serves pizzas, veggie & meat burgers, all-day b/fast, sandwiches & daily specials, mostly in the US$4–8 range. Kande is a hub of activities, with an on-site dive school (see *Activities, below*), windsurfers, sailing boats, catamarans, canoes, pedal-boats & snorkelling equipment for hire, & a games room with table tennis, pool table & dartboard. Internet access is available at a hefty Mk50/2mins. *US$15/30 sgl/twin beach chalet, US$50 en-suite dbl, US$80 family cottage (sleeping up to 5), US$10 pp dorm, US$5 pp camping.*

ACTIVITIES Kande is the site of two highly rated establishments offering activities to day visitors from other lodges and further afield:

Aquanuts Dive School m 099 1922242/088 1606078; e info@aquanutsdivers.com; www. aquanutsdivers.com. At the far end of Kande Beach Resort, this PADI resort offers 4-day open-water diving courses for US$350 pp, day dives for certified divers at US$45–50 depending on the site, night dives for US$50, & refresher courses including 1 dive for US$75. It also does snorkelling trips for US$15, & arranges transfers to/from Chintheche.
Kande Horse m 088 8500416/099 3164271; e info@kandehorse.com; www.kandehorse.com.

This impressive owner-managed stable houses 28 sleek horses, a floodlit gymkhana & the beginnings of a huge wine cellar. The bareback swim in the lake at the end of a ride through the bush & villages is a marvellous experience, & horses are available to suit all levels of ability, from novices to experts. Day rides with swimming cost US$40–80 for 1–3hrs, & there are longer-term volunteer opportunities available for those with a keen interest in horsemanship. Rides can be booked directly at the stables, or at their booking office (☉ 07.00–12.00, 14.00–18.00 daily) just outside Kande Beach Resort.

BANDAWE

For those with an interest in history and culture, the most interesting settlement on this part of the lakeshore is Bandawe, site of the Livingstonia Mission before it relocated to its present site on the escarpment in 1894, as well as the more recently established Chikumbuso Museum. The old mission site and its still functional church stand on a hilly peninsula about 2.5km from the M5 along a sandy road that also offers access to the museum. The mission and museum can easily be visited as a day trip from any of the lakeshore resorts between Kande and Chintheche, and Bandawe Point is also the site of Makuzi Beach Lodge, a lovely resort set on one of Malawi's most stunning beaches.

HISTORY In 1880, Dr Robert Laws relocated the Livingstonia Mission from its temporary site at Cape Maclear to a hill overlooking Bandawe Point. Back then, the lakeshore Tonga fisherfolk were terrorised by an Ngoni clan led by Chief Mombero, whose murderous annual raids frequently destroyed entire communities, razing villages to the ground and leaving hundreds of people dead. At first, Laws had an uneasy relationship with Mombero, but when one of the missionaries was asked to pray for rain during a severe drought and a thunderstorm ensued, the Ngoni chief became friendlier and Laws persuaded him to cease harassing the Tonga.

The mission site at Bandawe proved to be as unhealthy as its predecessor at Cape Maclear, despite Laws's practice of facing all buildings inland, in the belief that malaria was caused by 'miasma' rising from the lake. In 1894, it was abandoned for Khondowe on the Rift Valley Escarpment, where the Livingstonia Mission still operates today. Nevertheless, the Bandawe Mission had a lasting local influence in the field of education, and its graduates included Edward Kamwama, who founded the Ethiopianist Watch Tower Church in Bandawe in 1908.

WHERE TO STAY *See map, page 262.*

⌂ Makuzi Beach Lodge (11 rooms) m 099 9273287/9283980; e info@makuzibeachlodge. com; www.makuzibeachlodge.com. The only resort on Bandawe Point, this exclusive slice of paradise lies in sprawling gardens, thick with indigenous plants & birds, that run down to an idyllic sandy beach hemmed in by what is effectively a private bay. Accommodation is in hexagonal stone-&-thatch chalets with colourful but earthy décor, dbl beds with walk-in netting, & en-suite hot showers. The shady campground is superb & offers thatched gazebos, BBQ facilities, plug points & hot showers. There is a varied menu of aquatic activities on offer, from safe swimming & snorkelling to fishing & kayaking, as well as arranging PADI dives & horserides at Kande. The owners are involved in a local community project called the Shanti Trust, & have built a new school at the old Bandawe Mission Station. *US$85/140 sgl/dbl B&B, US$110/190 superior chalet B&B, additional US$35 pp FB, US$5 pp camping.*

WHAT TO SEE AND DO

Bandawe Mission The old mission site lies about 200m to the right of the feeder road to Makuzi Beach Lodge. The original hillside church, a somewhat warehouse-like brick construction built between 1886 and 1900, is still standing, and the priest welcomes visitors – he has in fact compiled a short history of the mission, illustrated with period photographs. There is no entrance fee but a small donation will be appreciated. Roughly 500m from the main mission building lies a small cemetery, a literal 'White Man's Graveyard', where several of the early Scottish missionaries are buried, most of them victims of malaria, many of them in their early twenties. A more recent grave is that of 'Mama' Jane Jackson, the owner of a nearby lodge who died tragically in a paragliding accident in Zimbabwe in 1997. Close by is the grave of an unidentified *mazungu* who drowned on the nearby lakeshore in 1986.

Chikumbuso Museum and Cultural Centre (*www.makuzibeachlodge.com/ shanti.html;* ⊕ *07.00–12.00 & 15.00–17.00 Thu–Tue; entrance US$5 pp*) This

small museum, situated about 1km from the mission, was established as a local community project under the leadership of Chief Yakucha (who died in 2008) with assistance from Makuzi Beach Lodge. A variety of local Tumbuka artefacts is on display, and the knowledgeable curator will elaborate on their purpose and significance. You can also ask to see demonstrations of traditional activities such as grinding millet, pounding cassava and building and paddling dugout canoes.

CHINTHECHE

The trading centre of Chintheche, set along a surfaced road that loops west from the M5, about 1km from the lake, isn't anything to shout about today. In colonial times, however, it stood closer to the lakeshore and was a fairly important settlement. Chintheche was earmarked for greater things in the Banda era, including the construction of a deepwater harbour and a paper-processing plant, which promised to create thousands of jobs. In order to accommodate this planned development, the residents of Chintheche were displaced inland in the early 1970s, and when finally the scheme was abandoned, they were forbidden from returning to their lakeshore homes.

Today, Chintheche is a forgettable little place, but quite well equipped, boasting a few guesthouses, restaurants and supermarkets, and even an internet café. More interesting than the town itself is the nearby lakeshore, with its scattering of lodges and resorts, among them the evergreen Chintheche Inn, a relic of the short-lived Banda-era building boom, now managed by Wilderness Safaris. Aside from the lake itself there are no specific attractions in this area, but it's a good base for day trips to Bandawe and Kande. Elsewhere, outside the lodges and main trading centre, facilities are limited to a small grocery store in the village of Malaza, which flanks the M5 about 500m north of the junction for Chintheche Inn.

GETTING THERE AND AWAY Chintheche lies immediately west of the M5, about 40km south of Nkhata Bay, 10km north of Bandawe and 17km north of Kande. Express and country buses between Nkhotakota and Nkhata Bay all stop in town, more-or-less opposite the People's Supermarket.

WHERE TO STAY *See map, page 262.*
Upmarket
⌂ **Chintheche Inn** (10 rooms) ☏ 01 771153/393; m 088 8729842; e chininn@africa-online.net or reservations@wilderness.mw; www.wilderness-safaris.com. One of the most tranquil upmarket retreats on the lakeshore, managed by Wilderness Safaris Malawi, Chintheche Inn lies in large grassy tree-studded grounds running down to a picture-postcard sandy beach. The spacious & stylish en-suite rooms line up in a narrow block next to the main building, & come with twin or dbl bed with walk-in netting, hot shower, fan & a private balcony with a lake view & direct beach access. With a swimming pool, tennis court & warm welcome for kids, Chintheche is an ideal family resort, while more adventurous visitors can snorkel in the nearby rocks, rent a

boat or borrow a mountain bike to explore the surrounding network of dirt roads. Organised excursions include a trip to the Bandawe Mission, bird walks & a community visit to a fishing village. The restaurant, with indoor & outdoor seating, serves substantial à la carte meals for around US$7, as well as a 3-course set dinner for US$25. Much of the food is grown in an on-site organic garden, & there's a highly successful tree nursery & reforestation programme. Tucked away to the right of the main building is an excellent campsite, with its own ablution block & a separate beach bar. *US$215/330 sgl/dbl inc dinner & b/fast, US$15 pp camping.*
⌂ **Sunga Moyo** (3 rooms) m 099 9964053/2; e stella@sunga-moyo.com; www.sunga-moyo.

com. Situated 2.3km from the M5 along a turn-off signposted 400m south of the one to Chintheche Inn, Sunga Moyo boasts a location of exceptional beauty even by the standards of Lake Malawi. Having undergone a period of intense neglect in recent years, the former Nkhwazi Lodge is under new management as of early 2013, & has been rechristened 'Sunga Moyo', or appropriately enough, 'that which must be protected'. The new owners are former overland travellers, & have embarked upon a programme of intensive renovations throughout the lodge. The rejuvenated campground is already operational & has *braai* & kitchen facilities, hot showers & plug points. The individually themed chalets & updated restaurant are all due to be finished in 2014, & there are plans for a new lounge & plunge pool as well. There's a lovely beach with exemplary swimming & snorkelling, & a small reef sits just offshore. *US$70 pp chalet B&B, US$10 pp camping.*

⌂ **The Beach House** (6 rooms) ☏ 01 876110; m 099 9960066; e centralafricana@africa-online.net or info@beachhousemalawi.com; www.beachhousemalawi.com. This beautiful self-catering beach house is situated about 3km north of Chintheche, along an unsignposted turn-off marked by 3 painted white lines at right angles to the road. The main house consists of 4 large en-suite twin or dbl rooms with nets, & there is a lounge furnished in colonial style, a terrace, an open conservatory & an equipped kitchen with fridge & freezer. A smaller & more basic house on the same property has 2 twin rooms. Both are available for serviced rentals of at least 2 days; advance booking mandatory. A returnable damage deposit is charged. *The main house costs the equivalent of £120/150 low/high season, & the smaller cottage costs £50, rates exclude 16.5% VAT.*

Moderate

⌂ **La Exotica** (12 rooms) ☏ 01 11930659/92566; m 088 8828758; e stan_nyirenda@yahoo.co.uk; www.la-exotica.com. While the name may be more Las Vegas than Lake Malawi, La Exotica is an ambitious new Malawian-owned lodge offering well-appointed double rooms in thatch-roofed brick duplexes set in a well-manicured compound. The lakeshore here is grassy & untamed, & while the rooms unfortunately

don't take advantage of the lake views, there are several thatch shelters dotted along the shoreline for beachgoers to relax underneath. There is a restaurant/bar with DSTV & billiards, & rooms have nets, fans & hot showers. Camping is also available, but they hadn't set a price yet when we visited. *US$31 dbl*

Budget

⌂ **Flame Tree Lodge** (6 rooms) m 099 9201987; e flametreemalawi@gmail.com; www.flametreemalawi.com. This attractive, easy-going place is on a shady wooded peninsula on the lakeshore immediately south of town. Flanked by 2 good swimming beaches, it offers accommodation in modest but spacious chalets with twin or dbl bed, framed nets & en-suite hot shower. The restaurant serves decent meals in the US$4–5 range. To reach the lodge, either walk for 15mins south along the beach from London Lodge (see below), or else follow the M5 south of Chintheche for 2km & take the signposted 1.8km turn-off to the left. *US$15.75/18.75 sgl/dbl, US$52 family house, US$3.25 pp camping.*

⌂ **Sambani Lodge** (19 rooms) m 088 8713857/099 3054761; e sambanilodge@gmail.com; www.sambanilodge.com. Signposted from the M5 about 5km south of Chintheche & another 2km over rough road, Sambani stands on a pretty beach in large grassy grounds dotted with indigenous & exotic trees. The 19 rooms, spread between 6 chalets, have dbl or twin bed, net, fan, TV & en-suite hot shower. Under new management since 2012, the restaurant/bar was under renovation when we visited, & improvements in the rooms can be expected as well. It's a lovely spot, & good value at the price. *US$16/25 sgl/dbl, US$37.50 family room, US$6.50 pp camping.*

Shoestring

⌂ **London Lodge** ☏ 01 11732882; m 088 1784096. The best cheapie in the area is this low-key beachfront lodge, situated about 700m from the M5, along a turn-off opposite the southern end of the loop road through Chintheche trading centre. *US$8.25/11.25 en-suite sgl/dbl with nets, US$2.50 per tent camping.*

⌂ **Mulunga Samana Resthouse** m 099 1803063. The pick of a few basic lodges in the town centre. *US$1.50/3.25 sgl/dbl.*

✕ WHERE TO EAT All the lodges listed on pages 267–8 prepare adequate to good food, with Chintheche Inn probably having the best reputation. There are a few eateries in Chintheche Town, the pick being **Mum's Restaurant** (\ 01 357499; ⊕ 07.00–20.00 daily), which serves a varied selection of Malawian staples as well as burgers and spaghetti for around US$2.

OTHER PRACTICALITIES
Internet L **Net Café**, in the town centre, has a fast connection and charges Mk40 for five minutes or US$1.25 per hour. Otherwise, the closest public internet is at Kande Beach Resort.

Exploring the wonders of our continent

AFRICA GEOGRAPHIC AND AFRICA – BIRDS & BIRDING
Award-winning magazines that draw you into the
natural heart of the continent

AFRICA GEOGRAPHIC EXPEDITIONS Tailor-made travel
into the wild places in Africa. Let us help you plan
your next trip to Africa – the place we call home.

AFRICA
Geographic
www.africageographic.com

18

The Lake Ferry and the Islands

There's arguably no more attractive way of exploring Lake Malawi than on the legendary MV *Ilala*, a ferry whose weekly circuit of Lake Malawi starts in the south at Chipoko, and heads as far north as Chilumba, stopping *en route* at Nkhotakota, Nkhata Bay and various lesser lake ports. One of Malawi's great travel highlights, the MV *Ilala* is something of a unifying factor between ports covered in numerous other chapters in this book. It also provides the only affordable access to Likoma and Chizumulu, a pair of inhabited islands that belong to Malawi, despite lying within Mozambican waters in the far east of the lake, and that have long held a special fascination for travellers. The present chapter thus breaks with the normal format of this book to include an overview of the MV *Ilala*'s itinerary, as well as fares and services, along with coverage of the two remote islands that it visits.

For local people, the MV *Ilala* forms the only connection between the mainland and the islands, and the crowded lower deck is testament to its importance to the islanders. For travellers, who mostly can afford to use the spacious first-class deck, the attraction of the ferry is primarily aesthetic. This is one of Africa's great public transport rides, a leisurely cruise on one of the continent's largest and most scenic lakes, offering fantastic sunsets and night skies, as well as a welcome break from the grind of bus travel. Although many travellers do use the ferry as a means of visiting one of the islands, a far greater number travel on it for its own sake, as an alternative means of transport between the popular lake resorts of Nkhotakota and Nkhata Bay further north.

Travellers should note that the MV *Ilala* was taken out of service for repairs in July 2012 and had yet to return as this book was going to print, but it should certainly be running by the time you read this. A series of deadlines for the ship's return were set and missed, but it appeared to be on the verge of returning to service in May 2013. On the bright side, when the *Ilala* does finally get back in the water, it will likely be a sparkling version of itself, having undergone a full cosmetic and mechanical makeover. Passengers can anticipate a more reliable, more comfortable, and possibly even faster trip.

THE LAKE FERRY

Since 1957, the MV *Ilala* has run up and down the lake once a week. Its present route is as follows: starting at Chipoko in the south, it runs up the lake's western shore to Nkhotakota, across to the Mozambican port of Metangula, then to the Malawian islands of Likoma and Chizumulu, back across to Nkhata Bay, right up the west coast to Chilumba, returning to Chipoko using the same route in reverse. Stops are also made at the smaller ports of Usisya, Ruarwe, Tcharo and Mlowe in the north. For the full itinerary see box *The MV* Ilala *timetable (2013)*, opposite.

Five ticket classes are available. Cheapest is lower-deck economy class, which is comparable in price to bus transport, but often very crowded and sweaty, with a real risk of theft. Many travellers use economy class, but, to quote one reader: 'vomiting children, chickens on your lap, cockroaches on your backpack and spiders on your legs without any space to move for 15 hours might sound very romantic, but it can cause frustration in the long run'. Next up, lower-deck second class is very comfortable for short trips to places like Ruarwe from Nkhata Bay, as it is not crowded and you normally get a big padded chair with table. The second-class option is not recommended for the journey between the islands and Nkhata Bay, even if you can sleep on your chair and there is access to the outside at the front of the boat, as it becomes very crowded. For many travellers, the compromise between cost

THE MV *ILALA* TIMETABLE (2013)

This timetable below has not changed significantly for the best part of a decade, except for the dropping of Tanzanian ports in favour of Mozambican ones and the recent deletion of Monkey Bay, but it might politely be described as flexible, and is prone to lengthy delays. For further details, to make bookings, or to confirm that the times given here still hold good, contact the Malawi Shipping Company office in Monkey Bay or Lilongwe (01 587361/411/221/203, 01 773738/9; e ilala@malawi.net or ilala.lake.malawi@gmail.com).

NORTHBOUND

Day	Port	Arrive	Depart
Saturday	CHIPOKA	–	16.00
Sunday	NKHOTAKOTA	01.00	02.00
Sunday	METANGULA [MZ]	06.00	08.00
Sunday	LIKOMA ISLAND	14.00	18.00
Sunday	CHIZUMULU	19.30	22.00
Monday	NKHATA BAY	01.00	07.00
Monday	USISYA	10.00	11.00
Monday	RUARWE	12.00	13.00
Monday	TCHARO	14.00	14.30
Monday	MLOWE	16.00	17.00
Monday	CHILUMBA	20.00	–

SOUTHBOUND

Day	Port	Arrive	Depart
Tuesday	CHILUMBA	–	02.00
Tuesday	MLOWE	05.00	06.00
Tuesday	TCHARO	07.30	08.00
Tuesday	RUARWE	09.00	09.30
Tuesday	USISYA	10.30	11.30
Tuesday	NKHATA BAY	14.00	20.00
Wednesday	CHIZUMULU	24.00	02.00
Wednesday	LIKOMA ISLAND	03.15	08.00
Wednesday	METANGULA [MZ]	14.00	15.00
Wednesday	NKHOTAKOTA	19.00	20.00
Thursday	CHIPOKA	06.00	–

18

and comfort is the first-class deck ticket, which allows you to sleep on the breezy, uncrowded upper deck, where there is a shaded bar, as well as a restaurant below. There is no need to book tickets for deck or first class, and if you embark anywhere but Nkhata Bay, tickets can only be bought once you are on the boat.

If you can afford it, the most comfortable way to travel on the MV *Ilala* is cabin class. There are seven cabins in total, with two single and four doubles using shared bathrooms, and a solitary double Owner's Cabin with private bathroom. Cabin space is limited, so it's essential to book in advance. Cabin bookings can be made through the Malawi Shipping Company office in Monkey Bay or Lilongwe (🌑 *01 587361/411/221/203, 01 773738/9;* e *ilala@malawi.net or ilala.lake.malawi@ gmail.com*). You could also try a tour operator but most of them are increasingly reluctant to make ferry bookings, because many customers have blamed them for delays that are totally out of their control. Either way, and at risk of stating the obvious, booking through the most reliable tour operator won't affect the ferry's punctuality (or lack thereof), and you probably shouldn't be using the ferry if you aren't prepared for the delays which are almost inevitable. Vehicles can be taken on the ferry at surprisingly reasonable prices (*around US$60 from Chipoka to Nkhata Bay, less for shorter journeys*).

SAMPLE FARES (These prices are per person in US$, introduced in May 2013 as the *Ilala* was poised to return to service.)

	Economy	Second	First	Cabin	Owner's Cabin
Chipoka–Likoma	8.75	15.00	27.50	67.50	90.00
Chipoka–Nkhata Bay	12.50	18.75	33.75	87.50	118.75
Nkhata Bay–Nkhotakota	8.75	15.00	27.50	67.50	90.00
Chipoka–Chilumba	12.50	18.75	33.75	87.50	118.75

So far as facilities go, there is a well-stocked bar on the upper deck, normally selling biscuits and other packaged snacks. The restaurant serves good three-course meals, but it is advisable to reserve lunch and dinner a few hours in advance. The first-class toilets are reasonable, and the communal showers have hot water. At ports other than Nkhata Bay, there are no jetties, and the bays are too shallow for the ferry to come in close, so passengers and goods are transported to and from the ferry on a smaller boat. If you are embarking at a port where the ferry docks at some distance from the town (for instance Nkhotakota) you might well want to bring along something to nibble and drink while you wait.

Aside from the *Ilala*, the only reasonably reliable ferry on the lake at the time of writing was the Tanzanian MV *Songea*. It connects two ports in Tanzania, Mbamba Bay (on the eastern shore) and Itungi Port (near Kyela on the lake's northwestern tip). The ferry leaves Itungi at 07.00 on Mondays and Thursdays and arrives at Mbamba Bay at around midnight the same day, after stopping at Lupinga, Manda, Lundu and Liuli. After arriving at Mbamba Bay, the ferry turns around almost immediately, to arrive back at Itungi at 17.00 the next day. The MV *Songea* does come to Nkhata Bay but not on a regular schedule, only once or twice a month and often less, arriving at Nkhata Bay on a Friday and leaving early on Saturday, though it is not so easy to find out in advance when exactly it will do this.

Additionally, the *Chambo* (yes, like the fish) is a new boat that promises to offer ferry services along the Mozambican shore and to Likoma. It's currently being built at the shipyard in Monkey Bay and though it is unclear when this would come into service, it could well be during the lifespan of this edition.

LIKOMA ISLAND

The island of Likoma, 8km long and 3km wide, lies within Mozambican waters but is territorially part of Malawi, mainly as a result of its long association with Scottish missionaries. Today, the island's main attraction for travellers is its isolation from the mainland and mellow atmosphere. This is no conventional tropical-island paradise, though the beaches really are splendid with the mountainous Mozambican shore rising above them, while the interior has a certain austere charm, particularly the southern plains which are covered in massive baobabs, shady mango trees and studded with impressive granite outcrops. Likoma has always generated a great deal of interest among travellers, but it remains surprisingly little visited. Above all, perhaps, Likoma has an overwhelmingly friendly mood, making it a good place to get to know ordinary Malawians.

HISTORY In 1886, Likoma became the site of an Anglican mission, established by Bishop Chauncy Maples with the help of his close friend and fellow Oxford graduate, the Reverend William Johnson. Maples was consecrated as the first Bishop of Likoma in London in 1895, but he never actively assumed this post as he drowned in a boating accident near Salima, caused by his enthusiasm to return to Likoma despite stormy weather. Maples was buried in the church at Nkhotakota. Johnson went on to become one of the most fondly remembered of all the missionaries who worked in Malawi. He arrived at the lake in 1882 and for 46 years he preached from a boat all around the lakeshore, despite being practically blind and well into his seventies when he died in 1928. Johnson's grave at Liuli (on the Tanzanian part of the lakeshore) remained for several decades a popular site of pilgrimage for Malawian Christians.

The Likoma Mission founded by Maples and Johnson remained the headquarters of the Anglican Church in Malawi until after World War II. During this period, the educational zeal of the missionaries ensured that Likoma was probably the only settlement in Africa with a 100% literacy rate. The most obvious physical legacy of the missionaries' work is the large and very beautiful **St Peter's Cathedral** (similar in size to Westminster Cathedral) designed by Frank George and built between 1903 and 1905 in a cruciform shape using local granite. The site of the church, chosen by Maples before his death, is where in 1889 he witnessed and was unable to prevent three witches being burnt to death. Notable features of the church include carved soapstone choir stalls, some fine stained-glass windows and a crucifix carved from a tree that grew near Chitambo (the village in Zambia where David Livingstone died in 1873).

GETTING THERE AND AWAY The most affordable way of reaching Likoma from the Malawian mainland is with the MV *Ilala*, which is scheduled to stop at Likoma on Sunday afternoon on its northbound trip and in the wee hours of Wednesday morning on the southbound trip. Allowing for delays, this means that you need to allocate at least five days to the round trip, spending three or four nights on the island. The MV *Ilala* docks a few hundred metres offshore at a beach about five minutes' walk from Chipyela. It is usually docked for at least three hours, which means, in theory, that ferry passengers who are travelling on could still hop off the boat and take a quick look around the cathedral. In practice, however, the complexities of transporting passengers between the MV *Ilala* and the beach make this inadvisable, unless you're prepared to risk the boat sailing away without you.

18

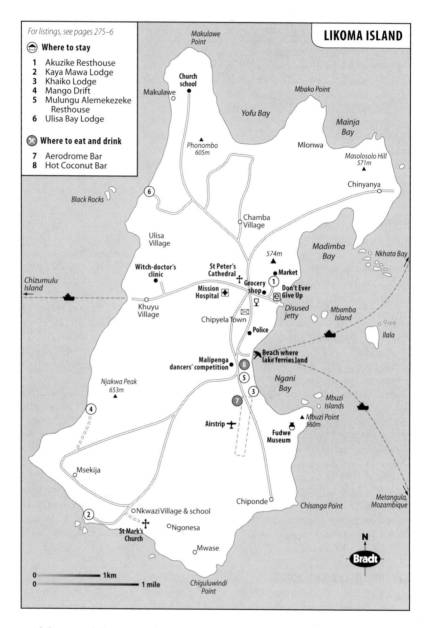

For listings, see pages 275–6

LIKOMA ISLAND

Where to stay

1. Akuzike Resthouse
2. Kaya Mawa Lodge
3. Khaiko Lodge
4. Mango Drift
5. Mulungu Alemekezeke Resthouse
6. Ulisa Bay Lodge

Where to eat and drink

7. Aerodrome Bar
8. Hot Coconut Bar

Makulawe Point
Church school
Makulawe
Mbako Point
Yofu Bay
Mainja Bay
Phonombo 605m
Mlonwa
Masolosolo Hill 571m
Chinyanya
Black Rocks
Chamba Village
574m
Madimba Bay
Nkhata Bay
Ulisa Village
Witch-doctor's clinic
St Peter's Cathedral
Market
Grocery shop
Don't Ever Give Up
Mission Hospital
Disused jetty
Mbamba Island
Chizumulu Island
Khuyu Village
Chipyela Town
Ilala
Police
Beach where lake ferries land
Malipenga dancers' competition
Ngani Bay
Njakwa Peak 653m
Mbuzi Islands
Mbuzi Point 560m
Airstrip
Fudwe Museum
Msekija
Chiponde
Chisanga Point
Metangula, Mozambique
Nkwazi Village & school
Ngonesa
St Mark's Church
Mwase
Chiguluwindi Point

0   1km
0   1 mile

N

Bradt

If the MV *Ilala* is out of service, as it was in late 2012 and early 2013, local boats pick up the slack, ferrying passengers and goods between Nkhata Bay and Likoma & Chizumulu islands for about US$6.25. These services all run on an ad hoc basis, but usually make 2–4 crossings/week, typically departing in either direction between 09.00–12.00 & arriving about 6 hours later. **Mulungu (m** *088 1704615/099 9700295*) is perhaps the most reliable operator (though this isn't saying much), and his boats have much-needed shade canopies. Bring snacks, sun protection and a sense of humour.

At the other end of the price scale, Ulendo Airlink (*www.flyulendo.com*) flies between Lilongwe and Likoma once or twice a day for US$295, and Nyassa Air Taxi (*www.nyassa.mw*) offers charters on the same route. All charter flights and boats to Likoma can be arranged through Kaya Mawa or their representative Ulendo Safaris. Additionally, the airstrip at Likoma now has international clearance, so direct flights can be arranged to/from Mfuwe in Zambia or destinations further afield.

The northern Mozambican shore of Lake Malawi, a rugged pile of rocks populated with far fewer fishing villages than the Malawian side, is cut off from the rest of Mozambique by vast tracts of emptiness, and is most easily accessed from Likoma. Boat transfers to Cobue and the delightfully remote Nkwichi Lodge (see box *Manda Wilderness Project*, page 277) cost US$60 per person and are easily arranged online (*www.mandawilderness.org*) or through the staff of Kaya Mawa.

It is also possible to travel between Likoma and Cobue on the Mozambican mainland using a local fishing boat. These boats make the short crossing regularly, but you'll have to ask around to find one. This is a good option for those without prearranged visas, as 30-day Mozambican visas are available for US$30 on arrival in Cobue for most European & North American passports. Malawi immigration is officially at the airport, but sometimes sets up near the disused jetty in town when boats are arriving and departing. Should you be crossing into Mozambique rather than paying a return visit, you might want to ask about the current transport situation on the road between Cobue & Lichinga.

WHERE TO STAY AND EAT *See map, opposite.*

Exclusive

Kaya Mawa Lodge (10 rooms) +44 7453 326398 (UK); m 099 9318359/60; e enquiries@kayamawa.com; www.kayamawa. com. This wonderfully laidback spot, near Nkwazi village facing the Mozambican shore, is arguably the most magical beach retreat anywhere in Malawi, set between two beaches on either side of an idyllic peninsula punctuated by large rocky outcrops & stands of baobab. 'Kaya Mawa' translates as 'maybe tomorrow', a name that could scarcely be more appropriate to a lodge where time seemingly stands still & visitors are encouraged to chill out & take things as they come. Sublimely isolated & ingeniously built into the local environment, the newly redesigned stone-&-thatch cottages are magnificently appointed, decorated with textiles hand-crafted on Likoma & feature walk-in nets, private balconies, outdoor showers & premium rooms have their own plunge pools. There are a number of family suites available, including the fabulous 4-bedroom Ndomo House, and a truly indulgent honeymoon suite on its own island. The food is world-class, and a wide range of activities includes waterskiing, wakeboarding, quad biking, mountain biking, fishing, kayaking & sailing, with qualified instructors for all watersports. If you do feel the need to connect with the real world, there's Wi-Fi, too. *US$335–US$495 pp all-inclusive, depending on time of year & room, with discounts for African residents.*

Moderate

Khaiko Lodge (5 rooms) m 088 8746262/8539678; e info@khaiko.com; www. khaiko.com. Set in sloping landscaped grounds running down to a lovely boulder-strewn sandy beach facing the Mozambican shore, this intimate lodge offers accommodation in spacious thatched cottages with twin or dbl beds with nets, modern furnishings, a private lounge & balcony, & en-suite hot showers. It's a great place to chill out, but tours of the island can be arranged, along with boats trips onto the lake. *US$50/60 sgl/dbl, US$60/70 deluxe, all rates B&B, camping permitted at a negotiable rate.*

Ulisa Bay Lodge (4 rooms, 2 under construction) m 099 4748707/088 4849988; e nyasalodges@nyasalodges.com; www. nyasalodges.com; see also advert on page 278. The newest lodge on the island, this tranquil set-up is under the same management as the highly regarded Nkhotakota Pottery on the mainland. Located in baobab-studded grounds on the sunset

18

side of the island, this is a low-key operation where swimming, snorkelling & kicking back at the sand-floored beach bar are the orders of the day. The restaurant serves a varied menu for about US$5–8, including locally caught *usipa*, chicken, lamb, & cheesecake for dessert. The comfortably furnished rooms are in whitewashed chalets with private balconies set along the beach, & deluxe rooms have en-suite hot showers. The lodge is about 3km from where the ferry docks, along a well-signposted series of roads. *US$32/44/48 sgl/ dbl/trpl, US$51/62/75 deluxe sgl/dbl/trpl.*

Budget

⌂ **Mango Drift** (6 rooms, 1 dorm) m 099 9746122/3048621; e enquiries@mangodrift.com or mailmangodrift@gmail.com; www.mangodrift. com. Under the same management as Kaya Mawa & set on a long stretch of beach about 1km further north, this idyllic resort is the unchallenged Mecca for backpackers & volunteers on Likoma. Accommodation is in simple bamboo beach huts or attractive en-suite chalets with walk-in nets & private balconies, along with an en-suite dorm & camping. There's always something afoot at the sociable bar & restaurant underneath a mango tree, & the pool table & darts have quite a view. Meals are tasty & reasonably priced, & there's a pizza oven to boot. Kayaks & snorkelling gear are free of charge, while waterskiing, wakeboarding, tubing & kitesurfing are all available for a fee. Their associated dive centre, Likoma Island Divers,

offers PADI open water courses for US$350. Back on shore, there's internet access, a book exchange & plenty of hammocks draped under the bougainvillea. *US$60/70 en-suite chalet sgl/ dbl, US$25/30 beach chalet using common showers, US$8 pp dorm bed, US$5 pp camping.*

Shoestring

⌂ **Akuzike Resthouse** m 099 4486282/088 4540590. This fairly rundown place is in Chipyela, facing the central market, about 5–10mins' walk from the beach where the ferry docks. There are basic but clean rooms with mosquito nets, & facilities include a flush toilet, running showers & a spasmodically functional generator. The restaurant prepares basic meals by advance order, generally fish, beans & rice, though you can also ask them to buy you a chicken. *US$2.25/4.75 sgl/dbl.*

⌂ **Mulungu Alemekezeke Resthouse** m 088 1169565. South of the Hot Coconut Bar, this is the closest accommodation to where the ferry docks, & would make a decent choice for anyone looking to minimise the length of their early morning trip to catch the boat, or simply for those who would rather stay closer to town. It consists of a handful of cramped en-suite cottages & a nondescript main building within a sandy compound along a busy fishing beach. Rooms are basic but clean with nets & fans, & there are meals & cold drinks available. *US$17.25 en-suite cottage trpl, US$8 en-suite dbl in main building, US$4.75/3.25 sgl/dbl with shared facilities, US$2.25 pp camping.*

EXPLORING LIKOMA Most visitors to the island are content to while away their time on the beaches or to explore **Chipyela**, the island's largest town. Chipyela (also known as **Mbamba**) lies between the **cathedral** (☉ *08.00–16.00 daily*) and the jetty, and is named after the spot where witches used to be burnt ('Chipyela' translates as 'the place of burning'). It is an unusual town: the neat, cobbled roads and stone houses have, according to one resident, led to it being nicknamed 'Half London', a strange epithet for a metropolis that not only lacks an underground but until recently boasted a grand total of only one car, the ambulance belonging to the **mission hospital**. (Today the total is closer to a gridlock-inducing 13.) The **central market** is dominated by a massive strangler fig with a hollow base large enough to stand in. Worth asking about are the occasional *malipenga* **dancing competitions** held on weekends about 500m out of town opposite the **Hot Coconut Bar** (see opposite) – these are generally held in the afternoon, and are rather boozy affairs, notable both for the interesting traditional instruments that are used and for the bizarre colonially influenced costumes the men wear. Continuing south from Chipyela and east of the airstrip, you'll find the **Fudwe Museum** (m 088 8736669/4039893), a (very) low-key affair where they have a small number of traditional crafts & tools on display, and you may be able to catch a dance performance as well.

Established on the Mozambican shore of Lake Malawi in 1999, the multiple award-winning Manda Wilderness Project (☎ +44 (0)20 3239 6253 (UK); e info@ mandawilderness.org; www.mandawilderness.org) is a 1,200km² game reserve managed in trust for local communities comprising some 20,000 Nyanja people. It protects a patchwork of habitats, including Brachystegia woodland and riverine forest, savannah, swamps, streams and mountains, all running down to the lovely beaches and crystal-clear waters of Lake Malawi (known as Lago Niassa in Mozambique). Game viewing is done on foot or from a canoe, and the most frequently seen large mammals are zebra, monkeys and otters, though others are present, including lion and wild dog. Though it falls within Mozambique, Manda operates mostly as an extension to the safari circuits in Malawi and Zambia, and is most easily reached by boat transfer from Likoma (US$60 per person).

Centrepiece of the wilderness project is the spectacular **Nkwichi Lodge** (6 chalets; US$395/660 sgl/dbl standard rooms inc all meals & non-motorised activities, US$450/720 luxury honeymoon chalets), whose chalets are widely spread on a rocky peninsula flanked by a powdery white beach and dense Brachystegia woodland. This ranks among the most exclusive lodges on Lake Malawi, comparable in standard to Kaya Mawa, Pumulani and Mumbo Island, and the designer chalets are ingeniously thought out to be both luxurious and environmentally harmonious. There's plenty to keep you busy, from tracking animals, birding and luxury camping excursions, to activities on the lake such as canoeing, snorkelling or sailing. Then again, you can just lie in a hammock.

Further afield, a half-hour walk eastwards from Chipyela takes you to the village of **Khuyu**, where visitors are normally welcome at the **witch-doctor's clinic**. Reputedly one of the most important 'witch doctors' in Malawi, he is regularly visited by people from as far away as Tanzania and South Africa, and his influence over the islanders is immense, despite the superficial trappings of Christianity associated with Likoma. Another good excursion is a boat trip to Cobue on the Mozambican shore of the lake, where there is a large ruined church – this is best organised through the management of Mango Drift or Kaya Mawa. Visas shouldn't be a problem for day trips; regardless, they are easily acquired in Cobue (see page 275).

The closest thing to a nightspot in Chipyela is the **Hot Coconut Bar**, an open-air bar with a fridge and shaded tables. It lies about ten minutes' walk from town, not far from the beach where the ferry lands. The newest addition to the Likoma nightlife scene is the **Aerodrome Bar**, inside the terminal building. There are cold drinks, a pool table, and it's consistently one of the busiest places in town (though this admittedly isn't saying much).

As far as internet goes, you've got precious few options. The **Don't Ever Give Up Internet Café** (m 088 1700183/1337438) in Chipyela seems to have given up on keeping regular hours, but when they are open there are two computers at US$2/hour.

CHIZUMULU ISLAND

Smaller than Likoma, and even more remote, the island of Chizumulu is noted for excellent diving and snorkelling in the surrounding waters, and for attractive beaches lined by large, ancient baobabs. Like Likoma, this is essentially a place to chill out, free of roads, cars and hassle, and widely regarded to offer the most beautiful sunsets in Malawi. Few travellers make it to Chizumulu, but those who do invariably regard it as a highlight of their time in Malawi.

GETTING THERE AND AWAY Most people travel to Chizumulu on the MV *Ilala*, which stops there between Likoma and Nkhata Bay on both the northbound and southbound parts of its weekly circuit. If the timing works, travellers who want to visit both islands can use the MV *Ilala* to get between them.

Alternatively, the **Lembemo** (m *088 4194771)* ferries passengers between Likoma and Chizumulu daily (exc Sunday) for US$1.50 per person. This boat leaves Khuyu Beach on Likoma between 05.00–06.00 and it arrives at Same Beach on Chizumulu at roughly 09.00, heading back to Likoma about an hour later. Timings are pretty vague, and it doesn't run at all in rough weather. A more romantic possibility is to charter a sailing dhow between the two islands. Contact Nick at Wakwenda Retreat for help with any transport arrangements.

Local boats like **Mulungu** (m *088 1704615/099 9700295)* will also ferry passengers between Likoma and Chizumulu on their way to/from Nkhata Bay for about US$2, but if you're coming from Likoma ask if they are stopping at Chizumulu, as they may not stop if they're full.

⌂ WHERE TO STAY

⌂ **Wakwenda Retreat** (3 rooms, 2 dorms) m 099 9348415 (SMS preferable); e chizinick@ gmail.com. For the better part of two decades, this labour of love has been the only place to stay on the island, & it's a seriously relaxed backpacker haven practically made for losing track of time. It's set on the beach a few hundred metres from where the *Ilala* stops & about 1km from Same Beach, where dhows & fishing boats from Likoma set anchor. Draped in bougainvillea & perched atop a rocky promontory, the picturesque restaurant/ bar offers good meals & veggie options to the tune of US$5–6, & multiple relaxation decks on which to enjoy them. The accommodation is simple but comfortable in thatched chalets with shared facilities, & there's plenty of room for camping. Scuba diving can be arranged for experienced divers (*US$30–50/dive*), there are canoes & fishing rods for hire, & snorkelling equipment is free. *US$16 dbl, US$6 dorm bed, US$4 camping.*

WHAT TO SEE AND DO Like Likoma this is a place to chill out, play *bao* (a board game involving competitive bean snatching), swim and watch the sunset with a Green in your hand. For the more active though there are plenty of options. A walk up the mountain takes about an hour and a half, or you can walk around it in just one hour. The walk around the whole island takes four to six hours and is rewarding for the contact you have with local people more than for any other reason. Swimming, snorkelling and diving are endlessly interesting, especially if you can find a fish expert, as there are many cichlid species here not found elsewhere. Wakwenda Retreat organises boat excursions and scuba-diving trips.

Ulisa Bay Lodge, Likoma Island www.nyasalodges.com
(+265) 0884 849988 or 0994 748707
nyasalodges@nyasalodges.com
Affordable Island Luxury

19

Nkhata Bay

Long one of the best-kept secrets on the African backpackers' trail, Nkhata Bay has steadily grown in reputation over the past two decades to eclipse Cape Maclear as the most popular traveller congregation point on Lake Malawi, if not anywhere between Zanzibar and Victoria Falls. It's not difficult to see why. Nkhata Bay has a gloriously lush and scenic setting, comprising a twin pair of bays enclosed by forested hills and separated by a long, narrow peninsula. And the small town itself, nestled between the hills and lakeshore, is as charming as it is uncategorisable – call it an overgrown Tonga fishing village, a venerable district capital, a bustling market port or an idiosyncratically laidback lakeside resort, one senses that few of its estimated 15,000 residents would be sure which of these labels wears best.

A big part of Nkhata Bay's appeal is the rare sense of traveller community that embraces the town and string of popular lodges running out towards Chikale Beach. The place is also addictively laidback, so much so that it habitually paralyses the will of travellers, and infuses their best-laid plans with an element of suppliant inertia. And while most visitors associate Nkhata Bay with lazy days and party nights, the town offers plenty of interest to more active travellers, including kayaking, snorkelling, forest walks, fish-eagle feeding, beach volleyball or simply joining in a local football match. Worthy of a special mention are the day/night dives and diving courses offered by Aqua Africa in a unique environment described by one experienced diver as 'fresh water with sea equivalents'.

So inherently likeable is Nkhata Bay that it feels churlish to raise any negatives. All the same, Malawi's most popular resort village won't be to everybody's taste. For one, the slow but sure drift of the backpacker scene away from the town centre towards Chikale Beach has made the more popular resorts feel somewhat insular, insofar as they offer limited opportunities to interact with those locals that aren't associated with the tourist industry. Furthermore, if it's pristine beaches you are after, then you might be better off at Chintheche, Kande or Chitimba, since the rapid population growth here in recent years means that urban development has all but swallowed the beaches on which Nkhata Bay built its reputation.

On a more positive note, the security problem experienced here some years back seems to be a thing of the past, with lodge owners and police now working together to contain crime against tourists. Nevertheless, it remains advisable to avoid dark areas on your own at night, especially the long unlit walk between the town centre and Mayoka village or points further south.

GETTING THERE AND AWAY

Nkhata Bay lies at the end of a surfaced 3km cul-de-sac running east from the M5 between Salima and Mzuzu. It's a 50km drive from Mzuzu, along a spectacular

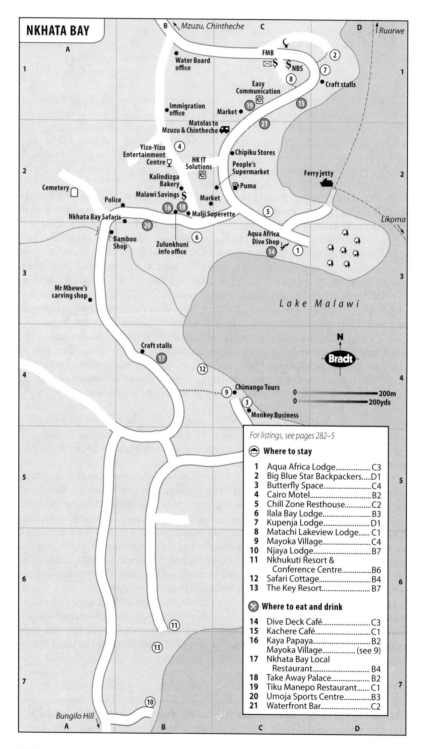

NKHATA BAY

Mzuzu, Chintheche

Ruarwe

FMB
Water Board office
NBS
Easy Communication
Craft stalls
Immigration office
Market
Matolas to Mzuzu & Chintheche
Chipiku Stores
Yizo-Yizo Entertainment Centre
HK IT Solutions
People's Supermarket
Ferry jetty
Kalindizga Bakery
Cemetery
Police
Puma
Malawi Savings
Market
Nkhata Bay Safaris
Malji Superette
Likoma
Bamboo Shop
Zulunkhuni info office
Aqua Africa Dive Shop
Mr Mbewe's carving shop
Lake Malawi
Craft stalls
N
Bradt
Chimango Tours
0 — 200m
0 — 200yds
Monkey Business

Bungilo Hill

stretch of the surfaced M5 that sees you whizzing down the Rift Valley Escarpment (or puffing up it) past expansive grassland and Brachystegia woodland, with the lake glittering in the sun hundreds of metres below. It shouldn't take longer than 45 minutes in a private vehicle, but may take twice as long on the regular minibuses and *matola* vehicles that link the two for US$3. Note that transport from Nkhata Bay to Mzuzu can be picked up from the main bus station [280 C2] or from a stage about 200m out of town past the courthouse.

Coming from the south, Nkhata Bay lies about 40km from Chintheche, and is connected to it by regular minibuses. There is also plenty of bus and *matola* transport along the 198km stretch of the M5 between Nkhotakota and Nkhata Bay. Coming from Lilongwe, the best option is the Axa Coach (see page 64) to Mzuzu; it's an easy hop down to Nkhata Bay from there.

For travellers heading on to Tanzania, the Taqwa/EasyBus (**m** *099 9334299/538*) buses between Lilongwe and Dar es Salaam no longer stop at Nkhata Bay to pick up passengers, instead departing Mzuzu just before midnight, once daily except Thursdays and Fridays. Tickets can be booked through Nkhata Bay Tours, which is also a good source of information about other bus routes.

When it's running, the MV *Ilala* (see pages 270–2 for full itinerary and fares) stops at Nkhata Bay, one of the few ferry ports to have a proper jetty [280 D2]. The ferry is scheduled to leave Nkhata Bay at 07.00 on Monday on the northbound leg and 20.00 on Tuesday on the southbound leg, but delays are commonplace. Smaller local boats also make the crossing from Nkhata Bay to Likoma and Chizumulu for US$6.25, running often when the *Ilala* is out of service, but sporadically otherwise. Other boats shuttle between Nkhata Bay and Mbamba Bay in Tanzania every few days for about US$8.50, and the MV *Songea* also visits Nkhata Bay on occasion (see page 272), connecting it with several ports on the Tanzanian lakeshore. Be sure to stamp out at the immigration office [280 B1] before leaving for Tanzania.

TOUR/ACTIVITY OPERATORS

For most travellers, activity in Nkhata Bay comprises mainly eating, drinking, sitting on the beach, recovering from hangovers and generally just hanging out. However, there is also plenty on offer for more active travellers, ranging from scuba diving and watersports to forest walks and hikes. Nkhata Bay is also a good base for overnight excursions, most popularly safaris to Livingstonia, Vwaza Marsh and Nyika National Park (which lie to the north of Mzuzu and can be quite tricky to explore without your own wheels), but also kayak trips to the remote beaches on the lakeshore north of the village. Most of these excursions and activities can be arranged directly through any lodge, but ultimately you'll probably be directed to one of the following operators, all of which are recommended.

Aqua Africa [280 C3] `01 352284; **m** 099 9921418; **e** divemalawi@gmail.com; www. aquaafrica.co.uk; see advert on page 290. The coast around Nkhata Bay offers superb all-weather diving, with a crenellation of coves offering protection from the occasional wind, & dozens of different cichlid species swirling around the rocks. Aqua Africa is the only dive operator in Nkhata Bay, with more than a decade's experience, & a good reputation for safety. Casual dives cost US$50 &

one-of-a-kind night dives US$70, inclusive of all equipment, while all-inclusive 4-day PADI Open Water certification courses cost US$375, with a maximum of 6 people per tutor.

Budget Safaris **m** 099 9278903/9268588; **e** info@budget-safari.com; www.budget-safari. com. Based in town, but no longer keeping a formal office, this Nkhata Bay stalwart, run by a German wildlife enthusiast & his Malawian wife, offers a good selection of wildlife & birding tours countrywide. The flagship 5-day tour to Livingstonia, Vwaza & Nyika costs US$435–865 pp, depending on group size.

Chimango Tours [280 C4] 01 994025; m 099 9268595/4547255; e mayokavillage@yahoo.co.uk; www.mayokavillage.com/chimango. Operating out of Mayoka Village, this dynamic local company specialises in aquatic excursions. Day trips include rock jumping, snorkelling & fish-eagle feeding, & most cost around US$10–25 pp. It also runs pricier 2–4-day kayaking or combined hiking/boating trips to Chikwina, Ruarwe, Usisya & hikes to Kawalazi Village & Tea Estate.

Monkey Business [280 C4] m 099 9437247/5357291. Operating from Butterfly Space, this company specialises in watersports &

local excursions, including highly popular kayak trips & deepwater fishing (inc all equipment) at US$15–20 pp. Overnight kayaking excursions go for US$40/day.

Nkhata Bay Safaris [280 B2] m 099 9265064; e daviemzungu@yahoo.co.uk; www.nkhatabaysafaris.com. Doubling as a free tourist information service, this local company has an office at the start of the road to Chikale Beach, & it also handles tours for Njaya Lodge. Day excursions on the lake or to Kalwe Forest typically cost around US$15–20 pp for 3 or more persons, while overnight trips cost around US$90 pp per day & include a 5-day Livingstonia, Vwaza & Nyika itinerary; there are also more wide-ranging safaris of up to 15 days in duration.

WHERE TO STAY *See map, page 280.*

Unlike Cape Maclear or Senga Bay, Nkhata Bay still caters almost entirely to the more budget-conscious end of the travel spectrum, and while there is no shortage of accommodation, with something to suit most tastes and budgets, there's little that could be described as upmarket. Many places in Nkhata Bay offer a range of private rooms at different prices, as well as dormitories and camping, so the categories used below do overlap slightly, especially as competition for tourist traffic has evidently placed a curb on the sort of inflation noted in room prices elsewhere in Malawi.

MODERATE

Nkhukuti Resort & Conference Centr
(35 rooms) 01 352286; m 088 8572469/099 9574646; e nkhukutiresort@gmail.com. This is the priciest establishment in Nkhata Bay, at least for non-residents, & one of the nicest, set right on the mango-shaded swimming beach at Chikale. Accommodation is in newly built duplex chalets with tile floors, AC, nets, balcony, en-suite bathroom & writing desk, all staggered in three tiers above the main beach. Superior rooms are closest to the beach & have DSTV & tea/coffee facilities as well. The restaurant offers Wi-Fi & a varied menu, with most dishes in the US$3.50–5.50 range. The resident room rate seems more in tune with the competition than the non-resident rate. *US$31.50/47/66 sgl/dbl/superior for non-residents, US$27/38/62.50 for residents.*

Safari Cottage (3 rooms) m 099 9278903/9268588; e info@budget-safari.com; www.safari-cottage.com. This lovely self-catering cottage just before Mayoka Village sleeps up to 5 people, & is rented out as a unit. It is fully fenced, with DSTV & a veranda with lake views, & the rate

includes a daily cleaning & laundry service. It's great value for groups. *US$65 for the whole cottage.*

BUDGET

Aqua Africa Lodge (4 rooms) 01 352284; m 099 9921418; e divemalawi@gmail.com; www.aquaafrica.co.uk. The nicest central option is the small lodge operated by Aqua Africa Dive School, which is used mostly by its guests, but open to all. The lodge has an attractive & convenient location on a low cliff on the same central peninsula as the ferry jetty, right next to the dive school & Dive Deck Café, & close to all other amenities. There's a small beach with hammocks, & the café has a breezy lounge with fantastic bay views. The comfortable en-suite twin rooms have a fan, safe, kitchenette & balcony, while deluxe rooms are larger & have AC & tea/coffee facilities. *US$35 dbl, US$80 superior dbl B&B.*

Butterfly Space (9 rooms, 2 dorms) m 099 9265065/9156335; e josieredmond@hotmail.com or blondieleap@hotmail.com; www.butterfly-space.com. Next door to Mayoka Village, this beautifully located lakeshore lodge is run by a pair of hands-on Brits in conjunction with a variety of local community projects offering opportunities to volunteers (see the website for details). It's not as smart & slickly managed as its neighbour, nor is it so nocturnally hedonistic, but the down-to-earth accommodation & food is a lot cheaper, the atmosphere is welcoming & sociable, & you can always pop through the gate to Mayoka if you're in a party mood. Facilities include regular day trips, free use of dugouts, snorkelling gear & guitars, bicycle hire, internet at Mk10/min, a waterfront bar, occasional concerts & movie screenings, & set meals every evening for US$3/4 vegetarian/meat. *US$7–10 pp stilted dbl room with balcony, US$5 pp dorm, US$3 pp camping.*

🏠 **Ilala Bay Lodge** (12 rooms) ☎ 01 352362; e info@ilalacrestlodge.com; www.ilalacrestlodge.com. Less than 5mins' walk from the bus station, this is the only lodge in the town centre with a private beach, & while the accommodation, in a dbl-storey face-brick building, doesn't quite match the setting, it is a very serviceable set-up with a decent & inexpensive beach restaurant/bar. Spacious en-suite standard dbl rooms come with net, fan & hot shower, & the executive rooms also have DSTV, a 2nd sgl bed & a writing desk. *US$17.50/22 sgl/dbl, US$20.50/25 executive B&B.*

🏠 **Matachi Lakeview Lodge** m 088 8522899/4527246; e lodgematachi@yahoo.com. Situated on the green slopes above the town centre, on the opposite side of the Mzuzu road to Big Blue Star Backpackers (see overleaf), this is one of the oldest lodges in Nkhata Bay. As of 2013, it was being completely rebuilt, but no details are available as to when it will reopen. Expect en-suite tiled rooms with hot water & lake views.

🏠 **Mayoka Village** (15 rooms, 2 dorms) ☎ 01 994025; m 099 9268595; e mayokavillage@yahoo.co.uk; www.mayokavillagebeachlodge.com. This inspiring lodge, built on the steep hill that falls into the lake about 1km from the town centre, is now firmly entrenched as the hub of traveller action in Nkhata Bay. Founded in 1998 in collaboration between local villagers & an energetic South African, Mayoka is well known for its lively party scene, with a bar that stays open late, & an excellent restaurant. The lodge is also well suited to more diurnal travellers, with free access to snorkelling gear & canoes, a small private beach enclosed by rocks, & regular day trips on offer. The small but stylishly decorated & well-equipped chalets perch on the slopes, while camping sites are tucked in next to the paths. It's a cosmopolitan place, where Chief Nyirenda installs himself in his chair in the bar with his mobile chocolate & sweet shop every night & will regale anyone with stories, while the 'worldwide' BBQ buffet on Friday nights is a sure crowd pleaser. Also on the premises is a woodcarving workshop. Other facilities include transfers to/from the ferry, laundry, book exchange & a safe, & there's a wireless internet dongle available for those with laptops. Overall, this is a fantastically well-run & laidback set-up, & justifiably popular, though this does mean that it can be rather cramped & crowded when busy, especially if you are camping. *US$15/28/30 sgl/dbl/trpl, US$20/40 en-suite sgl/dbl, US$8–10 pp dorm, US$5 pp camping.*

🏠 **Njaya Lodge** (16 rooms) ☎ 01 352342; m 099 9409878/9275297; e info@njayalodge.com; www.njayalodge.com; see also advert on page 287. Under the same ownership since it opened in 1993, it was Njaya that first established Nkhata Bay as one of Malawi's top party destinations. Of late, the backpacker party scene has refocused on nearby Mayoka, but Njaya remains a great choice for those seeking greater privacy & a more serene but still very sociable vibe. It has a lovely setting on Chikale Bay 2km from the town centre, spacious gardens running down to a small semi-private beach on the rocky lakeshore, a welcoming restaurant/bar with flat-screen DSTV, Wi-Fi, a library of more than 25,000 songs & hundreds of movies, engaging & flexible staff (many of whom have been here as long as the lodge has), & free snorkelling gear. The comfortable & airy accommodation (with nets, fans, & some rooms with AC) is spaced widely around the green gardens running down to the beach. Visa cards accepted. *US$10 pp rustic beach banda, US$13 pp beach house, US$25 pp en-suite chalet, US$32 pp en-suite cottage, US$5 pp camping, all rates bed only.*

🏠 **The Key Resort** (12 rooms) ☎ 01 352338; m 099 1270332; www.facebook.com/thekeyresort. About 1.5km from town on Chikale Beach, this scores highly on the location stakes, sharing the finest beach in Nkhata Bay with Nkhukuti Resort, but the semi-detached rooms with net & writing desk are nothing to write home about & could do with a facelift. There are a couple of newer rooms which are considerably smarter for the same price. The attractive beachfront bar has a pool table & serves adequate meals for US$4. They also host popular beach parties with local DJs on the first & last weekends of every month. *US$16/23.50 sgl/dbl.*

SHOESTRING

🏠 **Big Blue Star Backpackers** (10 rooms, 3 dorms) `01 352316`; m 099 9656987; e bigbluestarbackpackers@gmail.com; www. bigbluestarbackpackers.com. The best cheapie is this beautifully situated & very chilled backpackers' place, on a rocky beach below the main road from Mzuzu about 500m before you arrive at the town centre. Accommodation here consists of rickety bamboo huts with balconies, some of which stand on stilts right above the beach, & vehicles with rooftop tents can park right alongside the lake, too. Facilities include a bar with DSTV, Wi-Fi, use of kayaks & dugout canoes, & a restaurant serving wraps, baguettes, soups & mains in the US$3–4.50 range. *US$8/14 sgl/dbl hut, US$5–6 pp dorm, US$3.75 pp camping.*

🏠 **Cairo Motel** (30 rooms) m 099 5111072/5680064. Boasting a central location behind the market, this somewhat dingy &

atmospherically challenged trpl-storey monolith has acceptably clean rooms using common showers. The dbl rooms have king-size beds & all rooms have nets. *US$2.50/3.75/4.75 sgl/twin/dbl, US$11 en-suite dbl.*

🏠 **Chill Zone Resthouse** (14 rooms) m 099 9373753. This basic lodge along the road between the market & the ferry jetty has clean but no-frills rooms using common showers & toilets, though the bar next door could be noisy. *US$2.25/3 sgl/ dbl with nets.*

🏠 **Kupenja Lodge** (9 rooms, 1 dorm) m 088 4444064; e mkandawirejohn@yahoo.com. Just up the beach from neighbouring Big Blue Star Backpackers, this unpretentious & convenient lodge is the most affordable backpacker-oriented set-up in Nkhata Bay. Built into a treacherously steep hillside, it's a quiet spot to relax, enjoy the views, & play some *bao*. The rooms are relatively no-frills, but it's a great place to stay, particularly as you can watch the fishermen come in with their catch in the morning. It's undergone a number of improvements under the new Malawian owner-manager, & the new en-suite doubles are excellent value. There's a restaurant serving affordable local meals, or you can self-cater using the lodge kitchen. *US$4.75 sgl, US$8/9.50 en-suite sgl/dbl, US$2.25 pp dorm, US$1.75 pp camping.*

✗ WHERE TO EAT AND DRINK *See map, page 280.*

✗ **Dive Deck Café** `01 352284`; ⏲ 08.00–18.00 daily. Inside Aqua Africa, this smart & breezy café serves Italian & Mediterranean-inspired dishes including salads, pastas, hummus, bruschetta, sandwiches & a rotating menu of nightly specials. Cakes, baked goods & plunger coffee are available all day, & it's a seriously attractive place to use the complimentary Wi-Fi. They've also got juices, milkshakes & the usual range of alcoholic beverages.

✗ **Kachere Café** m 099 4349337; ⏲ 07.00–23.00. Though it wasn't yet open when we stopped in, this place has a beautiful setting on a terraced wooden balcony over the bay. The plan is to offer Thai dishes, pizzas, wraps, fish & more in the US$7–12 range. There's also a full bar with DSTV.

✗ **Kaya Papaya** m 099 3881188; ⏲ 11.00–22.00 Thu–Tue. This funky purple-&-orange restaurant/bar lies on the edge of the town centre towards Mayoka & Njaya. Set in a small

green garden, it's a 2-storey building with a cosy downstairs sitting area & covered seating on the upper floor or balcony. Soups, sandwiches, pizzas & salads supplement an excellent Thai menu. Most dishes cost US$4–5, & every Saturday evening there's a 3-course Thai dinner for US$5.75; call ahead to place your order. The well-stocked bar plays an eclectic selection of music.

✗ **Mayoka Village** `01 994025`; ⏲ 07.00–01.00 daily. The restaurant/bar at this popular backpacker haunt sprawls across a partially shaded wooden deck with lake views. The food is excellent, the menu is as cosmopolitan as the clientele, & it caters to vegetarians & meat-eaters alike, with vegetarian dishes costing around US$3 & meat around US$4.50. The lively bar, attracts plenty of locals & people staying at other lodges, & has a pool table, a good sound system, live music every Sun, & a popular BBQ every Friday evening.

✕ Nkhata Bay Local Restaurant m 099 3841055/7037151; ⏱ 07.30–evening. At the top of the hill along the road towards Njaya & Mayoka, this place has stunning views over the town & good local food & vegetarian options for about US$2, but ring in advance unless you're prepared to wait. They also offer a variety of informal drumming & art lessons starting at US$5/hour plus materials.

✕ Take Away Palace m 088 8390090; ⏱ 07.00–20.00 daily. Attached to the Malji Superette, this place offers good Indian curries, chapattis & grilled chicken, along with Malawian standards in the US$2.50–4.50 range.

✕ Tiku Manepo Restaurant m 099 4669866; ⏱ 06.00–21.00 Mon–Sat, 14.00–20.00 Sun. Hidden away in the market, this clean & friendly local spot is always busy, & is the best place in town for Malawian staples like chicken, fish, or beans with rice or *nsima* for US$1.25–2.

♀ Umoja Sports Centre m 088 1443333; ⏱ 07.00–22.00 daily, later during matches. This lively spot screens all major international football matches & other sporting events. The bar in front is the place to be, with flat-screen DSTV, a pool table & cold drinks at local prices.

SHOPPING

There's a good **People's Supermarket** [280 C2] in the town centre, and a well-stocked **market** [280 B2], though neither compares to its counterparts at Mzuzu, 50km distant. The **Malji Superette** [280 B2] is also reasonably well-stocked, and **Kalindizga Bakery** [280 B2] usually has fresh bread from 06.00 to 18.00 daily. The **Bamboo Shop** [280 A3] (⏱ *08.00–18.30 daily*) on the road towards Chikale stocks a great selection of inexpensive bead and leather jewellery, recycled paper products and the like, as well as paintings by local artists.

Nkhata Bay is one of the best places in Malawi for relaxed **craft shopping**, though the stalls that once lined the central market have relocated further out of town to three main sites. Of these, the cluster of stalls downhill of the Nkhata Bay Local Restaurant [280 B4] and the one next to Kupenja Lodge [280 D1] are the most convenient for travellers without their own transport. However, there's a greater selection on offer at the mass of stalls on either side of the roadblock at the junction of the Mzuzu and Chintheche roads a few kilometres out of town. Another option in town is **Mr Mbewe,** [280 A3], who sells his carvings outside his house on the Chikale road and comes highly recommended.

OTHER PRACTICALITIES

BANKING AND FOREIGN EXCHANGE NBS [280 C1] and **FMB** [280 C1] are the only two banks in town, both located on the Mzuzu road next to the post office [280 C1]. They both have ATMs that accept Visa, but for MasterCard or Maestro, you still need to head to Mzuzu.

INTERNET The most central internet café is **HK IT Solutions Café** [280 B2] (⏱ *07.30–17.30 Mon–Sat*), opposite the market, which charges Mk5/min. The internet café at **Aqua Africa** [280 C3] (⏱ *08.00–18.00 daily*) charges Mk10/min or US$3 for the whole day, and Wi-Fi is free for customers at the Dive Deck Café. For those staying on the beaches south of town, there's super-fast Wi-Fi at **Njaya Lodge** and an internet café at **Butterfly Space**.

IMMIGRATION The **immigration office** [280 B1] behind the Cairo Motel takes a few minutes to process visitors' pass extensions for Mk5,000 (about US$16 at the time of writing) per extra 30 days.

KALWE AND NKUWADZI FOREST RESERVES These two small reserves near Nkhata Bay support some of the last remaining lake littoral forest in this part of Malawi, and can be visited independently or on a guided day tour with Budget Safaris or Nkhata Bay Safaris, ideally in the early morning if you want to see wildlife. Kalwe Forest Reserve, the closer of the two to Nkhata Bay, straddles the Mzuzu road about 2km past the roadblock at the junction with the Chintheche road, and extends over almost 1km², though part of it, tragically, was cleared in 2009 as the site for a new district hospital. Much larger, the 6km² Nkuwadzi Forest Reserve lies about 15km from the same junction but along the road running south towards Chintheche, shortly after Vizara Rubber Plantation.

A fair network of roads and paths runs through both forests, and there is a good chance of seeing blue monkeys and (with luck) red duiker. The area also offers good but often rather frustrating birding, with more than 100 species recorded, many of them quite elusive. The main speciality is the very localised east-coast akalat, which is quite easy to locate, but you might also encounter crested guineafowl, Schalow's turaco, Narina trogon, trumpeter hornbill, barred long-tailed cuckoo, little spotted woodpecker and a wide variety of warblers and robins.

RUARWE Situated on the mouth of the Zulunkhuni River some 60km north of Nkhata Bay and a similar distance south of Chiweta, Ruarwe is among the most isolated lakeshore settlements anywhere in the country, inaccessible by proper roads in either direction. But the same mountains that render Ruarwe so difficult to access also lend the surrounding area a genuine wilderness character and swooning natural beauty, a landscape of tumbling waterfalls, lush riparian forest and steep wooded slopes teeming with baboons, fish eagles and other birds. The village is also the site of one of Malawi's most alluring and isolated tourist facilities, the legendary Zulunkhuni River Lodge, which started life in 2001 as a basic and eco-conscious backpackers called 'Wherearewe?'. Moderately more upmarket today, but no less environmentally aware, the rechristened Zulunkhuni River Lodge remains a wonderfully isolated retreat, and though it can only realistically be visited with a few days to spare, it attracts rave reviews from all who do make it there.

Getting there and away There are several options and, if you are coming from Nkhata Bay, it is worth talking them through with the **Zulunkhuni booking office in Nkhata Bay** (🕓 *07.30–16.00 Sun–Fri;* 📱 *099 9071914*), which is on the ground floor of Kaya Papaya.

Coming from Nkhata Bay or further south, the most popular option is the MV *Ilala*, which, when running, is scheduled to leave Nkhata Bay on the northbound leg at 07.00 on Monday, arriving at Ruarwe a few hours later, and passes back on the southbound leg on Tuesday. This is an inexpensive option (*US$5/9/21.25 economy/ second/first class*), but if you use it in both directions, you will need to choose between a one-night or eight-night stay, neither of which will be ideal for most visitors.

Another option is the Mkorongo boat-taxi, which leaves Nkhata Bay Wednesday and Sunday mornings heading north to Ruarwe, returning on Mondays & Fridays. Cancellations are frequent, however, so first check the situation with the Zulunkhuni booking office. Alternatively, a private boat to Ruarwe can be arranged anytime through the week, though the price fluctuates with the cost of fuel.

Coming from the north, the MV *Ilala* is scheduled to leave Chilumba on the southbound leg on Tuesdays, usually departing very early in the morning. It is also possible to hike in from the north over two to three days, taking public transport from Chiweta as far south as Mlowe, then following lakeshore footpaths and sleeping in local villages (this is a popular trip with Peace Corps volunteers). A boat connects Mlowe to Tcharo at 14.00 daily, returning at 18.00; from Tcharo you would have to walk four hours to Ruarwe or speak nicely to the captain to take you the rest of the way. A variation on this is a challenging but rewarding hike from Livingstonia offered by The Mushroom Farm and Lukwe Eco-Camp (see page 318).

Finally, coming from Mzuzu, a stunning road leads through the North Viphya Mountains to the lakeshore village of Usisya. Local *matolas* to Usisya leave from outside the Chenda Hotel in Mzuzu at around 11.00 daily, and it is also possible to drive yourself, though a 4x4 is required. Once in Usisya, the owner of the new **Usisya Beach Lodge** (see below) will help you on your way. If you're not taking the *Ilala*, you can either walk the 15km from there to Ruarwe (the path is quite flat all the way and porters are available for hire) or charter a boat (expect to pay around US$7 for a dugout or significantly more for a motorboat, assuming that you can provide fuel). The Mkorongo boat-taxi also calls at Usisya on its way to and from Nkhata Bay, and takes about 2–4 hours between Usisya and Ruarwe.

Where to stay *See map, page 242.*

⌂ **Usisya Beach Lodge** (2 rooms, more under construction) m 099 5636585/088 8717819 (SMS preferable); e d.kartscher@gmx.de. This beachside escape is simplicity itself, consisting of grass beach huts & standing tents in the remote fishing village of Usisya. The owner-manager also runs Kaya Papaya in Nkhata Bay, & the food here is also locally grown & Thai-inspired. It's an excellent waypoint on the way to/from Zulunkhuni, & you can make all onward transport arrangements here. There's a sandy beach flanked by granite boulders, outdoor showers & eco-loos, & a circular bar built around a mango tree. There are several more permanent chalets under construction scheduled to open in 2013. *US$15 dbl beach hut, US$5 pp standing tent, US$4 pp camping.*

⌂ **Zulunkhuni River Lodge** (4 rooms, 1 dorm) m 099 9071914/2148000, 088 4710952; e info@lake-paradise.com or zulunkhuni@yahoo.co.uk; www.lake-paradise.com. Practically all visitors to Ruarwe are headed to this peaceful retreat, which prides itself on having no electricity, very limited communications with the outside world & a stress-free natural environment. There's plenty to do here, though, whether you fancy snorkelling or swimming, walking through the riverine forest or paying a visit to one of several local community projects, chilling out with a book from the community library or braving the heart-stopping 8m cliff jump into the lake. There is a bar & restaurant, serving chilled drinks & imaginatively prepared vegetarian dishes. Long-term volunteer opportunities are also available, check out www.phunzira.org for details. *US$13–15 private room, US$8 pp dorm, US$6 pp camping.*

Njaya Lodge
Malawi

*Affordable simple
eco-accommodation
in exquisite surroundings*

For bookings, email:
info@njayalodge.com

+265 997 409 805
www.njayalodge.com

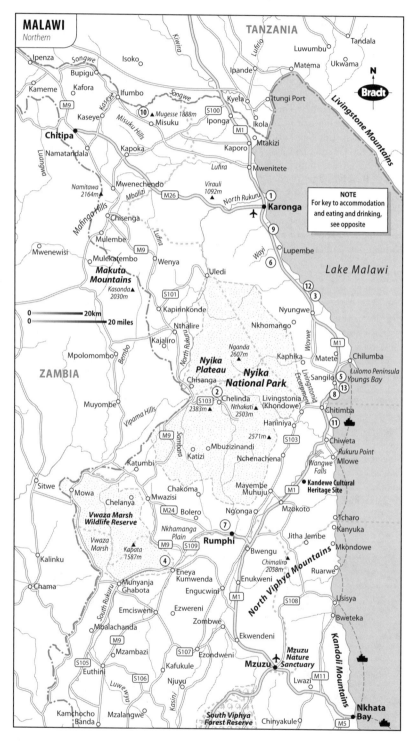

MALAWI
Northern

TANZANIA

ZAMBIA

Lake Malawi

Part Five

NORTHERN MALAWI

OVERVIEW OF PART FIVE

The following four chapters cover the far north of Malawi, a relatively thinly populated region dominated by the wild montane scenery of the sheer Rift Valley Escarpment towering above the northern lakeshore.

Chapter 20 covers the compact and well-equipped regional capital Mzuzu, situated at the junction of the M1 and M5, where it forms the main urban gateway to the region coming from elsewhere in Malawi.

Nyika, the country's largest and most northerly national park, protecting a remote highland plateau on the Zambian border north of Mzuzu, is the main focus of *Chapter 21*, which also incorporates coverage of the gateway town of Rumphi and the underrated but surprisingly accessible Vwaza Marsh Wildlife Reserve.

The region's dramatic topography means that the M1 north of Mzuzu only connects with the lakeshore as it approaches Chitimba, almost 100km north of Nkhata Bay. Chitimba and various nearby lakeshore resorts are covered in *Chapter 22*, along with the more remote highland mission of Livingstonia, which stands on the Rift Valley Escarpment almost 1km above the lake's surface.

Finally, *Chapter 23* covers the lovely Tanzanian border area, an area whose rich historical and archaeological heritage is explored in the new Cultural & Museum Centre in the port town of Karonga. Also included in this chapter are the little-visited but very scenic Misuku Hills, whose forest reserves protect several mammal and bird species unrecorded elsewhere in Malawi.

AQUA AFRICA,
NKHATA BAY,
MALAWI.
WWW.AQUAAFRICA.CO.UK
E-MAIL: DIVEMALAWI@GMAIL.COM
TEL: +265 (0) 999921418

LAKE MALAWI
A TOTALLY FRESH DIVING EXPERIENCE

20

Mzuzu

The capital of Northern Region, Mzuzu is the third-largest town in Malawi, and the fastest growing. An important route focus, it stands at the junction of the highland M1 and lakeshore M5, the two main south–north roads through Malawi. It's also the closest town of substance to the resort village of Nkhata Bay, and the main gateway for travel further north. Set at an elevation of 1,280m on a saddle between the North and South Viphya plateaux, it occupies a mid-altitude niche between the humid lakeshore and the breezy highland chill of the flanking mountains, while an average annual rainfall of 1,750mm ensures that the town and surrounding hills are green and fertile all year through.

Few would visit Mzuzu for its own sake, but if you do overnight there, it's a very friendly and likeable town. The compact, low-rise city centre is easily manageable on foot, and there's a strong people culture with many welcoming cafés and bars where you can sit and chat to locals. As for amenities, Mzuzu is well equipped with hotels and resthouses, restaurants and cafés, and supermarkets, internet and banks. It is somewhat more impoverished when it comes to tourist attractions, though the small central museum and readily accessible out-of-town nature sanctuary are both worth a look.

HISTORY

Mzuzu is very much a modern entity. For much of the colonial era, it was little more than the name of a stream running through the rural hillside, and the small settlement that stood here at the time of independence was practically inaccessible during the rainy season – they say that the highlight of the expatriate social calendar was the arrival of a Beaver plane from Lilongwe every Friday. Mzuzu took over from Mzimba as regional capital in the late 1960s, and it was granted official city status as recently as 1991. Its population has increased more than tenfold in the past two decades, from a mere 16,000 in 1987 to almost 200,000 today. The out-of-town Mzuzu University, established in 1997, is gathering pace and now has more than 1,000 students. In recent years, Mzuzu has also become strongly identified with the excellent coffee marketed by the Mzuzu Coffee Planters Cooperative Union, which represents more than 3,000 individual coffee growers in the highlands of Misuku, North Viphya, Phoka, Mzimba and Nkhata Bay.

GETTING THERE AND AWAY

Mzuzu lies 380km north of Lilongwe and 245km south of Karonga on the surfaced M1, and 50km northwest of Nkhata Bay along the M5. In a private vehicle, bank on about five hours' drive from Lilongwe, four hours from Karonga and 45

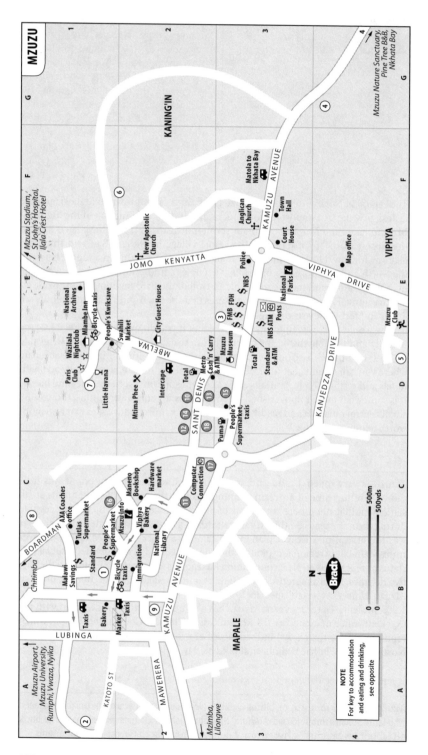

MZUZU

KANING'IN

VIPHYA

MAPALE

NOTE
For key to accommodation
and eating and drinking,
see opposite

minutes from Nkhata Bay. The best bus service to Lilongwe and most other main towns is Axa Coaches (✆ 01 931207/310785/310790), whose buses leave from the main bus station [292 B2], though tickets should be booked in advance at their office [292 C1] near Tutlas Supermarket.   Services include a daily Deluxe Coach to/from Blantyre via Lilongwe, and a daily northbound Deluxe Coach to Karonga and Chitipa. Otherwise, a steady stream of minibuses connects the bus station to most towns in northern and central Malawi, charging US$8 to Lilongwe, US$7 to Karonga, US$4 to Mzimba, US$3.50 to Rumphi and US$3 to Nkhata Bay. When you arrive at the bus station, you'll find plenty of taxis waiting outside and you can expect to pay about US$3 for a town ride. Taxi stands can also be found at the People's Supermarket [292 D3] on Kamuzu Avenue. It's worth noting that transport to Nkhata Bay can be picked up at a stage on the Nkhata Bay road about 200m past the Courthouse. A transfer by taxi to Nkhata Bay would cost around US$25. Taqwa/EasyBus (m 099 9334299/538) runs from Lilongwe to Dar es Salaam several times a week for US$38, picking up passengers from the main bus station in Mzuzu around midnight and arriving in Dar about 18 hours later.

TOURIST INFORMATION

If you visit the **Mzuzu Information Centre Café** [292 C2] (✆ 01 311166; m 099 4552531; e mzuzuinfocentre@yahoo.com; ⏰ 08.00–18.00 Mon–Fri) looking for tourist information, you'll be disappointed, but it's a nice spot for a pot of tea or to browse the internet at Mk10 per minute. More useful is the **National Parks office** [292 E3] (*Viphya Rd;* ✆ 01 332014; e Nyika@malawi.net), which stocks maps and brochures about Nyika and Vwaza Marsh, and can also provide up-to-date information about the status of accommodation in these reserves.

WHERE TO STAY   *See map, opposite.*

Note that the main cluster of local resthouse accommodation, which lies in the backstreets behind the banks and supermarkets, is none too salubrious, as the same area is also dense with nightclubs, pick-up joints – and dodgy drains. The options listed under *Shoestring* on page 295 stand out as the best.

UPMARKET

Mzuzu Sunbird Hotel (60 rooms) ✆ 01 310622; e mzuzuhotel@sunbirdmalawi.com;

www.sunbirdmalawi.com. The Sunbird is the only hotel in Mzuzu to approach international quality, though it's not quite comparable in standard to the same chain's premier units in Blantyre & Lilongwe. It is set in attractive suburban grounds within easy walking distance of the city centre, & has large, comfortable en-suite rooms with DSTV, AC, combined tub/shower, tea-/coffee-making facilities & 24hr room service. Facilities include a good restaurant & bar with pool table, airport transfers, hairdressing, car hire, internet, photocopy, fax & secretarial services, & foreign exchange at a good rate for hotel residents only. Air Malawi & DHL offices are here, as is the Mzuzu branch of Dedza Pottery, & residents get automatic day membership of the adjacent sports club & golf course. It's a Wi-Fi hotspot & Skyband cards are on sale. On Fri nights the Choma Bar is the place to go. *US$194/219 superior sgl/dbl, US$250/274 suite sgl/dbl, all rates B&B.*

MODERATE

🏠 **Ilala Crest Lodge** (29 rooms) \01 311834; m 099 3108721/088 8894196; e info@ ilalacrestlodge.com; www.ilalacrestlodge.com. About 2km from the city centre, in compact manicured gardens on Jomo Kenyatta Rd, past St John's Hospital, this popular hotel has spacious standard rooms with tiled floor, twin or dbl bed, net, DSTV, tea/coffee & cramped en-suite bathrooms, or executive rooms with fridge, kitchenette, private balcony & a larger bathroom. The restaurant serves meals for around US$7.50. *US$54/70 sgl/dbl, US$67/87 executive, all rates B&B.*

🏠 **Mimosa Court Hotel** (11 rooms) \01 312833; e mimosacourthotel@gmail.com. This functional 2-storey hotel, tucked away unobtrusively behind the museum & First Merchant Bank, is the top option in the city centre, but it's not quite to the same standard as the other out-of-town places listed here. The spacious tiled twin & dbl rooms come with DSTV, Wi-Fi, nets, tea/coffee & en-suite hot shower, while deluxe rooms in the annex are larger & have a fridge. *US$33.50/40 sgl/dbl, US$40.50/45.50 executive, US$47.50/58 deluxe, all rates B&B.*

🏠 **Mzuzu Lodge** (20 rooms) \01 332097; e info@mzuzulodge.mit.mw; www.mzuzulodge. mit.mw. Situated 1km along the Nkhata Bay road, this established lodge stands in large green grounds offering a panoramic view of the hills below the city. It is worth paying for one of the executive rooms in the new wing, which come

with queen-size or twin ¾ beds, net, DSTV, large en-suite bathroom with combined tub/shower, & in some cases a private balcony. The standard twins & superior dbls in the old wing have similar facilities but look very tired by comparison, & aren't that much cheaper. The restaurant charges US$8 for mains or US$14 for a 3-couse dinner. *US$40/53 standard sgl/twin, US$47/67 superior, US$57/77 executive.*

🏠 **Pine Tree B&B** (3 rooms, 1 dorm) m 099 5634395/9938721; e ptreemzuzu@hotmail.com. This attractive owner-managed lodge opened in 2009 & has since established itself as a favourite among travellers & local expats. It's about 3km along the Nkhata Bay road, just across from Mzuzu Nature Sanctuary. It's a very clean & homely set-up, with outstanding food (mains US$6–8) & a rustic setting with a wide veranda overlooking a valley. If you are coming from Nkhata Bay, ask to be dropped off at the State House stage, which is almost directly in front. *US$40 en-suite dbl, US$40 4-bed family room, B&B.*

BUDGET

🏠 **Flame Tree Guesthouse** (7 rooms) \01 310056; m 099 9511423. This appealing suburban lodge lies about 10mins' walk from the bus station in a calm quiet garden. Meals cost around US$5, there's a well-stocked bar & a selection of books to swap. *US$12.50 dbl, US$14 en-suite dbl B&B.*

🏠 **Chenda Hotel** (32 rooms) \01 312788; m 099 5432218. This long-serving & centrally located hotel is a reasonable fallback in this range, but it's looking a little tired & the ornate décor will appeal more to local business travellers than to tourists. All rooms have twin or dbl beds, TV & en-suite hot tub or showers. Overpriced. *US$23.50/33.50/53.50 sgl/twin/dbl B&B.*

🏠 **Mzoozoozoo Backpackers' Lodge** (3 rooms, 2 dorms) m 088 8864493. The 'Zoo' is undoubtedly the liveliest place in town & a popular choice with backpackers, with wooden 4-bed dorm & dbl rooms, & an ever-flowing bar with good music, a welcoming atmosphere & tasty food. It's also a useful source of up-to-date travel information for the region. Tucked away on a backstreet off Jomo Kenyatta Rd, it's not easy to find (there are no signposts anywhere in town) but the taxi drivers at the bus station know where it is. *US$16 dbl or twin, US$6.50 pp dorm, US$3 pp camping.*

Zikomo Lodge m 099 9409577/ 5441871/088 8683500. In a multi-storey building less than 300m from the bus station, this local lodge doesn't offer much in the way of character, but the upstairs en-suite rooms are bright, airy & spotless. All are tiled & have TV, hot showers & nets. Rooms include b/fast, but you can take US$3 off the room rates if you'd prefer to go without. *US$14/17.50 sgl/dbl, US$15.75/18.75 en-suite sgl/ dbl, B&B.*

SHOESTRING

Thandeka Resthouse (32 rooms) 01 11930402. Set amid the main cluster of nightclubs but far enough from the main road to be reasonably quiet, this has clean & secure rooms in the new wing, & it makes some effort to distance itself from the surrounding high jinks with a notice reading: 'The only recommended people to sleep is 2 only such as i. Mr & Mrs ii. Mr & Mr iii. Miss & Miss.' *US$3.25/4.75 sgl/twin.*

William Koyi Guesthouse (9 rooms, 4 dorms) 01 312333. In the CCAP compound off Boardman Rd, not far from the bus station, this is a good no-frills option, with clean accommodation, adequate canteen food & a quiet but central location. All rooms have nets. *US$12.50 twin, US$18.75 en-suite dbl with hot shower, US$3.25 pp 4-bed dorm, US$3.25 pp camping.*

✖ WHERE TO EAT AND DRINK   *See map, page 292.*

✖ A1 Restaurant m 099 5233445/ 088 8233445; ⏰ 10.30–22.00 daily. This comfortable restaurant is the best in the city centre, catering to vegetarians & meat eaters alike with its varied menu of Tandoori & other Indian dishes, supplemented by good pizzas & some Chinese options. It also has a well-stocked bar, DSTV & Wi-Fi. Mains work out at around US$5.50, with vegetarian options at US$4.

✖ Big Bite 01 311017; ⏰ 08.00–19.00 Mon– Sat, 09.00–19.00 Sun. This friendly Indian-run place is very popular at lunchtime for their burgers, subs (filled baguettes), pizzas & curries. Dishes are mostly in the US$2–4 range, & it also serves ice cream (when the machine is working). No alcohol.

✖ Green Vee Restaurant m 088 899666. This popular spot serves the usual Malawian staples for around US$1.50–2.50, & a lively bar is attached.

✖ Mark Restaurant m 099 9916635; ⏰ 08.00–22.00 daily. A sharp new fast food option in the city centre, this place has pizzas (topping choices include 'harm'), burgers, kebabs & other grills mostly in the US$3–5 range. Snacks, breakfasts & ice cream round out their offerings.

✖ Mzoozoozoo m 088 8864493; ⏰ 08.00–late daily. This suburban backpackers is a great place to meet travellers & volunteers based in Mzuzu. There's a lively bar & great home-style cooking, with breakfasts & sandwiches at around US$2–3 & more substantial dishes in the US$4.25–5.25 range.

✖ Mzuzu Coffee Den 01 311987; m 099 9957351; ⏰ 06.00–22.00 daily. This is Mzuzu's only proper café, & they offer a selection of coffee & tea to please the choosiest caffeine connoisseurs. Along with the cappuccinos & iced coffees, a variety of sandwiches & snacks are on offer for US$2. Customers are welcome to use their Wi-Fi all day for US$1.

✖ Nonhla's Restaurant m 099 9953855; ⏰ 06.30–19.00 Mon–Sat. Just opened at the end of 2012, this simple restaurant offers Malawian cuisine beyond the standard *nsima* & stew for US$1.50–4. There's a lengthy menu, but the daily specials on the chalkboard out front might be a better indicator of what's actually available.

✖ Nyika Restaurant 01 332622; ⏰ 06.00– 22.00 daily. This is the smartest eatery in town, situated on the ground floor of the Mzuzu Sunbird Hotel. It serves continental fare with African & Asian touches in a sedate atmosphere. Most mains are in the US$7–9 range, but there are cheaper vegetarian dishes & snacks.

✖ Obrigados Leisure Park m 088 8869696; ⏰ 11.00–late. This is a great place to hang out during the day or evening, with a shady garden, good Malawian fare for around US$2.50, & occasional live music. The garden also has a boxing ring, a stage, a children's play area & a pool table.

✖ Pine Tree B&B m 099 5634395/9938721. The restaurant here has a well-deserved reputation for serving some of Mzuzu's finest cuisine. Chalked up on the walls, the rotating menu features a wide variety of continental dishes including soups, steaks, duck, lasagne & an indulgent selection of desserts, all in the US$6–8 range. There is a sizeable wine list & casual outdoor seating on a shady veranda.

✕ **Sombrero Restaurant** \01 312833; ⊕ for b/fast, lunch & dinner daily. On the ground floor of the Mimosa Court Hotel, this has a good selection of meat, fish & vegetarian dishes in the US$3.50–5.50 range, including stir-fries & curries, & the steak comes recommended. There's an all-you-can-eat buffet on the last Saturday of the month.

NIGHTLIFE

The **Choma Bar** in the Mzuzu Sunbird Hotel tends to be quiet on week nights, when it closes at 22.00, but it is *the* place to go on Friday nights, staying open until the last customer leaves. There are several less flashy nightclubs, including the **Sports Café** and **BM Interland**, which are also busiest on Friday, but open every day, competing with each other in the amplified distortion stakes on opposite sides of St Denis Road, even when empty of clients. Another half-dozen clubs are dotted around Mbelwa Road north of the Swahili Market. **Mzoozoozoo** remains the backpacker hangout of choice, and the bar has been known to host some memorable (or not-so-memorable) parties.

SHOPPING

The **People's Supermarket** [292 D3] on Kamuzu Avenue is among the best stocked in the country, and has its own bakery and butcher. The **Tutlas Supermarket** [292 B1] is also good. The **Viphya Bakery** [292 C2] is probably the best in town, selling fresh brown and white loaves as well as scones and pastries. The **main market** [292 B2] is on the west side of town next to the bus station, but there's also a **hardware market** [292 C2] off Boardman Road and the clothing- and textile-oriented **Swahili Market** [292 D1] on Mbewa Road. Mzuzu offers surprisingly little in the way of handicraft shopping (Nkhata Bay is much better). An exception is **Mzuzu Pottery** (⋔ *01 310622;* m *088 8345401;* ⊕ *07.30–17.00 daily*) – the local branch of Dedza Pottery – in the foyer of the Mzuzu Sunbird Hotel, which sells various ceramic items, books, postcards and other curios, and accepts Visa payments. They also usually stock the Bradt guides to Malawi and neighbouring countries such as Mozambique, Tanzania and Zambia.

OTHER PRACTICALITIES

BANKS AND FOREIGN EXCHANGE The banks are mostly clustered along the east end of Kamuzu Avenue. All have Visa ATMs and forex facilities, and ATMs at the **Standard** and **National** banks also accept international Master and Maestro cards. Private forex bureaux have been slow to reopen in Mzuzu after a government-ordered shutdown in 2009, and there were none operating at the time of writing.

IMMIGRATION The **immigration office** [292 B2] around the corner from the main market takes a few minutes to process visitors' pass extensions for Mk5,000 (about US$16 at the time of writing) per extra 30 days.

INTERNET The two best internet cafés are **Computer Connection** [292 C2] (⊕ *08.00–17.00 Mon–Fri, 08.00–15.30 Sat*), which charges Mk5 per minute, and **Posts** [292 E3], attached to the post office on Kamuzu Avenue. The Mzuzu Coffee Den offers customers all-day Wi-Fi use for US$1. For Skyband Wi-Fi, head to the Mzuzu Sunbird Hotel.

SPORTS Founded in 1955, the **Mzuzu Club** [292 E4] (✆ *01 312597*) offers free day membership to residents of the neighbouring Mzuzu Sunbird Hotel (bring your key) and to anybody who arrives with a full member. Day membership costs US$1.50, and entitles you to use the nine-hole golf course at a charge of US$1.50 per person, with an additional US$1.50 caddy fee (negotiable) and US$1.50 for golf-club hire. All-comers are welcome at the restaurant (though the fare here doesn't look that tantalising) but the bar, which opens at 08.00 and keeps going until the last person drops or leaves, is strictly for full and day members only.

WHAT TO SEE AND DO

MZUZU MUSEUM [292 D3] (✆ *01 311455;* m *099 9386624;* ⊕ *07.30–12.00 & 13.00–17.00 Mon–Fri; free guided tours on request; entrance US$0.75*) Tucked away on the ground floor of the face-brick Mpico House on Mbelwa Road, this small museum is an excellent resource for local schools. A quick guided tour from one of the enthusiastic staff is worthwhile for the insight offered into the origin of *malipenga* dancing (which developed from the military parades of the King's African Rifles in the two world wars), the collection of traditional instruments and other artefacts used in local villages, and a series of old monochrome photos showing the installation of a Ngoni paramount chief. As interesting as the exhibits are the activities that can be arranged through the museum: traditional music groups and dancing is often put on by request, and there are also Zulu language lessons twice a week.

MZUZU NATURE SANCTUARY (✆ *01 301247;* ⊕ *07.30–17.00 daily*) Bordering the larger Kang'ina Forest Reserve, this sanctuary protects 30ha of indigenous Brachystegia woodland that has been rehabilitated from farmland since 1985. An information centre displaying skulls, horns and other artefacts stands near the entrance, and two short walking trails offer the opportunity to look for wildlife such as red duiker, yellow baboon, vervet monkey, elephant-shrew, bushpig, and a wide variety of woodland birds including Schalow's turaco, Boehm's bee-eater, Waller's starling, pygmy kingfisher and black-headed oriole. The reserve lies about 3km from the city centre and it is clearly signposted on the left side of the Nkhata Bay road, opposite Pine Tree B&B. A taxi from town will cost around US$4 one-way, or you can just head out along the Nkhata Bay road about 200m past the Courthouse, hop on any public transport, and ask to be dropped off at the State House bus stage. There's no entrance fee, but that might change during the lifespan of this edition.

21

Nyika and Vwaza

Northwest of Mzuzu, tucked up against the border with Zambia, stand two of Malawi's finest – and most geographically contrasting – reserves. Foremost among these is Nyika National Park, the country's largest conservation area, centred upon a wild chill highland plateau whose undulating landscapes provide a spectacular setting for rambling and hiking in the company of a variety of big-game species. Immediately south of this, the more torrid and low-lying Vwaza Marsh Wildlife Reserve, an eastern extension of Zambia's legendary Luangwa Valley, is a more stereotypical game-viewing destination, notable in particular for the large herds of elephant that traverse its wooded plains and wetlands.

The main urban gateway to Vwaza and Nyika is Rumphi, situated to the west of the M1 some 65km north of Mzuzu. For motorised travellers, Vwaza Marsh is easily reached from Rumphi using a back road to Mzimba, while for those dependent on public transport it is among the most accessible of Malawi's major game-viewing destinations. Nyika, by contrast, provides more of a challenge to independent travellers, as the road can be quite tough going without a good 4x4, especially after rains, and public transport is practically non-existent. However, several operators in Nkhata Bay offer reasonably priced tours to Nyika and Vwaza, and visits can also be arranged through Matunkha Ecotourism Lodge outside Rumphi.

Both parks have witnessed radical changes in recent years, precipitated by Malawi National Parks' 2008 withdrawal of Nyika Safari Company's long-standing concession to manage all lodging and camping facilities in both reserves. Nyika was taken over by the highly respected operator Wilderness Safaris Malawi (which also manages Mvuu Lodge and Camp in Liwonde National Park) in 2009, while Vwaza has remained under National Parks' management, and facilities have suffered as a result. It is expected that Vwaza will be awarded to a new concessionaire during the lifespan of this edition, and we will continue to provide updated information on the website http://updates.bradtguides.com/malawi.

RUMPHI

Attractively ringed by wooded hills on the north bank of the fast-flowing South Rukuru River, the small town of Rumphi (population 30,000) is the administrative capital of the eponymous district and main commercial centre for its declining tobacco industry. Of little inherent interest to visitors, the town nevertheless attracts a steady trickle of tourist traffic as the main springboard for visits to Nyika and Vwaza Marsh Wildlife Reserve, and the out-of-town Matunkha Eco-Tourism Lodge provides an excellent base for those who want to overnight *en route*.

As far as travel practicalities go, most essentials are to be found in Rumphi. In addition to a few resthouses and restaurants, it boasts a reasonably well-stocked

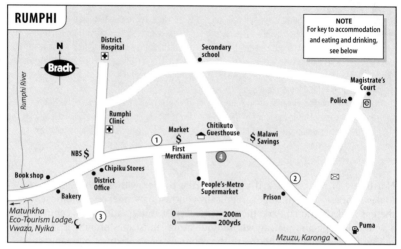

RUMPHI

NOTE
For key to accommodation
and eating and drinking,
see below

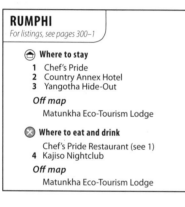

RUMPHI
For listings, see pages 300–1

🛏 **Where to stay**
1 Chef's Pride
2 Country Annex Hotel
3 Yangotha Hide-Out

Off map
Matunkha Eco-Tourism Lodge

✖ **Where to eat and drink**
Chef's Pride Restaurant (see 1)
4 Kajiso Nightclub

Off map
Matunkha Eco-Tourism Lodge

People's **Supermarket**, a busy **market**, several **banks** (with ATMs accepting Visa cards), a Puma **filling station** and **internet** access, respectively providing Nyika- and Vwaza-bound travellers with a last opportunity to stock up on groceries, buy fresh vegetables and fruit, draw money, fuel up or check email. That said, be warned that all these facilities are inferior or less reliable than their counterparts in Mzuzu, so best to take care of what business you can there, and treat Rumphi as a last-gasp fallback.

GETTING THERE AND AWAY Rumphi lies about 65km north of Mzuzu, and 7km from the M1, along a surfaced side road that follows the South Rukuru River westward before crossing a major bridge about 2km out of town. Minibuses between Mzuzu and Rumphi leave regularly in either direction on a fill-up-and-go basis, and cost US$3.50. Buses between Mzuzu and Karonga also generally divert to Rumphi. A daily bus connects Rumphi with Mzimba via Vwaza Marsh, and there are also a fair number of *matolas* heading this way. There is an option to walk from Rumphi to Nyika on an organised walk with Matunkha Ecotourism Lodge using local guides and taking only a maximum of five people per group.

🏠 WHERE TO STAY *See map, above.*
Budget
🏠 **Matunkha Ecotourism Lodge** (6 rooms) m 088 8203424/8202643; e eco-tourism@ matunkha.com; www.matunkha.nl. Situated on the right side of the Vwaza–Nyika road about 2km from Rumphi town centre (precisely 1.2km from where the tar ends), this hillside ecotourism camp

lies in the grounds of an impressive orphanage, & all proceeds go towards the support of the children living & learning there. Accommodation is in reasonably priced chalets, camping is permitted, & there's an attractively decorated restaurant. There is a small craft shop & internet access, & the grounds support indigenous vegetation inhabited by monkeys & a variety of birds. While you will find that lodges in Malawi are often quietly supporting a raft of community projects & orphanages, this is nevertheless a very impressive set-up & a stay here will be very informative. The lodge can also arrange a number of local tours, ranging from short community tours to a nearby village for US$8 pp to Nyika & Vwaza safaris in the range of US$90–400 pp depending on group size & duration (see website for further details). *US$25/30 sgl/dbl using common shower, US$30/35 en-suite sgl/dbl, US$4 pp camping, discount for residents.*

SHOESTRING

🏠 **Chef's Pride** ✆01 372428; m 088 8370893/8362882; e alfredlongwem@yahoo.com. Attached

to its namesake restaurant, this excellent new guesthouse is your best pick in Rumphi town. The tiled rooms are squeaky clean & surprisingly pleasant for the price, & the restaurant/bar is a welcoming spot for a quick meal. *US$6.50/8 en-suite sgl/dbl.*

🏠 **Country Annex Hotel** ✆01 372568. Another good option on the main road, offering clean dbl rooms in a secure compound near the Puma garage. Rooms in the new wing are significantly smarter but significantly pricier. *US$3.25/16 en-suite dbl in old/new wing.*

🏠 **Yangotha Hide-Out** This adequate cheapie is about 150m from the main road. *US$3.50/6.50 sgl/twin.*

🍴 WHERE TO EAT AND DRINK *See map, opposite.*

🍴 **Chef's Pride Restaurant** ✆01 372428; m 088 8370893/8362882. This central eatery serves typical Malawian fare in the US$2–4 range, & they also have fresh juices.

🍴 **Matunkha Ecotourism Lodge** m 088 8203424/8202643; ⏰ 06.00–21.30 daily. This out-of-town lodge has a great little restaurant with indoor & outdoor seating, serving pizzas & very palatable meals in the US$3–4 range, as well as cheaper snacks, beers & soft drinks.

☆ **Kajiso Nightclub** With its blaring sound system & flashing lights, this establishment wouldn't look out of place in downtown Nairobi on a busy night, particularly during the tobacco-harvesting season when local farmers roll into Rumphi to drink away their profits. Out of season, it's a lot more sedate.

NYIKA NATIONAL PARK

(⏰ *Early–18.00 daily (entrance gate); entrance US10 pp per 24hrs. Daily fee for private vehicles US$3)* Malawi's largest national park, Nyika was gazetted in 1965 and extended to its modern size of 3,134km² in 1978, though parts of what is now the national park have been under government protection since the 1940s. At the heart of the park, averaging over 2,000m in altitude, lies the gently undulating Nyika Plateau, where montane grassland and fern heather communities, notable for their prolific wild flowers during the rainy season, are interspersed with isolated stands of indigenous forest and exotic pine and eucalyptus plantations. Although the Nyika Plateau is very much the centrepiece of the park, and the only part that is readily accessible to tourists, the Brachystegia-covered lower slopes of the Nyika range also lie within its boundaries. The plateau is thus one of the coldest parts of Malawi, moderate in summer but subject to fierce winds and sub-zero temperatures often recorded on winter nights.

Nyika's main attraction is the wonderful montane scenery, a landscape unlike any other in Malawi, and one which reminds many visitors of Europe (an impression reinforced by the extensive pine plantations in the Chelinda area and the chilly winter nights characteristic of the plateau). The park was once notable for being one of the few African national parks with a stable and horseriding facilities, but it remains to be seen if and when this facility will return. Nyika affords visitors the freedom to explore a vast network of dirt roads and footpaths through an area rich

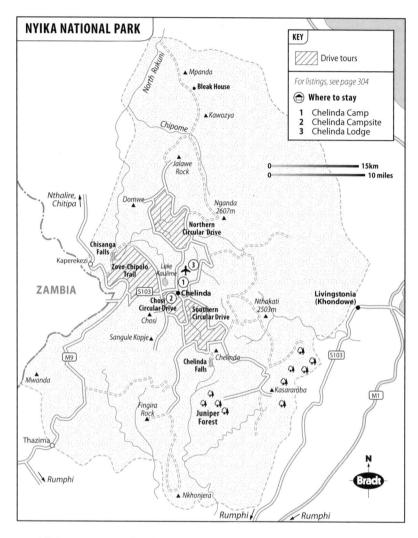

KEY

▨ Drive tours

For listings, see page 304

⌂ **Where to stay**
1 Chelinda Camp
2 Chelinda Campsite
3 Chelinda Lodge

North Rukuni

▲ Mpanda
● Bleak House

▲ Kawozya

Chipome

▲ Jalawe Rock

0 ─── 15km
0 ─── 10 miles

Nthalire, Chitipa

Domwe ▲

Nganda 2607m ▲

Northern Circular Drive

Chisanga Falls

Kaperekezi

Zovo-Chipolo Trail

Lake Kaulime

✈ ③
①

ZAMBIA

S103

Chosi ②
Chosi Circular Drive
▲ Chosi

●Chelinda

Southern Circular Drive

Nthakati 2503m ▲

Livingstonia (Khondowe)

Sangule Kopje ▲

M9

Chelinda Falls

Chelinda

S103

▲ Mwanda

Kasaramba ▲

M1

Fingira Rock

Juniper Forest

Thazima

↖ Rumphi

N

Bradt

▲ Nkhonjera

Rumphi ↙   ↙ Rumphi

in wildlife great and small. Of particular interest to botanists are roughly 200 orchid species, which generally flower in January and February; of these, 11 species are endemic to Nyika and a further 27 are found nowhere else in Malawi.

The long-standing lease for Chelinda Camp was withdrawn in 2008, leading to a period of uncertainty during which roads and facilities deteriorated, and poaching reputedly increased. Wilderness Safaris Malawi was awarded the concession in 2009 and there has thankfully been a complete overhaul of facilities and accommodation since.

WILDLIFE Nyika protects a rich diversity of mammals. Almost 100 species have been recorded, including an endemic race of Burchell's zebra (*Equus burchelli crawshayi*) and what is widely regarded to be the most concentrated leopard population in central Africa. In recent years a herd of more than 40 altitude-loving elephant have made their permanent home here, and they are now often spotted with young. Game viewing is good all year round, and the open nature of the plateau ensures excellent visibility. Owing to extensive poaching in more remote areas, animal populations are concentrated around Chelinda (sometimes spelt Chilinda) Camp, where visitors are practically guaranteed to see roan antelope, scrub hare, Burchell's zebra, reedbuck, bushbuck and eland, and stand a good chance of encountering one of the leopards that haunt Chelinda Forest. The Brachystegia woodland of the lower slopes supports significant populations of buffalo and elephant. Lion and cheetah are listed as infrequent visitors to the plateau, though neither has been seen in years, but visitors do stand a good chance of encountering spotted hyena and smaller nocturnal predators on night drives.

With well over 400 species recorded, Nyika supports the greatest diversity of birds found anywhere in Malawi, though this figure is rather deceptive as many of the species included on the checklist occur only in the inaccessible Brachystegia woodland of the lower slopes and are thus unlikely to be seen by visitors who stick to the plateau. Nevertheless, several tantalising birds inhabit the grassland around Chelinda Camp. Foremost among these is the internationally endangered wattled crane, a large, striking bird that is nowhere as likely to be seen as in the marshes around Chelinda. The dam in front of Chelinda is a good place to spot up the mountain marsh widow, an improbably long-tailed species restricted to a handful of montane areas in central Africa. Other grassland birds of note include the localised Denham's bustard and the exquisite scarlet-tufted malachite sunbird.

More rewarding than the grassland for general birding are the forests, particularly the large Chowo Forest, where localised species such as Sharpe's akalat, bar-tailed trogon, olive-flanked robin, white-breasted alethe and a variety of other robins and bulbuls may be seen. Four birds found at Nyika have been recorded nowhere else in Malawi (yellow mountain warbler, chirring cisticola, crackling cloud cisticola and mountain marsh widow), while the Nyika races of red-winged francolin, rufous-naped lark, greater double-collared sunbird and Baglafecht weaver are endemic to the plateau. There are also three butterfly species endemic to the plateau, and one species each of chameleon, frog and toad are found nowhere else.

GETTING THERE AND AWAY By road, Chelinda Camp is roughly 100km from Rumphi, and clearly signposted. The road there is highly variable in condition, depending on how recently it rained and when it was last graded, so a sturdy 4x4 may be required, especially in the rainy summer months. The route from Rumphi entails following the M24 westward for around 50km, then turning right onto the M9 to Chitipa. The Thazima Entrance Gate lies 8km along the M9, and it's about 30km further to the signposted turn-off right to Chelinda, another 16km away. If you are driving yourself, take note that the last place where you can buy fuel before reaching Chelinda is at Rumphi, and make a point of checking current road conditions with the National Parks office in Mzuzu.

Without private transport, getting to Chelinda cheaply by road is problematic, as no public transport runs all the way through. In the dry season, a twice-weekly bus between Rumphi and Chitipa can drop you at the last turn-off, from where you'll either have to walk the last 16km to Chelinda (it's reasonably flat!) or else hope to hitch a lift. In the rainy season, there is no bus, and *matola* traffic along the M24 from Rumphi to Katumbi would strand you more than 50km from Chelinda. There are irregular *matolas* year-round between Rumphi and Nthalire which could also drop you at the Chelinda turn-off, but there's no schedule; ask around in Rumphi for the next departure.

A more realistic option than either of these is to arrange a budget safari to Nyika and Vwaza out of Nkhata Bay through Budget Safaris or Nkhata Bay Safaris, which start at around US$90 per person per day, depending on duration and group size (see page 282 for further details). More adventurously, Matunkha Eco-Tours now offers a two-day hike up to Chelinda from Rumphi (see *Where to stay*, below).

For those without major budget restrictions, Ulendo Airlink (*www.flyulendo. com*) flies to Chelinda daily from Lilongwe via Likoma Island for US$485 one-way, with a minimum of two passengers. Nyassa Air Taxi (*www.nyassa.mw*) offers a charter service to Chelinda, and Wilderness Safaris Malawi can arrange all charter flights and road transfers. Safaris can also be organised through a number of operators based in Lilongwe or Blantyre.

WHERE TO STAY AND EAT *See map, page 302.*

There is only one area to stay on the Nyika Plateau unless you are on a guided safari which has overnight stops, and all the accommodation there is bookable through Wilderness Safaris Malawi (*01 771393/153*; e *info@wilderness.mw; www. wilderness-safaris.com*). Because room space is limited and the camp is a long way from any other accommodation, advance booking is highly recommended (unless you plan to camp); last-minute queries can be directed to the emergency mobile number (*088 8822398*).

Chelinda Camp (10 rooms) Booking details above. This picturesque cluster of old colonial forestry buildings lies downhill from the lodge, overlooking an attractive small dam & encircled by an extensive plantation of exotic pines. The camp operates as a separate entity from the lodge, & consists of 6 renovated self-contained dbl rooms, 4 private self-catering chalets & a cosy restaurant/bar with a children's playground out front. Each chalet has 2 dbl bedrooms, fireplace, a large lounge, an en-suite shower & toilet & a fully equipped kitchen. All soft furnishings have been upgraded following the takeover by Wilderness. *From US$330/480 to US$355/530 sgl/dbl rooms, depending on season, inclusive of all meals, activities & park fees, US$160/ unit (up to 4 people) self-catering chalets, with discounts offered to Malawi residents.*

Chelinda Lodge (8 rooms) Booking details above. The most upmarket option is this stone-&-timber lodge on the edge of the forest at Chelinda, which offers accommodation in luxurious en-suite log cabins that command stunning views across the montane grasslands of the plateau. Fully renovated in 2010, the handsomely appointed split-level rooms all have twin/dbl bed, upstairs lounge, fireplace, private balcony, bathtub & all-new furnishings. The sunny main lodge & dining area is equally impressive, with vaulted ceilings, tall windows, a wide viewing deck overlooking the plateau & a large central fireplace. *From US$400/600 to US$450/700 sgl/dbl depending on season, inclusive of all meals, activities & park fees, with discounts offered to African & Malawi residents.*

Chelinda Campsite About 2km from the main camp, this is one of the loveliest places to stay for the sweeping views over the undulating grasslands. It has welcome hot showers in a large ablution block & you can pitch your own tent. The walk back from the bar at night is a bit intrepid, given that hyena & leopard are around. There's a sign all campers should heed in the campsite, to tidy all belongings away as 'hyenas eat everything', & have even been known to gnaw on car tyres. *US$15 pp camping.*

What to eat Most people are accommodated on a full-board basis. Self-catering visitors in the chalets or campsite have the option of preparing their own food, but must bring *all* provisions with them or risk being very hungry. The nearest shops are four hours back in Rumphi, but the selection here is limited so you'd be better off stocking up in Mzuzu or Lilongwe. Should you want to eat in the camp dining room, try to book well in advance – typical prices are breakfast US$15, lunch US$20, dinner US$25 per person.

FURTHER INFORMATION For a broader introduction to the park and its flora and fauna, the best resource is the out-of-print 150-page *A Visitor's Guide to Nyika National Park, Malawi* (Mbabazi Book Trust, Blantyre) by Sigrid Anna Johnson. This book provides a detailed historical and ecological background to Nyika, 20 pages of special-interest sites and recommended walks and hikes, as well as complete checklists of all mammals, birds, butterflies and orchids recorded prior to its publication in 1989. It is not as easy to locate as it used to be, but you might still pick up a copy at bookshops in Blantyre and Lilongwe, and you can also refer to it in the library at Chelinda. A range of other books, pamphlets and maps relating to Nyika is sold at the shop in Chelinda Camp.

Another useful resource is the website of the **Nyika Vwaza Trust** (*www.nyika-vwaza-trust.org*), a UK-based organisation dedicated to preserving the wildlife and habitats of Nyika and Vwaza. The best source of current practical information is **Wilderness Safaris Malawi** (\ *01 771393/153;* e *info@wilderness.mw; www.wilderness-safaris.com*). Updates will also be posted at http://updates.bradtguides.com/malawi.

EXPLORING NYIKA Nyika National Park is rich in scenic spots, archaeological sites, mammals and birds, and the extensive network of roads and trails within the park gives visitors a practically unlimited number of hiking and driving options, and mountain bikes are also available for hire at Chelinda Camp (*US$20 per day*). All guided activities and night drives must be organised through Wilderness Safaris Malawi.

Walks around Chelinda
Plenty of roads radiate from Chelinda Camp, and it would be quite possible to spend four or five days in the area without repeating a walk. Unaccompanied short walks are no problem, but you're required to bring a guide along for trips beyond the dams or pine plantation. The marshy area immediately downstream of Chelinda Dam (which lies right in front of the camp) is a good place to see bushbuck and a variety of birds, and the dam itself attracts nocturnal predators such as hyena and leopard. A good short walk for visitors with limited time is to the **two dams** near Chelinda. The road here follows a *dambo* (a seasonal or perennial marsh) and the area offers good game viewing, as well as frequent sightings of wattled crane. The round trip covers 8km and takes two hours.

Another good short walk (about an hour) is from behind Chalet Four to the Kasaramba turn-off and then left along Forest Drive through the pine plantation back to Chalet Four. At dusk, there is a fair chance of seeing leopards along this walk, and daytime sightings are not uncommon.

A longer walk takes you to **Lake Kaulime**, which lies 8km west of Chelinda. This is the only natural lake on the plateau and is traditionally said to be the home of the serpent that acts as a guardian to Nyika's animals. More certain attractions than legendary serpents are migratory waterfowl (in summer) and large mammals, particularly roan antelope and zebra, coming to drink. It is also a very attractive spot, circled by indigenous trees.

Horse safaris
This used to be a great way of exploring Nyika, as well as getting in amongst the game – eland in particular allow horses to approach far more closely than they would a vehicle or pedestrian, as do the wary Nyika elephants. As of 2013, Wilderness Safaris was seeking an operator to re-establish the stables, but at this stage it's unclear if and when this will happen.

Game drives Both morning & night game drives are offered at Chelinda and are included in the guest rate, while campers can arrange them for $30 pp for parties of two or more. Spotlighted night drives out of Chelinda are highly recommended as they offer the best opportunity to see nocturnal predators. Leopard and serval are often seen on the fringes of Chelinda Forest, while spotted hyena and side-striped jackal are common in grassy areas, and the likes of honey badger are seen from time to time. Especially in winter, the plateau gets really cold at night, and you should take all your warm clothing with you in the vehicle.

Angling The rivers and dams on the Nyika Plateau are stocked with rainbow trout, and are thus popular with anglers. The dams are closed to anglers from April through to September, but the rivers are open throughout the year. Fishing permits must be arranged through Wilderness Safaris at Chelinda. Licences cost US$4 per day and rods can be hired for US$20 per day.

Guided wilderness trails Six wilderness trails have been designated within Nyika National Park, ranging from one to five nights in duration. Visitors wishing to use these trails must supply their own camping equipment and food, and are required to make an advance booking through Wilderness Safaris Malawi (for contact details, see page 96).

The most popular of Nyika's wilderness trails is the **Livingstonia Trail**, which leads from Chelinda all the way to Livingstonia on the Rift Valley Escarpment east of the national park. This three-day, two-night guided hike is recommended only in the dry season, and it costs US$80 for one or two people and another US$10 for every additional person. It is not permitted to hike this route in reverse, as a guide and park fees cannot be organised at Livingstonia, though this may become possible.

Of particular interest for wildlife viewing is the four-night **Jalawe and Chipome River Trail**, passing through the Brachystegia woodland in the northern part of the park and offering the opportunity to see elephants, buffalo, greater kudu and a variety of other mammals which are generally absent from the plateau. This and all other trails cost US$30 per person for the first night for the first two people and an additional US$20 per night for every additional person. Porters are available for all trails at a small extra charge.

FURTHER AFIELD

Many of the more interesting points in Nyika are too far from Chelinda to be reached on a day walk, though they are accessible to visitors with vehicles. Perhaps the most memorable viewpoint anywhere in Malawi, **Jalawe Rock**, lies about 1km (to be done on foot) from a car park 34km north of Chelinda. The views here are spectacular, stretching over a close range of mountains to Lake Malawi's mountainous Tanzanian shore. With binoculars, it is often possible to see buffaloes and elephants in the Brachystegia woodland of the Mpanda Ridge below. A variety of raptors, as well as klipspringer, are frequently seen around the rock, and the surrounding vegetation includes many proteas and aloes.

At 2,606m, **Nganda Peak** is the highest point in northern Malawi. It lies about 30km northeast of Chelinda, and can be reached by following the Jalawe Rock road for about 25km, then turning left onto a 4km-long motorable track. It's a steep 1.5km walk from the end of the track to the peak.

Kasaramba Viewpoint lies 43km southeast of Chelinda. You can motor to within 1.5km of the viewpoint and then walk the final stretch. When it isn't covered in mist, the views to the lake are excellent, and you can also see remnants of the terraced slopes built by the early Livingstonia missionaries. The most extensive rainforest in Nyika lies on the slopes below Kasaramba, and visitors frequently see the localised crowned eagle and mountain buzzard in flight. From Kasaramba, a 3km road leads to the top of the pretty, 30m-high **Nchenachena Falls**.

Further along the road to Kasaramba, also 43km from Chelinda, is a large **juniper forest**, the most southerly stand of *Juniperus procera* in Africa, and the first part of the Nyika Plateau to be afforded official protection back in the 1940s. A short trail through the junipers offers the opportunity of sighting forest animals such as leopard, elephant shrew, red duiker, bushpig and a variety of forest birds. The forest can also be explored from the verging firebreaks.

The **Zovo Chipolo Forest** lies on the Chitipa road near to where the Zambian Resthouse used to be. It is of special interest to birdwatchers, and harbours several mammal species, the most commonly seen of which are bushbuck, blue monkey and elephant shrew. An unmarked trail runs through the forest, which is best visited with a local guide, at least if you hope to pick up the calls of such elusive forest birds as the bar-tailed trogon. The larger **Chowo Forest**, which lies in the Zambian part of the park, used to be popular with people staying at the Zambian Resthouse, but it is now somewhat off the beaten track.

Fingira Rock is a large, granite dome lying 22km south of Chelinda. On the eastern side of the rock, an 11m-deep and 18m-long cave was used as a shelter by humans around 3,000 years ago – excavations in 1965 unearthed a complete human skeleton and a large number of stone tools. Several schematic rock paintings can be seen on the walls of the cave. A motorable track runs to the base of the rock, 500m from the cave.

The Brachystegia woodland around Thazima entrance gate is the most accessible in the park. The area is rich in birds, and noted for harbouring unusual species. Walking here, you are also likely to see mammal species that are rare at higher altitudes.

VWAZA MARSH WILDLIFE RESERVE

(⊕ *Early–18.00 daily (entrance gate); entrance US$5 pp per 24hrs. Daily fee for private vehicles US$2*) Proclaimed in 1977, Vwaza Marsh Wildlife Reserve covers an area of around 960km² along the Zambian border west of Rumphi and south of Nyika National Park, where it shares an open border with the Zambian reserves of the Luangwa Valley. This underrated reserve is, without doubt, Malawi's best-kept game-viewing secret, a highly attractive and surprisingly accessible and affordable target to anybody with an interest in natural history. Rich in wetland habitats, Vwaza is named after a rather inaccessible marsh in the northeast of the reserve, but the main focus for tourism is Lake Kazuni in the southeast, which is fed by the South Rukuru River, and lies on a public transport route and offers inexpensive accommodation and camping. By comparison with Nyika, this is a low-lying, hot and humid part of Malawi, especially during wet summer months, and mosquitoes and tsetse flies are abundant.

Vwaza Marsh is dominated by flat terrain at altitudes of around 1,000–1,200m, and it supports a mixed cover of Brachystegia and mopane woodland. Large mammal populations have suffered badly at the hands of poachers in the past, and are to some extent seasonal, but the reserve remains reasonably well stocked because animals can move freely between it and Zambia's contiguous Luangwa ecosystem. Some 2,000 buffalo and 300 elephant are thought to be resident, though the former have reputedly declined in number in recent years, probably through subsistence poaching. A variety of antelope is present, including roan, greater kudu, Lichtenstein's hartebeest, eland, puku and impala. Lion and leopard survive in small numbers, but sightings are rare. A few recent sightings of African wild dog suggest this endangered creature may be in the process of re-colonising the reserve from Zambia.

GETTING THERE AND AWAY Kazuni Camp, at the main entrance gate, is about 25km from Rumphi along the 'old' dirt road that connects to Mzimba. To get there, follow the M24 out of Rumphi towards Nyika for about 10km, and then turn left onto the S109, which is signposted for the reserve. You can normally reach the gate in a saloon car, but a 4x4 may be necessary after rain. Internal roads are generally closed during the rainy season. For those without a vehicle, day and overnight trips can be organised through Matunkha Eco-Tourism Lodge in Rumphi.

Access to Vwaza Marsh on public transport is surprisingly easy. In the dry season, there is at least one bus daily between Mzimba and Rumphi, apparently leaving Rumphi in the early morning and Mzimba at about 14.00. This bus doesn't stop right at the gate, but at Kazuni village, which is about 1km from the gate in the direction of Mzimba. A better option coming from Rumphi is to look for a *matola* lift to Kazuni. There seems to be a steady stream of pick-up trucks travelling between Rumphi and the tobacco farms in the Kazuni area, and you shouldn't have to wait longer than an hour for a lift. Private vehicles will generally drop you right at the gate, from where it is a five-minute walk to the camp. The best place to wait for a lift out of Rumphi is under the trees just west of the district offices.

WHERE TO STAY

Chigwere Cultural Village 01 334389. This cultural tourism project at Kazuni village, 1km from the entrance gate, offers simple home-stays, with all proceeds going to orphan care, & it also offers fascinating insights into the local culture of this mixed Tumbuka & Ngoni community – try your hand at maize pounding, just join in with whatever is going on at the time, or ask to see a traditional dance (US$5 pp). US$7 pp bed only, US$20 pp FB.

Å Kazuni Safari Camp [map page 288] (8 rooms) 01 332014; m 099 5427609/5472508; e andrew.kataya@gmail.com. Situated 500m inside the entrance gate, this tented camp sprawls attractively in a grove of evergreen woodland overlooking Lake Kazuni. The night-time atmosphere here is utterly compelling: just you, the trumpeting of elephants if you're lucky, snorting hippo, fluttering fruit bats & swooping owls. And, it must be said, rather a lot of mosquitoes – so cover up! Managed since 2008 by National Parks & bookable through their Mzuzu office, there have been a number of long-standing plans to bring in private management, but these have yet to materialise. Current facilities are basic, but include clean long-drop toilets, showers & a fireplace with grid, firewood & cooking utensils provided. You *must* bring your own food; the nearest place to stock up is at the supermarket in Rumphi, though there is a better selection of goods on sale in Mzuzu. The staff will cook for you on request. Beer & sodas are normally available at a kiosk just outside the reserve entrance, while a limited range of goods can be bought at Kazuni Village 1km back towards Mzimba. *US$19 per unit en-suite dbl/twin chalets, US$6 pp camping.*

Camping Camping is permitted at three other sites in the game reserve. None of these sites has any facilities worth speaking of, and they are accessible only in a private vehicle.

Å Khaya Camp On the Luwewe River
Å Turner Camp On Vwaza Marsh

Å Zaro Pool In the southwest corner of the reserve

EXPLORING VWAZA Because the camp looks over Lake Kazuni, you can see plenty of game just by sitting on the veranda of your hut. It is, in any case, an atmospheric and sumptuously African setting: an expanse of flat water surrounded by low hills and Brachystegia woodland, with hippo splashing, crocodiles basking and a steady stream of mammals coming down to the shore to drink. It is emphatically worth paying the small charge to take a guided game walk out onto the floodplain, where it's reasonably easy to approach animals on foot. The 1998 animal census estimated there to be 545 hippo living in the lake in 17 pods, and they are generally very approachable on foot (provided that they are already in the water). A couple of substantial elephant herds visit the lake on most days. Other large mammals that currently visit the lake include baboon, impala, puku and greater kudu, while three herds of buffalo are resident in the area. It should be stressed that walking out towards the lake without an armed ranger is forbidden, not to say foolhardy, as there is a real risk of being charged by buffalo or hippo.

More than 300 bird species have been recorded in Vwaza Marsh, and the Kazuni area also offers some good birdwatching. The lake itself supports a great many waterfowl, waders and storks, and I've seen osprey, fish eagle and palmnut vulture there on different occasions. The thick woodland around the camp is rattling with birds, especially in the morning – you might easily tick 50 species in a few hours, notably trumpeter hornbill, Carp's black tit, Hueglin's robin and a number of attractive small warblers. This is also a good site for the extremely localised white-winged babbling starling, a babbler-like relict species otherwise confined to a small part of Zambia. If you feel like taking an unguided stroll, you stand a good chance of seeing some animals by walking along the 1km stretch of public road between Kazuni Gate and the village (there's an electric fence, so it's safe to walk here unescorted). Even if you don't see much, it's quite interesting to look at the mudfish traps along the South Rukuru River as it flows out of the park near the gate.

Visitors with private vehicles can explore the limited network of internal roads within the reserve, though they are advised to check conditions with the warden at Kazuni before doing so.

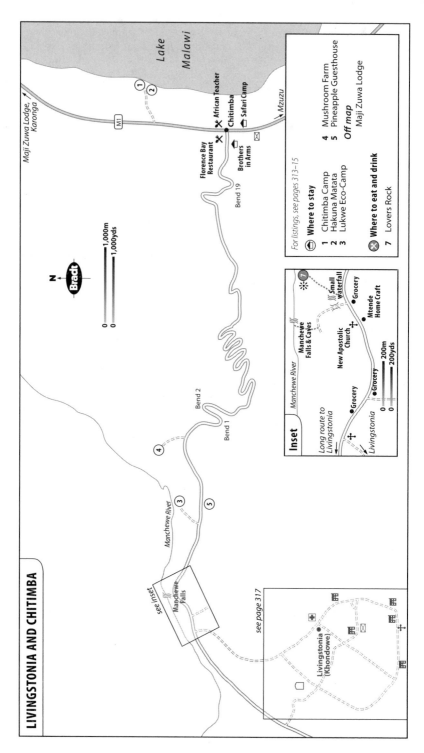

LIVINGSTONIA AND CHITIMBA

Lake Malawi

Maji Zuwa Lodge, ↑
Karonga

M1

Mzuzu

✕ African Teacher
● Chitimba
⌂ Safari Camp

Florence Bay ✕
Restaurant
⌂ Brothers
in Arms

Bend 19

Bend 2

Bend 1

④

③ ⑤

Manchewe River

see inset

Manchewe
Falls

see page 317

Livingstonia
(Khondowe)

N

Bradt

0 ____ 1,000m
0 ____ 1,000yds

Inset

Manchewe River

Manchewe
Falls & Caves

Long route to
Livingstonia →

New Apostolic
Church ✝

●Grocery

●Grocery

✝ Livingstonia

⛲ Lovers Rock ⑦
≈ Small
Waterfall
●Grocery

Mtende
Home Craft

0 ____ 200m
0 ____ 200yds

310

22

Livingstonia and the Northern Lakeshore Resorts

North of Rumphi, the M1 follows the South Rukuru River in a breathtaking descent of the Rift Valley Escarpment that brings you out at the lakeshore villages of Chiweta and Chitimba on Chombe Bay. Arriving here, it's immediately apparent – weather permitting – that this most northerly stretch of Lake Malawi is possessed of a unique scenic drama. Elsewhere, where the water is wider or the hinterland flatter, Lake Malawi can come across as a vast oceanic sheet stretching to a distant hazy horizon. Here, by contrast, the deep turquoise water and gorgeous beaches are hemmed in on both sides by a precipitous wooded escarpment that towers a kilometre above the shore, drawing vivid attention to the lake's containment within the immense tectonic scar we refer to as the Great Rift Valley.

For all its wild beauty, the northern shore of Lake Malawi is relatively undeveloped for tourism, largely because of its remoteness from Lilongwe and Blantyre. Not that there's any shortage of tourist accommodation in the area, but rather that the scattered small lakeshore resorts between Chitimba and Ngala all possess an isolated pioneering feel by comparison with the likes of Nkhata Bay, Salima and Cape Maclear. In short, the northern lakeshore forms an idyllic beach destination for those who want to get away from it all. What's more, it also provides an excellent springboard for energetic travellers to visit the 19th-century Scottish mission of Livingstonia, whose historical attractions are if anything outweighed by its magnificent highland setting atop the western escarpment overlooking the lake.

KANDEWE CULTURAL HERITAGE SITE

(*Entrance US$1.50/1 adult/child;* m *099 1499604/5533548*) Clearly signposted on the east side of the M1 towards Chiweta about 35km past the junction for Rumphi, Kandewe is best known as the site of the Zuwurufu Hanging Bridge, a basket suspension bridge that spans the South Rukuru River on the opposite side of the road. This bridge now forms the centrepiece of a government-sanctioned community project overseen by the likeably garrulous Abel Nyasulu, a natural entertainer and entrepreneur whose offbeat enthusiasm marks him out as the clear successor to the legendary Mr Ngoma (see box, overleaf), his erstwhile neighbour, in the eccentricity stakes. If you feel like stopping to check it out, the signpost is difficult to miss, and there's enough traffic along the M1 that backpackers could ask to be dropped by any vehicle bound for Chiweta and then hop on the next one when they've finished looking around.

Zuwurufu Hanging Bridge was initially constructed in 1904 to connect Kandewe to the village of Chigona Bweka on the other side of the South Rukuru, as well as giving them access to the ancestral shrine for which it is named. Made almost entirely from woven reed and bamboo (supplemented more recently by two wire ropes), the bridge literally does feel like a giant elongated basket dangling high above the water between two trees, and crossing it is not for the faint-hearted, though the local villagers still use it on a daily basis to carry everything from groceries to tobacco bales and furniture to/from Chigona Bweka, which remains otherwise inaccessible by road. The bridge was originally suspended closer to the river, but it was reconstructed at its present height of around 5m above water level after being swept away by floodwater. The bridge is also used by monkeys to cross the river, and locals claim a stray hippo somehow found its way onto it in 1998, and fell right through the base into the water!

The entrance fee also includes a visit to the museum and shrine maintained by the cultural heritage site. The former is an unexpected gem, dedicated to the local Phoka culture, and filled with a miscellany of traditional and semi-traditional artefacts, most intriguingly a functional record player that ingeniously uses a calabash as an amplifier/speaker. At the adjacent shrine, Mr Nyasulu might regale tales of the ancestors, ham a masked dance, sing a multi-lingual rain chant… and while it's difficult to say where tradition ends and showmanship begins, it's an engaging and erudite performance, and proceeds from the community project go towards the construction of a much-needed clinic for the 1,000 people of Kandewe.

There are plans to develop several other sites in the region for day visits and possibly overnight camping. These include the Tunduru Rain Shrine, a large rock where the Phoka used to pray to the ancestors less than 10km south of Kandewe, and, further north, the spectacular but difficult-to-reach Wongwe Falls, 25km from where the M1 bridges the South Rukuru River. The cultural group can also organise traditional Phoka dance performances, including the Vimbuza healing dance and Visekese wedding dance, with a couple of days' notice – call to make arrangements. Note that all guides associated with this project carry official identity cards.

THE LAKESHORE FROM CHIWETA TO NGALA

The 60km of lakeshore between Chiweta (where the M1 from Rumphi meets the lakeshore) and Ngala (40km south of Karonga) is a beautiful place to spend a few days, with marvellous beaches and fabulous scenery. It supports a scattering of

MR NGOMA'S HOUSE

For many years, the most famous landmark in this part of Malawi was the home of Mr S S Ngoma, a garrulous octogenarian whose morbid preoccupation with his own death once led to him being described as 'the greatest and most depressing raconteur of the north'. The most visible manifestation of this obsession was a two-storey mausoleum, made with various metal, wood and other scraps, and housing a coffin in preparation for the inevitable. Alongside this, he dug his intended grave, several metres deep, marked with a red tombstone reading 'S S Ngoma 1913–'.

Mr Ngoma fulfilled his long-standing fixation, aged around 90, but his house still remains – alongside the M1, about 15km south of Kandewe – and the family still welcomes visitors. Ironically, however, the elaborate burial plans to which Ngoma dedicated his latter years all came to naught, as bureaucracy intervened to ensure his coffin was not buried in his garden or mausoleum, but at another site altogether.

just over half a dozen resorts, generally less crowded than their more southerly counterparts, but collectively catering to most tastes and budgets.

The lakeshore between Chiweta and Ngala supports few settlements of substance. For visitors, the most strategic is Chitimba, which straddles the M1 about 10km north of Chiweta, and amounts to little more than a few homesteads and shops separating the beach from the main road. Chitimba, often but inaccurately marked on maps as Khondowe (the traditional name for Livingstonia), stands at the T-junction of the M1 and the dirt road to Livingstonia, and it is the best place to catch a lift there.

About 20km further north, the harbour village of Chilumba is situated on a peninsula several kilometres from the M1. Chilumba is not without natural charm, though rather surprisingly there is nothing in the way of tourist development, unless you count a few indifferent cheap local lodgings around the market, and there's no obvious reason to stop over there.

GETTING THERE AND AROUND The M1 between Chiweta and Karonga sticks within a kilometre or two of the lakeshore for most of its length, and is surfaced in its entirety. It's the busiest road in northern Malawi, so there is no shortage of public transport. All express and country buses between Mzuzu and Karonga stop at Chiweta and Chitimba. If you want to be dropped elsewhere along Chombe Bay, you need to use a country bus or minibus. Several other *matola* vehicles also operate between police checks. Most resorts lie alongside the M1, or within easy walking distance; details of access are given under the individual resort.

All buses between Mzuzu and Karonga divert to Chilumba, which also forms the northern terminus of the MV *Ilala* ferry service from Chipoka via Nkhata Bay, Nkhotakota and Likoma Island.

WHERE TO STAY *See map, page 310, unless otherwise stated.*
Broadly speaking the most upmarket lakeshore resort is the lovely Sangilo Sanctuary, set in scenic isolation on the eponymous peninsula, while the well-organised and sporadically lively Chitimba Camp is the northern lakeshore's closest approximation to the stylish backpacker lodges that proliferate in Nkhata Bay.

Chitimba Camp (8 rooms, 1 dorm) m 088 8387116; e camp@chitimba.com; www.chitimba. com. The main travellers' focal point in this part of Malawi is this sprawling camp 700m from the M1 along a sandy road signposted 1km north of Chitimba. Efficiently run by former overland truck drivers, the camp is on a huge white swimming beach next to a shallow river mouth, & it also offers a selection of activities ranging from village tours to guided hikes & 4x4 trips to Livingstonia. The thatched beach bar serves a good selection of snacks & meals in the US$4–5.50 range, & internet access is available. *US$17 rather gloomy en-suite dbl with net, US$15.75 brighter twin using shared showers, US$7.50 pp in 6-bed dorm, US$4 pp camping.*

FloJa Foundation B&B [map page 288] (2 rooms) m 088 4333023/099 9060185;

e flojamalawi@gmail.com; www.flojamalawi. nl. Situated 600m from the M1 exactly halfway between Sangilo & Karonga, this charmer of a place has its beginnings in the Dutch-run foundation & day-care centre located next door. There are two comfortable thatched cottages newly built from local materials, both with private bathroom, lounge area, tea/coffee, balcony & nets. The green lakeside gardens are nothing short of bounteous, & provide most ingredients for the home-cooked meals available for US$6.50. Campsites are equipped with plug points & *braai* facilities, & there is even a naturally fed hot spring if you're keen to have a soak. All proceeds go towards funding their day-care programmes for vulnerable local children, & guests can arrange to visit the remarkable centre. *US$25 pp ensuite dbl, US$20 pp twin, B&B. US$5 pp camping.*

22

⌂ **Hakuna Matata** (2 rooms) m 088 2297779/1262337; e hakunamatata.chitimba@gmail.com; www.hakunamatata-chitimba.com. Directly next door to Chitimba Camp, this new beachside lodge is a pleasant enough budget option, but neither 'half the price' nor 'twice as nice' as their rivalrous signposts proclaim. It is, however, a good place for those seeking lakeside peace & quiet, with spacious campsites in a large open setting. All rooms have nets & common hot showers, there is an on-site bar, & meals are available on request for US$5.50. It's also convenient for overlanders as the owner is a skilled mechanic. *US$8 pp twin, US$6.75 pp 6-bed dorm, US$5.75 pp standing tent, US$4 pp camping, all rates excluding b/fast.*

⌂ **Maji Zuwa Lodge** (12 rooms, dorm under construction) m 099 1767515/9778454; e matt@majizuwa.com. Perched on a hillside above the lakeshore, this recently opened lodge & 'economic centre' focuses on engagement with the local community, & visitors are free to get involved with an assortment of ongoing projects. For those seeking a more laidback approach, there are hammocks aplenty, DSTV, & the views from the bar/restaurant can't be beat. The menu includes burgers, pastas & the inventive chapatti tacos for

about US$4–6. Duplex rooms dot the hillside & are simply furnished with new beds, nets & fans, & the outdoor showers with lake views are a treat. *US$20 en-suite dbl, US$10 dbl, B&B. US$3 camping.*

⌂ **Mdokera Lodge** (8 rooms) m 099 7781110/5465782. This characterful place has a lovely beachfront location in Khwawa-Lulanga village alongside the M1 north of Chitimba. It offers winning Malawian hospitality & simplicity, with 1–3 beds & scattered furniture in reed & bamboo rondavels with a bucket shower to one side & an intriguing eco-flush toilet to the other. Even more intriguing is the full-sized bed wedged high in a tree; try it if you're feeling brave! There are local dugout canoes for guests, & they are happy to arrange guided canoe or fishing trips in the area as well. There is also a shop selling a fair selection of manufactured foods, but limited fresh produce, & meals are available by arrangement for about US$2. *US$8 pp B&B, US$2 pp camping.*

⌂ **Namiashi Lodge** (8 rooms) m 099 1565198/9421522; e nyadenani@yahoo.com. The first lodge you reach after Chiweta, Namiashi has a wonderful beachfront setting in shady gardens alongside the M1. Small, serene & secluded, it is not aimed at those seeking a lively backpacker scene or Westernised aesthetic, but feels more like

MV *VIPYA*

Chombe Bay was the site of the most serious boating accident recorded on Lake Malawi, when the MV *Vipya* sank in storm-related circumstances north of Chilumba. The *Vipya* was custom-built in Belfast by the British shipbuilders Harland and Wolff (the same company responsible for the RMS *Titanic* and HMS *Belfast*), shipped in pieces to Nyasaland in 1943 to be reassembled for a maiden naval voyage in 1944. More than 40m long, with a top speed of 12 knots, the boat embarked on its first scheduled passenger trip on 28 June 1946. Disaster struck little more than a month later, on 30 July, when a strong wind caused it to start rolling heavily on what was only its fourth voyage. The alarmed crew and first officer wanted to return to shore, especially when the ship started to take in water, but the captain ignored the danger and ordered them to keep sailing. Eventually, 12km out of Chilumba, just as the captain ordered the cargo hatch to be opened for an emergency evacuation, the ship was capsized by a massive wave, trapping most of the passengers and crew below decks. At least 145 passengers and crewmen died, and there were only 49 survivors. The MV *Ilala* was ordered as a replacement for the *Vipya*, whose hulk reputedly still lies submerged in the bay. The Queen Victoria Tower Clock in Mangochi was later dedicated to the victims of the tragedy, which also inspired Steve Chimombo's novel *The Wrath of Napolo*, about the sinking of the fictional MV *Maravi* on the same date.

an underutilised local budget lodge with a beach setting. The sgls are small, but dbls & twins are spacious & well maintained, & come with nets, fan & en-suite hot shower. Meals are in the US$2–3 range. *US$11/23/27.50 en-suite sgl/twin/dbl B&B, US$4.75 pp camping.*

⌂ **Ngara Resort** [map page 288] (13 rooms) m 088 4068855. This small lodge on the same side road as FloJa is certainly quiet & affordable, & it may well be a convenient overnight stop for people driving to/from Tanzania, but there are no activities on offer, seldom other guests, & the overall impression is that whoever owns the place has simply lost interest in it. There is a bar & restaurant with meals around US$4. The en-suite rooms come in a variety of shapes & forms, & the beachfront rooms are noticeably smarter. *US$6.25 sgl with ¾ bed & net, US$12.50/14 large sgl/dbl with fan & balcony, US$19/22 beachfront sgl/dbl with TV.*

⌂ **Sangilo Sanctuary** [map page 288] (8 rooms) m 099 9395203/088 8392611; e sangilo.sanctuary@yahoo.co.uk; www.sangilo.net. Undoubtedly the most stylish place to stay on the northern lakeshore, with a location to match, this owner-managed lodge is built into a secluded cove on the rocky Sangilo Peninsula. It lies 80km south of Karonga, some 2km from the M1 along a rough & in parts steep dirt road that requires decent clearance. The thatched dining area, built on a wooden deck alongside the small private beach, has a far-reaching reputation for the quality of its food (much of it grown in the lodge's own garden) & serves pizzas, pies & other mains for US$10, as well as snacks & sandwiches for US$5–6. Set on a rocky cliff above the restaurant, the airy stilted chalets, made mostly with organic materials, have nets, solar power & private verandas overlooking the lake. Activities include swimming, snorkelling, sunset cruises, water skiing, fishing trips & various watersports. *US$25 pp dbl, US$30 pp en-suite dbl cottage, US$150 family cottage, US$5 pp camping.*

LIVINGSTONIA

Perched on the Rift Valley Escarpment above Lake Malawi, the town of Livingstonia, founded by Scottish missionaries in the late 19th century, is one of the most scenic places in all of central Africa. The vertiginous views from the edge of this historic town – plummeting down the escarpment and across the lake to the Livingstone Mountains in Tanzania – are quite breathtaking. Indeed, on a clear day, and with sufficient imagination, the horizon is so distant that you'll swear you can see the curvature of the Earth.

Arguably the most intriguing settlement anywhere in Malawi, and certainly the most unusual, Livingstonia is a curiously unfocused place. Dotted along the escarpment, there is a resthouse, school, technical college and hospital, all dating to the turn of the 20th century. Elsewhere, separated by scattered patches of plantation forest and indigenous woodland, there is a low-key market enclosed by a few poorly stocked grocery shops, the vast mission church, and a cache of venerable administrative buildings and a clock tower overlooking a bizarrely redundant stone traffic circle surrounded by blooming flower beds. The overall impression is as if somebody started transporting a small Victorian village to the edge of the Rift Valley Escarpment, but got bored before they finished the job.

The combined scenic and historical interest of Livingstonia makes it one of the most popular non-lakeside tourist destinations anywhere in Malawi. True, it's not that easy to reach on public transport, but for many the uphill hike from Chitimba is an attraction in itself. And once you've ascended the escarpment, there's the choice of several very different but equally likeable places to stay, while amusements include a tour of the village and its museum, the walk to the spectacular Manchewe Falls, and the wide range of hikes that are possible around the escarpment.

HISTORY In 1875, Lt E D Young led a party of seven Europeans and four ex-slaves from the coast to the southern shores of Lake Malawi to found the Livingstonia

Mission for the Free Church of Scotland (later the Church of Central Africa Presbyterian or CCAP). Named in honour of Dr David Livingstone, the mission was established in order to enact its namesake's belief that the introduction of Christianity and legitimate commerce to Lake Malawi would be the most effective way to end the slave trade that had caused so much suffering in the region.

The original site chosen by Young was at Cape Maclear, but the high number of malarial fatalities here persuaded his successor Dr Robert Laws – a member of the founding party – to relocate further north to Bandawe in 1881. While at Bandawe, Laws and his fellow missionaries played a pivotal role in curbing raids on local villagers by Swahili slave traders and the recently arrived Ngoni. Unfortunately for the missionaries, however, malaria proved to be just as prevalent here as it had been on the southern lakeshore, and eventually Laws decided to move the mission away from the lakeshore.

The Livingstonia Mission found its permanent home at the small village then known as Khondowe when Laws and two colleagues set up camp there in October 1894. Situated a full 900m above the lakeshore, Khondowe was blessed with a healthy climate, fertile land and abundant supply of water, and within ten years the new mission site housed a small village of brick and stone buildings, including a church, a school, a hospital, a post office and several workshops, many of which are still in use today.

Overseen by Laws for five decades (he assumed leadership in 1878 and retired in 1927), the Livingstonia Mission initiated many social projects in the early colonial era, and it also offered medical assistance and higher education to many future members of the African nationalist movement in Malawi and neighbouring territories. Furthermore, Laws played a large role in the formation of the Native Associations that later amalgamated into the Nyasaland African National Congress, precursor to the Malawi Congress Party, which led the country to independence in the early 1960s (indeed, former president Hastings Banda once referred to Livingstonia as the 'seedbed' of the Malawi Congress Party).

Laws's long-term vision for the mission included the establishment of a university, an ambition that went unfulfilled during his tenure and was not seen as a priority by his more conservative successors. In 2003, however, the CCAP Synod of Livingstonia opened the University of Livingstonia, with an initial enrolment of 25 students from all parts of Malawi. Six years later, the university comprises a Technical College and College of Education at Livingstonia itself, and Colleges of Commerce, Nursing and Theology at Ekwendeni, serving more than 500 students.

GETTING THERE AND AWAY Livingstonia is connected to Chitimba on the M1 by the S103, a spectacular 15km dirt road that gains some 700m in altitude over the first 9km, following a series of 20 hairpin bends so tight that the last of them is only actually 4km from Chitimba as the crow flies. Passing through dense Brachystegia woodland, with spectacular views back to the lake, it is often described as one of the most exciting roads in Africa, particularly if the vehicle you are in has dubious brakes! In 2006, concrete was put down over the steepest sections of this road, but other sections remain very rough, so it is only a realistic prospect for tough high-clearance vehicles, and a 4x4 might be necessary after rain. Taken at a sensible speed, the ascent takes the best part of an hour, and the descent should be tackled in low gear to prevent brakes overheating.

There is no public transport between Chitimba and Livingstonia, but a few vehicles switchback up and down every day, and with an early start you can be reasonably confident of finding a *matola* lift. Alternatively, Chitimba Camp

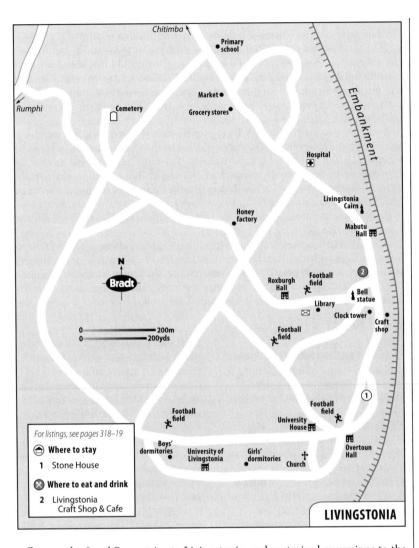

For listings, see pages 318–19

🛏 **Where to stay**

1 Stone House

✖ **Where to eat and drink**

2 Livingstonia
   Craft Shop & Cafe

LIVINGSTONIA

offers regular Land Rover trips to Livingstonia, and motorised excursions to the mission can be organised at Nkhata Bay. You could also call the Mushroom Farm to arrange a pickup.

The walk to Livingstonia is popular with fit travellers. You'll enjoy the walk a lot more if you leave as much luggage as possible at the base (Chitimba Camp would be your safest bet). And do resist the temptation to make use of the steep short cuts that plunge between the switchbacks, not so much because of the environmental degradation caused by using short cuts (over 99% of the pedestrian traffic on this route is local people, so a couple of tourists is neither here nor there), but because they are impossibly steep. And don't get overexcited when you pass Bend 20 – you still have around six (admittedly relatively flat) kilometres to cover before you reach Livingstonia, though if this seems too daunting, there's always the option of stopping at the Mushroom Farm (about 500m past the last bend) for refreshment or an overnight stay.

Another option is to arrange a guided day trip through Chitimba Camp (see page 313), which lies close to the base of the road to Livingstonia. The camp offers two alternatives. A 4x4 excursion taking in Livingstonia and Manchewe Falls costs US$100 for up to four people, leaving at 10.00 and returning at 16.00. A hiking trip involves walking in both directions (a total of around 30km) and costs US$4 per person, departing at 06.00 and getting back around 16.00, depending on your walking speed.

There are two other routes to Livingstonia, each of them long and extremely scenic. The one of key interest to visitors is the dirt road from Rumphi, inadvisable in anything but a 4x4 and impassable in the rainy season. Ask around in Livingstonia about the twice-weekly truck service to Rumphi, an experience not to be missed at the cost of a few dollars in either direction. In theory, the truck leaves Livingstonia on Tuesdays and Thursdays at 06.00, reaching Rumphi at about midday, where the driver reloads ready to leave Rumphi at 14.00 from outside the People's Supermarket.

Another walking route to Livingstonia often forgotten about is the path down from the Nyika Plateau. It takes two days to walk it, so you will need camping equipment. The most popular trek is between the Mushroom Farm and Chelinda Camp and then on down to the lakeshore. Both will organise a guide and a game scout for you. It is one of Malawi's most wonderful walks.

WHERE TO STAY *See map, page 310.*
Budget and camping

Lovers Rock Restaurant At the viewpoint over Manchewe Falls, this friendly little eatery serves a range of affordable snacks – chips, pancakes, tea, coffee – & it also allows camping. *US$4 pp.*

Lukwe Eco-Camp (4 rooms) m 099 9434985; e lukwe@live.com; www.lukwe.com. Permaculture first came to Livingstonia at Lukwe Eco-Camp, an owner-managed lodge, situated about 500m from the main road to Livingstonia, along a side road signposted to the right 1.3km past the turn-off for the Mushroom Farm. Accommodation is in small cliffside chalets with balconies & dramatic views, all using common showers & eco-toilet. The setting is lovely, & you are only 1km from Manchewe Falls. The food is highly regarded, with much of it grown in their lush permaculture garden. Mains are about US$6, & don't skip what could be Malawi's best salad. *US$12/20 sgl/dbl, US$5 pp camping, US$6 tent hire. All rates excluding b/fast.*

Mushroom Farm (4 rooms, 1 dorm) m 099 9652485/088 8591564; e themushroomfarmmalawi@gmail.com; www.themushroomfarmmalawi.com; see also advert on page 321. This is the first accommodation you'll reach coming from Chitimba, situated about 200m from the main road to Livingstonia, just after

Bend 1, some 9.6km from the junction with the M1. Friendly & informal, it has stupendous views over the lake, & offers accommodation in 3 basic but clean solar-powered huts & a new en-suite room, as well as camping & tent hire. It is a very eco-friendly set up, with toilets & showers built by permaculture aficionados, & an imaginative locally sourced menu with dishes in the US$5–7 range. The managers are outdoor enthusiasts, & this is a good place to arrange hikes, complimentary bike hire, volunteering & other activities. It's also one of the only places in Malawi you can greet the day with sunrise yoga. *US$30/40 en-suite sgl/dbl, US$15/20 sgl/dbl (US$20/30 for the superior 'top hut'), US$5 pp camping, US$5 pp extra to hire a tent, mattress & bedding.*

Pineapple Guesthouse (2 rooms) m 099 4802194. More of a village homestay than a conventional lodge, this locally run operation is to the left of the main road just before you reach the Lukwe turn-off. Offering two rooms in mud-&-thatch houses as well as camping space, it's carefully looked after, & certainly the cheapest place to stay near Livingstonia. Hikes could potentially be arranged, & you're sure to receive an authentically warm welcome. Malawian meals are available on request for about US$2. *US$2.50 pp, US$1.50 pp camping.*

Stone House [map page 317] (3 rooms) 01 368223; e house.stone@yahoo.co.uk; www.

malawiguesthouse.com. The only accommodation in Livingstonia itself is in the CCAP-run Stone House, which was built as the residence of Dr Laws in 1903 & retains a wonderful period feel with its stone walls, hardwood floors, tall ceilings, fireplaces, wide balcony offering a wonderful view to the lake almost a kilometre below, & furnishings that recall an Edwardian vicarage. Room 1 is a triple, while the others are 4 & 8-bed-dorms.

There are common hot showers in the basement, & it has a sporadic internet connection for Mk10/min. A limited selection of meals is available in the US$1.50–2.50 range (best order early), there are cold soft drinks on sale (but no alcohol), & the inexpensive pancakes make a great b/fast. *US$7 pp room 1, US$4.75 pp dorm bed, US$3 camping. Room 1 B&B, all others excluded.*

✘ **WHERE TO EAT AND DRINK** There are no bespoke restaurants or bars in Livingstonia (the closest thing being Lover's Rock at Manchewe Falls; see opposite), but day visitors are welcome to eat at the Stone House and the vegetarian food at Lukwe and the Mushroom Farm is also very tempting. The **craft shop** (⏰ *08.00–17.00 Mon–Sat*) opposite the bell statue carries a delicious selection of scones, doughnuts, coffee, tea and even homemade ice cream. There are several poorly stocked **grocery** shops around the **market**, but look out for freshly baked bread at an unsignposted **bakery** in the area, as well as the **shop** next to **Tiwange Grocery**, which stocks the only beers in town.

EXPLORING LIVINGSTONIA AND SURROUNDS The Livingstonia Mission is a place where you could spend many hours wandering around soaking up the views, admiring the time-warped architecture, and chatting to the friendly locals, most

---

EPHESIANS 2:14

The bed of whitewashed stones on the lawn outside the Stone House looks like a jumble from the ground, but it carries a clear and powerful message when viewed from the air. The stones were laid down there in February 1959, at a time when the struggle for independence had led to several outbreaks of violence in Rumphi and Karonga districts. The colonial government, concerned about the European missionaries at Livingstonia, flew a plane over the mission and dropped an unloaded gas canister containing a typed message. The message offered to evacuate the Europeans based at the mission if they felt they were in danger, and stated that the plane would return the next day, and the missionaries should lay stones in the shape of a Roman I on the lawn if they felt safe and a Roman V if they wanted to be evacuated.

The missionaries held a brief meeting that afternoon, and decided not only that they were going to stay, but also that they wanted to send a clear message to the world that even in tense times, people of different colours and backgrounds can choose to live in harmony. And so, when the plane flew over the next day, the pilot was greeted not with the single Roman numeral he had expected, but with a longer and more cryptic sequence of characters marked out in whitewashed stones on the lawn. It read 'Ephesians 2 v 14', and the photograph taken by the pilot appeared on the front cover of the *Rhodesian Herald* the next morning, and was published in the *Manchester Guardian* a few days later. And the stones remain there on the lawn to this day, a symbol of the mission's commitment to peace, progress and harmony: 'For He is our prince who has made us both one, and has broken down the middle wall of partition between us.'

22

of whom speak good English. If you prefer guided tours to casual wandering, contact Thomas Chisambi (m *099 9435091*), an articulate Livingstonian who offers short village tours for US$1 per person, as well as longer excursions to the likes of Manchewe Falls and Chombe Mountain for US$1.50–3.50 per person.

Around town

Stone House Museum (⊕ *08.00–17.00 daily; entrance US$1*) The obvious place to start any exploration of Livingstonia is this small museum, which is marvellous not so much for its contents, but for the fact it's there at all. Set in the house inhabited for 28 years by Dr Robert Laws, the museum provides a good overview of the mission's history and local tribal customs, illuminated by many photos dating to the late 19th and early 20th centuries. Exhibits include a letter from David Livingstone to his son, telling him of Mary's Livingstone's death from malaria, Laws's amazingly antiquated anaesthetic machine (the first in central Africa) and the various bits of early 20th-century entertainment equipment, an early cine camera and a collection of glass plates for slide shows.

Livingstonia Church and University Close to the Stone House, the mission church is a massive construction, started in 1916 but not completed until a full 30 years later due to lack of funding. As with so many of Malawi's mission churches, it is a feat of architecture and building skill, and is used by many hundreds each Sunday, including about a dozen choirs. The exterior is rather plain, but there is an interesting stained-glass window depicting Livingstone inside, and the caretaker will gladly take you to the top of the steeple, which offers a good view over the town. Around the corner is the main university building, which started life as a secondary school in the early 20th century.

Clock tower, craft shop and library The clock tower, which looks like it might once have been part of a church, overlooks what passes for the main traffic junction in Livingstonia, a large traffic circle that might be used by half a dozen vehicles on a hectic day. On the opposite side of the circle, a small **craft shop** (⊕ *08.00–17.00 Mon–Sat)* sells locally produced jewellery, woodcarvings and basketwork, along with a delicious variety of homemade baked goods, tea/coffee & ice cream. About 100m downhill from the circle is a library that stocks a good range of reading material including a rare copy of James W Jack's *Daybreak in Livingstonia: The Story of the Livingstonia Mission in British Central Africa*, first published in 1900.

Mission Hospital The focal point of Livingstonia these days is the large hospital complex, whose main building dates to 1910, and stands on the escarpment between the traffic circle and the market. Close by, you'll find **Mabutu Hall**, also known somewhat prosaically as House #1, as it was the residence of Dr Laws prior to the construction of the Stone House in 1903. The **Livingstonia Cairn** in front of the hospital marks the spot where Laws first camped at Khondowe in October 1894, accompanied by Dr Elmslie and a local convert Uriah Chirwa.

Further afield

Manchewe Falls Situated about 4km from Livingstonia, the Manchewe Falls crash down the Rift Valley Escarpment in one sheer 125m drop. Surrounded by lush rainforest, this waterfall is truly spectacular, and crawling to its edge is a vertigo-inducing experience. The main viewpoint over the falls, also the site of the Lovers Rock Restaurant, stands some 200m from the main road from Chitimba near the village of Manchewe about 1km past the junction for Lukwe Eco-Camp. The footpath to the viewpoint (on the right, coming from Chitimba or Lukwe) is not signposted, but it is easily recognisable as it lies directly opposite a small nameless grocery and about 20m before the junction with a dirt road leading down to a wooden bridge.

To visit the top of the falls, follow the dirt side road over the bridge and around a bend, then take a footpath to your right and follow it along a rocky stream to the caves behind the waterfall, which is where local people used to hide from slavers in the late 19th century. The caves are only ten minutes' walk from the main road, but it won't be easy to find them without a guide and there are plenty of kids around who'll show you the way for a small tip.

Lukwe Permaculture Garden The Lukwe Permaculture Garden next to the eponymous eco-camp makes for an interesting visit; here all manner of fruit and vegetables are grown on terraces with streams and ponds between them. The otters apparently love it, and in terms of irrigation, there are many people in Malawi who could learn from this place.

Adventure activities Currently no qualified climbing instruction is available, but there are countless opportunities for hiking, climbing, abseiling and even bungee jumping around Livingstonia, so this could change during the lifespan of this edition. Previously, the Mushroom Farm led a number of these activities, so it would be worth asking if they are once again offering them. The Mushroom Farm remains a good contact for hikes, however, including the two- to three-day trek to Chelinda Camp in Nyika National Park.

RELAX WHILE LIVING LIFE ON THE EDGE

THE MUSHROOM FARM

● ● ● ● ● ● ● ● ● ● ● ● ● ● ● ●

ECO-LODGE & CAMPSITE

- Outdoor Cinema
- Cliff-Top Restaurant & Bar
- Complimentary Mountain Bikes

- Free Wi-Fi
- Energizing Sunrise Yoga
- Volunteer Opportunities

WWW.THEMUSHROOMFARMMALAWI.COM

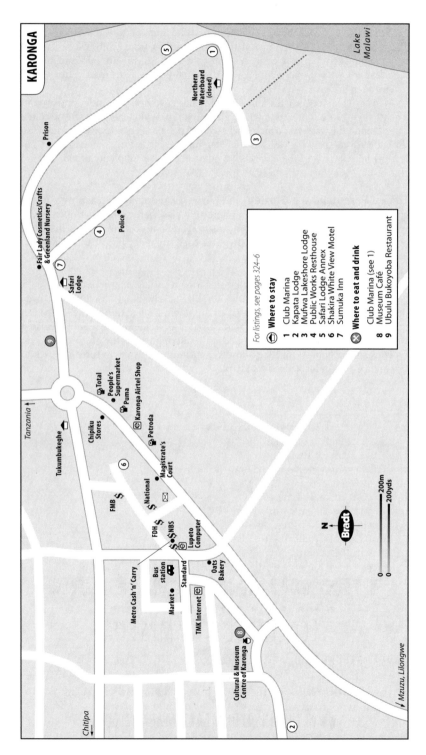

KARONGA

Lake Malawi

Northern Waterboard (closed)

Prison

Fair Lady Cosmetics/Crafts & Greenland Nursery

Police

Safari Lodge

Tanzania ↑

Tukumbukeghe

Chipiku Stores

Total
People's Supermarket
Puma
Karonga Airtel Shop
Petroda

Magistrate's Court

FMB
National

FDH
NBS
Lupeto Computer

Metro Cash 'n' Carry
Bus station
Market
Standard
Oats Bakery

TMK Internet

Cultural & Museum Centre of Karonga

Chitipa

↙ *Mzuzu, Lilongwe*

N

Bradt

0 — 200m
0 — 200yds

For listings, see pages 324–6

Where to stay
1 Club Marina
2 Kapata Lodge
3 Mufwa Lakeshore Lodge
4 Public Works Resthouse
5 Safari Lodge Annex
6 Shakira White View Motel
7 Sumuka Inn

Where to eat and drink
Club Marina (see 1)
8 Museum Café
9 Ubulu Bukoyoba Restaurant

322

23

Karonga and the Far North

The two main towns of the Tanzanian border region are Karonga and Chitipa, capitals of their respective namesake districts, but otherwise starkly different in character. Karonga, straddling the M1 on the northwest shore of Lake Malawi, is the country's seventh-largest town, a stickily tropical lake port that serves as the gateway to Tanzania to many northbound travellers, while providing an amenable introduction to Malawi for those heading in the opposite direction. Chitipa, in the remote northwest, is a dusty mid-altitude town that sees little passing tourist traffic, despite being the site of the main border post between northern Malawi and northern Zambia. The main attractions of this region are the lakeshore around Karonga, which also houses the country's most modern museum, and the little-known Misuku Hills north of Chitipa, which offer ample opportunity for off-the-beaten-track rambling through scenic mountain passes and forests inhabited by rare birds and monkeys.

KARONGA

The gateway for overland crossings into Tanzania, Karonga is the largest and oldest town in the far north of Malawi, stretching westward from the reedy lakeshore some 40km south of the Songwe border post. It was established in 1883 as an African Lakes Corporation (ALC) outpost, and went on to play an important role in the suppression of the slave trade and World War I hostilities with neighbouring German East Africa. Karonga remained somewhat isolated until 1981, when the surfaced M1 was extended this far north, and it enjoyed significant economic benefits when the first bridge across the Songwe River on the Tanzanian border was constructed in 1988. The town received another economic shot in the arm in 2008 with the opening of the controversial Kayelekera Uranium Mine 40km to the west. Today, Karonga – rather surprisingly – ranks as the largest port town anywhere on the shore of Lake Malawi, with a population estimated at 45,000. For all that, it is no metropolis, and while its urban amenities make it a useful first stop for fresh arrivals from Tanzania, the only real tourist attraction is the Cultural & Museum Centre, which focuses on the region's fascinating history and prehistory.

GETTING THERE AND AWAY Karonga lies on the M1 about 225km north of Mzuzu and 590km from Lilongwe. The road from Lilongwe and Mzuzu is surfaced in its entirety and covered by a steady stream of buses and minibuses, including a daily Axa Coach to/from Mzuzu (see page 64). The minibus fare from Mzuzu is US$7.

Matola pick-up trucks and minibuses ply back and forth all day between Karonga and the Tanzanian border post at Songwe. After crossing into Tanzania, it is easy to get a lift on a bicycle-taxi through to the main Mbeya–Kyela road, where you can pick up a bus in the direction of your choice. If you're heading towards Zambia, you must first aim for Chitipa (see page 328).

WHERE TO STAY *See map, page 322.*

Upmarket

Mikoma Beach Lodge [map page 288] \01 632666/998616; e mikomalodge@yahoo. com; www.mikomalodge.mw. Located off the M1 about 10km south of town, this new beachfront lodge is the most upmarket establishment near Karonga. Set in carefully manicured grounds, the atmosphere is a touch businesslike, but the swimming pool, spacious sundeck & inviting beachfront will surely please tourists as well. Rooms are all tiled & en-suite, with double beds, AC, DSTV, tea/coffee facilities, large nets & a wardrobe. There is a restaurant & thatch-roofed bar on site, replete with snooker table. Non-guests can use the pool for a few dollars. *US$82/100/150 sgl/dbl/family, all rates B&B.*

Moderate

Beach Chamber Hotel [map page 288] (15 rooms) \01 11997129; m 099 9134223. With a beachfront location 200m from the M1 only 5km north of town, this friendly lodge is good value & compares favourably with anything in town. The tiled en-suite rooms are comfortable & neatly furnished, with DSTV & AC, & there's a good bar/restaurant serving meals for US$3–5. Compared to most other resorts in Malawi, the reedy beach is nothing to write home about, & crocodiles have been reported here, so be sure to ask before you go for a dip! Back on land, the leafy courtyard offers plenty of shady spots to sit back & watch the fishermen haul in their catch. Any transport heading between Karonga & the Songwe border post can drop you at the hotel. *US$27 en-suite dbl, US$30 deluxe dbl, all rates B&B.*

SLAVERY IN NKONDELAND

The agriculturist Nkonde (or Nyakyusa) people have inhabited the fertile slopes of Karonga and Chitipa districts (as well as the neighbouring southern highlands of Tanzania) since the late 16th century. The first European visitors to Nkondeland were deeply impressed by its peaceful, hospitable and industrious character. Indeed, Consul Elton described it as the 'finest tract of Africa [he] had yet seen', comparing its climate and fertility favourably to Natal in South Africa, while the explorer Joseph Thomson, who passed through in 1878, described it as 'an enchanted place' and 'a perfect Arcadia'.

Elton's and Thomson's elegiac early reports of Nkondeland reflect the fact that it was then one of the few parts of central Africa left unscarred by the coastal slave trade or the Ngoni incursion. All that was to change from 1880 onwards, when a Swahili trader called Mlozi arrived in the area from the Luangwa Valley in Zambia. In 1886, Mlozi set up base about 10km from the ALC trade outpost at Karonga, and his militant slave-raiding parties, known as the Ruga-Ruga, proceeded to raid the surrounding villages for human booty.

Monteith Fotheringham, manager of the ALC's Karonga outpost at the time, described the devastation: 'If you could picture the beautiful villages desolated, and see the cruelties of these Arab slave traders – women carried away captives, separated from husbands and children, children separated from their parents, husbands who would stand up for their homes and those near and dear to them murdered and their bodies mutilated.' Fotheringham attempted to negotiate with Mlozi in order to stop the raids, but to no avail, and soon the Karonga area became the setting of a largely forgotten war between the ALC and the Ruga-Ruga.

This war was initiated on 27 October 1887, when Mlozi ordered the massacre of more than 1,000 defenceless Nkonde villagers that his spies had lured into the

Sumuka Inn (24 rooms) \01 362468; m 099 9444816; e sumuka.inn28@gmail.com. This new hotel, 500m east of the main traffic circle towards the lake, is easily the best in the town centre, offering clean en-suite accommodation in attractively furnished rooms with DSTV & AC. The setting is indifferent, but there is a popular cocktail bar & decent restaurant. *US$37 dbl, from US$40 deluxe rooms & suites B&B.*

Budget

Club Marina (12 rooms) \01 362302; m 099 1424724. This place certainly looks the part, set in a leafy green enclosure facing the lakeshore about 1.5km from the town centre, but the en-suite rooms with nets are nothing special at the price, though the AC will be welcome in summer, assuming it works, & the restaurant is as good as it gets in Karonga. *US$17.50/20.50 sgl/dbl, US$ 20.50/23.50 superior sgl/dbl B&B.*

Kapata Lodge (10 rooms) m 099 9283888. This homely lodge, in a lovingly tended suburban family garden 500m from the museum, has far better rooms than other options in this category – very spacious, with new furniture, AC, TV, fan & hot shower. The on-site restaurant serves the usual fare for US$3–4. Excellent value. *US$12.50/14 sgl/dbl, US$15.50/17 chalet sgl/dbl, all rates B&B.*

Mufwa Lakeshore Lodge (23 rooms) m 099 9600992. Set in a large compound whose tall brick walls disguise its proximity to the lake, this is cheaper than the other budget options, but also more rundown, & the bar & restaurant seem to be only nominally operational. The basic rooms have fans & nets. *US$6.25/11 en-suite sgl/dbl, US$5/10 using common showers, US$2 pp camping, rates exclude b/fast.*

Safari Lodge Annex (22 rooms) \01 362340. The pick of a somewhat overpriced bunch of otherwise adequate budget hotels in Karonga, this annex to the original (& now rather rundown) Safari Lodge lies in large peaceful gardens close to the lakeshore & 1.5km from the main traffic circle. The rooms are rather dingy, but spacious enough,

marshy Kambwe Lagoon at the mouth of the North Rukuru River. A distraught Fotheringham watched the massacre helplessly: 'The war whoops of the Ruga-Ruga smote the Nkonde heart with terror. The reeds were soon red with the blood of the dying, as the Ruga-Ruga speared those who stuck fast in the mud. They then fired the reeds, and as the flames rose, the yells of the poor creatures behind might be heard above the steady discharge of the guns. Those who did not perish by the rifle or the spear were either burnt to death or devoured by the innumerable crocodiles.'

A month later, Mlozi declared himself Sultan of Nkondeland and tried to capture the ALC fort in Karonga. In June 1888, a British raid on Mlozi's stockade was repulsed and almost resulted in the death of its leader, Captain Lugard (who 30 months later was to be instrumental in Britain's capture of Kampala in Uganda, for which effort he was made Lord Lugard). In 1889, Harry Johnston restored temporary peace to the region by signing a treaty with Mlozi. But, over the next six years, even as Johnston managed to conquer or negotiate with every other slave trader in the land, Nkondeland remained in the terrible grip of its self-styled sultan, who became more prosperous and powerful than ever in the first half of the 1890s.

In 1895, Johnston returned to Karonga, and on 3 December he led a successful attack on Mlozi's fort. When Johnston's troops entered the fort, it was littered with Nkonde bodies, victims of Mlozi's most recent raid, while more than 500 captives were imprisoned in a stockade, awaiting shipment to the coast. The next day, Mlozi was tried by a group of Nkonde elders, and Johnston had him hanged from a tree in Karonga, effectively ending the era of organised slavery in Malawi.

with dbl bed, net, fan, TV & hot shower. There is a restaurant, but the Club Marina around the corner is a better bet. *US$17.50 dbl, US$20.50 chalet.*

Shoestring

🏠 **Public Works Resthouse** (5 rooms) No phone. Situated in a green compound alongside the Sumuka Inn, this government resthouse, which has 4 en-suite twins & 1 dbl with TV, fan &

net, is very good value for money. Tracking down someone to check you in can be a neat trick, though. *US$3.50/8 twin/dbl.*

🏠 **Shakira White View Motel** (16 rooms) m 099 9074013. The pick of the local resthouses, this family-run place has a quiet location 5mins' walk from the bus station & clean, bright en-suite rooms with net & fan. *US$8 dbl.*

✕ WHERE TO EAT AND DRINK *See map, page 322.*

✕ **Club Marina** ☎01 362302; ⏲ 07.30–22.00 daily. The quiet restaurant in the grounds of this hotel serves the best food in town with a variety of Malawian & Western dishes at US$4–6, but choose elsewhere if you're in a hurry. The shady outdoor bar at the entrance is a popular spot for a lakeside drink.

✕ **Museum Café** m 088 8515574; ⏲ 06.30–22.00 Mon–Sat. Part of the museum complex, this unpretentious & popular place serves cold drinks & the usual Malawian staples in the US$2–3 range.

✕ **Ubulu Bukoyoba Restaurant** This is a friendly local eatery serving chicken/fish with rice/chips/*nsima* for around US$3.

SHOPPING The best place for general shopping is the **People's Supermarket** near the main roundabout, where craft sellers also congregate on occasion. A more reliable bet for handicrafts is the **Fair Lady Cosmetics/Craft Shop & Greenland Nursery** (m *088 1116579*; e *greenlandmw@gmail.com*; ⏲ *07.00–17.00*) which sells a variety of clay sculptures, carvings and beauty products just opposite the Sumuka Inn. There is additionally a very limited selection of handicrafts at the museum. It's also worth asking about the beautiful clay pots made by the potters at Matema Beach in Tanzania. Used by local people to cook and carry water, these well-crafted and wonderfully decorated pots are occasionally brought across the lake by dugout canoe to the beach opposite Club Marina for sale in Karonga.

OTHER PRACTICALITIES

Banks and foreign exchange There is no private forex bureau, but the **NBS Bank** changes money during normal banking hours. **National Bank** and **Standard Bank** both have ATMs where local currency can be withdrawn against Visa, MasterCard and Maestro, and the ATMs at **FMB** and **NBS** also accept Visa. If you don't have a suitable card and arrive from Tanzania outside banking hours, try to get hold of some Malawian currency at the border.

Internet The best internet connection is at the delightfully air-conditioned **Lupeto Computer** (⏲ *08.00–20.00 Mon–Sat*) which charges Mk10 per minute. **Karonga Airtel Shop** (⏲ *06.30–17.30 Mon–Sat*) along the Mzuzu road offers the same service minus the AC. The museum also has an internet connection during business hours.

WHAT TO SEE AND DO Few relics of Karonga's history remain. The grave of James Stewart, commissioned by the ALC to build the Stevenson Road between lakes Malawi and Tanganyika (the road was abandoned after Stewart's death), is in the mission cemetery. The Armstrong gun in front of the District Commissioner's Office is the one used by Captain Lugard in the abortive 1888 raid on Mlozi's fort. British and German war graves from the Battle of Karonga lie in the small cemetery behind the District Council Office. Another World War I relic is a large baobab tree (outside the old post office) which was used as a gun platform and which now has a mango tree growing out of it.

Cultural & Museum Centre of Karonga (m *088 8515574/099 9436427*; e *uraha@malawi.net; www.palaeo.net/cmck;* ⊕ *08.00–17.00 Mon–Sat, 14.00–17.00 Sun; entrance US$1.50*) Karonga's newest and most worthwhile attraction, this thoroughly modern and commendably informative installation deserves an hour or two of your time. The central exhibition entitled 'Malawi from Dinosaurs to Democracy' focuses on the rich prehistory and history of northern Malawi, from 240 million years ago to the present day. The astonishing main exhibit, about 12m long and 3m tall, is a life-size replica skeleton of the famous *Malawisaurus*, whose virtually intact 120-million-year-old fossil skeleton was discovered in 1924 at Mwakasyunguti in Karonga District (several other fossils of this dinosaur were unearthed nearby in the 1980s). There is also a superb sequence of displays on human evolution, including a replica of the 2.5-million-year-old *Homo rudolfensis*

THE BATTLE OF KARONGA

During World War I, Karonga was the focus of hostilities between the adjoining German East African Colony (later Tanganyika) and British Nyasaland. War in the region commenced with a 'naval victory' that was almost certainly the first of the war, and without doubt the most comic. When the British Commissioner in Zomba received news of the declaration of war, he decided the first priority must be to sink the *Hermann Von Wessman*, Germany's only ship on Lake Malawi. HMS *Gwendolyn* was dispatched into German waters under Captain Rhoades, its only gun manned by a Scotsman who hadn't seen battle in over a decade. Rhoades found the *Wessman* docked in Liuli Harbour and, when finally the rusty aim of the Scottish gunner and a live shell coincided, the German boat was sunk. Rhoades was then startled to see his enraged German counterpart and old drinking partner, Captain Berndt, leap into a dinghy and climb aboard the *Gwendolyn* screaming curses and questioning Rhoades's sanity. It transpired that news of the war had not reached Liuli. Rhoades sat Berndt down with a whisky, explained the situation, then led away his angry prisoner of war – who was by now loudly berating the German officials at Songea for not having informed him of developments in Europe.

The Germans at Songea did indeed know of the war. Immediately after securing his naval victory, Rhoades was dispatched to Karonga to repulse the German troops gathered at Nieu Langenberg (now Tukuyu). The Battle of Karonga of 8–9 September 1914 proved to be almost as farcical as the naval battle – the opposing troops marched straight past each other on the Nkonde Plateau and when they finally met the next day they were facing each other in the wrong direction. However, the skirmish resulted in tragic loss of life, mostly on the German side, with 19 out of 22 German officers being killed in the most bloody battle, and even heavier losses among the African conscripts. That Britain won was more a matter of luck than judgement (it so happened that the British troops accidentally stumbled on the Germans from behind, forcing them to flee into an ambush which would otherwise have been ineffective) but win it they did, and after the Battle of Karonga, Nyasaland was never again seriously threatened by the neighbouring German territory.

23

jawbone – the world's oldest-known relict of the genus *Homo* (the same genus as modern humans) – discovered near Chilumba by Tyson Mskika under the leadership of Professor Friedemann Shrenk in 1991. Other exhibits cover the traditional cultures of northern Malawi, the slave trade and colonial era in Karonga, as well as the advent of independence and democracy at a national level. There is also a traditional café and an internet café. Don't miss it!

Malema Camp and walking trails (m *099 9322974; other contacts as for the Cultural & Museum Centre;* ⊕ *dusk–dawn daily*) Situated about 3km west of the M1 along a clearly signposted turn-off 10km south of Karonga, this attractive bush camp is operated by the museum, primarily to house archaeologists and groups visiting or working on a nearby gorge where several hominid and other fossils have been unearthed, but it is also open to the general public. Several walking trails emanate from the camp, including a roughly 300m walk to the start of the gorge, and a longer trail to the Luwasho River and bird-rich woodland lining its banks. Day visitors are welcome, but a trio of stone-and-thatch chalets, though sometimes occupied by archaeologist or other museum-related groups, offers pleasantly rustic accommodation for US$5 per person, and camping is permitted for US$1.50 per person. Note, however, that there is no electricity as the solar panels were under repair at the time of writing, and no fridge, food or drinks are available on site; visitors must be fully self-sufficient to self-cater. If you plan to overnight, it is advisable to check room availability (and the electricity situation) through the museum before heading out this way.

CHITIPA

Arguably the most remote town in Malawi, dust-blown Chitipa lies in the far northwest close to the tripartite border with Zambia and Tanzania. As the most northerly border crossing between Malawi and Zambia, it was an important overland route focus in the 1980s, when the direct border between Malawi and Tanzania was closed owing to the former's associations with the apartheid regime in South Africa. While still not exactly a hive of activity, Chitipa has been enjoying something of a resurgence thanks to the recently completed surfacing of the M26 to Karonga. It also forms the northern terminus of the (very much unpaved) M9 from Mzimba/Rumphi via Nyika. It is a reasonably substantial town by Malawian standards, with a population of 11,000, and facilities include a People's Supermarket, a couple of banks, a district hospital and an internet connection.

GETTING THERE AND AWAY Chitipa lies 99km northwest of Karonga along the newly surfaced M26. This little-trafficked new road (brought to you largely by the nearby Kayelekera Uranium Mine) has quickly become one of Malawi's most enchanting drives. The mountainous scenery is stunning, and the landscape is so thinly populated and pristinely vegetated you might think you are passing through a national park or wildlife reserve. Axa coaches depart Chitipa at 06.00 daily, charging US$3.50 to Karonga and US$8.25 to Mzuzu. Other minibuses ply back and forth to Karonga throughout the day for about US$4.

The border post for Zambia lies on the northern outskirts of Chitipa, and from there it is about 90km along a poor road to the Tunduma/Nakonde border on the surfaced main highway between Dar es Salaam and Lusaka – no formal public transport is available, only *matola* rides. Dustier and rougher still, and definitely requiring a 4x4, despite being shown as a trunk route on some maps, is the 275km M24/M9 connecting Chitipa to Rumphi via Nyika National Park.

WHERE TO STAY

Butuzyo Motel (10 rooms) m 099 9088533. This unexpectedly pleasant hotel lies in a green compound along the Nyika road 1km from the main T-junction in the town centre. The quiet, clean rooms have tiled floors, nets & en-suite hot showers, while the unpretentious bar offers cold drinks at local prices. The restaurant is no more, but the lodging is still good value. If the prices are too high, a few indifferent cheaper lodges are dotted around the junction near the People's Supermarket. *US$4 sgl, US$8/10 sgl/dbl en-suite, rates exclude b/fast.*

Chitipa Inn ☎ 01 382228. Located about 1km towards Zambia from the main T-junction, this place was opened in 1976 by Kamuzu Banda & seems to have not changed a bit since. The décor is time-warped & the modestly attractive grounds are mostly deserted, but the bar & restaurant is fully up to date with the latest football & movies on DSTV. Malawian favourites are dished up for US$3–4. *US$19/25 sgl/dbl, B&B.*

OTHER PRACTICALITIES

Banks and foreign exchange NBS Bank and National Bank both have branches in Chitipa that exchange forex, as well as ATMs accepting Visa. For Mastercard and Maestro you'll have to head to Karonga.

Internet Globe Internet (⊕ *08.00–17.30 Mon–Sat, 12.00–16.00 Sun*) charges just under US$1/hour and is tucked about 100m behind the main T-junction. Walk straight through the junction (between the competing Airtel and TNM-painted buildings) and look for a large satellite dish.

MISUKU HILLS

Running along the Tanzanian border to the north of the M26 between Karonga and Chitipa, the wild and remote Misuku Hills form an ecological extension of Tanzania's southern highlands, from which they are separated by the steep valley carved by the Songwe River. Scenically, Misuku is somewhat reminiscent of the Western Usambara in northern Tanzania, its fertile and steeply terraced slopes supporting a hotchpotch of subsistence farms where tropical cultivars such as bananas and papayas are juxtaposed against pine and eucalyptus plantations. The area is regarded to produce the best coffee in Malawi, thanks to its rich soil and high rainfall (up to 2,000mm per annum), and it accounts for more than half of the produce marketed by the Mzuzu Coffee Cooperative.

Comprising four parallel ridges with an altitudinal range of 1,700–2,050m, the upper slopes of Misuku support a cover of lush montane rainforest that has been protected within two forest reserves since 1948. These are the very accessible Mughese Forest Reserve, which extends over 7.5km² near Misuku trading centre, and the more westerly 24km² Wilindi-Matipa Forest Reserve, centred on Matipa Peak, at 2,050m the highest point in the range. The forests of Misuku are regarded to support the country's most diverse flora, with more than 150 tree species recorded, including several types of strangler fig. It is also rich in epiphytic orchids.

Strong affiliations with the southern highlands of Tanzania mean that Misuku is the main or only Malawian stronghold for several East African forest species including Derby's flying squirrel, Tanganyika forest squirrel, three types of butterfly and five types of tree. For the casual visitor, the most alluring of these Misuku specials is the Angola colobus, a beautiful leaf-eating monkey notable for its flowing black-and-white coat and dashing arboreal acrobatics. Other large mammals include bushbuck, red duiker and blue monkey. Misuku is particularly alluring to birdwatchers, with a checklist of more than 100 forest specialists including three species found nowhere else in Malawi, namely spot-throat, Shelley's greenbul and forest batis. The *rungweensis* race of green barbet, easily seen in Mughese, is confined to Misuku and Mount Rungwe in southern Tanzania.

GETTING THERE AND AWAY The trading centre of Misuku lies about 30km off the M26 along a patchy dirt road branching north at the village of Kapoka, which is 76km from Karonga, 23km from Chitipa, and home to a prominent police roadblock at the time of writing. The road isn't in great condition, but it's a lovely roller-coaster ride over undulating hills covered in indigenous Brachystegia woodland and protea shrubs, but giving way to cultivation as you climb deeper into the hills. As you enter the trading centre, turn left, then right, and it's another 2–3km to the headquarters of the Mwalingo section of the Mzuzu Coffee Cooperative, where you'll find the Mwalingo Guesthouse. It is difficult to reach without private transport, though with patience you might pick up a *matola* ride at Kapoka.

 WHERE TO STAY *See map, page 288.*

🏠 **Mwalingo Guesthouse** (4 rooms) \01 382708; m 088 8554250. Run by the Mzuzu Coffee Cooperative, this cosy & very reasonably priced guesthouse offers superb views over the surrounding hills. Accommodation is in clean en-suite rooms with twin beds & en-suite hot showers. Ideally, you need to bring all food & drink with you, but there is a cook to prepare the food, & basic provisions can be obtained from the nearby trading centre. It's seldom full, but best to ring in advance just in case (though if you are stuck they can put you up in the inferior but adequate hostel a few hundred metres down the road). *US$8 dbl, plus US$1.50 service fee for the cook.*

EXPLORING MISUKU There are many possibilities, but a great starting point is the 12km drive from Misuku trading centre to Chinongo Coffee Drying Station via the Mughese Forest Reserve. From Mwalingo, first drive back to Misuku, then follow the main road through the village for 1km before taking a turn to the left. Follow this road for 3.7km to a T-junction where you need to turn left again past a cluster of buildings. After another 2.5km, you'll see St Michael's Secondary School, where you need to turn right. After climbing uphill for a short way, this road follows a high ridge offering great views over the forested slopes and valleys, reaching the signposted entrance to the forest reserve after 1.5km.

Lined with giant lobelias and ferns, the road now runs through the forest for about 2.5km, and it is worth stopping regularly (or even walking the whole way through) to increase your chance of hearing and seeing wildlife. Among the more vocal and conspicuous birds are silvery-cheeked and trumpeter hornbill, Schalow's turaco, green barbet, Fülleborn's boubou and black-headed oriole, while mixed bird parties often include several species of greenbul, apalis and other small leaf gleaners. Squirrels are common and conspicuous, red duiker less so, but the main mammalian attraction is the presence of Angola colobus and blue monkeys, both of which are common in the forest canopy, and most likely to first draw attention with their call – a quiet bird-like chattering in the case of the blue monkey and a harsh nasal boom for the colobus.

The road emerges from the forest at the first of several wonderful viewpoints over the Songwe River, which forms the border with Tanzania. Another 1.5km brings you to the Chinongo Coffee Drying Station, an open-air set-up with a relaxed attitude towards visitors, offering a good opportunity to watch the first phase of the coffee-production process from start to finish, at least in season. There are more views of the Songwe here, and you could hike down to the river itself, ideally with a local guide to show you the best trail.

Appendix 1

LANGUAGE

CHICHEWA Chichewa, the national language, is also the lingua franca of the Southern and Central regions (a role it shares with Chitumbuka in the north). Chichewa is classified as a Bantu language, a linguistic group that had its origin in the Congo Basin about 2,000 years ago, and which now includes practically every language spoken in sub-equatorial Africa, including all 40 indigenous to Malawi. Bantu languages share a common pronunciation and grammar, and many have closely related vocabularies – if you speak any other Bantu language, be it Swahili, Shona or Zulu, you will recognise many similar and identical words in Chichewa.

The overall standard of English in Malawi is possibly the highest of any country in Africa, so unless you plan on spending a long time there, the motivation to learn a local language is small. That said, it is polite to know the basic greetings and to be able to respond to them, and it is always true that even the clumsiest attempt to speak a local language will go a long way to making friends in Africa. Most Malawians will be more than happy to oblige you with an informal Chichewa (or Chitumbuka) lesson and they will greatly appreciate your interest in their native tongue. However many words you learn, the most current language is always going to be smiles and laughter.

Pronunciation In Chichewa, as in most Bantu languages, almost all words and syllables end with a vowel. There are five vowel sounds, represented by a, e, i, o and u. These vowel sounds have no close equivalents in the English language; they are, however, practically identical to the vowel sounds of a, e, i, o and ou in French. Where two vowels follow each other, they are not compounded but instead each retains its pure sound. Consonants generally have a similar sound to their English equivalent, though 'j' is always pronounced as 'dj'; 'ch' is far softer than the English 'ch'; 'ph' is pronounced as a breathy 'p' as opposed to an 'f'; and 'r' is often interchangeable with 'l'. To give some examples, Rumphi is pronounced more like Rumpi than Rumfi, and Karonga may sometimes be pronounced in a way that sounds closer to Kalonga.

Grammar and tenses The grammar and tense usage in Bantu languages is very different from that of English or any other European language. It is not something that tourists wanting to know a few basic words and phrases need concern themselves with. People who want to familiarise themselves with Chichewa grammar and tenses are advised to buy a copy of Revd Salaum's *Chichewa Intensive Course* (Likuni Press), which was first published in 1969 and went into a third edition in 1993. Alternatively, the newer and better (but pricier) *Tiyeni: Chichewa Language Course for Newcomers to Malawi* by Celia Swann and Max Sato is available through online booksellers and includes an audio CD. For those already in Malawi who would like a reference, *Chichewa for English Speakers* by Nathaniel Maxson was published in 2011 and is widely available.

Greetings and phrases

Hello	*Moni*
How are you?	*Muli bwanji?*
Fine (and you?)	*Ndiri bwino (kaya inu?)*
Thank you	*Zikomo (or ziko)*
What's your name?	*Dzina lanu ndani?*
How much (price)?	*Ndalama zingati?*
I don't understand	*Sindikumva*
Where are you going?	*Mukupita kuti?*
I'm going to Lilongwe	*Ndikupita ku Lilongwe*
I want... /I don't want...	*Ndikufuna... /Sindikufuna...*
Goodbye	*Khalani Bwino*

Some useful words

animal	*nyama*	hyena	*fisi*
arrive	*fika*	journey	*ulendo*
baboon	*nyani*	large	*kula*
banana	*nthochi*	meat	*nyama*
buffalo	*njati*	milk	*mkaka*
cattle	*ngombe*	mosquito	*udzudzu*
chicken	*nkhuku*	mountain	*phiri*
egg	*dzira*	name	*dzina*
elephant	*njobvu*	near	*pafupi*
English (language)	*chizungu*	no	*ai*
enough	*basi*	person	*munthu*
European	*Mazungu*	rain	*mvula*
far	*kutali*	salt	*mchere*
fish	*nsomba*	small	*ngono*
food	*kudya*	swamp	*dambo*
friend	*bwenzi*	tent	*hema*
goat	*mbuzi*	today	*lero*
god	*mulungu*	tomorrow	*m'mawa*
government	*boma*	water	*madzi*
hippo	*mvuu*	yes	*inde*
honey	*uchi*	yesterday	*dzulo*
house	*nyumba*		

SPEAKING ENGLISH TO MALAWIANS English is the official language of education, and many urban Malawians speak it with great fluency. Even in rural areas, you'll seldom encounter the linguistic communication barriers you might in other African countries. That said, not all Malawians speak English, and those who do often possess a relatively small vocabulary, or use phrasings and pronunciations derived from Bantu grammar. For this reason, adjusting your use of English to reflect Malawian norms is arguably a more important communication skill than picking up a few phrases of Chichewa.

The first rule when speaking English to those less fluent is to talk slowly and clearly. Phrase questions as directly and simply as possible, as it's easy to confuse people with excess words or slang. In most Bantu languages, a question is often phrased as a statement, but in an enquiring tone of voice, so bear in mind the tendency to use the grammatical phrasing of your home tongue when you speak a second language. 'There is a room?' is more likely to be understood by a Bantu-speaker than 'Do you have a vacant room?', and 'This bus is going to Lilongwe?' is better than 'You don't happen to know whether this bus is going to Lilongwe?'

Listen to how Malawians pronounce words. Often, they will use Bantu vowel sounds even when speaking English (in the same way that many English speakers use English vowel sounds when attempting to speak a Bantu language), and they may also carry across the Bantu practice of stressing the second-last syllable. For instance, a word like 'important' may be pronounced more like 'eem-POT-int'. Another common habit is inserting vowel sounds between running consonants (for instance 'penpal' might be pronounced 'pin-EE-pel') or at the end of words (*basi* for 'bus').

Certain common English words are readily understood by Malawians, while other equally common words draw a complete blank. For instance, practically anybody will know what you mean by a resthouse, but they may well be confused if you ask where you can find accommodation. Another example of this is the phrase 'It is possible?' which for some reason has caught on almost everywhere in Africa. 'It is possible to find a bus?' is more likely to be understood than 'Do you know if there is a bus?' Likewise, 'Is not possible' is a more commonly used phrase than 'It is impossible'. This sort of thing can occur on an individual level as well as on a general one, so listen out for words which are favoured by somebody with whom you have a lengthy conversation.

In terms of etiquette, every conversation should start with an exchange of polite greetings, however much of a rush you think you are in. 'Hello, how are you?' must be responded to and the question asked of the other person – and watch out for oddly formal phrasings such as 'May I know you?', which sounds unintentionally suggestive in the wrong context, but is actually a charming way of asking 'What's your name?'

GLOSSARY OF VERNACULAR AND SCIENTIFIC WORDS

Acacia	A genus of thorny trees dominant in many parts of Africa, but not in Malawi, where Acacia woodland is largely replaced by Brachystegia.
bakkie	South African word for a pick-up truck.
banda	In some African languages, this literally means home, but in hotel-speak it can refer to any detached accommodation unit.
boma	In Malawi and other parts of central Africa, the *boma* is the administrative part of town, often a discrete entity from the commercial centre of that town. Some game lodges use the word *boma* to refer to a stockaded outdoor dining area.
braai	Afrikaans word meaning 'barbecue', used widely in southern Africa.
Brachystegia	The type of woodland that is dominant in Malawi, characterised by trees of the genus Brachystegia and often referred to as '*miombo* woodland'.
buck	Any antelope.
chamba	Marijuana.
chambo	The main eating fish caught in Lake Malawi.
chiperone	Heavy mists that occur seasonally in highland areas such as Mount Mulanje.
chitenga	Sarong-type cloth worn by most Malawian women.
dambo	Seasonal or perennial marsh, normally fringing a river.
endemic	In the context of this guide, a race or species found nowhere else but in the area or country to which it is allocated.
exotic	A term that may cause some confusion as it is often abused in travel literature. An exotic species is one that has been introduced to an area; in Malawi, the pine plantations in Nyika are exotic, the palms that line the Shire River are indigenous.
koppie	Small hill, an Afrikaans term widely used in this part of Africa.

matola	A light vehicle or truck that carries paying passengers, often informally.
mazungu	Term used throughout East Africa for a white person, plural *wazungu*.
mielie	Term used throughout southern Africa for maize (corn).
nsima	Maize porridge that is the staple diet of most Malawians.
nyama	Any meat, but especially beef.
rondavel	Used by hotels to refer to a *banda* built in the round shape of an African hut.
south	South Africa – a lot of Malawians will tell you they used to work 'south'.
trading centre	Any village large enough to have a market or small shop.

Appendix 2

FURTHER INFORMATION

Please note that books can be expensive in Malawi, so it's best to get hold of them before you arrive. For rare or out-of-print titles mentioned below, try online sellers such as www. amazon.co.uk, or Central Africana Ltd (*www.centralafricana.com*).

BOOKS

Travel guides Several quality coffee-table books on Malawi have been published in recent years:

Johnston, Frank and Ferrar, Sandy *Malawi: The Warm Heart Of Africa* Central Africana Ltd/ Struik-New Holland, 2012. The best and most widely available pictorial introduction to Malawi, with an expanded edition reprinted in 2012.

Johnston, Frank *Malawi: Lake of Stars* Central Africana Ltd, 2012.

Kelly, David *Malawi – Endangered Beauty* David Kelly, 2005. A lavish book celebrating Malawi's natural heritage with paintings by David Kelly and text contributions from conservationists around Malawi. An entertaining and informative read.

As a second source of practical travel information:

Douglas, John and White, Kelly *Spectrum Guide to Malawi* Spectrum, 2003. A lavishly illustrated and informative guidebook written by two Malawi experts.

Several guidebooks to specific regions or places of interest in Malawi exist, though many are now out of print and difficult to locate in the country or outside it. They are:

Eastwood, Frank *Guide to the Mulanje Massif* Lorton Communications, 1988.

Johnson, Sigrid Anna *Visitor's Guide to Nyika National Park, Malawi* Mbabazi Book Trust, 1983.

Mundy, H and K *Zomba Mountain: A Walkers' Guide* Montfort Press, 1975.

The Wildlife Society of Malawi used to publish a range of inexpensive booklets and bird checklists covering all the main national parks and game reserves, as well as Judy Carter's *Day Outings from Lilongwe* (1991) and Peter Barton's *Day Outings from Blantyre*, the latter updated in 1997. Again, these booklets appear to be out of print and difficult to locate.

History and background

Ransford, Oliver *Livingstone's Lake* John Murray, 1966. One of the better general books written about Malawi. Ransford's accessible writing style and anecdotal approach to history make this book a pleasure to read, even if some of the views expressed by the author seem a little culture-bound 40 years after they were written. This book is out of print but is easily found in libraries or online booksellers.

Overview of central African and Malawian history

Muluzi, Juwayeyi, Makhambera and Phiri *Democracy With A Price: The History of Malawi Since 1900* Heinmann, 1999

Needham, Mashingaidze and Bhebe *From Iron Age to Independence: A History of Central Africa* Longman, 1974 and 1984.

Phiri, D D *History of Malawi From the Earliest Times to the Year 1915* CLAIM, 2004.

Tindall, P *History of Central Africa* Longman, 1985.

Wilson, D *A History of South and Central Africa* Cambridge University Press, 1975.

All these books are slightly on the dry side, but the two complementary Malawi-specific titles combined give the best overview of the country's history.

Biographies of Livingstone and books about slavery and the Zambezi Expedition

Hibbert, Christopher and Livingstone, David *The Life and African Explorations of David Livingstone* Cooper Square Press, 2002. A first-person retelling of Livingstone's travels, a good aeroplane novel and a gripping if slightly elaborated read.

Jeals, Tim *Livingstone* Heinemann, 1973. A better book, which was updated in 2001 and reprinted in paperback.

Liebowitz, Daniel *The Physician and the Slave Trade: John Kirk, the Livingstone Expeditions, and the Crusade Against Slavery in East Africa* W H Freeman & Co Ltd, 1998. A recent biography about one of Livingstone's fellow travellers, later the English Consul at Zanzibar.

Stuart-Mogg, David *Mlozi of Central Africa: Trader, Slaver and self-styled Sultan* Central Africana Ltd, 2010. A history of the British campaign against Mlozi, and against slavery in Nkondeland, near present-day Karonga.

Colonisation, politics and culture of Africa

Hartley, Aidan *The Zanzibar Chest* Harper Perennial, 2004. A passionate account of Africa's hotspots as seen by an African news correspondent; insightful and compelling.

Packenham, Thomas *The Scramble for Africa* Weidenfeld & Nicolson, 1991. You can't do better than Thomas Packenham's award-winning and wonderfully readable book.

Russell, Alec *Big Men Little People* Pan, 1999. A wry look at Africa's leaders.

Malawi

Buckley, Bea *My Malawi Journal* Athena Press Ltd, 2003. Written by a Peace Corps volunteer about her life in a Malawian village.

Gibbs, James (ed) *Nine Malawian Plays* Popular Publications, Limbe, 1976.

King, Michael and Elspeth *The Story of Medicine and Disease in Malawi: The 130 Years Since Livingstone* Arco Books, 1992 and *The Great Rift* Arco Books, 2000. Two compelling books written by a surgeon-and-wife team about their experiences in Malawi's hospitals.

Morris, Brian *The Power of Animals, An Ethnography* Berg, 2000. A somewhat dense but fascinating book showing how closely Malawian culture is related to wildlife.

Ó Máille, Padraíg *Living Dangerously – A Memoir of Political Change in Malawi* Dudu Nsomba Publications, 1999. A dark but highly readable book covering Banda's last years.

Schoffeleers, Matthew and Roscoe, Adrian *Land of Fire: Oral Literature from Malawi* Popular Publications, 1985. An interesting book if you want to know more about traditional Malawian beliefs.

Shepperson, George A and Price, Thomas *Independent African: John Chilembwe and the Nyasaland Rising of 1915* CLAIM, 2000.

Theroux, Paul *Dark Star Safari* Penguin Books Ltd, 2003. Retracing his footsteps through Africa and through Malawi, the author comes to depressing conclusions.

Wildlife and field guides
Birds

Dowsett-Lemaire, Françoise and Dowsett, Robert *The Birds of Malawi – An Atlas and Handbook* Tauraco Press, 2006. This long-awaited book, including comprehensive atlassing details of all bird species known from Malawi, is an essential purchase for dedicated birders. Be warned, however, that it lacks illustrative plates for identification, so is of limited use to more casual visitors unless used in conjunction with one of the field guides below.

Newman, Kenneth *Birds of Malawi* Southern, 1999 and *Birds of Southern Africa* Southern, 2002. The first book checklists every bird recorded in Malawi, with comprehensive details of distribution and status, and pictures of all species not illustrated in the second book (which deals with Africa south of the Zambezi). For Malawi-specific birding, especially for visitors familiar with southern African birds, these two books combined make a more focused package than the Sinclair and Ryan guide listed below, but unfortunately the Malawi title is long out of print (though available at a cost through online booksellers).

Roberts Multimedia Birds of Southern Africa CD-ROM Southern African Birding, 1997–2003. Superb multi-media alternative to the southern African title above, but needs to be supplemented with a Malawi guide.

Sinclair, Ian and Ryan, Peter *Birds of Africa South of the Sahara* Struik, 2003. This is a well-laid-out field guide with useful maps and good illustrations, and comprehensive for the sub-Saharan region, cramming a vast amount of information into one relatively portable tome. As things stand, it's the only option for anybody wanting to carry one field guide that includes all bird species recorded in Malawi.

Mammals

Este, Richard *The Safari Companion* Russell Friedman Books, South Africa; Chelsea Green, USA; Green Books, UK, 1999. Rather more bulky than any of the above guides, but highly recommended if weight isn't a consideration, most aptly described as a field guide to the behaviour of African mammals.

Kingdon, Jonathan *Field Guide to African Mammals* Academic Press, 1997. For those whose interest extends to small mammals, this wonderfully detailed guide is highly recommended.

Morris, Brian *The History and Conservation of Mammals in Malawi* Kachere, 2006. Excellent comprehensive overview of the decline of mammal populations in Malawi and of its most important protected areas.

Stuart, Tilde and Chris *Southern, Central and East African Mammals: A Photographic Guide* Struik, South Africa, 1992. This is the one to go for if weight is a consideration and you're content to stick with identifying large mammals. Despite being very compact, it covers 150 large mammal species found in the region.

Stuart, Tilde and Chris *The Larger Mammals of Africa* Struik, South Africa, 1997. A more comprehensive tome by the same authors, and a better buy for those who aren't carrying their luggage on their back.

Fish

Lewis, Reinthall and Trendall *Guide to the Fishes of Lake Malawi National Park* World Wide Fund for Nature, 1986. A field guide to the fish of Lake Malawi which is comprehensive within the confines of the national park, and pretty useful elsewhere on the lake. It is now out of print and difficult to locate, though you might be able to locate a secondhand copy on www.amazon.co.uk.

McKaye, Wiklund, Shawa et al *Lake Malawi National Park: World Heritage Site* HEED, 2008. This guide can be bought at several lodges in the area for around US$20, and (despite its rather tacky and clumsy spiral binding) is a detailed introduction to the park and its wildlife, in particular the fish, doubling as a useful field guide to fish anywhere in Lake Malawi.

Flora

Baumann, Gunter *Photographic Guide to Flowers of Malawi* Wildlife Society of Malawi, 2006. Glossy and informative book on Malawi's flora.

La Croix *Malawi Orchids Volume 1: Epiphytic Orchids* NFPS, 1983. For orchid enthusiasts.

Moriarty, Audrey *Wild Flowers of Malawi* Purnell, 1975. Now a rare book, but the best field guide.

Shorter, Clare *An Introduction to the Common Trees of Malawi* Wildlife Society of Malawi, 1989.

Novels

Theroux, Paul *Jungle Lovers* Ballantine Books, 1989.

Theroux, Paul *My Secret History* Penguin, 1990.

van der Post, Laurens *Venture to the Interior* Vintage, 2002.

Autobiography

Kamkwamba, William and Mealer, Brian *The Boy Who Harnessed the Wind: Creating Currents of Electricity and Hope* William Morrow, 2009. The story of a young Malawian boy who built a functioning windmill out of discarded materials.

Mapanje, Jack *And Crocodiles Are Hungry at Night* Lynne Rienner Publishers, 2011. A memoir of years spent as a political prisoner under the Kamuzu Banda regime.

Poetry

Mapanje, Jack *Beasts of Nalunga* Bloodaxe Books, 2007.

Mapanje, Jack *The Chattering Wagtails of Mikuyu Prison* Heinemann, 1991.

Health

Wilson-Howarth, Dr Jane *Healthy Travel: Bites, Bugs and Bowels* Cadogan, 2006 (4th edition).

Wilson-Howarth, Dr Jane and Ellis, Dr Matthew *Your Child Abroad – A Travel Health Guide* Bradt Travel Guides Ltd, 2005 (2nd edition).

WEBSITES

Tourism sites *(see also under safari companies' individual listings)*

http://updates.bradtguides.com/Malawi

www.malawitourism.com

www.go2malawi.com

www.malawi-tourism-association.org.mw

www.visitmalawi.mw

www.malawi-tourism-association.org.mw

www.explore-malawi.com

Book sites

www.centralafricana.com Malawi-based African book specialist.
www.africabookcentre.com For all published books about Africa.
www.nhbs.com Specialist bird book distributor.
www.amazon.co.uk/www.amazon.com Amazon stocks most current books on Malawi and often lists out-of-print books through other sellers.

Wildlife, parks and conservation sites

www.wildlifemalawi.org Wildlife & Environmental Society of Malawi.
www.birdlist.org/malawi Complete bird checklist for Malawi.
www.malawicichlids.com Great site to find out more about Lake Malawi's unique fish.
www.wag-malawi.org Wildlife Action Group.
www.malawi.gov.mw/information1/main.info.parks Home page for the Department of National Parks & Wildlife.
www.africanconservation.org General site with links to Malawi conservation projects.
www.mountmulanje.org.mw Information on Mount Mulanje.
www.nyika-vwaza-trust.org Information on Nyika National Park and Vwaza Marsh Wildlife Reserve.
www.projectafricanwilderness.org Information on Mwabvi Wildlife Reserve.
www.rhino.malawi.net Information on J&B rhinos in Liwonde National Park.
www.compass-malawi.com Community Partnerships for Sustainable Resource Management in Malawi.

THE AFRICA
IMAGE LIBRARY
TRAVEL & WILDLIFE PHOTOGRAPHY

wildlife • landscapes • culture • architecture • nature • people • cities • ceremonies • beaches • travel • forests • seascapes • adventures • mountains • flowers • birds • scenics • habitats • animals • activities • tourism • seascapes • village life • tribes • children • monuments • cityscapes • deserts • art • crafts • holidays • transport • reptiles • festivals • religions • costumes • museums • places • birds • savannas • migration • portraits • dancing • marine wildlife • safaris • art • activities • lodges • rivers • vegetation • food • wilderness • fauna • flora • scenes • **www.africaimagelibrary.com** • cities • ceremonies • beaches • environment • travel • forests • seascapes • adventures • mountains •

If you would like information about advertising in
Bradt Travel Guides please contact us on
+44 (0)1753 893444 or email info@bradtguides.com

Index

INDEX TO ADVERTISERS